THE CRUISER'S HANDBOOK OF FISHING

Praise for *The Cruiser's Handbook of Fishing*

"This is the ultimate guide to harvesting the sea. It should be aboard every cruising boat."
—Steve Dashew

"Now there is no excuse not to catch breakfast, lunch, or dinner while underway. Plenty of good advice garnered while fishing the world's oceans."
—*Latitudes & Attitudes*

"This is *the* definitive book for cruisers on the topic of what the authors call 'successful seafood procurement.' Whether one is trolling or fly-fishing, drifting or anchored, wading or diving, the Bannerots make fishing an adventure that involves both science and art."
—*Cruising World*

"Having fished with Scott and Wendy many a day, I've witnessed their uncanny abilities firsthand. This future classic is destined to be on every sailboat and motor cruiser."
—Peter Jenkins, best-selling author of *Along the Edge of America* and *A Walk across America*

"Every culture has its bible, and until now, there wasn't one for the voyager who had a passion for catching fish. This is now the definitive source on the various gear that is practical on small offshore vessels and a reference guide to the hundreds of species available to eat in the world's oceans. . . . The Bannerots' background in marine biology affords them the knowledge to provide a whole picture of fishing from a voyaging boat: fish habitat, population abundance, toxicity issues, and tips on catching the different species in many circumstances."
—*Ocean Navigator*

"I couldn't put this amazing book down. It's packed with information, photographs, diagrams, and illustrations . . . and would make a useful addition to any angler's library."
—John Eichelsheim, *New Zealand Fisherman*

"So complete and so thorough, it contains more than most of us could ever digest. But that is part of its charm and why it should be on every offshore sailboat and cruising boat. . . . Scott and Wendy are giving their fellow sailors the gift of an abundant life on the sea."
—*Blue Water Sailing*

"In one attractive volume, *The Cruiser's Handbook of Fishing* has a ton of helpful information."
—Stuart Cawker, *Boating New Zealand*

"This book is written primarily for yachties as a guide to enjoying fish and fishing, and comprehensively covers almost every fish extraction method from harpooning to fly fishing, but even the most hard-core knowledgeable angler could learn a lot from this book. The authors' exposure to the multiple fishing cultures across the oceans they have traveled has given them a broad base of experience and knowledge as well as enormous insight into traditional methods for catching and preparing fish. And, the section on fishing ethics shows a maturity and common sense that everyone can learn from. If this book can teach a yachtie to catch a fish—surely a very difficult task—then a true fisherman will really benefit from reading it." —David Green, Field Editor, *Fishing World* (Australia)

"It's hard to imagine anyone else in the world writing this book this well. The Bannerots combine their remarkable sailing and cruising experience with a tremendous knowledge of fish and love of catching them." —Doug Olander, Editor in Chief, *Sport Fishing Magazine*

"On top of all their other fishing advice, Scott and Wendy Bannerot include here a fine introduction to fly-fishing for the experienced cruiser."
—Jim Butler, Editor in Chief, *Fly Rod & Reel Magazine*

"One of the most comprehensive, easy-to-read, 'how-to-fish' books I've come across."
—Wade Whitelaw, Fisheries Research Scientist, Secretariat of the Pacific Community

"This is more than a first-class instruction manual on fishing for ocean cruisers. It is a wonderful reference work that will make fishing easier and more productive regardless of the equipment you have available or the exotic location you choose to wet a line."
—Gary Caputi, *The Big Game Fishing Journal*

"Cruising and fishing coincide in most coastal locales, so why not keep some fishing tackle aboard your boat—and a copy of *The Cruiser's Handbook of Fishing* with it?" —Joe Healy, Editor, *Saltwater Fly Fishing Magazine*

THE
CRUISER'S
HANDBOOK OF
FISHING

Scott Bannerot
Wendy Bannerot

International Marine / McGraw-Hill

Camden, Maine ◆ New York ◆ San Francisco ◆
Washington, D.C. ◆ Auckland ◆ Bogotá ◆
Caracas ◆ Lisbon ◆ London ◆ Madrid ◆
Mexico City ◆ Milan ◆ Montreal ◆ New Delhi ◆
San Juan ◆ Singapore ◆ Sydney ◆ Tokyo ◆
Toronto

The McGraw·Hill Companies

12 13   QFR/QFR   5 4

*The Library of Congress has cataloged the cloth edition
as follows:*
Bannerot, Scott P., 1959–
    The cruiser's handbook of fishing / Scott
    Bannerot, Wendy Bannerot.

        p.   cm.
    Includes bibliographical references (p.   ) and
index.
        ISBN 0-07-134560-4
    1. Saltwater fishing. 2. Boats and boating.
    I. Bannerot, Wendy. II. Title.
    SH457.B35 1999
    799.1'6—dc21   99-047114
Paperback ISBN 0-07-142788-0

Questions regarding the content of this book should
be addressed to
International Marine
P.O. Box 220
Camden, ME 04843
www.internationalmarine.com

Questions regarding the ordering of this book should
be addressed to
The McGraw-Hill Companies
Customer Service Department
P.O. Box 547
Blacklick, OH 43004
Retail customers: 800-262-4729 (within U.S.)
    609-426-5436 (outside U.S.)
Bookstores: 800-722-4726

Illustrations by Jamie Downing

All photographs © Scott P. Bannerot or W. S. Bannerot
unless otherwise indicated.

*To Palmer, Betty Ann, Chub, Nancy,
and Bonnie—thanks for your love and support,
and for always being there in every way,
regardless of the conditions; to our dear
friend Lea'aetoa Tavake; and to Ryan.*

Contents

Preface

The purpose of this book is to condense expert advice from a wide range of maritime commercial, scientific, and subsistence disciplines in order to provide cruisers, seafarers, and, indeed, any aspiring individual with a "one-stop reference" for successful seafood procurement. We present detailed information sufficient to transform the raw beginner—with a variety of budgets, levels of interest, and geographical locations—into a proficient provider, processor, and consumer, as well as to augment the knowledge of more experienced seafarers. Expert fishers, divers, and gatherers should find new information from their own or related fields to productively incorporate into their personal strategies and systems. Whether you're out on the water for the day or undertaking a longer journey, the skills presented here should maximize your chances of consistently having fresh seafood for dinner.

The prevailing fishing ineptitude of many boaters aboard sailboats and power cruisers can only be a temporary condition, caused by social isolation and lack of effective communication between expert commercial and sport fishers and this growing group of seafarers. Cruisers tend to be thinkers, learners, and adventurers. Perhaps only for a few hours at a time or for a lifetime, they seek to immerse themselves in and become a part of their natural environment. They soon realize that survival and sustenance compel them to participate in the food web, learning to be efficient, finely tuned predators who understand how to select and procure prey.

No portion of society has better reason to learn how to fish than cruisers, and no one better appreciates the rewards. We fervently hope this book may help reduce the imbalance of fishing knowledge and, in so doing, contribute to the happiness and well-being of many.

We chose to write this book in the first-person singular from Scott's point of view for convenience in describing anecdotes—including experiences that occurred both before and after we met and married—and unabashed accounts of Wendy's exploits through the eyes of her greatest admirer. Wendy took the lead for preparing large portions of this book, making us equal partners, as with the rest of our activities and our life together aboard *Élan*.

Acknowledgments

We thank Jon Eaton, Constance Burt, and the staff at International Marine for supporting this project, and for all their patience, advice, flexibility, hard work, and assistance. Special thanks are also due to Herb McCormick, Lynda Morris Childress, Bernadette Brennan Bernon, and the editors of *Cruising World* magazine for encouraging us to write a book based on a series of articles about how to catch fish from sailboats and other cruising vessels. Herb took special interest and time stimulating our efforts, for which we are extremely grateful. Michel Savage did a fine job editing the final products and coordinating artwork.

The friendship, inspiration, and guidance of Peter Jenkins comprise the cornerstone for our writing and ideas for future projects, and we thank you too, Rita, for your kindness and patience.

We appreciate the publishing support of Tim Queeney *(Ocean Navigator)*, Barry Gibson *(Salt Water Sportsman)*, David Ritchie *(Marlin)*, Gary Caputi and Len Belcaro *(The Big Game Fishing Journal)*, Ken Schultz (Schultz Associates), Joe Healy *(Saltwater Fly Fishing)*, Glenn Law and Vic Dunaway *(Florida Sportsman)*, Jim Butler *(Fly Rod & Reel)*, Bud Bendix *(Pacific Magazine)*, Doug Olander and Doug Kelly *(Sport Fishing)*, Albia Dugger (World Publications), Denver Bryan (Images on the Wild Side), Peter Van Gytenbeek *(Fly Fishing in Salt Waters)*, and very special thanks to Scott Boyan *(Salt Water Sportsman)*.

We thank Steve and Linda Dashew, John Neal, and Amanda Swan-Neal for supportive and timely comments and interactions that influenced our path to completing this project.

Paul Mead (in Tonga) openly shared his vast knowledge of fishing in the Indo-Pacific region, and provided invaluable sea time and fishing adventures by allowing us to join him aboard F/V *Dora Malia* and access to his personal library. Kim Andersen (Dive N' Fish Kiribati) generated hundreds of hours of invaluable fishing and diving time in the central Pacific by including us in his operations aboard F/V *Spinner* and F/V *Spirit of Christmas* for three months, and has supported and aided our writing efforts since that time. Wade Whitelaw kindly reviewed a pre-publication manuscript, generously provided highly useful information, and facilitated permissions to use selected materials from the many useful publications of the Secretariat of the Pacific Community (SPC) (New Caledonia). We thank everyone at the SPC for his or her help and generosity. Dr. Michael H. Owens kindly reviewed portions of the medical information, Dr. Joanne Ebesu provided references and ciguatera test-kit information, and Dr. Bruce Halstead guided our summaries of poisonous and venomous marine life. Drs. William W. Fox Jr., Joseph E. Powers, C. Bruce Austin, James A. Bohnsack, C. Richard Robins, Roger T. Hanlon, the late Ray Hixon, and Jerald S. Ault, along with many other mentors and colleagues at the University of Miami Rosenstiel School of Marine and Atmospheric Science, U.S. National Marine Fisheries Service, and University of Texas Marine Biomedical Institute, greatly influenced and shaped our knowledge and ideas about life in the sea.

Fish Catching Methods of the World by Andres von Brandt and *Poisonous and Venomous Marine Animals of the World* by Dr. Bruce Halstead were major references, as well as the following papers contained in Editor G. M. Hall's *Fish Processing Technology:* "Preservation of Fish by Curing (Drying, Salting, and Smoking)" and "Canning Fish and Fish Products" by W. F. A. Horner; "Biochemical Dynamics and the Quality of Fresh and Frozen Fish" by R. Malcolm Love; "Surimi and Fish Mince Products" by G. M. Hall and N. H. Ahmad; "Chilling and Freezing of Fish" by G. A. Garthwaite; and "Application of Lactic Acid Fermentations" by L. Han-Ching et al. The SPC generously permitted adaptations of selected material from several publications, including *On-Board Handling of Sashimi-Grade Tuna*, written by Michel Blanc and illustrated by Jean-Pierre LeBars; and *Trolling Techniques for the Pacific Islands* by G. L. Preston et al. Steve Darden kindly provided interesting material on cookie-cutter sharks from Peter Goadby's *Saltwater Game Fishing: Offshore and Onshore.*

The Food and Agricultural Organization of the United Nations (FAO) kindly permitted the use of illustrations from the *FAO Fisheries Synopsis* series. We especially thank Shalini Dewan, Jacek Majkowski, and Pere Oliver.

Ken Jaspers, Rich Beers (Rich Beers Marine, Inc.), Andy and Pam Wall, Pat Griffin, Jeff Braun, Graham Proctor, Lance Manson (Offshore Rigging), John Lucas (Seaquip Marine Engineers), Steve Trevurza (Trevurza Sails), James Doll (Doll Marine Metal Fabrication), Ken Kiddie and Grant Gurau (Peninsula Engineering), Norseman Rigging (Fort Lauderdale), Craig Nickalls, and Dave Kilpatrick all made substantial technical contributions to *Élan.*

Captain Harry's Fishing Supply, Offshore Angler, Atlantic & Gulf Fishing Supply Corporation, Ocean Producers International, Alvey Reels Australia, Penn Fishing Tackle Manufacturing Company, Austin's Diving Center, Trimble Navigation, West Marine, and Defender Industries all contributed information and assistance useful to this work. Bobby Boskivic at Seamart and Glennis King at Moana Fisheries, Ltd., and staff at both locations, went out of their way to furnish specimens for photos. Vitor Medina, Ken Larner, and Ilene Byron provided gear-supply information for South Africa and Great Britain.

Matthew Thompson and Cathy Moir (Kiwitech Marine Solutions, Ltd.) patiently and tirelessly dispensed computer support throughout. We gratefully acknowledge the cheerful and able printing and copying services of all the crew at Copy Cottage, Ltd. Debbie and Rob McLean loaned us a second computer, along with their home and endless hospitality, to expedite progress. Everyone on staff at Gulf Harbour Marina went out of their way to be helpful—thanks!

Palmer Bannerot initiated, aided, and abetted large portions of our personal journey to fishing success. Much of the blame for this book rests squarely on his shoulders. His passion for fishing, the sea, the people who live on and near it, and the styles of music they send wafting across to anchored cruising boats in exotic ports continues to inspire us. The other culprit is Bruce Austin, who introduced me to cruising under sail, free-diving with a Hawaiian sling, and to the spirit of adventure. He even found *Élan* for me and instigated my purchase of her. Betty Ann Bannerot; Chub and Nancy Smith; Bonnie Smith; Paul and Norma Glanville; Roz Crosby; Jack Glanville; Gregg and Jennifer Homola; Jimmy and Judy Doll; Lynn, Marshall, and Byron Kohr; Tony, Errick, and Shannon Fuller; Mike Owens; the late Buddy Austin; Fred Austin; Dave, Liz, Kenneth, and Bobby Kilpatrick; Fred and Rick Bannerot; Jon Broadhurst; Dave Lowe; Elizabeth McCutcheon; Eric Vogt; Mark Krajcar; Hans Dahlseng; Hans Swete; Ken and Jenny Kiddie; Steve, Leslie, Annie, and Ellie Leopold; Steve, Joanne, Juliet, Olivia, and Simon Palmer Bannerot; Sally Cousins; Kristi and Terry Newth; Tom Thomson; Chris and Diane Gardner; and Barry Smith have all either spent some serious time at sea with us or contributed significantly and unconditionally in other ways to our time away from land.

Each of the following individuals bestowed something special on our learning process—whether it was taking the time to answer questions after a long day when we were scruffy little kids hanging around the docks; having the patience to help us over a hurdle when we were young, inexperienced, struggling apprentices; showing us the ropes in environments new to us; spending time on or near the water with us; or adopting us into a foreign culture without prejudging us based on our skin color, race, gender, nationality, or any other superficial characteristic—we'll remember and salute each one of you, always: the late Earl Gentry; Max Register; Rick Ruhoff; Gary Register; Jamie Brody; Sarge Werner; Dick Williams; Hank Brown; John and Bonnie Maull; Dale and Olda Parsons; Ray Hathaway; John and Marcia Malloy; Rick Resto; Steve McKenny; Corey Christie; Alex Bueno; Wayne Rushworth; Drew Whitmer; Nitro; Malcolm; Tessa; Mel Walker; Mike Needham; Teddy D'Esposito; Don Gurgiolo; Kenny and Kymie Hum; Larry Dukehart; Carlos Delvalle; Skippy Nielsen; Alex Adler; Scott Stanscyk; Ralph Ratliff; George Hommel, Jr.; "Hoppy" Hopwood; Ray Green; Scottie Kingsley; Charlie Stivers; Bill White; Ricky Olsen; Jay Rieber; Curt Deuel; Warren and Mildred Servatt; John and Mary Magursky; Chuck Schimmelman; Billy Harbaugh; Dave Purdo; Jane and Anne Greenblat; Tommy Nielsen; Dr. Jorge, Krista, Julián, Fernanda, and Mariana Jiménez; Bonefish Bob; Kenny Knudson; Billy Knowles; the late Ken Doubles; Rich Hellmuth; Tim Klein; Rick Miller; Al Polofsky; Kerry "Zilla" Price; Brendan Burke; Roy Lindback; Clyde Upchurch; the late Ray Jensen; Michael "PI" Owens; Robbie Reckwerdt; Skip Bradeen; John Gargan; Jack Falcuchi; Kenny Collette; Gregg Waugh; Conner Davis; Larry Williams; Joy and Rick Francis; Ady Ordiales; Arthur Albury and family; Hogarth and Felina Lucas and family; Harry DeFerrari; Paul and Alisi Mead and children; the late Tiny Turcek; Hollis and Freddie John; the late Veronica John; Archie and John Harding; Kim, Totinnang, and James Andersen; Patrick, Natasha, and Vincent Rogers; Julian St. John; Kenly Franklin; Cecil Xavier; Franklin Thomas; Lenora Bell; Granny and Grandpa Bell; Rose Lee Brown and everyone in the Brown family; Diane and Rollin Bertrand; Junior "Scrap" Lightbourne; Terii and Titana Loyat and family; Guy and Lelani Lejeune and family; Joseph and Tracy Tauira and family; Peau and Letia Halahingano and family; the late Dick Entwhistle; Roger Lextrait; Jim and Barb Bohnsack and family; Ron and Elisapeti Cherry and family; Maurice and Thomas Doris; Francois Mauati, Sr., and family; Hubert Uraina; Leonard Tufaunui; Neri Peni-ikiua; Marie Manufui; Stuart Griffiths and family; Maurice "Mahaja" Clarke; Brother Butch and everyone in the One Love Rastafarian Tribe; Foster and Dwayna Derrick; Jerry and Lynn Bardoe; Kung Fu; Robbie Smith; Lorenzo Johnson; Joa Chim Lucas and family; Max and Simone Dominique and family; Lea'aetoa and Paea Tavake and family; Steve and Jenny Hart and family; the late Virginia Hart; John Leask; Campbell and Alison Brenton-Rule; Fiona Kirk; Jeremy Barnett; and Michael Salvaneschi.

We would be remiss if we did not extend our deep gratitude to the huge number of cruisers aboard both sailboats and powerboats out there we have met in our travels, and who have done so much to focus our efforts. There're hundreds of you, including some close friends . . . you know who you are, and we must salute you all as one large, far-flung group.

Last, we wish to thank Captain Butch Green for the following gift. Unbeknownst to Butch, I watched a downcast, lonely looking young kid approach him at Holiday Isle Charter Dock, Islamorada, in the Florida Keys. It was the end of an extremely rough, stormy day during the peak season, when all the charter-boat crews were exhausted from fishing for many days on end. The boy had a problem with a cheap, poorly maintained reel. Butch stopped what he was doing and spent almost an hour, standing in the wind and rain, to completely dismantle and repair the reel. He reloaded it with fresh line, tied on a rig, gave the kid some bait, and pointed him to a spot under a nearby bridge where he might catch something. The young guy was utterly transformed, and the warm glow that lit his features as he looked back at Butch one last time represented something far beyond fishing.

Introduction

The impetus for this book came from twenty years of periodic contact with sailors and power cruisers who were highly frustrated fishers. We have encountered these folks everywhere from the eastern United States to the Bahamas and Caribbean, Central America, and the far-flung islands of the tropical and temperate Pacific and Indo-Pacific regions. Having earned our living from commercial and charter fishing, diving, marine biological research, and aquaculture, it seems we're always catching, processing, or studying fish and invertebrates—and the stream of questions from would-be fisher folk is never far behind. Pointing people in the right direction, we've learned, frequently has a pervasive influence on their entire cruise, and sometimes on the overall confidence and self-esteem of the crew.

Female cruisers and children often become the resident fishing experts. Sorry, fellas, but despite all of those male-oriented fishing magazines, you can ask any experienced charter fishing captain who listens better, learns more quickly, and, therefore, performs better, frequently landing the biggest fish. Husbands on cruising boats sometimes settle into the role of boat handler, content to watch their wives and offspring assume the dominant role of catching fish and other seafood.

Whether we're trolling, drifting, or anchored; whether casting, using nets, or spearfishing; whether diving for shellfish or simply collecting seafood by hand from the shallows, success sharpens the senses, increases environmental awareness, and inevitably sparks interest in a much broader spectrum of topics. Few people, regardless of gender, age, or background, can fail to be overwhelmed by a close view of a sleek, brilliantly colored oceanic fish being brought alongside their vessel. And later, the aroma of fresh marinated fish steaks wafts from the grill as you slip silently along, hundreds of miles offshore, or swing comfortably at anchor in a balmy, tropical lagoon lined by white beaches and coconut palms—now *that's* living. The resulting crew enthusiasm may ultimately pervade the entire cruising lifestyle, perhaps channeling new intellectual energy into your child's correspondence courses or giving you more in common with native seafarers on far shores. And what better way to do something for others? Nothing is more appreciated by a fellow seafarer or a local resident than a gift of fresh seafood.

Why do many cruisers have less than desirable fishing success? It *should* be just like every other aspect of cruise preparation: get detailed professional advice, apply it to your personal budget and degree of interest, practice a little before you go, and start getting your own experience. The problem: nowhere previously has a complete spectrum of gear and techniques—for the pursuit of everything from big billfish to more humble targets—been presented in a manner tailored specifically for cruisers and the variety of situations they encounter. We hope this book is the solution.

Compared with many recreational and commercial fishing vessels, sailboats and power cruisers in general travel more slowly and stay at sea longer. Fishing tends to be a secondary rather than a primary objective of the trip, and the motivation is often immediate personal consumption. Yet a high percentage of the voyagers lacks significant fishing experience and expertise. This combination of factors results in a fishing environment that differs substantially from that found on most dedicated fishing vessels. Maximum success in the cruiser's environment requires some adaptations and modifications of conventional techniques, in addition to mastering fundamental skills drawn from a wide variety of fishing-related activities.

The keys to teaching these skills successfully are to provide sufficient detail so the reader can duplicate each *exactly*, and to present a simple distillation of highly effective gear, knots, tackle, and techniques most applicable to the cruiser from the wide—frequently bewildering—world of professional and commercial fishing and diving. This book provides abundant line drawings and photographs essential to this task.

After procuring sufficient gear commensurate to space and budget and mastering the technology for effective deployment, the cruiser must then locate, attract, and capture the quarry. Detailed discussion of how to read environmental signs, optimal fishing strategies relative to local conditions, and the distribution and behavior of target species and their prey, for a variety of different situations, provides cruisers

with a sound framework for sharply enhanced fishing success.

This success quickly exposes the cruiser to an array of unfamiliar experiences. For example, how does one safely battle, land, subdue, and prepare for consumption large, strong fish and other organisms variously armed with sharp fins, teeth, barbs, and other potential dangers, without sustaining personal injury or damaging their vessel? How does one identify potentially toxic species that should be avoided, along with other venomous or dangerous sea life sometimes encountered while fishing? Detailed, comprehensive descriptions and instructions address each of these issues.

We also cover prevention of and first-aid treatment for various injuries and afflictions incurred occasionally by active fishers; processing (i.e., cleaning) the catch; preparation for consumption (raw or cooked) and techniques for preservation; and application of this new expertise to survival-gear preparations and other aspects of the cruising lifestyle. Finally, we direct the reader to sources for recommended equipment (all prices are U.S. dollars), further reading, and periodicals and organizations of potential interest.

In short, this book endeavors to fill a significant void in the existing literature by thoroughly covering fishing for sailboat and power cruisers and their unique operating conditions.

1

Fishing Success under Power or Sail: A Preview

Development of fishing prowess requires patience with technical detail. Regardless of the fishery—a commercial swordfish longline fleet; an offshore or inshore sport charter-fishing industry; a billfish tournament circuit; or an artisanal handline, net, or diving fishery operating from dugout canoes from some remote coastline—the top performers, inevitably, are those who pay the most attention to detail. These folks get up earlier, stay out later, reinvest a greater portion of their return in more advanced gear, and spend more time on research and exploration rather than following the same daily routine. Many develop their own unique systems and approaches to fishing. The result? These top fishers consistently outperform their peers in reading the environment, predicting the presence of various organisms, and producing catches under conditions that would completely stump others. These are the offshore charter captains and skiff guides you have to book months in advance, the commercial highliners who make big money, the prosperous island fishers who provide well for their families and command the respect of their communities, the cruising sailors who seldom lack for fresh seafood and often have enough to share with others.

How did they get this way? Somewhere along the line, they developed a passion for fishing, a passion that carried them through endless detail that would bore the "uninfected." Second, they had, or created for themselves, circumstances that permitted them to spend thousands of hours on the water in the pursuit of seafood, for profit or for fun. While

exposure to aspects of fishing ignites the enthusiasm of a surprisingly high percentage of people, it's this second condition that poses a barrier to the competence of most. If you have a job unrelated to fishing and other normal demands on your time—like a family—it is very difficult to spend enough hours on the water to gain the desired level of expertise solely from experience. How do you overcome this barrier? No problem: get professional advice.

If you are fortunate enough to be preparing for a cruise, whether by sailboat, power trawler, or some other efficient, long-distance vessel, you will soon have the time and circumstances to further develop your fishing skills. Perhaps some past experience piqued your interest in catching a few fish, if only the culinary delight of a fresh seafood dinner at your favorite restaurant. You've maybe heard an interesting story or two, but you have no personal ambition to become some wild fishing captain—you just want to provide a little seafood from time to time with minimum hassle. You are possibly vague on what fishing success means relative to your upcoming trip, and the gear you wish to carry on board. What can you expect?

Your expectations should be directly correlated to your preparations, which involves purchasing some items and learning a few skills—whatever is consistent with your current degree of interest and how much money you can allocate to fishing. Before diving into the technicalities, we give you some vicarious exposure; a taste, if you will, of what attention to details can produce: fishing success under power or sail.

Trolling in the South Pacific

We were lost in our own thoughts, gliding silently westward along the rugged southern shore of Nuku Hiva, Marquesas Islands, French Polynesia on the 5 nautical mile (NM) trip from Taiohae to Hakatea Bay aboard our 41-foot (12.25 m) aluminum sloop, *Élan*. Surreal volcanic formations, giving way to steep cliffs and heavily jungled valleys, were patchily illuminated by late afternoon shafts of sunlight poking through the dense cap of clouds over Mount Muake.

A sudden, sharp, metallic scream obliterated our reverie. Wendy leapt to the deeply bent stand-up trolling rod, snatched it from the holder, and snapped the rod tip back sharply several times to ensure the hook point of the 5¼-inch (133 mm) Drone spoon drove through the jaw of whatever had grabbed the silvery, flashing lure. As I raced forward to drop the jib, the reel drag on the starboard trolling outfit began to protest loudly as a second fish grabbed the 8-inch (203 mm), skipjack-colored Australian Runner swimming plug and headed for the horizon. Wendy slammed the port rod back into the rod holder and nimbly danced across the tiller to set the hook on the second outfit, as I trimmed the mainsail and started the engine to facilitate our maneuverability during the fight. I jumped to the starboard rod and we both began working on our fish, first lifting the rod tips slowly and evenly, and then dropping smoothly while quickly winding the reel handle. Then again raising the rod tip for another short stroke in a steady rhythm, occasionally interrupted as the fish dashed off on another run.

My fish had hit on heavier tackle—a Penn International 50W reel loaded with 60-pound (27 kg) test monofilament fishing line; consequently, the double line broke the surface 20 feet (6 m) back in the wake after ten minutes of hard work. Wendy quickly placed her Penn 30W outfit (using 40 lb./ 18 kg test monofilament) in the rod holder, donned gloves, and came over to leader my fish. By the time she arrived, I had the double line on the reel and was just winding on the last few feet of shock leader, the black-barrel swivel just approaching the rod tip. I dipped the rod tip to her gloved hand and she began gingerly handlining the 50 feet (15 m) of single-strand, #8 stainless steel wire (93 lb./42 kg test

breaking strength). She grasped the wire carefully, thumb up at first, taking the pressure across her palms by turning them slowly toward her body as if she were showing herself a hitchhiker's sign, 90 degrees to the taut wire. Wendy gradually worked the fish up from the shadows, dropping the dangerous loose coils of wire on deck at her feet, ever careful not to entangle a finger or a toe, always ready to ease the pressure or even let go if the fish surged suddenly. Meanwhile, I backed the drag lever off a little (if Wendy had to release the wire, the fish wouldn't break off as it abruptly came tight on the reel again), carefully set the rod in the holder (mindful not to entangle Wendy or get a loop of leader wrapped around the rod tip), and grabbed the 6-foot (1.8 m) Aftco gaff with the 4-inch (102 mm) hook.

The boat was moving forward at a knot and a half, perfect for keeping the fish away from the propeller and oriented at a favorable shallow approach angle. Finally, the elongated torpedo shape—deep indigo with neon stripes—emerged from the gloom; it was a sizable wahoo, maybe 45 pounds (20 kg). Wendy expertly applied pressure to the leader, slowly and steadily easing the fish to within inches of the surface. I oriented the gaff hook down, passed it out beyond the thick area just aft of the fish's head, *behind* the leader, and stroked smoothly inward (the reverse of a strong pool shot) and upward, lifting the fish out of the water and over the lifeline on the follow-through. Wendy immediately immobilized the potentially dangerous, still-lively fish (one slash of the razor-sharp teeth of this species can open a serious wound) with several well-placed blows to the back of the head using an aluminum fish billy. She applied the coup de grâce with a stab to the brain, using a stainless steel ice pick we keep handy for this purpose. Leaving me to lash a tail rope to a nearby cleat, she then dashed back to her rod to resume battle.

This fish turned out to be a second wahoo, half the size of the first. This time, I leadered and she gaffed and lashed the fish to the starboard transom cleat. By now we had drifted west to an area offshore of our destination, so I dropped and secured the mainsail and went forward to prepare the anchor and provide a lookout as Wendy steered us into the anchorage under power. Shortly after dropping the hook, I transformed our catch into mouth-watering steaks, some of which were dropped directly into a plastic container of marinade (vinegar, olive oil, teriyaki, lime juice, and various seasonings, including thyme, parsley, and lemon pepper) prior to a quick sizzle on the grill. We carefully bagged the remaining steaks and placed them against the holding plates of our refrigerated hold below for later distribution to fellow cruisers and to the lone Marquesan family living in this isolated portion of the bay.

Darkness had fallen by the time we cleaned up the carnage. The first tantalizing wisps from the grill began permeating the cockpit. There was still an occasional swirl and gurgle audible from beneath the afterdeck fish-cleaning table as several hefty gray reef sharks simmered down from their frenzied feeding

Wahoo (*Acanthocybium solanderi*) caught by trolling an 8-inch (203 mm) skipjack-colored Australian Runner on a wire line outfit at 4.5 knots. Leader is 50 feet (15 m) of single-strand #8 stainless steel wire (Tonga).

on wahoo scraps. We took a moment to sit together under the stars, clinking our freezing-cold bottles of local Hinano beer in a solemn toast. As the saying goes, it doesn't get any better than this.

Adrift *Way* Offshore

About fifteen hundred nautical miles (NM) west of the Galapagos Islands, the sun was getting low and the light, barely detectable puffs of breeze weren't enough to ripple the glassy sea surface. The boat was nearly dead in the water, rocking gently to the long, slow rise and fall of the spent remnants of some far away Southern Ocean storm. I scrambled up the anodized aluminum arch for a look at the menagerie swimming around us. Seven school-sized (6 lb./ 3 kg) mahi mahi remained—we'd caught and cleaned thirteen the night before. The dark, fusiform shapes of slowly circling skipjack and small (10 lb./5 kg) yellowfin tuna could be seen moving in the darkening depths behind the transom. Suddenly, the school tuna disappeared, and a larger (40 lb./18 kg) yellowfin swam nervously to within a foot of the transom, packing itself next to the oversized outboard rudder, followed closely by the seven mahi mahi. I strained to make out the source of their discomfort in the late afternoon glare. An immense shadow eased deliberately from the inky depths and assumed the shape of a massive blue marlin, nonchalantly ghosting along in a gentle circle, not 25 feet (8 m) from the starboard quarter. Several remoras were clearly visible around her head. Based on her substantial girth, I conservatively estimated that she weighed 800 pounds (363 kg).

I shouted to Wendy to come have a look. She scrambled up beside me, and we both told the other to get the video camera. The big fish slowly receded into the glare as Wendy ran for the camera, and we ended up with footage of only the school tunas, the mahi mahi, and the larger yellowfin packed fearfully up behind the hull. After ten minutes or so, this tuna relaxed and meandered off. I went below and grabbed a 20-pound (9 kg) class spinning-rod and reel outfit and tied a ³/₈-ounce (10 g) white Millie's Bucktail jig to the end of the 50-pound (23 kg) monofilament shock leader. I couldn't convince Wendy to do the catching this time, so I opened the reel bail and pressed the line to the reel stem with

Blue marlin (*Makaira nigricans*) of comparable size to the fish that circled *Élan* 1,500 NM west of the Galapagos Islands. The fish in this photo was inadvertently caught on a swordfish longline offshore of Antigua, West Indies, and landed only after attempts to revive and release it failed. The meat fed many Antiguans for the next three months.

my forefinger. I then released the line while snapping the rod forward sharply, causing the lure to fly out in a shallow arc 45 feet (14 m) from the boat. I left the bail open after the lure landed with a plop and began to sink, peeling loops of line steadily off the end of the spool. When an estimated 80 feet (24 m) had run off, nearly straight down, I turned the reel handle (which automatically closes the bail) and began winding the handle as fast as I could, interspersed with abrupt, erratic, upward jerks of the rod.

The third or so upward jerk stopped in midstride as something substantial inhaled the jig, doubled the rod, and began screaming line off the Penn 850SS spinning reel. The fish sounded 100 yards

(91 m) toward the seafloor before the pressure of the drag convinced it to halt. I slowly pumped the rod, winding the reel handle on each drop, without allowing the line to get slack. More fast runs punctuated steady progress, causing repeated loss of painstakingly gained yards of line. Relentlessly working the rod, however, eventually took a toll. When we flicked on the bright arch light, we could see the silvery glow and distinct lemon-yellow fins of the tuna as it pulsed tiredly in a circle, getting inexorably closer to the sea surface. I raised the rod one last time and held it high on the outside of one swimming circle, pressuring the fish to the surface, around and to within range of Wendy's gaff. She stroked expertly, handed me the handle, then grabbed her camera and shot a few photos before descending the companionway to whip up a quick marinade for the grill. The yellowfin weighed 42 pounds (19 kg)—an average catch for heavy spinning tackle from a drifting vessel, but enough to feed a small army of hungry crew.

Anchored in Different Latitudes

Malden Island, Line Islands, Republic of Kiribati We recently anchored on the narrow shelf in the lee of uninhabited Malden Island to rest en route to Christmas Island from Bora Bora, French Polynesia. I had turned in for a nap following sunrise, after hoving-to during the night. Just past noon, I was awakened from a deep slumber by Wendy's shouts of excitement, the screeching of a spinning-reel drag, and, moments later, loud splashing immediately outside my porthole. Donning polarized sunglasses and cap, I staggered up the companionway just in time to see a fat gray reef shark noisily engulf a hooked 7-pound (3 kg) rainbow runner boatside, bucktail and all. As the shark zipped off into the depths, a vast school of similar-sized rainbow runners closed back over the opening they had made. We enjoyed their company—and eating those we could wrest from the many sharks—for five days.

The last evening at Malden, while preparing a rainbow runner for the grill at the afterdeck fishcleaning table, a big, chunky yellowfin tuna began aggressively eating scraps as they hit the water a few feet below me. I couldn't resist impaling a scrap on

NADINE GEORGES

a double-strength hook and chucking it out on the 300-pound (136 kg) test monofilament handline we keep handy in the cockpit. The scrap sank slowly for ten seconds; then the line suddenly picked up speed. I let the tuna run off loose loops of line for five seconds, then turned both palms inward with the line across them to set the hook hard, and the fight was on. About twelve minutes later, I called to Wendy to interrupt her work canning fillets in the galley, because I was nearly ready for her to gaff the fish. She jumped up and grabbed the gaff just as I muscled the fish's head into position, only to watch as the hook fell out of the corner of its mouth. I was already joking about the tuna's close call when, much to the fish's and my surprise, Wendy flopped down on her belly and free-gaffed the unfortunate tuna, then got to her knees and ordered me to "hold this." She grabbed another gaff and nailed the stunned yellowfin a second time, just in back of the head, handed me the second gaff handle, and calmly headed back to the galley. Holding two gaffs and staring at the now lifeless, easily 70-pound (32 kg) tuna, I stammered something about not believing what I had just seen. Halfway down the steps, Wendy paused long enough to reflect, "Well, you said you wanted it, didn't you?" and then casually disappeared below. We carefully processed and packed every scrap of the delicious pink meat into cold storage, providing weeks of great eating for ourselves and several guests.

Great Barrier Island, New Zealand The anchor finally budged slightly as 50-knot williwaws heeled *Élan* over repeatedly, despite our position over deep mud in a shallow arm of Port Fitzroy, one of the most protected anchorages in the entire country. A subtropical low had deepened and descended south from near Norfolk Island and was now abutted to a sharply strengthened high-pressure system to the east, directing 45-knot-plus easterlies, gusting to 82 knots, onto the northeastern coast of North Island. We upped anchor and motored around to a more protected cove, reanchored, and helplessly listened to the Auckland side of rescue communications involving two American cruising sailboats on the verge of sinking offshore less than 100 NM to the north. We had three guests aboard for the weekend, and everyone had been bottled up below, hiding

from the wind and driving rain. It was time to do something to salvage the trip.

A brief lull lured Campbell Brenton-Rule, an expert trout fly fisher who had recently acquired an interest in saltwater fishing, out to the afterdeck, bundled in foul-weather gear and armed with a 20-pound (9 kg) spinning outfit rigged for bottom-fishing. His cut bait, a plug of pilchard, hadn't been down long when we heard a happy shout, shaming me into joining him, just as he landed an iridescent, silvery pink porgy (locally called "snapper"). No sooner than this delicious pan fish was on the ice, Cam was rebaited, free-spooling for the bottom, and quickly hooked up again—this time with a small frisky trevally, another fine eating fish. Now the washboard was out, and Wendy, Mike, and Alison cheered Cam on as he quickly landed enough fish to feed us for two days (with help from Alison when she could no longer resist joining the fray). Firm, white, boneless fillets were soon on the skillet; we popped open a bottle of good local wine and did our best to set aside, for the moment, tragedies we could not change.

Dinghy Adventures

South of Bimini, Bahamas, nearly two decades ago As Jeff Kenney pulled at the oars, bringing our small fiberglass dinghy into the shadows of a large, semi-submerged wreck, commonly known as the "concrete ship," I hooked a small fish called a grunt on 6 feet (2 m) of 100-pound (45 kg) monofilament leader and sent it overboard, suspended by a round cork. "Think they're still around?" "I don't—oof! . . ." The butt of the makeshift "heavy outfit"—a stumpy, broken rod with a tiny revolving spool-reel hose clamped to it—had slammed into my gut as the rod jerked downward onto the gunnel, threatening to capsize us. The miniature reel drag squealed loudly in uneven bursts, begrudgingly giving up short lengths of the mere 60 yards (18 m) or so of 100-pound (45 kg) line packed onto the spool (despite being locked in full on position). This piercing sound was nearly drowned out by Jeff's hysterical laughter as the dinghy rocked wildly and began to pick up speed and head for the stern of the wreck. With much groaning and bailing, we zigzagged erratically around the wreck, much to the entertainment of the remaining crew of five watching from the deck of S/V *Small Hope* nearby. We finally tired the 35-pound (16 kg) amberjack enough to slip a hand in its gill and slide it aboard, along with 10 gallons (38 L) or so of seawater. Dinner was secured!

Raroia, Tuamotus, French Polynesia "Well, honey, I think we have some canned chili . . ." *zing* went the light-spinning reel drag. After some deft maneuvering among the shallow coral heads, Wendy eased the mottled-brown, 6-pound (3 kg) marbled grouper into the waiting landing net.

San Salvador, Bahamas "OK, Klaus, drop it about now." The vertical array of small barracuda chunks had no sooner touched bottom 450 feet (137 m) below, immediately offshore of the coral

Jeff Kenney with 35 lb. (16 kg) amberjack (*Seriola dumerili*) landed near Bimini, Bahamas (May 1980), from a small, oar-powered dingy.

wall outside the anchorage, than the rod tip started to jump. After seven minutes of intense cranking of the Penn International 30W, two brilliant pink yelloweye snappers and a blackfin snapper broke the surface.

Mopelia, Leeward Society Islands, French Polynesia The bright-blue-banded wahoo looked like a Polaris missile as it rocketed vertically into the air, the momentum of its upward rush to slam the pink-and blue-skirted jet-head lure carrying it 10 feet (3 m) skyward. Had it been night, the glow of Bernard Mauahiti's smile could have been seen in Tahiti—he had moments earlier told me this was the part of the reef wall where we would catch our wahoo for the feast that evening in the village.

Rio Coto Colorado, Near Golfito, Costa Rica We idled the dinghy quietly against the languid, swirling, caramel-colored current of the river beneath the dense green jungle canopy. We'd seen lounging iguanas, monkeys, several species of parrots, and a small crocodile that slithered down a muddy bank and submerged when we got too close. The battle-scarred Shakespeare Ugly Stik spinning rod, armed with a Penn 4500SS spinning reel loaded with 10-pound (4.5 kg) monofilament, bent for what could easily have been the thousandth time in its life. A fat dog snapper was soon in the cooler, fooled by the ½-ounce(14 g) Rat-L-Trap sinking plug we were lazily trolling.

Palmyra Atoll, Line Islands, United States A silvery tail broke the placid surface of the sand-flat shallows as commercial albacore fisher Mike Needham cast his fly 10 feet (3 m) in front of the shadowy forms of the fish school. He stripped twice and then raised the fly rod sharply to hook his first bonefish.

Christmas Island, Republic of Kiribati Outside in the gathering darkness: a dying outboard, loud whispering, the nudge of Hypalon against the hull, an intensely excited voice. "Hey, you guys, I'm sorry to bother you, but you've got to come see this; I'm just a little excited." We popped up on deck to find our neighbors, Jens and Allyson of S/V *Indigo*, holding on to the north and south ends of a stout, still-struggling yellowfin tuna that would later weigh in at 81 pounds (37 kg). They had just two days before received their first massive order of fishing gear after becoming seriously infected by the cruising seafarer fishing bug.

Bonefish (*Albula vulpes*) caught fly-fishing, Palmyra Atoll, Line Islands, United States.

Beneath the Waves and along the Shore

The last of six divers hit the water and joined the group of bobbing heads suspended in 35 feet (11 m) of water near the steep coral drop-off. "Ça va? Everyone set?" asked Hogarth, the burly good-natured Polynesian fishing-boat captain who had invited us on a spearfishing outing with his mixed Tahitian-Tuamotun crew. "Oh, yes, uh, Wendy, go to shallows and shoot small red fish—good to roast on fire." I stifled a smile and looked over to confirm what I already knew was occurring: a deep, quiet stare and subtle squaring of the shoulders as Wendy silently absorbed this well-intentioned advice from her friend. The muscular brown-skinned crew began fanning out along the reef, attired only in tattered shorts and weathered-looking fins, masks, and snorkels, but also armed with lethal, band-powered spearguns.

Our dive gear wasn't much less used, although we did have thin full wetsuits. The main difference was our weapons—simple Hawaiian slings, constructed of a cylindrical wood handle with a central hole for a stainless steel shaft. They are hand-fired like a modified slingshot or subsea bow and arrow, using a single band of elastic surgical tubing bound to either side of the handle. A small metal cup secured to the middle of this length of tubing accepts the butt of the spear. In a reversal of the common phenomenon of "better equipped, 'rich,' developed-country visitor

awing the locals with shiny new gear," our slings were understandably viewed with polite skepticism by our "better-armed" hosts, as was the presence of a woman on a diving foray.

Scarcely after Hogarth's last words, Wendy eased to a horizontal position and began finning purposefully for the deep reef edge. Hogarth and I exchanged glances, I smiled and shrugged, and then turned to follow. The nearly unlimited visibility afforded a clear view of Wendy's first free dive. She stopped moving her fins, breathed deeply and slowly—while relaxing every muscle in her body—took one last huge breath of air, bent 90 degrees at the waist, and then straightened both legs together vertically above her, their weight providing the initial downward thrust. She slowly moved her fins as she descended 10 feet (3 m), 15 feet (4.6 m), 20 feet (6 m); she conserved oxygen by letting her weight belt take over—no kicking, just a controlled glide—30 feet (9 m), 40 feet (12 m), 45 feet (13.7 m). Finally, I saw the target, a bulky, 12-pound (5.4 kg) saddleback grouper (also called "coral trout"), wagging slowly toward an overhang with one eye on the strange creature approaching from above. Wendy looked away from the target and altered her glide slightly to a parallel course, visibly easing the grouper's discomfort. Then she half-rolled, cocked the sling, and sent the razor-sharp spear blazing across the 10-foot (3 m) distance between her and a spot 3 inches (76 mm) behind the fish's eye. The dull thump of steel penetrating bone, accompanied by a sharp clang as the tip emerged from the other side and whacked the coral wall, were audible at the surface. She had aimed perfectly, "stoning" the grouper with a kill shot to the brain, freezing all motion—no frantic vibrations, no blood—which sharply reduces shark risk. I descended halfway to "ride shotgun," peering out into the endless deep blue beyond the drop-off, to cover her ascent.

Hogarth had seen the whole episode and was there to take the fish at the surface, his eyes wide, laughing and ebullient ("Bon pêche!"). I handed Wendy my shaft so she could get back into action. Soon the whole crew was watching her performance—carousing, joking, exclaiming at the irony—and occasionally diving down to help out or finish off the odd fish. Later, sharing some home-brewed coconut beer at the rustic fish camp on an uninhabited atoll, we wished our Tahitian, Tuamotun, or French was better as we caught snippets of the stories about "La Championess." We did manage to catch the phrase, *le petit poisson rouge*, followed several times by laughter.

The next year at the same atoll, relatives of this fishing crew showed us how to wade the reef flat at night for spiny lobsters and snorkel the inner lagoon for spider conch. This reminded us of many productive days in the Bahamas and Caribbean, picking up large queen conch in relatively shallow water. Other mollusks of various groups, crustaceans, and other invertebrates, both tropical and temperate, occur worldwide and can often be collected by wading the shallows or walking the shoreline, usually at low tide.

What's Best for You?

Experiences like these, or at least some subset of them, are easily within the grasp of the cruising sea-farer. If at any time you feel mired in technical detail later in the text, keep in mind that although some of the skills are laborious to describe sufficiently for duplication, and may appear arduous at first reading, none is particularly difficult to perform. After an overview, you may choose types of fishing that best fit your personal circumstances, and then focus mostly on what you need to know to execute these skills successfully. Be careful, however, because you *will* taste success, and this seems inevitably to transport previously inept and apathetic fishers to entirely new levels of cruise fishing. Stick with the details, repeat knots and other procedures until you have them right, and you will be on your way to fishing success under power or sail.

With Power Comes Responsibility

When you are flushed and perhaps a little stunned at newfound mastery of a once elusive skill, it is essential to prevent exuberance from translating into excess. People are placing unprecedented pressure on the world's marine resources, killing sea life as they endlessly scramble for protein, polluting once-pristine ocean environments, and altering world climate with a barrage of self-centered activity. The signs envelop us, even cruisers seeking escape in the

Fresh seafood caught diving and wading: spiny lobster (left, *Panulirus penicillatus*, uninhabited South Pacific atoll) and hogfish (right, *Lachnolaimus maximus*, Northwest Channel Light, Central Bahamas).

farthest corners of the globe: plastic refuse; oil globs; stressed, unhealthy coral reefs; depleted, unbalanced fish communities; record warm spells and associated weather. We're to the point where an individual fish or invertebrate *does* matter. When you kill something you don't need, you do yourself and your planet a disservice. Take a photo; a vibrant, live animal makes a much better picture than a vanquished carcass accompanied by a foolishly grinning warrior. Do you really need to transform the beautiful, complex organism before you into brown fecal matter within twenty-four hours?

The answer to this question may well be "yes." The practical side of the question is that we need protein to survive, and it surrounds those of us on the sea. Furthermore, when we go cruising, however temporarily, we become part of the natural food web. By exercising modest restraint and common sense, it *is* possible to participate in a balanced, responsible manner. Cruisers are accustomed to being their own electrician, plumber, mechanic, navigator, and watch-keeper; now they must become their own fishery manager and conservation officer. Guess what? It's incredibly simple and unrestrictive: don't kill anything more than you need for consumption and reasonable provisioning, never harm any threatened or endangered species unless your survival depends on it, and follow all local and international fishing regulations. This leaves plenty of room to have a great time, capture all kinds of spectacular marine organisms, and eat lots of fantastic seafood.

2

Gear, Tackle, and Connections for Hook-and-Line Fishing

The ability to catch fish and other seafood consistently can play an important role in the self-sufficiency and adventure of life afloat. Most cruisers have some sort of hook-and-line fishing gear aboard, which they may use diligently, usually to troll a lure while underway. The majority also carries dive gear, and often a speargun or similar devices, with the idea of adding fresh seafood to the menu from somewhere near the anchorage at their destination. A smaller number might carry a net or two of some kind.

Of these options, hook-and-line fishing is probably the most commonly attempted. It's the least strenuous, you don't have to get in the water, it can work unattended, and the gear is compact for stowage. The practice also has an inescapable allure, similar to a lottery: you get that lure out there behind the boat, drag it around long enough, and there's at least a *chance* you could hit the jackpot. The odds of this happening are certainly enhanced by the more remote areas that cruisers traverse, often well beyond the range of weekend warriors, charter fishing boats, or even local commercial fishing vessels. Why, then, are cruisers usually not as effective at fishing as they could be?

The single biggest detriment to the hook-and-line fishing success of cruisers is Mickey Mouse gear: cheap hooks; inappropriate leader hardware and lures; incorrect length, material, and construction of leaders; clumsy, poorly tied knots and improper crimps; low-quality fishing reels with sticky, rough, uneven drags that cause frequent break-offs; trolling rods with fixed rather than roller guides causing chafed monofilament fishing line;

and so on. To paraphrase a proverb, the bitterness of cheap quality lingers long after the sweetness of the initial low price of the fishing gear first purchased by many cruisers.

Let's assume you've been realizing less than satisfactory fishing success. You're tired of trolling mile after mile without a strike. Then, when something finally hits, there's often that loud snap and it's gone—or the hook comes out—or the fish is lost boatside, beaten off the hook by a fumbling, inept attempt with some short, toy-like gaff. Now you're angry and frustrated. You come across a couple of fishing catalogs and feverishly page through the morass of equipment. Some of the stuff looks good, some looks like it's designed more to seduce fishers than fish. You begin adding up prices, and realize how rapidly a careless mass order could bust your budget, not to mention take up more space than you have available onboard. So what works, what doesn't? How much must you spend? Where do you begin? We first review the options and then make specific recommendations.

Handlines

Let's start our gear discussion with the most common fishing mode: trolling a line off the back of your sailboat or power cruiser. At one end of the spectrum is the simple snubber line, a handline featuring an in-line elastic section made of surgical tubing, bicycle-tire inner tube, or various other kinds of stretchy rubber sections designed to dampen shock loads—in this case, of striking or surging, hooked fish (fig. 2-1). The advantages are simplicity, low cost, com-

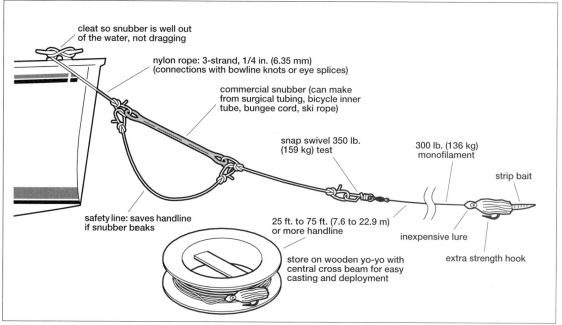

cleat so snubber is well out
of the water, not dragging

nylon rope: 3-strand, 1/4 in. (6.35 mm)
(connections with bowline knots or eye splices)

commercial snubber (can make
from surgical tubing, bicycle inner
tube, bungee cord, ski rope)

snap swivel 350 lb.
(159 kg) test

300 lb. (136 kg)
monofilament

strip bait

safety line: saves handline
if snubber breaks

25 ft. to 75 ft. (7.6 to 22.9 m)
or more handline

inexpensive lure

extra strength hook

store on wooden yo-yo with
central cross beam for easy
casting and deployment

Fig. 2-1. Snubber line—a handline, usually deployed for trolling, with a shock-absorber. Snubber lines can be fastened to cleats or suspended from makeshift outriggers, such as downwind poles, allowing multiple-line trolling at minimum initial cost.

pact size for storage, not having to stop or slow down to land fish, and the ability to confer occasional success for smaller-sized fish. The disadvantages are that the leader and hook must be relatively heavy and therefore more visible, because there is no mechanized drag device to take over and ease the strain after the elastic is at the end of its stretch. At this point, it becomes an all-or-nothing situation, severely limiting the array of presentations and, therefore, potential strikes. Fish that do strike are often ripped from the hook under the strain; over time, the cost of all the lures (even cheap ones) and hooks lost by larger fish breaking the line can add up.

An attended handline fished while drifting or anchored, on the other hand, can be one of the most effective, least expensive, and simplest means of catching fish. Large, strong fish still present a problem better handled from a cruising boat with devices featuring greater line capacity and a mechanized drag, but you can whip some sizable quarry using professional handlining techniques. Did you know, for example, that high-seas swordfish longliners handline every fish once the leader is detached from the

mainline? Granted, most of these fish have been struggling for hours and are usually tired, yet it is still an unforgettable experience to raise a 1,000-pound (454 kg) class marlin, swordfish, mako, or tiger shark with simple hand pressure on a 300-pound (136 kg) monofilament handline. This same line, in trained hands, can make fast work of a freshly hooked 50-pound (23 kg) mahi mahi or 100-pound (45 kg) yellowfin tuna that might take a considerably longer time to boat with a rod and reel.

Although attended handlines are more effective than those trolled with a snubber, they still suffer the drawback of needing to be heavier grade than would be possible for the same fish species and size targeted with other gear. Heavier gear is more visible underwater and may seriously curtail the number of strikes, especially if you are fishing in an area that receives any appreciable pressure from other fishers. We experienced many days of reef fishing for large yellowtail snapper off the Florida Keys, for example, when any leader size larger than 12-pound (5 kg) test resulted in refusal, and we can cite similar examples involving other reef, coastal pelagic, and pelagic fish

Yo-yos loaded with various sizes of monofilament fishing lines can be efficiently hand-fished. Keep these handy in the cockpit for opportunistic use.

species. Most have excellent eyesight and may refuse unnatural-looking offerings, regardless of location.

Another disadvantage of handlines is the inability to impart as much speed to lures and baits as would be possible with devices geared for this purpose, like fishing reels. Fast, erratic action often makes the difference between eliciting a strike and having a fish follow your offering, only to lose interest and swim away.

Rail-Mounted Reels

The next step up is a rail-mounted revolving-spool reel, the biggest and largest capacity that you can afford. It can be virtually any model designed for use on a fishing rod, or you might choose a commercial-fishing deck winch. For example, for many years we have used a Penn Senator 12/0 sport fishing reel (capacity 800 yds./732 m of 80 lb./36 kg monofilament fishing line), loaded with 200-pound (91 kg) test monofilament, simply attached to the aft rail with the standard mounting hardware supplied with the reel. More recently, we acquired a commercial deck winch for this application, an Alvey 1225RM Reef Master (capacity 1,083 yds./1,000 m of 80 lb./36 kg monofilament fishing line). It has the

added advantages of a swivel mount, a short fiberglass boom with roller guide, faster retrieve, larger industrial-grade drag system for smoother performance and lower maintenance, and more rugged construction designed for heavy-duty users.

The adjustable-drag feature of a rail-mounted reel has numerous advantages over a snubber line, including no more break-offs during the initial strike, resulting in more successful hook-ups and fewer lost lures and hooks; greater flexibility for deploying different types of lighter leaders and more lifelike lures, thereby eliciting more strikes; and the ability to tire and eventually land much larger fish by taking advantage of drag adjustability and greater line capacity. (In 1998 a commercial fisher landed a 708 lb./321 kg blue marlin on an Alvey in Hawaii.) Thus, your potential for fishing success is increased exponentially, in terms both of number and size of fish, over snubber lines.

Disadvantages? Although rail-mounted reels should probably have a place in the repertoire of virtually any cruising boat's fishing gear, they do have the shortcoming of being fixed in one place. This requires positioning the boat to always be clear of the line during a fish fight, which is occasionally inconvenient for short-handed crews operating with limited maneuverability. Also, both handlines and rail-mounted reels generally attach the fisher more directly and with stronger line to potentially very large, fast, strong fish, which increases the possibility of danger. An accidental loop of line around the end of a fishing rod can result in a broken rod tip. That same errant loop of 300-pound (136 kg) line around a finger can easily remove it if the fish is large and surges quickly. Stepping into a loose coil of line or tangling it around your hand or wrist can be fatal, as it was recently for a sportfishing mate off North Carolina. He was last seen by his horrified shipmates being hauled off into the depths behind

Attended handlines. Barbadian commercial fishers using 300 lb. (136 kg) test monofilament handlines to catch mahi mahi *(Coryphaena hippurus)* and yellowfin tuna on whole flying-fish baits in the southeastern Caribbean. Casting to *(top)* and landing *(bottom)* a nice bull mahi mahi.

a blue marlin that sounded suddenly near the boat at a moment when he had the leader looped around his hand.

Stand-Up Outfits

A stand-up outfit is just what it says—a rod and reel designed for use while you are standing up, rather than sitting down in a fighting chair. This arrange-

Rail-mounted reels. Penn Senator 12/0 *(top)* and Alvey 1225RM Reef Master *(bottom)*. The hand crank for the Alvey is on the opposite of the spool, not visible here (see photo page 33).

ment allows the fisher to move freely around the boat as needed during the battle; for example, in response to a sudden, fast, sustained change in direction or depth on the part of a strong fish. The line strength is lower than what is generally used with handlines and rail-mounted reels, the rod (not your hands) controls line pressure and trajectory, and the reel compactly stores the line, removing the hazard of loose coils on deck or around body parts. These factors reduce the strain and directness of the connection between the fisher and the fish. Stand-up outfits solve the fixed-position drawback of rail-mounted reels, and reduce potential hazards and inefficiencies associated with heavier, more direct connections.

All things considered, one could make a strong case that by far the most versatile and effective fishing tool for cruisers is one of the heavier-grade stand-up outfits. This tackle is specially designed for efficiently subduing large, offshore gamefish by changing the distribution of strain compared to longer boat rods that require a fighting chair. The strain from these short, compact rods is transmitted to the lower hips and shoulders via a harness-and-belt combination (see fig. 3-20). This allows the fisher to apply pressure comfortably and effectively to the fish in short, rhythmic, raised strokes of the rod, followed by smooth drops of the rod and simultaneous winding of the reel handle to gain line. The design originated from the southern California long-distance party-boat fishery. It has been subsequently promoted and popularized by well-known angler Marsha Bierman, who spends much of her time fishing for giant billfish at various world hot spots, using stand-up gear to land marlin up to 1,000 pounds (454 kg) and more in amazingly little time.

Stand-up outfits feature the same conventional (i.e., revolving-spool) offshore game reels as their boat-rod counterparts. The most common sizes of matched rod-and-reel combinations are for use with 30-pound (14 kg), 50-pound (23 kg), and 80-pound (36 kg) monofilament line. We recommend a 50-pound (23 kg) class stand-up rod and a high-quality, matching conventional reel with maximum line capacity as the best combination of strength, versatility, and ease of handling in this range. This is probably the most expensive outfit you will consider. It will set you back initially but, if properly maintained, will easily provide a lifetime of service, and it is compact enough to deploy from your dinghy. It's capable of catching everything from tuna, wahoo, mackerel, jack, cod, halibut, grouper, snapper, and mahi mahi (also called dolphin or dorado) to large marlin, swordfish, and sharks—you name it.

Wire-Line Gear

The last heavy rig you should strongly consider is a wire-line outfit, developed in southeastern Florida for deep-trolling and bottom-fishing. This often consists of a Penn 9/0 or similar reel loaded with 100-pound (45 kg) Monel trolling wire and mounted on a shortened, compact, bent-butt rod with a specialized swivel tip. Alternatively, you could use the rail-mounted Alvey 1225RM Reef Master already described. We strongly recommend the use of

The versatile 50 lb. (23 kg) stand-up outfit. Jon Broadhurst with bohar snapper *(Lutjanus bohar)* caught trolling a Rapala Countdown Magnum from an inflatable dinghy *(top*, Tonga). Ken Kiddie subdued *(bottom)* this striped marlin *(Tetrapterus audax)* en route from Tonga to New Zealand.

Monel, *not* stainless steel wire, which tends to corrode down in the spool and then later breaks at those weakened spots. The lower initial cost isn't worth it.

Wire line represents the simplest, most direct way to troll lures and baits deep, enabling you to wreak havoc on wahoo, tuna, mackerel, jack, grouper, snapper, and many others offshore, inshore, and near reefs, wrecks, and seamounts. It's simple to use—no setting the hook, no removal from the rod holder, no belt and harness—all you do is crank the reel handle whenever the fish is not taking line off the spool until you get it boatside. The Monel is impervious to the elements. It's not considered very "sporty," but it will out-catch your monofilament surface rigs two to one over time. Shortcomings of trolling wire line are that it is generally not as effective for mahi mahi, and it may not handle the really big ones, especially larger billfish. But when we need a good eating fish, particularly nearing port or some significant fish-producing area, we often deploy only the wire line because of its effectiveness (see the photo of the wahoo on page 5).

Wire is superior for deep (150 ft./46 m plus) bottom-fishing while drifting or anchored. Its high density, small diameter, and weight greatly assist direct, vertical drops on specific bottom features that are holding fish. It is less affected by current, which may cause other line materials to belly and angle off away from the target area on the seafloor. Another important feature is lack of stretch, so that bites are transmitted more directly from great depths to the rod or boom, giving the operator more information about what is happening to the baits than would be possible with monofilament, for example.

Spinning Tackle

Thus far we've discussed only revolving-spool (conventional) reels, the normal choice for most hook-and-line fishing pursuits using any line strength in excess of 30 pounds (14 kg). We focused only on reels designed for trolling and other applications that involve deployment by releasing the tension on the spool and letting the line run out (or down, as the case may be), rather than casting a bait or lure through the air at a target. Although entire categories of conventional casting reels exist, it's fair to

Lyretail grouper (*Variola louti*, also called coral trout) caught deep-dropping with wire line at a depth of 490 ft. (149 m), South Minerva Reef, Tonga.

say that, at least for saltwater applications, fixed-spool, open-face spinning reels are most widely used for light-tackle casting. They also work well for light-duty trolling, bottom-fishing, drifting, and reef-fishing.

Why might a cruiser consider adding a spinning outfit or two to the vessel's complement of fishing gear? These outfits are highly versatile, light, compact, easy to handle, and feature smooth, adjustable drags, high line capacity, fast retrieve rates, and the ability to cast baits and lures a considerable distance through the air to a sighted fish, sign of fish, or likely looking lair. They are capable of catching some fairly large fish. For example, heavy (20 lb./9 kg) spinning tackle is standard charterboat gear for pursuing sailfish averaging 45 pounds (20 kg) and tarpon to well over 100 pounds (45 kg) in the Florida Keys, and giant trevally to 100 pounds (45 kg) at Christmas Island, a Central Pacific atoll. A lighter spinning outfit (e.g., 10 lb./4.5 kg) is perfect for effectively presenting small, light, delicate lures and baits to a wide range of fish species and sizes. It is one of the best choices for dinghy and shallow-water, shore-fishing expeditions made from cruising boats.

Fly-Fishing

We believe it's safe to say that fly-fishing gear is not a necessary component of a cruiser's fishing arsenal. This mode of fishing may cause you to imagine a stuffy guy dressed in waders and a goofy-looking hat, smoking a pipe, and flicking a light wisp of a rod back and forth in an effort to artistically present a microscopic fake bug to a tiny trout. What's this got to do with cruising? Well, the sport of fly-fishing has broadened its horizons considerably during the last two decades. Saltwater fly-fishing has become very popular and commonplace, with magazines and large sections of fishing catalogs dedicated to it. Under rare circumstances, it is actually the most efficient means of capturing some desirable marine and freshwater fish species. Most people, however, do it just for fun.

JENNIFER HOMOLA

Blue smalltooth jobfish (*top, Aprion furca*, Family Lutjanidae, Tonga) and Gregg "No Mercy" Homola fighting *(bottom)* a 47 lb. (21 kg) bull mahi mahi offshore of Islamorada, Florida, both on spinning tackle.

Fly casting is fundamentally different than casting with spinning or other tackle. Instead of the weight of whatever you have tied to the end of your line carrying the cast, the weight of the line itself propels a fly cast to the target. This allows the presentation of extremely delicate imitations of, say, shrimp, crabs, and small fish on light leaders to wary fish with good eyesight, like bonefish and various large members of the jack family. Your voyage might also take you to some of the world's great trout-fishing destinations, like Alaska, New Zealand, or Chile. It's not as hard as it looks, the gear takes little space (we have four fly rods aboard), and you might enjoy it. We give you all the information you need to get started in appendix 3.

Selecting Tackle

Snubber lines, other simple handlines, rail-mounted reels, and stand-up rods and spinning outfits of various descriptions can all be used effectively by cruisers for drift- and bottom-fishing, as well as for

Rainbow trout (*Oncorhynchus mykiss*, 5¼ lbs./2.4 kg) caught on fly gear from an inflatable dinghy, Lake Aniwhenua, New Zealand.

trolling. We usually lean toward the heavier end of each tackle spectrum for two reasons: (1) we're more interested in successfully landing a fish than in a lengthy, epic battle by virtue of ultralight gear; and (2) our boats tend to be slower and less maneuverable than, say, many purpose-built sportfishing vessels, reducing our ability to recover line on a hooked fish.

What's right for you? We strongly recommend buying the highest quality tackle your budget can stand because, over the long run, you'll save money. Nevertheless, don't despair if you've already spent most of your money on other gear—you can still do well with some inexpensive arrangements. For example, a single handline, homemade snubber, and some hooks (even one) are enough to get started. Effective lures can be fashioned from scrap materials, natural baits from flying fish or squid that end up on deck overnight. The other extreme is a full complement of rail-mounted reels, wire-line outfits, stand-up conventional outfits, and spinning outfits—maybe even a fly rod or two—and a bunch of store-bought lures and accessories.

We start with a set of simple recommendations covering every cruiser fishing situation and budget, distilled from the massive array of fishing gear on the market (table 2-1). This is professional gear we can specifically recommend based on hard-earned commercial experience. Numerous alternative brands and equipment certainly work just fine, but we have personally abused everything listed in the table over the years, and we know it's rugged and rebuildable, has good worldwide parts availability, represents good value for the money, and will serve you well.

You will learn much more about when and how to use the different outfits in table 2-1 for trolling, casting, drifting, and bottom-fishing in chapters 3, 4, and 5, enabling you to decide what best suits your personal aspirations and finances. For now, let's go ahead and assume you have purchased some shiny new gear and appropriate line for loading your reel(s) or handline spool.

Connections

Before we go further, let's review exactly how to make the same strong, reliable connections used by professional fishers the world over. Many beginners

No Offense to Competing Brands!

Our particular brand recommendations throughout this book bear no negative connotations for competing manufacturers. Yet, highly specific advice is critical for new fishers, and those of us in the professional fishing business with experience helpful for dispensing such advice have inevitably settled on a subset of what may be equally good brands. This choice doesn't imply that other brands are inferior, only that we were highly successful with those recommended.

find this subject intimidating or bewildering, sometimes after reading entire books dedicated only to fishing knots. We have good news: the professionals keep it simple. Wander down to the docks at any charter or commercial fishing port and start asking about the fifty-seven knots you just read about, and no one will know what you're talking about.

Individual systems vary and, not surprisingly, top fishers tend to be independent and highly opinionated. Despite variations between fishing operations, you could probably imitate the system of any seasoned pro and be successful. We've dis-

tilled this information to a minimum set of knots and other connections, which is all you need to know (table 2-2). We present a few other specialty knots later.

Briefly review these connections now without trying to tie them and then forge ahead. Each time you encounter a new knot or connection—for example, in the sequential instructions that follow on setting up your gear—refer back to the specific connection required and learn it. Keep in mind the following axioms of successful knot-tying and—with a little practice—you will be able to accomplish each connection quickly, easily, and professionally.

- There's nothing especially complicated or difficult about it.
- Pay attention to proper setup—general orientation (i.e., what to hold in which hand, and with what fingers) to create the right twists, tensions, or insertions.
- Pay close attention to proper tightening, making sure the finished product is neatly and correctly finished. It helps to prelubricate monofilament knots with saliva before tightening.

TABLE 2-1. **GEAR OPTIONS FOR BASIC HOOK-AND-LINE FISHING EQUIPMENT**
(SEE APPENDIX 1 FOR SUPPLIERS)

Item	Specific Recommended Options	Approximate Price
Handline	20 lb./9 kg Ande monofilament	$6
	100 lb./45 kg Ande monofilament	$6
	300 lb./136 kg Ande monofilament	$6
Handline storage spool	Capt. Harry's wood yo-yo, small (6 in./15 cm I.D.)	$22
	Plastic yo-yo, small (alternative)	$1
	Capt. Harry's wood yo-yo, large (9 in./23 cm I.D.)	$32
	Plastic yo-yo, large (alternative)	$3
Rubber snubber	commercial, made for fishing	$7
Backing/safety line	¼ in. (6.35 mm) three-strand polyester	$0.15 per ft. (305 mm)
Handline/snubber/spool	Turbo Dog Fishing Handline	$10
Rail-mounted reel	Penn Senator, largest you can afford	$59 to $355
	Alvey 1225RM Reef Master Reel	$350
Wire-line outfit	Capt. Harry's Combo (Penn 115L/CHSWC)	$460
Stand-up outfit	Penn 50TW International/5-ft., 6-in. Gold Cup Combo	$625
Spinning outfit—heavy	Penn 850SS/2-piece (20 lb./9 kg) spinning rod	$185
Spinning outfit—light	Penn 4400SS/Gold Cup Model GCS60610 rod	$122

TABLE 2-2. SUMMARY OF CONNECTIONS FOR HOOK-AND-LINE FISHING

Connection	Application
Bimini twist	forming monofilament double line for leader construction
Uni-knot	joining monofilament, either line to line or line to terminal tackle
Albright special	joining monofilament to single-strand wire
Improved clinch knot	joining lighter monofilament to terminal tackle
Haywire twist	joining single-strand wire, either wire to wire or to terminal tackle
Crimp	joining heavier monofilament or any multistrand wire to terminal tackle

---

♦ Leave a ¹⁄₁₆-inch (1.6 mm) or so tail of bitter end when you trim your connections. Trimming *too* close can cause problems.

♦ Carefully discard all monofilament and other trimmings in your garbage bin. Fishing line that ends up in the bilge may become entrained in bilge pump impellers, causing at best a blown fuse or popped circuit breaker, and often a damaged pump. *Never discard monofilament overboard—it is nonbiodegradable and hazardous to marine life and birds.*

BIMINI TWIST

The Bimini twist (fig. 2-2) is the strongest knot for formation of that all-important double line. A double line is just what it says it is—instead of a single strand of line leading out to your offering, you now have folded the single line back upon itself, braid-

ing it neatly along a considerable length, and secured this braid with a knot. It's twice as strong, twice as abrasion-resistant. Most often you'll use another knot to add a further length of heavier single-strand line to the end of the double line to create a shock leader. The double line is usually closer to the strength of the shock leader material, which results in a stronger line-to-line connection.

There are a few alternatives to the Bimini twist. One is the spider hitch, faster to tie but weaker. We recommend keeping it simple by learning the best knot. Beginners probably find this knot more intimidating than any other, which is why we are presenting it first. *This is a very simple knot—essentially, a series of five half hitches.* Proper setup is the key for smooth execution. Take the time to measure a few distances first, tie it a few times, and you'll get perfect results.

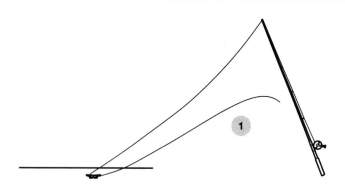

(1) Start your Bimini twist by placing your fishing rod in a rod holder. Locate a nearby handy projection, such as a cleat. Loosen the reel drag and strip out an amount of line approximately equal to double the distance between the rod tip and the cleat.

Fig. 2-2. The Bimini Twist.

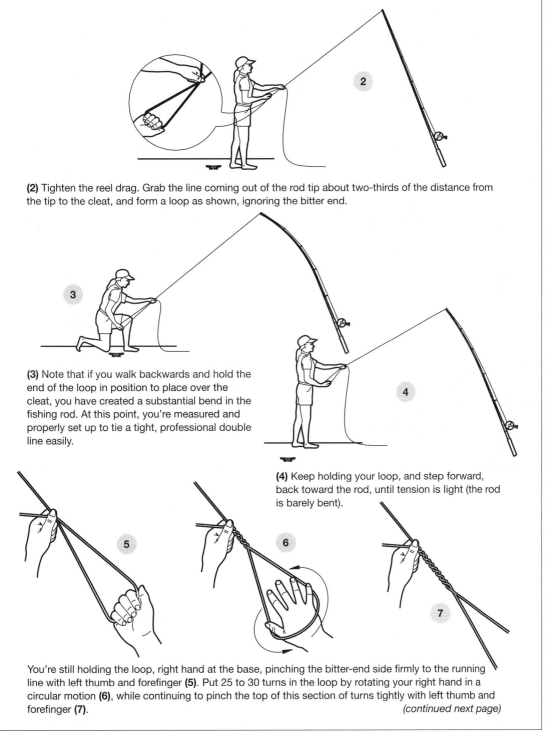

(2) Tighten the reel drag. Grab the line coming out of the rod tip about two-thirds of the distance from the tip to the cleat, and form a loop as shown, ignoring the bitter end.

(3) Note that if you walk backwards and hold the end of the loop in position to place over the cleat, you have created a substantial bend in the fishing rod. At this point, you're measured and properly set up to tie a tight, professional double line easily.

(4) Keep holding your loop, and step forward, back toward the rod, until tension is light (the rod is barely bent).

You're still holding the loop, right hand at the base, pinching the bitter-end side firmly to the running line with left thumb and forefinger **(5)**. Put 25 to 30 turns in the loop by rotating your right hand in a circular motion **(6)**, while continuing to pinch the top of this section of turns tightly with left thumb and forefinger **(7)**. *(continued next page)*

Fig. 2-2. The Bimini Twist (*continued*)

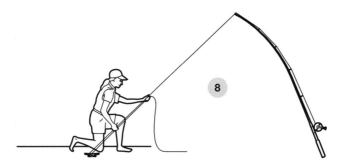

Hold onto your work firmly, and put the end of the loop over the cleat **(8)**. You should now have re-created that substantial bend in the fishing rod. Keep your right hand in between the two loop legs, and continue to grasp the top of the turns with your left hand. Without releasing tension on the turns with your left thumb and forefinger, carefully transfer these two fingers so that they now hold only the bitter end above the section of turns, under tension.

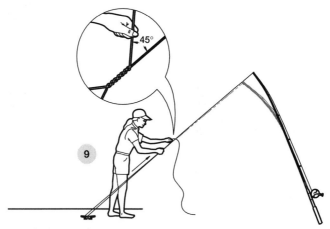

Form an angle of about 45 degrees between the bitter end and the running line, and keep tension on the bitter end **(9)**. Slide your right (loop base) hand up to the bottom of the section of turns, and continue to press upward, spreading the two loop legs as you push your right open palm between them toward the rod tip. Hold tension on the bitter end with your left hand as you move it along ahead of your right hand. *This step draws that long bitter end down through the upward-moving section of turns, under tension, and the bend in the fishing rod decreases as this occurs. Let this long bitter end travel (under tension) through your left thumb and forefinger. You'll feel the spin imparted by its descent through the turns and into the double line or loop. (Don't accidentally release the bitter end!)* Stop while you still have a moderate bend in the rod (and, therefore, moderate tension in the line in your hands).

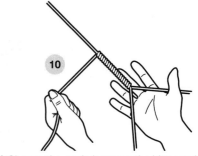

(10) Change the angle between the bitter end and running line to 90 degrees. Begin to push upward with your right palm.

Fig. 2-2. The Bimini Twist (*continued*)

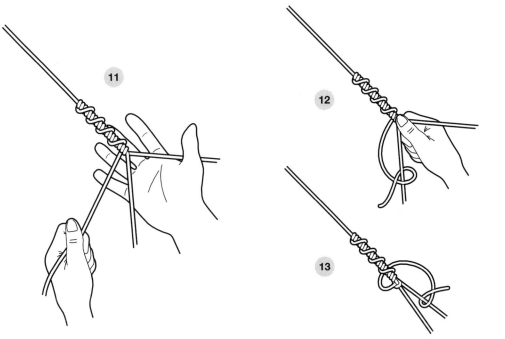

Here's the magic step. As you force your right palm up farther, the 25 to 30 turns begin, from top to bottom, to pack successively tightly together. The bitter-end side, although under tension from your left thumb and forefinger, begins to spin neatly in tight, even wraps back down the column of packed turns—like stripes on a barber pole—facilitated by increasing the angle between the bitter end and running line beyond 90 degrees **(11)**.

When these bitter-end turns reach the base of the column, at the juncture of the two loop legs, pinch firmly between your right thumb and forefinger. With your left hand, tie a half hitch on first one leg and cinch tight **(12)**, then the other leg of the loop, and cinch tight **(13)**.

(14) Finish by tying three half-hitches around both loop legs, sequentially cinching each one tight as completed.

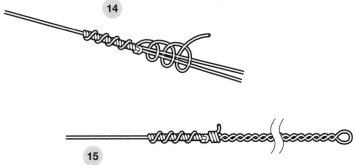

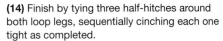

Let go of everything, and twang the whole affair like a guitar string **(15)**. Your double line will spin together into a beautiful, tightly braided leader. Trim bitter end.

Fig. 2-2. The Bimini Twist (*continued*)

UNI-KNOT

The uni-knot (figs. 2-3 and 2-4) is the single-most versatile and useful fishing knot. The same knot can be used to tie your line to terminal tackle or to join two lines together, and it has a breaking strength almost equal to that of the line. You could conceivably learn only this knot and fish effectively for a lifetime. It is also one of the easiest to tie. If it has a quirk, it's that you must tighten it properly.

ALBRIGHT SPECIAL

The main application of the Albright special (fig. 2-5) is to attach monofilament to single-strand stainless steel wire leader material without using hardware, such as a barrel swivel, thereby creating a leader that is lighter and less visible to fish. It's fast to tie and is in widespread professional use, particularly in lighter-tackle fisheries for species with sharp teeth, abrasive bills, or other rough anatomy

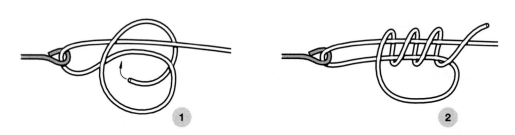

We find it easiest to form the initial loop and then hold this work in the left thumb and forefinger while making the passes of the bitter end through the loop using our right thumb and forefinger **(1)**. Make three passes, draw the bitter end through and out the last time **(2)**. Let go with your left thumb and forefinger, using them now instead to hold the terminal tackle.

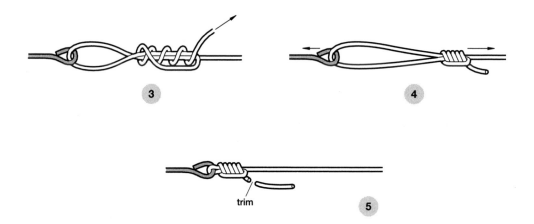

Holding the terminal tackle firm, tighten by pulling the bitter end slowly and firmly until the loop closes and the turns begin to grip the running line lightly **(3)**. Wet with saliva, and then pull the bitter end enough to bring the turns together, again lightly so that the knot can still slide easily along the running line in the next step **(4)**. Release the bitter end, grasp the running line with your right hand and the terminal tackle with your left, and pull your hands apart in opposite directions, steadily and firmly. Your lubricated uni-knot should slide down to the terminal tackle and stop; and the turns should tighten into a neat stack as you pull soundly **(5)**. Trim the end.

Fig. 2-3. Uni-knot, line to terminal tackle.

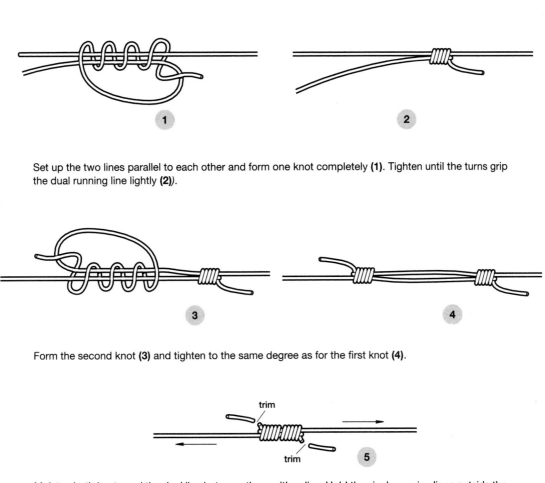

Set up the two lines parallel to each other and form one knot completely **(1)**. Tighten until the turns grip the dual running line lightly **(2))**.

Form the second knot **(3)** and tighten to the same degree as for the first knot **(4)**.

Moisten both knots and the dual line between them with saliva. Hold the single running lines outside the knots in both hands, then pull your hands apart steadily and firmly. The two knots will slide toward each other, abut, and the turns of each will stack neatly as you continue to apply pressure **(5)**. Trim the end.

Fig. 2-4. Uni-knot, line to line.

that's hard on monofilament. Rigs constructed with Albright specials instead of bulkier, more visible hardware often catch more fish, particularly in clear water live-bait fisheries, because the reduced weight and resistance may also allow live baits to swim more freely.

Like other line-to-line connections, this knot is strongest when the lines to be joined are of reasonably similar strength. This knot also requires a little extra attention to proper tightening.

IMPROVED CLINCH KNOT

Also known as a fisherman's knot, the improved clinch knot (fig. 2-6) continues to see widespread use, despite the fact that the uni-knot makes it unnecessary. We still find it handy for attaching monofilament less than 20-pound (9 kg) test to terminal tackle because it is easy to tie and tightens properly with little special attention in this line-size range. For approximately 100-pound (45 kg) test and larger monofilament, you may have to exert heavy pressure

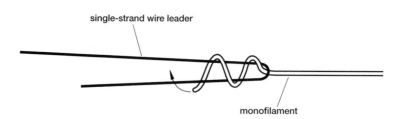

single-strand wire leader

monofilament

Form the tight, elongated loop depicted in the single-strand wire first, then run the monofilament through the end of the loop of wire, and begin wrapping it firmly, under light tension, all the way around both loop legs.

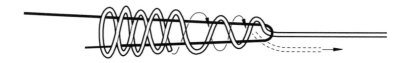

Continue this process away from the loop end for about seven turns, then start wrapping back over these seven or so turns toward the loop end, keeping this series of turns tight and approximately equal in number. Exit the loop with the bitter end of monofilament *the same way you went in*. Take any slack out of the series of monofilament wraps by pulling smoothly on the bitter end.

Lubricate with saliva, and tighten the knot with steady, opposing tension on monofilament running line and wire. The turns should pull down into a neat stack, as shown. Trim both monofilament and wire ends.

Fig. 2-5. Albright special.

to attain proper tightening, usually by attaching the terminal tackle to something solid and pulling with both hands to get the top turn flat onto the stack of lower turns. We find the uni-knot faster to tie and easier to cinch for any but lighter monofilaments.

HAYWIRE TWIST

The haywire twist (fig. 2-7) connects stainless steel single-strand leader wire or Monel wire to terminal tackle, or Monel wire "line to line." Because of the large number of desirable target species possessing sharp teeth, the low visibility of single-strand wire,

and the effectiveness of using wire lines for trolling and deep bottom-fishing, you'll likely use this connection often.

The need to connect Monel to Monel wire is relatively rare—perhaps a tangle occurred that kinked and damaged the running wire, or you want to top up a reel that is getting low on wire. Refer to figure 2-7.1, blending first one bitter end and running line, then repeating for the other bitter end so that you have one continuous section of blended turns. Barrel-wrap and break off the two bitter ends (fig. 2-7.2).

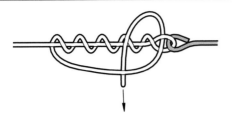

Tie as shown, using five to eight turns (more for lighter line). Grasp bitter end in your teeth, lubricate knot with saliva, and pull bitter end through while holding opposing pressure on the running line and terminal tackle.

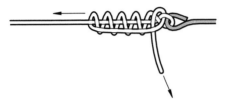

Continue pressure in these three directions. The turns will tighten and begin to descend toward the terminal tackle.

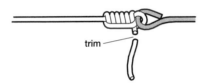

Release the bitter end from your teeth, and pull the running line and terminal tackle steadily and firmly apart. The turns should stack tightly, with no spaces or irregularities, *including* the top turn. Trim the end.

Fig. 2-6. Improved clinch knot.

CRIMPS

Because knots are more difficult to tighten properly, use crimps (fig. 2-8) with heavier monofilament (150 lb./68 kg to 400 lb./181 kg) and for strongest connections with multistrand-wire leader material of any strength. Crimps are fast to make and extremely handy for constructing a variety of heavy-duty fishing gear—handlines, leaders, deadly custom hook rigs. You will also find them useful for a range of nonfishing applications aboard your boat (e.g., lanyards, courtesy-flag halyards, tie-downs). Here again, you could buy a crimping tool, learn how to

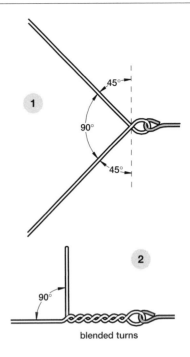

The key to a good result is to start the bitter end and running wire at 45 degrees from vertical, 90 degrees relative to each other **(1)**. Maintain these angles while you twist the two legs into tight, equally blended turns (five to eight, more for lighter wire), then bend the bitter end 90 degrees to the running wire **(2)**.

Hold the section of blended turns firmly between thumb and forefinger or with fishing pliers, and make a neat series of "barrel wraps" (equal in number to the blended turns), maintaining that 90-degree angle of bitter end to running wire **(3)**. *Do not trim by cutting with fishing pliers—this inevitably creates a very sharp burr that can slice your hand open as you are handling the leader.* Instead, bend the bitter end 90 degrees to itself, and use this "handle" to work it back and forth until it breaks off neatly, right at the end of the barrel wrap.

Fig. 2-7. Haywire twist.

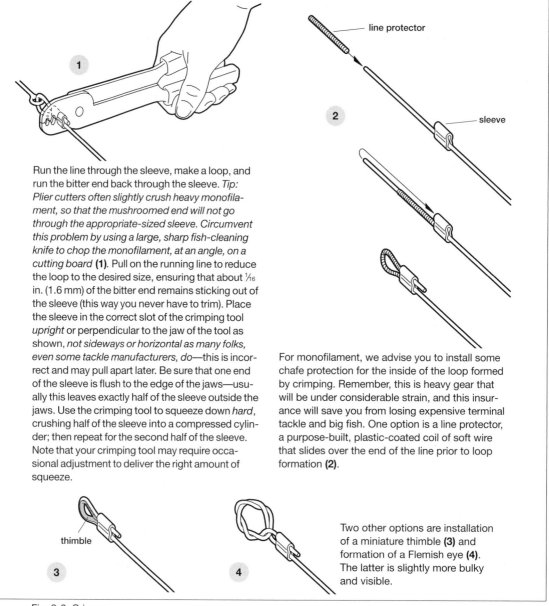

Run the line through the sleeve, make a loop, and run the bitter end back through the sleeve. *Tip: Plier cutters often slightly crush heavy monofilament, so that the mushroomed end will not go through the appropriate-sized sleeve. Circumvent this problem by using a large, sharp fish-cleaning knife to chop the monofilament, at an angle, on a cutting board* **(1)**. Pull on the running line to reduce the loop to the desired size, ensuring that about ¹⁄₁₆ in. (1.6 mm) of the bitter end remains sticking out of the sleeve (this way you never have to trim). Place the sleeve in the correct slot of the crimping tool *upright* or perpendicular to the jaw of the tool as shown, *not sideways or horizontal as many folks, even some tackle manufacturers, do*—this is incorrect and may pull apart later. Be sure that one end of the sleeve is flush to the edge of the jaws—usually this leaves exactly half of the sleeve outside the jaws. Use the crimping tool to squeeze down *hard*, crushing half of the sleeve into a compressed cylinder; then repeat for the second half of the sleeve. Note that your crimping tool may require occasional adjustment to deliver the right amount of squeeze.

For monofilament, we advise you to install some chafe protection for the inside of the loop formed by crimping. Remember, this is heavy gear that will be under considerable strain, and this insurance will save you from losing expensive terminal tackle and big fish. One option is a line protector, a purpose-built, plastic-coated coil of soft wire that slides over the end of the line prior to loop formation **(2)**.

Two other options are installation of a miniature thimble **(3)** and formation of a Flemish eye **(4)**. The latter is slightly more bulky and visible.

Fig. 2-8. Crimps.

use it properly, and conceivably fish efficiently for a lifetime without ever learning a fishing knot.

Getting Started

Suppose you selected a 50-pound (23 kg) stand-up outfit and 20-pound (9 kg) spinning rig from table 2-1, and they've just arrived. You open the packages

and extract the reels and rods. Now what? Handliners, not so fast—you should at least skim over this section because a few tips affect you.

TACKLE PRETREATMENT

Your Penn International 50TW needs only a light spray of Corrosion Block, WD-40, or similar anticorrosion product. Wipe off the excess with a rag. Applying this protective film *before* your reel gets loaded with line or sees the environment, and subsequently maintaining it, will save you headaches later on with the many small side-plate and other stainless steel screws that must be removed for periodic disassembly. If you let these freeze up from salt deposits, you'll have to drill them out or use other onerous techniques to remove them, transforming a simple job into a painstaking experience. Spray and wipe the roller guides of your stand-up rod, the reel seats of both stand-up and spinning rods, and your new Penn 850SS or other spinning reels the same way.

Several additional procedures enhance the performance of your Penn SS series spinning reel.

1. *Replace the bail roller lock washer.* Refer to figure 2-9: use a small slot-head screwdriver to remove the bail stud screw (part 36) and underlying star-style lock washer (part 36A). Take this washer to the local hardware store, select a small stainless steel lock washer of the same O.D. and sufficient I.D., and substitute it for part 36A. Part 36A may occasionally allow the bail stud screw (36) to become loose. This in turn creates a gap at the bail roller (part 35). Inevitably, the line falls into this gap, usually during a fast run by the fish, and the line binds and breaks. Replacing part 36A completely solves this pitfall.

2. *Replace the standard fiber drag washers with Teflon drag washers and lubricate the drag.* Refer again to figure 2-9: unscrew the drag knob (part 52) and remove the spool (part 47) from the crosswind shaft (part 39). Use a small slot-head screwdriver to pry the retainer ring (51) out of the spool, keeping a finger over the spool to prevent the retainer ring from flying out and getting lost. Insert the screwdriver into the center of the spool, gently pry out the stack of alternating fiber and metal washers that constitute the drag assembly, and lay them out flat, side by side, in order. Replace the fiber drag washers with the appropriate-sized Teflon drag washers (available from World Wide Sportsman, see appendix 1). Apply a *very* thin film of grease (Penn Muscle

Grease, Super Lube, or Daiwa Blue Grease) to each metal and Teflon drag washer by rubbing it between your thumb and forefinger (*do not overgrease*). Stack the washers in order, replace the assembly in the spool, lever the retainer ring back into its groove, and place the spool back over the crosswind shaft. Wiggle it a little to make sure it seats properly, dropping into position, and thread the drag knob onto the end of the crosswind shaft. The entire job takes only a few minutes after you've done it once, and you'll get longer, smoother service out of the Teflon washers. Whenever the drag starts operating unevenly, disassemble and clean it, replace any warped or distorted washers, regrease, and reassemble. You won't have to do this very often, and this small maintenance procedure plays a crucial role in the capture of many fish that would otherwise break the line due to a rough, sticky drag.

3. *Grease the internal mechanisms of the reel housing.* Refer once more to figure 2-9: with the anti-reverse lever (6E) on, unscrew and remove the reel handle (15) from the housing (1), unscrew the knurled bearing cover (232) from the side of the housing cover (45), use a small slot-head screwdriver to remove the housing-cover screws (46), and lift off the housing cover (45). Use a small brush to grease the main gear (8) and other internal mechanisms liberally, smearing everything with a protective coating, and reassemble. Stop short of filling the whole housing cavity with grease, which would inhibit the free, fast movement of the reel's retrieve. Reassemble, remembering to grease each housing-cover screw (46) for easy removal next time. This quick, easy job significantly lengthens the service life of your reel under harsh conditions.

Can you skip all of this and use your new tackle straight out of the box? After all, isn't it supposed to be ready to go? Sure, and it will even work fine for a while. The cruiser's environment, however, tends to place extra demands on equipment—we may not have gallons of freshwater available for flushing and spraying off gear, which may reside outdoors in a rod holder for days at a time. When equipment fails, we're not always right down the street from the

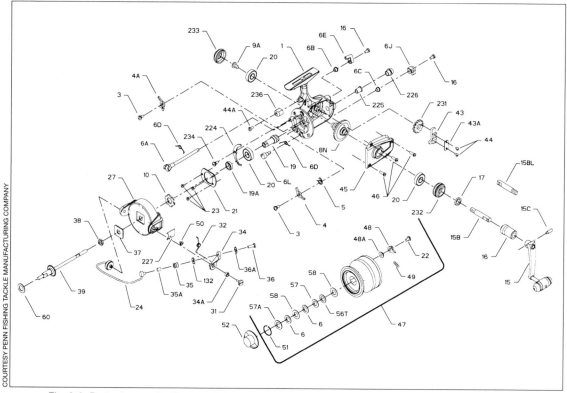

COURTESY PENN FISHING TACKLE MANUFACTURING COMPANY

Fig. 2-9. Parts diagram for Penn models 750SS and 850SS, typical of the Penn SS series skirted-spool spinning reels.

tackle repair shop, and the budget doesn't always permit us to throw money at our repair problems. Often, if something fails, we must either fix it ourselves or it stays broken. This atmosphere encourages more attention to preventive measures such as those already described.

MOUNTING THE REELS

Start by clamping the reels onto the rods. Most conventional reels, like Penn Internationals, have a bottom bracket, called a *reel clamp*, which is secured by two bolts with lock nuts. Remove these lock nuts, then remove the reel clamp from the two bolts and set it aside. Open the reel seat on your rod by backing off the two knurled locking rings enough so the reel seat will accept the reel's stand. Slide the forward end of the reel stand into the upper reel seat hood, slide the lower reel seat hood up over the back end of the reel stand, and secure firmly with the knurled locking rings. Slide the reel clamp back

over the two reel clamp bolts, which now straddle the reel seat, flush against the bottom of the reel seat. Start the two lock nuts. Tighten these lock nuts gently and evenly—take care not to tighten the nuts overzealously or you'll splay the bolt shafts, possibly enough to warrant replacement. Your reel may have a forward reel clamp secured by turnbuckles; if so, position it forward of the reel seat, usually on the foregrip of the rod, and tighten the turnbuckles evenly.

Spinning reels have only a stand on the end of a stem, no reel clamps, bolts, or nuts. Lock the stand onto the spinning rod's reel seat by the same method just described for conventional reels, tightening the two knurled locking rings successively by hand.

Alvey commercial deck winches have three mounting options (the photo at right shows two of these). Power cruisers may elect to install the flush deck mount somewhere on the aft cockpit covering board. Sailboat owners will likely select either the

G-clamp or spigot mount for attachment to railing somewhere near the transom. All options permit easy removal for stowage below when the reel is not in use.

LOADING REELS WITH LINE

The next step is to load your conventional and spinning reels, yo-yos, and/or commercial deck winches *properly* with suitable fishing line. Most pros select monofilament over the alternatives (i.e., Dacron, micron, braided nylon, linen) for general-duty use, whether trolling, drifting, or bottom-fishing above 300 feet (91 m) or so. For some bottom-fishing below this depth, and for certain trolling specialties, Monel wire may be the best alternative for revolving-spool devices (e.g., conventional sport reels, commercial deck winches). Monofilament is almost unanimously chosen for any spinning reel. Its ability to stretch also makes it the best handline material. Therefore, most cruisers should begin by selecting an appropriate strength and spool size of monofilament (see table 2-1).

Load any revolving-spool apparatus directly from the line spool. Place an axle (e.g., a stick, dowel rod, or taut line) horizontally through the spool of line. Run the bitter end through the roller guides of the fishing rod and to the reel, and attach it to the spool with a uni-knot. Put a glove on your left hand, grasp the line between your left thumb and forefinger, and wind the monofilament onto the reel. It's critical to maintain steady, firm pressure by squeezing your left thumb and forefinger while moving the line evenly back and forth across the spool. The line needs to pack level and under moderate tension—you should not see any loose loops or pile-ups, or be able to slide bunches of line back and forth with your thumb. Why? Because when you hook a fish on the appropriate drag setting, the pressure on the outer line will carry it into any loosely packed interior turns, causing it to bind and break. Continue winding the reel handle and, in the case of a Penn 50TW, 850 yards (777 m) or so later about ¼ inch (6 mm) or less of bare spool edge will be showing. Cut the line when the spool is filled to this point.

Loading Monel wire line on a revolving-spool reel is the same, except that a haywire twist is used for attachment and the spool of wire must also be

Mounting options for the Alvey commercial deck winch. Spigot *(left)*, G-clamp *(right)*, flush deck mount not shown.

kept under tension so that it does not overrun. Have a second person apply light hand pressure to the sides of the spool, or do it yourself by arranging the spool low and sufficiently close to apply similar pressure with the sides of your feet (fig. 2-10). When the reel is full, hold tension on the wire as you cut it, then secure, to avoid a bird's nest.

Remember that spinning reels have a fixed spool and must be loaded from *off the end* of the line spool to avoid twisting (fig. 2-11). The trick is to wind the monofilament onto the reel spool *in the same direction (rotation)* it comes off your spool of new line. Accomplish this by viewing the reel spool from *behind* the reel housing (yielding an end-on view of the spool *base*) and turning the handle (forward). Most brands (including the Penn SS series from table 2-1) deposit line counterclockwise. Place the line spool vertically on the deck, pull the end of the line upward, and note the direction it comes off the spool. If counterclockwise, you're set; otherwise, flip the line spool onto the opposite end. Run the end of the line through the rod eyelet nearest the reel, under the reel bail, and attach to the reel spool with a uni-knot.

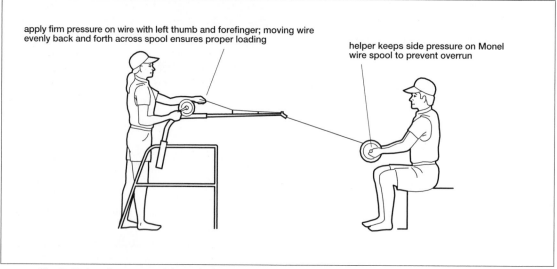

apply firm pressure on wire with left thumb and forefinger; moving wire evenly back and forth across spool ensures proper loading

helper keeps side pressure on Monel wire spool to prevent overrun

Fig. 2-10. Loading any revolving-spool reel with line.

Tighten the drag, pinch the line firmly between your right thumb and forefinger, and wind the reel handle until the spool fills to within ⅛ inch (3 mm) of the upper spool flange. Your spinning reel moves the spool out and in to distribute line evenly, so you won't have to move your right hand to accomplish this task; however, you still must provide appropriate tension to avoid loosely spooled line.

SETTING THE REEL DRAGS

Properly setting the reel drag is critical to fishing success. The fundamental purpose of the drag is to prevent the line from breaking, which may happen if the drag is too tight. Too loose, and there may be insufficient tension to hook and play a fish to the boat. If reel drag is

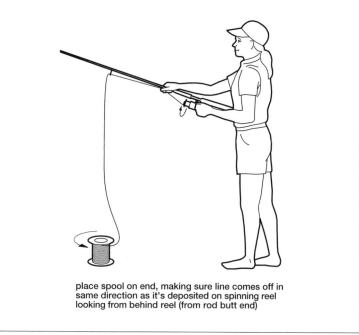

place spool on end, making sure line comes off in same direction as it's deposited on spinning reel looking from behind reel (from rod butt end)

Fig. 2-11. Loading a spinning reel with line.

very loose, the mere tension of your trolled lure will cause all the line to run off the spool.

Regardless of type, reels with adjustable drags are equipped with a convenient means of changing the amount of tension the drag device exerts on the reel's line spool. Fishers frequently need to check or change this setting, depending on the situation. Spinning reels have a drag knob on the end of the spool, usually turned clockwise to increase drag, counterclockwise to decrease drag. Less expensive conventional reels (e.g., Penn Senators) feature a star wheel at the base of the reel handle that increases the drag when rotated clockwise. Higher-end conventional reels (e.g., Penn Internationals) use both a drag control lever and preset control knob. Pushing the drag lever forward increases drag, pulling back decreases the drag tension, and rotation of the preset control knob determines the maximum drag setting possible to exert by use of the control lever. Some heavy-duty specialty reels (e.g., Alvey Reef Master and Elec-tra-mate) control all drag settings, from free-spool to full drag, with a single large knob.

What's the correct setting? As a general rule, 25 percent of the breaking strength of the line. How do you determine this? Attach the end of the line to a spring scale that is hooked onto something solid or held by someone. Back off a little, and raise the rod to a 45-degree angle, as though you are fighting a fish. Tighten the drag and back up, putting a bend in the rod. Adjust tension, for example, so that the scale reads 12.5 pounds (5.7 kg) for 50-pound (23 kg) test monofilament. As you walk backward (or as the scale holder steps steadily away from you), the bend in the rod should remain nearly constant and the line should flow smoothly, under tension, from the reel spool. This smooth drag action, at the proper setting, permits the capture of fish many times the weight of your line's breaking strength, as well as prevents line breakage due to snagging bottom or some other object. You will quickly develop a feel for the correct approximate drag settings for your tackle and be able to set the drag properly by estimating after pulling some line off the reel by hand.

Adjust the drag above and below this 25 percent value as you gain experience. Higher speed and wire-line trolling require lightening the drag setting to compensate for the increased shock of the hook contacting the fish's jaw, in order to avoid ripping the hook out rather than attaining a secure set. Experienced fishers often back the drag off almost completely after hook-up under the following circumstances.

♦ When a very large, fast fish hooked while trolling makes a long run, in order to reduce the possibility of a break-off due to increased water drag if the fish turns suddenly and creates a belly in the line.

♦ A shark or other predator homes in on the fish you are battling, to increase the chances of your quarry escaping the predator and, consequently, the possibility of it becoming your dinner instead.

♦ Two fishers are fighting fish at the same time, and the lines become tangled—taking all strain off one decreases the chance of line breakage while you get things sorted out.

♦ A hooked fish tangles the line around the anchor rode or a downrigger line—reducing the tension again buys time and prevents a fast chafe and break-off.

♦ An unanticipated species takes an offering on light leader, such as a sailfish eating a school-tuna bait on 30-pound (14 kg) monofilament; less tension may prevent an abrasive bill, jaw, gill plate, or other anatomical feature from wearing through the leader before you can boat your catch.

♦ A bottom fish becomes entangled on some structure—releasing the drag may fool it into relaxing enough to swim back out, whereupon quick tightening of the drag and sudden heavy pressure may allow you to wrest the fish to the boat.

♦ The crew is short-handed, a fish is boatside, and the reel operator must abandon station to assist the landing process; loosening the drag considerably before moving will save a broken line if the fish finds new energy and dashes off again suddenly.

Other circumstances demand tightening the drag beyond the 25 percent breaking-strength benchmark.

♦ Bottom-fishing usually dictates an initial drag setting of up to 40 percent of the line's breaking strength, both to drive the hook through the fish's jaw and to prevent a quick sprint of the panicked quarry back home to the inside of a wreck, cave, or other bottom feature from which extraction by line pressure may prove impossible.

♦ Increasing the drag to the vicinity of 33 percent of line strength for slower trolling speeds (e.g., below 4 knots) can sharply increase the rate of successful hook-ups, provided your offering has sufficiently strong hooks to withstand the additional drag without opening or breaking.

♦ Large fish that have sounded deep may sometimes be raised only by drag settings that risk breaking your line, from 66 to nearly 100 percent of the breaking strength.

♦ Experienced fishers nearly always temporarily increase drag later in prolonged battles to raise tiring fish and pressure them to the boat more rapidly, frequently by using hand or finger pressure on the spool, enabling quick release if the fish surges suddenly.

Remember, for now, the setting of 25 percent of line-breaking strength and see what it feels like at least once on a spring scale. That'll get you started, and you can come back later to some of the more advanced applications of varying drag settings as needed.

CREATING SHOCK LEADERS

Shock leaders are lengths of line stronger than the line on your reel, tied to the end of the line coming off the reel. Creating a double line usually makes the connection with the shock leader stronger (fig. 2-12). Shock leaders resist the chafing action of often violent contact between the leader and the head, shoulders, and wagging tails of struggling fish, as well as abrasion and other trauma more likely to occur close

to the boat. They prevent the loss of many fish, for example, that create inadvertent line-boat contact by making quick, last-minute dashes deep under the hull. They enable the crew to handle the leader with the fish at a greater distance from the boat, which can bring a much faster end to fish fights than would be possible by gently playing the fish all the way to the gaff with only the rod and reel.

You don't need shock leaders for gear already loaded with heavy monofilament line (over 130 lbs./59 kg) or for Monel wire line. Otherwise, create double lines using a Bimini twist, for example, on both your new stand-up and spinning outfits. Then use a uni-knot to tie the 50-pound (23 kg) double line of the stand-up outfit to about 50 feet (15 m) of the biggest monofilament that will pass through the roller guides after knotted (probably 80- to 100-pound/36 to 45 kg test for a noncustom fishing rod). Put a 15-foot (4.6 m) length of 50-pound (23 kg) test monofilament on your 20-pound (9 kg) spinner, again by attaching the double line to the leader with a uni-knot.

Now you're nearly armed, although probably not yet particularly dangerous. Use a uni-knot to tie something to the business end of your new shock leaders—a snap swivel for trolling use or perhaps a hook or lure. Otherwise, secure the unadorned line end to a rod eyelet or somewhere on the reel pending further instructions.

Gear Checklist

Table 2-3 lists specific tools, parts, and materials needed to perform procedures described in this

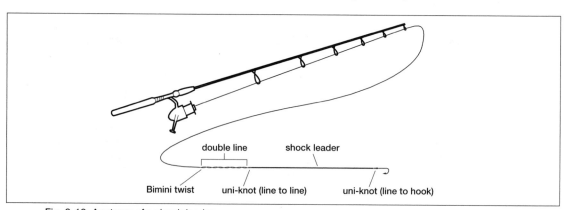

double line   shock leader

Bimini twist   uni-knot (line to line)   uni-knot (line to hook)

Fig. 2-12. Anatomy of a shock leader.

chapter—exclusive of crimps, lines, and tools for making connections, which are given in detail for specific rigging applications in the next chapter. The checklist feature is repeated in subsequent chapters, so if you want to execute specific actions or acquire particular terminal tackle or other gear, read through the procedure and then refer to the Gear Checklist.

Want to Set a World Record?

Formed in 1939, the International Game Fish Association (IGFA) meticulously maintains world records for a wide variety of marine and freshwater fish species. The organization is truly international, with official representatives in most countries you are likely to visit. Anyone is welcome to join this organization, whose primary objective is the promulgation of sportfishing and associated sound conservation practices. IGFA publishes and sends to all members a bimonthly newsletter and an annual book entitled *World Record Game Fishes*, which features a comprehensive, updated list of all records for various line strengths and other categories, and a wealth of other information about fish and fishing. This book also contains IGFA angling rules and a world-record application form. You should read all of this material carefully if the possibility of holding a world record appeals to you and your crewmates, and closely adhere to the specified hook arrangements, leader lengths, and other details.

We mention this now because many fundamental fish-catching tips and specifications given in this book may be highly effective but do not necessarily comply with IGFA rules. For example, the total length of double line and shock leader, or any other leader, may not exceed 15 feet (4.57 m). So, if you create shock leaders according to our instructions, go out for a day sail, and land some monster that you'd like to enter for the IGFA record book, you'll be disappointed. However, you can follow our instructions and then tailor specific measurements and rigs to IGFA directives so you're all set to play the world-record game. You might also find Jeanne Craig's *Fishing Fame: How to Catch a World-Record Fish* helpful and inspiring.

Unless fishing in a tournament or for the specific purpose of seeking a world record, many professional sportfishing captains emphasize tackle-rigging details that maximize the customer's chances of having a successful outing. Our instructions follow this same philosophy of increasing your odds of catching fish, regardless of the rules of any organization. Nevertheless, I have been a member of IGFA since childhood and highly recommend this stimulating and fun organization. After some experience, you may enjoy paging through the record book based on the fish species and sizes you are seeing at various locations you visit. You will find that line class records for specific categories are frequently swimming around your boat, should you care to seek them. We find that this particularly appeals to cruising kids (with all due respect to the many adult record-seekers out there).

Sound like fun? See appendix 2 for contact information for the International Game Fish Association.

TABLE 2-3. **CHECKLIST FOR GEAR AND TACKLE PROCEDURES, HOOK-AND-LINE FISHING**
(SEE APPENDIX 1 FOR SOURCES)

Item	Specifications
Anticorrosion spray oil	Corrosion Block, WD-40, Pennz-Guard, or CRC
Soft rag	
Screwdriver	slot-head, small (suitable screwdriver comes with new reels)
Stainless steel lock washer	match to star washer removed from your model of Penn SS reel
Teflon drag washers	match to fiber drag washers from your model of Penn SS reel
Reel grease	Penn Muscle Grease, Super Lube, Daiwa Blue Grease
Small grease applicator brush	
Wrench	suitable wrench comes with new reels

3

Offshore Trolling

For the purpose of this chapter, we define offshore trolling as follows: dragging any artificial
or natural presentation behind your boat while
underway with intent to catch a fish. Our discussion,
therefore, encompasses a full range of depths, habitats, and representative target species, from the
moment you untie the dock lines or raise anchor
until you return, whether from a half-day coastal
outing or a major ocean passage.

Your motivation is usually some combination of
food, entertainment, and education. Your personal
perspective and local conditions influence the specific trolling strategy you select. Subsistence may
prejudice your tactics—how full is your food storage locker or refrigerator? What is the current sea
state, wind velocity, level of crew fatigue and interest, boat condition? On the other hand, suppose
you've got plenty of fish for food. Might you still
wish to troll a line or lines? Quite possibly, for example, if the weather is nice and the kids are bored, or
you have never experienced the unforgettable sight
of a billfish pirouetting in midair, or you are curious
about what fish species might be available, for your
own knowledge and later reference.

This chapter provides you with a complete tem-
plate from which you may tailor an approach best
suited to the specific conditions of your current situation. The information should give you the maximum possible chance at catching a fish by trolling,
regardless of your vessel type, boat speed, location,
crew size, trip duration, and weather.

General Preparations and Perspective

At this point, we assume you have either a handline
with snubber, rail-mounted reel, stand-up outfit,
spinning outfit, or wire line rig—maybe more than
one—and that you have created shock leaders if
required for your tackle (see chapter 2). So far, so
good. Now you're standing there with the end of
your line, and you'd like to put something on it *that
works*; that is, some offering that will attract fish,
elicit aggressive feeding behavior (bites), securely
hook the attacker, and withstand the strain of escape
attempts long enough to subdue and extract your
quarry from the water.

How can we possibly help you with this question? After all, we don't know exactly where you are.
Furthermore, Class Osteichthyes (bony fishes) contains far more living species than any other class of
vertebrates (current best guess is twenty-one thousand), and Class Chondrichthys (cartilaginous
fishes, like sharks and rays) includes almost another
eight hundred species. These species do everything
imaginable—nip microscopic plankton from midwater; root in the mud for shellfish and other invertebrates; attack and eat large squid, other fish, even
mammals. Species composition varies wildly among
freezing polar seas, temperate zones, and the balmy
tropics, all environments frequented by modern
cruising vessels.

Despite this great diversity, the aquatic food
web of most locations features niches occupied by

predatory fishes. Some sit camouflaged on the bottom, waiting for hapless prey items (like your bait or lure) to venture close enough to engulf in a sudden rush. Others cruise at different depths—just off the bottom, midwater, or right at the surface, sometimes with pieces of fins and tails sticking out of the wave tops as they seek prey. Many are sleek and fast, capable of swimming for short bursts of at least 60 miles per hour (97 kph), often depending on raw speed to capture their prey. More bottom-associated species may depend on adjustments to color scheme, favorable current conditions, and low ambient light to get close to prey.

What does most of this huge variety of predator fish, inhabiting completely different aquatic environments, have in common? They tend to be opportunistic generalists—if they sense something that has roughly the right shape, size, or wiggle, the tendency is to pounce first and ask questions later. This, of course, is their downfall when subjected to the right trolling presentation, and also the reason we can dispense highly effective advice for application almost anywhere.

Nevertheless, your decision of what to tie on the end of the line will be most effective if you have knowledge, or at least a reasonable guess, of what you are seeking. How big and how fast are the potential targets, and what is your expected boat speed? Do the fish have sharp teeth, requiring wire leaders, or dentition that permits the use of more flexible, less visible monofilament? What sort of prey items do they tend to eat at your location—small fish, big fish, crustaceans, or mollusks—and what color are these prey items? Is the water murky or clear, deep or shallow, rough or calm, and is the sky sunny or overcast? If you are new to fishing or to your current area, what generally effective rigs, lures, or baits can you put out to "test the waters"? Keep these questions in mind as you review the remainder of the chapter.

Rigging for Trolling

Why do we construct "rigs" for trolling or other modes of fishing—what exactly are we talking about? Rigging is the assembly of quality components into an entity that is highly effective, tailored precisely to your intended use, and seldom commercially available in finished form. Sometimes we can tie a hook or lure directly to the end of our shock leader and dump it over the side into the wake. More often, a snap swivel and leader of specific length and material precedes the bait or lure. Let's focus first on the business end of your trolling rigs.

LURES

Good tackle, proper setup, and mastery of knots, connections, and leader construction are necessary, but not sufficient, for sustained fishing success. You must also know the right stuff to put on the end of the line for the prevailing conditions. Selection and effective presentation of potent artificial trolling lures represent the most attractive fishing options for seafarers—no hassle with capture, preservation, and preparation of smelly natural baits; no vigorous manual labor to impart lure action; no active hunting required. Drop them overboard, let them out, and they do all the work for you while you eat, sleep, navigate, keep watch, perform a repair, or relax and read a book. Like all other specific recommendations made in this book, we by no means imply that other brands, types, and methods don't work, only that what we present has attained *unequivocally deadly* status from extensive professional exposure. That doesn't stop us, nor should it discourage you, from constant experimentation and learning, but you may wish to acquire some surefire selections to accompany lesser known quantities.

Two fundamental categories of trolling lures are those with built-in hooks and those predrilled for inserting the leader through the body of the lure for attachment to a hook or hook rig selected and purchased separately by the fisher. Many lures in the former category are intended for relatively light-duty use and have the attractive characteristic of being ready to go. Those in the latter category may be rigged for everything from light to extremely heavy duty, requiring slightly more knowledge and time. Sometimes this factor may cause beginning fishers to attempt the use of lures with built-in hooks for situations that dictate stronger gear, contributing to lost fish from bent and broken hooks and other hardware failures.

Lures with Built-In Hooks

We have divided lures with built-in hooks into three fundamental categories: jigs, spoons, and plugs. My dad, Palmer, once told me that if he could have only one lure for anywhere in the world, it would be a white bucktail jig. He carries a light spinning rod armed with this lure almost everywhere he goes, and proceeds to catch a huge variety and size of marine and freshwater fishes with it. I once returned to a commercial wharf with supplies for a swordfish longline trip in Antigua, West Indies, to find him landing his second 20-pound (9 kg) tarpon. My brother-in-law and I have many times had to stop our fishing boats and clear large spreads of baits so Palmer could land something he'd hooked after sneaking his beloved bucktail out into the wake. Recently, we returned from a hike in New Zealand to find that Palmer had just landed a stunning 16-pound (7.3 kg) rainbow trout on . . . you guessed it.

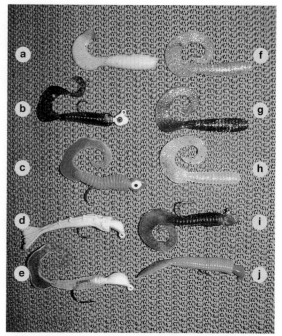

Fundamental types of jigs suitable for trolling. These light-duty lures are often used with spinning and light to medium conventional tackle. Jigs are more commonly used for casting or dropping and "jigging" near the bottom. We describe the vast variety of jigs for these purposes in chapter 4. These lures average 3½ in. (89 mm) in length: **(a, f, g, h)** plastic grubs in various colors (many similar products available); **(b, c, i)** flathead jig heads armed with plastic grubs in assorted colors; **(d, e, j)** Capt. Hank Brown's Hookup Lure armed with a plastic shrimp tail, a plastic grub, and a flat tail plastic bait body.

You should probably have a few of these aboard, and we discuss more details about jigs in subsequent chapters, but the new and increasing variety of plastic bait bodies deployed on plain jig heads are deadly for many fish species available to the trolling cruiser. These plastic baits thread easily off and on the hooks with molded lead heads (i.e., Captain Hank Brown's Hookup jigs, or jigs designed expressly for different bait bodies), which makes it easy to change color or style and to imitate a variety of invertebrate and baitfish species. Unlike bucktail jigs, most of these plastics have good wiggling action as they troll, even at slow speeds, with no manual jigging action applied to the trolling line (some types can easily be added to bucktails for enhanced action). Blackfin, skipjack, and yellowfin tuna, for example, sometimes pound black or dark worm and eel imitations trolled slow and deep on light tackle long after they are no longer feeding aggressively at the surface, and we could fill a small book with other examples.

Spoons are less subtle than jigs. They have a wild, flashy, erratic action particularly attractive to aggressive piscivores (i.e., fish that focus on other fish for a significant part of their diet)—especially in areas frequented by silvery, shiny baitfish species. Spoons work extremely well at slow speeds, allowing

seafarers to produce highly dynamic lure activity even when they are barely ghosting along. Larger spoons (e.g., Drone or Tony Accetta over 3½ in./890 mm) trolled deep are highly effective for wahoo, bluefish, mackerels, jacks and trevallys, salmons, tunas, barracudas, sea basses, groupers, and many other reef and bottom species. Smaller spoons (e.g., Clark and Krocodile under 3½ in./890 mm) trolled on light tackle can work well in the inshore shallows, rivers, and bays, and along the coast, as well as offshore in some situations.

All of these spoons, however, suffer the drawback of twisting the trolling line as they inevitably dance more on one rotation than the other, requiring the use of quality barrel and snap swivels.

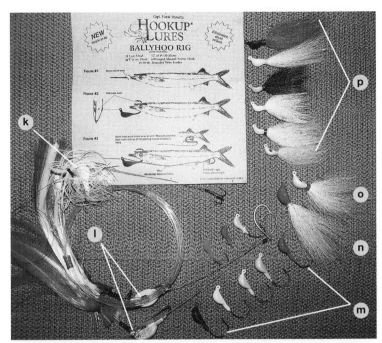

Other assorted Capt. Hank Brown's Hookup products: **(k)** model 01 Lure Rig (a form of stinger rig effective for slashing feeders like mackerel and wahoo);**(l)** Ballyhoo Rigs (note sea-witch-style skirts); **(m)** various lures for use with natural or plastic baits; **(n)** model 116 Bucktail (length approx. 4½ in./114 mm); **(o)** model 115 Bucktail (length approx. 3½ in./89 mm); **(p)** various model 110 and 112 Bucktails (avg. length 3 in./76 mm).

Strength of hook arrangements varies by brand, with many suitable only for light or medium duty, below 50-pound (23 kg) test tackle, sometimes no more than 10-pound (4.5 kg) tackle. Furthermore, the fixed, inflexible hook attachment of the Drone, Clark, and Tony Accetta spoons contributes to higher frequency of de-hooking because the leverage of the lure sometimes works against the set of the hook in the fish's mouth. Regardless, numerous situations exist where the high strike rates induced by spoons over-whelm any disadvantages.

Plugs, in general—almost always hard-material imitations of baitfish—suffer the same lack of hook strength common to most lures with built-in hooks. Improvements continue to be made as people realize their ability to attract some of the largest predatory fish species. Like spoons, many plugs have excellent action at slow speeds,

A selection of highly effective spoons for trolling: **(a, i)** Clark spoons (2 in./51 mm and 4 in./102 mm); **(b)** Reflecto spoon (1¾ in./44 mm); **(c, f, g, h)** Krocodile spoons (2⅝ in./67 mm and 3½ in./89 mm); **(d)** Johnson spoon (2½ in./64 mm); **(e, j)** Drone spoon (3¼ in./83 mm and 6⅛ in./156 mm).

often the key to success for power and sailing voyagers. This compels us to lighten the reel drag and make other adjustments to facilitate their use.

The sheer number of different plugs available on the tackle market is staggering. Many have hardware inappropriate for marine use (e.g., weak hooks, split rings, and attachment wires that easily corrode and break). Others are more ruggedly constructed, have good action, and elicit strikes, but have problems with hook arrangements that seriously curtail the number of successful hook-ups. Some just plain don't work—one manufacturer gave me a case of large well-made plugs that even glowed in the dark; to the best of my recollection, I never got a single strike on those lures.

Plugs are among the more expensive lures, so if you pick a dud it's more painful. Fortunately, several companies are now producing rugged, corrosion-resistant plugs that are both durable and highly effective for application in the cruiser's environment. The photo below illustrates a selection of proven killers that swim below the surface. The photo at right shows topwater plugs, designed to pop, gurgle, chug, and splash, drawing strikes with the appearance of a wounded baitfish and with the attendant sound and disturbance at the water surface.

Plugs armed with strong single and double hooks can handle open-ocean duty on up to 80-pound (36 kg) tackle, although all begin to have

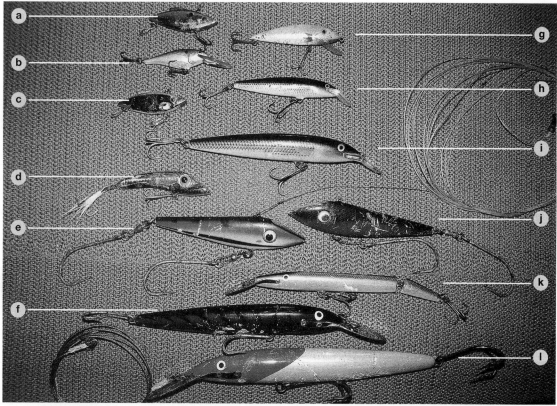

Swimming plugs that work well for trolling in a wide variety of cruising environments: **(a, c)** Original Rat-L-Trap, ½ oz. (14 g) sinking model; **(b)** small (2¾ in. 70 mm) floating shad-type swimmer (similar models made by Rapala, Lazer Eye, and others); **(d)** Invader plug (5 in./127 mm, 2 oz./57 g); **(e, j)** Australian Runners (8 in./203 mm, 3½ oz./99 g); **(f, l)** Rapala Countdown Magnum sinking plugs (9 in./229 mm, 3½ oz./99 g, and 10½ in./267 mm, 4½ oz./128 g); **(g)** small (3 in./76 mm) floating minnow-type swimmer by Cotton Cordell; **(h, i)** Rapala Countdown Magnum floating plugs (5½ in./140 mm, ¾ oz./21 g, and 7 in./178 mm, 1½ oz./43 g); **(k)** Rapala Sliver (7¾ in./187 mm, 1⅜ oz./39 g).

problems with successful hook-up and outright breakage when subjected to the rigors of crushing strikes from billfish and the largest wahoo, tunas, and sharks. We landed a 200-pound (91 kg) black marlin, for example, on an 8-inch (203 mm) skipjack-colored Australian Runner during an experiment under sail off the Pacific coast of Panama. However, the next day a larger marlin summarily broke both hooks off a 9-inch (229 mm) Australian Runner with one strike. A friend had three successive large, rugged plugs utterly destroyed by big dogtooth-tuna hits near an uncharted seamount off of Vanuatu (southwestern Pacific). To remedy this problem, some offshore professionals are experimenting with removing the standard hooks on plugs and rigging large single hooks to them with 400-pound (181 kg) test multistrand wire. This is difficult to do, however, without either interfering with the balance or action of the lure, or negatively influencing hook-up rates.

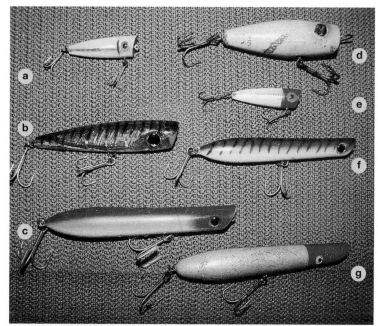

Surface or topwater plugs, normally cast and retrieved manually, but also suitable for slower-speed trolling under specific conditions: **(a, e)** Trouble Makers (2½ in./63 mm); **(b)** Yo-Zuri Hydro Tiger (5¼ in./ 133 mm, 1¾ oz./50 g); **(c, f)** Yo-Zuri Surface Cruisers (7 in./178 mm, 2⅛ oz./60 g, and 6 in./152 mm, 1⅜ oz./ 39 g); **(d)** Fred Arbogast Scudder (4½ in./127 mm, 1 oz./28 g); **(g)** Cotton Cordell Pencil Popper (6½ in./165 mm, 1 oz./28 g)—the nearly identical-looking Williamson Popper (6 in./152 mm, 3½ oz./99g) is an effective sinking-type surface plug. (All plugs shown are floating models.)

Nevertheless, for many cruisers, this end of the target spectrum is not of immediate interest, and an average range of captures possible on production plugs straight out of the box would more than satisfy their goals. At any rate, they could effectively challenge the giants using other types of baits and lures. Plugs armed with double hooks are stronger than those with treble hooks, which require lighter drag settings to prevent the hooks from opening. Both doubles and trebles effectively hook most species other than billfish, for which single hooks do far better. Match your tackle and your plug size, hook type, and strength to the target species.

Lures Designed for Custom-Hook Rigging
The majority of lures used for open-ocean trolling and a considerable amount of coastal trolling leave the decision of hook size, strength, style, material, position, number, and orientation up to the purchaser. This has the decided advantage of allowing us to create and maintain strong, lethal arrangements that can take great punishment (*Hark,* all of you handliners!) and are designed for specific target species. Rigging your own hooks demands additional expense and labor, but promises substantial rewards. The figure and photo on pages 44 and 45 illustrate a spectrum of top lure selections suitable for a full range of target species and sizes. We can make analogies between some of these lures and their lighter-duty cousins with built-in hooks.

Octopus skirts and trolling feathers, like jigs, may imitate either invertebrate or fish prey species and, therefore, are broadly effective. Trolling feathers have a lead head. Octopus skirts can either be fitted over trolling feathers or rigged with egg sinkers placed inside the bulbous head to provide the necessary

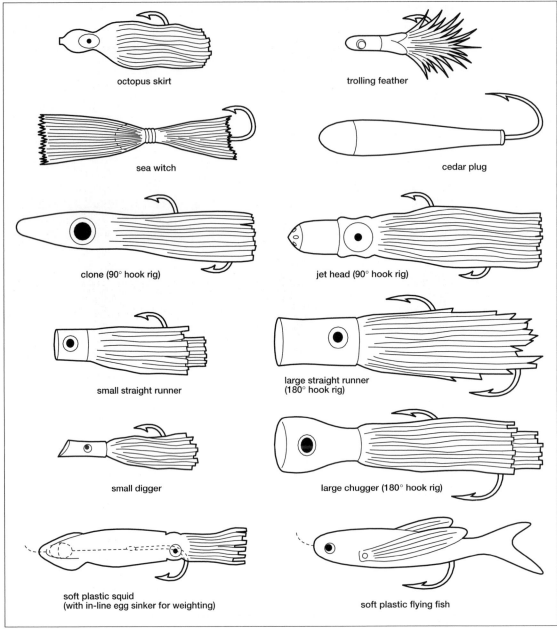

octopus skirt

trolling feather

sea witch

cedar plug

clone (90° hook rig)

jet head (90° hook rig)

small straight runner

large straight runner
(180° hook rig)

small digger

large chugger (180° hook rig)

soft plastic squid
(with in-line egg sinker for weighting)

soft plastic flying fish

A selection of highly successful trolling lures that require fishers to rig their own hooks, showing appropriate hooks and hook positions. **In the photo on the next page: (a)** Octopus skirt pushed down over a ¼
oz. (7 g) trolling feather, rigged with 30 lb. (14kg) test monofilament and 6/0 Mustad 7691 hook.
(b) Small digger similar to C&H Lil' Swimmer (we call the one in the photo a "Hawaiian jig"), with 4½ in.
(114 mm) skirt, rigged with 80 lb. (36 kg) test monofilament and a 7/0 Mustad 7691 hook. **(c)** Mold Craft
Hooker Softhead (5½ in./140 mm) rigged with 100 lb. (45 kg) monofilament and an 8/0 Mustad 7691 hook.
(d) Ultimate Junior (6 in./152 mm) rigged with 8/0 Mustad 7691S hook—100 lb. (45 kg) test monofilament
would be a common leader choice. **(e)** Yo-Zuri Flying Fish (6 in./152 mm) rigged with 7/0 Mustad 7691S
hook—100 lb. (45 kg) test monofilament would be a common leader choice. *(continued next page)*

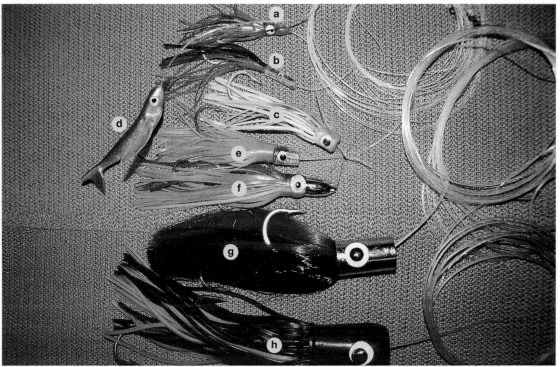

(f) Offshore Jet Head (8½ in./216 mm) rigged with a 180° hook rig, Mustad 7691S hooks (8/0 front, 7/0 rear)—use #8 stainless wire leader with this. **(g)** Iland Express (10½ in./267 mm) rigged with two 9/0 Mustad 7732 hooks at 180° and 300 lb. test monofilament. **(h)** Mold Craft Super Chugger (12½ in./318 mm) rigged with two 9/0 Mustad 7732 hooks at 180° and 300 lb. test monofilament—this is the same lure you see in the mouths of the shortbill spearfish (page 80) and of the striped marlin (page 17).

weight to make them swim realistically. They work well over a range of speeds, although their potency can be greatly enhanced—particularly at slower trolling speeds—by adding a strip of natural bait to the hook.

Cedar plugs represent an excellent way of capitalizing on the attractiveness of plug swimming action and appearance without many of the problems associated with those featuring built-in hooks, and at a fraction of the cost. These plugs are now available in various sizes and colors, or simply as old-style unpainted wood with lead heads. Adapting size and hook style to your target species can result in the capture of everything from pan-sized mackerel to large marlin (like the 440-lb./200 kg black marlin caught in 1997 by Captain Paul Mead on a 7 in./ 178 mm light green cedar plug rigged with a single hook near Vava'u, Tonga).

Clones and jet heads tend to run subsurface to deep, primarily imitating cephalopod (i.e., squid and octopus) prey items that dominate the diets of many predator fish more than most fishers realize. These lures, especially in color combinations ranging from pink or red to purple and black, wreak havoc with many species from near shorelines, reefs, and seamounts to the open ocean, particularly when trolled deep and fast (7 to 12 knots or more). For example, I have found logs, pallets, and other debris far offshore, climbed into the tower, and counted up to a dozen wahoo stacked under the object. I then proceeded to elicit the corresponding number of strikes on successive trolling passes by the object using an 8½-inch (216 mm) jet head on a wire line.

Sea witches are a "backwards" permutation of a trolling feather. Note that the long end of the skirt faces the boat when trolled, so that water pressure exerted by trolling folds it back over the lead head in a mushroom-shaped plume that pulsates with boat motion and the slightest of speed changes.

Fish love it, and the durable skirt material takes many strikes without falling apart.

Diggers, straight runners, and chuggers are all variations of lure heads developed largely from the recreational billfish fishery at Kona, Hawaii. All are designed to pop, smoke, and swim along the surface when trolled. Manufacturers worldwide now produce endless variations in every imaginable color and size. They catch almost any predator fish attracted to a splashy offering at the sea surface by trolling throughout temperate, subtropical, and tropical regions of the planet.

The slanted face of diggers causes them to wobble and throb as they zip from side to side, often throwing a little spray of water in front of them. These are extremely effective for pelagic and some coastal species in smaller sizes (i.e., 5¾ in./146 mm) on light (60 to 80 lb./27 to 36 kg) monofilament leaders, deployed from a relatively high angle (e.g., from a release clip attached to your arch, backstay, or bridge). Billfish are equally excited by the larger-size lures, but hook-up rates suffer. This may be because the fish is unable to get an accurate bead on the lure and simply misses it, or the fish tries to kill the lure rather than engulf it, and loses interest as the lure continues (unnaturally) to swim even after being nailed hard.

Straight runners and chuggers solve this problem by tracking in a steady line. Adjust size and hook rig to your intended quarry and make sure the lure breaks the surface at least once every five seconds or so, yet doesn't hop completely out of the water; once again, you have an offering that will effectively catch a huge array of species. These lures generally require enough boat speed to create the desired surface action and may be enhanced by adding a strip of natural bait. The primary targets of larger-sized (over 9½ in./241 mm) straight runners and chuggers are large billfish, so don't buy these for your snubber line or if you have no desire to tangle with these animals—stay with smaller sizes or other lures. No matter the size, we find that the soft-headed versions of these lures out-catch many of those manufactured with hard-material heads. This may be due to the more natural initial feel of the lure in the fish's mouth and the consequent fractionally longer time before rejection.

This may also be a contributing factor to the success of the relatively new soft-bodied replicas of various bait species, primarily squid and flying fish. Similar to current trends in realistic plastic bait bodies designed for use on jigs, the number of larger soft bodies designed for trolling with custom hook rigs is growing. Squid versions may be trolled on or below the surface, while the flying fish should be trolled skittering along on its outstretched wings. Note that at the time of this writing, we can recommend only the 6-inch (152 mm) size of flying fish due to apparent balance problems with the chin weight on larger models, which causes them to tumble and twist in an unsatisfactory manner. Both flying fish and squid can be devastating under some conditions but surprisingly impotent at other times. The squid are a good choice for trolling among a high density of scattered sargassum or other weeds and debris because they tend to snag less than most other lures, requiring less frequent clearing.

RIGGING LURES

You now know about some good lures, proper tackle preparation, professional connections, and shock leaders. Only two pieces of the puzzle remain: selection of trolling hooks, and construction of appropriate leaders using the correct materials, strengths, and lengths to suit your particular trolling tackle and intentions. Once again, let's start at the business end first.

Hooks are the downfall of many frustrated cruisers, especially in trolling mode. Think about the load that must be borne by a hook traveling along at 7 knots when it suddenly becomes snagged in a massive object traveling 60 mph (97 kph) in the opposite direction, reel drag setting notwithstanding. Little wonder that frail, inexpensive hooks straighten out, snap off, or disconnect due to the opening

---

Making and Repairing Your Own Lures

On a stringent budget? Wondering as you look over these fancy, sometimes expensive, commercially produced lures, why you or your kids can't make up some effective lures yourselves? The answer: *of course you can!*

Cedar Plug

To make a form of cedar plug (see figure on page 44), carve, whittle, and sand a stick, piece of dowel, or other piece of wood **(1)** to approximate its shape **(2)**. Drill a hole straight down the middle, entering at the center of the nose and exiting at the center of the tail **(2)**. Cut in half longitudinally, then dig out a depression inside the nose of each half to allow an egg sinker to fit with room to rattle **(3)**. With the egg sinker encapsulated between the two halves, glue the two pieces back together with two-part epoxy, wiping off the excess glue, and running a length of line through the channel to ensure it's open. Don't get any glue into the egg sinker, so it's free to rattle **(4)**. Finish by sanding and painting the plug.

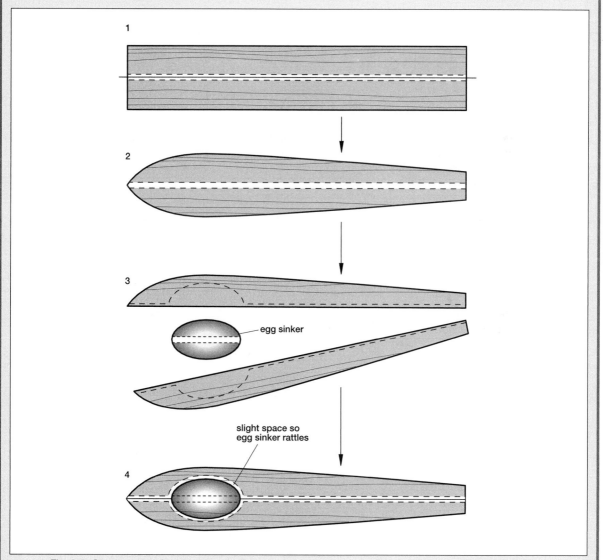

Fig. 3-1. Construction of a cedar-type trolling plug. **1, 2.** Shape and drill the cedar. **3.** Cut the plug in half and shape hollow for egg sinker. **4.** Epoxy the halves back together, encapsulating egg sinker between.

Bowling-Pin Plug

Again, find an appropriate piece of wood. Shape it as shown here. Take care to create a comparable angle for the face of the lure, which causes it to dig down erratically and wiggle side to side as it is trolled. Painting it white or silver on the belly and dark blue or black on the sides and back is helpful but not necessary. Drill and rig as you would a cedar plug for smaller versions (6 in./152 mm); try the multistrand wire harness for lures up to 14 inches (356 mm).

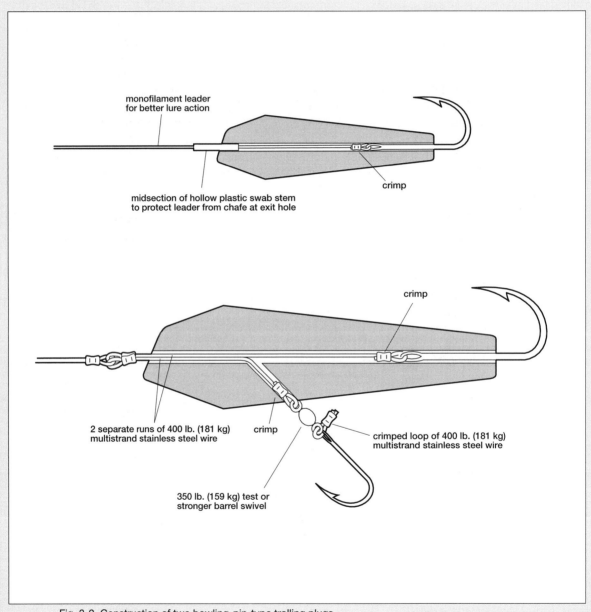

monofilament leader
for better lure action

crimp

midsection of hollow plastic swab stem
to protect leader from chafe at exit hole

crimp

2 separate runs of 400 lb. (181 kg)
multistrand stainless steel wire

crimp

crimped loop of 400 lb. (181 kg)
multistrand stainless steel wire

350 lb. (159 kg) test or
stronger barrel swivel

Fig. 3-2. Construction of two bowling-pin-type trolling plugs.

of unwelded hook eyes. The purchase of quality double-strength hooks with welded or solid eyes will constitute a quantum leap in your fishing power.

Figure 3-6 depicts an array of trolling hooks fitting this description. Mustad models 7982HS, 7732, and 7691S are stainless steel, good for longevity and ease of maintenance, but more brittle than the tinned mild steel of models 7731, 7691, and 7754. This brittleness causes stainless steel hooks to occasionally break under extreme conditions, usually under the strain of a large billfish, although they sometimes sustain even these situations. We recommend the Mustad 7982HS (or anything similar) double hook in sizes 6/0, 7/0, and 8/0 as an alternative for rigging general-duty trolling lures (any but lures g and h in the photo on page 45) under a length of approximately 7 inches (178 mm), except if you wish to hook billfish. If you are willing to accept a slightly lower hook-up rate for other species and want to hook billfish successfully, use Mustad model 7731, 7732, 7691, or 7691S.

The 7731 and 7732 have a straight bite, meaning the point is parallel to the hook shank, which is better for hooking billfish. The 7691 and 7691S have a closed bite, with the point angled in toward the hook shank, better for hooking and holding slashing feeders with relatively soft mouths (e.g., wahoo and mackerel). The 7691 and 7691S will miss more billfish strikes than the 7731 and 7732, due to both the closed bite and a slightly thickened hook diameter that retards penetration in hard bony structure but performs well for most other species. After successful hook-up, however, the holding ability of the 7691 and 7691S is superior.

The Mustad 7754 is a strengthened straight-bite hook best suited for heavier gear to drive its thickened diameter through bony structure. This model is a good choice for 80-pound (36 kg) and heavier tackle, including snubber lines. An alternative strategy for snubber lines, especially if you are traversing an area with a significant number of big fish that will break you off regularly, is to reduce cost by using cheap

Skirted Lures

Consider purchasing plain purpose-manufactured heads, available at a fraction of the cost of a finished lure, in every style: jet head, trolling feather head, Kona head—all the shapes you see in the photo and figure on pages 44 and 45, and many more. If you're *really* on a budget or having fun doing it from scratch, imitate these heads or shape your own innovations from wood, plastic, aluminum dowels, wine corks, fiberglass, bottle caps—virtually any material. You also can use an egg sinker. Be sure to create a flared base similar to commercial heads for the skirt attachment.

(continued next page)

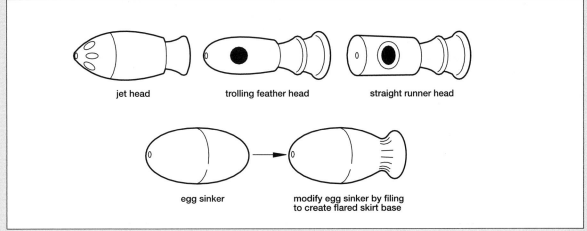

jet head   trolling feather head   straight runner head

egg sinker   modify egg sinker by filing to create flared skirt base

Fig. 3-3. A selection of heads for homemade lures and repairs.

Skirted Lures (cont.)

Your imagination is the only limit to materials for lure skirts: feathers, hair, cloth strips, frayed fibers of nylon or polypropylene rope, frayed synthetic twine, strips of aluminum foil, shiny wine-bag material, cloth, rubber, plas- tic—you name it. (A contemporary fly-fishing magazine advertisement shows a guy at an upscale cocktail party maneuvering for a surreptitious snip of material from a lady's mink coat.) Tie these on as shown in figure 3-4.

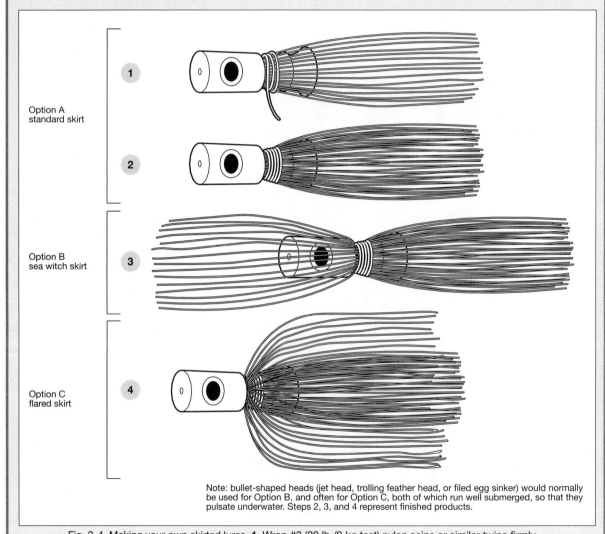

Option A
standard skirt

Option B
sea witch skirt

Option C
flared skirt

Note: bullet-shaped heads (jet head, trolling feather head, or filed egg sinker) would normally be used for Option B, and often for Option C, both of which run well submerged, so that they pulsate underwater. Steps 2, 3, and 4 represent finished products.

Fig. 3-4. Making your own skirted lures. **1.** Wrap #3 (20 lb./9 kg test) nylon seine or similar twine firmly around the skirt keeper of the lure head as you successively and evenly add strands of material. **2.** Continue wrapping until the skirt has the desired fullness; tie off with a series of half-hitches to finish. **3.** To create a sea witch, tie on strands that extend well forward of the lure head and again finish with a series of half hitches (these will flow back in a plume that pulsates underwater when the lure moves forward). **4.** Fold back forward-pointing longer section of strands of your sea witch and tie once more near the forward end of the skirt keeper for a flared skirt, which will have a different pulsating action than the sea witch. (Adapted from Preston et al., 1987, courtesy of the Secretariat of the Pacific Community)

Skirted Lures (cont.)

Repeated strikes will demand occasional replacement of rubber skirts on your favorite lure heads.

Replacements are available in a wide range of color combinations and sizes.

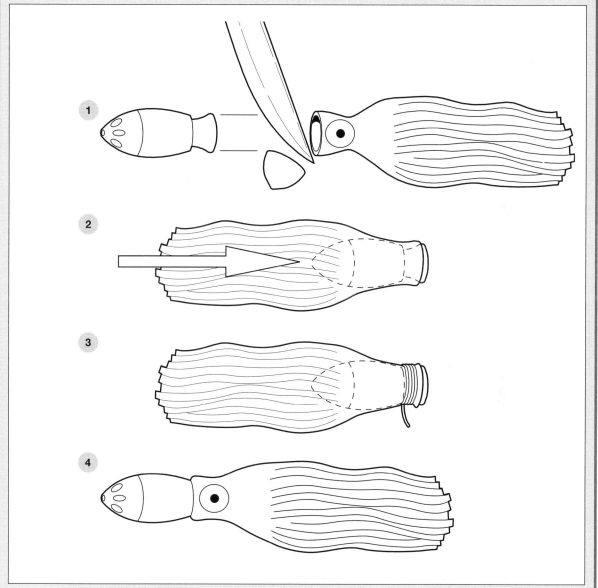

Fig. 3-5. Replacing rubber lure skirts. **1.** Cut the nose from the octopus skirt so that the skirt barely fits over the flared base of the lure head. **2.** Turn the skirt inside out and insert the head as shown, pulling the skirt over the flared base (skirt keeper) of the lure head. **3.** Secure with firmly wrapped light twine or dental floss, finishing with half-hitches. **4.** Fold skirt back right side out. (Adapted from Preston et al., 1987, courtesy of the Secretariat of the Pacific Community)

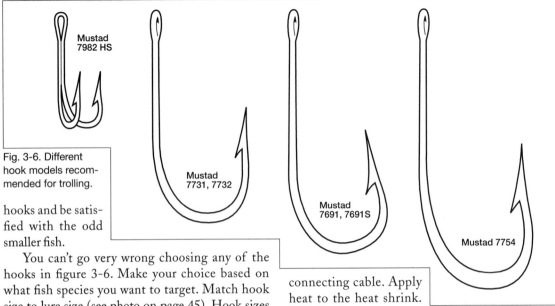

Fig. 3-6. Different hook models recommended for trolling.

hooks and be satisfied with the odd smaller fish.

You can't go very wrong choosing any of the hooks in figure 3-6. Make your choice based on what fish species you want to target. Match hook size to lure size (see photo on page 45). Hook sizes 6/0 to 10/0 should cover most of your trolling needs. Use sizes 3/0 to 5/0 for the smallest trolling feathers and the other delicate presentations sometimes necessary to catch fish tuned in on tiny prey items.

Hook-up rates for lure sizes above 7 inches (178 mm) may be drastically improved by using double-hook rigs (fig. 3-7). These may be purchased, if you can find rigs that suit your specifications; however, we recommend that you construct your own because it's less expensive, you can be sure it's done right, and you can customize precisely to fit your lures and target species. We use Mustad 7691S hooks at 90 degrees for subsurface lures like jet heads and clones, and Mustad 7732 and 7754 hooks at 180 degrees for the larger straight runners and chuggers.

Refer to figure 3-7 as we review some important details about proper rig construction. Start by crimping the 400-pound (181 kg) multistrand stainless steel leader cable to what will be the back hook, and slide a tight-fitting section of heat shrink down the cable to the bend of the hook. Orient the back hook to the desired angle and distance behind the forward hook before making the crimp fast to the forward hook. Slide the original heat shrink forward over the crimped loop of the back hook, then pass a larger-diameter section of heat shrink over the full length of the shank of the front hook and

connecting cable. Apply heat to the heat shrink. *You're done!* The heat shrink makes the hook rig "stiff," holding the back hook rigid at the desired angle. Lacking heat shrink, you can do the same thing with amalgamating tape or electrical tape. For an added touch, use tape colors that blend well with your lure color. Retape after strikes rip the back hook loose. Double-hook rigs perform exceedingly well for both hooking and holding fish of all species.

OK, now what kind of leader should you pass through your lure to these hooks or hook rigs, or attach to your lure with built-in hooks? How fishers answer this question demonstrates the artistic side of fishing. Leader length, material, and size depend on tackle strength, lure size and weight, water clarity, and the visual acuity, feeding behavior, and morphology of the target species. The more precisely you adjust your leaders to the conditions, the more effective you will be.

Table 3-1, pages 54–55, is an overview of leader recommendations for most of the fish families you may exploit, whether by trolling or other methods, using lures or natural bait. Apply the following general rules to table entries.

♦ For each given range of leader size, use larger sizes for heavier tackle and bigger individual target fish.

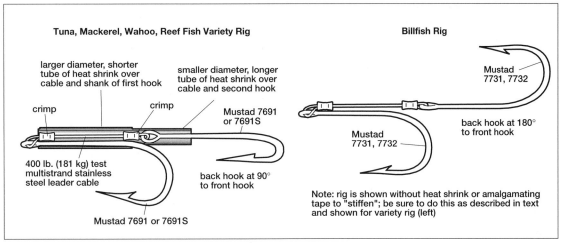

Tuna, Mackerel, Wahoo, Reef Fish Variety Rig

larger diameter, shorter tube of heat shrink over cable and shank of first hook

smaller diameter, longer tube of heat shrink over cable and second hook

crimp

crimp

Mustad 7691 or 7691S

400 lb. (181 kg) test multistrand stainless steel leader cable

back hook at 90° to front hook

Mustad 7691 or 7691S

Billfish Rig

Mustad 7731, 7732

back hook at 180° to front hook

Mustad 7731, 7732

Note: rig is shown without heat shrink or amalgamating tape to "stiffen"; be sure to do this as described in text and shown for variety rig (left)

Fig. 3-7. Construction of double-hook rigs for larger trolling lures.

♦ You may always use heavier-than-recommended leader sizes for your target species; if they won't bite, reduce leader size.

♦ You may always substitute wire for monofilament, something you may want to do when you start getting cut off. Remember, however, that any wire is more visible, may inhibit the action of your lure or bait and, in the case of single-strand wire, is more difficult to handle than monofilament. Single-strand wire also carries the risk of break-offs due to kinks imparted by the fish or from errors on the part of the fisher. (This is most likely to occur with fish that jump actively and thrash on the surface; for example, billfish, mahi mahi, tarpon, barramundi, and snook.) Sometimes sustaining a certain number of cut-offs is a necessary part of catching the species you are targeting, but this rule does not normally apply to the use of lures because of the expense.

♦ All recommended wire in table 3-1 is single-strand stainless steel because it is far less visible than multistrand stainless steel. Feel free to substitute multistrand stainless steel leader for either monofilament or single-strand wire, knowing that fish see it better, which may seriously curtail the number of strikes. The only common physical failure of multistrand wire is during long battles with mako and other shark species when the points of their teeth penetrate the braid, which gradually frays and eventually breaks it.

♦ For more reliable shark leaders in the 15–19 size range, form a braid of two lengths of single-strand leader wire and make haywire twists as if one strand.

♦ Any time you have questions about optimal leader material, strength, and length, perform a simple experiment: run the recommended leader side by side with whatever you want as a test to see which one catches more fish.

♦ Many big-game anglers now use a special knotless leader that obviates the need for hand-lining lengths of monofilament or wire that lie between a barrel swivel and the hook, and the risks this entails. They're called wind-on leaders, formed by inserting the running line off the reel into a special sheath that grips it tightly under pressure. These are available from specialty catalogs (see appendix 1).

You have arrived! Figure 3-8 shows sample rigs for a variety of trolling applications. Pay attention to leader length, size, and material for each as we walk you through. We begin at the top with some light-tackle, low-visibility rigs generally suitable for inshore shallows, coastal, and open-sea trolling for many smaller species and individuals—school mahi mahi, mackerel, tuna, jacks, reef fish, bottom dwellers, small wahoo—just about anything. Substituting an

TABLE 3-1. **RECOMMENDED MATERIAL AND STRENGTH RANGE OF LEADERS FOR COMMONLY EXPLOITED FISH FAMILIES OF THE WORLD**
(TO SPECIES OR GROUP LEVEL WITHIN FAMILIES, WHERE NECESSARY)

Fish Family and Species	Monofilament, lb. (kg) test	Single-Strand Wire, size
Albulidae: bonefishes	2–20 (1–9)	
Alopiidae: thresher sharks		15–19
Arripidae: kahawai	15–50 (7–23)	
Balistidae: triggerfishes	20–50 (9–23)	
Monacanthidae: filefishes, leatherjackets		2–4
Belonidae: houndfish, needlefishes		2
Bothidae: lefteye flounders	30–100 (14–45)	
Bramidae: pomfrets	30–100 (14–45)	
Carangidae: jacks, trevallys, pompanos, permits	2–100 (1–45)	
Carcharhinidae: requiem sharks		4–19
Centropomidae: barramundi, snooks	50–80 (23–36)	
Cheilodactylidae: morwongs	30–50 (14–23)	
Clupeidae: herrings, pilchards	2–15 (1–7)	
Coryphaenidae: mahi mahi	30–80 (14–36)	
Dasyatidae: stingrays	30–100 (14–45)	
Elopiidae: tarpons, ladyfish	20–100 (9–45)	
Engraulidae: anchovies	2–15 (1–7)	
Exocoetidae: flying fishes	2–15 (1–7)	
Gadidae: cods, pollocks, haddocks, hakes	50–100 (23–45)	
Haemulidae: sweetlips, grunts, margates	10–50 (4–23)	
Hemirhamphidae: halfbeaks, ballyhoos	2–15 (1–7)	
Hexagrammidae: lingcod	50–100 (23–45)	
Istiophoridae: sailfish, spearfishes, marlins	50–400 (23–181)	
Kyphosidae: sea chubs, drummers	10–30 (4–14)	
Labridae: wrasses, hogfishes, humpheads	10–100 (4–45)	
Lamnidae: mackerel sharks		15–19
Lampridae: moonfish	100–300 (45–136)	
Latridae: trumpeters	30–100 (14–45)	
Lethrinidae: emperors	20–50 (9–23)	
Lobotidae: tripletails	15–30 (7–14)	
Lutjanidae: snappers	10–100 (4–45)	
Malacanthidae: tilefishes	50–100 (23–45)	
Moridae: morid cods	50–100 (23–45)	
Mullidae: goatfishes	10–30 (4–14)	
Mugilidae: mullets	2–20 (1–9)	
Myliobatidae: eagle rays	50–100 (23–45)	
Nematistiidae: roosterfishes	15–50 (7–23)	
Nemipteridae: coral breams, spinecheeks	20–50 (9–23)	
Nototheniidae: icefishes, polar cods	50–100 (23–45)	
Orectolobidae: nurse sharks	30–100 (14–45)	
Pentacerotidae: boarfishes	50–100 (23–45)	
Percichthyidae: temperate basses, hapuku, wreckfishes	20–100 (9–45)	

TABLE 3-1. **RECOMMENDED MATERIAL AND STRENGTH RANGE OF LEADERS FOR COMMONLY EXPLOITED FISH FAMILIES OF THE WORLD (cont.)**
(TO SPECIES OR GROUP LEVEL WITHIN FAMILIES, WHERE NECESSARY)

Fish Family and Species	Monofilament, lb. (kg) test	Single-Strand Wire, size
Pleuronectidae: right-eye flounders (halibuts)	150–300 (68–136)	
Pomatomidae: bluefishes		4–8
Rachycentridae: cobia	100 (45)	
Rajidae: skates	30–80 (14–36)	
Salmonidae: salmons, trouts	2–50 (1–23)	
Scaridae: parrotfishes	15–30 (7–14)	
Sciaenidae: drums, sea trouts, croakers, corvina	15–100 (7–45)	
Scombridae: mackerels, wahoo, tunas		
Mackerels		2–5
Wahoo		4–8
Dogtooth tunas		4–15
Other tunas	20–300 (9–136)	
Scorpidae: stonebreams, maomao	8–15 (4–7)	
Serranidae: tropical basses, groupers, coral trout	30–100 (14–45)	
Sparidae: porgies, sea breams	20–50 (9–23)	
Sphyraenidae: barracudas		2–8
Sphyrnidae: hammerhead sharks		4–19
Squalidae: spiny dogfishes	30–50 (14–23)	
Stromateidae: butterfishes, rudderfishes	50–100 (23–45)	
Trachichthyidae: roughies	50–100 (23–45)	
Triglidae: gurnards	20–40 (9–18)	
Xiphiidae: swordfish	300–400 (136–181)	
Zeidae: dories	20–50 (9–23)	

Monofilament strengths are pound (kg) test, single-strand wire by standard size number.

Albright special for a barrel swivel allows a shorter length of wire while maintaining low visibility.

You could run the next three rigs—the Drone spoon, Australian Runner, or jet head—on either monofilament or wire trolling line. These are subsurface presentations that work well offshore or in coastal waters for the same array of targets; however, they will handle much larger individuals, easily to 200 pounds (91 kg) and more depending on your tackle. Recall that the spoon and swimming plug work effectively at slower speeds, whereas the jet head does best from 7 to 12 knots. We have caught literally hundreds of wahoo on 8½-inch (216 mm), 2½-ounce (71 g) jet heads rigged with Mustad 7691S hooks at 90 degrees in this speed range. All sizes of tunas, trevallys, jacks, groupers, snappers, and many others are equally fond of this lure. You can run Australian Runners this fast and experience good success, and Rapala Countdowns (floating or sinking) that have a very hard wiggle at even lower speeds (2 to 3 knots). Spoons like the Drone are good also in this lower speed range, particularly when you need some flash to penetrate turbid water and you arm yourself with quality swivels to prevent line twist.

The middle section of figure 3-8 illustrates surface and near-surface rigs featuring small (6 in./152 mm or less) to medium (6 in./152 mm to 9 in./229 mm) lures. Use monofilament leaders when possible to greatly enhance the action of these lures, which are intended to catch everything from mahi mahi and tuna to smaller billfish. These offerings work particularly well in any situation where fish are active near the surface—splashing, feeding schools marked by

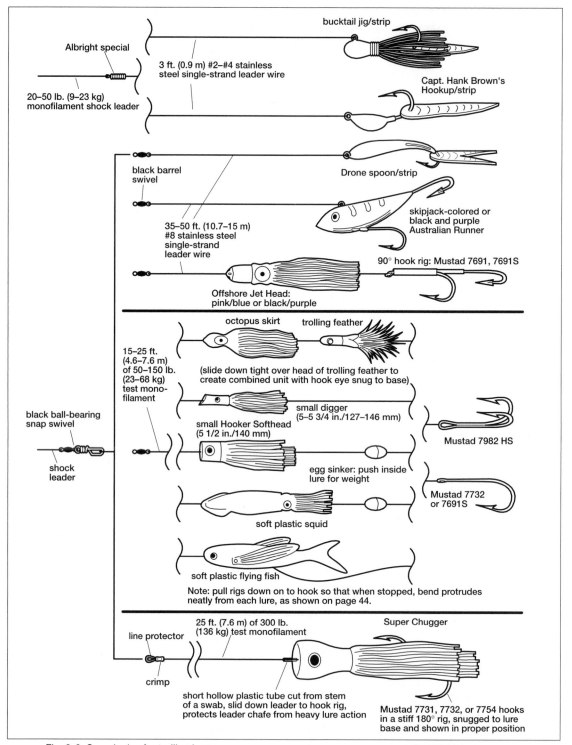

Fig. 3-8. Sample rigs for trolling lures.

birds, current rips, seamounts, tidal plumes. You will catch large individual fish using this class of presentations. For example, we have had blue marlin well over 250 pounds (113 kg) piling all over 5½-inch (140 mm) Hooker Softheads, ignoring other more appropriate lures and repeatedly attacking the small lure. This forced us to remove the small lure from the water and put another bait right in the fish's face in order to secure a hook-up.

The bottom of figure 3-8 shows rigging specifications for a standard, medium to large (8 in./203 mm to 12½ in./318 mm) offshore lure. *Warning:* If you pull something like this behind your boat while offshore in many areas from the equator to temperate seas, you will eventually hook a billfish, sometimes several in one day. This is the main weapon of all those globe-trotting marlin aficionados. You will catch large tuna, mahi mahi, mako sharks, and other odds and ends too, but you can target these with other methods. So we repeat our warning: *do not* purchase and put something like this out unless you want to do serious battle, and *never* deploy these on a snubber line.

These large offshore lures fall outside the purview of many cruising crews; on the other hand, they could create some of the most memorable experiences of your life. You can always release the fish after photos—you may even wish to tag the fish to help fishery biology research—and your 50-pound (23 kg) class stand-up outfit has a chance of handling most marlin you hook. We know several sailors who enjoy catching marlin and other billfish, and fish for them on a regular basis. After all, there must be some reason certain people spend thousands of dollars each year trying to catch one, and you are in the unusual position of being able to do it "for free" as a casual sideline to other activities.

NATURAL BAIT RIGGING

Properly rigged natural baits can do more than any other single factor to overcome lack of action due to slower boat speeds characteristic of many power and sailing cruisers, relative to their fishing-vessel counterparts. Furthermore, the most pleasant time to fish from cruising vessels is during relatively calm conditions, which frequently may be associated with less speed in the case of sailboats.

The world of natural bait rigging is vast and has had numerous books dedicated solely to it. This is another stumbling block for aspiring fishers, similar

Big Fish on Small Lures

We were bound for Tahiti from the Tuamotus in idyllic, settled weather. The sun was dipping low toward the faint silhouette of our destination, although still 45 NM west of our position. The wind had come from nothing to between 12 and 15 knots over the starboard quarter, filling the sails and pushing us forward at 5 knots. The outriggers were folded out, and our full spread of lures began to pop, gurgle, and show some life behind us. The sun was just touching the horizon when the right outrigger bait—a 6-inch (152 mm) black and purple Ultimate Junior, rigged with a single 8/0 Mustad 7691 hook and baited with a silvery strip of queenfish—disappeared in a large, almost quiet boil of surface water; no part of the predator broke the surface. The Penn 50W screamed as the stand-up rod bowed deeply in the rod holder. I grabbed the rod and gave it a couple of jabs, set it back in the holder, and ran around dropping sails and starting the engine so we could maneuver. Wendy woke up from yet another violation of her off-watch naps, and the fight was on.

Thirty minutes later, we had a sizable yellowfin tuna alongside—perhaps 180 pounds (82 kg)—long yellow streamers seemingly aglow in the last of the daylight. We leadered the fish up to the transom platform, still 4 feet (1.2 m) above the sea surface, and I struck home the first of two straight gaffs. The fish had plenty of life left, and I confess to receiving a sound beating and nearly going overboard while trying to dodge the rigging and get around to the port side from the afterdeck. Wendy had to hang over the side and tail-rope the thrashing tuna so we could get some help from one of the halyard winches, finally getting our catch over the lifeline and onto the deck. We were glad we'd built a 300-pound-capacity fish hold amidships, as were many Tahitian and cruising friends when we got settled in the next day in Papeete.

Large yellowfin tuna caught trolling near sunset east of Tahiti, French Polynesia. Note tail rope and noose around body to hoist it aboard.

to the Bimini twist. They see the pros do it, and it looks difficult. We intend to break this subject down into some very simple trolling-bait preparations that you will have no problem creating, yet will prove to be some of the deadliest options in your growing arsenal of fishing skills.

Like the Bimini twist, bait rigging is made easy by proper setup. Select hook sizes and leader material commensurate to bait size and target species. The next step, particularly for rigging whole baits, is to lay the bait out on a flat surface, preferably waist-level, and premeasure various distances. Following these pointers contributes significantly to the ease and fun of bait-rigging.

Consider putting a lure on the nose of your rigged bait, such as a sea witch, trolling feather, straight runner, clone, jet head, or simply an octopus skirt. Lures can give rigged natural baits a larger, noisier profile, submerge them beneath the surface, increase action, help retard washout and deterioration, and make them less susceptible to snagging weeds and debris. Lure-bait combinations account for a high percentage of trolling hook-ups from

professional fishing boats. Plain rigged natural baits can sometimes outperform their adorned counterparts when fish are focused and feeding on specific prey items, such as squid or flying fish, so don't ignore this option.

Strip Baits

Strip baits are extremely easy to prepare. Use them alone or in combination with a lure and you'll have something even the best professional bait riggers find hard to beat. Enhancing a spoon, octopus-skirt/feather combination, jet head, or other skirted lure with a strip sharply increases the number of strikes, especially at slower speeds (fig. 3-9).

Cut strips from virtually any kind of larger fish, squid, or fillets of smaller species such as flying fish, needlefish, halfbeaks, and members of the jack family. Match size to hook and lure. Make the strips symmetrical so that the strip will not spin when trolled, with blunt head tapering to a thin, pointed tail (which can be split for extra action). For fish strips, form the blunt end from aft of the tapered end relative to the body of the fish you are cutting. This results in the muscle fiber of the strip flowing with, rather than in opposition to, the flow of water as it is trolled. It will not wash out as soon or form asymmetrical lumps of flesh as easily. Trim the meat side to a uniform thickness of approximately ⅛ inch (3 mm). Place the strips in a zippered plastic bag, pour in a bunch of salt, and shake thoroughly. Now lay the strips out flat on any surface (the bottom of a plastic container works well), meat side up, sprinkle heavily with salt, and refrigerate if possible. By the next morning, you'll have toughened natural baits that will last all day and can be stored for a long time in a refrigerator for later use.

Squid and octopus are naturally tough, and strips of either give more durable performance than untreated fish. Nevertheless, don't hesitate to troll fresh fish strips while your main supply is toughening in salt. They will work fine, but will require more frequent changes. Salt-treated squid strips seem to last almost indefinitely!

Whole Squid

Find a flat surface and lay your squid out on it. Select a Mustad 7754 from size 7/0 to 10/0 that matches the size of your squid and install a line protector and

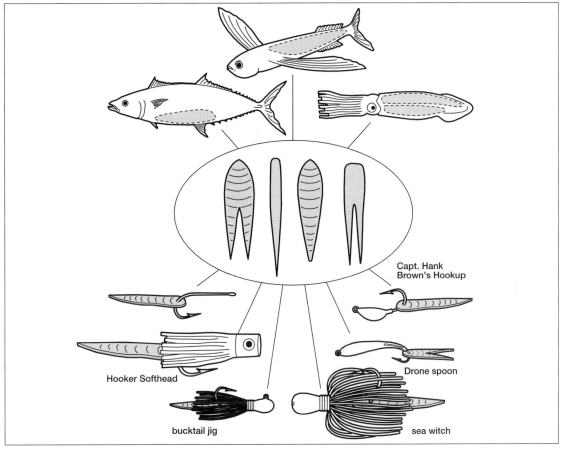

Fig. 3-9. Formation and use of strip baits.

crimp, leaving a bitter end longer than the mantle length of the squid (fig. 3-10). Slide a second crimp down the leader and over the bitter end to a position that leaves just enough space for the stopper (e.g., egg sinker for subsurface; wine cork for splashy surface-swimming bait), crimp, and slide the stopper down flush to this second crimp. For 300- to 400-pound (136 to 181 kg) monofilament leader, trim the rod end to a sharp point, and work the leader up through the squid's mantle and out the apex. Pull it all the way through, until the stopper rests snugly up inside the apex of the mantle (use a rigging needle, if needed, to run lighter monofilament leader material up through the mantle). Finish by pushing the hook point through the middle of the squid's head, midway between the eyes.

This bait should swim straight, without spin-

ning. The tentacles flutter behind the hook, and the bait exudes a strong-smelling oily slick (you'll see this streaming out behind your bait for hours). I once fell overboard at night from a swordfish long-liner, luckily catching another crew member's attention as I slipped off the gunnel and splashed into the water. I will always remember the distinctive thick aroma of the squid oil in my nostrils as I clumsily swam back up the gear to the waiting vessel. Fish love this, and you will often get strikes on trolled squid when nothing else is working. This holds true particularly in slick calm conditions, when fish are lazily basking or moving slowly near the sea surface.

Ballyhoo (Halfbeaks)
Use the same salting procedure described for strip baits to toughen whole ballyhoo, laying them belly-

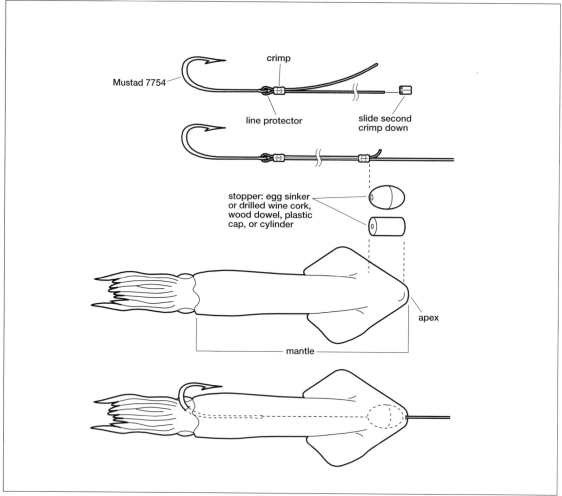

Fig. 3-10. Rigging whole squid for trolling.

up prior to application of the last heavy sprinkling of salt. Leave them overnight and they'll be ready for durable service the next morning. Grasp one by the head with one hand and squeeze hard just behind the gills with your other thumb and forefinger, sliding this hand aft to eject the guts from the vent. Now hold the bait belly-down, back to the sky, in the palm of one hand and successively pinch the back muscles from head to tail with thumb and forefinger of your other hand. As you feel the sections of muscle crush, stop each pinch before you break the skin. Ejecting the guts and internally crushing the dorsal musculature prior to rigging makes the bait limber, causing it to wiggle

and undulate enticingly when trolled.

Premeasure and construct your rig as shown in figure 3-11, either from monofilament or single-strand stainless steel wire, ensuring that the head spike and hook are in the same vertical plane. Start the hook into the gut cavity just behind the gill rakers, lever the hook shank in an arc while threading it into the bait, and finish with the hook bend protruding precisely from the midline of the belly. The leader rests underneath and exactly between the undersides of the gill plates after the head spike has been driven upward, completely through the head approximately half the distance between the eyes and the mouth. Finish by running the rigging wire through the eyes, firmly in

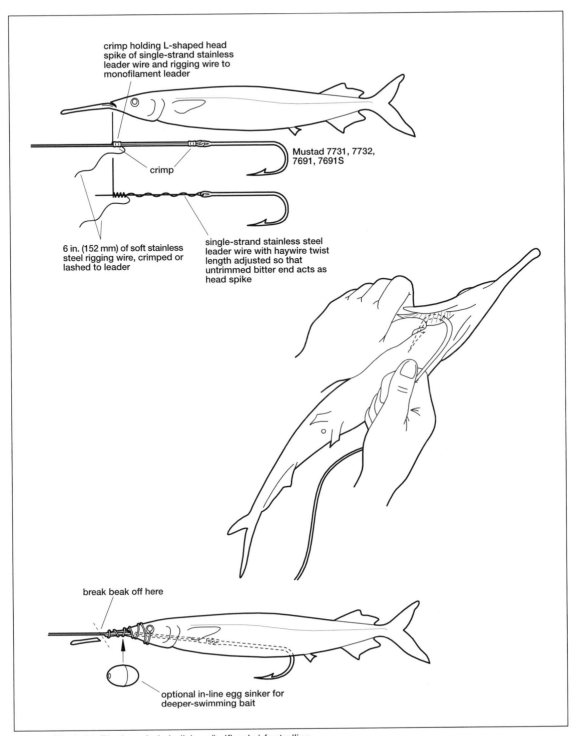

crimp holding L-shaped head
spike of single-strand stainless
leader wire and rigging wire to
monofilament leader

crimp

Mustad 7731, 7732,
7691, 7691S

6 in. (152 mm) of soft stainless
steel rigging wire, crimped or
lashed to leader

single-strand stainless steel
leader wire with haywire twist
length adjusted so that
untrimmed bitter end acts as
head spike

break beak off here

optional in-line egg sinker for
deeper-swimming bait

Fig. 3-11. Rigging whole ballyhoo (halfbeaks) for trolling.

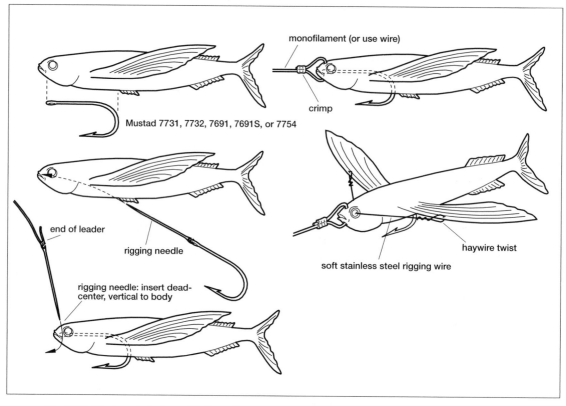

Fig. 3-12. Rigging whole flying fish for trolling.

back of the head spike, forward across the mouth, and a short distance up the beak in tight wraps. Break off the beak just forward of the last wrap. For a subsurface swimming action, add an egg sinker by running it down the leader and securing it in place with rigging wire at the chin of the bait.

Always be careful to rig exactly on the midline of the bait body to attain balance and perfect symmetry. This causes the bait to swim in a lifelike, natural manner, without spinning. If your bait spins when you first begin trolling it, bring it back in and try again. Sometimes you can make minor adjustments without having to start again from scratch—look for misalignment between the hook and head spike, remembering that they should be *exactly* in the same vertical plane.

Flying Fish

Two methods work well for rigging whole flying fish, by either "ballyhoo style" or the simple loop method illustrated in figure 3-12. Whichever you choose, limber the bait up by ejecting the guts and crushing the back muscles as for ballyhoo. Be sure to execute the last step, tying the wings out at 90 degrees to the lengthwise profile of the body. Use rigging wire haywire-twisted to the leading wing spine and run it tightly through the head via the eye socket. View the bait head on to ensure that each wing is also at approximately the same 90-degree angle relative to the body cross section, like an airplane. This bait will realistically splash, flutter, skip, and take short flights over the surface. It's so attractive, you might have to keep your back to the water while preparing it!

Mackerel, Small Mahi Mahi, Tuna, Scad, and Other Larger Whole Fish

Using larger baits often encourages bigger fish to bite, but sometimes large baits also work best on average-sized quarry. The size and commotion can

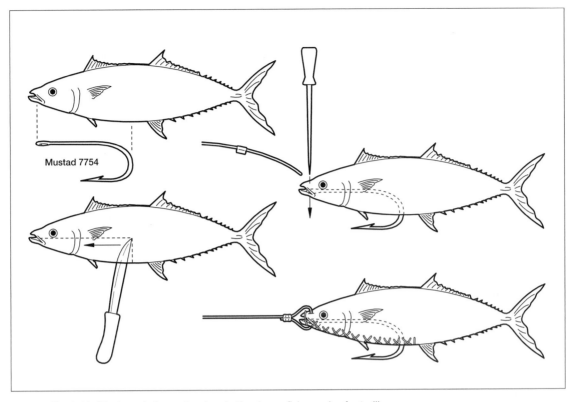

Fig. 3-13. Rigging whole mackerel and other larger fish species for trolling.

stir fish into an attack that might otherwise pass on a more subtle presentation. Excited fish strike baits bigger than they can swallow whole; improbably large prey items turn up regularly in predator fish stomachs. Thus, you may want to occasionally prepare larger whole-fish trolling baits even if you are not seeking a 1,000-pound (454 kg) marlin, shark, or other behemoth.

Pretreat your 10- to 15-inch (254 to 381 mm) or larger whole-fish baits with salt as described for smaller fish baits. Go heavy on the salt, especially on the upturned bellies. The pros "sauce" them overnight by submerging them in formalin solution for greater longevity (not a reasonable option for most cruisers due to the smell and toxicity of the chemical). Leaving them in the salt for two days or more, perhaps adding a heavy fresh sprinkle after the first day, results in a reasonably durable bait. Limber up the bait by bending back and forth in a swimming motion prior to rigging.

Figure 3-13 demonstrates the simple loop rig for big baits. Select an appropriately sized Mustad 7754, probably 10/0, 11/0, or 12/0. Lay the bait out and position the hook so the eye ends up in the bait's mouth. Make an incision dead on the centerline, from just behind the projected exit of the hook, up through and splitting the lower jaw exactly in half. Position the hook inside the body so that the eye is centered in the mouth. Use an ice pick to make a vertical hole through the middle of the head. Pass the single-strand wire (12 to 19), heavy monofilament (best bait action, least visibility—300 to 400 lbs./136 to 181 kg), or multi-strand leader (300 to 400 lbs./136 to 181 kg) end into the hole, through the hook eye, and out the lower jaw. Complete the loop with a haywire twist (wire) or crimp (monofilament, multistrand wire) just in front of the nose. Suture the incision with bait needle and nylon lacing or rigging floss. *Note: viewed head on, the loop should be centered and vertical on the midline of the bait's body.*

These baits alternately skip and swim or wiggle subsurface with a sufficiently heavy lure on the nose. If you follow the rigging directions carefully, it will look as if you could stop the boat and the bait would continue swimming right past you. Baits with this appearance eventually tend to disappear in violent white explosions of seawater.

Deploying Trolling Gear

Attention to small details contributes exponentially to fishing success. None is more important than ensuring that every hook going into the water is razor-sharp. Test sharpness by gently moving the hook point across your thumbnail; it should leave a distinct white scratch. If not, whip out your file (or sharpening stone for smaller hooks) and touch it up. File from point to barb to create a triangulated point with a shallow angle of attack (fig. 3-14). Thinning the sides of the barb on extra-strength hooks like the Mustad 7754 facilitates penetration. Stainless steel hooks tend to hold sharpness and require less attention than other hooks, most of which require sharpening straight out of the box before use.

Many other nuances contribute to effective trolling: correct distance in back of the boat; angle of attack, depth, and spacing of lures; optimal use of release clips; use of teasers; and maintenance of trolling rigs and tackle. This section reviews the entire drill.

HOW FAR BACK SHOULD WE RUN OUR LURE OR BAIT?

The question of correct distance to deploy trolled baits and lures may be asked more than any other. The short answer: a boat length and a half to three boat lengths will usually do. A thorough, more accurate response depends on many factors. Engine noise and boat presence tend to spook fish more inshore and in shallower water, demanding greater distance between boat and lure, whereas pelagic species may actually swim right up to the transom to eat trolled offerings. On the other hand, engine noise frequently causes surface-feeding tuna and other fish schools offshore to sound more quickly than when the engine is not running, and many other oceanic species alternate between bold and shy behavior. So what's best?

If you are running only one line, letting it out 35 yards (32 m) or so will cover you for most situations. Multiple lines allow more flexibility of lure distance and spacing. Regardless, ensuring proper lure or bait action determines the question of the right distance back for each line, which in turn depends on size,

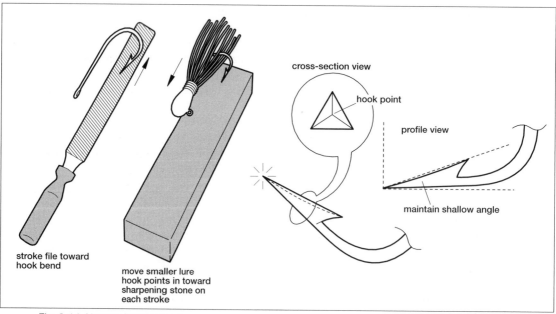

stroke file toward hook bend

move smaller lure hook points in toward sharpening stone on each stroke

cross-section view

hook point

profile view

maintain shallow angle

Fig. 3-14. How to sharpen hooks.

type, weight, and action of the offering; boat speed; and angle of entry between trolling line and sea surface. Use the following guidelines to set correct distances for surface lures like straight runners, chuggers, and diggers; for specialty lures rigged to run on the surface, like rubber squid and flying fish; and for any natural baits rigged for surface action.

♦ The bait or lure should "pop" or break the surface at least once every five seconds, without hopping completely out of the water.

♦ For a given boat speed, larger and heavier baits and lures will have to run closer and smaller offerings farther from the boat for proper action.

♦ Increasing the angle between trolling line and sea surface increases the surface action of any given lure or bait, and consequently increases the correct distance back for that specific lure or bait.

♦ Always run lures and baits on the *face* of any standing waves created by your hull in the wake, *never* on the crest or "back side"—try this, and note the enhanced swimming action of an offering positioned to surf on a wave face as opposed to any other position. Over time, you will learn the specific wake wave for each of your lures at given boat speeds. The next time you overhear professional fishers discussing the first, second, third, fifth, or whatever wave relative to a given lure, you'll know what they're talking about.

♦ Baits and lures run better downsea than upsea, and worst directly upsea. Thus, any time you are maneuvering on suspected fish or signs of fish, try to present your trolling lines as much *off* the seas as possible.

Subsurface baits and lures are less picky about where they run. As long as they stay submerged, never popping out of the water, and wiggling nicely, you may let other considerations determine distance back, such as sensitivity of target species to boat and engine noise or positions of other presentations in your spread. Some lures or lure/bait combinations (e.g., octopus-skirt/feather combinations and jet heads) can be run either on the surface or submerged, while lures like swimming plugs and spoons usually do not break the surface. Other lures, such

as small diggers and rubber flying fish, should skitter and skate along the surface essentially full time for the best effect (you may want to run whole rigged natural flying fish in this manner also).

EFFECTIVE USE OF RELEASE CLIPS

Several devices facilitate optimal deployment of multiple trolling presentations. All depend on adjustable-tensioned release clips to hold various lines originating from different locations around the back of the boat at desirable positions in your wake, liberating them when fish strike. This has the added advantage of providing "drop-back," or a small amount of slack line, which allows the fish a fraction more time to swallow the lure or bait, thus increasing the chance of a successful hook-up.

Release clips may be suspended laterally from the boat with outriggers; vertically up by a center rigger or attachment to superstructure; vertically down by attachment to a cleat, scupper, or other low deck feature; or subsurface with a downrigger (fig. 3-15). These arrangements permit tangle-free trolling of numerous offerings in a "bait spread" and confer added flexibility for setting bait and lure distances by allowing changes in the angles between trolling lines and the sea surface.

Create optimal bait spreads using the following guidelines.

♦ Stagger your lures and baits so that sharp turns and orientation relative to the prevailing wind direction will not cause tangles (fig. 3-16).

♦ Run teasers and big baits and lures close, smaller presentations farther back in the spread (fig. 3-16).

♦ Position release clips to allow running windward flat lines and outrigger lines lower to the sea surface than leeward lines (fig. 3-16).

♦ Deploy heavier lines with more wind resistance to leeward of lighter lines.

♦ Run wire line to windward of monofilament trolling lines.

♦ Run heavier surface lures in higher wind and rougher conditions.

♦ Use at least some darker lure colors (e.g., black, red, or purple) on overcast days, at least some brighter lures (e.g., pink, blue, or white) on sun-

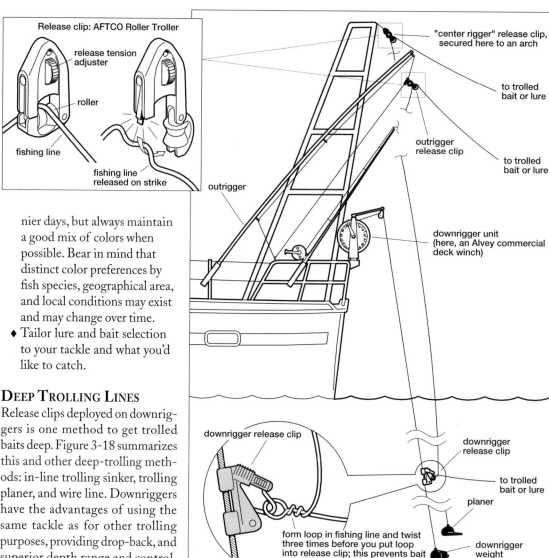

Fig. 3-15. Use of release clips to deploy trolling lines.

nier days, but always maintain a good mix of colors when possible. Bear in mind that distinct color preferences by fish species, geographical area, and local conditions may exist and may change over time.

♦ Tailor lure and bait selection to your tackle and what you'd like to catch.

Deep Trolling Lines

Release clips deployed on downriggers is one method to get trolled baits deep. Figure 3-18 summarizes this and other deep-trolling methods: in-line trolling sinker, trolling planer, and wire line. Downriggers have the advantages of using the same tackle as for other trolling purposes, providing drop-back, and superior depth range and control. The disadvantage is having to clear an extra line from depth after hookups to prevent tangles. Downrigger lines can use trolling planers or weights to maintain depth.

The in-line trolling sinker option is simple and effective for some fisheries, but suffers from the drawback of having an unwieldy weight on the line during the fish-fighting and -landing process. These weights tend to swing around and promote de-hooking, and represent a leader-handling inconvenience near the boat.

Trolling planers rigged in-line suffer the same pitfalls, although they too represent a simple, inexpensive way to troll at depth. When a fish hits, the trip ring pops forward on the towing bracket, angling the device toward the surface, also assisting fish up from the depths. This is a good snubber line option as long as you use significantly greater line strength from boat to planer than from planer to bait, so that the planer is not lost when big fish break the line.

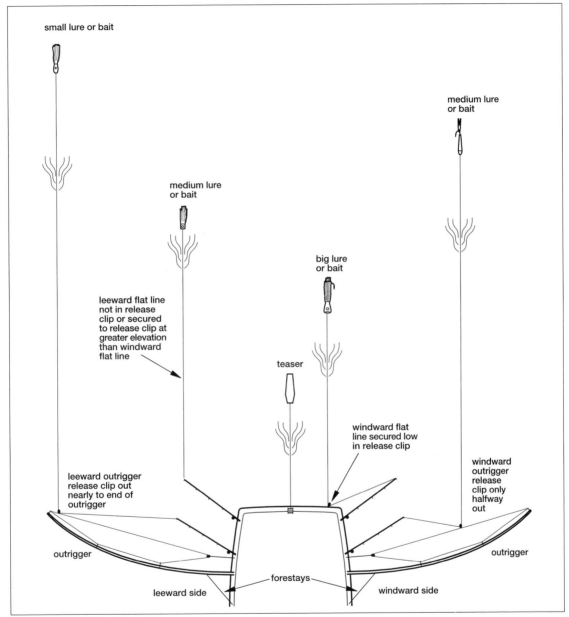

Fig. 3-16. How to deploy trolling spreads that will not tangle from sharp boat turns or wind. Ripples indicate point of trolling-line entry into the water, which should always be aft of the next closest lure to the boat.

Wire lines are initially expensive, heavy, and specialized. The high price of the wire demands highly inconvenient extrication measures if you accidentally snag the bottom. No method can beat them, however, for certain applications desirable to many

power and sailing cruisers: deep, unencumbered trolling offshore, near reefs and other bottom structures, and bottom-fishing below 450 feet (137 m). Count on a minimum of 10 feet (3 m) of bait or lure depth per 100 feet (30 m) of wire (mark with den-

What Are Teasers?

A teaser is something you drag behind your boat to cause added commotion and attract fish. Teasers often are larger than normal lures, lack hooks, and are run close behind the boat on heavy lines. Their job is to thrash, splash, and stir up the emotions of fish that you want to bite your hooks. Even if you have no interest in billfish, the most common target of teaser deployment, do not underestimate the extreme influence these devices can have on a variety of smaller species.

You can buy ready-made teasers. Our all-time favorite is the bonito-colored Lulu, a bowling-pin shape that does amazing things over a wide range of boat speeds and generates pronounced reactions from tuna, wahoo, mahi mahi, mackerel, reef fish, sharks, and billfish. We have one Lulu with a broken off marlin bill stuck in the end, and another covered in teeth and bill marks from many kinds of attacks. We often let Lulu do her thing even with no fishing lines out, just to watch the show. Recently, a 50-pound (23 kg) wahoo responded to her flirtations by rocketing vertically, snatching her in its mouth on the way up, firing easily 15 feet (4.6 m) into the air as our crew of four stared up, mouths agape, at this magnificent fish soaring above us. Following that frozen moment, it dropped Lulu and arced back down in a graceful swan dive. It's also a wonderful way of observing big, highly excited marlin at close range without risking an unwanted hook-up.

If you *do* want to catch marlin and other bruisers, run a 9½- to 12½-inch skirted lure or rigged natural bait 6 to 8 feet (1.5 to 2 m) behind Lulu or some other teaser. Usually, it will all happen so fast that before you can blink, the fish has been teased, attracted, veered onto the lure, hooked itself on the strike, and is now streaking away from you at blinding speed. Occasionally, you'll need to "bait and switch"—remove the teaser and put the lure in the face of the excited fish to tempt a strike.

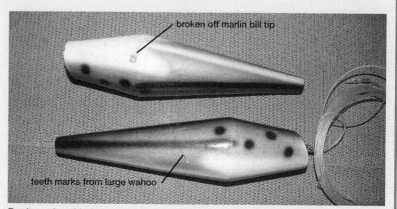

Bonito-colored Lulu teaser with broken marlin bill tip imbedded *(top)*, and wahoo teeth marks *(bottom)*.

Large lures with no hooks, plastic liter soda bottles weighted with sand, a chunk of wood—anything can work. Spreader bars rigged with multiple rubber squid work very well for sailfish, tuna, and other predators. "Bird" teasers, either alone or in line ahead of a chugger or straight runner, are very effective for numerous species (fig. 3-17).

tal floss or paint) behind the boat while trolling, more for deep-diving swimming plugs or heavy clones, jet heads, and trolling feathers and very slow trolling speeds (below 3.5 knots).

Most of the top wire-line captains tend to troll approximately 300 feet (91 m) of wire. This, of course, is a lot of work to clear if you hook a sizable fish on another line. Also, if you have an interest in billfish, many experienced captains believe that wire lines negatively impact billfish strikes on other baits and lures in the spread (our experiments support this

contention). You will likely catch more wahoo and tuna on wire than on any other lines, even in the absence of visible surface activity, and your ability to catch all manner of reef and bottom species by trolling will be substantially enhanced with a wire-line setup.

TROLLING-GEAR MAINTENANCE

When you bring your trolling rigs in the last time each day, detach them from the snap swivels, coil them neatly, and check them over carefully for chafe

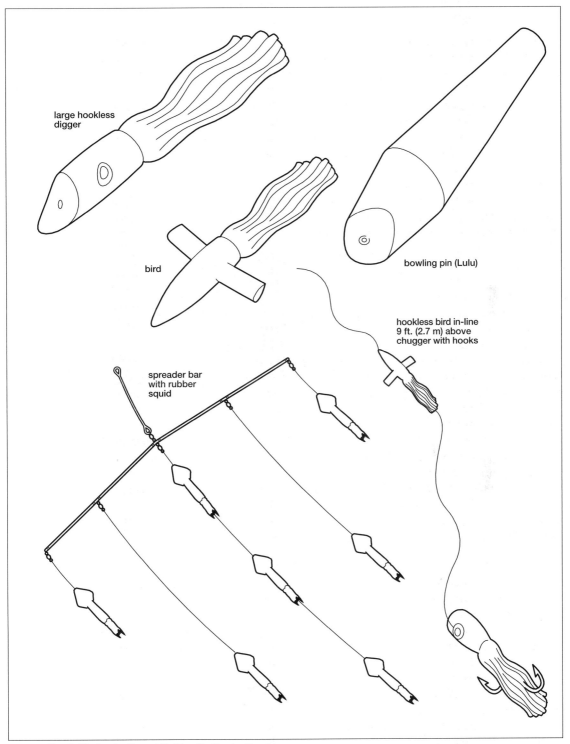

large hookless
digger

bird

bowling pin (Lulu)

hookless bird in-line
9 ft. (2.7 m) above
chugger with hooks

spreader bar
with rubber
squid

Fig. 3-17. A selection of highly effective trolling teasers.

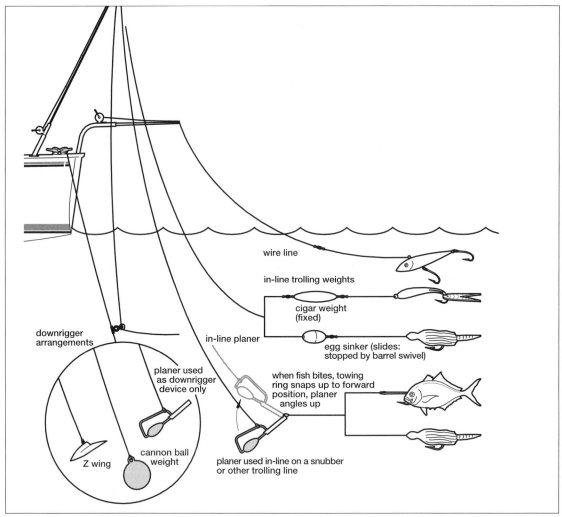

wire line

in-line trolling weights

cigar weight
(fixed)

downrigger
arrangements

in-line planer

egg sinker (slides:
stopped by barrel swivel)

planer used
as downrigger
device only

when fish bites, towing
ring snaps up to forward
position, planer
angles up

Z wing

cannon ball
weight

planer used in-line on a snubber
or other trolling line

Fig. 3-18. Arrangements for trolling lines at significant depth.

or damage. Straighten light leader wire with a wire straightener, cut out any damage (i.e., abraded or knotted monofilament, kinked single-strand wire), reconnect them, rinse with freshwater, and hang them up to dry (fig. 3-19). Use a small spray bottle for this purpose to economize on freshwater usage at sea.

Rinse all roller guides, reel seats, and reels with the same spray bottle. Occasionally scrub reels and reel seats with freshwater and light detergent to defeat salt deposits. Dry with a rag and spray lightly with anti-corrosion oil, stow below or strap on a protective reel cover and leave in the rod holder. Ultraviolet light waves oxidize monofilament, so keeping reels covered

while outside greatly prolongs time between line changes. Be sure a safety lanyard is attached to the outfit. Store your now-dry trolling rigs below to prevent deterioration from salt spray. (See appendix 4 for detailed periodic reel maintenance procedures.)

Safely Boating Your Catch

Let's suppose a desire to improve your fishing skills carried you energetically through the discussions of fishing equipment, connections, lures, baits, rigging, and deployment schemes, and you've finally gotten the chance for a test run . . . perhaps an early summer day off a subtropical coastline. The new gear is

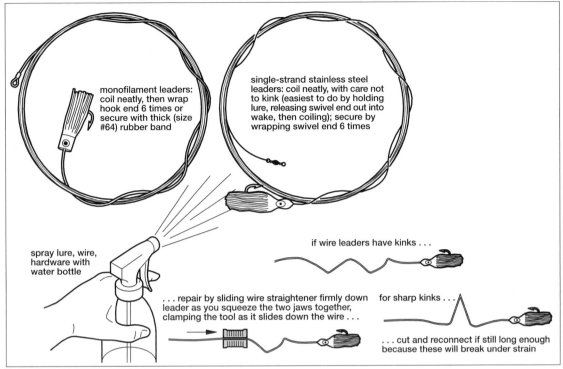

monofilament leaders: coil neatly, then wrap hook end 6 times or secure with thick (size #64) rubber band

single-strand stainless steel leaders: coil neatly, with care not to kink (easiest to do by holding lure, releasing swivel end out into wake, then coiling); secure by wrapping swivel end 6 times

spray lure, wire, hardware with water bottle

if wire leaders have kinks . . .

. . . repair by sliding wire straightener firmly down leader as you squeeze the two jaws together, clamping the tool as it slides down the wire . . .

for sharp kinks . . .

. . . cut and reconnect if still long enough because these will break under strain

Fig. 3-19. Care and maintenance of trolling rigs.

gleaming in the afternoon sunlight. The drag is set and razor-sharp hooks slice through the water beyond the transom, rigged on a seductive offering. A gentle, balmy, 12-knot breeze kisses your beam as you move comfortably over an easy swell. Two hours pass and you've all but forgotten the lively bait or lure swimming frantically in the wake. A languid glance aft at just the right moment to see it disappear in a wild detonation of flying seawater becomes a bug-eyed look of surprise, and the line begins melting off your shiny new reel at an alarming pace. What now?

Particularly in the case of larger fish like the one that is now heading for the horizon with your lure, you and your crew need to do the following.

1. Set the hook by removing the rod from the holder and imparting a few sharp jabs. (Omit this step for your wire line or rail-mounted reel. Some experienced fishers would say never do it on the troll. We do—you can't hurt anything, and at slower boat speeds setting the hook

could easily finish driving it through a tough part of the jaw, resulting in a successful hook-up instead of a lost fish.)
2. Slow or stop the boat.
3. Start the engine/adjust or drop sails.
4. Strap the stand-up belt and harness onto a fisher (if it's the stand-up outfit that got hit), who should immediately start the short-stroke pumping technique when the fish stops taking line (fig. 3-20).

If the fish threatens to run all of the line off the spool, and you want it, you'll have to turn the boat around and follow it to regain some line. Tire the fish with relentless pressure . . . remember the old fishing guide's axiom: If you rest, the fish rests.

As the battle moves into closer quarters, keep the boat moving downwind, forward, and away from the fish, thus preventing entanglement with the prop and rudder. Don't get caught upwind of the fish. Continue to keep the boat moving forward as you begin the leadering process, speeding up if the fish starts to head under the boat, slowing back down, stopping, even reversing temporarily if you begin to lose line as the fish drags aft. *Never wrap the leader completely around your hand.* Handline across your palms, fingers up and wrapped over the leader, thumbs out, turning your palms to your chest—always ready to let go if the fish suddenly surges away. If necessary, give your biceps a break from this style by turning both palms down—note that you are still taking the pressure across the outside of each palm, but now your triceps are taking the load (see photo, right). *Keep your fingers, feet, head—everything—clear of loose coils or loops of leader material.* Have a high quality gaff, fish billy (i.e., club), and ice pick ready.

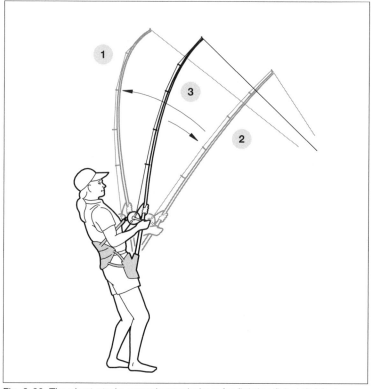

Fig. 3-20. The short-stroke pumping technique for fighting fish. Lift **(1)**, drop and wind **(2)**, and lift again **(3)**.

Always gaff using an overhand stroke *behind* the leader so you do not risk de-hooking the fish on a missed shot, and try to gaff in or just behind the head. Always orient the hook down. You can get away with body shots on some fish more reliably than others. For example, gaff shots to the body hold fairly well on tuna, but you should try hard for a near-head shot on mahi mahi because they often tear off of a body shot. Think twice before you gaff a fish much over 100 pounds (45 kg), perhaps less. Make sure it is as tired and played out as possible, and consider using a gaff hook to loop on a tail rope attached to a cleat or winch. Welcome your catch aboard with some sharp blows to the head using the billy, and finish matters with a stab to the brain using the ice pick; a shudder followed by slight trembling and general immobilization, often accompanied by a sudden color change, indicates a successful hit. Tossing a towel or wet burlap sack over the fish's head (shielding the eyes) will often quell flopping and struggling while you finish matters. *Watch out for sharp teeth, fin spines, scutes, and other hazardous fish body parts.* Dispatch fish quickly

Correct leadering technique is critical to personal safety.

Tools for Landing Fish

Having the right tools for the job will boost your fish-landing success rate (see photo below). Purchasing *all* of these items would go far beyond the needs, if not the budgets, of most cruisers. Select a subset of items applicable to your situation. You can save money by constructing your own gaffs (fig. 3-21). Make two—one with an 8/0 and the other with a 12/0 fishhook—following the instructions, and you're covered for a variety of fish sizes. The smaller size is called a picker gaff and is extremely handy for landing small mackerels, tunas, mahi mahi, jacks, trevallys, snappers, and similar fish that otherwise frequently shake off the hook as you attempt to lift them bodily from the water by the leader.

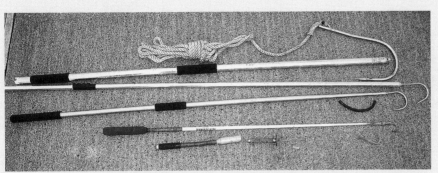

Bottom to top: Fish billy and ice pick 6 ft. (1.8 m) AFTCO gaff with 4 in. (102 mm) hook, 8 ft. (2.4 m) gaff with 6 in. (15 cm) hook, Pompanette flying gaff.

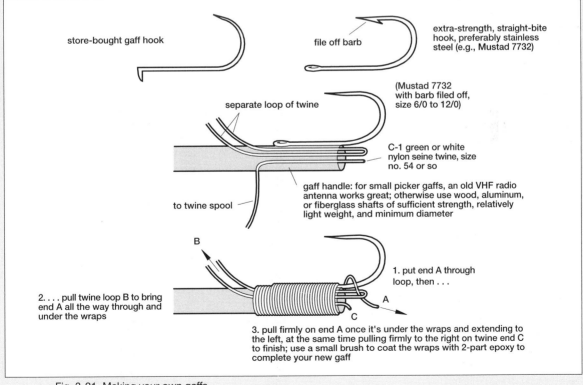

store-bought gaff hook

file off barb

extra-strength, straight-bite hook, preferably stainless steel (e.g., Mustad 7732)

(Mustad 7732 with barb filed off, size 6/0 to 12/0)

separate loop of twine

C-1 green or white nylon seine twine, size no. 54 or so

to twine spool

gaff handle: for small picker gaffs, an old VHF radio antenna works great; otherwise use wood, aluminum, or fiberglass shafts of sufficient strength, relatively light weight, and minimum diameter

B

1. put end A through loop, then . . .

2. . . . pull twine loop B to bring end A all the way through and under the wraps

A

C

3. pull firmly on end A once it's under the wraps and extending to the left, at the same time pulling firmly to the right on twine end C to finish; use a small brush to coat the wraps with 2-part epoxy to complete your new gaff

Fig. 3-21. Making your own gaffs.

before they inflict damage on you, your crew, or your vessel. Even a 15-pound (7 kg) mahi mahi or tuna can dish out significant punishment.

Be especially careful of the *incredibly* sharp rows of teeth on wahoo of any size. Light contact—for example, accidentally brushing your heel across the jaw of a motionless fish on deck—can easily slice you to the bone. A strong slash across an artery from a live wahoo coming aboard could have extremely serious consequences on a slow cruising boat far from help.

Billfish and sharks require special handling. Most cruisers decide to release these animals unharmed after bringing them boatside for photos and perhaps a scientific tag. Control played-out billfish by grabbing the bill (be sure to wear gloves) and carefully removing the hook rig. *Do not* bend over so that your body is across the direction the billfish is pointing—people have been literally skewered by last-minute leaps. If you can't get the hooks out, cut the leader as close to the jaw as possible; this is usually also the best strategy for releasing sharks.

Steve McKenny shows perfect form gaffing this mahi mahi.

Selected Trolling Specialties

Cruising seafarers who use good technique often catch all they want en route to their destinations. Sometimes, however, we hit dry spells—sections of coastline or ocean spaces with little apparent fish activity. If we spot signs of fish at times like these, we suddenly become more interested in making a deviation from the rhumb line. We can taste those

A Near Miss

One blustery winter day, 200 NM south of St. Croix, U.S. Virgin Islands, a small (165 lbs./75 kg) blue marlin amply demonstrated the power, speed, and potential danger of leadering billfish. Dale, my beefy, tattoo-covered crewmate aboard the high-seas swordfish longliner *Rush*, was vigorously handlining this particular individual to the boat for release so that we could continue hauling gear. The fish's head was pointing toward our beam as it wagged slowly closer in response to firm pressure on the 300-pound (136 kg) test monofilament leader. Without warning, the fish erupted from the sea and began tail-walking across the water, straight for the opening in the bulwark used for hauling fish aboard. Dale alertly dropped the leader, but the sheer speed of the panicked, airborne rush made an imminent collision and possible impalement seem certain. The fish's tail smacked the lip of the deck as it came flying aboard, dropping the onrushing bill to Dale's waist level. Somehow, like a matador in a bullfight, he managed to leap aside and spin laterally as the fish flew directly at him—but not quite fast enough. The bill caught the outer 2 inches (50 mm) of his beer belly and got just enough traction on the

exposed skin to spin him like a top as it crashed by and slammed hard into the mainline reel spool.

I had dived aft and the two other crewmen had dived forward toward the wheelhouse. My relief at not seeing the gaping, bloody hole I expected in my friend's stomach was quickly dissipated by the stoic, pathological expression on his face and the rapid exit of the other crew to the protection of the wheelhouse. Dale quietly picked up the meat cleaver lying at the butcher's station, and suddenly hurled it forcefully across the deck in the direction of the flopping marlin. Incredibly, the flying meat cleaver buried itself neatly in the fish's brain, causing it to abruptly freeze, stone dead. The other guys emerged from hiding and matter-of-factly resumed work, with no words spoken.

I later asked the butcher, who'd been fishing with Dale for ten years, "How'd you guys know to run inside the wheelhouse so quickly?" He replied, "Any time we see that expression, we know he's about to do something really out of hand." "Oh. Well, what about that throw, does he practice it or what?" "Naw, he just got lucky."

Reading the Signs

Fish are not evenly distributed offshore. They congregate along specific oceanographic features and bottom topography, and may associate with floating debris and even other animals. Their presence can be detected, directly or indirectly, by the alert cruising seafarer armed with some fundamental knowledge.

♦ *Current shear*. This is a zone where adjacent water masses are moving past each other at different velocities, sometimes evident as a color change, surface slick, or a pattern of ripples, eddies, or swirls. Pelagic weeds (e.g., sargassum) and debris collect along these zones, with a myriad of prey items for pelagic predator fish. If you spot such a condition either near an island or shallow bank, such as an outgoing tidal plume, or far at sea during a passage, this is a prime area for trolling.

♦ *Floating debris*. Tuna, wahoo, mahi mahi, sharks, billfish, and a variety of smaller species may all be found in the vicinity of objects that have spent some time afloat offshore—tree parts, freight pallets, and other lumber lost overboard by ships; bundles of tangled fishing gear; floats; pieces of hawser; small boats or rafts—anything, even your own sailboat or power cruiser on longer offshore passages. Trolling around anything like this, or simply deploying your presentations if it's you they're hanging around, can quickly result in fresh fish for dinner.

♦ *Bottom topography*. While planning your next passage, take note of any steep drop-offs near islands that you pass or offshore banks and seamounts in the vicinity of your intended rhumb line. These features tend to deflect nutrient-rich deeper waters to sunlit surface layers, precipitating pockets of biological activity founded on enhanced local phytoplankton production, and, consequently, elevated predator fish concentrations. Watch out for large, breaking seas around the seamounts when it's rough, however.

♦ *Bird and baitfish activity*. Swarms of seabirds feeding on bait items pushed to the surface by predators below often occur over an offshore seamount, although pockets of bird and bait activity also may

be present far from significant bottom topography. With a little practice, you can frequently deduce both the presence and identity of some predator fish based on seabird behavior. Erratically diving terns and boobies—moving rapidly in sometimes quickly changing directions—often indicate surface schools of tuna. Smaller groups of terns, hovering and dipping vertically over a steadier, slower-changing trajectory, frequently indicate mahi mahi. Similarly, frigate birds holding to a fairly slow steady course, occasionally interrupted by a swoop to the sea surface, are often tracking pods of larger mahi mahi or even a single tailing billfish. Dense packs of terns hovering low over the water near Indo-Pacific atolls regularly indicate the presence of rainbow runners and juvenile skipjack tuna. If you need a fish, maneuver your trolled offerings near and under the birds.

♦ *Marine mammals, sharks, and turtles*. The association, particularly in the equatorial Pacific, of dolphins with yellowfin tuna has become infamous due to its use by tuna purse-seiners. Unlike purse-seining, trolling in the vicinity of dolphin herds can't hurt the dolphin and may allow you to bag a nice tuna or two, perhaps a marlin. We have found both skipjack and yellowfin tuna in association with small whale species in the Bahamas and Caribbean. On several occasions, we have caught mahi mahi that were swimming along the surface in association with whale sharks off the Florida Keys. Similarly, one of the best ways to find mahi mahi offshore throughout

(continued next page)

Boobies and terns swarm over a surface-feeding school of mixed skipjack and yellowfin tuna east of Tahiti-Iti, French Polynesia.

Reading the Signs (cont.)

the tropics is to locate a sea turtle basking on the surface. Approach with care, however, because if you spook the turtle, the mahi mahi usually dive down with it.

♦ *Direct sightings.* If you wear polarized sunglasses and a billed cap, and particularly if you have a transom arch, crow's nest, flying bridge, or other structure that allows you to spend some time elevated above the deck while offshore, you will be surprised at the number of directly visible, free-swimming pelagic fish you can spot with some practice. Sharks, marlin, sailfish, and many other species spend a certain amount of time right at the sea surface, sometimes actively tailing down the face of waves with bits of fins and tail sticking out, other times basking nearly still or lazily moving. We have on two occasions observed small blue marlin come wagging right up to the steering-vane servo-rudder, spotted while we sat side by side facing aft on our transom arch (with no baits out). Getting as far

above deck as you can around debris or weed lines can result in sighting and capturing mahi mahi, wahoo, tripletails, rainbow runner, and other species.

♦ *Time of day.* Early morning and evening are prime feeding times for many offshore species. Having a line or lines in the water at first light and until well after the sun disappears often results in spectacular catches. Many pelagic species also feed all night, particularly on a bright or full moon, and can be caught trolling if you need some excitement on the graveyard shift.

♦ *Atmospheric condition.* Overcast conditions are normally far more productive for offshore trolling—use darker lure colors for better contrast. Rough, windy conditions also induce higher levels of near-surface fish actively offshore. A bright, clear, and calm sunny day is generally a more difficult fishing condition, but can be overcome by reading signs and finding some pocket of activity, or by deploying your wire line.

fish fillets before we change course and get the gear in the water. Enthusiastic crew may even request more focused fishing efforts, extra passage time be damned. When you are no longer satisfied only with the fish that find *you*, how do you go about finding *them*? Read the signs.

Aside from general signs, numerous species-specific tricks of the trade can sharply enhance your ability to put fresh fish on the table. We review several of these applicable to widespread areas of the world traveled heavily by cruising powerboats and sailboats.

Mahi Mahi

Mahi mahi *(Coryphaena hippurus)* are highly migratory and occur worldwide in tropical and warm subtropical seas. Smaller individuals swim in sometimes large schools, often near the sea surface. Larger individuals, from 16 pounds (7 kg) or so to the maximum size for the species (90 lbs./41 kg), normally travel in smaller groups of two to seven, occasionally more. They are fast, colorful, often strike readily, and have delicious, firm white meat.

Target mahi mahi with splashy surface lures and

baits, preferably on monofilament leaders. Leaving one hooked individual in the water may keep other school members in the vicinity of the boat, allowing additional captures. If they follow trolled offerings but won't bite, try increasing the speed by reeling or pulling in line and imparting more erratic action by sweeping the rod tip sharply in short, fast arcs or, with handlines, by sharp tugs on the line. Present natural baits to them—adding a fluttering thin strip to the hook of a skirted lure or letting back a nicely rigged whole flying fish can make the difference.

Mahi mahi are extremely generalized feeders but, like other species, may become focused on specific prey categories according to local availability. One example is flying fish—groups of mahi mahi that are chasing these fleet baitfish tend to be moving fast and may be more difficult to tempt with lures bearing no resemblance to flying fish, especially at low boat speeds. Obviously, whole rigged flying fish are ideal for this situation, although any higher-speed fish imitations in blue, white, and silver may suffice. The complete opposite is mahi mahi casually traveling along dense sargassum weed lines, feeding on juvenile jacks, crabs, shrimp, puffers, filefish, trig-gerfish, and myriad other weed-associated prey, most of which are yellowish-brown in color. This is when amber rubber squid, as well as bucktail jigs, octopus skirts, trolling feathers, and various skirted lures in yellows and greens, have maximum attraction. Mahi mahi hanging around seamounts and current rips may be predisposed toward the same lures in pink, red, orange, and white, reflecting a high proportion of cephalopod prey items in the area.

Stay tuned for more mahi mahi tricks in the next chapter.

WAHOO

Wahoo *(Acanthocybium solanderi)* may reach at least 183 pounds(83 kg) and are sometimes solitary, but usually occur in groups, often in greater numbers for smaller-sized individuals, worldwide in tropical and warm-temperate oceanic waters. They associate strongly with floating debris, steep drop-offs, and seamounts, and may also be caught offshore in open water. In many respects, they are ecological oppo-sites of mahi mahi, preferring the cooler sea sur-face temperatures of winter months in the tropics and greater average feeding depths.

Target wahoo with flashy or dark-colored sub-surface offerings trolled at speeds near the upper range for specific lures and deep on light, long, low-visibility wire leaders. Swimming plugs, jet heads, clones, large spoons, octopus/feather/strip combina-tions, sea witches, and whole baits rigged to swim below the surface top the list. Use of a downrigger, wire line, or other means of trolling your presenta-tion at a 30- to 60-foot (9 to 18 m) depth vastly increases the number of wahoo captures.

LARGE MACKEREL

King mackerel (tropical Atlantic/Caribbean, *Scomberomorus cavalla*) and narrow-barred mackerel (Indo-Pacific, *Scomberomorus commerson*) are similar ecologically to wahoo except that they are coastal rather than oceanic and attain a smaller maximum size (100 lbs./45 kg). These fish are susceptible to the same presentations that work well for wahoo. Reduce the size of leader wire, lures, and hooks for maximum number of strikes. Troll outer reefs, wrecks, and shelf breaks. If you get too many "short strikes" from these

The sharp teeth of the Indo-Pacific dogtooth tuna *(Gynmnosarda unicolor)*, like most mackerel, dictate the use of wire leader.

slashing feeders, install a "stinger," consisting of a short length of single-strand leader wire attached from the eye of the existing hook on your lure or bait to a small treble hook (e.g., Mustad 3561E). See instructions in chapter 4, page 99.

TUNA

This large, ecologically diverse group of fish includes small coastal bonitos (genera *Euthynnus, Sarda*), small oceanic species (skipjack tuna, *Katsuwonus pelamis*; blackfin tuna, *Thunnus atlanticus*; albacore, *Thunnus alalunga*), medium to large species that support large fisheries worldwide (yellowfin tuna, *Thunnus albacores*; bigeye tuna, *Thunnus obesus*), and giants that may reach 1,500 pounds (680 kg) (bluefin tuna, *Thunnus thynnus*). Tuna-feeding ecol-ogy encompasses everything described for mahi mahi and wahoo; thus, any of the methods for tar-geting those species work well for tuna. One Indo-Pacific species, dogtooth tuna *(Gymnosarda unicolor)*, is very similar to the large mackerels and susceptible to the same fishing techniques, including the use of wire leaders to defeat their sharp teeth.

Use mahi mahi–style surface presentations adjusted to tuna target species size near surface-feeding schools, in rough and overcast weather, and during early morning and late afternoon hours. Target tuna with subsurface wahoo-style gear in the absence of visible surface activity, during calm and sunny conditions, especially during midday hours. Remember that some tuna frequently swim in mixed-species schools; therefore, trolling larger baits and lures near groups of apparently small individuals may often draw a strike from a much larger fish swimming below the little folks.

Tuna can be very sensitive to engine noise but will slowly become accustomed to a trolling vessel in their midst if you adjust your engine rpm to match the swimming speed of the school *and then do not vary it.* Surface schools accept the presence of sailing vessels even more quickly. In either case, it is common for tuna in open water to begin swimming along with your vessel, feeding on flying fish and squid spooked into flight by the hull, and packing closely to the hull during periodic visits by larger predators such as marlin. This may supply you with a ready source of fresh fish on longer passages.

> ### Skipjack Tuna, Tahitian Style
>
> Acclimating fish schools to engine noise is the key to success in a unique fishery for skipjack tuna operating throughout French Polynesia. Fast, locally built, wood flying-bridge fishing boats powered by single, turbo-charged diesels head offshore in search of surface-feeding tuna schools marked by birds. The boat slows down to lure speed (about 5 knots) and drives gently into the center of the school, adjusting to a steady rpm that causes the boat speed to match the swimming speed of the school. The crew deploys skipping spoons made from pearl oyster shells, trolled close to the boat on short lengths of 300-pound (136 kg) monofilament from 20 feet (6.1 m) bamboo or fiberglass poles.

REEF AND BOTTOM FISH

Virtually any midwater or bottom-dwelling predator fish species associated with seafloor features is susceptible to trolling with lures and natural baits. These fish will attack surface lures in shallow, clearer waters. More often, you should target these groups with deep trolling methods and relatively heavy tackle to counter their propensity to dive for bot-

Pearl oyster shells and Polynesian tuna lure. Fishers take advantage of subtle differences in the hues of individual shells to make various lure colors. When the tuna stop biting one color, fishers grab another bamboo pole armed with a slightly different-colored lure from the bundle lashed to the bridge (see next page, top), deploy it, and the bites often start again. Note the barbless hook on the lure.

The first skipjack tunas *(Katsuwonus pelamis)* bite as the school becomes accustomed to the presence of the boat. Each tuna is snatched bodily into the air, and de-hooks as it hits the deck. Soon they're striking two at a time.

One crew member works full-time gutting and racking the fish as they come aboard, sloshing them periodically with fresh seawater to keep them cool and fresh.

tom structure, once hooked. The presence of multiple species, some of which possess sharp teeth, normally dictates the use of wire leaders. As usual, use of leaders with sufficient length and minimum strength and hardware to reduce visibility sharply increases the number of strikes. Adjust boat speed and lure or bait size to target species for your area. Quite low boat speeds may be relatively more effective for some species, but do not underestimate the ability even of bottom dwellers to capture faster-swimming objects in fast rushes from their lairs.

BILLFISH

Marlin include a species that may reach a maximum size approaching 2,000 pounds (907 kg) and occur worldwide (blue marlin, *Makaira nigricans*), an equally large (possibly larger) species limited to the Indo-Pacific (black marlin, *Makaira indica*), and other smaller species with less than worldwide distributions (striped marlin, *Tetrapterus audax*; and white marlin, *Tetrapterus albidus*). Blue and black marlin are limited to tropical and warm temperate zones, while striped and white marlin range farther into temperate seas during summer months (sometimes 40

Jon Broadhurst with a lyretail grouper that charged off the bottom to take a large swimming plug trolled from an inflatable dinghy (Tonga).

Shortbill spearfish *(Tetrapterus angustirostris)* caught trolling a Mold Craft Super Chugger 325 NM north of New Zealand. We released this fish unharmed just after taking the photo.

degrees latitude or more from the equator). All are highly migratory oceanic fishes and voracious predators, and may occur close to land or in the open sea. Therefore, regardless of what lures you troll, you have an excellent chance of someday getting a bite from one of these species over a large area of the planet, whether you want it or not.

Marlin are best targeted with larger, splashy lures and baits on heavy monofilament leaders and heavier tackle. They also readily eat a variety of subsurface presentations. They exhibit a general preference for faster trolling speeds (7–8 to 15 knots); however, they can be effectively enticed at medium cruising boat speed (3 to 6 knots), and occasionally are caught trolling lower speed presentations, particularly those involving natural bait. The same color themes discussed for other oceanic species work. It's hard to go wrong with pink or black and purple, but if you're serious, keep a full range of the myriad color combinations available and rotate them regularly through your bait spread. Large, splashy teasers can enhance strike rates.

Sailfish *(Istiophorus platypterus)* occur worldwide in tropical and subtropical seas, normally but not exclusively in association with land masses (see photo page 306). Maximum size is likely not more than 250 pounds (113 kg). Sailfish feeding protocol normally differs significantly from marlin in that they often more deliberately approach, firmly grasp and crush, then swallow prey rather than wild, high-speed engulfing. Thus, marlin-style "drag and snag" lure trolling catches fewer sailfish than other methods, even if they are abundant in a given area. Sailfish exhibit a distinct preference for smaller baits and lures trolled at slower speeds, and multiple teaser arrangements, such as spreader bars, which consist of numerous smaller items like rubber squid. Troll natural baits and *soft material lures*, like products from Mold Craft, with reels in or near free-spool, and clicker on. Allow ten seconds or so of drop-back before you throw the drag to strike position (or close the spinning-reel bail), quickly reel up any slack, and set the hook.

Spearfish consist of three documented species: longbill spearfish *(Tetrapterus pfluegeri,* Atlantic), shortbill spearfish *(T. angustirostris,* Indo-Pacific and southwestern Atlantic), and Mediterranean spearfish *(T. belone,* Mediterranean). Maximum size for longbill spearfish, apparently the largest, is 100 pounds (45 kg). Spearfish morphology is intermediate between sailfish and marlin. They are uncommon over most of their ranges, occurring almost exclusively in deep offshore waters. Trolling captures occur on small baits and lures up to marlin-sized gear, indicating aggressive feeding tactics of sometimes small (20 lbs./9 kg) individuals. Rarity makes spearfish difficult to target—put out some splashy skirted lure/bait combinations well offshore and don't hold your breath waiting for the first one to bite.

A Few Last Tricks and Tips

Let's examine a few situations, routine and rare, where a little know-how can make a big difference.

♦ *Somehow your line becomes badly twisted.* A swivel locks up while trolling a spoon, a bait or lure fouls and spins for a time unnoticed, an inexperienced fisher cranks the handle of a spinning reel without gaining line—all of these events can cause monofilament to become so twisted that any slack produces an instant "hair ball." Cut above the double line and let out the twisted running line into the wake while under way. Be sure to allow the full length that became twisted off the reel. Troll this plain, unadorned line 5 or 10 minutes, then retrieve it, and it will be like new.

♦ *A fish is just about to run all of the line off the spool.* Grab a second outfit with the highest available line capacity. Clip the snap swivel onto the outfit about to be spooled, or tie the end of the line to it, anywhere solid around the reel seat. Adjust the drag of this second outfit to approximately half or less the drag setting of the first outfit. When the fish gets near the end of the spool, throw the first outfit overboard, continue the fight with the second outfit until you recover the first, fight the fish again on the original outfit, and repeat if necessary. In lieu of a second outfit, tie a life jacket or poly ball onto the rod and reel, and toss it overboard just before the spool empties. Let the fish tire and then retrieve the outfit; recover the line normally, repeating as necessary. This fairly standard charterboat trick accounts for many an oversized fish on light tackle. The submerged reel will need thorough service after the trip (see appendix 4).

♦ *You lack a reel with a drag but would still like to catch some big fish.* Rig a poly ball to the end of your trolled handline and attach it to the boat with light monofilament (one loop, strength equal to about 25 percent of the breaking strength of your mainline; e.g., a 50 lb./23 kg test breakaway for a 200 lb./91 kg mainline). When the fish hits, the poly ball breaks free under enough tension to firmly set the hook, but not break the trolling line, and goes flying overboard. Turn the boat around, give the fish some time to tire, then pull alongside of the poly ball, retrieve the line with a gaff or boat hook, and handline the fish to the boat. We elaborate on this topic in chapter 4.

♦ *What about landing really big fish?* Your straight gaff won't do for monsters, with maximum size suitable for straight gaffing determined by your strength and experience. The majority of cruisers decide to release such specimens; however, if keeping one is consistent with your needs, storage capability, and conservation ethics, you'll need a strong stainless steel meat hook with a welded, closed handle and rope attached, or a flying gaff, the head of which detaches from the handle with a twisting motion under pressure and secures to a cleat with a length of strong rope (see sources in appendix 1).

♦ *Everyday gear vigilance.* At the end of each day, early the next morning, and periodically during fishing, cast a sharp eye on your gear. Run your fingers along the line—do you feel any chafing or powdery white oxidation from ultraviolet exposure? If so, change the line and carefully inspect your rod guides for any grooves or damage that could be causing chafe. Also check outrigger and downrigger release pins for similar defects. What if the line *looks* OK but you experienced an unexplained break-off or suspect it's getting old? Grasp the line tightly with each hand, and pull apart sharply (use gloves for heavier monofilament)—if it breaks easily, oxidation has taken a toll. You'll get used to the right feel for different line strengths by trying this with fresh line. When in doubt, change the line. Also check leaders for chafe and nicks, single-strand wire for kinks (straighten these—see instructions in figure 3-19—or change the leader), and examine all hook points after each capture or snag on any object. Did the point hit bone and break off or deform? Is the hook slightly opened? Return all salvageable hooks to original condition with a file or by bending back into shape, or reject them for a fresh one.

Check Those Hooks, Dummy

The day that commercial tuna fisher Mike Needham asked me to play bonefish guide for him at remote Palmyra Atoll (Line Islands, U.S.A.), I got him started with a spinning rod before moving into fly-fishing gear. He soon caught a small bonefish on a light brown Phillips Wiggle Jig and was getting used to spotting, casting, and working the lure. Minutes later, he cast to a pair of larger bonefish coming up the deep edge of the flat, only to have a bluefin trevally race up from the emerald lagoon depths and hit the jig hard before the bonefish could get to it, putting a brief strong bend in the rod, and then swimming off unhooked. This happened again ten minutes later after a nice bonefish engulfed the jig, and one more time fifteen or so minutes later. I started to give Mike a few hints and a little ribbing about timing. He didn't say much, then quietly reeled in and closely examined the lure. The entire hook had snapped off right at the bend, almost certainly from that bluefin trevally. Of course, this led to an hour or so of commentary about the difficulty these days of finding good guides.

Gear Checklist

Table 3-2 is a selection of lures, hooks, leader materials, leader hardware, tools, materials, and accessories for completing tasks described in this chapter, with specific recommendations and approximate prices for each. This list is a distillation of gear selected on the basis of value, durability, and effectiveness. The intent is to save you time, frustration, and money, and to provide you with a reliable foundation for offshore trolling success. Refer to table 8-1, page 233, for recommended outriggers, downriggers, rod holders, and other boat modifications for trolling.

TABLE 3-2. CHECKLIST OF OFFSHORE TROLLING GEAR
(SEE APPENDIX 1 FOR SOURCES)

Item	Specific Recommendation	Approximate Price
Stand-up belt	Braid Power Play Tuna Kit	$84
Stand-up harness	Braid Power Play Harness	$120
10 lb. (4.5 kg) test monofilament	Ande Premium, ¼ lb. spool (1,350 yds./1,234 m)	$6
20 lb. (9 kg) test monofilament	Ande Premium, ¼ lb. spool (600 yds./549 m)	$6
50 lb. (23 kg) test monofilament	Ande Premium, 1 lb. spool (1,000 yds./914 m)	$22
100 lb. (45 kg) test monofilament	Ande Premium, ½ lb. spool (250 yds./228 m)	$12
200 lb. (91 kg) test monofilament	Ande Premium, ½ lb. spool (100 yds./91 m)	$12
300 lb. (136 kg) test monofilament	Ande Premium, ½ lb. spool (67 yds./61 m)	$12
110 lb. (50 kg) test Monel wire	Capt. Harry's solid Monel trolling wire	$19 per pound
#8 stainless steel leader wire	Malin, ¼ lb. spool	$8
#4 stainless steel leader wire	Malin, ¼ lb. spool	$9
#2 stainless steel leader wire	Malin, ¼ lb. spool	$9
Barrel swivels	barrel swivel kit (always in black)	$21
Snap swivels	barrel snap swivel kit (always in black)	$18
Crimps	1.9 mm mini double sleeves (100)	$6
Loop protectors	1.5 and 2 mm	$2 per 10
Hand swager (crimp tool)	sufficient for 1.9 mm sleeves	$19
Stainless steel multistrand cable	Duratest 49 Strand, 400 lb. (181 kg) test, 30 ft. (9 m)	$8
Heat shrink	assortment for hook rig construction	$10 to $20
Tape	vinyl ¾ in. (191 mm) x 20 ft. (6.1 m), various colors	$1
Rigging wire	Malin soft stainless steel	$16
Rigging needles	ring eye, hook eye	$1 each

TABLE 3-2. **CHECKLIST OF OFFSHORE TROLLING GEAR (cont.)**
(SEE APPENDIX 1 FOR SOURCES)

Item	Specific Recommendation	Approximate Price
Bait rigging floss	1,000 ft. (305 m) dispenser	$9
Waxed nylon lacing	170 yd. (155 m) spool	$5
Egg sinkers	¼, ½, ¾, 1 oz. (7, 14, 21, 28 g) (12 each)	$8
Lure heads	Mold Craft Hooker Bubbler Heads	$2 to $4
Wine bottle corks	your choice	highly variable
Stainless big-game hook	Mustad 7691S, 6/0, 7/0, 8/0, 9/0	$2–$3
Stainless big-game hook	Mustad 7732, 9/0	$3
Tinned big-game hook	Mustad 7754 (7/0 to 12/0, match to bait)	$1–$3
Stainless steel double hook	Mustad 7982HS, 3/0, 4/0, 5/0, 6/0, 7/0, 8/0	$2
Tinned triple-strength treble hook	Mustad 3561E (2/0 to 5/0, match to bait)	$0.16–$0.32
Swimming plugs	Australian Runner, 8 in. (203 mm)	$12
	Rapala Countdown Magnum, 7 in. (178 mm)	$11
	Rapala Countdown Magnum, 9 in. (229 mm)	$13
	Rapala Floating Magnum, 7 in. (178 mm)	$10
	Rapala Sliver, 7 ¾ in. (197 mm)	$10
	Rapala Super Shad Rap, 5 ½ in. (140 mm)	$7
	Original Rat-L-Trap, ½ oz. (14 g) sinking	$4
Surface plugs	Yo-Zuri Surface Cruiser, 8 in. (203 mm)	$19
	Pacific Island Lure Innovations, Pili Sinker	$8
Cedar plugs	Sea Striker, 6 in. (152 mm) and 8 in. (203 mm)	$5–$8
Clone	Sevenstrand Tuna Clone, 6 in. (152 mm)	$5
Small digger	C & H Lil' Swimmer, 5 ¾ in. (146 mm)	$5
Straight runners	Mold Craft Little Hooker, 5 ½ in. (140 mm)	$6
	Mold Craft Wide Range, 9 ½ in. (241 mm) standard	$12
	Mold Craft Super Chugger, 8 ¼ in. (210 mm)	$11
	Mold Craft Super Chugger, 11 ½ in. (292 mm)	$20
Teasers	Lulu Teaser, bonito color	$25
	Mold Craft Hooker Soft Bird, 9 ½ in. (241 mm)	$12
Rubber squid	Mold Craft or Yo-zuri Squid, 6 in. (152 mm)	$2
Rubber flying fish	Yo-Zuri Flying Fish, 6 in. (152 mm)	$15
Octopus skirts	Boone or Yo-Zuri, 4 in. (102 mm)	under $1
	Boone or Yo-Zuri, 7 ¾ in. (197 mm)	$2
Trolling feathers	No-Alibi or any other, ¼, ½, 1, 2 oz. (7, 14, 28, 56 g)	$2–$4
Sea witch	No-Alibi Sea Witch, ¼, ½, 1 ½ oz. (7, 14, 21 g)	$1–$2
Spoons	Drone Spoon, 5 ¼ in. (133 mm)	$4
	Tony Acetta Pet Spoon, 2 ¼ oz. (64 g)	$7
	Clark Spoon, RBM Model, 3 in. (76 mm)	$3
	Krocodile Spoon, chrome 2¹¹⁄₁₆ in. (68 mm)	$3
Jet head	Offshore Jet Head, 8 ½ in. (216 mm)	$15
Jigs	Millie's Roundhead Jig, ⅜ oz. (11 g)	$3
	Capt. Hank Brown's Hookup Jigs, ¼, ⅜, ½ oz. (7–14 g)	$1
	Saltwater Assortment plastic bait variety kit	$30
Fishing pliers	Sargent Sportmate, 6 ½ in. (165 mm)	$28

(continued next page)

TABLE 3-2. **CHECKLIST OF OFFSHORE TROLLING GEAR (cont.)**
(SEE APPENDIX 1 FOR SOURCES)

Item	Specific Recommendation	Approximate Price
Fishing pliers belt case	Ruff 'n' Ready, leather	$6
Hook file	Sharp 4 in.	$6
Sharpening stone	#10 bench stone, 8 in. (203 mm)	$8
Gaff	Aftco 4 in. (102 mm) hook, 6 ft. (1.8 m) handle	$62
Picker gaff	Aftco 2 in. (51 mm) hook, 4 ft. (1.2 m) handle	$39
Box hook	Reliable Handy Hook	$21
Gloves	cotton work gloves, or orange polyester	$3/pair
Fish billy	No-Alibi	$15
Stainless steel ice pick	West Marine	$7
Hook removers	10 ½ in. (266 mm) Offshore Angler hook remover	$5
	9 ½ in.(241 mm) stainless steel Hook Out	$11
Wire straightener	Capt. Harry's medium (#5–#15)	$8
Polarized sunglasses	any	$12 to over $100
Billed cap	any	free to over $20
Release clips	Aftco Roller Troller, outrigger style	$33
	Aftco Roller Troller, flat line clip	$17
Trolling planer	HS 8 Sea Striker	$20

4

Adrift or Anchored

Offshore trolling accounts for a high percentage of whatever fish are caught by many cruising seafarers. Few, however, are aware of the full spectrum of highly productive possibilities available when the boat is no longer moving quickly through the water. Indeed, many situations exist where persistent, continued trolling is actually counterproductive. In this chapter, we discuss stationary techniques from a logical voyaging perspective, beginning with the transition from offshore trolling mode, continuing with how to catch fish while becalmed at sea or restfully residing in protected anchorages. Finally, we look at more energetic, directed pursuits such as power-drifting or anchoring over and near wrecks, reefs, and other bottom features for the purpose of fishing.

Before this sequence of fishing scenarios, we arm you with knowledge and specific fishing techniques applicable to very slow-moving, drifting, or anchored vessels. These techniques require varying amounts of effort. The decision of how much energy you have available and want to expend on the pursuit of fish is highly personal and tends to vary widely. One axiom of fishing is that if you're willing to go to enough properly focused effort, you can *make* things happen regardless of substantial adversity. Some cruising folks might go no further than dangling an untended line while they snooze in the hammock under an awning; others become full-blown cruise-fishing fanatics. A dose of knowledge, a taste of success frequently propels formerly casual dabblers hurtling down the path toward the enthusiastic, energetic end of the fishing activity spectrum.

What is the fuel that ignites this journey? *Fun* . . . and the anticipation that further sacrifice may result in even *more fun* . . . in many ways the most fundamental people-driver. This chapter summarizes a range of methods and their application to fishing while adrift or anchored, within a range of budgets and level of effort, that can amplify the amount of *fun* you have when you are not underway. This fun will be a combination of fresh seafood dinners and cruise-fishing aesthetics made possible by your new expertise.

Attracting Fish to Your Boat

Cruising vessels often have a passive feel while underway. Think of the many instances when you may have observed—and perhaps tried to maneuver and intercept—fast, erratic surface schools of fish. It becomes quickly obvious that the farther you are below a maximum vessel speed capability of at least 12 to 15 knots, the less your ability to force yourself and trolled offerings on rapidly swimming fish. This passivity is at no time greater than when you are adrift or anchored. Except when you have searched for and located fish, and positioned your boat accordingly prior to becoming stationary (or nearly so), you will *only* get a shot at fish that swim near or under your vessel.

The good news is that fish generally tend to be strongly attracted to drifting and anchored floating objects, including your boat. Fishers, fishing organizations, and government agencies worldwide capitalize on this well-known propensity by constructing, deploying, and maintaining a variety of floating and suspended devices, usually moored but in some cases drifting, to attract and concentrate desirable fish species. These are called fish aggregating devices (FADs). You may be familiar with one common type of FAD in widespread use near islands and coastlines: floating steel rafts or buoys moored in depths of 1,500 to more than 2,500 feet (457 to 762 m) that demand your attention for safe navigation.

Why do people go to so much trouble and expense? Because FADs *really* work. And guess what? The moment you drop sail, take the engine out of gear, or come tight on the hook, you become a full-fledged FAD. The longer you drift or stay anchored, the greater the accumulation of organisms on and around your hull, with no further effort on your part. Frequently, some of this menagerie will be edible species of fish.

The rate and degree of this accumulation process varies widely according to location and is usually related to your proximity to human populations. A polluted anchorage in a major port may produce no significant aggregation useful for food and fishing. More pristine inshore anchorages that receive heavy fishing pressure, or drifting in oceanic zones featuring low biological productivity, may occasionally yield slow-developing, modest results. Remote anchorages—for example, near steep oceanic drop-offs outside sparsely inhabited coral atolls, or drifting in highly productive ocean areas—may feature rapid, spectacular, possibly overwhelming aggregations of fish and other sea life, including numerous sharks. For all but the latter, you may wish to accelerate or enhance the accumulation process by using some combination of three major attraction techniques: chumming (using chum, also called berley, which is usually a ground mix of oily fish), night lighting, and deploying additional FADs.

PUTTING OUT FADS

Deployment of additional FADs is the least likely option you will use to attract fish to the vicinity of your stationary vessel, yet potentially dramatic results make this technique worth knowing about. Possibilities include FADs that are either free-floating or attached to your vessel.

Successful short-term deployment of free-floating FADs by solitary vessels is not common and, in some cases, is more rumor than fact. The idea is to toss overboard something that floats, return to it at a later time, and catch all the fish that have congregated around it over a brief period. Stories include East Coast Florida charter captains spreading rafts of newspaper and other expendable floating material on the sea surface as a hedge against slow conditions farther offshore, returning later to save the day for their clients by catching school-sized mahi mahi now swarming around the material. One could envision more easily located, reusable devices (e.g., a radio transmitter buoy or radar-reflecting high flyer, both used by commercial longline vessels for gear-finding), but this carries the risk of loss and high expense, and it is highly unlikely to conform to a cruising vessel's activities. Furthermore, if local fish density is sufficient for such short-term effectiveness (seldom a reasonable expectation), the likelihood of more efficient means of capture is high. Finding free-floating FADs from other origins that have been in the water for a while is usually superior to expecting success from your own temporary device.

On the other hand, vessels that expect to be adrift offshore for hours or days *might* be motivated to attempt to increase the probability of collecting fish to their vicinity as they slowly traverse open seas. The basic strategy is to let out a floating object(s) on a line to windward, periodically retrieving it to draw any fish that have accumulated around the object(s) to within range of your vessel's fishing gear. Thus, instead of sweeping only one vessel length of ocean as you drift, you can sweep twenty times or more the distance using this method. Commercial fishers use this technique to drift open ocean waters in the southeastern Caribbean with striking results.

THE USE OF CHUM (OR BERLEY)

Commercial chum is normally sold as frozen blocks of ground, oily fish and other organisms and dispensed from submerged or semisubmerged mesh bags or other porous containers attached to the boat. More broadly defined, chum can be any substance released by fishers to attract fish. Entrails, blood, and other scraps from processing fish and invertebrates, tail-roped fish carcasses, fish oil, whole or cut dead baitfish, live baitfish or other small organisms, plate scrapings from meals, rolled oats, cooked rice or pasta . . . there is a huge variety of organic material that attracts fish. Yes, that's right, each time you wash the dishes, you are also chumming, further increasing the fish-attracting power of your stationary vessel.

Several techniques go beyond suspension of marine organism remains from a cleat or rail, or dumping, scraping, and ladling other unpackaged items into the water. These are normally variations intended to dispense chum at depth.

♦ Suspending a weighted chum dispenser on a length of line to the desired depth (e.g., placing a dive weight or stone inside a mesh chum bag), usually from somewhere forward of the stern to keep the line as far as possible from fishing lines.

♦ Attaching a chum dispenser to the anchor rode (not recommended; inconvenient to add new chum, possibility of a shark bite severing a nylon rode).

♦ Attaching smaller chum dispensers just above baited portions of bottom-fishing rigs (most often done for deep bottom fishing, in depths over 200 ft./61 m).

♦ Chum balls: mixtures of sand, oats, ground-up organisms, or scraps, packed into a ball that sinks to considerable depth before completely breaking apart.

♦ Dropping unattached, weighted packets of chum overboard (e.g., conch shells, paper bags, banana-leaf packets), often arranging for a baited hook to descend with the chum.

Attracting Fish with FADs

Fishers from the island of Barbados let out long lines of three evenly spaced FADs constructed of floating lashed bundles of dry sugar cane as far as 900 yards (823 m) to leeward of their drifting vessels offshore. Groups of flying fish accumulate under each bundle, usually depositing viscous egg masses and commonly stuffing themselves into the interior of the bundle. Periodically, the fishers retrieve the FADs, strip them of flying fish and egg masses so that they do not sink from the additional weight, and let them back out again to windward. Each such retrieval causes the free-swimming flying fish associated with individual FADs to join the growing school remaining immediately around and under the hull. A suspended basket of mashed flying fish further attracts more fish to the boat. The flying fish are harvested with gill nets and hand scoop nets. Using baited 300-pound (136 kg) test monofilament handlines, the fishers catch larger predators like mahi mahi, tuna, and billfish opportunistically as they respond to the abundance of flying fish and general commotion. These vessels commonly stay at sea for ten days or more at a time. This fishery has many concepts, adaptations, and implications for voyaging seafarers adrift at sea. *(continued next page)*

John Harding lets out a FAD on a longline to windward of the drifting vessel.

Attracting Fish with FADs

(continued)

Flying fish and egg masses found in a retrieved FAD.

Flying fish become numerous around the boat, and John Harding begins catching them with a simple scoop net made of split bamboo and mesh.

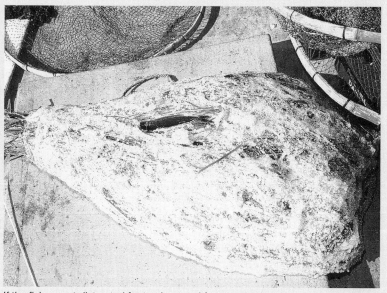

If the fishers get distracted for too long and forget to retrieve them periodically, the FADs may begin sinking from the weight of flying-fish egg deposits. Sticky egg masses completely envelope this FAD. Note one of many flying fish trapped in the FAD (*center*) and closer views of scoop nets (*upper left and upper right*).

The purpose of these chumming techniques is not only to attract fish to the vicinity of your vessel, but also to whet the palates of your visitors. This makes them less cautious, more aggressive, and therefore more likely to make the mistake of biting your baited line or swimming into the range of a net. Chumming practices can make a significant difference in your catch anywhere, but the end result is usually most evident in areas that receive more fishing effort.

In these more heavily exploited regions, resident fish may not be as abundant or naive as they are in locations where they see few or no fishing lines. Professional fishers hone the practice of chumming to a fine art. They instigate, sustain, adjust, and control the behavior of fish attracted to their vessel. The idea is to orchestrate chumming activity in a manner that keeps the fish excited for the longest time feasible, and then translate this excitement into the maximum possible number of captures. By the end of the fishing day, the catch difference between the chumming experts and the less experienced (although they may have fished the same reef or seamount), is monumental. Accomplish this by using the following guidelines.

♦ Develop a keen eye for nuances in the swimming behavior, coloration, and aggression of any individual fish you can see in the chum slick, and constantly monitor this compendium of clues.
♦ Don't over-chum or "feed" your guests—control chum flow sparingly, enough to maintain their attention and hold them in the near vicinity, but not enough to satiate.
♦ Bait your fishing lines with more desirable offerings than those used for chum. For example, use baitfish fillet meat for baited hooks, chopped sections of backbone for chum. One exception to this rule can be chumming with handfuls of live baitfish, when the bait on the hook is the same as the chum.
♦ To the extent possible, never dispense "free" handfuls of chum—always accompany such doses with a baited fishhook somewhere in the midst.
♦ When relevant and available, particularly in clear water, use sand and other substances to reduce visibility in the immediate vicinity of chum doses. This can significantly enhance strike rates by obscuring the leader from interested but wary fish. For example, toss in a handful of scraps, simultaneously cast a baited hook into the midst of the chum, and then toss a scoop of sand on top.

We explore further subtleties of chumming later in this chapter in specific fishing scenarios.

NIGHT LIGHTING

Like chumming, most cruising vessels inadvertently attract fish and other predators to some degree through normal use of cabin and other lighting at night, whether adrift offshore or anchored. Why do lights attract fish? Ambient light level profoundly influences the activity of most marine organisms, none more interestingly than zooplankton, the tiny microscopic and macroscopic animals that play such an important role in fish distribution. These little species, many of which are crustaceans, exhibit negative phototaxis; that is, they migrate vertically down in the water column by day over distances as great as 3,282 feet (1,000 m), returning to surface layers to feed on phytoplankton (tiny, free-drifting plant life) by night. Nevertheless, when you flick on an arch or spreader light, zooplankton eventually appear in visible swarms, followed by planktivorous small fish, and, consequently by larger predators including fish and squid. Obviously, response depends on location, and once again may range from barely detectable to sensational.

Pronounced results are normally more likely to occur offshore or in outside anchorages, although at least some response occurs almost anywhere. If you can afford the amps or don't mind performing battery-charging duties or running a generator at night, switch on some strong deck or cockpit lighting for a while after sunset. Find a comfortable seat and settle in for the show. You will likely be surprised, and what you see may spur you into some fishing activity.

Research ships and commercial fishing vessels that run extremely bright quartz-iodide deck lighting all night while adrift offshore or anchored on seamounts often attract incredible, unforgettable menageries of sea life. Cruising vessels can also attract considerable aggregations under some conditions. We spent three months anchored outside the lagoon aboard *Élan* at Christmas Island, Republic of Kiribati, at the same time a La Niña condition enhanced the trade winds and therefore equatorial upwelling. We customarily adjusted our daily routine to facilitate running our powerful arch light at night to enjoy the extraordinary "evening show." Featured were clouds of pinkish zooplankton, followed by small silvery plankton-eating fish of various species, squid, occasional flying fish, large planktivorous milkfish, then bigeye, bluefin, and giant trevallys, and occasional yellowfin tuna and spinner dolphin. The latter two developed a protocol of sending panic-stricken flying fish into reckless flights that ended abruptly against the hull, then rushing in to gobble the stunned baitfish as they dropped into the sea beside us.

Casting a ¼ oz. (7 g) white bucktail jig on light (10 lb./4.5 kg test) spinning gear out beyond the lit area, letting it sink 30 feet (9 m) or more, and then retrieving it rapidly and erratically through the school resulted in this bigeye trevally.

Small bluefin and bigeye trevally (*Caranx melampygus* and *C. sexfasciatus*) swarm into the glow of *Élan's* arch lights at anchor off Christmas Island, Republic of Kiribati.

Fundamental Techniques of Stationary Hook-and-Line Fishing

OK, you've got 'em attracted to the boat now, either by accident or through some effort. The boat, however, is no longer moving fast enough to create significant lure or bait action. This is a fundamental change from trolling. You *see* the fish you want on the grill—it's swimming around the boat. What's the best way to catch it?

This section reviews the hook-and-line techniques that will optimize your efforts. Supplied with this array of knowledge, you can execute the appropriate action dictated by specific situations. Other methods are covered in chapter 7.

CASTING WITH HANDLINE OR ROD AND REEL

Casting is one of the deadliest means of capturing fish near the sea surface close to the boat. Use a handline stored on a yo-yo, with line and hook size matched to the quarry, or a spinning rod and reel outfit that is up to the task. The latter type casts farther and permits the use of lighter line, smaller leader size, and a faster retrieve, all of which could make the difference in getting your target to bite. These characteristics generally make a spinning rod superior for lure presentation and many bait presentations; handlines cast to fish on the surface are usually more effective when limited to natural bait. Also, once successful hook-up occurs, handlines can whip many fish long before any rod and reel could get them to the boat.

Figure 4-1 demonstrates casting technique for both styles of gear. Because of its greater flexibility, the average cruiser should reach first for a spinning outfit (10 lb./4.5 kg or 20 lb./9 kg test) in most situations involving fish to 45 pounds (20 kg). Begin to consider handlines (or heavier rod and reel) for fish 45 to 100 pounds (20 to 45 kg) or so; use heavier tackle for heavier fish. If your budget does not permit spinning tackle, keep some lighter monofilament handlines armed with smaller bait hooks handy (say a 20 lb./9 kg test line with a hook size in the vicinity of 2, 1/0, or 3/0, and a 50 lb./23 kg test line with a size 5/0, 6/0, or 7/0 hook). Go easy on the hand pressure as you set the hook and battle the fish.

DEEP-JIGGING

Deep-jigging involves either casting or simply free-spooling jigs and other lures and letting them sink deep, either to some midwater depth or all the way to the bottom. Depending on the target species, you may then be able to leave the lure at depth and *jig* it up and down, with sharp tugs by hand or abrupt upward sweeps of the rod tip. More commonly, you should impart this same jigging action while retrieving the lure upward at a rapid rate.

Special lure types facilitate this method (see photo page 92). Heavy, fast-sinking lead jig heads

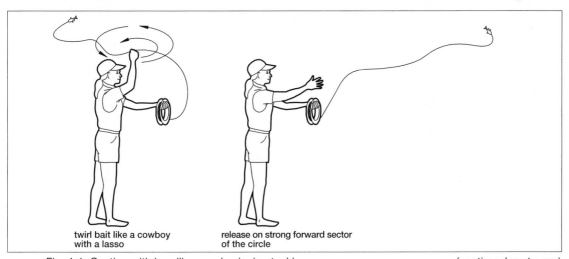

twirl bait like a cowboy with a lasso

release on strong forward sector of the circle

Fig. 4-1. Casting with handlines and spinning tackle.   *(continued next page)*

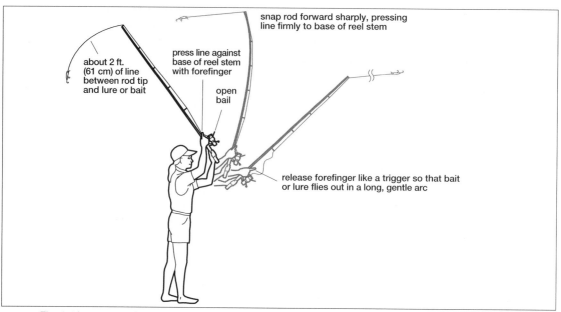

Fig. 4-1*(continued)*. Casting with handlines and spinning tackle.

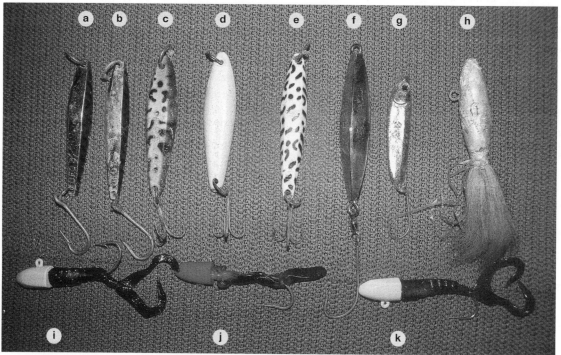

Lures for deep-jigging tend to be heavy and shaped to facilitate rapid descent: **(a, b, e)** UFO #3 lures (4⅞ in./ 124 mm, 3 oz./85 g); **(c, d)** California-style jigs similar to Ironman Jigs (4¾ in./121 mm, 4¼ oz./ 120 g); **(f)** Bead Diamond Jig (5½ in./140 mm, 8 oz./227 g); **(g)** Luhr-Jensen Crippled Herring Spoon (3½ in./89 mm, 3 oz./85 g); **(h)** Capt. Harry's Deep Jig (10 oz./283 g); **(i, j, k)** Offshore Angler Bullet Head Jigs (3 oz./85 g) baited with 4 in. (102 mm) Shrimpi Twin Tails and a multicolored Gummy Bear candy **(j)** —fish love this.

in bullet or vertically compressed shapes—either bucktails, plastic bait bodies, or naturally baited—work well on many bottom-dwelling and other fish species. Other deep-jigging lures fashioned from torpedo-shaped, heavy pieces of metal can be equally effective: diamond jigs, crippled herrings, hammered spoons, and California jigs like the Ironman. Some are painted in various colors, others are bright shiny metals.

Because casting is unnecessary for deep-jigging, any of your tackle is potentially useful for this technique. However, fast retrieve and enhanced action from sweeping a fishing rod tip in an arc probably confers a general advantage on rod and reel outfits compared to handlines and rail-mounted reels.

Free-Lining

Free-lining is allowing your baited hook to drift, naturally and unencumbered, out and away from you into the water column. Accomplish this by freely hand-feeding line off the spool of any reel, yo-yo, or deck winch at a rate that matches the speed of the prevailing current or, in the absence of current, the natural sink rate of your bait. The idea is for the bait to drift and sink in a manner identical to that of sur-rounding chum scraps with no hook and line attachment (whether or not you are chumming). Any resistance imparted by the fisher from feeding too slowly tends to unnaturally retard the progress of the hooked bait relative to chum scraps—a dead give-away that something is suspicious. Conversely, over-feeding the line (i.e., stripping off loose coils faster than the drifting bait takes up loose slack) causes problems with bite detection and knowing whether your bait has come to rest on the bottom. Table 4-1 gives details for various unweighted free lines.

A study of the influence of catch distribution among anglers as a function of fish abundance provided the opportunity to spend hundreds of hours submerged with scuba gear in chum slicks behind partyboats anchored on reefs in the Florida Keys. We observed the reactions of yellowtail snappers to different free-line presentations. The fish would rise en masse in response to each pulse of chum dispensed by the partyboat crew; each average, well-presented bait would receive numerous inspections and refusals. (Baits were mostly 1 in./25 mm strips of squid or fish on size 2 Mustad 9174 hooks, with 12 to 15 lb./5 to 7 kg monofilament leaders.) Occasionally, individuals would take particularly natural-

TABLE 4-1. **HOOK AND LEADER ARRANGEMENTS FOR FREE-LINING**

Hooks	Leader Arrangement	Application
Mustad 9174 for dead baits, Mustad 94150 for live baits (sizes #6 to 5/0)	No leader—tie hook directly to monofilament line coming off the reel spool	Use to drift small dead or live baits to midwater snappers, jacks, finicky mahi mahi, and other species whose teeth do not require use of wire leader (see table 3-1).
Mustad 3561E treble hook (sizes #2 to 1/0)	Light (#2 to #4) wire leader (2 ft./61 cm) tied directly to monofilament line coming off the reel spool, using an Albright special	Use to drift small dead or live baits to mackerel, bluefish, dog tooth tuna, small wahoo, and other slashing feeders with sharp cutting teeth (see table 3-1).
Mustad 7691 or 7691S for dead baits, Mustad 94150 for live baits; match hook size to bait size over the full range available.	Tie a Bimini twist on the end of the monofilament line coming off the reel spool, add a shock leader (fig. 2-12), then use either a uni-knot (line to line) or a barrel swivel to attach a 15 to 25 foot (4.6 to 7.6 m) length of 30 to 300 pound (13.8 to 136 kg) test monofilament or #5 to #19 wire depending on target species (see table 3-1).	Use to drift any size dead or live bait to virtually any potential target species.

looking baits that *exactly* matched the flow of free-drifting materials; no other baits stood a chance. Back at the dock, the most experienced anglers among the twelve to forty-five passengers would invariably have the highest catches regardless of total catch for the boat (which varied according to fish abundance). Why? The most successful fishers pay more attention to free-lining their baits to match the current perfectly.

Free-lining normally involves natural bait rather than lures, although fish occasionally take lures—particularly soft plastic and rubber imitations—that are dead in the water. Free-lining works very well with live bait. Several variations of free-lining exist for situations where unweighted drifts simply do not get the bait deep enough or quickly enough to the strike zone of the target species.

- ◆ *Split-shot sinkers.* Clamp one or more small split-shot lead sinkers onto the line 1 to 3 feet (30 to 90 cm) above the bait.
- ◆ *Sliding rigs.* Construct and deploy sliding rigs, where an in-line egg sinker is stopped by a barrel swivel attached to a 5- to 20-foot (1.5 to 6 m) leader.
- ◆ *Chum balls.* Wrap a dozen or more turns of unweighted line around a firm, tightly packed chum ball of mixed sand and chum, with bait inserted into the middle; then feed slack line freely after dropping it overboard to carry the bait to depth in a cloud of sand and fish bits.
- ◆ *Drop stones.* Wrap a weighted or unweighted line a dozen or more times around a stone or stone-like expendable object, secure with a slip knot, and drop freely to depth, giving a tug to free the baited line from the stone at the desired depth.
- ◆ *Live baits.* Hook live baitfish under the chin or just above the anal fin, which causes them to swim down rather than laterally away from the boat. When predator fish are staying deep and this live bait suddenly comes flashing into their midst from above, they often eat it.

Figure 4-2 summarizes details for each method of getting free lines to depth. Deploy lines weighted with split-shot sinkers or sliding rigs just as you would an unweighted line, slowly feeding loose coils out into the water column, attempting to match natural drift and sink rates. Unlike unweighted free-lining, your rig is now intrinsically unnatural, and will less often truly match the sink rate of chum. These weighted offerings sink down into the strike zone on their own—although not surrounded by a cloud of chum, they may still be effective by virtue of reaching the depth where the fish are hanging out rather than skating over them in the current. Be sure to stop feeding line if you feel the bait come to rest on the bottom. Bring the bait up a few yards or meters if you are over rocks, coral, or other types of seafloor that may snag your bait as the boat swings on the anchor.

Chum balls and drop stones require more effort but promise greater rewards by increasing the attractiveness of the bait by surrounding it with chum at depth. Careful attention to viscosity while mixing sand, water, and chum can result in a mixture that permits creation of chum balls, approximately the size of an American softball, that will get baits as deep as 150 feet (46 m) or so. Drop stones carry baits much deeper than this—the only limit, really, is the amount of line you have available. Island fishers in the tropical Pacific commonly fish for bigeye tuna and albacore to depths of 900 feet (274 m) using this method.

Bottom-Fishing

Bottom-fishing consists of lowering rigs sufficiently weighted to make contact with the seafloor as vertically as possible relative to the boat, and holding this position regardless of current or boat drift. This generally requires more weight than rigs used for deep free-lining, and mostly targets fish species that live in close association with the seafloor. The same egg-sinker sliding rig used for deep free-lining, more heavily weighted, is one of the most effective bottom-fishing rigs because the line slides through the sinker when fish eat the bait, making it less likely that they'll detect the unnatural drag of the sinker. Other rigs attach various style sinkers to the end of the line, and suspend multiple baits in a vertical array between the sinker and the boat. This tends to be effective for smaller schooling species, in surf conditions where pyramid sinkers help anchor the array in shifting sand, and for fishing greater depths (over 150 ft./46 m). Figure 4-3 shows a variety of useful bottom rigs.

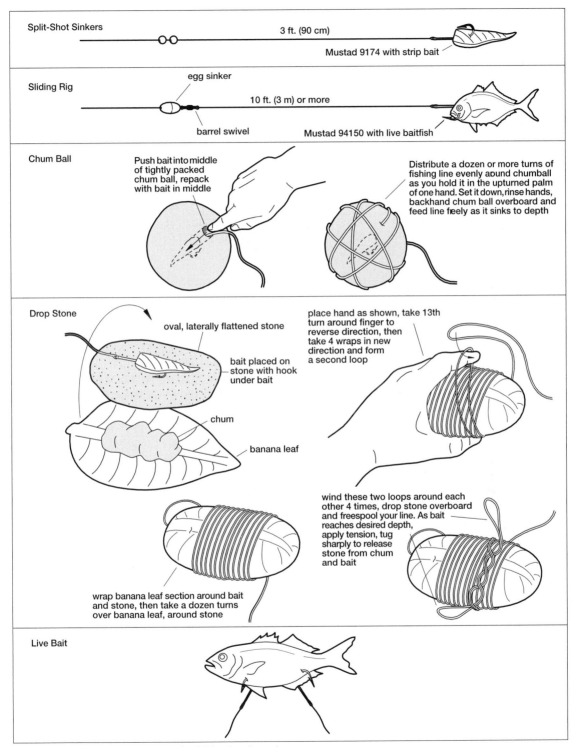

Split-Shot Sinkers

3 ft. (90 cm)

Mustad 9174 with strip bait

Sliding Rig

egg sinker

10 ft. (3 m) or more

barrel swivel

Mustad 94150 with live baitfish

Chum Ball

Push bait into middle of tightly packed chum ball, repack with bait in middle

Distribute a dozen or more turns of fishing line evenly around chumball as you hold it in the upturned palm of one hand. Set it down, rinse hands, backhand chum ball overboard and feed line freely as it sinks to depth

Drop Stone

oval, laterally flattened stone

bait placed on stone with hook under bait

chum

banana leaf

place hand as shown, take 13th turn around finger to reverse direction, then take 4 wraps in new direction and form a second loop

wind these two loops around each other 4 times, drop stone overboard and freespool your line. As bait reaches desired depth, apply tension, tug sharply to release stone from chum and bait

wrap banana leaf section around bait and stone, then take a dozen turns over banana leaf, around stone

Live Bait

Fig. 4-2. Different methods for fishing free lines deep.

A few additional tricks can sharply boost success. Pay close attention to bait species preference of your targets. One pilchard species with slightly more slime and looser scales, for instance, may elicit far more strikes than a member of the same genus with tougher scales. Also, regardless of bait species, scraping some scales off the sides before sending live or dead bait to the bottom gives your offerings a distinct edge. Keep in mind also that dead split-head baits are particularly lethal in murky conditions as the sweet juices and fluids emanate downcurrent. Another trick is effective in locations where more aggressive species like jacks and trevallys are outcompeting desired catches like snapper: substitute a big, juicy, tough strip of bonito or other oily bottom bait for smaller live or dead baits that are quickly getting engulfed whole by the marauders.

This gives slower-swimming snappers and other species enough time to wander over, disperse the cloud of jacks, and sedately swallow the bait. Now you're selecting exactly the fish you want from a multispecies assemblage.

One common term for specialty bottom-fishing at great depth (450 to 1,000 ft./137 to 305 m and more) is deep-dropping. This practice usually involves the heaviest weights, vertical arrays of circle hooks, and use of a wire-line outfit, either rod and reel (sometimes with a 12-volt power attachment such as an Elec-tra-mate) or commercial deck winch. Depending on depth and conditions, low-stretch Dacron line and sometimes heavy monofilament can substitute for wire without intolerable loss of efficiency. Sea state, current velocity, and bottom features may permit deep-dropping from an anchored vessel equipped with a

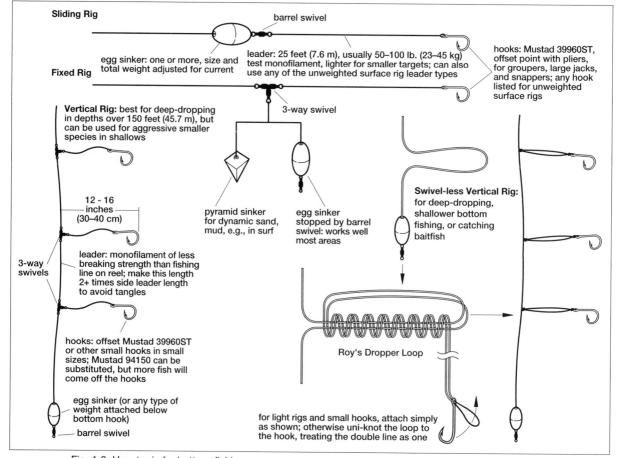

Fig. 4-3. How to rig for bottom-fishing.

grapple and long anchor rode (see fig. 4-8). Otherwise, it is necessary to power-drift—position for a drop, use power to maintain an optimal drift of the desired bottom area, and then reposition for the next drift.

FISHING WITH FLOATS

Floats accomplish the purpose of suspending baits at the desired depth—near the surface or far below the waves. Floats are an easy, direct way to deploy and keep track of live or dead baits, they serve also as strike indicators, and sometimes act as fish attracters. Remember those small, plastic, red and white clip-on bobbers ubiquitous in almost every tackle and variety store? You could put them on a cane pole or on a dinky little pushbutton reel and rod and fish for freshwater bluegills, bass, and catfish with worms or other bait, lifting and reeling any time the bobber disappeared from the surface. This same concept underlies standard techniques used by professional fishers to catch everything from baitfish on tiny hooks to fishing for giant tarpon, swordfish, and everything in between.

Those red and white clip-on bobbers are still around and work well on smaller fish. Larger baits—for example, a 10-inch (254 mm) live mullet—require a larger, more buoyant float, like a round, in-line, 2-inch (51 mm) diameter, natural-colored cork with a hole drilled through the middle and plastic stopper pin to secure it to a fixed position on your line. Cylindrical corks with cupped faces may be "popped" and chugged like a surface plug, attracting the attention of fish to the vicinity of the bait below. Toy-store balloons have many uses as fishing floats, with size adjusted to the mass and vigor of the bait. At the opposite end of the fishing float spectrum are round, thick-walled PVC buoys up to a 32-inch (81 cm) diameter, commonly called poly balls, used by swordfish longliners and other professional fishers to suspend commercial gear. Poly balls also serve as dock fenders, anchor buoys, and sea-anchor and trip-line floats. They store well on deck and are deflatable, making them one of the most versatile and useful items a cruising vessel can carry.

Figure 4-4 summarizes a selection of float fishing arrangements potentially useful to cruisers. The concept for all is similar: regardless of size, floats are in-line and fixed, and may be used on lines connected to yo-yos, reels, winches, or cleats, or on fishing lines

designed to float free, unattached to the vessel. Poly balls deployed on heavy gear have buoyancy sufficient to resist the struggles of very large fish, which can then be handlined more easily to the boat.

USING RELEASE CLIPS ADRIFT AND ANCHORED

The release clip setups described in chapter 3 for trolling (outriggers, upriggers, and downriggers) can work equally well adrift or anchored. Orient these lines so that they stream out to windward when adrift and downwind/downcurrent at anchor, ensuring that they do not pass under the boat. This requirement may make it possible to deploy release-clip arrangements only from part of the vessel, often the windward side. Release clip devices—for example, outriggers—may be useful for placing float lines or free lines out of the way of other lines. Downriggers can work well for getting baits down to the desired depth in high current that would make sufficient in-line weights too heavy to be practical.

Fishing kites are release-clip devices used to present baits enticingly at the surface. Think of a fishing kite as a long vertical outrigger, an uprigger, that sticks up from the sea surface at 45 degrees and can easily suspend your bait vertically out 60 feet (18 m) or more away from the boat. Live or specially rigged dead baits deployed from in-line release clips on the kite line struggle and swim at or just below the sea surface. The leader passes straight up into the air from the bait toward the release clip, minimizing the length of leader below the surface, and often making it essentially invisible to the target fish. Like other more advanced techniques, this method is more work but promises rich rewards. Plus, it can be lots of fun—you get to fly a kite and fish at the same time (fig. 4-6).

Fishing kites are intended for use while adrift, power-drifting, anchored, or slow trolling, and are available in models designed for specific ranges of wind speed from less than 4 to more than 20 knots. Their construction encourages stable and easy flying behavior. They pop up, rise steadily under tension, and park themselves at altitude—falling slightly if the wind lightens, rising with wind increases. In a steady breeze, they are nearly stationary. Fishing kites make it possible to have extremely dynamic bait action at zero boat velocity and no manual

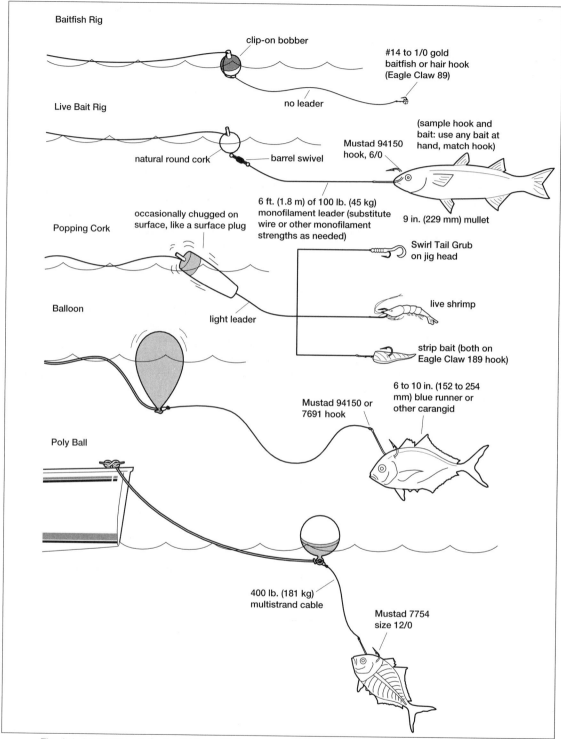

Baitfish Rig

clip-on bobber

#14 to 1/0 gold baitfish or hair hook (Eagle Claw 89)

no leader

Live Bait Rig

(sample hook and bait: use any bait at hand, match hook)

Mustad 94150 hook, 6/0

natural round cork

barrel swivel

6 ft. (1.8 m) of 100 lb. (45 kg) monofilament leader (substitute wire or other monofilament strengths as needed)

9 in. (229 mm) mullet

Popping Cork

occasionally chugged on surface, like a surface plug

Swirl Tail Grub on jig head

Balloon

light leader

live shrimp

strip bait (both on Eagle Claw 189 hook)

6 to 10 in. (152 to 254 mm) blue runner or other carangid

Mustad 94150 or 7691 hook

Poly Ball

400 lb. (181 kg) multistrand cable

Mustad 7754 size 12/0

Fig. 4-4. A selection of rigs for fishing with floats.

labor by the fisher. In steady trade winds, you can put out the kite, turn the reel clicker on to let you know when you've got a bite, and then take a nap, read a novel, or do maintenance. Like teasers, some of the greatest shows in fishing are created by fish raised and excited—in full view close at hand—by kite baits. We have actually had customers get wet from the violent splashes of fish crashing kite baits set out close to the boat.

Fishing Scenarios

There's no better teacher than experience: exposure to actual situations, application of skills and technology to specific conditions on the water. The best

Stinger Rigs

Regardless of whether you're fishing the surface, midwater, or bottom, you may experience "short strikes," where toothy, slashing feeders (e.g., mackerel, wahoo, and barracuda) chop off the back of your bait and miss the single hook. This is the time to employ a stinger rig. Scale the hook, leader, and barrel swivel size to bait and target sizes and species. For a western Atlantic king mackerel (*Scomberomorus cavalla*) or an Indo-Pacific Spanish mackerel (*Scomberomorus commerson*) from 5 to 50 pounds or more, the least visible stinger rig would be 20-pound (9 kg) or less spinning tackle with a 6-inch (15 cm) live or dead cigar minnow (*Decapterus*), and featuring a #2 wire leader, a 5/0 Mustad 9174 lead hook, and a #4 Eagle Claw L774 treble hook. The stinger length should be such that the treble hook sits two thirds of the way from the head to the tail of the bait. Such mackerel rigs are best fished with bail closed (spinning tackle) or drag in strike position (conventional tackle); that is, no drop-back.

The stinger can swing free or be hooked lightly through the aft portion of the natural bait. Slow-trolled live baits usually work best not impaled by the stinger. Scale this idea up for wahoo, going to larger hooks and #5 wire, and use a 12-inch (30 cm) live mackerel scad or tuna, or a dead squid or strip bait. The idea also works for large shark baits, using #19 wire and same-sized, 9/0 or larger Mustad 7691 or similar hooks, where wire leader length exceeds body length of the targeted sharks. Monofilament stinger rigs employing two single hooks find favor with some billfishers. Consult IGFA on regulations regarding double-hook use if you seek records—stingers are allowed, but stringent rules control specifications and use.

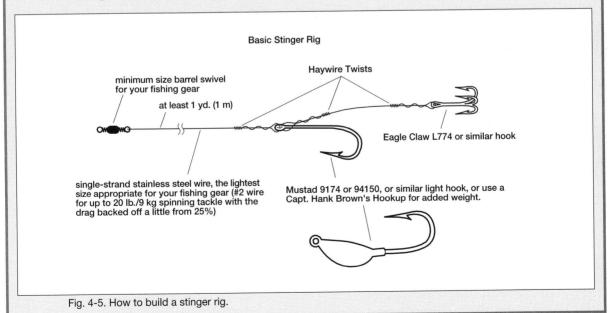

Basic Stinger Rig

Haywire Twists

minimum size barrel swivel for your fishing gear

at least 1 yd. (1 m)

Eagle Claw L774 or similar hook

single-strand stainless steel wire, the lightest size appropriate for your fishing gear (#2 wire for up to 20 lb./9 kg spinning tackle with the drag backed off a little from 25%)

Mustad 9174 or 94150, or similar light hook, or use a Capt. Hank Brown's Hookup for added weight.

Fig. 4-5. How to build a stinger rig.

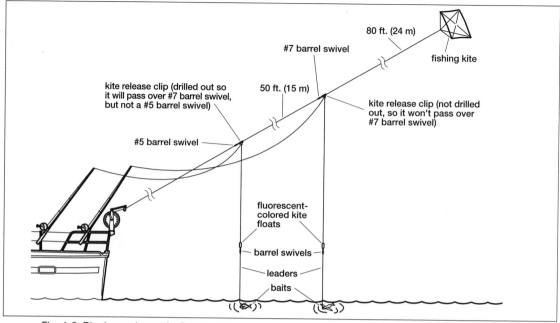

80 ft. (24 m)

#7 barrel swivel

fishing kite

kite release clip (drilled out so
it will pass over #7 barrel swivel,
but not a #5 barrel swivel)

50 ft. (15 m)

kite release clip (not drilled
out, so it won't pass over
#7 barrel swivel)

#5 barrel swivel

fluorescent-
colored kite
floats

barrel swivels

leaders

baits

Fig. 4-6. Rigging and use of a fishing kite.

thing we could do for you, the reader, is have you meet us somewhere to go out fishing. The next best thing we can do for you, particularly in the case of a chapter that attempts to teach the broad range of methods effective for drifting and anchoring, is to immerse you in a selection of instructive situations with words. Experience the action and the fun and pay attention to the technical detail imbedded throughout each scenario, then choose those relevant to your particular circumstances and duplicate them.

Regardless of scenario, compared to trolling, natural bait often plays a relatively larger role for best fishing success adrift or anchored. The fish have more time to inspect what you offer; fresh dead or, even better, live bait can pass inspection more frequently than a fake. This becomes particularly true in the case of untended lines. Review figure 4-7 before we plunge into fishing together will bring you up to speed on natural bait-rigging for drift and anchor fishing.

THE TRANSITION FROM TROLLING

Suppose you've been on an offshore passage for a couple of days now, trolling nicely prepared offerings, diligently scanning for signs of fish. Perhaps in your enthusiasm to do well, you busted the budget on new gear after making convincing predictions of how much fishing prowess would enhance the voyage. Your spouse eventually yielded, even believed you. The weather has been settled, the crew is hungry, ready to light the grill. At least one set of eyes follows your every move. The pressure is on, to the point of a few fun-poking remarks. Suddenly, in the late afternoon glare, you spot a sizable section of a semi-submerged tree, change course, and artistically circle it, splashing your baits within a few feet of the tree. Several neon-blue shadows appear fleetingly in the spread, but nothing happens. Now what do you do?

Don't lose sight of the debris. The mahi mahi and other pelagic species will continue to orient to it. Bring in the trolling lines, possibly leaving only one out at a distance (especially if it's a natural bait), and maneuver to within casting range. Slow or stop the boat. Toss a bucktail jig (⅜ oz./11 g, size 3/0 Millie's roundhead jig) or weighted strip bait (⅜ oz./11 g, Captain Hank Brown's Hookup jig with squid or fish) on a 20-pound (9 kg) test spinning rod out toward the log. Leave it in free spool and let it sink 60 feet (18 m) or so. Now close the bail, reel fast, and

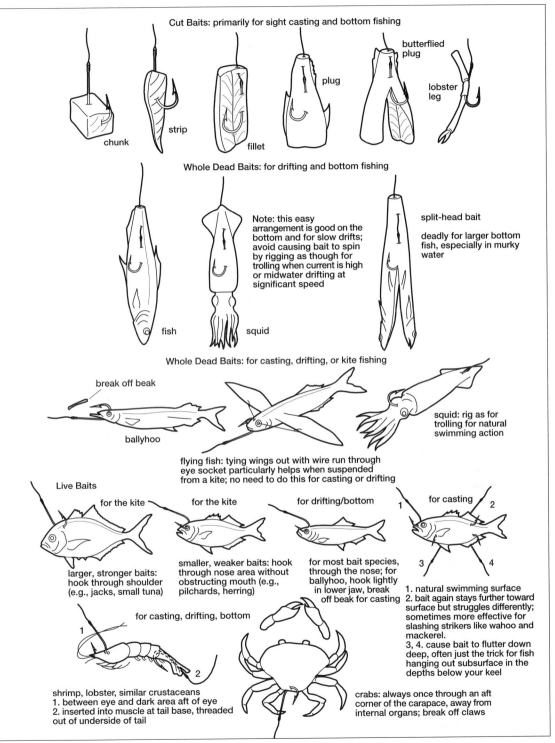

Fig. 4-7. Natural bait rigging for cruisers adrift or anchored.

retrieve the jig rapidly upward using sweeping jerks of the rod and fast winding of the reel handle. If you have attached a 12-inch (305 mm) trace of #4 single-strand stainless steel leader wire at the end of your 50-pound (23 kg) monofilament shock leader (using an Albright special knot), you have only slightly decreased the action of your lure. However, you have covered the possibility of a strike by a toothy wahoo or silky shark, both delicious table fare and common under debris worldwide in tropical and subtropical latitudes. More likely your first strike will be one of the aggressive mahi mahi you initially glimpsed darting into the lure spread, or perhaps a colorful rainbow runner. Leave the former in the water until you have hooked another (if you have enough cold storage space available). Use this same casting technique each time you are landing a tuna, wahoo, mahi mahi, or other schooling pelagic species: cast out beyond the hooked fish, let the presentation sink, and retrieve. Even if you don't see the others, they are frequently lurking somewhere in the vicinity of the school member you have hooked. Also try this "blind" after you have been becalmed a while, day or night. *Remember:* your drifting vessel becomes a mecca for a variety of open-ocean sea life, much of which may not be readily visible.

Other lures that cast and sink well can be used effectively in the same manner. These include various plastic bait imitations hooked on either bucktail or plain jigs; also flashy metal lures like diamond jigs and crippled herring spoons. What if, despite trying several of these different lures, the fish follow but still won't bite? Natural baits often do the trick. Chunks of fresh tuna, flying fish, squid, or other fish all work well. You may want to keep a small plastic container of these baits handy in your refrigerator or freezer. Match hook size to the baits and target fish: if they *still* won't bite using a 3/0 to 7/0 Mustad 7691, go to a Mustad 9174 or 94150 and a lighter monofilament leader; toss whole flying fish or squid baited on 8/0 Mustad 7691s for tuna, mahi mahi, wahoo, and other species 15 pounds (7 kg) and up. If you are near debris and desperate to catch a mahi mahi or two that seem to have lockjaw, use light line and #10 gold hair hooks baited with tiny pieces of fish or squid or baitfish quill lures to catch small fish from under the debris (jacks, file-fish, triggerfish, and puffers). Now hook these live baits onto your 20-pound (9 kg) spinning rod (or handline) and pitch them out in front of your quarry. Be sure to let them eat the bait well while still in free spool—for a count of "three to ten one thousand"—before reeling up all of the slack and raising the rod tip sharply several times to set the hook. Set the hook on handlines by grasping the line firmly *without taking a wrap* and letting the surge of the fish drive the hook through the jaw. Gain additional leverage on heavier handlines by breaking the line over the gunnel, railing, or other solid boat part.

And if they still won't strike? Tease ... harass ... frustrate ... incite ... persevere. Hook a whole dead flying fish in the side, just aft of the wing. Toss it out and immediately begin retrieving rapidly, snapping the line hard, which will cause erratic sideways darts accompanied by flexing of the wings. Take the bait away from the fish the first few times they rush it. Don't let them get too close. When their feeding colors light brightly, pause and see if they'll eat. Alternatively, throw a surface plug (Pacific Lure Innovations and Yo-Zuri make some beauties) out a distance and retrieve fast and erratically, making it pop and chug. The mahi mahi or other fish usually flash their feeding colors and follow closely; one may take the plug. If not, cast a second lure or natural dead or live bait right behind the plug and you will often get a strike. Otherwise, continue the surface plug retrieve right along the side of the hull and free-gaff the fish with a fast overhand stroke behind the head. *Remember that free-gaffed fish are normally very "green"*—fresh and full of energy since they haven't been battling against a reel drag or handline—and should be immediately subdued before they inflict serious damage on your boat and crew. With a little practice, free-gaffing is not as difficult as it sounds and can be the difference between fresh fish and canned food for dinner.

Let's rewind this game tape to when you were trolling along, still looking for signs. Instead of debris, you spot a small black spot near the horizon. You grab your powerful binoculars, and the spot takes the form of a frigate bird low on the water, attempting to swoop and catch flying fish being chased by something below. You change course to intercept, and note over the next ten minutes that each time the frigate returns to a hover, it's on a relatively straight course downsea, indicating that it's probably over a pod of large mahi mahi. You've found them. How do you capitalize?

Get a bearing on the group of fish marked by the frigate bird. Clear your billfish teaser and downrigger, and leave out one natural rigged bait or soft-bodied lure, from an outrigger if available. Don't lose track of the bird(s). When you get close enough to easily see the birds without binoculars, have someone wearing polarized sunglasses get on the highest safe station on your vessel and start scanning hard for the fish. To maximize casting distance and visibility, angle for a position upwind and up-sun of their estimated path. Turn the boat to a course parallel to and in front of the group of fish. If you see the fish, consider bringing in the last trolled bait. You'll hook and land a higher percentage of large mahi mahi that eat baits cast on monofilament leaders and are hooked after a sufficient drop-back than those striking trolled baits. If visibility is poor, you can attempt the first hook-up on a bait trolled blindly in front of and under the birds.

Keep the boat moving at the same speed and course as the fish, staying in front and to the side of the group, and maintain that upwind, up-sun position. The spotter should direct casts with simple hand signals giving the bearing for the *cast* (not to the fish) as individuals come into view. If you need more than one, or for insurance in case the first fish comes off the hook, chuck a second bait back blind behind the first fish you hook (you can always release the second fish unharmed). Are they reluctant to eat? Another trick is to throw repeated "freebies"—plain baits with no hook—right in front of the fish, until they finally weaken and eat one. Feed them another and then toss them the bait on the hook. If you can get stubborn mahi mahi to eat *just one* free bait, they're yours.

PASSIVE FISHING

Did all of that casting and maneuvering wear you out, seem like too much work? How about some relaxing yet productive scenarios for fishing that can work unattended? You already have the knowledge for most of these: fishing kites, outriggers, downriggers, fixed midwater or surface lines, float lines, and bottom lines. Deploy these on a snubber line or, more effectively, on a rail-mounted reel or stand-up rod and reel outfit in a rod holder with appropriate natural baits (see fig. 4-7), and the possibilities are endless. Be sure to set the drag in "strike position" (i.e., 20 to 25 percent of the line's breaking strength) and put the click lever on if you are using a reel.

Other methods require more activity but can be used opportunistically. For example, you come up on deck and notice that the natural attractiveness of the hull or, at night, normal lighting, has drawn a desirable food fish to the vicinity of the boat. Or you see nothing. Pick up your rod and reel or handline, the former all set up with a generalized lure, and make a cast, free-line a bait back, drop down a deep jig, maybe a fresh bottom bait. Many times you'll get a quick strike, and you may land a fish sufficient to feed your crew for a day, maybe more. If not, put your gear back in the holder or storage locker and try later.

One passive approach that can be entertaining and educational is to set out a poly-ball float line for sharks. Tie a length of dock line to your biggest poly ball, suspend a fish carcass on a length of heavy (at least 400 lb./181 kg test) multistrand stainless steel cable or chain and a large sharp hook. Secure the dock line to a transom cleat (*do not omit* the poly ball—this takes the bulk of the strain of hooked sharks and helps avoid broken stanchions, cap rails, and personal injury). Scale down hook and bait size to target smaller sharks. When the boat lurches suddenly, perhaps spilling your coffee or beer, you'll know that a big shark swam in, ate the bait, and has come tight on the line. Stand by and watch the fireworks as the poly ball cuts a rug, zigzagging and throwing a white wake behind it until the shark tires. To avoid harming it, handline the shark boat-side while it's still swimming and not overly exhausted. Be ready to let go in an instant if it surges suddenly away. Photograph, tag, dehook if at all possible (otherwise, cut the leader as close as possible to the hooks without risking a bite), and gently release the shark. The kids will be thrilled by close-hand views of these magnificent animals. The practice also provides an index of what's swimming around near the anchorage so that you can adjust your aquatic activities accordingly. Many anchorages are truly safe, others are fairly shallow, innocent-

Gray reef shark *(Carcharhinus amblyrhynchos)* circles fish carcasses suspended as chum at night, South Minerva Reef, Tonga.

looking areas but warrant staying a little closer to the boat or shore.

Another opportunity occurs most often when drifting offshore, sometimes anchored, and most commonly at night: the chance to have fresh calamari, or squid, for dinner. The most productive condition for better-sized squid tends to be dark, moonless nights when they hunt in packs near the surface. When the moon rises, they usually disappear to the depths, probably a predator-avoidance strategy. Tie a special squid jig, usually a cylindrical body with a sharp ring of barbs around the base, onto a light monofilament handline or 20-pound (9 kg) spinning rod, cast out well beyond the sphere of light, and retrieve rapidly while twitching and jigging. Squid dart forward, ensnare the lure by shooting out two long feeding tentacles, and quickly pull it into a ring of eight arms. The barbs become impaled in these ten appendages. Pressure it into the boat as you would a fish, using the short-stroke pumping technique. Land it with a dip net as you would a smaller fish to prevent the possibility of losing your catch; lifting it bodily by the leader may cause the hooks to pull out. Carefully unhook the squid and place it in a cooler or bucket, remembering that squid can deliver a nasty bite with their concealed parrot-like beak.

DIRECTED EFFORT

Suppose most of your effort so far has been dragging in fish that bite trolling gear, or opportunistically catching fish attracted to the immediate vicinity of your relatively stationary cruising vessel while adrift or anchored. Possibly you stopped on debris encountered while trolling but, for the most part, you haven't found them ... they've found you. The most trouble you have taken to this juncture has perhaps been switching on a few lights at night. This makes for fairly easy fishing: when the fish show up, you dip into your growing bag of tricks, and soon the first tasty fillets are ready for the table.

What about the times when you are moored or anchored in an unproductive area near a large human population, or a low-current backwater that doesn't hold many fish? Night lighting produces only a few small baitfish at best and, furthermore, you may have legitimate concerns about eating anything bigger if you are in a large port with questionable water quality. The fishing opportunities you almost began taking for granted during stops at more remote areas have evaporated, and your refrigerated seafood supply is long gone. The novelty of eating ashore has worn off, not to mention the bite it is taking out of your cruising budget. The remedy for this situation, if you know how to go about it, may be a day trip to a nearby reef, wreck, or other bottom structure that can combine a pleasant mini-cruise with other activities, including some productive directed fishing. Of course, you can always troll for starters and, if the area is known, you can proceed to a predetermined spot. Otherwise, you must read the signs to search for and locate pockets of productivity, just as you learned to do while trolling offshore (see Reading the Signs, next page).

Catching Baitfish on Hook and Line

Now that your surroundings have spurred you into more fishing effort, you may consider catching a few fish to use for bait, customarily en route to the fishing

---

Landing Smaller Fish with Nets

Landing nets save you from losing many fish that are a little too small for gaffing, but may drop off the hook and plop back into the water if you attempt to lift them into the boat by grasping the leader. Instead, the fisher pressures the fish along near the surface to within range. Decisively plunge the front of the landing-net rim underwater immediately in front of the fish's head at a 45-degree angle as the fisher continues pulling the fish in a line straight into the net. Make sure that the rim is well below the head, and scoop forward and up as the middle of the body passes over the rim.

Keep the following hints in mind.

- *Net the head.* Never attempt to scoop the fish from behind, tail-first, or from the back or belly; these orientations allow it to kick forward and away from the net.
- *Submerge the net at the last moment.* Don't hold the net underwater waiting for the fisher to drag the fish to it. Fish see the net and will muster their last energies to thrash away from it, possibly coming unhooked at the last minute. Surprise them.
- *Think of netting as a passive act.* Let the fish's momentum—created by a combination of directional line pressure and perhaps some vestiges of swimming action—carry it into the net as you position and move it forward easily, deliberately. You're not swiping or wildly scooping as if trying to catch a butterfly.

---

grounds. Professional fishermen from many different fisheries—sport and commercial—expend immense effort ensuring they have a satisfactory variety and amount of natural bait before they begin to fish for the target species. The reason? Natural bait, particularly live bait, can contribute more to fishing success than any other single variable in the productivity equation. Thus, the pursuit of live bait regularly becomes as refined and hotly competitive as the fishery itself, spawning highly creative search-and-capture protocols and occasionally entire mini-industries.

Wait a second, right? What's all this got to do with a laid-back cruiser? That depends on how easy the target fish are to catch in your area, and your own cost-benefit energy analysis. Would you rather troll for hours with lures and *maybe* catch a fish, or is it actually easier to anchor briefly in the shallows, procure some natural bait, and then bag dinner in a much shorter time and use less fuel? Is this an accurate assessment of your situation? The answer depends strongly on location and target species—you might never need to concern yourself with natural bait, or it may best suit your purpose to pursue bait relentlessly.

Obviously, you need a bait maintenance system of some kind to keep live animals efficiently over time. Small collapsible holding pens store compactly, can be tied off to a cleat, and keep many bait species alive when drifting or anchored, but cannot be used underway. Built-in bait wells of various kinds are easy additions to many power cruisers but are not as practical for most sailboat designs. We address such modifications in detail in chapter 8. Non-hook-and-line methods may be necessary for efficient capture of large amounts of bait, particularly for the purpose of live-bait chumming. You'll learn about mass bait-catching methods in chapter 7.

In the meantime, even with no bait maintenance system and no cast net, you may have ample reason to capture live bait on hook and line: for immediate use either live or dead from your present position, or to be treated and stored for any number of possible uses later.

We described catching bait around offshore debris on small hooks. This same strategy holds for most bait species: build miniature versions of rigs shown in figures 4-2, 4-3, and 4-4 (see also table 4-1), using small hooks commensurate to mouth size

Reading the Signs

Cruising seafarers adrift offshore have either found a sign and dropped sail or shifted to neutral to fish, or will themselves become a FAD even if their drift has been initiated for other reasons. We also know that anchored vessels, particularly near the open sea, often attract and hold fish in their vicinity. Chumming and night lighting can enhance rate and quality of fish attraction. None of this information helps the common occurrence of arriving in an unfamiliar area that features a secure but unproductive anchorage. Ready to target some fish on an excursion using your cruising boat? Dig out your most detailed charts, tune up your depth-sounder if you have one, and prepare to do a little exploring. Here's what to look for.

♦ *Wrecks and other man-made structures.* Ships, planes, cars and trucks, construction rubble, small boats, storm debris, virtually any submerged or semisubmerged object provides habitat for a variety of desirable fish species. Don't ignore lighthouse stanchions, navigation buoys and other markers, jetties, seawalls, docks, and piers.

♦ *Points of reef and shelf.* Examine your chart closely. Can you find an area along the reef or shelf break that juts out into deeper water? Almost without exception, such areas feature higher fish densities than other more uniform bottom contours.

♦ *Sharp vertical relief.* Whether in shallow or deep water, steep gradients near current project food items to predators in a turbulent flow. This principle can be applied to locating concentrations of everything from schools of planktivorous baitfish in 10 feet (3 m) of water to deep ledges and broken bottom holding schools of demersal species 850 feet (259 m) and more below the sea surface.

♦ *Isolated patch reefs.* Piles of rock, aggregations of hard and soft corals, and other natural features that form distinct entities located away from other structure on relatively uniform bottom (e.g., sand, mud, and seagrass) invariably attract and hold significantly higher densities of fish than surrounding areas. These may be located by eye to considerable depths in clear water. If you find an area of bank or

Alligator Light, Florida Keys, is home base for a menagerie of tasty panfish (mostly grunts, Family Haemulidae).

Reading the Signs (cont.)

lagoon scattered with many such patches, you can maximize your catch rate by fishing at each patch for a relatively short period (i.e., thirty minutes to an hour) and then moving on to a different patch.

School of sharpfin barracuda *(Sphyraena acutipinnis)* near a vertical coral wall in the Tuamotus, French Polynesia. Small dark fish in left center are black durgons or triggerfish *(Melichthys niger,* Family Balistidae), a species found world-wide in the tropics.

Isolated patch reef featuring high fish density (Belize).
(a) hogfish *(Lachnolaimus maximus,* Family Labridae);
(b) jolthead porgy *(Calamus bajonado,* Family Sparidae);
(c) doctorfish *(Acanthurus chirurgus,* Family Acanthuridae);
(d) spotted goatfish *(Pseudopeneus maculatus,* Family Mullidae); **(e)** ocean surgeonfish *(Acanthurus bahianus,* Family Acanthuridae); **(f)** mixed species daytime resting school of grunts (Family Haemulidae).

of targeted baitfish (a selection of sizes between 14 and 1/0 will cover most situations). Many baitfish species bite unbaited gold hooks, although capture rate is normally better with bait. Keep baits small, tiny squares of squid, fish, or other material whose sides are half the length—or strips approximately equal to the full length—of the hook shank. Commercially available bait quills, consisting of small flashy strands of material or bits of feather tied onto these miniature hooks, jigged and twitched in short, darting spurts, are potent baitfish lures that work worldwide on many species. Manufacturers frequently sell these baitfish quills as pretied multiple hook rigs that you can simply attach to the end of your line, possibly adding a split-shot sinker to help get the affair out or down, and you're in business.

Baitfish are commonly among the early arrivals to chum slicks and night lights. When you see these small species, including ballyhoo, needlefish, herring, pilchards, menhaden, flying fish, small jacks, sardines, grunts, and anchovies, get out your bait or hair-hook selection and free-line tiny baits on light monofilament out into the action (see table 3-1 for specific leader recommendations by fish family). Use a tiny clip-on bobber to float baits to surface-hugging ballyhoo and flying fish, a small split-shot sinker or two to drift the bait down into midwater, or a vertical rig with an egg sinker at the bottom to send it down deep for species near the seafloor. Gently set the hook in response to essentially any tug or other sign of life on the line—no dropping back to these small fry. Alternatively, use bait quills.

Shallow Bottom Structure (150 ft./46 m depth or less)

We'll assume you have left the anchorage, stopped and caught bait, and located a wrecked ship or other fully or partially submerged item, perhaps a natural formation of rocks or coral, that is well defined and isolated from similar areas on the open seafloor. The general strategy is to anchor so that the boat ends up a reasonable distance (10 to 40 yds./3 to 12 m or more) upcurrent and upwind of the target structure. The goal is to draw the fish out and away from the habitat, hook them, and get them to the boat by preventing their vigorous efforts to return home.

Let's review an all-out assault similar to that of a full-fledged charter fishing boat, far beyond the effort and amount of tackle likely to be on board most cruising boats, but highly instructive in that you can select those techniques most applicable or appealing to you. Attracting fish in the short term (over part of a day) is best accomplished by chumming. Start by bombing the structure with a few large chum balls prior to dropping the hook, and drop one or two blocks of frozen chum overboard, in large-mesh (2 in./51 mm) stretch bags that maximize chum flow, tied off to port and starboard transom cleats. Drop a float (an empty bleach bottle will do) moored with a sash or dive weight and monofilament to mark smaller, more-difficult-to-find structures (e.g., small wrecks in deeper water). Anchor, coming tight on a 3:1 scope calculated to place the transom 30 yards (27 m) directly upcurrent of the structure for the prevailing wind/current vector on the hull of the boat. Deploy the following.

- *Fishing kite.* With two release clips, each kite-fishing line rigged with short #4 to #8 wire traces connected by an Albright special to 50- to 80-pound (23 to 36 kg) monofilament shock leaders fished from tackle ranging from 20-pound (9 kg) spinning to 50-pound (23 kg) stand-up conventional. Hooks for these rigs are Mustad 94150, size adjusted to bait dimensions (normally 3/0 to 7/0), including #4 to #8 wire stinger equipped with Mustad 3561E (size 1/0 to 3/0) or Eagle Claw L774 (size 6 to 2) treble hook with live or rigged dead baits (if billfish

are expected or have priority, don't use a stinger).

- *Outriggers.* One live or dead bait in each, fished on #2 wire leaders from 20-pound (9 kg) spinning tackle with a single Eagle Claw L774 (size 6 to 2) treble hook and closed bail for mackerel, or with the 20-pound (9 kg) monofilament tied straight to a Mustad 9174 (size 6 to 3/0) for midwater snappers, or with 50-pound (23 kg) monofilament shock leader straight to a Mustad 94150 for billfish and other midwater species lacking sharp teeth.

- *Downrigger.* One live or dead natural bait using any of the other rigs, up to an 80-pound (36 kg) stand-up conventional and 80-pound (36 kg) monofilament leader straight to a Mustad 39960TS circle hook with barb offset from hook shank prior to deployment, using a vice and pliers. Target species are large midwater and bottom fish. Never set a circle hook. As increased tension makes the bite apparent, lower the fishing rod to horizontal, and then reel as fast as you can—don't jerk or snap the rod tip or handline.

- *Bottom baits.* One or two 50- to 80-pound (23 to 36 kg) stand-up outfits with sliding rigs and Mustad 39960TS circle hooks for large bottom fish.

- *Free lines.* At least two 10- to 20-pound (4.5 to 9 kg) spinning rods with line tied straight to Mustad 9174 hooks using dead or small live baits targeting small to medium midwater species.

This system undergoes considerable modification within the specified depth range, generally with lighter tackle and elimination of the downrigger (and often the kite), when fishing shallow patch reefs (30 ft./9 m or less depth) inside the main reef line, shelf break, or lagoon. Prevailing wind and current in deeper water may cut down on the number of rigs possible to have in the water without causing tangles. Special targets, like larger billfish and sharks, require the appropriate bait, leader sizes (see table 3-1), and hooks (single-strand stainless #19 wire and a razor-sharp 7691 sized to the bait will handle most of the larger sharks). Also, don't hesitate to try any of the techniques discussed so far, from surface to seafloor, while anchored and fishing shallow bottom structure.

Now let's continue discussing some finer points of the fishing methods most applicable to this depth range, tips that will give your fishing efforts a sharp, effective edge. Use fluorescent kite-fishing floats in-line above the barrel swivel on lines fished from the kite release clips. This makes it easy to keep track of the baits and will help indicate imminent strikes and the presence of predators as live baits panic, causing the floats to move around rapidly. Reel in or let out line in response to changes in kite altitude with changing wind speeds, keeping the baits near the surface (within 1 yd./1 m) for maximum effect. Generally fish kite lines with closed bail (spinning reels) or in strike position (conventional reels), possibly open bail or in free spool with clicker on when targeting sailfish and other billfish with larger baits (this also holds true for outriggers and downriggers). Use a soft, insulation-covered individual telephone cable wire, haywire-twisted to the reel stem, the other end formed into a shallow hook to hold the line from falling off your spinning reel when fished in free spool. The soft wire releases the line freely upon strike (the next time you see a phone company van, ask the technician for a scrap section of cable; the bundle of insulated, small-diameter wires inside will provide a lifetime supply of these handy spinning-reel devices). Small tension-adjustable clips, fixed just forward of the reel seat by a cable tie, are also commercially available.

Let bottom baits on sliding rigs down relatively slowly, so that the usually lengthy leader does not wrap up and tangle with the weight and shock leader above the barrel swivel. Accomplish this with fast bursts interspersed with periodic stops. Drop until you hit bottom, then reel the weight 15 to 20 feet (4.6 to 6.1 m) or so back up off the seafloor to prevent entanglement, unless your position is well out on featureless mud or sand. Fish baits bail closed/strike position, drag setting at least 25 percent of line-breaking strength.

Try unweighted free lines diligently before weighted free lines and chum balls. Make repeated bait drifts, giving fish some time to rise off the reef or other structure in response to your chum. Often the largest individuals of midwater species, such as snapper family members worldwide, fall victim to

this technique. Structure in the deeper part of this depth range (120 to 150 ft./36 to 46 m) may require fishing free lines via drop stone or chum balls to get baits into the strike zone. Whenever you are free-lining, remember that when the line suddenly speeds up as you are feeding it to match the current, a fish has taken the bait. Hesitate, letting the fish swallow the bait, then set the hook. Maintain maximum possible pressure after hook-up—without breaking the line or ripping the hook out—to prevent the hard-sounding fish from reaching the bottom structure.

Deep Bottom Structure (150 to 1,000 ft./46 to 305 m or more)

Deep wrecks, seamounts, ledges, and other features are more often drifted or power-drifted rather than fished from the anchor, particularly in the case of nondedicated fishing vessels like sailboats and power cruisers. Any of the techniques discussed so far can produce (including chumming and surface baits and lures). Many tend to think of fast-swimming pelagic species such as tuna, wahoo, and billfish as susceptible mainly to rapidly moving lures or live bait, but drifted stationary or free-lined dead baits can be extremely effective. These fish, although speedy and wide-ranging, will still orient—at least temporarily—to floating items or bottom-associated features. They will respond to chum and sometimes swim slowly up and suck in dead bait—just like a fat, lazy reef fish—if undistracted by fast-moving schools of baitfish or squid. Live and rigged dead baits presented using a fishing kite can be lethal, particularly flying fish with wings tied out and adjusted to skitter at the surface below the kite-line release clip.

Fish for big groupers, snappers, sea bass, wreck-fish, amberjacks, yellowtails, trevallys, and other large midwater and bottom dwellers using heavy (50 to 80 lb./23 to 36 kg test) stand-up tackle or hand-lines and a three-way sinker rig (see fig. 4-3) with heavy, long leader (20 ft./6 m or more of 50 to 100 lb./23 to 45 kg test or more monofilament or wire, if appropriate). Bottom-fish a sizable live bait, whole dead bait, or fillet or cut bait on a circle hook, just as you would on more shallow structure.

Catch most of the same species and some of the demersal fish targeted in shallower depths by deep-jigging. Drop 6- to 20-ounce (0.38 to 0.57 kg) baited or unbaited bullet-head jigs all the way to the bottom on medium to heavy gear (20 to 50 lb./ 9 to 23 kg), then retrieve madly in big, sweeping tugs. Re-drop when you have brought the lure above the strike zone for the target species. When big fish pile on to a deep jig, you'll feel a jolt as though someone abruptly tossed a load of bricks on the line. Other deep-jigging lures may work better dropped to the bottom, and then retrieved rapidly straight up, with no jigging action (e.g., Ironman Jigs and similar lures). Deep-jigging requires considerable energy but can yield stellar results in considerable water depth, no bait required—this is a good one for restless older kids with a few spare calories to burn.

More often than not, we bottom-fish the greater depths seeking the attention of selected deep-dwelling fish species—brilliant red snappers, exotic groupers, silvery pink porgies, tilefish with firm flesh that sometimes tastes like lobster, wreckfish, hapuku, roughys, cod—many species that live in cool, dark depths far below what we can experience during normal diving. The capture of these fish gives us a window on a completely different environment, a part of inner space few humans will ever see—not to mention some of the highest quality seafood on the planet. If you have invested in wire line, this is a circumstance where it will out-fish any other gear you have.

How to Extract Fish That Tangle on the Bottom

Inevitably when bottom-fishing, the time comes when a fish defeats your best efforts to keep it from reaching the seafloor. Your quarry dives into a hole, cave, or wreck, or possibly wraps one or more turns of line around a stalk of kelp, soft coral, tree branch, piece of a wreck, projection of rock, or other obstacle. Maybe you can still feel life on the line, although you are unable to budge it; other times you may feel only the solid, immovable resistance of your new connection to the planet. Should you give up, cut the line, rerig, and try again? Not before you try the following tricks.

♦ *Fool the fish into swimming back out.* Immediately halt all tension on the fishing line, and feed out enough slack with thumb and forefinger so that you're sure the fish feels absolutely no pressure; it will frequently regain sufficient composure to venture back out of a refuge. If you feel the line begin to move through your fingers, close the bail or throw the drag into gear, quickly wind up the slack, and apply maximum pressure.

♦ *Goad the fish into swimming back out.* Under maximum tension, pluck the tight fishing line like a guitar string. Twang it hard and repeatedly. This causes fish to panic and come bursting back out into the open. You can sometimes accomplish the same thing by twitching the rod tip, but this is not generally as effective.

♦ *Change the angle of line pressure.* Walk forward on your boat, sweeping the line low to the water, and apply pressure. If applicable or deemed worth the effort, move the boat forward, to either side or behind the snagged fish, as though trying to free a hung anchor. This might be enough to extricate the tangle or cause the fish to move to your advantage.

♦ *Handline.* Whether using handline, rail-mounted reel, or rod and reel, apply maximum tension and then grasp the line in your hands exactly as though leadering a fish. Apply increasing pressure—sometimes this will be enough to force your fish clear. If you decide it's time to terminate the situation, win or lose, crank up the hand pressure until you either get the fish coming or break the line. This situation is appropriate for taking a wrap or two of line around your hand if it makes the job easier.

♦ *Dive down and extract the fish.* This is a last resort. Have you been chumming or catching numerous fish at one spot? How deep and how clear is the water? Have any sharks been hanging around, either sighted or perhaps taking a bite out of hooked fish? What is the likelihood of encountering aggressive sharks or other dangerous marine life? Is it *really* worth it? If so, free dive or use scuba gear, and either undo the tangle and allow the fisher to bring the fish up on the line, or grab, gaff, or spear the fish and bring it up yourself.

You have already been briefed on how to set up for deep-dropping. Now you need to station your boat properly in order to make the drop. Use visual cues; for example, the position of rips and standing waves caused by current deflected up over the bottom feature, land ranges, or a marker float you dropped on top of the structure. For power-drifting, position your vessel upcurrent and as close to the target site as possible in order for the weighted deep rigs to fall onto the desired area of the seafloor. If current is light or negligible, get right over the spot. Drop vertical arrays of cut squid, tuna, or other fish on smaller-sized circle hooks (Mustad 39960ST for 8/0 and up, Tainawa and other Japanese brands for 7/0 and smaller; see appendix 1 for suppliers). Spice up the action with a small mesh bag of chum tied at the top of the array. Crank up fifteen turns or so of line immediately when you hit bottom—which takes some practice to detect at greater depths. The secret is to drop at good line speed and then note a sudden pause, sometimes accompanied by visible slack in the wire, quite subtle at great depths. The response is frequently immediate if you have managed to reach the seafloor on or very near the feature, because many such fish populations do not receive a fraction of the effort experienced by their shallow-water counterparts. Your wire rod or commercial deck-winch boom will start throbbing; when you get some experience, you will be able to gauge the number of fish hooked up. We normally start cranking them up at three. Deep-dropping is highly addictive, and you will soon want to purchase a hand-operated deck winch or 12-volt attachment for your conventional reel to do the cranking for you.

Wait a minute, you say, this is it! It's simple (pushbutton, no less), fun, and productive, the fish are beautiful and have firm, white meat—why do anything else? Well, there can be complications, even assuming you have found the fish and they're biting. With any appreciable current, you've got to become adept at power-drifting, watching your GPS and depth machine, leading the fish-holding feature, and starting your drop at just the right moment. Feeling the bottom also requires practice, and any time you over-drop, you risk hanging up and losing substantial lengths of expensive wire. Reduce this risk by always constructing the hook/sinker rig out

of monofilament of lesser strength (50 lb./23 kg test) than your Monel wire (100 lb./45 kg test). Heavy current and rough seas can make deep-dropping next to impossible. Last, many of the spots feature dense midwater shark populations, and they don't take long to home in on the activity. Despite all this, it does work out often enough to be well worth doing, and it's a technique applicable virtually anywhere in the world.

Some banks and shelf areas can be productively drifted for deep-dropping over large zones, obviating the need for precision power-drifting. One professional technique is to put out a parachute sea anchor—with size adjusted to desired drift speed—to increase the time and comfort of a drift. This frees the skipper from the control station, creating another pair of hands for assisting fishing activities.

Other bottom configurations make it possible to anchor and fish deep water. Prevailing wind and current, for example, may permit dropping the anchor in shallow water (say, 60 ft./18 m) upwind of a steep drop-off or gradient, letting out scope to hang at various depths to 1,000 feet (305 m) or more, and employing any combination of fishing techniques. Be sure you can either swing in a complete circle without coming to grief in hazardous shallows or that you have rigged your anchor rode with a poly-ball marker float that can be detached and cast off immediately, in case the wind changes (be constantly alert for this possibility).

Many cruisers seldom consider dropping anchor in depths greater than 80 feet (24 m). Possession of extra ground tackle, however, can enable effective anchoring in depths to 600 feet (183 m) or more, with no need to risk losing an expensive anchor. Carry a grapnel anchor, 30 feet (9 m) of chain, and 1,500 feet (457 m) of cheap polypropylene anchor line, all sizes being the minimum necessary for your boat tonnage. Shackle the chain to the welded eye at the *base* of the grapnel, lay it along the shank, and tie a link with breakaway material to the end of the shank (where you'd normally think of attaching an anchor chain— a half-dozen turns of 80 lb./36 kg monofilament will hold a 12-gross-ton fishing boat in reasonable sea conditions). Maneuver directly over the bottom feature, leading it a little if there's current, and drop the grapnel until you hit bottom. Monitor the descent by driving forward just enough to watch it on your depth recorder. Maintain light tension and back off to a scope of 2.5 or 3:1 (the minimum you can get away with), lock off the rode, and see if you can get it to hold. Rig with a poly-ball marker so that the rode can be quickly cast off and retrieved later in case of a rapid change in the weather. This is obviously a fair-weather strategy and should not be attempted in excessive current, wind, or dangerous breaking waves. When you are ready to leave, ease your boat forward and take up as much slack as possible, lock off the rode, and reverse to part the break-away. The chain separates from the boat end of the anchor shank and comes tight to the shackle at the anchor base; the pressure pulls the anchor out in reverse of the direction it went in. Retrieve by winch or by hand, or make it easy by putting a poly ball and anchor ring on the rode and driving forward in an arc—keeping the rode well away from the drive train—until a galvanized wire nonreturn barb that you have whipped onto the rode just above the chain passes through the anchor ring. The barb will suspend the anchor and chain near the surface. Now turn the boat around and bring in the weightless anchor line. Figure 4-8 illustrates this entire drill.

This technology has nonfishing applications, and you can make some compromises to make deep anchoring rodes more generally useful aboard your vessel. For example, we carry two main rodes for our 15-gross-ton cruising sailboat, 340 feet (104 m) of ⅜ inch (10 mm) chain and 1,000 feet (305 m) of ¾-inch (19 mm) three-strand nylon rode. We can use the latter with a grapnel exactly as described previously in up to a 400-foot (122 m) depth in settled conditions, or we can use it to anchor comfortably and securely for the longer term with a 45-pound (20 kg) CQR or 44-pound (20 kg) Bruce anchor in sand or mud to 200 feet (61 m) depth. It also gives us plenty of line for storm anchoring and other uses and could be valuable for any cruising vessel for emergency anchoring in the event of a sail or mechanical breakdown on a lee shore.

Too crazy for you? Professional fishers make it a regular habit. Let's take you to a seamount that rises to within 300 feet (91 m) of the surface in 8 to 12 knots of breeze and a 1-knot current, and drop the grapnel at the upcurrent lip of the pinnacle. This par-

ticular underwater mountain juts up from a surrounding platform of rough, broken bottom ranging from 600- to 1,000-foot (183 to 305 m) depths. It presents an obstruction to the prevailing oceanic current flow, causing the water to "squeeze" around and over it. The vertical component of this squeezing action sends water from deeper layers boiling to the surface, along with myriad organisms not normally concentrated near the sea surface (e.g., squid, preyed upon directly by predator fish, and zooplankton, fed upon by schools of flying fish, which in turn become prey for speedy surface-feeding fish). And you have just stationed your vessel in the middle of the action!

Cast and retrieve, free-line, bottom-fish, deep-jig, deep-drop, put out the fishing kite, outriggers, a downrigger—chum and night light—use your imagination, all the tools you now have at your disposal, and whatever bait or lures you have onboard. One deadly trick is to set out a daisy chain of live baits. Form this like a vertical bottom rig, using three-way swivels or dropper loops for each side leader and hook, and tie a hook on the end instead of a sinker. Hook baits on, and let it out 30 feet (9 m) behind the boat. Throw a few handfuls of live bait (e.g., pilchards, sardines, or herring) out on top of the teaser. The panicked free-swimming baits cluster tightly around those on the daisy chain, creating an irresistible, sphere-shaped silhouette of bait that tuna, wahoo, billfish, mahi mahi, and many other predators find impossible to ignore. Cast out live baits on Mustad 94150 hooks near the teaser as the big fish start rocketing vertically through the living chum, or free-line baits back into the vicinity while you are waiting for them to show. No live bait? Fish a daisy chain of rubber squid from your fishing kite, adjusting the baits so that they skate and swim back and forth at the surface. Just about the time you become absorbed in deep-dropping or some other pursuit, you'll hear the distinctive sound of the kite-line release pin popping open, followed by the screaming drag of the fishing outfit with the daisy chain.

Specialties for the Deep Blue (applicable inside or outside the 1,000 ft./305 m depth contour)
Suppose you have at this juncture mastered most of the basics of both offshore trolling and stationary

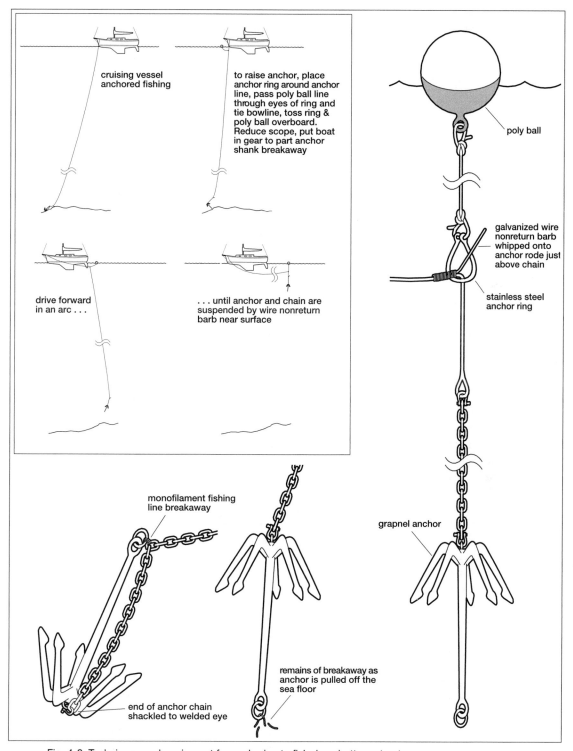

cruising vessel
anchored fishing

to raise anchor, place
anchor ring around anchor
line, pass poly ball line
through eyes of ring and
tie bowline, toss ring &
poly ball overboard.
Reduce scope, put boat
in gear to part anchor
shank breakaway

drive forward
in an arc . . .

. . . until anchor and chain are
suspended by wire nonreturn
barb near surface

poly ball

galvanized wire
nonreturn barb
whipped onto
anchor rode just
above chain

stainless steel
anchor ring

grapnel anchor

monofilament fishing
line breakaway

end of anchor chain
shackled to welded eye

remains of breakaway as
anchor is pulled off the
sea floor

Fig. 4-8. Techniques and equipment for anchoring to fish deep bottom structure.

sailboat fishing techniques. Your investment of time, money, and effort has been increasingly rewarded, resulting in the capture of mahi mahi, wahoo, tuna, various reef and temperate midwater and bottom species, squid, and perhaps a few billfish and sharks. You are beginning to feel experienced, and your crew has developed finely tuned palates for a growing variety of seafood and the experiences associated with procuring it. You have become comfortable with the use of a fishing kite, downrigger, and outrigger. Consider two intriguing options the next time you are adrift offshore, anywhere from the equator to temperate seas.

♦ Fly your fishing kite during the day with a live, small- to medium-sized tuna, mahi mahi, rainbow runner, or other baitfish caught easily on your spinning rod and a small lure, or dead-rigged flying fish, squid, or strip bait, for bait. The goal would be a shot at a big billfish, tuna, or other large pelagic species.

♦ Use the downrigger at night to drift a dead-rigged squid or fish bait deep for a broadbill swordfish, or try baits super deep during daylight hours.

Kite Fishing for the Big Ones

The action and lack of leader visibility associated with baits fished from kite release clips combine for a presentation that pulls fish from considerable depths to the surface, sometimes more than one at a time, to examine and frequently eat your offering. This can afford views of fish the likes of which you have never seen—massive mahi mahi over 50 pounds (23 kg), bruiser wahoo to 100 pounds (45 kg) and more, yellowfin tuna approaching the 200-pound (91 kg) mark and bigger, any size marlin, mako shark, and many others. Few people have the opportunity to view fish like this, much less hook one and actually see what it looks and feels like in battle. The use of large baits (12 to 24 in./305 to 610 mm) will generally encourage bites from bigger individuals and species.

Why might you wish to give this a try? Primarily for aesthetics and education, possibly food at the smaller end of the spectrum of potential catches.

Take photos, tag and release the fish if you are able to get it to the boat, give your kids an experience they'll tell their grandchildren about. Live a little. Do it in settled weather when everything is going smoothly and you are well rested.

A light-wind fishing kite will fly in as little as 4 knots of relative wind and will work either while drifting or slowly moving along under power or sail. If billfish are of interest, leave the reel in free spool with the clicker on. When a marlin eats a big bait, drop back to the fish for as long as thirty to forty-five seconds, less for smaller baits and for the size marlin, sailfish, and spearfish more apt to take these (say, ten seconds). Carefully monitor the speed and behavior of the eating fish by observing the line coming off the spool. A sudden burst of speed may indicate panic, true also whenever a fish begins jumping during the drop-back. In either case, immediately wind up all of the slack and set the hook because it has sensed that something is amiss and is trying to get rid of the bait (e.g., the leader brushed its eye or came tight somewhere on the body; it felt a hook). Slashing feeders like wahoo are best fished with the drag on strike position, and one could argue the merits of free spool versus strike position for big tuna and mahi mahi that swing in and attempt to engulf prey. A relatively short drop-back, again ten seconds or so, works well for sharks.

Use 15 feet (4.6 m) of 275-pound (125 kg) multistrand wire leader cable to cover any eventuality, 300-pound (136 kg) monofilament if you do not expect or want to catch wahoo or sharks. Crimp a barrel swivel to the rod end of the cable and install a fluorescent-colored kite fishing float on the shock leader above the barrel swivel. Use a Mustad 7754 hook sized to the bait (most likely 9/0 to 11/0), hooked in the shoulder meat between the head and dorsal fin of live baits. Remember to increase the tension on your kite-line release clip so it can handle the larger, heavier bait. Fish the bait close to the hull (20 ft./6 m out is plenty) for a good view, settle into your seat, be patient, and wait for the show to begin. Maximize the chance of a hook-up by quickly taking the rod out of the holder when you see signs that Godzilla has arrived, focus carefully on a proper drop-back, throw the lever into strike position, wind all slack, and set the hook. If you can get to the rod in time after seeing some submarine you *really* don't want any part of (e.g., a 2,000-lb./907 kg longfin mako shark), then quickly reel the bait so that it comes out of the water and dangles in the air high enough for the predator to lose interest.

Moonlight (and Daytime) Madness— Drift-Fishing for Broadbill Swordfish

Broadbill swordfish are the sole species in a different family (Xiphiidae) than marlin, sailfish, and spearfish (Istiophoridae). Viewed side by side with one of these species, the distinctive features of swordfish contrast sharply. The bill is a formidable weapon, much longer, heavier, and laterally flattened than that of any other billfish. The eyes are much larger, reflecting nocturnal feeding habits. The skin is similar to that of a shark, with tiny, peculiar, spiny scales that act like sandpaper—brush your forearm across the skin of a swordfish and you will instantly have a painful raw area. The dorsal, also as on sharks, is rigid and fixed in adults, and does not fold down. Free-swimming swordfish *look* more like a shark than a marlin, and project an aggressive demeanor that doesn't change when they are on the hook boatside. These fish will fix you with a baleful stare and take deliberate swipes at you with their sword. Records show several documented attacks by swordfish on submersibles.

Despite lowered abundance from considerable commercial fishing pressure worldwide, swordfish are widespread from the equator to temperate seas. They spend most of their time in midwater depths between 200 and 2,000 feet (61 and 610 m), rising with the nightly upward migration of zooplankton and other organisms(termed the deep scattering layer [DSL]) to feed. They spend more time at and near the surface in cooler temperate seas, a habit supporting traditional (but waning) harpoon fisheries off of New England and California in the United States. They are voracious, generalized predators, feeding on a variety of fish, squid, and other animals, including midwater stingrays. Scars around the head from altercations with large squid and pieces of spine from rays in the mouth and gut are common.

Throughout much of the world's oceans, the wide range and aggressive feeding behavior of swordfish make their capture quite likely by someone drifting offshore at night. Once again, cruising seafarers' normal activities fortuitously place them in a position to experience the aesthetics and culinary delight of a legendary gamefish, something others can only do by special arrangements and payment of large sums of money. Yes, swordfish can exceed 1,000 pounds (454 kg), but the average broadbill captured, for example, in the Caribbean weighs less than 100 pounds (45 kg)—easily manageable on 50-pound (223 kg) class stand-up tackle. You owe it to yourself to try some fresh swordfish steaks broiled or grilled, and the impressive sword can be treated and intricately carved for a souvenir.

Fishing for swordfish is simple. Rig the largest squid you can find, or any species of fish preferably 9 to 15 inches (228 to 381 mm) long, as though for

Broadbill swordfish with shark damage on the deck of a swordfish longliner (western tropical Atlantic).

trolling (see chapter 3). Many sportfishing charter captains use sinkers, just as you would for rigging subsurface trolling baits (see figs. 3-10 and 3-13). They tie elongated toystore balloons to the line at the surface as strike indicators. The balloon stands vertically from the weight of the suspended bait. If you see the balloon lie on its side, a swordfish may have ingested your bait on the rise, taking the tension off the line. In this circumstance, wind like crazy to get all slack out of the line and get tight to the fish. Other strikes pull the balloon under or move it around on or near the surface.

Several points speak against weighted baits, or in-line weights, as a means of getting the presentation to depth. First, fishers will likely miss fish that take or make contact with the bait, then release it—and can't find the unnaturally fast-sinking weighted bait that the angler above is free-spooling out in response to a detected bite. You can solve this problem by not dropping back; however, this may also negatively influence your hook-up rate. One solution is to present unweighted rigged baits using your downrigger, leave the reel in free spool with clicker on, and drop back as the fish eats the bait after the initial small taps characteristic of swordfish. Depending on the drift and what the fish does, this may increase the possibility of a tangle, but this is not usually a problem if you are only fishing one line. The other way to do it is to use a drop stone, tropical-Pacific style. Once you break the stone off with a tug, of course, there's no weight to hold the bait at depth, and any line drag from current or boat drift causes the bait to slowly rise. Of course, this is one way to check out a spectrum of depths. Reduce drag by backing down on your bait diligently with your boat, keeping the line as vertical as possible.

However you choose to fish, when the runoff becomes settled and steady or abruptly picks up speed (or the balloon lies on its side), throw the reel into strike position, wind like crazy to get all the slack out, and set the hook as soon as you get tension.

Rig details: Use a 300-pound (136 kg) monofilament leader with a chemical light stick attached 4 feet (1.2 m) above the bait with a size #34 rubber band. Bend the light stick sharply and shake to activate. Loop the rubber band onto the eye of the light stick, spin the light stick several times under tension around the leader, then pass it back through the rubber band, and cinch tight. It will stay firmly attached to this spot on the leader. Here's a commercial swordfisher's secret that *seems* to actually work, to such a degree that our longline crew would religiously take the time to embellish thousands of light sticks en route to the fishing grounds: wrap the light stick with black vinyl electrical tape in a spiral, like the striping on a candy cane or barber pole. The glow pattern thrown off by this spiral as the light stick bobs up and down from the motion of the sea surface above seems to result in higher swordfish catch rates. Also, green light sticks seem to outperform white or blue, although red light sticks occasionally work extremely well on deeper baits (250 ft./76 m) during dark moon phases in the tropics.

How deep should you set your bait? At night, anywhere from 60 to 450 feet (18 to 137 m) can work. Deeper baits are generally more effective for brighter moon phases, when higher ambient nocturnal light levels suppress the upward migration of the DSL and discourage squid and other prey items from cavorting too close to the well-lit surface layers. Sportfishing captains in some areas claim higher success around the full moon, but excellent catches of swordfish can happen on any moon phase, depending on the area and attention to detail when setting out the baits. A recent sport fishery focuses on catching broadbills during daylight hours.

Tire these fish thoroughly before attempting to land them. Like black marlin, swordfish have a tendency to fight until they die, rather than giving up and allowing themselves to be coaxed near the boat while still in relatively good health. Always try to gaff them in the head, preferably in the eye socket. Consider carrying a large hand gaff or flying gaff to use on larger individuals, attaching it to a cleat with rope. Remember also that a tail rope is highly effective for securing bigger fish. Always use one gloved hand to control the bill, and quickly subdue it once aboard. Cut into fresh steaks (see chapter 9). If you or the kids would like a showpiece, remove the bill with a hacksaw and suspend it overboard, submerged on a line, until marine bacteria have consumed the dark outer cover and oily interior, eventually leaving a white sword. This can take a while (over a week), so be patient, and you'll have a great conversation piece that won't stink up the boat. At a port with good bone carvers (e.g., the Kingdom of Tonga) or scrimshaw artists (New England), have your sword transformed into a masterpiece.

You'll catch other pelagic species when you fish for swordfish. Many sharks bite through the monofilament leader, saving the trouble of battling them to the boat. Swordfish techniques during daylight hours can be effective for delicious bigeye tuna because adults tend to spend most of their time feeding well below the surface. Albacore, assorted billfish, and other species are other likely possibilities. Good luck!

Vertical Longlines

Your trusty poly ball and a yo-yo or, better yet, a commercial deck winch, can be used to catch some of the same deeper-dwelling open-ocean fish targeted by a deep bait fished swordfish-style off a downrigger. Attach the poly ball to the end of a spool of 300-pound (136 kg) monofilament (your mainline), toss it overboard, and move the boat ahead slowly, allowing the mainline to spool off freely as you go. Affix longline snap-on connectors crimped to 6-foot (1.8 m) lengths of 300-pound (136 kg) monofilament or multistrand wire equipped with baited offset circle hooks at intervals. Then stop or slow the boat, cut the mainline, tie a dive or sash weight on the end, and toss the weight overboard. Keep the poly ball in sight as you troll around or drift—you'll see movement as fish get hooked. Give them time to tire if the sharks permit this luxury. Then swing over to the poly ball, gaff the mainline, begin hauling, and handline each fish to the gaff as it surfaces.

This technique can work particularly well near some fish-holding features, such as a seamount, purpose-built FAD, floating debris, or shelf break, in the vicinity of fish schools marked by birds or noted on your depth-sounder, or any generally productive area of open ocean. It is a simple way of presenting baits deep to catch something different from your normal fare, and you can always snap on a few shallow leaders as well. Obviously, this is most relaxing in calm sea conditions during the day; however, you can attach a floating dive flag, man-overboard pole, or similar arrangement on a short tether to the poly ball, and tie light sticks (one to three) to the top of the flagpole for night fishing. Monitor the glow of the light sticks as you drift in the vicinity, periodically motoring back when you get far enough away to risk losing sight of it.

Why not tie off this arrangement to the boat instead? For the same reason you must move slowly and spool line off fast enough when you are setting out your vertical longline: so that you do not pull or drag the mainline through the water—doing so causes the snap-on leaders to spin up around it and become tangled.

Break away Poly-Ball Lines

While your mind is still on the use of poly balls, let's revisit one last trick to take this fishing scenario section near where it began, with the transition from trolling. Remember the inherent problems with the all-or-nothing disadvantage of snubber lines? In the

Broadbills by Day

For commercial and recreational fishers, with the exception of harpooners and the odd sportfishing opportunity to bait usually reluctant, surface-basking individuals, swordfishing is a nighttime practice. Do they vanish during the day? No—they descend with the DSL (deep scattering layer) to the darkened depths. Recently, a combination of ingenuity and practical circumstances enabled Venezuelan charter-fishing captain Oscar Benito and colleagues to show the world how practical it can be to forget all of that Special Forces stuff and catch them during the day. They use 1½ to 2 pounds (0.7 to 0.9 kg) of in-line lead sinkers above the snap swivel (a sliding rig) and 400- to 500-pound (181 to 227 kg) monofilament leaders to fish the baits at 1,440 to 1,680 feet (455 to 517 m) over the 1,800-foot (553 m) depth contour, offshore of Caraballeda. It's dark as night down there, so they use Cyalume light sticks as usual. The bite rate is excellent (often in the first 15 to 20 minutes at this location in the late afternoon), and a high percentage of the fish seem to take the bait and rise rapidly to the surface, so watch for that balloon to tilt sideways! Deep daytime swordfishing is in its infancy, so give it a try on some calm day during your next cruise. Just remember to face Venezuela and salute Oscar as the first swordfish steaks start to sizzle on the grill.

last chapter, we introduced the technique of rigging heavy trolling handlines to a snubber, then rigging a poly ball with a light monofilament breakaway (a single loop of 50 lb./23 kg test mono is about right for a 200 to 300 lb./91 to 136 kg handline). Place the poly ball outside railings, stanchions, or lifelines so that when a fish hits, popping the breakaway line under just enough tension to set the hook, it can fall unobstructed into the water.

Keep the poly ball in sight—here again, you *could* rig it with a man-overboard flag for improved visibility (this is not necessary in reasonably settled conditions). Turn the boat around and head back to the poly ball, which should have a hooked, struggling fish suspended from it. Look around for more fish on the surface, and drive close to the poly ball with your depth-sounder on—multiple marks below the poly ball are your fish's colleagues. If you want more than one fish, break out your casting gear (or handline) and fire deep-jigging lures or baits down in the immediate vicinity of the hooked fish and out around the poly ball on the surface. You may hook other school members, especially if you have tuna, mahi mahi, wahoo, large mackerel, or other nonsolitary species of fish, even billfish, on the poly-ball line. Last, pull alongside the poly ball, gaff the line, and handline that fish to the boat.

Obviously, the breakaway poly-ball method should normally be employed only during daylight hours when sea conditions, your willingness, and your timetable (if you have one) permit turning the boat around to go back and pick up the gear. Avoid this technique at night or any time it's difficult, uncomfortable, or dangerous to come about. Sailors flying a spinnaker, running wing and wing with downwind poles and preventers, or blasting along in any configuration requiring heavy sail work to turn around will probably choose other options, as will most power cruisers and sailors in windy, rainy, or rough conditions. After all, we're *supposed* to be having fun!

A Word of Caution

If you choose to become adept at fishing from your sailboat or power cruiser while adrift or at anchor, the entertainment, activity, and seafood provided will likely encourage ever-slower passage times as you are tempted to enjoy hanging out longer offshore. Sailors may actually start to enjoy getting becalmed, and perhaps not raise sail when breezes do resume. Furthermore, for similar reasons, you may remain longer at the more exciting outer-reef anchorages than before. You might even begin to allow these factors to influence your selection of anchorages and, later, islands and possibly entire island groups. The last stage is planning lengthy passages in zones of light wind, fine weather, and a favorable drift toward the next group of islands.

Gear Checklist

Table 4-2 lists fishing gear for use when your boat is drifting or at anchor. Add to your tackle arsenal according to personal taste and budget. Although professional fishers are opinionated and will debate their pet theories and fishing systems as vigorously as cruisers discuss different hull types and rigs, the gear suggested here fits the fishing strategies in this chapter, without repeating gear listed previously. You'll eventually develop tricks and variations using this foundation, and alternative approaches are endless. Nevertheless, these additional items will at the least get you off to a good start, and help get you fishing successfully from a relatively stationary vessel.

TABLE 4-2. **CHECKLIST OF GEAR FOR FISHING ADRIFT OR ANCHORED**

Item	Specific Recommendation	Approximate Price
Fishing kite	Capt. Bob Lewis Fishing Kite	$55–$63
Fishing kite floats	Capt. Harry's fluorescent kite float	$0.65
Kite release clip	Capt. Bob Lewis Kite Release Pin Kit	$20
Dedicated kite line dispensers	handline spool or yo-yo	$3–$32
	cheap kite reel (e.g., Penn 285L)	$30 or less
	Capt. Harry's kite rod	$60

TABLE 4-2. **CHECKLIST OF GEAR FOR FISHING ADRIFT OR ANCHORED (cont.)**

Item	Specific Recommendation	Approximate Price
#19 stainless steel leader wire	Malin, 1 lb. (0.45 kg) spool	$21
Stainless steel multistrand cable	Duratest 49 Strand, 275 lb. (125 kg) test, 30 ft. (9 m)	$8
Egg sinkers	2, 4, 6, 8, 16 oz. (57, 113, 170, 227, 454 g)	$1 per lb. (0.45 kg)
Pyramid sinkers	choose according to tackle and environment	$1 per lb. (0.45 kg)
Split-shot sinkers	split-shot assortment (124 sinkers)	$2
Sash weights	or any 1–3 lb. (0.45–1.36 kg) scrap weight	variable to free
General-purpose hooks	Mustad 9174, sizes #6–5/0	$4–$8/100
	Eagle Claw 189, sizes #8–3/0	$7–$11/100
Small treble hooks	Eagle Claw L774, sizes #6–#2	$8/50
Live bait/general-purpose hooks	Mustad 94150 and 94151, sizes #2–7/0	$4–$10/100
Circle hooks	Mustad 39960ST, sizes 8/0–12/0	$12–$23/100
	Tainawa circle hooks, 7/0 and smaller	$8 to $15/100
Gold baitfish or hair hooks	Eagle Claw 89, sizes #14–1/0	$6–$7/100
Bait quills	Sabiki Hot Hook Bait Rigs, sizes #15–#4	$3–$7/six-pack
Bait-holding pen	Bait Motel, 65–130 g (246–492 L)	$66–$86
Bait dip net	available in many sizes	$9–$25
Floats	Round plastic red/white clip-ons	less than $1 each
	Natural round corks with plastic stopper	$0.65–$2.50
	Plastilite weighted slot Poppin' Bob	$1–$2
	Toystore balloons	cheap
	Poly balls, 20–60 in. (50–150 cm) circumference	$6–$36
Stainless steel anchor ring	Capt. Harry's Anchor Ring	$26
Grapnel anchor	Econo Grapnel	$38–$75
Polypropylene line	A & G, ½ to ¾ in. (13–19 mm), per 600 ft. (182 m)	$70–$150
Longline snap-on connectors	A & G heavy duty	$2
Chemical light sticks	Cyalume, green and red	$2
Rubber bands	#34	$5 per pound
Large hand gaff	Pompanette Meat Hook	$82
Flying gaff handle	Aftco Taper Tip, 6 ft. (1.8 m)	$110
Flying gaff heads	Aftco 6, 8, or 10 in. (15, 20, or 25 cm)	$88, $94, $147
Landing net	available in many sizes	$10–$35
Three-way swivels	Offshore Angler Three-Way Brass Swivels	$2 per 3–10
Squid jigs	Shrimp Chokka Jigs	$6
Deep jigs and lures	Deep Jigs, 6–20 oz. (170–567 g)	$3–$7
	Bullet Head jig heads, 1–3 oz. (28–85 g)	$0.60–$1.35
	Swirl Tail Grubs, 6 and 8 in. (152 and 203 mm)	$3 per 4–10
	Shrimpi Twin Tail, 4 and 6 in. (102 and 152 mm)	$4/15, $5/10
	AA's Swimming Eel, 12 in. (305 mm)	$3
	Ironman Jigs, 1¾–3¾ oz. (50–106 g)	$4–$6
	Bead Diamond Jig, 1–32 oz. (28–907 g)	$3–$13
	Crippled Herring Spoons, 1–3 oz. (28–85 g)	$4–$5
	No=EQL Lures, single hook, 6 oz. (170 g)	$7
Electric deep drop reel	Elec-tra-mate, many models for Penn reels	$115–$2,350
Chum bag	Nylon mesh	$3

5

Dinghy Techniques

Do you recall the Dinghy Adventures section of chapter 1, a medley of snapshots, in words, of diverse fishing experiences? What's the common thread in all of these incidents, other than adventure, camaraderie, education, and gourmet eating? They were made possible by understanding the many ways to catch fish from dinghies during cruises aboard various vessels. This chapter is a complete primer on the extensive melange of fishing techniques and opportunities made possible by something that virtually every cruising boat possesses, the dink: inflatable or hard; powered by oars, outboard, or sail—these craft are perhaps your most versatile, fun, and productive weapon.

Cruisers need dinghies to go where it is either inefficient or impossible to take the big boat, often at speeds not possible for their floating homes. This gives them access to coral-strewn shallows, marshes, sandy flats and beaches, rocky shorelines and kelp beds, creeks and rivers that penetrate jungles or rugged icy highlands, meandering estuarine tidal channels, occluded areas that can only be entered by small craft, and inland freshwater lakes and rivers. Weather permitting, dinghies provide more rapid, hassle-free transport to near-shore, reef, and offshore environments than if one were to up anchor and use the big boat. Properly outfitted, nearly any dinghy expedition can potentially include the efficient capture of fresh fish for dinner.

Liz McCutcheon plays a blue smalltooth jobfish *(Aprion furca)*, hooked trolling a ½ oz. (14 g) Rat-L-Trap swimming plug on 10 lb. (4.5 kg) test spinning tackle, to the net with Jon Broadhurst supervising (Tonga).

Suppose you were to do nothing more than install a single rod holder on the transom of your dinghy, take along an inexpensive, collapsible spinning rod made for backpackers (so you can carry it with you ashore rather than tempt theft by leaving it aboard), and carry a pocket-sized box with several lures. If you were to drag one of these behind you as a normal part of any dinghy trip, and choose your lures well, you *might* not need to do any other food fishing for much of your cruise.

Getting Started

As with any other area of fishing, you can sophisticate your efforts considerably beyond this introductory level, compelled by fish scarcity along your regular dinghy routes, curiosity, adventure, fun-seeking, or a slowly worsening case of fishing fever. More pristine and productive areas for exploration are often only a short dinghy ride from a secure, although relatively barren, big boat anchorage. Whether the approach is passive, trolling light tackle as a small part of other activities, or more actively focused on fishing, many of the most memorable moments of cruising for us have been instigated by or were related in some way to dinghy fishing. Cold, misty mornings catching firm, brilliantly hued rainbow trout on crystal clear inland lakes and swift-flowing rivers in temperate latitudes; languid tropical sunsets, the chatter of monkeys and parrots, and deep jungle greenery as a backdrop to

Collapsible spinning outfit.

Double-lined or shark mackerel (*Grammatorcynos bilineatus*) (Tonga).

casting for tarpon, snook, jacks, and snappers near the equator ... experiences like these may tempt you to step slightly beyond the bare minimum of dinghy gear and modifications.

WHAT TO TAKE

Safe and efficient fishing from dinghies involves several categories of gear. Like the dinghy itself, think of these categories as miniaturized versions of what you might carry aboard your cruising boat. Good seamanship, planning, personal safety, load-carrying capacity and distribution, comfort, and *fun* are all paramount. Retribution for mistakes and oversights can be quick and unmerciful on these small boats.

Normal Dinghy Gear for an Extended Trip

Consider the following items for any dinghy trip, especially to leeward of land and anchored vessels, out of sight of other mariners or local inhabitants, or when the destination involves traversing open water, potentially hazardous conditions, or significant distance:

◆ bailer
◆ oars
◆ anchor, chain, and *plenty* of rode
◆ portable VHF with fully charged battery
◆ emergency patch kit
◆ ample drinking water
◆ tool/spare-parts kit for engine
◆ fins and mask
◆ sea anchor (small drogue or bucket that can double as a high-volume bailer)

We're all guilty of omitting subsets of these items as a practical matter for various other dinghy trips, with good reason, and then forgetting to put them back on when we really should have them. Getting caught can range from inconvenient to fatal. For example, a friend collected me from *Élan* for an impromptu sunset offshore trolling expedition on the leeward side of an atoll in a fast inflatable dinghy. The outboard died just outside the steep outer reef wall about 2 miles from the anchorage. A steady 15- to 18-knot trade wind immediately began carrying us offshore (the distance to the next landfall was approximately 1,000 NM). The dinghy would

not row upwind, and we had only an hour of daylight remaining. A quick review of our options revealed no portable VHF, a few tools, and the tackle box. I had tossed aboard powerful fins and a diving mask, permitting me to go overboard and make good progress towing the dinghy upwind—swimming energetically with the bow line held over my shoulder—while my fishing partner examined the engine. We made it to a canoe mooring in the reef shallows. We were able to dismantle the carburetor and clear the main jet of a dried chunk of old fuel varnish with a piece of #2 fishing leader wire, reassemble it, and get back under power before dark. This tiny piece of wire and the dive fins provided a narrow and fortunate escape from our stupidity. What if there had been any appreciable offshore current, or a single aggressive tiger shark?

Another time we watched a newly infected fisher hook a marlin while trolling alone from an inflatable, again near a steep ocean drop-off immediately to leeward of land. Soon he was a tiny orange speck, threatening to disappear over the horizon. We were making preparations for a rescue when, through the binoculars, the orange dot began to grow larger and sported a visible white bow wave. A belated decision to terminate the engagement by locking the reel drag had produced the desired result and a fishing rod broken in half (it's better to cut the line with knife or fishing pliers).

More recently, two anglers fishing from an anchored, small inflatable dinghy near shore off North Island, New Zealand, became alarmed at the behavior of a small (7 ft./2 m) mako shark that was hanging around their position. Relocating slightly seemed to work, but only temporarily, as the mako reappeared and commenced to rush in and bite the bow. One guy cut the anchor line and stemmed the outrush of air from the torn forward section with his hand; the other guy started the engine, throttled hard, and threw his partner overboard. He scrambled quickly back on, now considerably behind on saving the deflated bow section. As they proceeded to run the partially swamped dinghy toward shore, they managed to place a cell-phone call to the police, complete with their Global Positioning System (GPS) position from a handheld unit. A rescue effort was ultimately rendered unnecessary by their unceremonious and damp arrival back at the boat ramp.

And here's one for anyone tempted to be smug about owning a hard dinghy. A friend's brother-in-law borrowed his new 12-foot (3.6 m) aluminum dinghy and brand-new outboard for an inshore bottom-fishing outing (off New Zealand's North Island). He inadvertently hooked a 6-foot (1.8 m) bronze whaler shark. During efforts to de-hook and release it, the shark somehow managed to flip *aboard*, crashed around violently in a melee of asses and elbows, and abruptly sunk the dinghy. The two fishers had little time to concern themselves about further revenge from their new swimming companion, as a nearby vessel quickly swung in for the rescue. Salvage efforts later revealed a gaping split in the hull.

The point is, dinghies are by nature small, frail, and therefore subject to events that wouldn't faze your big boat. Guard against the heady rush of your new fishing expertise. Yes, you can fully expect heavy action on your chosen outings, but try to anticipate the other unfamiliar positions in which this new power may place you. A little prudence, forethought, and planning can greatly improve the probability of a safe, routine outing, fully successful in all respects.

Finally, consider all other aspects of the length and duration of your intended voyage consistent with small-boat seamanship. What time do you expect to return? Inform a neighboring boat or another contact of your plans. What effect might the tidal state have on your journey? Will an outgoing tide transform passable shallows into dry land, preventing a timely return? Will the timing of tidal flows reverse current directions favorably or unfavorably for your intended route? Will they cause dangerous standing waves to form predictably in a narrow pass that is deceptively placid at other times? What's the short-term weather forecast?

It all sounds obvious, but cruisers continue to get caught by the same old things sooner or later, hopefully not repeatedly. We readily admit to occasionally subjecting ourselves to situations within each of the preceding categories.

Basic Fishing Gear

Fishing brings into sharper focus the timeless conflict cruisers must balance between ease of stowage and utility of the tender, frequently solved by owning an inflatable rather than a hard-material (rigid hull) dinghy. The fundamental problem, of course, is the ease and potentially grave consequences of puncturing an inflatable with the many sharp objects associated with fishing: fishhooks, gaffs, knives, teeth, bills, fins, and dorsal spines, to name a few. Nevertheless, it is possible to get many years of fishing service from an inflatable with no mishaps. We review precautions that will assist this endeavor as we go over basic gear that requires no modification of your dinghy. Most will also enhance safety aboard rigid-hull tenders.

- *Fishing rods.* Take anything from ultra-light spinning gear to 50-pound (23 kg) stand-up conventional tackle, even fly rods, on dinghy expeditions. Secure hooks carefully in the *bridge* of a rod guide or eyelet (never *inside* the area where the line passes because nicks, cuts, or small grooves in these surfaces can chafe and damage line as it passes through, eventually leading to break-offs). Ensure that the hooks cannot rattle into a position that could pierce an inflatable hull. Alternatively, cut off and stow hooks and lures inside a secure container until time for deployment.
- *Tackle box or bucket.* A standard small tackle box, clear-plastic hardware organizer, or similar closing box is handy for storage of lures, hooks, sinkers, and other terminal tackle. Avoid carrying more than the minimum amount of gear. A small simple box stored perhaps in a light daypack prevents the specter of a larger tackle box with stacking trays inevitably getting wet inside, subjecting a lot of gear to ruinous corrosion. Large conventional tackle boxes store poorly on cruising boats, and even worse on dinghies. For dinghy trips targeting larger species (e.g., on trolled lures), a 2-gallon (7.6 L) plastic bucket with V-shaped grooves notched around the rim for hanging the rigs and lures is a handy asset (a mini-grinder with a cutting wheel makes formation of the hook grooves fast and easy). Lengthy leaders coil neatly in the bottom of the bucket, and you can toss in gloves, hook remover, sheathed ice pick,

sunscreen, and other useful items as well. Set this bucket inside another bucket, which can serve as a sea anchor or high-volume emergency bailer. Small, slim-profile bailers and sponges are nice, but a bucket can sometimes make the difference in staying afloat. It may also permit continued travel to windward despite conditions that are depositing large quantities of seawater inside your small open vessel.

♦ *Gaff.* Place a length of close-fitting plastic hose over the point of the gaff, slide it firmly up onto the bend of the gaff hook, and trim at least 3 inches (76 mm) below the point. Remove only for gaffing fish, and replace promptly.

♦ *Landing net.* Don't forget this important piece of gear, useful not only for preventing loss of fish boatside, but also for keeping them away from inflatable hulls. Landing nets are especially good for avoiding situations where a fish falls off the hook at just the wrong moment *over* the hull, potentially driving sharp spines or teeth through hull material.

♦ *Fish bag or cooler.* Hard plastic insulated coolers work fine if you have the room, which is often not the case on cruising sailboats and smaller dinghies. Power cruisers with more deck storage space may be able to select a sizable cooler that also fits comfortably lengthwise in the tender. Mount an inexpensive swiveling chair on the lid, and you've got a wonderful elevated bow seat and fishing perch. Sailors will probably do better with one of the durable insulated fish bags now on the market. These stow neatly and, like coolers, can be stocked with plastic water bottles that have

But for a Bucket

Several years ago, I spent a blustery January day offshore of Tobago, West Indies, commercial fishing for flying fish, yellowfin tuna, and mahi mahi with my old friend Hollis John aboard his 28-foot (8.5 m) outboard-powered pirogue. We had something on the order of 1,000 pounds (454 kg) of fish by the time we'd drifted almost 30 NM west of the island, the wind was piping up close to 30 knots, and the sun was getting low. Hollis called a halt to the fishing, and we stowed the gear, bracing ourselves for a rough ride home. The narrow bow of the pirogue knifed gamely into the heavy swells and wind chop, displacing solid walls of water, much of which blew straight back into the boat. Hollis urged me and the young crewman, both armed with buckets, "C'mon, *bail*, mon . . . it's gittin' late, an' we 'lone 'pon the sea." The two of us bailed steadily and nonstop until the lee of Tobago finally eased the wind and seas. We arrived back at the beach and began off-loading our catch just as the sun touched the horizon.

A similar condition, featuring significantly more wind velocity, had prevailed on another winter day in the Caribbean six years earlier as we stood watch aboard the high-seas swordfish longliner *Rush*. We were pounding to the southeast from Puerto Rico,

roughly 150 NM west of Martinique. I was surprised to spot a pirogue motoring off sea toward us, the lone fisher waving frantically with one hand and guiding the outboard tiller with the other. The whites of his bulging, frightened eyes glowed strikingly as he skittered by on a wave crest, almost level with the wheelhouse, and took advantage of the following trough to swing sharply behind us into our wake, waving and yelling urgently. There were no targets on the radar, no other visible boats, definitely no one concealed below the gunnels in the pirogue, only genuine fear mixed with relief on the man's face . . . this looked like a genuine case of distress. I eased the throttle and awoke the captain. We helped the bedraggled French West Indian aboard and took his boat in tow. We determined from maritime authorities in Guadeloupe that he had been missing overnight, a search was underway, and they were greatly relieved at news that he was safe. What was the problem? He explained that when the wind came up, he could not by himself bail fast enough to make way against the conditions, and he was gradually forced farther from land as he did what he could to stay afloat. One or two crew and buckets *may* have been the difference between his uncomfortable predicament and our situation in Tobago.

been frozen or at least refrigerated to keep your catch cold and fresh. Unzip these "body bags" as you are ready to gaff or net your catch, place the fish in the bag, subdue, and zip the bag shut—your dinghy and crew are safe from errant spines and teeth. The only slight drawback with our models is the tendency for bloody fish water to ooze out through the stitching along the bottom seam of the bag.

♦ *Live bait bucket or hotel.* Live bait works much better under certain conditions than anything else, so it may be worth bringing along a simple means of keeping some temporarily at hand. Some bait items are hardy enough to last in your regular sea anchor/bailer bucket with no water or an occasional partial water change (e.g., hermit crabs, shore crabs, shallow-water crabs and shrimp, certain hardy fish species, sand fleas, bloodworms, conch, and other shelled mollusks). Others may tolerate short transport times in a bucket of seawater, and subsequent transfer to a semi-submerged holding pen of some kind (e.g., collapsible mesh bait hotels or purpose-designed "trolling" buckets). You may be able to catch bait on-site and transfer it directly to an overboard holding device, possibly allowing use of more sensitive species.

♦ *Transom-mount fish finders.* You're probably having the same reaction we did when a friend proudly announced the recent acquisition and intent to bring along a transom-mounted fish finder called the Fishin' Buddy II, powered by three C batteries, and complete with side-scanning sonar and temperature probe. Our skepticism completely evaporated over the course of a half-dozen outings, particularly when we had repeated opportunities to verify both vertical and side-scan readings. We're not saying you need it (we don't have one ... yet), but if your situation makes sonar capability particularly advantageous, it's inexpensive and it works. We did find the standard mounting bracket inadequate for leaving the unit deployed at anything above idle trolling speed; however, this could be easily remedied for somewhat higher speeds.

GENERAL MODIFICATIONS TO YOUR DINGHY FOR FISHING

You can catch plenty of fish without doing a thing to your dinghy. *However*, it won't be long before you start thinking of ways to make life easier ... more convenient ... more fun. The first step would probably be installing two rod holders on the transom, set as far apart as possible, and fixed at 45-degree angles so that the fishing rods splay outboard, maximizing distance between trolling lines. These free up your hands for other things ... holding a cold beer, pointing out a pretty sight ... and contribute significantly to your relaxation. You can make these yourself from aluminum pipe or PVC (only for light tackle) or buy commercial models. If you make your own metal holders, take the time to construct gimbals using ¼-inch-diameter (63.5 mm) stainless steel hex-head bolts so that you can use them for your heavier stand-up tackle. Through-bolt any rod holders, dabbing some West System epoxy resin into the holes just prior to installation for wood transoms. For metal transoms (usually aluminum), coat the bolts liberally with Duralac (a yellow insulating lacquer) to prevent galvanic corrosion (fig. 5-1). We have found the 9-inch (229 mm) Sea Dog model 325150-1 stainless steel side-mount holders (I.D. 1⅝ in./41 mm) to be inexpensive, durable, and adequate for all our dinghy fishing needs.

As long as you're installing rod holders, throw on a few stainless steel pad eyes, also through-bolted if possible. These are handy for attaching lanyards from various items you would like to prevent from going overboard (like your shiny new stand-up outfit), or as attachment points for snubber lines, other lines (e.g., a teaser line), small bailers, bait containers, and chum bags.

Once again, further elaboration might be tempting depending on the size of your tender, amount of tackle you have, and how much you like to fish. Small outriggers suitable for dinghy use are readily available. These require holders, so you'd need to fit another pair suited to the outriggers that you purchase. One way to take care of many issues simultaneously would be the fabrication or acquisition of a removable multiple-holder unit, commonly called a rocket-launcher, that fits into two vertical, transom-mounted rod holders (see photo on page 127). This

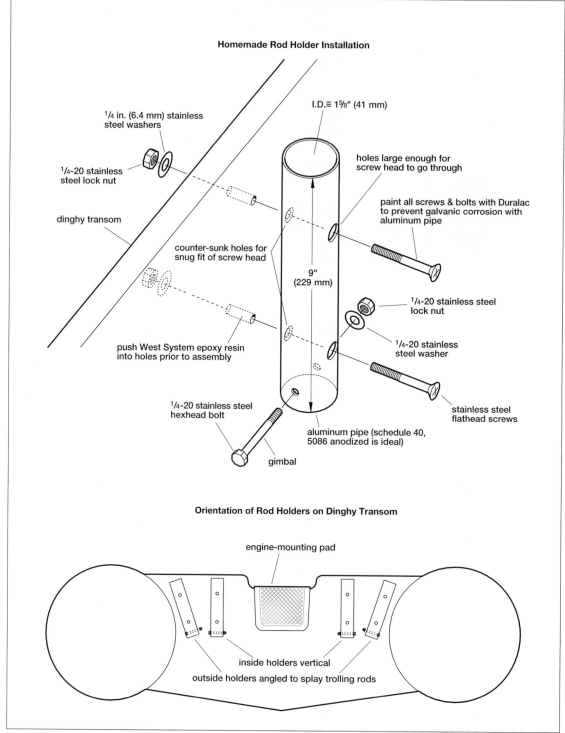

Homemade Rod Holder Installation

I.D. ≅ 1⅝" (41 mm)

¼ in. (6.4 mm) stainless steel washers

holes large enough for screw head to go through

¼-20 stainless steel lock nut

paint all screws & bolts with Duralac to prevent galvanic corrosion with aluminum pipe

dinghy transom

counter-sunk holes for snug fit of screw head

9" (229 mm)

¼-20 stainless steel lock nut

¼-20 stainless steel washer

push West System epoxy resin into holes prior to assembly

¼-20 stainless steel hexhead bolt

stainless steel flathead screws

aluminum pipe (schedule 40, 5086 anodized is ideal)

gimbal

Orientation of Rod Holders on Dinghy Transom

engine-mounting pad

inside holders vertical

outside holders angled to splay trolling rods

Fig. 5-1. Construction and installation of homemade dinghy transom rod holders.

Rocket launcher, with four rod holders and two outriggers, installed on inflatable dinghy transom.

would allow you to mount two outriggers and carry or fish up to four fishing rods at the same time.

THE ULTIMATE FISHING DINGHY?

Many power cruisers and larger sailboats have room for a substantial rigid-hull dinghy. Those who can carry a small fiberglass or aluminum skiff (e.g., an 11-foot/3.4 m Boston Whaler with a 25-hp outboard) can have at their disposal a formidable miniature fishing craft able to pull off substantial missions. This was the dinghy aboard a 48-foot (14.6 m) motorsailer I occasionally crewed on for years, very close to the trawler end of the sailboat spectrum, and great for coastal voyaging, but dangerous for extensive bluewater work. Other cruising friends who sail extensively offshore have a more compactly arranged, similar-sized dinghy consisting of a two-piece plywood pirogue that stows neatly on different sections of the deck. It's fairly convenient to assemble and disassemble, but the length of their cutter is 55 feet (16.8 m), somewhat longer than the average cruiser. A steel ketch owned and built by a Canadian pipeline welder has a slightly smaller one-piece aluminum dinghy, set up as a displacement-hull centerboarder that can be sailed or efficiently powered by oars or outboard. This ketch, however, is also around 50 feet (15.2 m).

Where does that leave the rest of us, particularly sailboats under 50 feet (15.2 m) with limited deck space, who want the option of safe long-distance ocean crossings? Usually with a very small hard dinghy that stows somewhere on deck, probably more often with an inflatable, increasingly with a rigid deck or at least a semirigid floor. Kayaks are also becoming more popular. While much can be done from all of these tenders, one could safely do more fishing in a dinghy with the following characteristics.

- *Rigid-hull material.* Inflatables are much too vulnerable to the everyday hazards associated with fishing to be considered ideal. Also, they don't row well upwind in the event of engine failure.
- *Capable of sailing, motoring, or rowing.* Fishing expeditions can carry you far afield. The ideal fishing dinghy could be sailed or rowed reasonably well to windward, yielding multiple options for an unassisted safe return from the fishing grounds without outboard motor power.
- *Centerboard.* Both to enhance windward sailing ability and for vessel stability in a seaway while fishing.
- *Self-bailing.* Traveling to windward in heavy conditions should not require a dedicated bailer. Also, heavy overnight rain should not be capable of sinking your dinghy.
- *Light total weight.* High strength-to-weight ratio to maximize seaworthy deck stowage by raising the cruising vessel's center of gravity as little as possible. This probably means using no more than ¼ inch (6.35 mm) 5086 marine-grade aluminum for construction material.
- *Ability to stow in pieces.* This is the only way many cruisers can afford the deck space for such a vessel. Making the portions double as low-profile deck stowage containers, possibly positioned aft for cockpit spray protection and optimal windage, would increase the utility of the arrangement. Dedicated deck fittings would accommodate each dinghy portion, facilitating fast, secure connection to the deck. Pilothouse and cockpit views would remain unobstructed. New cruising vessel designs would incorporate

these ideas into deck layout because the best fishing dinghy is also a superior tender for most other purposes. Assembly and disassembly would be quick, easy, and secure.

- ◆ *Built-in live well.* Many fishing boats have either fixed, perforated, partially submerged transom boxes or naturally aspirated wells built into the hull. The latter have angled openings facing forward and aft to encourage entry and egress (respectively) of fresh seawater as the boat moves along. The ideal bait well is circular, with a horizontal black line painted in a circle around the inside, two-thirds of the anticipated water depth from the bottom. This assists orientation of faster-swimming bait species and therefore reduces damaging contact between the marine organisms and the bait well walls. Some research suggests that this effect is further enhanced by adding a series of diagonal stripes from the horizontal line to the base of the live well.
- ◆ *Viewing port.* Consider the option of installing a ½-inch (13 mm) clear plexiglass viewing port or ports below the waterline in a convenient location. This "glass bottom" can be both entertaining and highly useful for locating good fishing and diving spots, particularly in clearer, shallower waters.

What else? Well, it would be nice if the dinghy was unsinkable and if everything, including mast base, rod holders, cleats, and pad eyes, were integrally welded. A small anchor locker forward could double as a bow platform for sighting, casting, and poling (i.e., using a pole to propel the boat silently in shallow water). This "ultimate" fishing dinghy would look something like figure 5-2. What do you think?

Fishing from Shore

Forget all of that theoretical fishing dinghy stuff for now. Assume you've already got *some* kind of tender, *anything* that'll get you from your boat to shore. That's all you need to pursue a mind-boggling number of fishing opportunities. We take a look at these from a logical voyaging perspective, based on general characteristics of anchorages most often selected by cruising vessels.

WALKING TO THE WINDWARD SIDE OF A LANDMASS

Prudent skippers make unfamiliar landfalls with plenty of daylight, check coastal bearings against electronic navigational aids using up-to-date charts, and proceed cautiously to a carefully selected anchorage with reasonable holding ground. The criteria for a "good" anchorage usually include maximum protection from as many wind directions as possible, particularly the prevailing wind direction. This frequently puts us on the leeward side of the landmass—we seek to repose peacefully in a placid, low-energy environment and let rocky cliffs, beaches, and reefs absorb the punishment of crashing, wind-driven waves. Biologically, however, the more robust, highly oxygenated waters of the windward environment may hold more promise than our quiet anchorage. This confluence of conditions makes a walk to the windward side with some fishing tackle an option worthy of consideration.

Rocky Shorelines

Travel light the first trip and do some reconnoitering. Fishing from high rugged cliffs is difficult. As you survey lower rocky promontories, gullies, and ledges that provide better access, be aware of the tidal stage and other factors influencing near-future tenability of your prospective fishing perch. Is the tide, say, halfway out—as indicated by algae growth on the rocks—and still falling, or coming back in? What's the tide range and what is the surf condition? Stand there and watch your spot for a while—does an infrequent, above-average wave smash forcefully across the rocks? How would you fare if you were standing there at the time the wave hit? Is there anything nearby to which you could fasten a rope to a safety harness just in case, for example, to increase the safety margin of leaving your kids unattended at the location? Do you have a rock-climbing device that could be made secure somewhere in the rocks for this purpose?

Getting washed off the rocks is the main hazard of fishing rugged, high-energy shorelines. If your normal cruising grounds feature this kind of topography, you might also consider purchasing relatively inexpensive cleats made for fishers who wish to traverse the slippery, algae-covered rocks of these

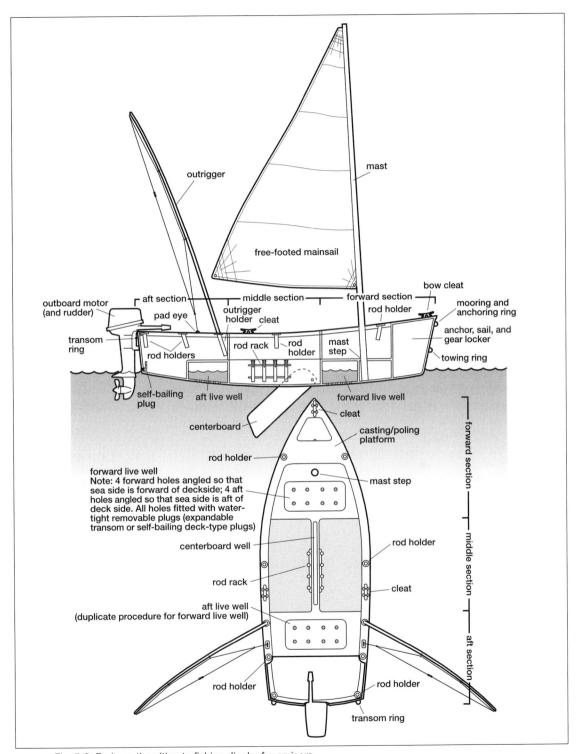

outrigger

mast

free-footed mainsail

bow cleat

aft section

middle section

forward section

outboard motor (and rudder)

pad eye

outrigger holder cleat

rod holder

mooring and anchoring ring

transom ring

rod holders

rod rack

rod holder

mast step

anchor, sail, and gear locker

towing ring

self-bailing plug

aft live well

forward live well

centerboard

cleat

casting/poling platform

rod holder

forward live well
Note: 4 forward holes angled so that sea side is forward of deckside; 4 aft holes angled so that sea side is aft of deck side. All holes fitted with water-tight removable plugs (expandable transom or self-bailing deck-type plugs)

mast step

forward section

middle section

aft section

centerboard well

rod holder

rod rack

cleat

aft live well
(duplicate procedure for forward live well)

rod holder

rod holder

transom ring

Fig. 5-2. Perhaps the ultimate fishing dinghy for cruisers.

An Ounce of Prevention

My dad used to allow my cousin Jack and me to stay roped onto the small light stanchion at the end of the north jetty at Indian River Inlet, Delaware, to fish the boiling surf at high tide for striped bass. Our tethers made it safe—we'd occasionally get gently knocked off our feet by largely spent tops of above-average breaking waves, but the relatively smooth, algae-coated granite platform was benign. We cast ½-ounce (14 g) white bucktail jigs with a red plastic side sleeve, tipped with commercially produced white strips of pork rind, as far as we could with 20-pound (9 kg) spinning rods. Then we retrieved them through the white, foaming cauldron of wave action. The 5-pound (2.3 kg) striped bass always seemed to pile on those jigs at the last second, right in the swirling suds at our feet, snatching the lures with great and sudden force, sharply doubling our rods. The bite would stay red-hot for the hour around slack high tide, and then abruptly stop. We felt like heroes as we made our way back down the jetty with our stringer of gleaming fish and filleted them for our family meal. It also taught us to be good mechanics, as we were forced to overhaul our seawater-soaked reels frequently.

A few years later, I got a dose of what can happen when you misjudge a rocky coastline. As an overconfident sixteen-year-old, I hiked alone at night to a rugged promontory on the windward side of Kauai, Hawaii, and immediately made my way down in bright moonlight to a conveniently low platform, ignoring signs such as abundant fresh seawater puddles all around, and began casting obliviously. It wasn't five minutes before a large breaker catapulted me backward across the rocky substrate. Fortunately, and purely by accident, the configuration of the platform did not lend itself to a deep, high-volume wash-off capable of sucking a body over the edge and into the sea. The loss of skin from elbows, forearms, and back was a small price to pay for such a grievous error.

areas. Rocky shorelines on tropical islands in many parts of the world have the opposite problem—*too much* traction—in the form of pinnacle rock. Selective weathering of exposed calcium-carbonate platforms (usually exposed backbones of ancient coral reefs) creates a densely pocketed latticework of razor sharp edges and pointy projections that demand sneakers or rugged dive boots for best protection. Focus on not spraining an ankle as your body weight teeters on very small edges of substrate, and never risk a wave knockdown on this shore type or you'll likely leave more than just skin behind.

Other fishing challenges of rocky windward shores include wind resistance to casting, highly turbulent underwater conditions that seek to uproot and move bottom-fishing rigs, and rocky snags and obstructions that claim lures and bottom rigs and make it difficult to land hooked fish. Combat these conditions by selecting heavier, more aerodynamic casting lures, pyramid sinkers that will firmly anchor bottom rigs in sandy areas between the rocks, and heavier tackle (e.g., if you have both 20 lb./9 kg and 10 lb./4.5 kg spinning tackle, bring the heavier outfit). Tighten the drag setting up over 25 percent of line-breaking strength, and exert heavy pressure as soon as you hook up. Use wave action to assist you during the battle—hold your rod high and hang on tight on the outgoing surge, which aids the fish's efforts to struggle away from shore, and lift hard. Then drop and wind in a rapid, short-stroke rhythm to gain line on the incoming surge. Time the finale with an arriving swell, using the boost from the arriving wave to pressure your fish up and onto the shore, or at least into the shallows. Get a foot under the belly and kick it the rest of the way to dry land, scoop the fish up in your landing net, or securely gaff.

A quick word on surface plugs . . . recall that these come in sinking and floating models. The sinkers are usually a better choice for agitated windward conditions. They stay down in the water better and can be made to dart, pop, and chug at high speed rather than becoming airborne, skipping and skittering ineffectively across the surface.

Surf Fishing from Sandy Beaches

You may discover that the windward side of the landmass protecting your anchorage has short sections of sandy beach interspersed along a rugged rocky shoreline, usually in small coves. Other wind-ward coastlines feature long, unbroken stretches of sand beach, often backed by sand dunes covered with sea oats or other salt-resistant vegetation. These beaches are generally far more benevolent, forgiving fishing habitats than rocky shorelines, and beach surf zones are major patrol areas for desirable target fish species worldwide.

Why? Fish scout the surf for the same reason they tend to frequent many other areas ... because food items are projected to them in a turbulent flow. Migratory schools of baitfish and, therefore, predator species that follow and feed on the smaller fish, frequently swim parallel to unbroken stretches of beach, meandering in and out of the surf zone. This happens from the equator to upper temperate latitudes. Other species reside permanently in the surf zone, often smaller invertebrate feeders.

Surf-fishing enthusiasts at famed locations like North Carolina's Outer Banks have transformed this specialty into an advanced art form. They patrol the beaches with custom-rigged four-wheel-drive vehicles fitted with rod racks full of long surf-casting rods, each rigged for specific possible encounters. Like other fishing specialists, they carefully read nuances of wind, weather, and bird and bait activity, and anticipate seasonal arrivals of various fish migrations. They catch bluefish, striped bass, channel bass (redfish), and other trophies, sometimes exceeding 50 pounds (23 kg). Their ability to cast long distance can be important for success, encouraging them to wade out chest deep and fling heavy offerings on very long fishing rods to score.

Humbler efforts in similar environments can produce plenty of good table fare on a consistent basis. Various members of the drum and croaker family, dogfishes (a small "toothless" family of sharks widely used for fish and chips), kahawai, skates, flounders, and many others can be caught by bait-fishing with pyramid sinkers rigged at the base of vertical arrays or on single-hook, three-way swivel rigs (see fig. 4-5 and table 3-1).

From warmer temperate seas to the equator, the potential number of fish species that can be wrested from the surf increases greatly. One strong example consists of pompanos and other members of the genus *Trachinotus*, a firm, silvery group of fish fond of shrimp, crabs, and other invertebrate baits. This genus occurs throughout tropical and subtropical zones of the world. Other examples include surf and sand perches, sea breams, more drums and croakers (including various sea trouts and corvina), snook, tarpon, bonefish, sharks, many species of jacks and trevallys, roosterfish, mackerel, groupers and sea basses, wrasses ... the list is long. Sight-casting is sometimes possible when the water is clear enough, but more often turbid conditions demand that you fish blind.

Wading to fish beach surf is generally less safe in the tropics than in more temperate waters, particularly in highly turbid conditions, due to higher incidence of large, potentially aggressive sharks. If the water is clear and the surf gentle, OK. The opposite end of the spectrum might feature selected turbid surf zones in tropical Australia or the Caribbean coast of Costa Rica, where chest-deep wading would constitute a life-threatening risk. In most latitudes, shuffling rather than stepping reduces the risk of your foot landing on top of a half-buried stingray, and suffering a serious, excruciating wound from the serrated barb that projects from the base of the tail. An alarmed stingray reacts by arching and abruptly raising its tail, causing the barb to lever out at a 90-degree angle and jab whatever is over it.

Several devices make beach surf-fishing more relaxing and fun. The most important of these is probably the sand spike, a plastic or metal rod holder cut on a long, sharp diagonal at one end so that it can be stuck either vertically or at a slight angle in beach sand. This frees you to nap on a beach towel, play Frisbee, or read a book while you wait for a bite. Tie a small, light bell to the rod tip for an audio alarm (a beer or soda can with a few pebbles in it works). Some fishers paint the rod tip fluorescent pink or orange to facilitate bite detection from a distance. Go light on the drag setting, or be sure your spike is secure, because if it topples over, your rod and reel will be heading out to sea if something big grabs the bait.

As usual, keep an eye out for signs of fish. Large shadows that look like a cloud may actually be schools of baitfish. Pitch a lure out along the margins or straight in to the school to attract the attention of predators following along. Watch for diving birds, splashes of surface-feeding fish, dark shapes backlit inside unbroken wave faces, or shadows cast on the bottom by nearly invisible fish that have adjusted their color to match the light hue of the sand. Sometimes the signs hit you over the head, like when big, excited fish chase bait out of the water so that the bait flops onto the beach, the fish occasionally even throwing themselves after the bait, then thrashing and slithering back to sea on the next wave. Pitch a heavy surface plug, swimming plug, diamond jig, or other good casting lure out in front of them; after hook-up, use the wave action to your best advantage, as described previously. Don't forget your senses and go running too far into the surf trying to grab or net your fish. If it's murky and highly aerated, you could hardly blame an excited shark for mistaking your foot or hand for the struggling, possibly bleeding, fish in the water next to you.

Windward Reef Crests and Flats

Cruises to the subtropics and tropics take you to islands that have beaches or other shore types where the surf breaks on a shallow, semi-exposed coral-reef margin, anywhere from a short cast to a long walk out from land. The water between this reef crest and shore might consist of clear, knee-deep shallows, or be nonexistent at low tide. This zone is the reef flat. Under normal conditions, the reef crest absorbs almost all the wave energy, so that shallow-reef flat waters lap gently at the shoreline. This constitutes a third fundamentally different shore-fishing situation you may encounter on your walk to the windward side of a landmass.

Here you have two choices. You can fish very light gear in the shallows of the reef flat between shore and the reef crest, or you can favor your heavy outfit, walk out to the reef crest, and fish in a similar manner to other surf-casting conditions. If you opt for the latter, watch more than ever the tide and wave action *and* your footing as you traverse the coral. You will almost certainly suffer serious abrasions and cuts from sharp coral if you take a hard spill; days of careful treatment will be required to avoid hazardous infections.

Casting out beyond the reef crest is exciting, and in the Indo-Pacific, this is prime habitat for the largest trevallys. Perhaps the most favored lure type is a large sinking surface plug, retrieved thrashing and spraying at maximum speed along the air-water interface. You can't reel too fast. The takes are spectacular surface explosions followed by brutal, long, deep runs. Frankly, you lose more than you catch, which is also the case worldwide with other large denizens hooked on 20-pound (9 kg) spinning tackle from this vantage point. They're extremely strong, and there's a lot of high-relief coral, so bring your oldest lures. You will land a higher percentage of more modest-sized fish, particularly midwater species to 7 or 8 pounds (3 to 3.6 kg). Fishing the bottom with crabs or other invertebrate bait will selectively target a variety of good-eating smaller reef fish that are easier to extract from the coral.

Light-tackle targets include mostly fleet, smaller fish that ascend to feed on the reef flat at higher tidal stages. As you walk along in these shallows, the most obvious will be beautifully colored parrotfish and surgeonfish, scraping the coral with specialized teeth. These fish occasionally take small baits fished on light line, although you may find other targets more worthy of your attention, including snappers, emperors, goatfish, small groupers, trevallys and other jack family members, porgies, grunts, and sweetlips . . . a real cornucopia of tropical panfish. Bonefish, barracuda, and small sharks are also common in this habitat.

The best time to fish the reef flat is the top half of the incoming tide and high tide, because the fish feed actively with no concern for moving back down off the reef flat. Sight-cast lures or bait either to fish that you can see or to likely looking holes, ledges, and other structure. Immediately upon hook-up, raise your rod high over your head to maximize the angle your line makes with the shallow bottom. Shuffle over and stand on a higher perch if possible. The idea is to keep the line away from the many sharp objects on the bottom in this habitat. Your best efforts will frequently fail, particularly when you hook stronger, larger specimens like bonefish. They take off at high speed, zigzagging across the uneven coral; the line angle inevitably decreases, touches bottom, and goes slack, cut as though by a sharp knife. Smaller fish are easier to catch, and if they dive into a hole, *do not* pressure them at all. Simply walk over, reeling slack line as you go, put on a glove, and extract them by hand (watch out for sea urchins and moray eels, abundant in holes on most reef flats—see photo page 341).

Here again, protect your feet with sneakers or heavy dive boots. Stepping unprotected on certain cone shells and stonefish, both limited to the tropical Indo-Pacific, is potentially fatal. More common concerns are cuts from coral and punctures from sea urchin spines. Keep an eye on small sharks that show persistent interest in your wading actions. Chucking a piece of coral rubble directly on them normally puts them off, although on one unusual occasion featuring several 4-foot (1.2 m) blacktip reef sharks, this seemed to egg them on. We were wading the reef flat on an uninhabited atoll in the Tuamotus, and Wendy laughed uncontrollably at the sight of me pumping along in a high-kneed sprint for the beach with two in hot pursuit of my splashing feet. She'd surely have tried to help, perhaps with an accurate toss of a chunk of dead coral, if she wasn't on her knees, incapacitated by her own convulsions. Mention of the incident still brings tears to her eyes.

LEEWARD-SIDE SHORE FISHING

The leeward side of landmasses can feature rocky shorelines, beaches, and reefs, but generally in a less rugged, lower-energy environment. You may have more opportunity to fish successfully with lighter tackle. Since you are now casting *with* the wind, you can use a wider variety of lures, including some of your more delicate, lighter imitations. The fish tend to be a little less frenetic … it's calm, they're often cruising slowly, taking more time to look things over—not like in the wild foaming surf, where if they spot a potential prey item, they must grab it quickly or the opportunity is lost.

Here, floating surface plugs, for example, may outperform sinkers. Chug and pop, and don't neglect the value of one- to four-second pauses. One calm spring night in the Florida Keys, I was guiding a tarpon trip, and I mentioned to my customer that it sounded as though his retrieve was too continuous. He had stopped reeling, first to say "huh?" and then to listen to my ten-second explanation. As if on cue, a 65-pound (29 kg) tarpon inhaled the motionless lure—floating quietly 5 feet (1.5 m) out from the customer's feet—in a loud surface deto-

nation that startled him so badly he yelped and nearly fell in the water.

Slow subsurface retrieves can be equally potent for selected species. My dad was riding along with me on a half-day scientific sampling trip for larval lobsters along the coast of Antigua, West Indies. We'd finished our collections and were casting white bucktail jigs to the mangrove shoreline of a small bay. He pointed out that my fast, erratic retrieve was probably ruining my chances of hooking a snook or tarpon, two of the more likely species we might encounter, and that I should try barely moving the lure, slowly and steadily. I dutifully complied, one-third of the way in on the current retrieve, and was rewarded with a small snook after only four or five more turns of the reel handle. Just to show it was no fluke, we each hooked small tarpon on our next casts.

This is not to say those faster retrieves and heavier lures don't work in calm or leeward conditions. Some species demand it. Your options, however, are generally more numerous with some protection from contrary wind.

Leeward conditions permit other intriguing possibilities in addition to lighter lures and different retrieves. You no longer have a problem with getting baits to whatever distance you wish. Float natural baits out on a balloon, letting the wind carry it offshore. Fly your fishing kite from shore, your fishing line perhaps baited with something fresh, small, and live that you have just caught close to land on light spinning gear. Fishers use both of these techniques extensively in Australia and New Zealand, and land everything from southern yellowtail (kingfish), large pink porgies (snapper), yellowfin tuna, mako and other large sharks, and even the odd striped marlin from shore.

Much of the rest of this chapter discusses dinghy-related fishing in fairly protected conditions. This is a perfect juncture to infuse you with a mindset and some general sign-reading knowledge that will help you become adept at inshore fishing as you assimilate the remaining material (see sidebar next page).

ESTUARINE SHORELINES

Estuarine shorelines can be the most difficult to fish from land, but maybe someone else needs to use the dinghy or you've selected a target zone inaccessible

Reading the Signs

Finding fish in shallow-water environments involves predicting and interpreting natural phenomena and their pronounced effects on patterns of movement and activity. Nowhere do tides, wind directions and velocities, rainfall, and atmospheric temperature trends have a greater impact on being in the right place at the right time. Proficient inshore fishers are keen observers of the interplay of every environmental nuance and the possible effect on their quarry, and have become adept at identifying areas likely to hold fish. They also tend to be students of the details of fish-feeding ecology, able to identify preferred natural prey items and whether feeding is taking place near the bottom, midwater, or surface. Enthusiasts spend lifetimes immersed in forecasting all of this dynamic interplay. Fortunately, a number of generalities apply that enable you to do just fine on a more casual basis.

♦ Tropical and subtropical flats. The fish often follow predictable, area-specific foraging patterns, ascending on the incoming tide to feed on mollusks, crustaceans, marine worms, and small fishes over substrate that may be exposed at low tide. Find points of shoreline (e.g., sand spits, mini-peninsulas, jetties, oyster beds) where the flat is narrower, concentrating the fish as they swim into the current and around the projecting land. Scan the area for telltale puffs of mud created as otherwise invisible individuals root and feed on the bottom. If the source turns out to be a ray or group of mullet, cast anyway—often bonefish, jacks, redfish, sea trout, and other species swim along with rays to feed on the prey items they disturb. Look for edges, such as grass-bed margins, calcareous algae beds, slight depth contours; fish often swim along these natural demarcations. They also tend to hug leeward flats and shorelines during elevated winds. Keep your eyes peeled for water movement and exposed tails as the fish orient nose-down to search out and feed on benthic prey items.

♦ Other shallow environments. Patches of various habitats, including kelp, seagrass beds, rocks, coral, ledges, mangrove prop roots, oyster beds, marsh edges, trees, holes, undercut banks, and wreckage, may serve as resting spots sought as refuge from predators or unfavorable water temperature, tide, time of day, or current, or they may provide good foraging areas (usually a combination of both factors). Identification of such areas and accurate presentation of an appropriate bait or lure will sharply enhance your catch rate. The specifics vary according to species sought. Learn about the habits of your quarry from local fishers, textbooks, and personal observation; as you explore, ask yourself where they might be, what they're doing, and why.

♦ Evaluating coral. One constant of a high proportion of tropical and subtropical voyaging destinations is coral. Clear water helps you identify the most productive of the many forms of coral habitat you will encounter. As you gain experience, you will reject suboptimal coral areas and become more selective about where you fish. Three types of highly productive coral areas visible from the surface are as follows:

♦ Various diameter (10 to 100 yds./9 to 91 m), often circular patches of habitat that include a combination of high-relief hard coral heads (these appear brown and frequently have a white halo of sand around them), seagrass, and soft corals, surrounded by relatively featureless bottom in depths from 10 to 40 feet (3 to 12 m).

♦ Continuous ledges that feature undercut caves, indentations, and internal chimneys and passageways.

♦ Open sand bottom dotted by high-profile coral domes and pinnacles, often deeper in the visible depth range (35 to over 100 ft./11 to 30 m).

When you find locations fitting these descriptions, you will very likely be able to put a bend in your fishing rod.

by dinghy. These shores border bays, sloughs, river deltas, and marshes, and the tributaries that feed them. Deep muck and impenetrable growth may render futile your attempts to walk or wade. Salt marshes, sawgrass estuaries, and mangrove swamps usually fall into this category. Also, when these habitats occur in the tropics, they might harbor crocodiles, alligators, and other dangerous critters. Rocky cold-temperate zones and sandy subtropical areas have a higher percentage of fishable estuaries.

If you find some firm footing, several general comments apply for large parts of the world. Think of presentations in each of three fundamental strata: near surface, midwater, and bottom. Adjust lure and bait type and weight to the portion of the water column you want to fish. For hard current, remember that fish can't make a living, bioenergetically, by swimming vigorously in the main force of the current. They can't ingest enough food to afford that kind of energy expenditure. Therefore, they position themselves behind obstructions that break the current, head facing upcurrent, and dart out briefly to nab prey items. Many such obstructions are on the bottom. When the tide slackens, they emerge and range more freely, feeding more actively throughout the water column.

Adjust your strategy to these principles. When the tide is running hard, cast weighted lures diagonally and upcurrent, let them sink to the bottom by applying no retrieve tension, only very slowly bringing in slack as the lure descends and begins bumping along the bottom just before it passes you in the current. Keep your rod at a 45-degree angle. Retrieve slowly, *feel* the lure as it slowly bumps past and gets downcurrent from you. Keep that rod tip up, and work the lure *across* the current, right on the bottom, *very slowly*. As the lure reaches your side of the current, and your line becomes parallel to the bank, speed up the retrieve slightly, but work the lure diligently all the way to the rod tip. Don't make the common novice error (for *any* type of lure fishing) of quitting the retrieve a short distance away and rapidly reeling the lure out of the water, thereby missing the many strikes that occur at the tail end of lure retrieves.

Repeat the entire sequence several times, then mix up the slow retrieve with a few faster ones featuring erratic hops. Any time you feel the lure pause—as though stopped on an obstruction—or feel slight pressure, immediately set the hook; this is how many takes feel when retrieving in this mode. Use weighted spoons, bucktail jigs, and jig heads baited with plastic bait bodies or natural baits, such as whole live fish or shrimp or small chunks or strips of fish, squid, shrimp, or shellfish. Sinking, deep-swimming plugs work well. Cast surface plugs, popping corks and other shallow presentations to back eddies and near obstructions when the current is flowing fast. Occasional stronger-swimming fish eat midwater and surface baits at peak tidal flow, but this will likely be your lowest percentage fishing option.

As the tide begins to slow, try more midwater presentations. For example, cut off your jig, tie on an Eagle Claw 189 baitholder hook, and install a small split-shot sinker just above the hook eye. Bait with a plastic imitation or a whole live shrimp or strip bait and use the same basic sequence described for full tidal flow, casting upcurrent, letting the bait sink, and retrieving. This time, however, initiate a slow, steady retrieve earlier in the sequence, causing your lure to swim and wiggle up off the bottom and track across the water flow at mid-depth. Switch to popping corks (again, baits can be soft plastic fakes or the real thing), surface plugs, and floating swimming plugs. If you have multiple fishers, keep one on the bottom, one in midwater, and one near the surface until you determine which stratum yields the most action. Float out a live bait suspended on a round cork and place this fourth line in a sand spike.

Light tackle will often suffice for shore-based estuarine fishing. That small, collapsible spinning rod discussed previously can be handy for longer hikes because it stows neatly in your pack. Don't forget bug spray, adequate drinking water, a landing net, and a short length of rope to string and transport your catch.

Wading the Shallows

The logical extension of standing on any shoreline to fish is stepping into the water, always with the idea that this will somehow improve your chances. We touched on this mode briefly for fishing surf and reef flats. Venturing into the water on foot can also enhance estuarine fishing success, if bottom type, current strength, and dangerous predator populations permit it. Wading is a veritable institution among tropical flats fishers. It may put you within range of a productive tide current rip, bottom feature, series of "lies" or fish lairs, passing bait school, broad target-fish patrol area, or individual targets giving away their position by any number of telltale signs. If you didn't wade, you might only watch helplessly from shore.

Wading in many cases lends itself to the use of light tackle of all descriptions. If you're ever going to try fly-fishing, some wading environments are the ideal place to start (see appendix 3).

ESTUARINE SYSTEMS

Fishers wade estuarine systems, with great success, to fish for spotted sea trout, redfish, and other species on the Gulf coasts of Texas and Florida; for striped bass, bluefish, and weakfish in the northeastern United States; and for salmon and sea run trout species in places like Alaska, elsewhere along the northwestern coastline of the North American continent, and at South Island, New Zealand, just to name a few examples.

Waterproof waders, often insulated, may be essential for colder water. Unfortunately, this specialized gear type doesn't stow compactly aboard, and thus will probably be omitted from any cruising boat not anticipating extensive travel in regions where they'll see a lot of use. Insulated waders *do* provide warm, dry, buoyant foul-weather-gear bottoms—justification for inclusion on temperate-zone cruising vessels with ample space—but they tend to be clumsy for moving around on deck. Most boats have dive wetsuits aboard, which may double as cold-weather wading gear for fishing.

When wading in swift water flows, minimize body resistance by maintaining a sideways orientation. Take measured, deliberate steps, keeping your feet shoulder width apart and close to the substrate, and visually pick footholds if the water is clear enough. Tie a belt of some kind tightly across the chest of waders to discourage rapid filling with water if you are swept off your feet by the current. If you fall and are propelled downcurrent, protect your head with your arms, take deep, opportunistic breaths and hold them during times you are sub-

merged by turbulence; don't waste precious oxygen on frantic efforts to swim with your waders on. Continue this form of "dead man's" float or drown-proofing until a quiet stretch or back eddy affords an opportunity to use a survival backstroke or breaststroke to ease across and out of the current. Remove your waders if necessary. The same mishap in a wetsuit features greater maneuverability and possibly earlier opportunity to swim your way out of trouble. Stay cool, take it slow.

Be especially careful wading creek and river deltas, the platform of sedimentary deposits at the mouth. Firm deltas afford the opportunity to wade out near the drop-off and work lures straight downcurrent, then retrieve them back to the base of the steep delta bank where fish often congregate. The problem is that the lips of most deltas are inherently unstable and will collapse if you stand close enough to them. Approach the edge with great caution, and keep back a conservative distance. Fatalities occur usually from fishers in waders collapsing the delta lip, falling, having their waders scoop a large quantity of cold water, getting sucked down by the current as it tumbles over the steep delta face, and inhaling water while still submerged.

Other estuarine environments suffer none of these hazards, and offer sanguine opportunity for relaxed, tranquil fishing experiences.

INSHORE FLATS

The words *tranquil* and *sanguine* are also among the many inadequate attempts humans make to fully capture in words the experience of hunting fish with light tackle while wading in shimmering, clear, tropical shallows, collectively named "flats." Some of the greatest thrills in the world of fishing—experiences that aficionados pay thousands of dollars to do even for a few days, and spend Saturday mornings watching TV shows about—are easily available to seafarers throughout much of the world's tropical cruising grounds, in less than 3 feet (0.9 m) of water. Bonefish, jacks and trevallys (some as large as 100 lbs./45 kg), snappers, triggerfish, barracudas, sharks, and many other species patrol these shallows for food, when the tidal stage permits it. Conditions often allow stalking and sight-casting to schools or individuals. Fish hooked in these meager depths fight particularly hard, and many provide firm, white meat for table fare. Anglers get hooked on this type of fishing to the point of obsession—it's quiet, peaceful (except when you hook up), beautiful, and challenging, and light tackle—spinning or fly—works well.

Check your tide tables. Usually, the incoming tide is most productive, although you will find areas that are most active on the falling tide. You don't need bait, but if you are taking beginners or kids that aren't yet polished casters, rustle up some shore crabs, hermit crabs, shrimp, conch or other mollusk, or any cut or strip bait. Lures depend on the target species—small bucktail jigs (⅛ to ¼ oz./3.5 to 7 g) with horizontally flattened heads will catch nearly every flats species. Heavier roundhead bucktail jigs, small

spoons, and swimming and surface plugs may be desirable for larger targets, like some of the jacks or trevallys. Wear polarized glasses and a billed cap. For best visibility and casting, anchor the dinghy upwind and with the sun behind where you will search, or get out and wade with the sun at your back (sit and wait for fish to come to you or hunt actively). Note the direction of any current, and remember that most of the fish will swim into the flow. Read the signs. If visibility is difficult, toss out a few pieces of bait without hooks for chum, and one or more baited lines and let them sit (bail closed for spinning gear), or cast and work your lure blind.

For sight-fishing, train yourself to look *through* the water surface. Develop a search image for silvery gray to olive, torpedo-shaped shadows. On light

---

A Taste of the Tropical Flats

Three grayish-green shapes, barely visible 60 feet (18 m) away in the hazy, mirrored reflection of an overcast tropical Pacific sky, ghosted slowly over the soft, tan sediment in loose formation. The lead fish paused, creating a small, puffy cloud of turbidity as it nosed into the substrate, its entire upper caudal lobe flickering out of the water, sending out tiny ripples over the glassy sea surface. A quick, firm double haul sent a sparsely tied, light tan fly called a Gotcha 8 feet (2.4 m) in front of the trio. The tailer, distracted in the endeavor for real food, jerked forward in response to the immediate rush of its squadron mates toward the sinking fly, but never had a chance. I couldn't tell which of the two scrapping bonefish inhaled the presentation, on the first small strip, as I set the hook in response to the distinctive, firm tap transmitted through the fly line to my fingers. The last few loose coils of line flew through the rod guides and began screaming off the reel, breaking the placid, deep silence of lush, remote Palmyra Atoll. The flat exploded as groups of startled bonefish, previously invisible in the difficult spotting conditions, responded to their panicky colleague. Then I heard the ripping sound of the wide arc of fly line being violently sucked out of the water, as the hooked fish took a hard right turn for the deep waters of the adjacent lagoon.

Other bonefish weren't the only denizens that noticed the disturbance—a chunky 4½ foot (1.4 m)

blacktip reef shark and 30-pound-plus (13.6 kg) giant trevally materialized immediately and began tracking back and forth in the wake of the fleeing bonefish. At the same time, they both seemed to draw a bead on the tiring, imperiled fighter, wildly surging ahead, throwing foaming, parallel wakes and scattering groups of bonefish across the flat. Despite a quickly released drag, my fish was no match for the charging tandem, the shark chopping the aft two-thirds of its body off in one flashing motion, leaving the trevally excitedly pirouetting around the perimeter. I quickly cranked the drag down and reeled rapidly, skittering the head along the surface while back-pedaling toward the shore of a small islet. The shark was now again in hot pursuit and the massive forehead of the trevally carved a deep furrow in the water as it followed close behind. I won the race, got the fly back, and pitched the head of the former 6½-pound (2.9 kg) fish to the two predators. The head splashed noisily, spooking the trevally, before it disappeared in the midst of a dense upheaval of snapping jaws, blood, shark, and water.

Breathing heavily, I flopped down on the rocky beach beneath a towering crown of coconut palms. Definitely time to let things settle down before wading off a bit. Seven consecutive hook-ups had the predators homed in on my position, and all I would do now is feed them bonefish and maybe a few flies from my waning supply.

sand flats, fish are more obvious. Visibility is tougher on darker bottoms of seagrass or other substrate and when it's overcast or windy. When you spot the fish, get a bead on direction of movement. Cast your bait or lure ahead of their path, far enough away not to spook them with the splash (this varies from 5 to 15 ft./1.5 to 4.6 m or more, with bright, sunny, windless conditions requiring the farthest lead distances). Work jigs in short, jerky hops with a slight pause in between. Raise the rod sharply once to set the hook, and hold the rod high as the line screams off the reel. This helps avoid cut-offs on the shallow bottom just as you did on the reef flat (bonefish may run over 100 yds./91 m before you can slow them down).

Sharks, usually only 2 to 4 feet (0.6 to 1.2 m) in length but sometimes much larger, are among the most common sights on the flats. They normally pose little or no threat and are themselves good light-tackle quarry and eating. Be cognizant of their presence and movements while wading, however, and remember that they can only see a small portion of your body below water. If you attract a crowd during a fish battle, consider backing over to the shore or your dinghy before bringing the hooked fish in around your feet. Recall that curious individuals can usually be spooked off with a rod tip or rock. If they get too persistent, leave the area.

The term *flat* also applies to tropical, subtropical, and temperate areas with mud, sand, or seagrass bottoms that may not be conducive to as much sight-fishing due to combinations of turbidity and, in the case of wading, unsuitable bottom (especially muck). This is more often the case along the shores of continents or, as we have seen, near estuarine systems. If the bottom is too soft, forget wading. Because most dinghies have very shallow drafts, one can effectively fish these areas blind or by sight-casting; for example, with a bucktail or other lure, while drifting, anchored, or propelling yourself slowly along using a push pole. Even in murky conditions, your targets still may make wakes, ripples, and swirls; stick pieces of fin or tail out of the water; and make splashes and other noise as they pursue prey items. Cast much closer to the fish in these situations—you can often plop it a foot or two from their heads without spooking them.

Intermediate Depths near Shore

Flats, regardless of latitude, are frequently bordered by channels, or drop-offs, to deeper lagoon or bay waters. Depending on location, they may be studded with coral, carpeted by grass beds of various descriptions, or consist of oyster bars, sand, mud, gravel, rocks, or kelp forests. These edges are productive for numerous fish species, as are some of the nearby habitats beyond. Work these areas with lures or bait by wading in the shallows to within casting range of the edge. It's often more efficient to stay in the dinghy and fish, either anchored, adrift, or by trolling, any of which can result in some epic catches. Let's review general techniques that apply worldwide, starting shallow and moving out to greater depths.

CORAL REEF SHALLOWS

Whether it's profuse, high-profile coral or lower-relief rocky ledges and associated soft corals, you will develop an eye for the habitats most likely to hold fish. One way to gain experience is to take advantage of your shallow draft and work around these areas trolling small spoons, jig heads with strip baits or soft plastic bait bodies, or small swimming plugs on a couple of light spinning rods in the outboard rod holders. All of these have good action at lower speeds, allowing you to putt around and weave through the mixed coral and sandy areas. It's easy "drag-and-snag" fishing—they hit, and they either hook themselves or they're off, and you're ready for the next strike. It's quite possible to catch a dozen or so different species in an afternoon, good action for kids, and there are some occasional real lunkers. *Check local knowledge before consumption to avoid ciguatera fish poisoning.*

You can also anchor and drift, chum, bottom-fish with bait, or drop jigs vertically down around the coral, applying the same techniques used from your cruising vessel, except usually on lighter tackle.

SURGE AND TIDE CHANNELS

Deep, winding grooves for the passage of surge and tidal seawater flows are typical of tropical island bays and lagoons, as well as continental estuarine systems in most latitudes. These conduits often drain and fill vast areas of shallows, transporting and distributing tremendous volumes of sea life. Predictably, they are used as highways for all types of predator fish movements, many related to feeding ecology. You can troll or drift, but anchoring in selected areas and working your lures or baits is most effective because the fish are usually already moving—you don't need to cover ground to find them if you get in the right spot at the right time.

Concentrate such efforts at the end of the outgoing tide, slack low, and beginning of the incoming tide. This is the time fish are down off the flats and in the channels. Anchor slightly downcurrent of side-channel entrances and outside margins of bends in the channel, especially when there is some rock pile, deep hole, or other bottom feature nearby. Fishing technique is similar to that described for shore fishing an estuary. Cast, say, a ¼- to ⅜-ounce (7 to 11 g) Captain Hank Brown's Hookup bucktail tipped with natural bait or a plastic swirl tail upstream at a 45-degree angle to the current, let it sink as it swings down past you, and begin retrieving when it is 45 degrees downcurrent from you. Vary your retrieve from slow and steady to faster and more erratic. Do the same thing with a Captain Hank Brown's Hookup jig baited with a shrimp or strip, slow and steady along the bottom. Work plugs and spoons similarly. Cast surface and swimming plugs to work the top and mid-depths, particularly if you spot surface activity.

CREEKS, RIVERS, CANALS, AND OTHER ESTUARINE WATERWAYS

Systems that distribute freshwater or salt water into the ocean from the interior or margins of landmasses are often vast, and usually best explored and fished from your dinghy rather than by walking or wading. The same anchoring technique described previously for tidal channels can be highly effective *after* the discovery of specific areas. In the meantime, it is often more feasible and productive to troll various sizes and weights of swimming plugs and plastic-baited jig heads—you can relax, explore, sightsee, and still catch enough to make things interesting. If you spot a particularly intriguing piece of shoreline, ease over, cut the engine, and anchor or drift the area while casting lures and baits

right up against the shore and under overhangs. Consider keeping one rod set up with a surface plug for throwing to any surface activity. We spent many wonderful afternoons taking jungle cruises through mangrove creeks in Central America, catching snook, dog snappers, sierra mackerel, and various jacks, and still had plenty of time to kick back and enjoy the parrots and other exotic bird life, iguanas, monkeys, crocodiles, and towering tropical forest. We used the same fairly casual combination of techniques one afternoon while exploring the distinctly different, temperate environment of the upper Waikato River in New Zealand, and caught a nice bunch of rainbow and one brown trout. It works, it's easy, and anyone can do it.

CHANNELS BETWEEN ISLANDS, AND PASSES BETWEEN ENCLOSED WATER BODIES AND THE OCEAN

Channels and passes typically feature significant depth and torrential current because they provide conduits for large volumes of water squeezing through relatively narrow spaces. Tidal-flow velocities in the passes of coral atoll lagoons can exceed 8 knots, and where strong wave action to windward constantly fills the lagoon, the flow is always out, just slowing down during the "incoming" tide. Near civilization, bridges may span passes and channels, and rock jetties often guard entrances from the ocean, along with channel buoys and lighthouses. This combination of variables presents fish with tremendous outflows of food items, as well as habitat to seek refuge from the full brunt of the flow. Little wonder that, worldwide, so many of them become the focus of intense, consistently prolific fishing activity.

Monitor the interrelated variables of bird activity, bait presence, and evidence of predator fish surface-feeding relative to tidal stage. Use your depth-finder to locate and watch groups of target fish. Search for undercut banks and walls, deep potholes, rubble piles, and other fish-holding features. Use your downrigger to troll swimming plugs and jigs that match the size, color, and action of baitfish and invertebrate species you see or that you suspect occur in the area, deep, across, and near these features. Power-drift the spots, bombing them with deep-jigging lures or weighted bait-fishing rigs with live or dead natural offerings. Fish midwater and surface presentations close to jetties, channel margins, and semisubmerged objects (e.g., bridge pilings, channel markers, buoys, and light stanchions) by either trolling or drifting and casting. *Learn* the daily and seasonal rhythm of your channel or pass. Know the timing and moods of both liquid contents and inhabitants, and pattern your hunting accordingly. Avoid conditions that produce dangerous standing waves, and have enough rode onboard to anchor in the event of mechanical failure on an outgoing tide.

The configuration of some channels and passes allows successful fishing while anchored or tied off to or between bridge pilings or other structures. Switch to techniques described for other high-current waterways, throwing weighted presentations upcurrent, and fishing them deep as they bump bottom back toward you, and fish midwater and surface as tide flows weaken. For example, John Malloy taught me how to fish for snook at night during the winter by tying off a skiff between the pilings of the old Rickenbacker Causeway in Miami, then hopping out onto the piling base, and setting out a bright Coleman lantern. We would dip-net live penaeid shrimp that swam close by in the light, and use them whole on plain jig heads called Troll-Rites (Captain Hank Brown's Hookup Lures weren't available yet). We hooked the shrimp once through the clear section of the head, between the brain and the mouth, and fished them back toward us along the bottom after casting upcurrent. Mine soon stopped, the rod tip bowed gently, then slammed downward as I belatedly set the hook. The line briefly poured off the 20-pound (9 kg) spinning outfit out into Biscayne Bay, then nearly went slack as the fish doubled back for the pilings, swung under the bowline of the skiff, and took a hard right down the middle of the parallel rows of pilings. I rushed to pass the rod under the line and clamber into the skiff. By sheer luck, it doubled straight back again and raced directly at us, a dark streaking missile exploding into the glow cast by the lantern, 3 feet (0.9 m) below the surface. Somehow John dove into the skiff beside me and stabbed the landing net vertically at the last possible instant. The big snook

powered straight into the mesh before it knew what had happened . . . and was snatched up quickly—hanging over the rim of the net—and slung flopping onto the deck. Thanks to John's expertise, we later weighed this very unlucky snook at Junior's Bait and Tackle. It was exactly 20 pounds (9 kg)—not *huge*, but I haven't been able to catch a bigger one in the ensuing twenty-two years, probably because John got too busy with law school to take me fishing.

Another method is to anchor *upcurrent* of bridge pilings near the end of either tide, and free-line unweighted live baits back toward the bridge. You can also anchor under the bridge or tie off to a downcurrent piling and float live baits out away from the bridge on a cork. This usually works best with live baits capable of swimming strongly enough not to twist and spin unnaturally in the current. Last, anchor downcurrent of the pilings, cast presentations up to the bridge, and work them back toward the dinghy. Around bridges, nighttime is generally more productive than day, and both sunrise and sunset, like almost anywhere, tend to be active feeding times.

The techniques given in this section will catch a very large variety of fish species, including bottom dwellers and midwater and surface feeders.

BAYS, LAGOONS, AND LAKES

Where the water is relatively shallow, 3 to 10 feet (0.9 to 3 m) or so, trolling or drifting can help cover ground and locate productive areas such as rich grass beds or rocky ledges, reefs, and isolated coral heads. Cast your bucktail jig, plastic bait body, swimming plug, or other offering into any pothole, drop-off, or edge habitat you see, let it sink, and then retrieve. Look for puffs of mud from feeding bait or target fish. Large schools of herbivorous mullet, for instance, root in the substrate and attract moderate-sized predators that feed on items they stir up. Under many such circumstances, you can get more strikes by stopping or returning to an area that produced a fish and either drifting again or anchoring. The pros mark such areas by sticking a push pole into the bottom substrate, drifting away, motoring back upwind quietly, giving the pole a wide berth in order not to spook the fish, and then setting up to drift silently back downwind to the action spot so they can work it over more thoroughly.

Farther from the shallows, anchor or drift and deep-jig or bottom-fish, troll deeply by using a downrigger arrangement, or troll surface presentations near signs of activity (diving bird flocks mark everything from schools of small jacks to mackerel, tuna, and many other species in these habitats). The light line and more delicate offerings possible on small spinning tackle, as well as the greater mobility of a dinghy, are often a highly effective combination in these situations.

Offshore Dinghy Specialties

You can use your dinghy to fish most of the ways that you fish off your cruising boat—offshore trolling, anchored, drifting or power-drifting; using a fishing kite, downrigger, or any other technique, with the probable exception of power deep-dropping—within the limits of prudent seamanship dictated by your particular dinghy and physical surroundings. What are some of the options that may be available specifically as a result of deploying your dinghy rather than the big boat? Most stem from speed, mobility, and maneuverability. You can use slow-action lures and bait to accomplish a great deal from a sailed or rowed dinghy, although most of the following options require a motor.

HIGH-SPEED TROLLING

Certain lures work best at 8 to 12 knots or more, like the jet heads so highly effective for big wahoo and many other species. If it's calm enough to comfortably permit these speeds, and your dink can do it, a quick early morning or dusk trolling expedition along the outer reef slope and any vertical walls can produce some beautiful steaks for the grill. Occasionally slow down in the vicinity of such features, let the lure sink until the line is nearly vertical, then hit the throttle to bring it rocketing back up toward the surface.

SURF BREAKS

Remember that turbulent conditions often allow predator fish to feed more efficiently, that surf breaking on obstructions or shorelines fits this description, and is therefore a major fish patrol zone. You can safely maneuver your dinghy into position for casting usually somewhat heavier, bigger lures with your

Cruiser Jens Yeager of S/V *Indigo* shows yellowfin tuna (in cooler) . . . and a nice wahoo caught trolling a black and purple Offshore Jet Head from his dinghy (Christmas Island, Republic of Kiribati).

medium or heavy spinning tackle parallel to the breakers near a point of land or isolated small islet, reef, or rocks. Sometimes you can safely anchor; more often, you should stay mobile so that you can move laterally away if larger individual swells arrive. In the tropical Pacific, for example, you can spot giant trevally actually surfing within the interior of waves and pitch big surface plugs (sinkers) to them from a safe distance outside of the break—30- to 60-pound (14 to 27 kg) individuals are not uncommon at some locations. This is heady stuff for most people, an experience they'll not soon forget.

Trolling along just outside sections of breaking waves can also be highly productive at many different latitudes and locations. Don't take chances with getting in too close to the breakers, and keep an eye to seaward for spotting the telltale over-sized lumps of an incoming, unusually large, wave set.

HEAVY-TACKLE REEF-TROLLING

Pronounced bottom features near shore such as rock ledges and ravines, kelp forests, walls and drop-offs, and spur-and-groove coral reef formations become temporary, and sometimes long-term, habitats for large predator fish. Lightly exploited areas in the continental subtropics can harbor grouper species that may reach 1,000 pounds (454 kg) in as little as 15-foot (4.6 m) depths. Hammerhead sharks to this size have been observed chasing tarpon in even shallower water.

Obviously, these extreme examples should not be the focus of cruiser fishing. We *are* interested, however, in more typical situations, which usually involve seasonal habits of sexually mature members of the grouper, snapper, jack and trevally, porgy, and similar families moving near or into the shallows, usually during winter months, to feed and, in some cases, spawn. At these times, it's possible to capture individual bottom fish to 100 pounds (45 kg), more commonly from 5 to 30 pounds (2.2 to 14 kg), on relatively shallow-water dinghy expeditions that would require fishing at much greater depths at other times of the year. You may get a surprise from a large mackerel, tuna, or another more open-water species.

Employ any of the bottom, live bait, or casting techniques discussed to this point for drift or anchor fishing. Our personal favorite, because it's so easy and hassle-free, is to have one fisher sit amidships and hold a 50-pound (23 kg) stand-up outfit at a 45-degree angle, with the rod butt secured in the belt gimbal and stand-up harness attached to the reel. Clip a 35-foot (10.7 m) #8 wire leader onto the shock leader's snap swivel, and haywire-twist a large (8 to 10½ in./203 to 267 mm), hard-wiggling swimming plug to the other end (usually a sinking, deep-diving model like the Rapala Countdown Magnum, Australian Runner, or similar model). Big spoons baited with a strip bait are great too. Troll the lure, while the other fisher drives the dinghy, maneuvering along ledges, ravines, drop-offs, and in and out of surge channels in reefs that would be impossible or dangerous to fish in the big boat.

Be prepared for whopping strikes and heavy strain. Driver, keep motoring, swinging the dinghy away from the bottom structure to help pull the hefty denizen into deeper, obstruction-free water. Don't ease off the throttle until you're well clear. Fisher, apply maximum pressure, short stroke, and wind that reel handle like you're possessed. Tire the big fish thoroughly and ease it to net or gaff.

PASSING SURFACE SCHOOLS

How many times have you been anchored near a steep ocean drop-off, looked up from your novel while relaxing in the hammock, and seen bird activity marking a school of fish, maybe just a few hundred yards (meters) away? What if your dinghy has a motor, a couple of appropriate rods set up in the rod holders, and your safety and other gear? You can jump in, blast over, and nail a beauty or two for afternoon sushi. If you wish to select for larger yellowfins in a mixed tuna school, use the same surface plug as for surf-fishing, maneuver near the school, cast right under the birds, and retrieve rapidly with lots of violent pops.

DEEP-DROPPING

This is another good one for when you're anchored near a steep drop-off, and a short hop in the dinghy can result in a delicious fish dinner. Grab your 50-pound (23 kg) stand-up rod or a similar strength handline. Go to the drop-off, and drift or power-drift to an estimated depth of 180 to 600 feet (55 to 183 m), then drop a vertical rig of small circle hooks baited with chunks of fish to the bottom. Bites will be subtler to detect, due to the distances involved and to the stretch of the monofilament compared to wire. When you feel some life on the line, crank up hard. This might not be fun to do for hours, but in more lightly fished locations, one drop will suffice for a delicious meal.

BAIT SHOWERS

We've saved the most exciting for last. Worldwide in the main "cruising belt" you will see, in a fairly broad range of conditions where deep open water abuts to shallows, hundreds of silvery baitfish greyhounding and skittering out of the sea as they are hotly pursued by large fast predators, including sailfish, large tuna (30 lbs./14 kg to well over 100 lbs./45 kg and more), oversized mackerel, jacks, and a host of other species (salmon and other cold-water species also push bait to the surface). Frequently in warmer waters, the bait species are ballyhoo or houndfish, but there are many others—blue marlin and large wahoo, for example, can make schools of mahi mahi behave in this manner offshore. Bait showers that occur outside the reef break tend to be more ephemeral, but often those that occur in as little as 20 feet (6.1 m) or less of water tend to be much more sustained and fishable. A significant number of anchorages feature this sort of activity quite often, usually most pronounced early in the morning and later in the afternoon, and often marked by swooping frigate birds trying to snag airborne ballyhoo on the fly.

Alone or with one other person, set up a couple of throwing rods—20-pound (9 kg) spinning tackle will work. Bait one rod with a ballyhoo, flying fish, or strip bait, another with a large surface plug, and idle out near but not on top of the activity. Scan carefully; large patches of ripples caused by frightened bait schools usually precede a shower, as does a strong anticipatory dip on the part of a hovering frigate bird. The moment the shower starts, head onto an interception course at full throttle, stop on arrival, wing your plug and/or bait into the middle of the melee, and start retrieving. If you spot one of the predators, cast 10 feet (3 m) or so in front and start working it. If it's a sailfish eating your natural bait, try to open the bail and drop back to the fish on the take. For the surface plug, regardless of species, dip the tip on the strike and then wind and set the hook. These surface strikes are violently spectacular, and you will be in for a wild battle on your light gear.

One of our memorable cruising experiences involved a frantic forty-five minutes of chasing bait showers just off the beach in Taiohae Bay, Nuku Hiva, in the Marquesas with my close friend Joseph Tauira. We were roaring from shower to shower, casting a surface plug and getting an enthusiastic response from little tunnys, 10- to 15-pound (4.5 to 7 kg) giant trevally, and one 35-pound (16 kg) yellowfin tuna. No one had ever seen anything like it, and the frenetic mix of broken French, Marquesan, and English we were using to get the job done was carrying loudly across the water to the growing crowd of spectators, contributing mightily to their merriment. Joseph carried the catch up the beach to

a hero's welcome that eventually transformed into a substantial feast; to this day, he displays the scarred-up lure on the wall in his house.

How did that ancient Chinese proverb go? This version is a little crude and oversimplified:

If you want to be happy for fifteen minutes, have sex.

If you want to be happy for an hour or two, get drunk.

If you wish to be happy for a lifetime, *learn how to fish.*

Rigging Tips for Dinghy Fishing

You are at this point a professional-grade rigger. You have exposure to a full spectrum of fishing rigs for every depth stratum and which hooks, leader size and material, swivel types, knots, baits, and lures to use for different situations anywhere in the world. Local knowledge should always be considered, but you could sail to *any* shore and *without a doubt* supply yourself with fish caught on hook and line.

All of the rigs you use for offshore trolling and fishing from your stationary cruising vessel can be applied to dinghy fishing. Your dinghy is better suited to lighter tackle than is efficient for much of your big-boat fishing activity, and it allows access to environments unreachable with the "mother ship." The addition of several rigs to your repertoire will maximize your effectiveness for lighter, shallower fishing challenges and some offshore activities uniquely suited to fishing from your dinghy (fig. 5-3).

Gear Checklist

Virtually all of the fishing gear you have previously acquired can be used from your dinghy. Adding some light spinning tackle and appropriate hooks and lures can transform your tender into a highly efficient fishing platform. If you lack the space, budget, or desire to take on some of the more vigorous offshore fishing, you could limit yourself to a small amount of this less expensive, more compact gear and stay well supplied with fresh fish by focusing most of your effort on dinghy fishing. Both the tackle and the more shallow, protected environments are the easiest to handle, especially for younger kids.

The sheer amount of light tackle and accessories on the market today can be more bewildering than

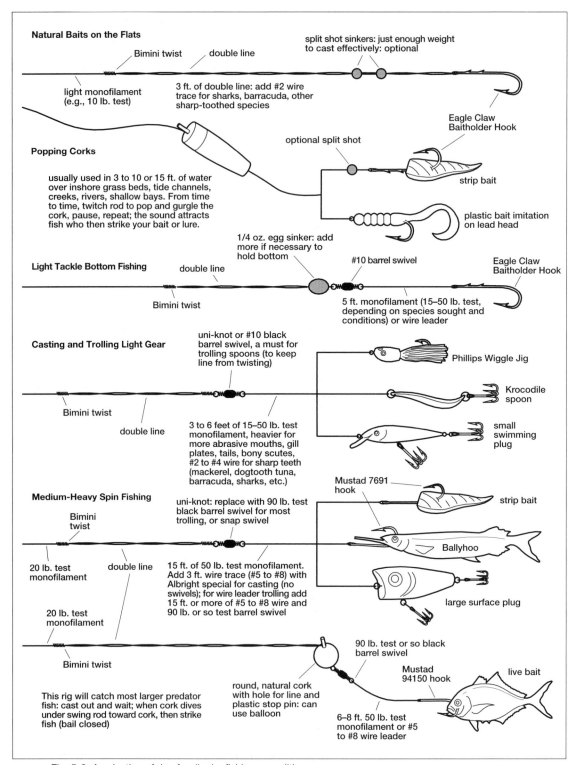

Natural Baits on the Flats

Bimini twist   double line

split shot sinkers: just enough weight
to cast effectively: optional

light monofilament
(e.g., 10 lb. test)

3 ft. of double line: add #2 wire
trace for sharks, barracuda, other
sharp-toothed species

Eagle Claw
Baitholder Hook

Popping Corks

usually used in 3 to 10 or 15 ft. of water
over inshore grass beds, tide channels,
creeks, rivers, shallow bays. From time
to time, twitch rod to pop and gurgle the
cork, pause, repeat; the sound attracts
fish who then strike your bait or lure.

optional split shot

strip bait

plastic bait imitation
on lead head

Light Tackle Bottom Fishing

double line

1/4 oz. egg sinker: add
more if necessary to
hold bottom

#10 barrel swivel

Eagle Claw
Baitholder Hook

Bimini twist

5 ft. monofilament (15–50 lb. test,
depending on species sought and
conditions) or wire leader

Casting and Trolling Light Gear

uni-knot or #10 black
barrel swivel, a must for
trolling spoons (to keep
line from twisting)

Phillips Wiggle Jig

Krocodile
spoon

Bimini twist

double line

3 to 6 feet of 15–50 lb. test
monofilament, heavier for
more abrasive mouths, gill
plates, tails, bony scutes,
#2 to #4 wire for sharp teeth
(mackerel, dogtooth tuna,
barracuda, sharks, etc.)

small
swimming
plug

Medium-Heavy Spin Fishing

Bimini
twist

uni-knot: replace with 90 lb. test
black barrel swivel for most
trolling, or snap swivel

Mustad 7691
hook

strip bait

20 lb. test
monofilament

double line

Ballyhoo

15 ft. of 50 lb. test monofilament.
Add 3 ft. wire trace (#5 to #8) with
Albright special for casting (no
swivels); for wire leader trolling add
15 ft. or more of #5 to #8 wire and
90 lb. or so test barrel swivel

20 lb. test
monofilament

large surface plug

Bimini twist

90 lb. test or so black
barrel swivel

Mustad
94150 hook

live bait

This rig will catch most larger predator
fish: cast out and wait; when cork dives
under swing rod toward cork, then strike
fish (bail closed)

round, natural cork
with hole for line and
plastic stop pin: can
use balloon

6–8 ft. 50 lb. test
monofilament or #5
to #8 wire leader

Fig. 5-3. A selection of rigs for dinghy fishing expeditions.

going Christmas shopping at Toys 'R Us. Some of it works; some of it snags more fishers than fish. Table 5-1 constitutes a no-frills, professional-grade distillation of extremely effective gear. You will undoubtedly experiment and discover many other products that catch fish, but you might as well start out with proven killers. Any previously listed items are not repeated. (See appendix 1 for sources.)

TABLE 5-1. **GEAR CHECKLIST FOR DINGHY FISHING EXPEDITIONS**

Item	Specific Recommendation	Approximate Price
Dinghy bailer	West Marine Dinghy Bailer	$4
Dinghy anchor	folding grapnel anchor	$10–$24
Dinghy sea anchor	The Drifter, 24 in. (61 cm)	$18
Dinghy outriggers	Dot Line telescoping, with parts kit	$105
Pad eyes or eye straps	stainless steel, pick appropriate size for your dinghy	$1–$10
Epoxy resin	West System 101 Handy Repair Kit	$8
Dissimilar metal isolator	Duralac Jointing Compound	$11
Fish finder	Bottom Line Fishin' Buddy II	$200
Rod holders	Sea Dog Side-Mount, Model 325150-1	$24
Fish storage bags	Canyon Tournament King Cooler	$75
	Canyon Original Soft Cooler	$24
Live bait container	Flambeau Trolling Bucket	$12
Cleats	Korkers Safety Sandals	$40
Waders	pick from Cabela's huge variety	$35–$120
Telescoping rod	inexpensive backpacker's spinning rod	$18–$40
Small tackle storage boxes	MFS Waterproof Modular Fishing Systems	$3–$6
Small circle hooks	Eagle Claw Circlesea, sizes 8–1	$8 per 100
Flats jigs	Phillips Wiggle Jigs, ⅛ and ¼ oz. (3.5 and 7 g)	$2
Plastic crustacean lures	Twitchin' Shrimp, 3½ in. (89 mm)	$3
	D.O.A. Shrimp, 3 and 4⅛ in. (76 and 105 mm)	$2 and $3
	Crippled Crab, 3½ in. (89 mm)	$3
General-purpose jigs	Capt. Hank Brown's Hookup jigs, ⅛–¼ oz. (3–7 g)	$1
	Capt. Hank Brown's bucktail jigs, ⅛–¼ oz. (3–7 g)	$3
	Millie's Bucktails, ⅛–¼ oz. (3–7 g)	$3
	Offshore Angler Round Head Jigs, ¼–⅜ oz. (3–11 g)	$2 per 5–10
Deep/casting jigs	Buzz Bomb (salmon, trout), 3–5 in. (76–127 mm)	$3–$5
Plastic bait bodies	Scamper Shrimp, 3 in. (76 mm)	$3 per 25
	Kalin Evil Eel, 8 in. (203 mm)	$3 per 10
Small spoons	Clark Squid Spoon, RBM model, 2 in. (51 mm)	$2
	Johnson Sprite Spoon, ½ oz. (14 g)	$3
Swimming plugs	Trader Bay Baby Slayer, 3½ in. (89 mm)	$8
	Rapala Countdown Magnum, 2¾ in. (70 mm)	$7
	Rapala Magnum Floating, 4⅜ in. (111 mm)	$8
	Cordell Broken Back Red Fin-CJ9, 5 in. (127 mm)	$5
Swimming/surface plug	Super Zara Spook, 5¼ in. (133 mm)	$6
Surface plugs	Trader Bay Baby Chugger, 2⅜ in. (60 mm)	$7
	Trader Bay Chugger, 4½ in. (114 mm)	$8
	Yo-Zuri Surface Cruiser, 6 and 7 in. (152 and 178 mm)	$15 and $17
	Pacific Island Lure Innovations, Pili Floater	$8
Small barrel swivels	Berkley McMahon Swivels, size 10, black	$6 per 100
Egg sinkers	¼ oz. (7 g)	$1 per dozen
Landing net	Scoop Net, 24 in. (61 cm) handle *and* net depth	$9

6

Walking, Wading, and Diving

Watching Harry DeFerrari dive is mesmerizing, not to mention inspirational and educational. Great free divers appear to do the impossible. I'd been introduced to the practice during my first opportunity to crew on a five-week cruise to the Bahamas, where I purchased a Hawaiian sling and a few stainless steel spear shafts and had a number of other subsequent opportunities to use it. At first, the bottom looks like it's several miles away. You get halfway down, and your throat feels tight. You kick harder, and by the time you reach the seafloor it's *past* time to come up. Your lungs feel like they'll burst as you pump those fins and *finally* break violently through the surface, gasping for air in massive, sputtering gulps. Things got better over the course of that first voyage and improved somewhat on a research cruise with an experienced tournament spearfisher to collect specimens for the University of Miami. But it wasn't until Harry invited me to accompany him on a short trip to Bimini, Bahamas, that I finally began to understand.

Harry wasted no effort, ever. He floated softly, descended gently, repeatedly, to depths between 60 and 80 feet (18 and 24 m). He had lots of time on the bottom—he would artistically control his movements and body posture in ways that made his victims feel unthreatened, setting up shots from considerable distances—underhand, side-arm—whatever suited the situation. His shots seldom missed their mark, the unattached, free-flying shafts arcing with deadly accuracy straight into the brain or spinal cord of big, strong, black, yellowfin, and Nassau groupers. No thrashing, no rapid escapes into impenetrable reef structure. . . . Harry would ease over, look around for signs of sharks, gently pick up the motionless fish, and kick slowly to the surface. Determinedly, I'd push down after a target in between his dives, shoot something, go crashing after it, and surface half-dead, too breathless to be triumphant. Harry was a good twenty years my senior. How did he do it?

After one particularly ugly excursion, where I'd gut-shot a mutton snapper that'd wriggled free (requiring Harry's partner Roger to make a quick dive down to finish it off), Harry appeared beside me. "You know, Scott, if I made just *one* dive like you've been doing all day, it'd kill me. . . ." Then he quietly told me *exactly* how to do it. By the end of the day, everything felt different. My dives began to resemble the description of Wendy's exploits related in the Beneath the Waves section (page 9).

Does it take some fantastic physique or weird lungs to do this kind of diving? No. Is this a pastime reserved for the "young"? Absolutely not. What's wrong with scuba tanks or a hookah rig and band-powered spearguns? Not a thing, unless it's illegal (like in the Bahamas, Turks and Caicos, and Kingdom of Tonga). Aren't there some easier alternatives a little farther removed from sharks and other dangerous predators? Yes, many. The purpose of this chapter is to present a wide range of hunting activities available to cruisers who may or may not be involved with hook-and-line fishing, but who don't mind jumping overboard with mask and fins or walking and wading the shorelines and shallows to sample the cornucopia of fresh seafood that awaits them.

You can walk, wade, or dive and collect a considerable variety and amount of edible organisms by hand. Sometimes, simple hand tools, such as pry bars and gigs, and spears of several types greatly facilitate collecting efficiency. Many other more elaborate devices, including nets, traps, and harpoons, can be set up to fish unattended, require two persons to operate, or special skills to deploy. These are covered in the next chapter. For now, take the next logical step in the fishing sequence of your cruise...you began by dragging a line or two behind the boat after you left port, maybe stopped to drift or anchor en route, arrived and put the dinghy in the water ... *now* it's time to step or dive out of the dinghy and leave hook-and-line gear behind.

Dive-Assisted Trolling

Trolling light tackle near coral inevitably results in cut-offs when larger fish grab the lure and dive in or behind the reef. This happened to Wendy and me twice on one isolated lagoon pinnacle at Raroia, Tuamotus, in French Polynesia late one afternoon. We returned with snorkel gear and spears in bright sunlight the next morning, free-dove meticulously, peering into likely dens and ledges. Within twenty minutes we had speared the preceding day's culprits, two marbled groupers (*Epinephelus polyphekadion*). We retrieved our lures, each still firmly implanted in the jaws, prior to processing the fish into fillets and grouper chowder parts.

Many years before, Dick Entwhistle and I were trolling a large swimming plug on 20-pound (9 kg) test spinning tackle from the tender to the University of Miami's R/V *Calanus* off Rose Island, near Nassau, Bahamas. Something big ate the plug, burned off 25 yards (23 m) of line, and "rocked up" in the bottom. Dick swung around, I went to the bow, reeling as we motored to a vertical position over the taut line. I dove down, followed the line through a ravine, under a coral arch, and into a cave, where a huge, square, black tail protruded. One hour, many free dives, and seven Hawaiian sling spear shafts later, we extracted a 51-pound (23 kg) black grouper (*Mycteroperca bonaci*), a perfect specimen for the ciguatera research project that was our mission.

Where Do You Start?

Let's rewind this movie a little. Remember the last time you were using the dinghy to troll around the coral shallows with your light tackle? Kind of hot, wasn't it? And the kids, although they're doing much better, created a couple of monofilament tangles that grew into big "hairballs" that had to be cut out ... and then there were those two bigger fish that engulfed your best lures, took off like freight trains for the coral, and dove into holes or otherwise cut you off...got kind of expensive, didn't it? Frustrating, too—you can see many of the details of the coral patch a mere 10 feet (3 m) below, and you know your quarry is sitting down there somewhere close by with your favorite lure dangling from its mouth. This is an excellent time to slip overboard with mask, fins, snorkel, and your trusty Hawaiian sling to rectify the situation.

On the other hand, maybe you have now worked the area around the anchorage with hook and line, and gained familiarity with the topography and local fish community, but you're still ready for a break from tossing around in the dinghy or big boat in the bright glare of the sun, fussing with all of the baits and lures, and their proper presentation. Furthermore, perhaps you don't even feel like getting wet and salty again—if you had the option of putting on your straw hat, sipping an exceptionally cold beer, and walking along collecting a nice meal in a more leisurely fashion, you'd jump at it. We start with this approach, then work our way gradually to more strenuous pursuits.

Walking and Wading

Effective seafood collection from the shore and shallows requires knowledge about the variety of edible inhabitants, the ability to identify the specific habitats in which they reside, and sometimes a few tricks for their successful capture and processing. Daytime forays to various intertidal-zone areas—sand, mud, rocky shorelines, near-shore shallows, reef flats—can produce an assortment of mollusks (clams, mussels, oysters, top shells, conch, octopus), crustaceans (land crabs, shore and reef crabs, spiny and slipper lobsters), echinoderms (sea urchins, sea cucumbers), and other edible creatures. Accessibility makes this form of gathering a way of life among maritime native cultures. Many of the target items are often consumed raw, on the spot, and are unfamiliar to the visiting cruiser's palate—sea urchin eggs, shore crabs, most mollusks, the long, spaghetti-like intestines of sea cucumbers. Accompanying your native friends on such outings allows you to sample and learn more about easily gathered near-shore seafood than you can possibly learn from books or by trial and error. You may be surprised at the appeal of some of these items, and you can apply your new expertise to similar environments that you encounter on your own. Your self-sufficiency will improve another notch, and with it, your survival knowledge. Some items that you couldn't imagine consuming, particularly raw, might start to look pretty good if you were shipwrecked and starving on an uninhabited island or coastline.

Night expeditions are most effective for a number of near-shore invertebrates. Crabs, lobsters, octopus, and many others emerge from daytime resting lairs to forage under cover of darkness, affording a hunting opportunity for the wading cruiser armed with a light source and perhaps a gig or pole spear. This category of forays includes everything from subsistence collection of small invertebrates to activities that comprise high-production commercial fisheries for valuable commodities such as live lobsters.

To this point, we have tried to not overwhelm you with scientific names in the text. The detailed knowledge helpful for seeking more cryptic, less "mainstream" food items, however, would make an attempt to use only common names too vague to be of value. Latin names, like mathematical symbols, are a universal language. They confer the ability to discuss the habits and biology of specific groups of organisms succinctly and without confusion. Most species have numerous common names but only *one* scientific name. Don't be put off by these—pronounce them phonetically as you read them, with the confidence that most of the brilliant scientists whose life's work revolves around them do no differently. The more you know about the biology of the species you seek, the better you will become at catching them.

One more thing. Look, we know most of you didn't buy this book to learn about sucking on the south end of a sea cucumber for nutrition. You want to catch, prepare, and sample fresh gourmet seafood that appeals to you personally, to share intimate sunsets in exotic destinations, perhaps with a chilled bottle of white wine and steaming, fragrant aromas that rival the finest restaurants anywhere in the world. Nevertheless, we implore you to open your mind to a review of new possibilities and tastes, to explore through the knowledge of other cultures' seafood categories that may not be familiar menu items in your home port. To this end, our selection of seafood procurement opportunities available through walking, wading, or diving includes mainstream delicacies interspersed with multicultural and survival selections.

DRY LAND

Two of the most successful invertebrate classes, Class Gastropoda (the largest class of mollusks) and Class Crustacea (the only mostly aquatic, large class of arthropods), include representatives that are both good to eat and do not require getting wet to capture. Gastropods, basically, are snails. (*Not so fast* . . . conch and abalone are gastropods, too!) Terrestrial and freshwater snails are consumed with relish in widely separated parts of the planet, from Asia to Europe (witness *escargot*), and occur most of the places you might visit on a cruise. Tropical versions tend to be small. Do not carry any acquired propensity to consume marine gastropods raw along with you inland, as you can develop severe problems with parasites found in uncooked nonmarine snails.

Terrestrial snails fail to arouse the culinary interest of some folks. OK, then, what about all of those delicious crabs, shrimp, freshwater crayfish, and lobsters you "paid through the nose" for the pleasure of eating prior to your cruising life? They all belong to the largest order of crustaceans, Decapoda. The fossil record indicates numerous incursions on land and freshwater by decapods, with the only widespread example of success being freshwater crayfish. This still leaves several terrestrial representatives that have captured the tastes of humans. The strongest examples fall into the general category of land crabs.

Crabs inhabiting land usually stay in burrows or under or inside rocks, rocky structure, or trees by day and become more active at night. Most have good eyesight, can move quickly when alarmed, possess formidable claws, and live within a reasonable distance of the water.

Superfamily Coenobitoidea includes the widely distributed land hermit-crab genus *Coenobita*, occurring throughout the Indo-Pacific and West Indies, and the closely related coconut crab *Birgus*, whose distribution is limited to the Indo-Pacific. Both genera live in coastal areas. *Coenobita* includes most of the various-sized land hermits common from the equator to the subtropics, some of which are big enough to consume without having to collect a large number. They tend to be one of the easiest land crabs to catch due to their tendency to depend on the adopted shell they carry on their back for shelter from the sun and refuge from harm. Although they are more active at night, if you leave some coconut shell fragments with the meat attached scattered around and go take a walk, upon your return, the area is likely to be swarming with crabs, even at midday.

This would certainly not be true of the more reclusive and much larger coconut crab. Juveniles adopt a shell, hermit-crab-style, after emerging from aquatic larval development. They abandon the shell as adults and construct burrows farther from the ocean, coming forth at night to forage. They're omnivorous and will eat fresh or decaying matter. They do indeed eat coconuts and have the ability to climb towering palm trees using the spike-like ends of their legs for purchase. One sign of a coconut crab abode is shredded coconut husks near a burrow, log, or abandoned structures, such as World War II–era gun revetments on South Pacific islands. Natives capture them by hand, often with the aid of a stick, when they're cornered in accessible habitats. They are induced to emerge by bait, or by baited pit traps designed to seduce the crab into a buried bucket or other concavity from which it cannot emerge. Another trick, which varies from island to island, is to attach a wreath of grass or leaves high on the trunk of a palm tree after the crab ascends, causing it to release its grip on the trunk and fall to the ground on the way back down.

A string tied to a leg secures captive crabs, which may be fed and maintained for a while before consumption. These animals are long-lived, slow-

Hermit crabs, Family Coenobitidae (Tuamotus, French Polynesia).

growing, and highly revered for food throughout their range, a combination of factors that has led to severe depletion in most areas anywhere near human populations of any size. You can still view some impressive specimens at uninhabited or sparsely inhabited tropical Pacific atolls; however, we should limit ourselves to photographs, unless we are in a survival situation or have been invited by a native inhabitant to eat a captive coconut crab.

Amphibious and land crabs belonging to the Superfamily Brachygnatha are generally a different story. They tend to be prolific and widespread, and sustain considerable exploitation without catastrophic depletion, so *go for it*. Amphibious crabs constitute a huge array of species that depend to varying degrees on fresh, brackish, or salt water for periodic immersion and breeding. These include inhabitants of freshwater rivers, rice paddies, swamps, marshes, mangroves, estuaries, rocky shores, and beaches. They bury, burrow, and climb. The group includes fiddler, soldier, ghost, Chinese mitten, river, and mangrove crabs. Many are smaller than you'd normally think of eating, but they may provide important sustenance for native inhabitants. They tend to be very fast and are much easier to catch at night by freezing them in the beam of a strong flashlight. Ease a hand slowly into position, and make a quick move—usually open palm, pressing the crab to the substrate—and then secure it with the help of your other hand. Drop them into a burlap catch bag.

The most popular terrestrial brachyuran food crabs may be those belonging to the genera *Cardisoma* and *Gecarcinus*. These large, round-bodied crabs with big, fat claws are what many people think of when they hear the term *land crab*. Representatives live in tropical and subtropical North, Central, and South America; Africa; the West Indies; and throughout the Indo-Pacific. These crabs live in burrows near the shoreline, because the females must return to the sea to deposit their eggs. Natives of different coasts pursue them with varying degrees of enthusiasm, particularly during mass movements or "runs" correlated with moon phase,

Coconut crab, *Birgus latro* (Palmyra Atoll, Line Islands, United States).

Ghost crab, Family Ocypodidae (Tonga).

rainfall, and season. Interestingly, favored preparation and body-part utilization varies sharply between human populations over some relatively short geographical distances (see chapter 13).

One of the most popular and productive ways to catch land crabs is to ride along unpaved or paved tracks and roads at night, on either a bicycle or motorized vehicle equipped with at least one headlight. Each time a nice-sized crab freezes in the lights, stop, jump out, and catch the crab. Natives often grab them by hand, even reaching blindly into burrows to seize desirable individuals that made it home, but we've seen enough mutilation and scars to discourage us from anything braver than the old stick-and-bag routine. Try to press the crab to the substrate while it remains motionless or is at least above ground. They nearly always grasp the stick in their claws. Use their grip and pressure on the stick to sweep them into the bag. We are seldom able to extricate holed-up crabs with only a stick, so we leave those for next time.

STREAMS, RIVERS, PONDS, AND LAKES

Cruisers, whether seeking fish on hook and line or fish and invertebrates via other means, understandably focus on marine organisms for sustenance. We ventured slightly inland from the coast in the last section in pursuit of terrestrial invertebrates, most of which are still linked to the sea. Let's carry that thought one step further. Imagine anchoring just

---

An Unlucky Land Crab

Many Bahamian and West Indian friends are confirmed land-crab fanatics. Maurice "Mahajah" Clarke, my Rastafarian research assistant in Antigua, would never let us pass a sizable crab, no matter how late it was or how tiring our day at sea. One dark night, about a third of the way to his house in St. John's from the west coast, I groaned inwardly at the sight of a monster frozen in the headlights. We were both soaked and exhausted after a full day's winter pounding in a small native boat, but Mahajah instantly became animated. I dutifully slammed on the brakes, then begged, "C'mon, Mahajah, you know you're tired, and when we get to your house you'll wanna leave the thing in the car like usual. I'm tired of those damned things nipping at my heels after we've both forgotten all about 'em—the last one just about caused an accident." "*No*, Scottie, me gon' put 'im in the pot *tonight*!" "That's what you said last time" . . . the passenger door was already open as he stealthily slid out, oblivious to anything other than the crab, whispering for it not to move. Just then, the crab shook off the dazzle of the headlights enough to tentatively scuffle sideways a few steps, prompting a mad sprint by Mahajah—massive mane of dreadlocks flying, casting wild shadows over the scene. The crab's uncertain shuffle accelerated into a high-speed dash for the bushes, where it disappeared a microsecond ahead of my lurching friend. Mahajah didn't break stride, crashing full tilt into the bush, followed by at least twenty seconds of resounding cracks, rustlings, and reverberating shouts and one-sided conversation.

My rising hopes were dashed by the radiant smile illuminating Mahajah's brown, finely sculpted features through his tousled locks as he popped headfirst out of the underbrush, holding his hapless captive by the claws. He eased to the back door and tossed it laconically into the back of the small station wagon. Moments later, you wouldn't have known anything happened as he dozed periodically to the pulse of reggae and soca from the local radio station.

"OK, you promised." "Scottie, look, mon, m' *can't* see 'im, an Bunny jus' say she got us a nice soup all ready. C'mon, nah, don' be dat way." "Yeah, alright, I just hope it bites your ass tomorrow morning and not mine."

The crab fulfilled my wish shortly after I collected Mahajah the next morning, and spooked him again that night as it scrabbled loudly under the front seat, though it quickly scuttled into an inaccessible space and evaded casual efforts at recapture. I happened to have a collision late that night; several days later, while torch-cutting the ruined front end of the car off in the course of welding on a replacement grill made of steel construction reinforcing rod, Junior George and I looked at each other at the same time. *What* was that smell? A peek under the front seat revealed Mahajah's crab, legs and claws pointing stiffly skyward.

offshore of a mountainous island or coastline that features a small waterfall near the beach. Cool, freshwater plummets into a rushing stream that either runs down a steep incline into the sea or perhaps terminates in a short, lazy, brackish slough prior to entering the ocean. If we hike past the steep incline or waterfall, we enter a freshwater stream or small river environment, possibly punctuated by pools, and perhaps ponds and lakes. What culinary opportunities await us here? Over a broad range of latitudes, three possibilities are freshwater crayfish, shrimp, and eels.

Freshwater Crayfish

Freshwater crayfish consist of more than five hundred species that live all over the world. They belong to Superfamily Nephropidae, along with the clawed marine lobster genus *Homarus*, which includes the well-known Maine lobster. Crayfish look like miniature clawed lobsters, and usually attain a length of approximately 4 inches (10 cm). One genus found in Australia, *Euastacus*, attains the size of a marine lobster. Most live in burrows, excavated in the beds of a variety of water bodies. Anyone who has been to New Orleans, Louisiana, or other areas in the Deep South of the United States cannot have missed the steaming trays of whole boiled, seasoned crayfish served at bars and restaurants of every description.

These small crayfish are omnivores. They respond strongly to any scrap-meat bait such as chicken necks or fish heads. One easy method of capture is to set out a series of lines tied to sticks stuck vertically in the sediment along the bank, each baited with a piece of bony meat scrap. Steadily and slowly handline those that pull tight. Place a small dip net in the water and ease in the line, leading the crayfish hanging onto the bait into the net, and scoop them up before they release their grip. Keep your catch in a plastic bucket full of water, and change the water occasionally to keep them alive. When the action slows down in one area, move to a new section of the water body and start again. This method is very simple and the action is fast, which makes it feasible for and very popular with young children. They can do it *themselves!*

Freshwater Shrimp and Prawns

Most members of the handful of freshwater shrimp families are small. These are the little darting crustaceans that snap up off of the sediment in swarms as you wade upstream. The Family Palaemonidae, however, includes economically important freshwater prawns that are indigenous to many areas and that have also been the subject of a considerable amount of aquaculture. The genus *Macrobrachium* includes species that range in length from 4 to 8 inches (10 to 20 cm).

If you befriend Polynesians in the Marquesas or Society Islands, for example, they may invite you to participate in a *chevrette* (freshwater prawn) expedition, which occurs at night. You will probably hike well inland, possibly driving part of the way, and then walk deep into an interior valley and descend to a clear, cool stream. The favored weapon is a mini-harpoon, not much over a yard (meter) long, with three prongs about 5 inches (13 cm) long. The hunter walks stealthily upstream, illuminating the waters ahead with a headlamp, searching for nocturnally active prawns foraging out on open bottom. The prawns are striking, with bluish-gray to pale bodies, long antennae, and thin, elongated claws. The better fishers seldom miss impaling their target with a quick, deft thrust.

Freshwater Eels

Eels of the Family Anguillidae occur from the equator to temperate regions throughout the world. Adults spend most of their life in freshwater, often far from the coast, and then migrate back to the sea to spawn. Males of one species are known to take eleven to thirty-four years in freshwater to reach sexual maturity; females of the same species take even longer, twenty-four to forty-seven years. Individuals of most species seldom exceed 48 inches (1.2 m) in length, although records document some 78-inch (2 m) monsters weighing over 111 pounds(50 kg). Little is known about the location and mode of spawning, except that it appears to be a one-time event, like most salmon (except that adult and juvenile habitats are reversed). Fertilized eggs hatch and gradually develop at sea into distinctive, elongated eel larvae (called a *leptocephalus*), likened to a long thin leaf in shape. The leptocephali rely primarily on ocean currents to travel *back* to their place of genetic origin. They eventually metamorphose into juveniles (elvers) close to shore and in estuaries, entering rivers sometimes in great masses. The small (2.5 in./64 mm) elvers swim upstream, scaling rapids and small waterfalls to arrive inland, settle, and grow to maturity. This process may span thousands of nautical miles of ocean.

Adults are considered a delicacy when smoked, particularly in Europe and Japan, and to indigenous peoples such as the Maori of New Zealand. Larger-scale fisheries exploit adults heading downstream to spawn, usually with dam-like fence traps called weirs. Cruisers can catch individual adults with gigs or handlines using any meat for bait. These eels are nocturnally active, and may be seen in considerable numbers by using a powerful light to search stream and lake beds devoid of visible individuals in daylight.

ROCKY INTERTIDAL ZONES

Myriad edible marine organisms inhabit different parts of rocky intertidal zones distributed throughout the latitudes of the world. Some are among the best-known, most popular seafoods. Other delicacies seem to be overlooked by almost everyone except local native people and military survival instructors.

Chitons

Chitons are a prime example of a little-known, palatable group of about six hundred mollusk species inhabiting rocky intertidal zones throughout the world. Most range in length from just over 1 to 5 inches (2.5 to 13 cm). They constitute the sole members of Class Polyplacophora, named for the eight segments that make up their flattened, oval-shaped shell. These animals attach strongly to the substrate with a snail-like foot, and

move extremely slowly, scraping algae and small organisms with a roughened sort of "tongue" called a radula. They are most active at night, particularly when submerged by the tide, emerging from daytime hiding to forage, literally, at a snail's pace. This, consequently, is the best time to get them.

Walk and wade with a light source. Pry suitable-sized chitons off the rocks with sudden, forceful leverage using a dull stainless steel butter knife or similar thin, strong tool. If the initial effort fails, the chiton has become alarmed quickly enough to suck onto the rock with its girdle. They grip the rock with this outer ring of the body, then raise or hump the inner-body margin to create a vacuum, making them very difficult to remove.

Gastropods

Descending from dry land to the rocky intertidal zone, we encounter gastropods of increasing culinary popularity. Many belong to the Order Archaeogastropoda, a primitive, mostly marine group with numerous small members. For example, dense populations of the intertidal snail genus *Nerita* virtually litter tropical and subtropical shore-

Chiton, an underrated delicacy found worldwide in rocky intertidal zones.

lines around the globe but provide only small tidbits of meat for the effort.

Top shells are widely distributed and morphologically similar to nerites, except that they attain much larger sizes. This makes them highly sought-after food items throughout their range. The West Indian top shell *(Cittarium pica)*, for instance, has been exploited to extinction in South Florida and Bermuda. It remains second only to queen conch *(Strombus gigas)* in economic value among gastropods in the Bahamas and Caribbean. Indo-Pacific top shells such as *Trochus niloticus* are equally important and have been the subject of successful mariculture in Palau.

Size and abundance of top shells tend to be directly related to distance from human populations. They're easy to find and collect. Daytime is fine. Walk and wade pinnacle rock shorelines. Check smoother pockets and depressions from the wave spray zone to well below the high-tide mark. Unless the animal is deep inside a close-fitting hole, you can usually pull it free of the rock by hand. Use a prying implement for tough cases. Growth rates are faster in zones with less severe wave action, so quieter sections of shoreline that don't bear the full brunt of prevailing seas may harbor the biggest individuals.

While top shells are probably the best rocky intertidal gastropod prize in the tropics and subtropics, abalones (genus *Haliotis*) capture this distinction in cooler climates. More than a hundred species of abalone occur worldwide, with some ranging from inshore shallows into the intertidal zone. The low-profile shell is often encrusted with growth and blends cryptically with the surrounding habitat, sometimes requiring a sharp eye and specific search image for best success. Lever abalone off the rocks with a strong prying tool. Like other large gastropods, abalone are relatively slow-growing and easy to overexploit. These characteristics underlie their scarcity in more accessible environments near human populations.

Bivalves

Class Bivalvia contains the largest number and widest distribution of commercially important food mollusks. All possess hinged, laterally compressed shells composed of two halves that completely

Indo-Pacific pyramid topshell *(Tectus pyramis)*, similar to the better-known *Trochus*.

encase the body. They feed on small particulate matter, usually phytoplankton, which they pump through filtering apparatuses with inhalant and exhalant siphons when submerged. As a result, population size and density, and size of individuals, are often greatest in cooler areas featuring high primary production (i.e., lots of plankton) rather than clear, relatively sterile tropical seas.

The two most popular groups of bivalves exploited in rocky intertidal zones are mussels and oysters, both members of Subclass Lamellibranchia, Order Anisomyria. Mussels (e.g., *Mytilus, Perna*) frequently secrete tough byssal threads by a gland in the foot to attach to the rocks or other hard substrate; many of the desirable oysters (like *Crassotrea virginica*) orient sideways and cement one valve to hard surfaces. Both mussels and oysters may require tools such as a hammer and chiseling device for easiest removal. These animals can regularly be found in clusters attached to each other, so that detaching the few individuals at the base rewards the hunter with a big clump of delicious seafood.

Mussels and oysters are easy to locate and procure due to their usual fixed position between the low- and high-tide marks. Their feeding habits and habitat also make them sensitive to contamination from some kinds of algal blooms, pollutants, and sewage-born pathogens, so exercise caution near possible sources of these entities. Once again, consulting local knowledge can save you from mishap. See chapter 10 for more details.

Crustaceans

The rocky intertidal zone is not prime habitat for the most desirable food crustaceans. Members of Family Portunidae (swimming crabs) and various temperate and tropical lobster species will *occasionally* pop up to the vicinity of the low-tide mark, but this is generally an exception. The most numerous visible crustaceans in this habitat are usually shore crabs belonging to Family Grapsidae. They're mostly small, light on meat, and fast. Hand-capture at night in the beam of a strong light is relatively efficient. We have visited areas where natives avidly sought these crabs—despite the low food return and abundant alternatives—for the sweet taste of the leg and claw meat.

Cephalopods

Class Cephalopoda includes octopods, squid, cuttlefish, and nautili. Of these, only octopuses (genus *Octopus*) are regularly found in and near the intertidal zone along rocky shorelines. The octopus chooses a lair, usually a hole or crevice in the rocks, and emerges at night to feed. They are masters of camouflage, capable of precisely matching the color and pattern of the substrate. They ambush fish, gastropods, and crustaceans, grasping them with the aid of their eight arms, haul them into the den, and consume them. Powerful jaws tear into the prey, and poison secretes from glands in the mouth cavity, which drains into the torn flesh and immobilizes struggling victims. They extract gastropods by using their specialized radula to drill a hole and inject poison directly into the flesh of the snail (now you know the origin of the tiny holes visible in many of the dead shells you find along the shoreline).

Night is the best time to catch an octopus. Walk and wade the tidal pools and rocky shallows with a flashlight, headlamp, or lantern. Carry a sharpened stick, gig, spear, or small gaff. Your targets in this habitat could range in length from less than 12 inches (30 cm) to well over 40 inches (102 cm), depending on location, so be prepared for a scrap. Impale the octopus and subdue it with a knife stab to the brain, which is best accomplished with a short incision between the eyes. Don't store a live octopus in a bucket because it will climb out and crawl away.

To Kill an Octopus

Many years ago I was out pulling lobster traps in the Florida Keys with a commercial fisherman friend. He was telling me how he'd seen a TV show the previous evening about a European trap fishery for octopuses. He was particularly intrigued by a scene showing the fishermen instantly killing each octopus with a quick, precise bite right between the eyes of each animal. Octopuses are frequent, undesirable occupants of lobster traps, and my friend was determined to put his new knowledge to use at the first opportunity. It wasn't long before a trap came up with a stout, 20-inch (51 cm) *Octopus briareus*. "Here, watch this." The burly fisherman deftly grabbed the octopus and quickly chomped it somewhere on the head. I was impressed by this open-minded, bold initiative . . . it looked fast and professional. The octopus, however, seemed relatively unaffected, and rapidly sucked onto Wayne's face, wrapping all eight arms around the back of his head in an intimate embrace that knocked off his baseball cap. I could see Wayne chewing away beneath the flurry of wiggling, clutching arms, with suction cups stuck firmly to his cheeks and the bulbous, pulsating body covering his face. I couldn't quite make out the content of his gargled exclamations. The octopus ejected a wad of ink, which immediately began to squeeze out from beneath the melee and drool down from Wayne's chin and onto his shirt in creeping, elastic, mucus-like blobs of black. By this time my paroxysms had transcended laughter, every muscle in my abdomen burned, and I couldn't see for the tears. I believe the last movements of the octopus occurred just before Wayne succeeded in gnawing it nearly in half. There's no substitute for perseverance.

INTERTIDAL SEDIMENT FLATS

Spacious, gently sloping or relatively level areas, paved by firm mud, sand, and other sediments and lying between the high- and low-tide marks, comprise one of the most prolific categories of seafood hunting grounds in the world for cruisers on foot. Although flounder and other fish, octopods, portunid crabs, and occasional lobsters may be grabbed, gigged, or hand-speared, the real bounty of this habitat is gastropod and bivalve mollusks.

Gastropods

The most commercially important gastropods found on intertidal sediment flats are probably conch (genus *Strombus*). These large marine snails have representatives from the equator to the subtropics in the Indo-Pacific and Caribbean regions, and also inhabit grass beds, reefs, and deep sediment flats to at least 160 feet (50 m). Queen conch (*Strombus gigas*), found from Florida and the Bahamas through the Caribbean, have undergone heavy exploitation leading to various states of depletion in different areas. Fishing moratoriums were declared in Florida, U.S. Virgin Islands, and Bermuda, and bag and size limits have been imposed in the Bahamas and elsewhere. Nevertheless, cruisers can sometimes find legal-size queen conch for dinner while wading the shallows or even walking on fully exposed sediment flats at low tide. A large number of smaller species sometimes found in the same areas also provide good table fare: milk conch *(Strombus costatus)*, hawkwing conch *(Strombus raninus)*, fighting conch *(Strombus alatus* and *Strombus pugilis)*, and roostertail conch *(Strombus gallus)*.

The Indo-Pacific lacks a single, large, widespread analog to *Strombus gigas*, but it's possible to satisfy your taste for conch with other members of Family Strombidae. Many smaller *Strombus* occur in this zone (*S. lentiginosus, S. gibberulus, S. mutabilis, S. erythrinis*, to name a few), and various species of spider conch (particularly *Lambis lambis* and *Lambis crocata*) can rival the size, meat content, and quality of Caribbean queen conch.

Conch are usually easy to spot in the shallows, especially those that periodically bury in the sediment, which tends to keep the shells relatively free of growth. Conch in some areas may have algae, tubeworms, and other growth that camouflages them to a degree. Capturing them is easy—just reach down, pick them up, and place them in a mesh dive bag secured with a drawstring.

Burrowing Bivalves

Soft, penetrable sediment affords subterranean protection from predation. Although details and specialized adaptations vary, burrowing bivalves feed and breath while buried through elongated inhalant and exhalant siphons extended to the sediment surface.

This extremely successful strategy underlies the staggering number of families and species and prolific populations of cockles, clams, lucines, and buttercups available everywhere from freezing polar seas to the equator in intertidal sediment habitats. Density and individual size tend to peak in cooler, nutrient-rich seas, but tropical areas also produce enough for a tasty meal with a little extra search effort.

Digging for clams and other burrowing bivalves is easy and fun. Wait for the last half of the outgoing tide. Take off your shoes and squish on out across the flat. Different species thrive in assorted sediment granule sizes and types, and live at different depths in the sediment; for example, habitually very near the surface, quite deep, or at intermediate levels. Others move up and down or have the ability to rapidly descend to shallow depths in more dynamic, shifting sediments. Look for siphon holes, and watch and listen for gurgling bubbles made by bivalves withdrawing siphons and closing their shells as they sense your approach. Feel with your bare feet and toes, and extract individuals by hand or with the aid of a small digging implement. Some people use steel clam rakes. When you find a few, concentrate on that specific area for a while rather than a random scattering because their distribution is usually patchy. Store your catch in buckets, nylon mesh dive bags, burlap sacks, or other suitable containers. Once again, use common sense and consult local knowledge regarding the possibility of contamination.

Unattached Sediment Surface Bivalves

Among the relatively few bivalves adopting this lifestyle, the most important for our purpose belong to Family Pectinidae, the scallops. The ranges of some species encompass sediment bottom as shallow as the low-tide mark. They rest on their sides, scanning with a multitude of tiny, beady blue eyes located on the sensory lobe of the mantle. Scallops have the ability to actively swim by rapidly opening and contracting their valves to eject seawater, creating enough thrust to skip a yard (meter) across the bottom, or even to go flapping off in the water column away from danger.

Attune yourself to the precise characteristics of the sediment type most favored by the species in your area. Often this consists of a relatively firm, fine- to medium-grain sand bottom with reasonable current flow and exposure to wind wave action, causing persistent, shifting ripple patterns on the bottom. One frequent clue to finding the right bottom type is the size and material of adjacent shore rocks or sediment. Look for consistent patterns correlated to the presence of scallops. Individuals may be lightly buried—keep a sharp eye out for the faint outline of the animal in the sand. You can readily catch those that dart off because their swimming ability largely serves to evade slow predators such as carnivorous starfish, not hungry, fast cruisers and their kids.

Marshes and Swamps

Like the intertidal sediment flats, marshes and swamps offer various opportunities to walk and wade for dinner when the footing permits. Flounder, mullet, and many other fish species can fall prey to gigs, small hand spears, even band-powered spearguns fired from above the water surface. Catfish and others can be effectively harvested with unattended trot lines, basically miniature longlines with short leaders and small hooks. Smaller brackish-water species of turtles, frogs, iguanas, snakes, and alligators or caimans all provide valued sustenance for locals in different coastal areas of the world. Most of these food sources and hunting styles are, for assorted reasons, in little danger of becoming the focus of mainstream cruiser activities.

Our selected seafood superstars for cruising-boat pedestrians armed with simple hand gear in this environment: crabs. Amphibious and swimming crabs thrive in the salt and brackish waters of coastal marshes and swamps—they literally swarm here. We've mentioned previously the true land crabs and variety of smaller amphibious crabs; our focus for this section is portunid crabs, such as *Callinectes*, which includes the well-known North American blue crab and similar species. Over widely disparate marsh and swamp coastal zones, you can step to the water's edge, chuck out a chicken neck or fish head on a piece of twine, and soon feel the tugs and pulls signaling the arrival of a portunid crab of some kind. Gently retrieve and hand-net, and you're on the way to another tasty dinner of fresh seafood.

Reef Flats

The living and dead calcium-carbonate platform between shore and outer reef crest on tropical and subtropical islands provides an incredible array of seafood for the walking hand-collector. Many marine invertebrates described from other environments, including conch, octopuses, crabs, and lobsters, also range onto the reef flat. Many others are found primarily in this specific habitat, as well as on similar substrates submerged at different depths, including boring, attached, and some unattached surface-dwelling bivalves (e.g., mussels, oysters, and certain scallops and clams); chitons; a huge array of hard-surface and coral-dwelling gastropods, often small; a large assortment of reef crabs, some large enough to warrant our attention (e.g., *Mythrax* and *Carpilius*); and sea urchins, sea cucumbers, and other echinoderms unlikely to appeal to most Western palates.

Bivalves tend to be small and scattered on the reef flat, with the notable exception of the giant clam genus *Tridacna* of the Indo-Pacific. Some species of these famous clams reach epic proportions (remember how Lloyd Bridges was always getting stuck in those monsters in the TV series *Sea Hunt*?). Despite heavy exploitation, driven in part by excessive prices paid by Asian buyers for the adductor muscle for resale as an aphrodisiac, *Tridacna* of more modest proportions are still a relatively common sight in many areas of the tropical Pacific. However, you only have to visit one of the more pristine, isolated, and uninhabited submerged atolls, reefs, or islands to get a true feel for how much depletion has actually occurred elsewhere. We feel fortunate to have visited two reefs in particular where these animals were extremely abundant, with shell length of individuals commonly exceeding 12 inches (30 cm); several were more than 22 inches (56 cm). Some are weakly attached to the reef and may be pulled off by hand, others bore into the reef and become firmly immersed and surrounded by living coral; thus, collection of boring *Tridacna* can be quite destructive. Considering this and the prevailing rates of widespread depletion, we urge cruisers to put all *Tridacna* clams on their personal list of protected species, along with coconut crabs, sea turtles, and other slow-growing animals having difficulty with the onslaught of humans. Save these for survival situations only.

Indo-Pacific giant clam *(Tridacna)* on shallow reef flat photographed on an uninhabited South Pacific atoll.

The giant oyster *Hyotissa hyotis* (superficially similar to *Tridacna* clams but with shell lips consisting of a sharp-cornered, deeply triangular zigzag) still supports sizable harvests near some inhabited areas of the southwestern South Pacific. These bivalves occur in tidal creeks and shallows, and require removal from the substrate with a sledge-hammer. Err on the side of caution and accompany a native friend, rather than risk offending locals by collecting a batch yourself.

Cheer up, because Indo-Pacific reef flats are the perfect environment for the spectacular experience of collecting spiny lobsters by wading at night. This practice has been refined to a lucrative art form on some of the more lightly populated tropical Pacific atolls. The targets are panulirid lobster species that migrate vertically at night from the depths, up over the reef crest, and out onto the reef flat to forage, sometimes in considerable numbers, during very specific moon phases that vary from atoll to atoll. Standard equipment includes footwear capable of traversing sharp coral for hours, a bright Coleman lantern (yes, you can use a dive light or other device, but your catch rate will be minimal compared to

that possible with much brighter illumination), a dive bag (or, if you're really serious, a tin-covered plywood box "backpack" with shoulder straps), and heavy gloves. Find an expanse of reef flat with water level waist deep or less, wait until darkness falls, light the lantern, and start searching. If the water is not much more than knee-deep, ease over and quickly, decisively, and firmly grab the lobster, by the carapace if possible. Don't let go! Toss it into your container. If the water is deeper, approach stealthily and step on the lobster, hold it pressed to the bottom with your foot, then reach down and grasp tightly with your hand to secure it. Don't neglect lower tidal phases out near the edge of the reef crest—this can be easy pickings as the lobsters crawl around with the upper parts of their carapaces and tails exposed. Just be mindful of getting knocked down or, worse, carried completely off the reef by a larger-than-average breaking wave. Other potential hazards, usually easy to avoid with reasonable vigilance, include sea-urchin spines and bites from moray eels or small sharks. Before venturing out at night, get a feel in daylight hours for the reef flat you want to try.

Diving for Dinner

Whether we choose to free dive, use scuba gear, or use a surface compressor of some kind to deliver air at depth via long hoses, descending below the sea surface submerses us, literally and figuratively, in a new world. We come face-to-face with life forms that utilize the same essential gases and nutrients that sustain ourselves, but which live in an entirely different medium. Here, our anatomy relegates us to the status of temporary visitors, where we float, weightless and isolated from the sounds and sensations of our normal environment. The view through our face mask provides us with a firsthand glimpse of minutiae invisible from above the water's surface, and subjects our bodies to an unfamiliar regime of physical phenomena.

Diving usually permits far greater target selectivity and efficiency than fishing gear deployed from above the surface. Properly executed, an underwater excursion can be the most efficient means of procuring seafood of any method cruisers might consider, with the lowest environmental impact. It is entirely possible to dive overboard and take a single shot or pick up a handful of less mobile invertebrates, and come back aboard without having touched or disturbed *anything* other than the animals chosen for dinner—no crunching around stepping on live coral;

no killing dozens or more baitfish in the hopes of catching something bigger; no breaking off hooked target fish so that they are left to swim around with a hook or lure dangling from their mouth, trailing a long string of monofilament behind; and no "catch and release" of undesirable species, some of which inevitably die from deep hook wounds, ruptured gill filaments, or exhaustion.

Some of the larger invertebrates catchable by hand while wading also occur in deeper water nearby (e.g., various species of conch, scallops, and lobsters) and can also be caught sans sling, speargun, or other equipment. Other organisms may require tool-assisted prying or other removal from the substrate—oysters, mussels, some clams, and abalone. Animals with a broad vertical distribution (e.g., queen conch in the subtropical western Atlantic and Caribbean) may be considerably larger and more abundant at greater depths (25 ft./8 m to over 100 ft./30 m), farther from easy grasp in the shallows. Successful location of these and other benthic invertebrate seafood requires a keen eye for both precise details of preferred habitat, and the usually well-camouflaged individuals themselves. This also holds true for hunting a number of fish species. It's the same familiar story: search, read the signs, locate, and capture.

Bruce Austin free-diving at the mouth of Thunderball Cave (Staniel Cay, Exuma Islands, Bahamas).

SEARCH STRATEGIES

How do you do all of this efficiently in diving mode? Start by using many of the same techniques employed to locate fish for hook and line capture, using either the cruising boat or dinghy and some combination of prior knowledge, depth-sounder, and eyesight to locate prime areas. Take along a glass viewer or put on your face mask and dip your head overboard for a closer look. Local shark population permitting (usually it's no problem, but some places are unsafe), tow one or more divers behind the search vessel on a dock line (make a bridle for multiple divers by attaching the ends to port and starboard transom cleats). Allow them to drop off and pursue individual targets they spot, circling back gently without approaching the area where surfacing divers may pop up. If they need extra time, get downwind/downcurrent of the area, and periodically reverse into the conditions to stay close (be sure to retrieve your towline first). Drop anchor—again, downcurrent of the divers, if they've found structure or encountered a situation that requires more time. If no boat driver is available, set up the anchor for easy deployment, then drift along with your vessel (usually the dinghy) or tow it as you swim along, scanning the area. Whatever you do, keep the boat as close as possible, especially when spearfishing.

INDIVIDUAL SKILLS AND EQUIPMENT

Let's discuss individual skills and equipment from the standpoint of free-diving with minimal gear (i.e., no dive tanks or other underwater breathing apparatus). These skills are important for those who scuba dive or use hookah rigs as well, and hunting and shooting techniques and precautions are virtually the same. As usual, the right equipment makes a huge difference in your learning curve and ultimate performance. Get a low-volume, three-panel dive mask with flexible nosepiece (easy to clear, good peripheral vision); a pair of long, very low resistance fins for maximum thrust with little or no oxygen demand; a weight belt with just enough lead to make your buoyancy neutral or *slightly* negative at the surface; and some form of full-body protection commensurate to the water temperature (even if it's warm, wear a full ⅛ in./3 mm wetsuit or thin Lycra suit for protection from coral scrapes—including a hood if possible). Choose a snorkel with a large I.D., boomerang as opposed to U shape, no corrugated flexible section, no purge valve, and a comfortable mouthpiece (some have soft pads that can be heated to conform exactly to your teeth).

Work yourself into free-diving gradually, starting shallow and progressing out to greater depths. Execute proper surface dives to get an effective "free

Basic gear for free-diving.

boost" from your vertically raised legs (see fig. 6-1). *Do not kick hard* to get to the bottom—it may seem counter-intuitive at first, but you will have more bottom time with a slower descent made with the absolute minimum of muscle flexure. Use your fins *very gently* during the first part of the descent, until you feel the momentum of your increasingly negative buoyancy take over. Then use your fins, an outstretched arm, and body angle only to control your glide into "inner space." Keep one thumb and forefinger on your nose, and clear your ears as you descend—stop immediately and come back up slightly if one or both fail to clear. (If you cannot efficiently clear your ears, your free-diving will be limited—try *very* slow descents with a scuba tank or regulator attached to a hookah unit, *but don't force it.*)

See if you can lie down, sit, or stand for a time once you reach the bottom. Focus on the smallest details of the new world that surrounds you. Let your mind go free. You may feel a tightness of the throat, or a sensation of not having much air, from the increased pressure compressing your air spaces. That's normal, and you will eventually forget about it. Now start the ascent (you can bend your legs and spring off the seafloor to get a start). You'll need to kick firmly at first, in steady, sweeping strokes to overcome your negative buoyancy. It gets progressively easier as you rise. Hold one hand toward the surface, and look up near the end to avoid surfacing into a boat bottom, propeller, stinging jellyfish, or other hazard. Use the displacement method to clear your snorkel: a few feet below the surface, with head facing skyward, puff some air into the tube, break the surface with your face, then tilt your head forward and back down. *Voilà!* No water in the snorkel, and your face is submerged and looking at the seafloor again.

Alternate dives with your partner, and watch over each other. Excessive hyperventilation prior to your free dive can depress the levels of carbon dioxide that trigger the urge to breathe without increasing available oxygen. Thus, you are "fooled" into

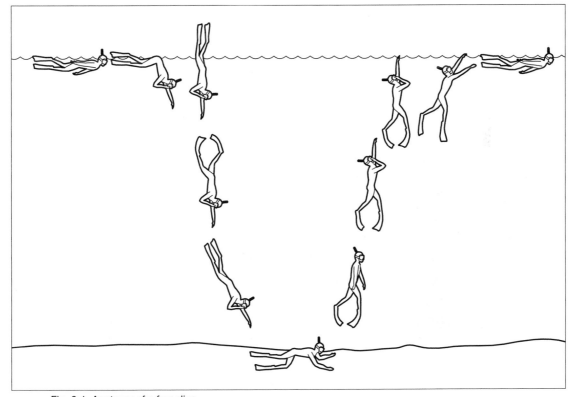

Fig. 6-1. Anatomy of a free dive.

staying submerged too long, and you may lose consciousness on the way up (this is called "shallow-water blackout"). If you experienced a form of tunnel vision near the surface upon ascent, usually accompanied by a cool sensation around your eye sockets, you were getting close. Back off your deep breaths prior to the next dive. If your partner blacks out, descend at all costs, retrieve the person quickly, and get and keep their head above water (discard the weight belt). Don't push the hyperventilation and you shouldn't have this problem.

How deep can you effectively go shooting? This is highly dependent on many factors, obviously, but most people in reasonable physical condition can easily and quickly develop a comfortable working depth between 20 and 40 feet (6 and 12 m). This is plenty, and with more practice you can break into the 40-to 60-foot (12 to 20 m) range, which in many areas results in sharply enhanced fishing success. The number of free divers who can work consistently below 65 feet (20 m) or so is not large, and most do it for a living or at least as a serious hobby. Some artisanal professions feature free divers who regularly exceed 100 feet (30 m); these are special people. Wherever you end up on this spectrum, you will undoubtedly surprise and enjoy yourself, and get a pleasant and excellent workout.

HOW TO RIG UP
FOR FISHING UNDERWATER

Choice of diving and fishing tools suitable for your intended destinations and fishing activities, cruising vessel type and size, physical condition and age, and personal tastes will vary. We offer here an objective outline of the possibilities and review disadvantages and advantages of different options. Our goal is to help you make the best decision.

Dive Gear

Free-diving requires the least gear and therefore the lowest cost. The advantages are less to stow, carry along in the dinghy, and strap on your body. Underwater, your movements are free, unencumbered. It's the best exercise, it is seldom illegal to collect at least some seafood by free-diving, risk of decompression sickness is minimal (only likely with extensive, very deep free-diving followed by a plane ride, but mild

cases have occurred), no license or special training is required. The limitations are restricted, discontinuous bottom time, far greater three-dimensional exposure to sharks, the need to repeatedly and rapidly equalize pressure in your sinus and inner-ear spaces both on descent and ascent, enhanced risk of shallow-water blackout, and less time to extricate yourself from any sort of entanglement while on the seafloor.

Hookah diving consists of breathing air that is pumped by a special gas or electric compressor unit, usually delivered to depth with a long hose attached to a regulator held in the clenched teeth of the diver. Both the gas engine and electric-powered versions of Brownie's Third Lung, for example, have found favor on some cruising boats. Advantages include potentially increased bottom time (certainly over free-diving and often more than with scuba tanks depending on the depth), less cumbersome body gear than scuba, reasonable portability, and possibly less weight and volume of stowage than a rack of scuba tanks. Possible disadvantages include possession of one more bulky engine or other fairly complicated device to maintain and keep dry; unsuitability for use in surf and other agitated sea conditions; drag exerted by the hose and possibly the floating unit on the diver; potential for long, cumbersome hoses to entangle with submerged objects; depth limitations; the requirement to make a life-threatening emergency ascent if the compressor stalls or runs out of fuel; and the ability to support a maximum of not more than two divers who are also restricted in the distance they can range from each other.

Scuba-diving capability shares with hookah the advantage of sustained bottom time and the drawbacks of any breathing-apparatus failure requiring an emergency ascent—and the fact that at least several of the world's top cruising destinations forbid visitors to use the gear to collect seafood. Tanks are bulky to wear, but permit far deeper excursions, with no intrinsic horizontal range restriction and no drag from being attached to a compressor via a long hose. With this comes more potential for diving accidents involving nitrogen narcosis and decompression sickness, although the latter can easily occur using hookah below a 33-foot (10 m) depth. Scuba gear is suitable for use in agitated sea conditions, surf, windward surge channels, and other situations not feasible for hookah. Filling your own tanks, however, requires a heavier-duty compressor than hookah. The heavier compressor usually requires more space and power, weighs more, and often needs more maintenance. Many cruisers get around this by adopting an opportunistic policy of filling tanks at land stations, available at most seaside resort areas and many villages and towns with commercial fisher residents. Possession of at least one full scuba tank and regulator on board is excellent for emergency work below the waterline and, with the appropriate attachments, for numerous jobs requiring compressed air. Both scuba and hookah involve relatively high initial equipment cost and should include a commitment to formal training.

Ideal situations exist for free-diving, hookah, and scuba diving. You can't go wrong, if you do no other diving, by at least giving free-diving a try in safe, shallow conditions. The aesthetics alone are worth it.

Miscellaneous Tools

Regardless of dive-gear type, several simple hand tools can greatly assist your efforts. Prying tools are essential for collecting some attached gastropods and bivalves. A dive knife that fits neatly into a sheath strapped to your leg or arm might do fine. Bring a nylon mesh dive bag to store invertebrates. Wear at least one protective glove. Take along a gauge for measuring various captured organisms to see if they exceed the minimum legal size. Some gauges are conveniently marked and designed for several species.

Hand tools can be highly effective for catching lobsters, either where regulations forbid spearing or for selected habitat types regardless. The first is a "tickler stick," 1 yard (1 m) or a little more in length, combined with a nylon mesh dive bag. Select a commercially produced fiberglass tickler, cut yourself a piece of wood or aluminum dowel rod, or use a spare sail batten. Most lobster dens feature some sort of back-door exit or opening and are deep enough to allow individuals to back away out of hand's reach. Position your partner at the back exit, with nylon mesh bag placed open against the rear aperture. Push your stick in the front of the den, and try to tap or prod the lobster between the antennae. This usually induces a panicked thrust out the back door and into your waiting partner's bag. If the lobsters in the den choose to bounce around inside rather than shoot out the back, increase the vigor of the stick action until they are sufficiently agitated to attempt an exit.

Sometimes this becomes ridiculously easy, such as during one research project conducting visual fish community samples in the Florida Keys. Fish weren't the only sea life colonizing the artificial reefs we'd constructed of neatly stacked rows of cinder blocks. The reefs looked like high-rise lobster condominiums, with antennae bristling everywhere from the holes in the blocks, each compartment big enough for one lobster. After the fish count, Jim Bohnsack would get behind the condo, choose particularly fat, tasty-looking tenants, and flash me the address by holding up fingers representing column and row number. I'd flick each selection in the face, prompting a short, rapid flight backwards into Jim's waiting dive bag.

Another highly effective lobster hand tool is an all stainless steel snare, consisting of an adjustable loop of multistrand steel cable delivered to the back of the lobster den by a long, small-diameter tube. A push/pull control at the other end effects snare opening and closing. This permits the diver to extend the loop far into the back reaches of the den (much deeper, and in smaller confines, than would be possible by hand), pass it over the tail and forward to the carapace of the lobster, tighten the noose, and extract it unharmed from deep within the reef or rocks. Sublegal-sized individuals and egg-carrying females can be released. These devices are widely used in New Zealand (see top photo page 164).

Pole Spears and Hawaiian Slings

Pole spears and Hawaiian slings are simple "hand-operated" devices powered by a single length of surgical-type tubing. Hook your thumb under the rubber loop lashed to the base of the pole spear, slide your hand forward on the shaft and grip it tightly, aim, and let go (see bottom photo page 164). Note that the spear end releases from close to or beside your face mask, a big advantage for working in the close quarters and dim lighting under a ledge or inside a cave. You can sight the target and, rather than having to back out and guess at the aim, fire

Lobster snare.

Shooting a pole spear

accurately by direct visual reference. Excellent for lobsters (where legal) and for extracting wounded fish that have wedged themselves into a small, dark confine. The threaded spear end allows attachment of different heads most appropriate for specific situations, including three-point "grains" or elongated prongs and standard, flexible-barb spearheads. Shooting requires only one hand, leaving the other free to steady or hold yourself in position. Limitations include fairly short effective range and less velocity than other spearing devices.

Hawaiian slings feature a free-flying spear shaft launched by a loop of surgical tubing bound with twine to a cylindrical wood handle through which

the spear ejects. Shooting requires both hands (fig. 6-2). This implement can deliver deadly, high-velocity shots over considerable distances (easily 20 ft./6 m) in the hands of a powerful diver. It reloads very rapidly and can therefore be used for multiple fish, lobsters, or other animals on a single dive, like a "kebob." It's simple, requires no special maintenance, stores compactly, and because it is not automatically loaded or precocked, it poses no threat to fellow divers. Multiple shafts can easily be utilized where needed to finish off a large specimen or to ward off sharks. Limitations include the potential for large fish to swim away with the shaft if not debilitated by the shot, and thus the requirement to dive deeper and position more carefully for shots; and consequent target limitation according to size and position relative to steep drop-offs and slopes. Lack of an attached line also obligates the diver to secure the catch in very close quarters, usually by grabbing either side of the shaft, which increases vulnerability to sharks and barracuda that may have difficulty distinguishing between you and the struggling prey item.

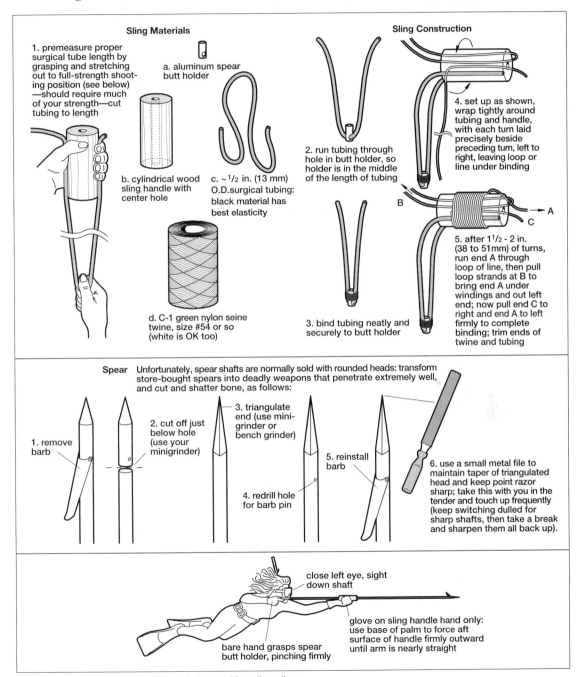

Sling Materials

1. premeasure proper surgical tube length by grasping and stretching out to full-strength shooting position (see below) —should require much of your strength—cut tubing to length

a. aluminum spear butt holder

b. cylindrical wood sling handle with center hole

c. ~1/2 in. (13 mm) O.D. surgical tubing: black material has best elasticity

d. C-1 green nylon seine twine, size #54 or so (white is OK too)

2. run tubing through hole in butt holder, so holder is in the middle of the length of tubing

3. bind tubing neatly and securely to butt holder

Sling Construction

4. set up as shown, wrap tightly around tubing and handle, with each turn laid precisely beside preceding turn, left to right, leaving loop or line under binding

5. after 1 1/2 - 2 in. (38 to 51mm) of turns, run end A through loop of line, then pull loop strands at B to bring end A under windings and out left end; now pull end C to right and end A to left firmly to complete binding; trim ends of twine and tubing

Spear Unfortunately, spear shafts are normally sold with rounded heads: transform store-bought spears into deadly weapons that penetrate extremely well, and cut and shatter bone, as follows:

1. remove barb

2. cut off just below hole (use your minigrinder)

3. triangulate end (use minigrinder or bench grinder)

4. redrill hole for barb pin

5. reinstall barb

6. use a small metal file to maintain taper of triangulated head and keep point razor sharp; take this with you in the tender and touch up frequently (keep switching dulled for sharp shafts, then take a break and sharpen them all back up).

close left eye, sight down shaft

bare hand grasps spear butt holder, pinching firmly

glove on sling handle hand only: use base of palm to force aft surface of handle firmly outward until arm is nearly straight

Figure 6-2. How to make and shoot a Hawaiian sling.

Both Hawaiian slings and pole spears are legal in at least one vast, prime cruising destination that does not permit spearguns—the Bahamas—but are now illegal for cruisers to use in the nearby Turks and Caicos Islands.

Band-Powered Spearguns

Band-powered spearguns use the same principle as pole spears and Hawaiian slings. The more serious models, however, harness more power by utilizing two or more stout surgical-type rubber bands that clip into notches on the spear shaft (see photo below). A trigger releases the clips, firing the shaft at great velocity with mere finger pressure. A safety latch prevents accidental firing, and a considerable length of line connects the butt end of the shaft to the gun. Models storing this line on a fishing reel complete with adjustable drag are available.

These spearguns empower the undersea hunter with the ability to seek large, strong quarry. The extreme end of the spectrum involves diving in open ocean waters to shoot big tuna, wahoo, mahi mahi, and other pelagic species. Attaching the spear line to a length of line fixed to a poly ball allows complete release of the fish line after the shot, boarding of the dinghy or other vessel with speargun in hand, and collecting the catch after it has become fatigued by fighting the buoyancy of the float. This is a viable strategy for cruisers targeting larger individuals in passes, deep lagoons, and near outer reef slopes. Bold spearfishers do this offshore around seamounts

and in open water; for example, in order to shoot at tuna and other predators slashing through balled-up schools of bait fish.

Band-powered spearguns confer the same power on any diver strong enough to pull a light trigger, and allow many shots too risky for a Hawaiian sling, such as those aimed at a background of deep water and shots from above and behind large fish heading over a deep wall or ledge. They also permit the diver to hang motionless in midwater and take careful aim from greater distances at undisturbed subjects. After the shot, the diver can maintain a safe distance from the animal while handlining and getting it to the boat. Drawbacks include slow time to reload, danger from accidentally leaving the safety off when loaded, less flexibility in situations requiring multiple shaft use, and their illegality for use by cruisers and other visitors to at least the Bahamas and the Turks and Caicos.

Over the years, several incidents document cruisers utilizing band-powered spearguns for self-defense against intruders aboard their vessels in countries that remove and hold firearms, which could be considered another possible advantage.

Powerheads

Powerheads, or bangsticks, are underwater firearms that usually use 12-gauge or .357-Magnum rounds. Sharp contact from a thrust against a solid object activates a heavy, spring-loaded, stainless steel firing pin, which detonates the round from a short barrel. Much

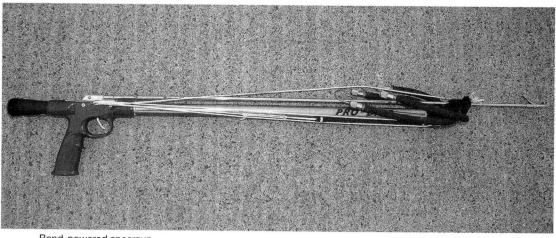

Band-powered speargun.

of the devastation inflicted on the target comes from the rapidly expanding gases forced into the body by the barrel end pressed at that moment against it. These weapons have proven capable of immediately dispatching extremely large sharks. They have been used to decimate some shallow-water species of giant groupers such as the jewfish *(Epinephelus itajara).* One small group of commercial fishers, using mixed gas to dive to 300 feet (91 m) on seamounts off the east coast of Florida, employs powerheads to dispatch gags *(Mycteroperca microlepis)* and other groupers efficiently and to fend off big sharks.

Powerheads might be helpful to cruisers for shark protection, but one could argue that if you really need to carry a bangstick, you should consider safer ways to catch seafood for dinner. I carried a small .357-Magnum bangstick in a compact rack on my scuba tank for two years while diving alone doing fish census work in partyboat chum slicks off the outer reef of the Florida Keys. I'd tested it several times on sponges, and it gave me smug reassurance when the occasional shark appeared. One day I surfaced, climbed on board my small skiff, and noted a lot of white water and thrashing alongside the partyboat. I called over to Steve McKenny, the skipper, and he answered that a customer had brought in a bull shark and was determined to keep it, but they didn't have any firearms on board to kill it. I said no problem, I'd come over and take care of it with the bangstick. I got the anchor up, motored over, tied up, leaned down, popped the devastating weapon sharply against the shark . . . the firing pin clinked dully and nothing happened. A brief slide show of recent shark encounters (all completely benign) flickered through my mind, with the realization that I had had no protection after all, slapping like a cold, wet fish tail across my face. I called the manufacturer later that afternoon. "You *did*, of course, seal all of your rounds with nail polish *(dummy)*, like it says in the instruction manual *(idiot)*?" I'd missed that somehow. Subsequently coating the bullets and then regularly testing veterans of multiple dives proved the manual correct. Using a powerhead above water will work once, but destroy the machining of the barrel.

STALKING, SHOOTING, AND AVOIDING MISHAP

Your journey into the world of fishing while cruising will immeasurably increase the intimacy of your relationship with the sea. This intimacy is probably at no time greater than when you slip into the ocean, spear in hand, to go hunting beneath the waves. The decisions you make based on the accuracy of your perceptions, capacity for astute observation, and knowledge of your environment will nowhere have more direct consequences for your success and personal safety.

Reading the Signs

Interpretation of the subtleties of habitat gradations and types; camouflage schemes; ephemeral sightings and movements; and the identification, biology, and behavior of targets, potentially dangerous predators, and other hazardous marine life will profoundly influence the course of your diving and wading endeavors for seafood. You have immersed yourself in the environment that you intend to exploit. You must not only decipher and anticipate the actions of your intended prey, but also the effect your own movements and behavior will have on those of the target as well as animals that may occasionally compete with you for the target. Your choice of action may influence the outcome of encounters with animals that are scrutinizing *you* as potential prey.

♦ *Daytime resting schools.* Worldwide, many of the smaller species of grunts and sweetlips (Family Haemulidae) and snappers (Family Lutjanidae) aggregate during daylight hours near reefs and other structures to rest, then disperse to forage over adjoining, less-sheltered habitats at night. Their reluctance to leave the vicinity of the structure during daylight may allow repeated shots despite the general agitation caused by stalking and shooting. Location of one such school can result in enough fish for dinner.

♦ *Attracting targets.* It is common to locate an optimal habitat for large, desirable target species (e.g.,

(continued next page)

Reading the Signs (cont.)

groupers in an area of open sandy bottom dotted-with high-profile coral heads in 55-foot/17 m depth) and make a number of free dives without spotting a target. Often, targets can be induced to show themselves. On your next dive, settle down on the bottom and tap the reef sharply with your spear, or shoot a small fish so that it struggles and makes noise. Look around—frequently one or more heads will emerge from caves and crevices to see what's going on. If you stay long enough, one may approach close enough for a good shot. If not, mark its spot, go up, and then dive down on the location and attempt to get a shot. When you do shoot a fish, even if you get a kill shot, other individuals will appear to check out the action. You may be able to shoot a second fish on the same shaft if you are using a Hawaiian sling—just wind up and shoot with the other fish still impaled, then retrieve and surface with both fish in one dive. An area that looked dead initially may suddenly come very alive. Scan for the arrival of sharks before each shot.

♦ *Interpreting and influencing target behavior.* Throughout the animal kingdom, a squared-shoulders, face-on, eyes-staring body posture is a threat, while shoulders sideways, eyes averted or looking elsewhere is a nonthreatening posture. Your posture near prey can grossly affect their tendency to flee out of range, or allow you to approach close enough to shoot. Avoid square-on approaches and heavy eye contact. Sidle up obliquely, watch from the corner of averted eyes. Cock and aim your sling or swing your speargun on line slowly; be as subtle as possible. With certain species (e.g., some of the large snappers), you can transform initial flight into an approach by heading straight for the bottom, turning your back on the fish, and gently scratching the sand in front of you. Stay long enough and they might turn around and approach closely from behind, allowing you to cock and turn slowly for a close shot.

♦ *Shot selection and timing.* You will become familiar with the idiosyncrasies of the species you hunt during your voyage . . . whether you are taking your shot by hand, with a Hawaiian sling, pole spear, snare, net, speargun . . . and develop a sense of when to make your move. Spiny lobsters initially may step outward from the den and briefly expose themselves to easier capture, or speed up as they become aware of your presence as they walk on the reef flat. Squid, octopuses, and Indo-Pacific cuttlefish exhibit specific postures just as they are ready to disappear in a cloud of ink. Some fish species freeze behind a soft coral, as if they think you don't see them, and allow you an excellent shot through the flimsy growth. Others leave their head exposed from a cave, hole, or crevice, feeling secure with their body inside, thus permitting an easy shot—but not if you approach too close. Some swim away in a ritualized zigzag that, with proper anticipation, may create an opportunity for a long, looping shot through the shoulder and into the head.

♦ *Predator identification and behavior.* Know your shark species and their general tendencies. Increased speed and directional changes, closer approaches, and erratic movements all signal elevated excitement. One unequivocal danger sign by Indo-Pacific gray reef sharks (*Carcharhinus amblyrhynchos*) is an arched-back, pectoral-fins-down posture, accompanied by exaggerated head movements and swimming motion. Due to strong territorial behavior, this can occur whether or not you are spearfishing; it is your cue to vacate the area immediately or risk an unprovoked bite. Rarely, great barracuda (*Sphyraena barracuda*) exhibit similar behavior, and though we have never witnessed a subsequent attack, we keep a close eye on such individuals and usually move off to another area rather than challenge them. Other obvious signals that the situation is getting out of hand with sharks are repeated circling or close approaches; any sort of nudging, bumping, or rubbing contact; or fast, head-on approaches, especially open-mouthed. Attempt never to allow the situation to develop to this stage. You should not be in proximity to a dead or wounded fish with aggressive sharks or larger barracuda nearby. Both are extremely fast and may flash in on the fish you are holding, inadvertently grabbing part of you. The arrival of larger shark species that show any persistent interest in you, or show up after

---

Reading the Signs (cont.)

some shooting activity, deserves your respect and full attention, if not an exit from the water.

♦ *Other hazardous marine life*. Cone shells, stonefish and other scorpionfish, half-buried stingrays, toxic sponges, fire coral, Portuguese man-of-war and many other hydrozoans, jellyfish, and sea snakes, to name a few, can cause the wader or diver everything from mild discomfort to death. Perhaps the most dangerous known venomous marine animal is the relatively innocuous-looking cubomedusae *Chi-*

ronex fleckeri, or sea wasp, a shallow-water Indo-Pacific jellyfish whose sting may cause death in seconds to several minutes. Also, many invertebrates and fishes can be toxic to eat for a variety of reasons. The primary defense against this entire category of mishaps is knowledge (see chapter 10 and appendix 2 for more details). Local knowledge is also particularly indispensable in the case of hazardous marine life and is more useful if you know what questions to ask.

The first decision is whether to dive at all. Rarely, you will encounter coastal shark populations featuring numbers, sizes, and a degree of aggression sufficient to discourage getting in the water for any reason. Some locations harbor other dangers—a European cruiser went overboard in 1998 to check his anchor in murky conditions in the Solomon Islands and was killed by a crocodile. Other factors are depth, turbidity, proximity to deep water, current, time of day, availability and competency of a dive partner, support vessel and equipment, weather, and local knowledge. Best environmental conditions for spearfishing are good sunlight, underwater visibility significantly greater than depth, and manageable current and sharks. These conditions vary by latitude and locality, but when you start to push these, safety margins can plummet. If you have never been to the area, do some explorations, watch what goes on, take your time . . . ask questions if there are any inhabitants or other mariners.

The next decision is how, what, and when to grab or shoot. Apprise yourself of all local regulations (e.g., marine reserve boundaries, size and bag limits, closed seasons, and protected species) and purchase proper licenses. Understand and be sensitive to local culture and mores—what are the unwritten laws governing exploitation of near-shore resources? Consult local knowledge—what fish and invertebrate species and sizes are known to be ciguatoxic or otherwise dangerous? Are there other hazards to consider, and how are these best avoided or handled (e.g., seasonal stinging jellyfish and poisonous sea snakes)? Once this is all taken care of and

you're in the water, apply the same how, what, and when questions to potential targets as they come into view.

Carefully and continuously analyze your target, situation, and shot as you descend. Scan around 360 degrees at least once on the way down. Don't hesitate to hold off if things change . . . a kill-shot angle is transformed into a suboptimal shot . . . the fish moves into a darkened cave, or down a deep wall . . . will shooting create a situation where you will be making repeated dives to extract a noisy, bleeding, wriggling fish? Not good. When there's less time, as in the case of faster-moving, less bottom-oriented species (i.e., some snappers and wrasses, jacks, trevallys, mackerel, tuna, perhaps a wahoo or mahi mahi), consider other debilitating shots, aimed at the lateral line/spine, through-the-shoulder head shots, and vertical shots (usually from above the fish). Try never to gut-shoot a fish; it is very likely that it will tear off and eventually die, bleeding profusely, after swimming away too rapidly for you to recover it. Anticipate your post-shot position—will you be able to subdue a wounded target and get back to the surface? Remember that with a sling you must follow and grab the spear shaft, engage the fish, and then ascend. Spearguns afford the luxury of shooting and heading back up, holding the gun with the impaled fish struggling well away from the diver; however, be aware that some fish in this position may retaliate for shooting them by swimming over and biting you. Dogtooth tuna and sharks both have this tendency.

Regardless of weapon, again scan 360 degrees as you ascend after the shot. If you spot a shark approaching purposefully, don't be proud or stingy, just quickly donate the fish (drop the shaft and everything else if things are happening fast—you'll probably be able to retrieve it from the bottom after things settle down). Cover your partner throughout each dive, and descend immediately if he or she is approached by a shark. If you aren't up to rushing down and getting between your partner and the shark, and shooting it at close range if necessary, then you should not be spearfishing together.

Once on the surface, get the fish out of the water quickly. Storing fish underwater on a stringer or hooked to a float is asking for trouble. Always keep the dinghy or cruising boat nearby. Be cognizant of other predators that may come in for a bite of your fish, larger morays (rarely) near the bottom, and barracudas throughout the water column. Too much melodrama? Not a chance. Spearfishing is inherently dangerous, and as you inevitably get more proficient, you'll go deeper and shoot larger, more challenging quarry; sooner or later, you'll face some interesting situations. Even a relatively small bite far from medical care can have permanent consequences.

Two other temptations that may befall the increasingly competent, as yet unscathed hunter/ diver are nocturnal seafood collection and a dip into blue open-ocean water. You can get away with either under specific conditions. As a general rule, however, engaging with struggling animals in either darkness or anywhere you can't see the bottom (like around floating debris offshore) ranges from mildly risky to decidedly dangerous. Your chances improve greatly if you can go with an experienced local or get in with only the camera and swim around quietly without attempting to shoot or capture anything. The safest option, depending on circumstances or when in doubt, may be simply to remain on board.

SHARK STORIES

There's no substitute for experience. We offer the following true accounts for the lessons that they teach.

♦ *Near Hopetown, Abacos, Bahamas.* Excited about learning a new skill two decades ago, I remained in the water much too late hunting for groupers in the reef shallows. I shot a small

yellowfin grouper *(Mycteroperca venenosa)* in the rapidly fading light and surfaced with it dangling on the end of the shaft below me. A stout gray shape brushed between my legs and hit the spear shaft with such force that the grouper came off, whereupon the confused 4½ foot (1.4 m) reef shark *(Carcharhinus perezi)* excitedly bumped and nuzzled my ankles and fins, oblivious to the blows I was landing with my spear shaft. Finally, the barb fell out perpendicular and poked the shark sharply in the gill slits, causing a short dash off and a fast, tight circle, whereupon it caught sight of the sinking grouper and pounced on it.

♦ *Offshore of Sandy Point, Abaco, Bahamas.* At the same inappropriate time of day a couple of years later, a young teenager from Islamorada, Florida, was in the water with a fish he'd shot. He and his father were cruising the area in their sailboat. A small reef shark *(Carcharhinus perezi)* came barreling in and bit the boy on the back of a leg, removing a sizable chunk of flesh and severing an artery. The VHF radio wasn't working well, and the father had no recourse but to sail as fast as possible to Sandy Point, the nearest settlement, which took hours. His son was dead by the time they arrived.

♦ *Tobago, West Indies.* My friend Hollis John was free-diving recently, trying out a new speargun. He shot a small (4 ft./1.2 m) shark and noticed that the line had gone slack as he ascended to call for the boat. In the next instant, he felt a hard jolt and excruciating pain as the shark bit him forcefully on the inner hip, narrowly missing his genitals. Hollis survived the loss of considerable blood and a piece of flesh and muscle.

♦ *Central Bahamas.* A commercial spearfisher shot a large grouper with his Hawaiian sling and rushed in to secure the catch. Just as he engaged, a massive bull shark *(Carcharhinus leucas)* moved in and engulfed the grouper, spear shaft, and diver; only his lower legs remained visible. His partner immediately descended at full speed and shot the shark, causing it to cough out the diver in distress. He got the gravely wounded man to the surface, the boat crew hauled him aboard, and a fast radio call to a nearby island by chance caught an airplane preparing to take off from the small runway for Nassau. The fishing boat blasted in and got their unconscious victim on the plane. By the time he got to the hospital, the diver had suffered extreme blood loss from massive, deep lacerations over most of his body. His survival following a mass blood transfusion and many hundreds of stitches was described as miraculous. He still resides in Spanish Wells.

♦ *Berry Islands, Bahamas.* The 7-pound (3 kg) hogfish *(Lachnolaimus maximus)* was dimly visible, lying on its side far under a coral head that towered up over a deep, undercut ledge, pumping out clouds of typically green-looking blood from a gut shot that had punctured the heart. I was backing out in preparation for drawing a bead with the sling when I was suddenly slammed to the roof of the narrow cavern by a very excited reef shark *(Carcharhinus perezi)* that was stuffing itself enthusiastically inward toward the source of the blood. My face mask was pressed to the top of its snout, then shoulders and back, and both of us were squirming hard, the shark forward, myself in reverse. I finally broke free in the enlarged outer part of the opening and began to rise. I was able to clear and center the mask in time to see the confused 6-foot (1.8 m) shark come flying back out of the hole to rejoin me, frenetically bumping my legs and fins in search of the fish. My clumsy blows to its head and body with the spear shaft appeared to go unnoticed. This continued during our initial rise from the bottom, until suddenly we emerged from the cloud of fish blood; the shark immediately disengaged and slammed back into the hole.

♦ *The next day, Berry Islands, Bahamas.* I spotted a fat 15-pound (7 kg) Nassau grouper *(Epinephelus striatus)* gliding slowly along the lip of a steep drop-off 45 feet (14 m) down. The fish turned, descended the wall, and entered a large cave at 65 feet (20 m) as I approached from the surface. Looking in from the entrance, I could make out the pale outline of the fish hovering comfortably, tail down, at the back of the cav-

ern 15 feet (4.6 m) away. The shot thumped through the fish just behind the head, missing the spine, so that the stunned grouper began kicking back and forth. Still on high alert from the previous day's incident, I took a quick glance around . . . no predators. I squirted in, grasped the shaft; then I noticed a chimney leading out the back of the cavern and eased up into this tunnel, hoping not to have a shark encounter in the tight quarters. I popped my head out of the chimney and again scanned in all directions—still clear, now 45 feet (14 m) to go, so I wriggled out of the hole with the fish and began ascending steadily, spinning and looking as I went. Just as my field of view shifted to the infinite blue offshore of the wall on the second revolution, a bulky shadow materialized in my peripheral vision through a side panel of the mask, causing my head to snap around. A burly, pot-bellied reef shark *(Carcharhinus perezi)*, about 8 feet (2.4 m) long, was tracking up from the depths, angling up directly for me, tail wagging and head swinging side to side. Still 35 feet (11 m) below the surface, the only choice was to unload the fish, fast— I slammed my right palm against its head and pushed it quickly off the butt of the spear. The shark snapped its head up, accelerated like a rocket, and was literally in the blink of an eye, inhaling the grouper 3 feet (1 m) from my knees. The momentum of the upward rush carried it to eye-to-eye level with me. The jaws popped loudly as they hit the grouper's spine, distended once more; the fish disappeared into the hunched body of the shark immediately in front of my face, blood puffing out of the gill slits. All in the same motion, the shark whirled off and sped out of sight, leaving a strong swirl of turbulence.

♦ *Cocos Island, Costa Rica, eastern Pacific.* I eased over the side of the dinghy and tried to be happy about the fact that all I could make out below me in the gloom were the backs of large scalloped hammerhead sharks *(Sphyrna lewini)*. A friendly long-distance-dive charter captain had explained how to experience this incredible aggregation. We motored to the adjacent rocks,

MICHAEL H. OWENS

Excited Caribbean reef shark *(Carcharhinus perezi)* swings by close to the transom as we clean fish at anchor (Carters Cay, Abacos, Bahamas).

anchored, and descended with scuba tanks to sit on a rocky perch and watch these majestic animals mill around off the deep wall, occasionally swinging in for a closer look at us through dark eyes mounted at the ends of the strangely protruding lobes of the hammer.

♦ *Palmyra Atoll, Line Islands, United States.* Drifting slowly in the gentle tide of the pass, I snorkeled along holding onto a 20-foot (6 m) painter attached to our inflatable dinghy, occasionally free-diving for closer views of coral and fish. A few fat, lazy blacktip reef sharks *(Carcharhinus melanopterus)* swam by from time to time, minding their own business. My peripheral vision registered a larger shadow midwater in the pass, sweeping its long tail in a slow, deliberate cadence; the blunt, squarish head swept gently side to side as it pushed into the current. I began to hoist myself into the dinghy but held off for a better view as the faint, distinctive stripes of the 9-foot (2.7 m) tiger shark *(Galeocerdo cuvier)* became visible. This fairly small (for this species) individual never changed course, swimming by less than 15 feet (4.6 m) from me, the oversize, solemn

black eye calmly appraising the stranger. Once past me, the shark slowly exaggerated one sweep of its head for a parting glance, and continued on for a night of foraging for smaller sharks inside the lagoon.

♦ *Middle Tuamotus, French Polynesia.* We had several spearfishing encounters with gray reef sharks *(Carcharhinus amblyrhyncos)* during different visits to an uninhabited atoll. Our commercial-fisher diving partner ended one by shooting the shark through the spine from above and behind with his speargun (the point of entry just behind the dorsal, the exit midline from the forward part of the abdominal cavity), resulting in instant immobilization. With a forceful poke of her spear shaft at close quarters into the side of their heads, Wendy repelled two gray reef sharks long enough for us to exit the water.

Sharks aren't sinister. You have entered their world and chosen to share items from their regular menu, right in front of them. Bear in mind the fierceness of the struggle to "make a decent living" and survive in the ocean. It's only reasonable to forgive apparent rudeness at times when they don't wait for an invitation to join you.

With the exception of territorial reef sharks and the largest, most voracious species, it is rare to have unprovoked problems. Think about your other diving experiences . . . it's cute when an angelfish, or even a 50-pound (23 kg) amberjack, curiously moves in for a bold, close inspection. If a shark does *exactly* the same thing, is this a dark, villainous act? Not necessarily . . . unless you possess a struggling animal, it is often merely a benign, passing, inquisitive look.

You can spearfish for many hours, even days, in some locations and never see a shark. Remaining vigilant, minimizing exposure to high risk such as the moment you engage a struggling fish or time spent "blind" inside enclosures with wounded fish, and diving with a competent partner all make the difference between a controlled encounter and a close call. My last close call was the second Berry Islands incident described previously, which occurred fourteen years ago. Since that time I have learned to take far fewer chances of any kind and pass on more shots. Most important, I acquired a fantastic, brave dive partner, and I virtually never go shooting without her. We watch over and protect each other at all times.

Gear Checklist

Top quality hook-and-line fishing gear appropriate for sailboat use can be purchased at discount prices through a combination of several catalogs that together constitute a "one-stop" international tackle supply shop. Given sound advice, a novice fisher can order a list of specific items sight unseen and soon be properly outfitted. This is not true for many of the items you will need to successfully dive for fish and other seafood. Facial bone structure varies widely among individuals, so specific dive masks must be tested in person for a proper seal before purchase. Likewise, wetsuits, hoods, dive boots, and even snorkels should be carefully tested for fit and comfort, and can frequently be found on sale with some shopping around. Take your time, try several of each before you make final decisions. The following guidelines are intended to steer you toward gear that will enhance your wading and underwater performance, and therefore your seafood-

gathering capability. Where possible, we give specific models that can be ordered without prior personal fitting. Otherwise, the intent is to at least get you to the right part of the rack at your local dive-gear outlet and to ask questions that will focus the efforts of the sales staff on your precise needs. Once again, the first step to success is the right gear—if they don't have it, try elsewhere. Remember that not all salespeople are competent free divers, so don't be talked into buying substitutes.

What if you are outfitting in an area not blessed with a number of competing dive shops? The bind created by the need for personal fitting

A shark swiped part of this yellow jack *(Caranx bartholomaei)*, hooked trolling a feather on a handline from a small sailboat (Mores Island, Abacos, Bahamas).

can sometimes be handled by knowing an exact mask model that seals perfectly to your face, or by sending measurements for a custom wetsuit. Check out ads in dive magazines; fax or call for information. Probably the best arrangement is a relationship with a local dive-equipment outlet that carries a full inventory of quality gear at reasonable prices. If you're not having much luck on your own, talk to equipment experts Terry and Kristi Newth at Holiday Isle Dive Shop or contact Austin's Diving Center (see appendix 1 for contact information). Both shops carry or can get nearly every brand of top gear, including a wide range of spearfishing equipment, and they routinely ship worldwide. (See appendix 1 for other gear sources.)

TABLE 6-1. **GEAR CHECKLIST FOR WALKING, WADING, AND DIVING**

Item	Specific Recommendation	Approximate Price
Lantern	Coleman Dual Fuel Lantern	$45–$90
Dive light	Ikelite Super C-Lite	$40
Headlamp	UK Mini Q40	$19
Dive mask	3-panel, low-volume, full nosepiece	$45–$100
Snorkel	large I.D., boomerang shape, no flex section, no purge valve	$8–$25
Fins	Cressi-Sub Rondine Gara	$109–$129
Gloves	orange nylon fishing gloves, or neoprene for colder water	$3–$25
Dive boots	neoprene with heavy treaded soles for reef walking	$15–$45
Wetsuit	⅛ in. (3 mm) one-piece for maximum mobility and protection	$40–$200
	¼ in. (6.4 mm) for colder water	$40–$250
Hood	with neck/shoulder skirt	$10–$45
Weight belt	any kind	$7–$22
Dive weights	standard lead or new soft weights	$1–$2 per lb.
Shooter	Hawaiian sling with straight cylinder (not tapered) hand grip	$18–$30
Spear shafts	spring stainless steel only—*not cold roll galvanized*	$23–$35
File	6–8 in. (15–20 cm)	$5–$10
Spear shaft storage tube	PVC pipe, I.D. sufficient to house at least 6 shafts, with caps	cheap
Mask sealant	Vaseline—smear around face, especially under nostrils, if necessary	cheap
Nylon mesh dive bags	24 in. (61 cm) x 36 in. (91 cm) or larger for gear and seafood	$8–$12
Plastic water jug	water for drinking and rinsing stinging ctenophores	free
Pry bar	flattened bar for removing mollusks from substrate	cheap
Dive knife	For prying or general use—any sharp, compact model	$16–$65
Lobster snare	available from Coast Dive Centre, New Zealand (see appendix 1 for contact information)	$20–$30
Pole spear	long (about 6 ft./1.8 m), 2-piece for easy storage	start at $20
Speargun	choose according to anticipated targets and personal taste	start at $90
	Seahornet from AB Biller (Australia), available worldwide	$120–$230

7

Hand Tools, Traps, Nets, and Other Assorted Gear

Have you ever seen those romantic photos of a native fisher effortlessly flinging an impossibly large cast net . . . the net stretches in an immense circle, perhaps silhouetted against a sunrise or sunset? Would you like to learn how to do this, no problem?

Or how about taking a shot at the following true or false questions.

1. A method exists for catching all the fish you need, unattended, with a single bed sheet, which will never touch the water.
2. Tie a bowline to form a tight loop in a small-diameter rope, put the end through the loop to form a lasso or noose, and you have all the gear necessary to consistently catch one of the fastest open-ocean fish on the planet.
3. Under the right conditions, you can catch all the lobsters you want without so much as getting your feet wet.
4. Custom-built speedboats designed to chase down and harpoon lightning-fast mahi mahi form the basis for a commercial fishery.
5. A specially carved piece of cow bone dipped near the bottom on a string proves irresistible to octopuses—they grasp it and can be lifted to the boat for capture.
6. Your toenail clippers are actually a deadly weapon which, deployed at sea anywhere in the world, will result in the capture of giant squid to 60 feet (18 m) in length.

What were your answers? If you said *true* to each question, you were wrong only once. (C'mon, you didn't *really* take the bait on the last one, did you?). And for open-minded cruisers, unfettered by preconceived notions about what is "sporting," uninvolved in social conflicts promulgated by political lobbyists for different fishing groups, heedless of "status" or what someone else might think regarding personal decisions about how to fish . . . this is just the beginning. Cruisers are beholden only to a responsibility to respect, conserve, and have the least possible impact on the environment they've chosen to call home.

We touched on some effective hand implements in the last chapter and promised to expand on the general subject of non-hook-and-line methods. Most of these come from artisanal and larger-scale commercial fishing industries, where the very livelihood of the participants absolutely depends on successful catches. This is not a playful pastime, hobby, moment for quiet reflection, or form of contrived entertainment . . . this is often serious, difficult, dangerous work.

What falls into this category? Trawls, dredges, harpoons, seines, drift nets, gill nets, traps . . . some of it so brutally effective that it has been outlawed, the mere mention capable of sparking environmental outcry (occasionally with good reason). Is anything in this subject area worthy of a cruiser's consideration? Absolutely. Even some of the most fervent conservationists and sportfishers use selected items of commercial origin, and so can the most environmentally sensitive cruiser without losing a moment's sleep.

Without being overly judgmental—there's a time and place for most gear and techniques—let's quickly review mostly non-hook-and-line fishing methods of the world for the many lessons to be learned from subsistence and commercial fishers. Some methods are candidates for incorporation into the cruiser's normal repertoire; others may come into play during survival situations. A quick look at the variety of approaches should provide both entertainment and stimulation for your imagination.

Certain of these practices are unsound regardless of the circumstances; for instance, the use of dynamite or bleach. Others are unreasonable based on size, weight, and manpower, such as most trawls and all but the smallest nets of any kind. Cruisers should probably also eliminate most dredges, too, and any sort of bottom trawl, based on detrimental impact to the seafloor. That still leaves us with a full chapter's worth to talk about in various detail. We go out on a limb and promote and describe precisely how to use one particularly flexible, versatile, compact, and fun piece of gear: the cast net.

Gathering by Hand and with Simple Tools

The path from subsistence to mechanized, high-volume commercial fishing spans the existence of our species. Feeling and catching with the feet and hand-picking naturally lead to the invention of devices to extend the reach of human appendages and to broaden the capability of the hands and feet. We've touched on many hand implements used directly to procure the target—prying tools, hooks with handles, scoops, spears, gigs, rakes, and hand nets for use by walkers, waders, and divers. These may assist the capture of prey located at rest or moving normally, or prey that has become stranded usually by stampeding into the shallows, either in pursuit of bait items or fleeing from fishers. Sometimes fishers immobilize fish trapped in tidal pools or other restricted areas by removing the water with hand bailers.

These fundamental tools evolved into a variety of longer-handled implements mostly for catching invertebrates and eels, often in cooler temperate and polar latitudes where they are most abundant. Fishers from Europe, Russia, North and South America, and Asia invented clamps, tongs, rakes, and wrenching gear for taking shrimp, lobsters, mollusks, sea urchins, seaweed, and even edible jelly-fish. Variations of special combs, scythes, and forks dragged through soft sediments—effectively impaling or wounding eels enough to enable collection—see use from upper temperate zones to the equator.

Plummets of different forms further extend the reach of fishers from northern Europe, Asia, and the South Pacific. These consist of weighted barbed prongs in various arrangements, sent down a vertical line to impale slow-moving bottom dwellers, particularly sea cucumbers and flatfish. Glass-bottomed buckets or divers facilitate aiming. Weighted snatch hooks are the reverse of plummets, usually consisting of a large treble hook with lead molded around the shank, operated by casting on a line into a fish school, and jerking rapidly up through the group in an attempt to impale individuals from below or the side.

Many variations of the simple hand spear also extend the reach of humans, but allow capture of faster prey than plummets (fig. 7-1). Fishers either jam these into the quarry without releasing the handle or free-throw the device through the air. Non-vertical shots require practice to adjust for the refraction of light in water, which makes fish appear higher in the water column and farther from the hunter than their actual position. Night lights exacerbate this illusion. Casting mechanisms, consisting of a short lever that greatly increases the range and velocity of the spear, saw widespread use prior to mechanically powered harpoons.

We previously discussed one category of such devices—gigs—that are essentially small harpoons intended for stabbing without leaving the grip of your hand. The most common targets are invertebrates and fish in the shallows. Night hunting with a headlamp is often best. Search for the reflected glow from the eyes of your targets, sneak up on them, and stab forcefully to drive the barbs deep into or through the animal. Firm bottom assists this process.

Harpoons

Harpoons are the next step up from gigs. These weapons are larger, featuring a long, counterbalanced handle and a detachable head joined to a strong running line stored neatly in a container affixed to a float (usually a poly ball) at the other end (fig. 7-2). Active harpoon fisheries still exist for broadbill

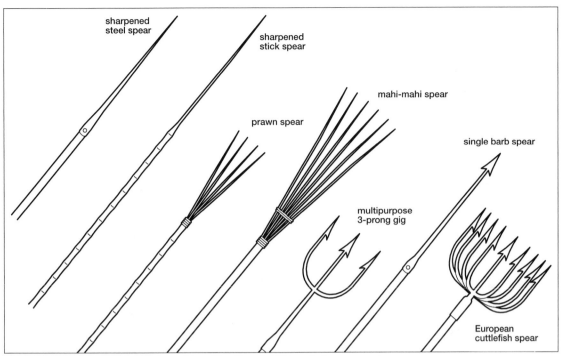

Fig. 7-1. Hand spears (adapted from Von Brandt 1984 and other sources).

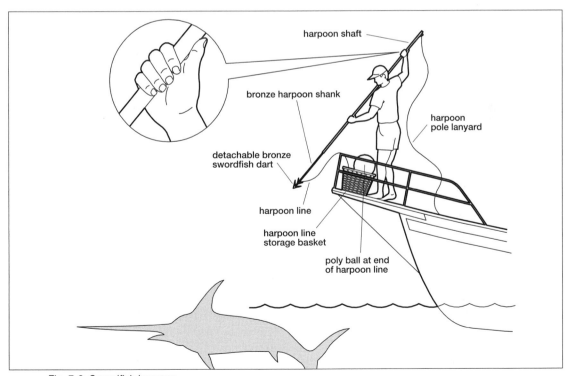

Fig. 7-2. Swordfish harpoon.

swordfish and giant bluefin tuna; the method works for lesser prey, such as smaller pelagics basking near the surface, and for assorted species of rays in deep or shallow water that make delicious table fare.

The best method is to use two hands, one low on the harpoon shaft to aim and guide, the other high to supply the power thrust. Ideally, with a detachable head, you can thrust and hold the handle. You should attach a lanyard to the end of the handle, nonetheless, which also permits the option of longer tosses. Successful shots are nearly always *downward* into an animal swimming beside or immediately forward of the bow. The ideal scenario is to accomplish this positioning slowly and cautiously, although wild maneuvering on alarmed animals, either unable or unwilling to sound, also works.

This is the case for a Polynesian fishery targeting mahi mahi. Purpose-designed skiffs have a unique, far-forward steering station consisting of a vertical bar operated by pushing it side to side. This confers strong one-handed boat control, leaving the other hand free to throw the harpoon, a multipronged affair with a handle much shorter than those used for swordfish and tuna. Fishers chase mahi mahi relentlessly on the surface at high speed, turning sharply to stay right on their tails. Most don't sound. Eventually, they tire and appear to become demoralized, a state signaled by body color suddenly flushing a very dark, opaque, greenish-black, except for a distinctive splotch of almost-white on the lips and nose. A turn back *toward* the chase boat, or turns that no longer respond to the maneuvers of the pursuer, often accompany this color change. This is the time the fisher aims for the head and throws, killing the fish with the tight pattern of prongs, at least one of which is likely to penetrate the brain or spinal-cord termination. These boats are especially numerous throughout French Polynesia's Society Islands.

Larger quarry will rip all of the coils of harpoon line rapidly out of the basket or other container, and should be left to tire suspended from the poly ball float. Top swordfish boats have 25-foot (7.6 m) bowsprits with hydraulic controls that allow the harpooner to adjust angle and distance off the water as the vessel approaches fish on the surface. A good boat might have several fish tiring on poly balls on a sunny day off the North Atlantic's Grand Banks.

One pair of boats brought their own lightweight miniature airplane out with them to assist spotting. Harpoon outfits similar to those used for swordfish adorn vessels based in Maine and elsewhere in New England in the hope of catching a giant bluefin tuna that they can sell to the Japanese sushi market for exorbitant prices.

From the cruiser's standpoint, harpooning is just one more option to have onboard. We've had yellowfin tuna to 50 pounds (23 kg) accompany *Éian* for days on long passages, and often they were close enough to harpoon. Mahi mahi sometimes approach cruising vessels or allow cruisers to get near enough to them for harpooning without wild high-speed maneuvers. Rays in the shallows are also susceptible. Remember, as always, don't harm or harass anything you don't need for consumption and, certainly, please do not apply this method to sea turtles except in survival situations.

Shooting through the Air

Ancient shooting devices, still used to fire projectiles through the air into fish and other prey, include blowguns and various bow-and-arrow arrangements, peaking with the modern crossbow. Harpoon guns became infamous for their role in the decimation of world whale populations yet continue to see limited use. Rifles and shotguns can effectively dispatch fish near the water's surface, more likely from the concussion caused by detonation of the round than by physical penetration of the bullet or pellets.

One exception to this is shooting airborne fish. For instance, a little afternoon skeet-shooting can be effective for capturing flying fish as food or bait. I worked for one captain who would choose calm afternoons far offshore to position himself comfortably near the bow—with his rusty old shotgun, cigar clenched firmly in his teeth, and stained coffee cup of unrefrigerated beer at his side—and plink at flying fish spooked into flight by the hull. A slight change in course was usually all that was necessary to collect downed fish with a long-handled dip net. One day he asked if I'd like to give it a try. Soon a large batch flew in scattered directions in front of us and, unthinkingly, I swung the barrel toward a big one flying off to leeward. I was starting to squeeze the trigger when, by sheer luck, the jib obliterated the target from view just in time—and I narrowly avoided the ignominy of blowing a hole in the sail, or worse, obliterating the forestay. That ended my brief fish-shooting career.

Stunning Methods

Dynamite and other charges, like firearm rounds, concuss fish, but usually on a larger scale. Industrial chemicals like sodium hypochlorite (bleach) can be almost as lethal, cauterizing the gill filaments and therefore the ability to breathe. Both methods are outlawed virtually worldwide.

Natural ichthyotoxins are also usually illegal or heavily regulated. They occur in hundreds of plant species around the globe. Some are indigenous to temperate zones. The majority, however, are tropical. Fishers of varying latitudes discovered and utilized their properties to stun fish, often in limited water bodies like pools and ponds. The active ingredients are protoplasma poisons that have pervasive effects on the nervous system and break down red blood cells, causing suffocation. The general technique is to grind poison-rich plant parts, frequently the roots, and throw the extract into the water. One of the best known and most widely used poisons, rotenone, comes from the tropical twining plant *Derris elliptica*. Operating under strict special permits, scientists use it to collect cryptic species from reefs and other inaccessible habitats.

Other toxins that see significant use are quinaldine, pesticides like paraquat, and sodium cyanide. The practice of divers squirting cyanide solution in and around reefs, particularly in Southeast Asia, Indonesia, the Philippines, Maldives, and the western tropical Pacific, is the most widespread and devastating stunning method. The objective is collection of live ornamental and food fish to supply high-dollar Hong Kong and other Chinese markets; however, the practice kills coral, thus ruining the very habitat necessary to sustain reef-fish target species. Regulations and restrictions are slowly evolving to curb this destructive fishery.

Electricity sees some use for stunning, disorienting, or influencing the swimming direction of fish. Application of DC current between a cathode and anode, to either a fixed or moving area, can prove effective in limited, less saline water bodies. The high conductivity of seawater tends to reduce the tendency of current to pass through fish bodies, mitigating the ability to affect the prey.

Less sophisticated means of stupefying fish include depriving them of oxygen by vigorously stirring up muddy bottom, hammering rocks to shock fish that may be under them, beating ice to mesmerize fish moving sluggishly just below, directly striking fish with clubs or sticks, or hitting them with hand-thrown projectiles like rocks and boomerangs. People in underdeveloped regions continue to feed themselves by these means, and this knowledge could play a potential survival role for a stranded or shipwrecked cruiser.

Using Animals

Dogs, birds, otters, remoras, porpoises, and even horses continue to play a role in human fishing activities today. Trained otters, dogs, and some birds herd fish into the shallows or toward traps, nets, or other set gear. Wild porpoises appear to become conditioned to human herding activities and may play a beneficial role at certain times and locations. Horses pull trawls in the shallows and, in the past, have carried riders in fish-herding and disorientating operations.

Primarily in Asia, a family of swimming seabirds called cormorants physically captures fish for their masters following months of training. A string around the neck prevents them from swallowing the catch. The practice persists only as a tourist attraction in Japan. It remains a commercial enterprise in parts of China.

Perhaps the most improbable documented, widespread utilization of an animal for fishing involves capturing various sucker-fish species; for example, a remora, passing a line through the tail region, and turning the tethered fish loose in sight of a turtle or shark. The remora swims to the new host, attaches firmly with the suction-cup device, and consistently sustains (within a limited target-size range) enough line pressure to retrieve the larger animal to the boat.

Hookless Line Fishing

Recall the old "meat on a string" routine for portunid crabs and freshwater crayfish from chapter 6? The same method applies to clawed cold-water lobsters (the Finnish are big on this), predatory gastropods such as whelks, a Hawaiian crab fishery marking baits suspended near the seafloor with surface floats, and European fisheries for cuttlefish and octopuses.

Unbaited, hookless lures also work for octopuses. These seem to be most widespread in Oceania, and often appear to be inspired by the legendary hatred of rats by the octopus. You may have heard the story of the octopus carrying the drowning rat to safety, only to have the rat ungraciously defecate on its head, creating perpetual, global animosity. Some lures constructed of seashells, sticks, and fiber actually imitate rats, whereas others are more abstract bone carvings. Tongans should perhaps win the gold medal for cow-bone octopus lures. Patterns are usually flattened oval frames enclosing arcing cross members and tapered terminations. Stylized necklace pendants imitating the real thing are common, although the manufacture and utilization of the actual lures are slowly dying with aging artisans. Fishing technique is a variation of deep-jigging, and the specific nuances of the upward and downward motions imparted by the fisher reportedly determine success. The octopus grabs the offering and holds on tenaciously while being brought within range of the landing net.

Other baited or unbaited attractors suspended on lines depend on entanglement rather than holding tenacity of the target. They utilize frayed nylon or other artificial fibers, wool, hemp, hair, and even spider webs to attract and entangle teeth or other roughened or horny projections of the target species. Such lures capture eels, needlefish and houndfish, billfish, and lobsters. One now-illegal New Zealand version of this method was to toss the head of a slaughtered sheep on a line into the sea. Spiny lobsters attracted to the flesh became enmeshed in the wool, permitting capture of multiple individuals per haul.

Another category of hookless devices includes gorges and other precursors of modern fishhooks, usually baited with natural substances. Gorges are relatively straight and baited parallel to the line for easy ingestion, depending on the pull of the line to lodge sideways in the fish's throat or mouth cavity. More strongly bent primitive hooks made of wood, stone, bone, or thorns are designed to penetrate the

wall of the mouth, throat, or gut. These preceded modern hook designs, and remain in active commercial use in some areas today. One strong example is the simply bent stainless steel hook fixed to the pearl-shell lures currently used for commercial skipjack-tuna-fishing in French Polynesia (see chapter 3).

More Tricks for Attracting and Aggregating

We have previously discussed the use of the following.

- ◆ Various purpose-built fish aggregating devices (FADs), including those moored in deep water, attached to drifting vessels, unattached (drifting), and structures resting on the seafloor (artificial reefs).
- ◆ Chum, a concentrated chemical attractant consisting of ground fish, for example.
- ◆ Discontinuous reflection of natural light from shiny lure parts.
- ◆ Chemical light sticks.
- ◆ Night lights.

Brief elaboration on additional attraction methods, some related to these prior subject areas, could be interesting for cruisers. For example, several other types of shelters are effective. The use of brushwood bundles strung along the seafloor in Japan works like surface bundles of sugar cane in the Caribbean—fishers retrieve the FAD lines, lift the bundles from the sea, and shake out the fish stuffed inside. The same method is widespread throughout Asia, Africa, North America, and Europe for collecting eels, herring roe, shrimp, crabs, cuttlefish, and small fish. Other shelters include bamboo or wood tubes set out for eels and multiple vase-like pots or jugs deployed in lines on the bottom for octopuses. In both cases, the animals take up residence, and extreme reluctance to abandon the habitat allows fishers to haul them to the water surface.

Still other shelters attract multiple occupants. Cuba has long boosted spiny-lobster production by placing habitats suitable for residence by juveniles and adults at various depths on the reef shelf, reducing predation and aggregating individuals for capture. The presence of some individuals attracts additional residents, a strong factor also in some lobster and fish traps.

Fishers exploit social aspects between male and female individuals in order to capture other species. For example, trolling or placing female cuttlefish in a basket attracts males, which are then speared or dip-netted in the Mediterranean and in East Asia. This theme also works for fish—either females or rival males, or sometimes artificial replicas—placed in traps to induce other males to enter; examples include burbot in Germany, catfish in Nigeria, and salmon in various locations.

Noisy water-surface disturbance and distress-like vibrations effectively attract fish, as we learned from the use of teasers and surface corks and plugs. Splashing or beating the water can produce a similar effect. Swishing a fishing-rod tip violently back and forth through the water, for example, can immediately agitate and excite sluggish mahi mahi into taking baits or lures. Conversely, systematic splashing by multiple fishers in the shallows can spook fish into waiting nets or other gear. Vibrations from rattles inside all sizes of fishing lures, from large straight runners for marlin to small, light-tackle swimming plugs, may result in significantly greater success. Other fishers design and use rattles to attract specific fish to the vicinity (e.g., sharks in Oceania, groupers in New Zealand, and catfish in Africa).

Last, V-shaped barriers consisting of stacked stone, rigid mesh, or flexible netting, and most often built in rivers, estuaries, narrow passes, and sometimes on tidal flats, act to guide and concentrate moving fish into mazes or waiting fishers. People use this technique worldwide to exploit, for example, migrating eels and salmon, groupers moving en masse through lagoon passes during specific moon phases to aggregate for spawning, and smaller numbers of various species transiting areas on routine daily feeding forays.

Single-Event Snares and Traps

Spring-loaded, triggered aquatic versions of terrestrial traps and snares abound worldwide. Fishers continue to use assorted preset designs that work unattended. Disturbance of the bait triggers the closing of doors and shutters or setting of hooks, due to the harnessed forces of gravity, bent flexible poles or rods, twisted fibers, or springs.

Other devices require manual operation. Pacific Islanders utilize nooses, either plain lasso-style lengths of rope or nooses created by a loop suspended from passing a line to the end of a pole that can be closed by quickly tugging the line at the boat end of the device (fig. 7-3). Noosing pelagic fish basking or moving slowly at the sea surface is popular. Micronesians, particularly the I-Kiribati,

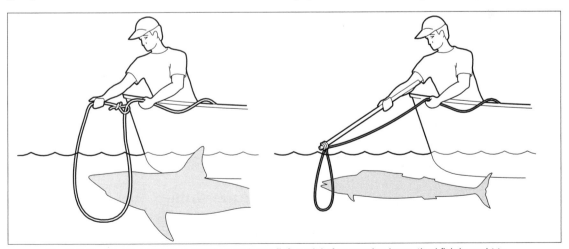

Fig. 7-3. Pacific island nooses: simple rope lasso (*left*, mainly for securing large, tired fish brought to the boat on hook and line; note that noosing large, free-swimming sharks is extremely dangerous) and pole noose (*right*, used to extend the reach of the noose to catch basking wahoo and other species).

are the masters of this method. The primary target, believe it or not, is the speedy wahoo. Sharp-eyed fishers are constantly on the lookout for individuals that are apparently in a state of restful torpor, motionless near the surface like a barely submerged log. They drift or paddle quietly alongside and slip the noose over head or tail, then snatch it rapidly tight. The same method works for excited individuals that have followed a hooked fish, bait, or lure boatside. Sharks and other species also fall prey to this method. A tail rope, of course, is the same technique and may be useful for securing hooked fish that have been battled to the boat. Free-gaffing is effective for almost any situation appropriate for a noose.

Static, fixed rings of wire can also be effective for certain species of fish and spiny lobsters. Unbaited strings of wire rings suspended vertically from bridges or boats, particularly at night, catch large numbers of pilchards under some conditions in the tropical western Atlantic. For some reason, the fish have a tendency to swim head first into small-diameter rings and become firmly stuck halfway through. A Hawaiian lobster snare consisting of two wire rings, side by side with a bait in the middle, works the same way.

Catching Seafood in the Air

We won't keep you waiting any longer on the bedsheet method mentioned in the quiz at the beginning of the chapter. This technique is good for collecting flying fish at night. Select a white sheet and suspend it vertically, like a wall, stretched tightly lengthwise on any makeshift frame in your dinghy. Anchor the dinghy off a beach, reef, other area of known flying-fish abundance, or leave it tied off to your cruising boat's transom. Direct light from a dive light, lantern, or other illumination source onto the sheet, perhaps lashing it in place with duct tape or cord. Leave it deployed after dark. Flying fish attracted to zooplankton in the reflected glow of the light on the sheet will, for various reasons, take short flights, often hitting the sheet and landing in the dinghy. This technique is popular in parts of the Pacific coast of Costa Rica.

Much farther west, Polynesians, Micronesians, and Melanesians seek flying fish at night by more active means. They ride through target-rich areas in small, maneuverable powerboats equipped with a spotlight, and sweep or scoop the quarry in flight with long-handled dip nets. Gill-netting has largely replaced traditional fisheries for netting airborne flying fish in Taiwan and Madagascar.

Elaborations on the Costa Rican boat trap for flying fish abound in India, China, Indonesia, and Southeast Asia. Fishers suspend a white board at a steep angle the length of the vessel to form a *submerged* barrier, then usually move slowly near shore. Fish, shrimp, and prawns encounter the alarming underwater wall, leap to clear it, and land in the boat, sometimes with the help of a screen backstop positioned on the opposite side of the boat.

Broad floating rafts are a popular means of capturing mullet in coastal areas of the Indian and Pacific oceans, and particularly in the eastern Mediterranean, Black Sea, and Caspian Sea. The method always involves getting the mullet to jump onto the raft(s). Russian fishers, for instance, spook mullet from the interior of a circular arrangement of rafts, causing them to leap up and fall onto them.

Other Mediterranean fishers deploy untended verandah nets, which consist of an underwater fence extending from surface to bottom, backed by a wide, angled net above water for catching fish that attempt to leap over the fence barrier. Another variation, designed for salmon, is to construct a transverse fence across a stream or river and suspend round catch baskets on poles above and near it; leaping salmon fall into the baskets.

Pit traps, like those described previously for coconut crabs in the South Pacific, are employed to catch fish that migrate overland at night between water bodies in African swamps and Asian rice paddies. Chinese fishers bait hooks, suspend them in the air over water, and allow them to fish untended— fish that leap up to grab the bait become hooked by the velocity of their own falling bodies.

Long-Handled Dip and Bully Nets

Long-handled dip nets, similar to those described for catching airborne flying fish, work well for submerged, near-surface flying fish, shrimp, crabs, and squid attracted to night lights displayed by anchored

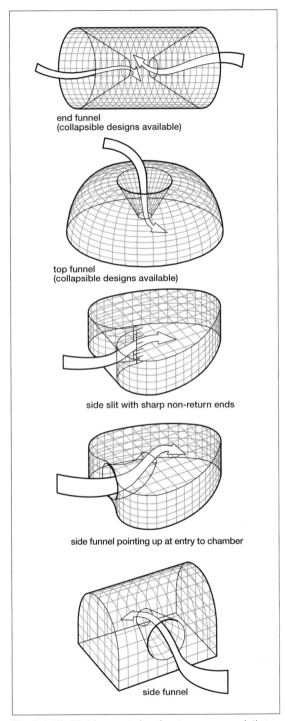

end funnel
(collapsible designs available)

top funnel
(collapsible designs available)

side slit with sharp non-return ends

side funnel pointing up at entry to chamber

side funnel

Fig. 7-4. Worldwide, most chamber traps are a variation of one of these fundamental fish and invertebrate designs.

vessels. Acquiring such a net with a soft, small-meshed, knotless nylon bag and long, multiple-piece handle enables any of these options.

Bully-netting is also a night activity, highly effective for collecting spiny lobsters and other benthic invertebrates. This type of net could also prove helpful for night-walking the reef flats. Bully nets have a 6- to 12-foot (1.8 to 3.7 m) handle. The frame is perpendicular to the handle. Fishers normally pole or drift in small boats over the shallows with a strong light source, thrusting the net down over lobsters (and sometimes crabs) out walking the open bottom in search of food. The alarmed invertebrates thrash up off the seafloor and into the inverted net bag, permitting the fisher to deftly sweep the handle to the surface to complete the capture.

Traps

Traps are highly effective for some fish, lobsters, crabs, shrimp, and octopuses. They are the principal gear for numerous important high-volume commercial fisheries throughout the world. At the same time, their use in subsistence fisheries is equally pervasive. Fish traps have proven *too* effective for sustainable commercial use in Bermuda, Florida, and many Caribbean islands. They have been the center of considerable debate and emotional controversy, particularly among user groups in highly exploited areas.

Nevertheless, several cruising situations permit unobtrusive, completely responsible use of specific small traps over a broad geographical range. Design details tend to be highly regionalized, as do regulations concerning mesh size, degradable panels that prevent ghost traps (those lost at sea by fishers) from continuing to fish, and reserves where trap use is illegal. *Be sure* to check the rules before using a trap, because penalties can be severe.

Let's get ideas for traps suiting specific cruising environments by taking a brief tour of various designs from around the world (fig. 7-4). Huge, heavy steel traps catch Alaskan king crabs in the Bering Sea. Wood-slat traps of different styles procure cold-water clawed lobsters, spiny lobsters, and stone crabs. Traps made from wire, bamboo, plastic, net mesh, reeds, and other materials reap everything from deepwater shrimp, various crabs, groupers, snappers, salmon, sardines, herring, and eels to assorted reef fish and baitfish. Fenced trap systems consisting of variously shaped wings to funnel fish into mazes and chambers combine the principles of barriers and individual trap units. Weirs and pound nets fall into this category and are frequently used to capture large numbers and schools of fish, sometimes focusing on smaller species.

Traps best suited for use by cruisers are relatively small, ideally collapsible, and effective for a variety of invertebrates and fish. Most traps operate on the principle of behavioral disorientation of the target species following entry. Figure 7-4 illustrates various openings that accomplish this purpose. Baits, either tough, long-lasting material or strong-smelling substances encased in perforated containers, induce animals to enter. The presence of one or more individuals already in the trap often compels others to enter. Florida fishers are permitted to leave limited numbers of sublegal-sized spiny lobsters inside traps for this reason.

Cruisers successfully and routinely employ com-pact traps for subsistence seafood collection in North America's Pacific Northwest and Alaska (often for various shrimp and crabs), New Zealand (mostly for spiny lobsters), the southeastern United States (mostly portunid crabs), and many other mostly temperate and subtropical areas. Purchase traps locally or construct them yourself. Ask questions, learn the local species and techniques, and experiment with trap designs from other areas. Who knows, the locals may soon be coming to you for advice!

Dredges and Beam, Bottom, and Midwater Trawls

Dredges are heavy baskets, sometimes with rake-like projections, dragged relatively slowly through unobstructed bottom types mostly for mollusks and crustaceans. Hand-operated units or versions small and light enough to tow by dinghy or cruising vessel might suit seafarers who have sufficient storage area and a love of mussels, cockles, clams, and scallops.

Fixed traps in lagoon passes, featuring V-shaped fence wings leading to a maze of chambers, are common in the South Pacific. These fishers are ejecting sharks from a trap chamber in the Tuamotu Archipelago, French Polynesia, prior to herding and extracting their catch.

Beam trawls are similar to some dredges. Generally, they are designed to skim the seafloor more lightly, permitting faster towing speeds and enabling the capture of fish as well as invertebrates. The catch unit is flexible mesh, held open by a beam the length of the mouth. A tickler chain may disturb the target animals from the bottom and into the trawl.

Rather than a beam, bottom and midwater trawls usually use a combination of paddle-like boards, floats on the upper lip, and weights on the bottom lip to keep the mouth of the unit open. Additional floats, diving planes, and weights control trawl depth so that variations of the fundamental design may capture organisms throughout the water column. Side- and forward-scanning sonar units enable commercial vessels to aim trawl paths to intercept massive schools and aggregations of fish, cephalopods, and crustaceans.

What's this got to do with cruising? Well, small, compact midwater trawls can be very useful and productive under some conditions. One good example combines commercial trawl design ideas, is cheap and easy to build, can be easily towed from the dinghy, and might enable an exciting and productive evening of shrimping (fig. 7-5). The best time to deploy this gear is at night, during the right season (usually winter or early spring), at the proper moon phase (often the darker phases), and on the best tidal phase (frequently outgoing) to collect penaeid shrimp that are migrating well off the bottom. Fish-ers attempt to augment the catch by directing strong lights forward of the trawl, attracting more of these positively phototaxic animals to the mouth of the gear. Members of this shrimp family occur worldwide in tropical and subtropical regions, particularly near continental estuarine systems.

Nets for Scooping and Lifting

Woven baskets designed to scoop or push through the water, sometimes with a handle, are still used extensively in Africa and Asia. Scoop nets, more advanced devices featuring various opening configurations, handle types and lengths, and mesh materials, see widespread use in the same areas and nearly everywhere else in the world (fig. 7-6). We described using scoop nets for the midair capture of flying fish, securing various invertebrates brought in with hookless baited lines, and for landing fish brought boatside on hook and line. Natives of North and Central America, Europe, India, Asia, Africa, and Oceania catch salmon, mullet, eels, shrimp, crabs, cephalopods, bivalves, and many other edible organisms by dragging, pushing, or dipping with scoop nets.

Scrape nets are generally larger, often flatter cousins of scoop nets. The biggest versions have reduced or no handles and use the bow, transom, or gunwale of the boat as a fulcrum.

Stow nets apply the idea of scoop nets primarily to rivers and estuaries, letting the current do the

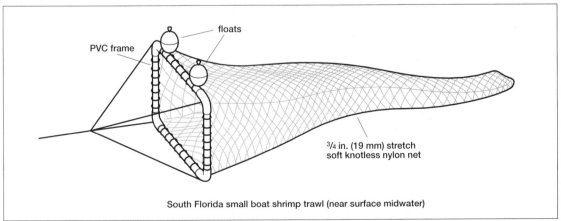

floats

PVC frame

3/4 in. (19 mm) stretch
soft knotless nylon net

South Florida small boat shrimp trawl (near surface midwater)

Fig. 7-5. South Florida small-boat penaeid-shrimp trawl, a midwater design intended to run near the surface. These trawls also work deployed in current from stationary structures like bridges, docks, and anchored cruising boats.

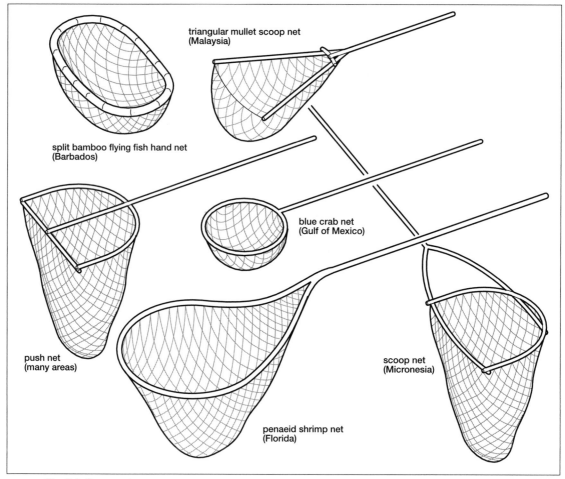

triangular mullet scoop net
(Malaysia)

split bamboo flying fish hand net
(Barbados)

blue crab net
(Gulf of Mexico)

push net
(many areas)

scoop net
(Micronesia)

penaeid shrimp net
(Florida)

Fig. 7-6. Scoop nets.

scooping. The general construction is essentially the same as the South Florida recreational shrimp trawl. Fishers station these nets with poles, with anchors, or in concert with fenced wings and allow them to fish unattended.

The same scooping principle applied vertically upward explains the idea behind lift nets. Like scoop nets, lift nets come in all sizes from small hand-operated designs to giant stationary, blanket, and boat lift nets. Several of the smaller versions have proven useful to cruisers, as well as the closely related star trap (fig. 7-7). Used with bait, or while chumming or night lighting, various lift nets are used to catch snails, crayfish, crabs, lobsters, and many species of planktivorous fish.

Seine and Encircling Nets

Seine and encircling nets endeavor to wall off and entrap aquatic organisms without entangling them; therefore, mesh size tends to be small. The float line suspends the net from the surface, and the lead line holds the bottom of the net at depth. Some are simple, elongated rectangles, others consist of two wings and a catch bag (fig. 7-8). Even the smallest seines normally require a minimum of two fishers for most efficient use. Most beach and boat seines of any size employ multiple fishers and vessels. Community social life on many islands and in coastal areas may revolve around morning or evening beach seining activities, where men and women, young and old, all join in to give a hand. Cruisers

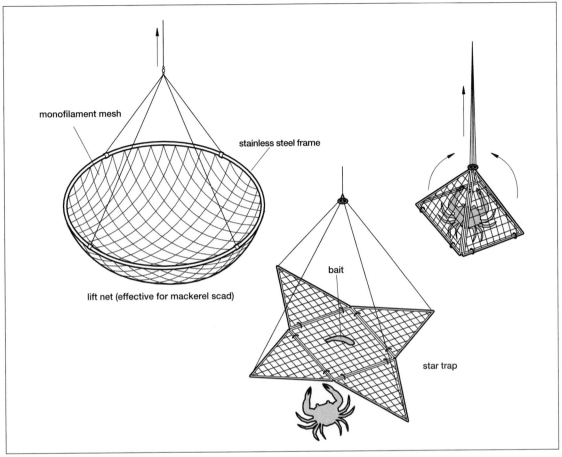

Fig. 7-7. Lift net and star trap.

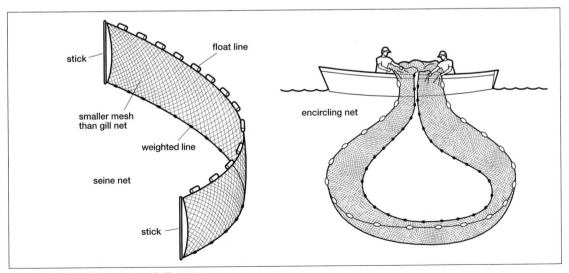

Fig. 7-8. Seine and encircling nets.

willing to pitch in with the labor will be rewarded with a share of the catch, just like everyone else, and it's also a great time to make jokes, laugh, learn a new language, and make new friends.

Small-boat seines attempt to encircle fish but usually depend on a section of shoreline or shallow depth to help seal escape routes. More specialized encircling nets, such as lampara nets, purse seines, and ring nets, enclose the captured fish by sealing off the bottom after surrounding the school. These devices are well beyond the purview of most cruisers, although power cruisers could stow and use miniature versions if they had a good enough reason to do so.

Gill and Entangling Nets

The advent of monofilament fishing line nowhere had a greater impact on world fisheries production and, in some cases, overexploitation, than in the con-struction of gill and entangling nets. Both depend on lack of visibility and behavioral mistakes to ensnare fish and other animals in the mesh, the size of which is generally large relative to seine and encircling nets, and adjusted to species sought.

Lists of specific devices employing these principles are long. Fishers may set gill nets fence-like along the bottom, floating at the surface while held in place by anchors, or drifting freely, or they may drag them along like a seine net. Entangling nets might consist of single walls similar to a gill net, trammel nets that entrap fish in pockets formed in a small mesh sandwiched between two large mesh walls, or set in front of a single wall of large mesh in cases where all fish enter from one direction. Other entangling nets consist of various arrays of material on frames or connecting lines.

Gill and entangling nets catch virtually every-thing that swims, and some things that don't, like

Monofilament gill nets see extensive use around the world. Here, long-range commercial fishers from Barbados use a gill net to catch flying fish that have been attracted to a drifting vessel with FADs in the southeastern Caribbean.

specialized mop-style devices for dragging through, breaking off, and entangling valuable corals. If you are wincing at this point, you're on the right track. This entire net category is riddled with outlawed and heavily regulated members; for example, pelagic drift nets, deplored in various treaties and conventions due to their unselective and highly deleterious nature.

Smaller-scale monofilament gill nets deployed by a single small skiff in coastal waters are one of the most universal artisanal fishing gears in the world today. Most of these are too large and bulky for practical cruiser use, but the smallest versions can be efficient, easily stowed gear. Consider, for instance, a short length of Kiribati-style gill net (e.g., 20 by 4.2 ft./6.1 by 1.3 m). Set and leave to fish temporarily unattended in near-shore shallows, especially across a small tidal channel, creek, estuary, or pass, or carry the net while wading in search of activity. Set across the anticipated path of sighted fish schools, and attempt to drive them into the net by herding, splashing, or throwing objects. It's also possible to effectively throw these nets almost like a cast net (fig. 7-9). Here again, check local regulations and

social mores *very carefully* before you whip out your gill net. It's another one that can quickly land you in hot water with the locals due to the potential abuse from nonselectivity and high efficiency.

Not a sound possibility for cruisers? We don't carry one, but I have had the opportunity to use the nets of many native fishers. The judicious seafarer who develops the skill to throw or set a small gill net under carefully selected circumstances, catches a half-dozen fat mullet, and then puts the net away would certainly be acting responsibly.

Cast Nets

Cast nets do not suffer from the regulatory and social stigma of gill nets. Quite to the contrary, natives who spot you artistically throwing a big net tend to respond warmly, respecting and identifying with your skill, as long as you are not irresponsibly hammering lots of fish. The sight of a cruiser throwing a cast net also seems to be a complete novelty, at least at the locations we've visited. Cast nets are very effective fishing tools for capturing baitfish, food fish, and other seafood for dinner, and yet they are generally

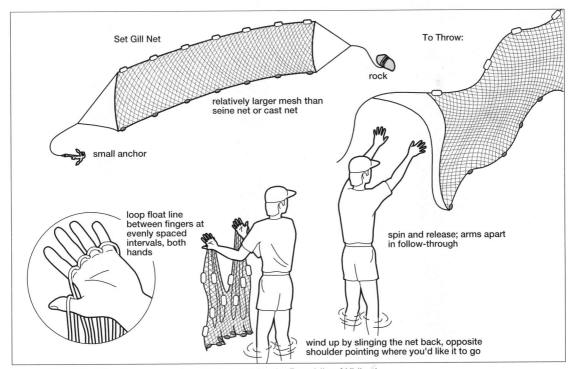

Set Gill Net

relatively larger mesh than seine net or cast net

small anchor

To Throw:

rock

loop float line between fingers at evenly spaced intervals, both hands

spin and release; arms apart in follow-through

wind up by slinging the net back, opposite shoulder pointing where you'd like it to go

Fig. 7-9. Gill-netting as practiced in Gilbert Islands, Republic of Kiribati.

quite selective. These nets do little if any damage to the environment; are applicable in most areas you choose to cruise; are deployable from a big boat, a dinghy, or shore; stow compactly; and are great fun to use. For these reasons, we feel that teaching you all about this particular gear could have a significant positive impact on your cruising enjoyment.

To this point, we've discussed numerous nets and their precursors that dip, scoop, lift, encircle, entangle, and wall off organisms. Like these other nets, the idea behind the cast net is a logical extension of a simpler gear still in widespread use in less developed areas: the cover pot. These devices are bottomless pots or barrels, often fished blind in turbid water, which come down vertically on top of the target species. Extraction is usually by hand through the opening made in the upturned bottom of the pot. Lantern nets operate exactly the same way, but lighten the weight of the gear by substituting a frame and mesh for the solid walls of the pot or barrel. Cast nets vastly increase the range and diameter of the catch zone relative to cover pots and lantern nets.

WHY ELSE SHOULD YOU CONSIDER A CAST NET?

The biggest single barrier to many kinds of offshore fishing success is the ability to catch live bait. This is particularly true of winter and spring oceanside pursuits in a popular area like the Florida Keys. Sport fisheries for sailfish, king mackerel, blackfin tuna, wahoo, cero mackerel, sharks, amberjacks, and even various reef and wreck species including yellowtail, gray, and mutton snappers and groupers depend strongly on the use of various live baits for best success. You'd be hard-pressed to cruise in a more active or developed fishing area, so a detailed look at bait availability in the Florida Keys should further demonstrate the important role of the cast net. All bait species in the following discussion occur or have close relatives worldwide.

In most cases, the live bait species are not for sale at the local bait shop or anywhere else. Some shops are now consistently carrying live pinfish (*Lagodon rhomboides*, Family Sparidae) and crabs (small portunids), in addition to shrimp (mostly *Penaeus duo-*

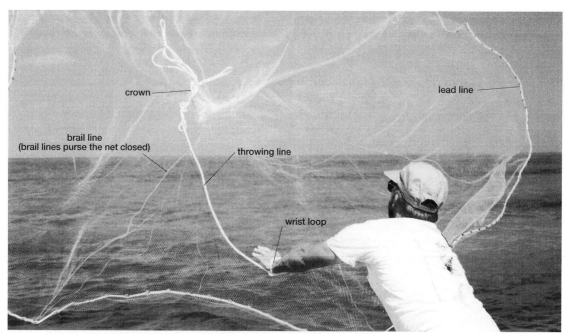

Throwing a cast net inshore of Crocker Reef, Florida Keys, in 15 to 20 feet (4.6 to 6.1 m) depth on white sand bottom interspersed with patches of turtle grass and low-relief coral patch reefs. This habitat supports numerous bait species, including ballyhoo (*Hemiramphus*), cigar minnows (*Decapterus*), and pilchards (*Harengula*).

rarum, Family Penaeidae), and it is possible to purchase live mullet (Family Mugilidae) during tarpon season at very specific times and places. A better-established bait industry for bigeye scad (*Selar crumenophthalmus*, Family Carangidae) operates farther north on the eastern coast of Florida. Professionals catch these in the early morning darkness, maintaining them for days at a time in large holding pens in order to supply offshore sportfishers, especially during the winter and spring. This has not become established in the Florida Keys, where the primary offshore bait target species are ballyhoo (mostly *Hemiramphus brasiliensis*, Family Hemirhamphidae), pilchards (*Harengula*, Family Clupeidae), and cigar minnows (*Decapterus punctatus*, Family Carangidae)—all caught, maintained, and used in quantity for various endeavors—and, to a lesser extent, blue runners (*Caranx crysos*, Family Carangidae), grunts (*Haemulon*, Family Haemulidae), and mackerel scad (*Decapterus macarellus*, Family Carangidae). While this section uses the Florida Keys as an example, the technique described can be used almost anywhere in the world to enhance fishing success.

This is the reason that nearly all professional and serious amateur fishing expeditions in the Keys begin with catching live bait. The bulk of the bait, particularly ballyhoo, pilchards, and cigar minnows, are captured with large cast nets. Other skills and equipment are necessary—knowing where and how to find the bait under different conditions, possession of the proper electronics and a high-volume bait well—but the most formidable obstacle to the aspiring fisher is probably the ability to successfully throw these nets.

SELECTING THE RIGHT NET

First let's talk about cast nets. This is not a good area for penny-pinching. Also, don't make the common mistake of going for a miniature version as a "starter"—a small, Mickey Mouse net from the local variety store doesn't throw like a real cast net, and it won't catch you any serious bait. Get a good net and learn how to use it.

Cast nets are sized according to their radius: Half the diameter of a fully circular opening, or the vertical height from the crown (i.e., the plastic ring that secures the tops of the brail lines and is the center point of the fully opened net) to the lead line (the weighted line to which the brail lines attach, and which also forms the outer rim of the fully opened net; see photo page 190). Mesh sizes are measured by the distance from knot to knot of a single opening, stretched closed. The most commonly used offshore cast net in the Florida Keys is probably a 12-foot (3.7 m), 1-inch (254 mm) stretch. This will get you by in most situations, although a 10-foot (3 m), ¾-inch (191 mm) stretch is good for smaller pilchards on shallow grass flats. A 14-foot (4.3 m) or 16-foot (4.9 m), 1-inch (254 mm) stretch mesh can make a big difference catching deeper bait out in channels or near the reef's edge. Mullet nets, on the other hand, range from 1⁵⁄₁₆- to 2-inch (333 to 508 mm) stretch mesh. Note that for the same lead-line weight, net sink rates are faster for larger mesh due to less resistance.

The importance of purchasing a high-quality, sweet-throwing cast net cannot be overemphasized. For years, many South Florida professionals favored the nets made and distributed by "Frank the Net." When Frank recently ceased to do business in the area, everyone began searching for new quality net sources. The Upper Keys market void was serviced largely by Captain Fred King; West Coast Nets, marketed by Captain Harry's Fishing Supply in Miami, has more recently entered the fray. Both sources produce excellent, durable, smooth-throwing products. (See appendix 1 for contact information.)

Be specific about the net you order. You will be spending $250 to $350 or more on a new net, although Fred sometimes has used ones in reasonable condition. If this is your first and perhaps only cast net, get a 12-foot (3.7 m), 1-inch (254 mm) stretch (commonly called a *ballyhoo net*)—add a 10-foot (3 m), ¾-inch (191 mm) stretch and a 14-foot (4.3 m), 1-inch (254 mm) stretch later. You can order specific lead-line weights for faster or slower sinking action, but the standard total weight, in pounds, is usually approximately equal to the radius, in feet. Specialty nets can be ordered for glass minnows (a generic local term referring to small schooling anchovies and silversides) and mullet. Check the latest regulations governing the area you plan to catch your bait *before* you buy your net—frequently, specific rules limit maximum net sizes, and some areas are entirely off-limits.

SETTING UP FOR THE THROW

Now that you've got your shiny new professional-grade cast net out of the bag and into a plastic bucket, you're wondering how you'll ever manage to get that big wad of mesh, rope, and lead to fly open in a beautiful, perfect, circular throw—a "pancake." Like everything else in the world of fishing, you'll do it by attention to detail.

Fishers employ many styles to successfully throw cast nets. Specific throwing style is unimportant as long as the net opens fully at the right time and distance. I've seen people throw a mean net *Cuban style, Keys style, Caribbean style, Polynesian style,* and all variations in between. Rather than confuse the issue, I will describe in detail what is commonly known as *Keys style,* using a standard 12-foot (3.7 m) ballyhoo net. Whatever other methods exist, I have never seen better results, whether you need to wing it *way* back for those extra spooky ballyhoo, or pancake a heavily weighted 16-foot (4.9 m) net on pilchards hugging the bottom in 30 feet (9 m) of water.

First, "stretch" the net. Pull it out of the bucket by the crown, and make sure the brail lines are straight and the lead line has no tangles. If you've got a flying bridge, hand the crown up to the captain and have him or her suspend the net vertically while you "pick it out"—this means plucking out any tangles in the lead line and ensuring that the net is hanging straight and free. Lacking a bridge, suspend the net overboard by the crown. With practice, you can simply pull the net out of the bucket or storage compartment by the crown, grab the neck in one hand and the midsection in the other, and shake it out (photo 1). Now gently set the stretched net on the deck, cinch the wrist loop securely to your left wrist, and coil the soft, ¼-inch (6 mm) throwing line clockwise in same-sized loops, stacking them outward from the thumb toward the base of your fingers in your palm (photo 2). Grab the net 2 to 3 feet (61 to 91 cm) below the crown with your right hand, and lay it across the still-open palm of your left hand (photo 3). Close your left hand, and again grab the net fully in your right hand about 40 percent of the way back from the piece in your left hand to the lead line. Place this piece of net overhand into your left hand (photos 3 and 4a). This loop that you form is called the *bag.*

The bottom of the bag should normally be a few inches (centimeters) above the lead line. However,

3

adjustments to bag length can be made for various types of throw. Lengthen the bag so that the bottom dangles below the lead line for super distance throws or if you are wading in deeper water. Shorten the bag for popping the net open right behind the transom. For 14- and 16-foot (4.3 and 4.9 m) cast nets, form a double bag by grabbing the net just below the crown and overhanding two equal-sized bags into your left hand. I once watched a commercial fisherman friend triple-bag his 18-foot (5.5 m) net, sending it out beautifully on a school of Spanish sardines.

Now you've formed your bag, either a single or a double, and you're ready for the next step. To guard against fatigue, many professional mates stop the setup right here and rest the lead line on the gunwale or deck if the captain is cruising around looking, or if the ballyhoo are still too far back. They are still able to fire through the rest of the protocol quickly for a throw. As the bait gets closer, raise everything with your left hand and pick a small handful from the suspended mesh directly below your left thumbnail with your right hand (photo 5).

bag

4

5

Pass this between the suspended net and your body, around the outside of your left elbow, and toss it up over your left shoulder onto the crease of your neck (photos 6 and 7). Throughout the rest of this procedure, make sure that piece of net stays firmly in place—don't let it slip out onto your left shoulder.

Pick up the lead line closest to your body (i.e., the inside lead line, photo 8); place it in your mouth (between the leads) and place your right hand under the net, palm toward you (photo 9); and flick successive pieces of net up over your right shoulder, stopping when approximately half of the lead line remains suspended from your left hand (photos 10, 11, and 12). It often helps to spin slowly in a circle, clockwise, during this sequence to help the net folds toss neatly and evenly over your right shoulder and into the crease of your neck. Dip your right shoulder

and drop this accumulated half of the lead line off and into the waiting open palm of your right hand (photos 13 and 14). Last, and this is very important, extract your right thumb and forefinger, holding the net you've just shrugged into your hand in your remaining three fingers, and grasp the lead line (photo 15). Now flick the lead line to your left, so it comes to rest on the outside and left of the net held in your right hand (photo 16). Congratulations—you're now ready to throw (photo 17).

ATTENTION TO DETAIL

Believe it or not, the hard part is over. No matter what people will have you believe, the biggest part of throwing a cast net is meticulous attention to the precise details of a proper setup. When you have finished doing this, you have pretty much preordained the quality of the throw. Given a good setup, anyone with reasonable upper-body strength can execute a respectable toss of a 10- or 12- foot (3 to 3.7 m) net in a very short time. Masterful throws of a spectrum of net sizes, over the full range of conditions, takes more practice.

A good example of the big difference made by small details involved the acquisition of my first 14-foot (4.3 m) net, purchased during my first year of full-time charter operation. We'd gotten in late with a nice catch of blackfin tuna when Frank the Net pulled up behind the slip with the new net. I couldn't clean fish and help scrub the deck fast enough. Then I grabbed a bucket and the net and hurried around the corner to a grassy area near one of the swim-

ming pools at Holiday Isle Resort Marina, in Islamorada, Florida, and quickly set up for some throws. I'd first learned thirteen years before and caught bait professionally hundreds of mornings, but every toss of the new net was the same—a good opening of the back two-thirds of the net, weak distance, and a big dip in the leading edge of the lead line. Thoroughly frustrated, I returned back to the charter dock and caught sight of Kenny Hum, who is easily the best cast-net thrower I've worked with. I told him about my problem, and it only cost me a sixpack of cold beer to get him over to the practice spot. He had me throw three times, all with the same result. Not one to mince words, he popped a second beer and said, "Your hands aren't tight enough—set up so they end up 6 to 8 inches (152 to 203 mm) apart,

do everything else the same, and that'll give you the lead-line velocity or speed that you're missing." By now it was well after dark, the net was back in the bucket, and we were sipping cold beer as we headed back to the offshore charter dock. I couldn't resist stopping (no one was around) and giving it a shot right there in the mostly empty parking lot. I did exactly what Kenny said, wound up, and cut loose. The net flew open in a 28-foot-diameter (8.5 m) pancake, nearly to the end of the throwing line, loudly catching the bed of a shiny new pickup and breaking several decorative lights on the corner of Mickey Rat's Bar. I hardly noticed Kenny's loud cheers as I rushed to inspect the damage and reassure the cowering barmaid that she was not under attack.

THROWING THE NET

So, remember to set up so that your hands are tight. This is done at the time you drop the net off your right shoulder and into your right hand. Make sure that your right hand is no more than 8 inches (203 mm) from your left as you grasp this section of net. The "wide-hands error" will relegate you to the average range of throwing skill. At first, keeping the hands tight feels a little uncomfortable, but you'll end up swearing by it.

It's time now to throw. Point your right shoulder where you want the net to go, or even a little to the left of the target zone, spread your feet, bend your knees slightly, and raise the net up and away from your body (photo 18). Swing the net aft, then forward, getting the lead line out and away from your legs and body (photos 19 and 20). Now rotate your upper body counterclockwise as you swing the net strongly aft in one motion at about a 45-degree angle to the deck, letting it arc fully in this direction

(photo 21). A good strong back swing is critical to imparting the momentum necessary for a good throw.

Rotate your upper body, put your weight on your back foot, and extend the lead line fully behind you—just like feeling a fly rod "load up" on the back cast (see appendix 3). At this precise moment, drive your lowered right shoulder forward and sling the net strongly with your arms in a forward arc, shifting your weight to your forward foot and releasing the net with both hands (photos 22 and 23). You'll only forget to let go of the lead line with your mouth once. A full follow-through, just like shooting a basketball or swinging a golf club, ensures a nice smooth motion and, in the case of throwing a cast net, finishes with arms apart (photos 23 and 24). The back of the lead line hits first (photo 25), followed closely by the forward or leading edge to form a perfect circle, with the crown centered on the target.

HOW TO PRACTICE, AND A FEW EXTRA NET-THROWING TRICKS

A few words about practice. Loosen up a little first, do some stretches so you don't pull something. Don't overdo the number of throwing attempts. Get your net out and throw it about six times, then put it away until the next day. Your performance will deteriorate quickly with fatigue and repetition, especially when you're just getting started. You'll also find that what went smoothly with practice throws at paper plates in the backyard during the Sunday barbecue is quite a different story on a cramped, wet, pitching deck offshore in 20 knots of salt spray and breeze. Get reasonably proficient in the yard, then get out on the water and try the real thing. Yes, it takes months to get really good, but you can study the setup, throw a few times on land, and go out later the same day and get good enough openings to catch some bait. I've done this with friends and relatives, and they're always surprised at how easy it is to get started.

A few last tricks of the trade before you get out on the water. Sometimes bait responds so aggressively to chum that the problem becomes getting a full opening *close* enough to the boat to catch them. Throw more gently and, at the point of release (photo 23), briefly grab the back of the lead line with both hands and drop it at the transom.

On very windy days, your boat may swing back and forth on the anchor so dynamically that the crosswind collapses your net while it is airborne, if thrown normally. Counter this by standing as high as you can comfortably balance (e.g., on a fish box or wide enough covering board) and slinging the net in a forward arc nearly parallel to the deck (instead of a more normal 45-degree angle between the net and your body; make it almost 90 degrees) and down, so full opening occurs just as it hits the water. Throwing into the wind, on the other hand, is futile in all but the lightest of air.

What about distance? The main issue here is getting those leads well out and away on the back swing (photo 22), getting a full-bodied wind-up, and slinging the net forward with as much ferocity as you can. Focus forward energy by elevating the angle the net makes with your vertical body from 45 to about 60 or 70 degrees, so you're slinging it a little

more sideways. Psychology can be important too. One excellent captain told me he envisions an excellent long-distance opening just as he is making the throw. Others use a nasty, aggressive approach—one of my favorite mates used to turn beet red and growl like a rabid dog as he was winging the net way back for particularly skittish ballyhoo, but nobody laughed and we were one of the few boats able to catch bait on several of those days. Some boats carry a lightly weighted 10-foot (3 m) net with an extra long rope for such occasions.

TIPS FOR CATCHING BAIT WITH CAST NETS

The behavior of different bait species dictates appropriate chumming and netting techniques for successful capture. Some species, such as ballyhoo and needlefish, tend to swim and feed mostly near the surface. Others, like pilchards and sardines, may flip at the surface when undisturbed under the right sea conditions (usually in light or no wind and calm water), descend to midwater, or hug the bottom at other times. Cigar minnows, mackerel scad, and their relatives tend to surface and feed on chum in fast, frantic bursts, punctuated by rapid dives deep or to the bottom at the slightest hint of danger. Unalarmed mullet swim near the surface but respond to the smallest shadow or movement by rapid lateral flights and by sounding. What does all of this mean? You can be a great net-thrower and still not catch a single fish for food or bait under many conditions without using the right stalking or attraction techniques.

A few general comments apply to most target species.

♦ *Read the signs.* Wind velocity, wind direction, moon phase, tidal stage and flow, air and water temperature, time of year, time of day, bird presence and behavior, water clarity, cloud cover, recent weather events, barometric pressure, current weather pattern, wave action, phytoplankton blooms, predator fish location and abundance, and many other variables determine the position and behavior of baitfish at any given time. The more you understand about every nuance of the biology and ecology of the baitfish you seek, the more successful and consistent will your efforts be at finding them. For future reference, you may wish to log the specifics of each condition when you find bait.

♦ *Use your electronics.* Switch your depth-finder to a higher frequency, usually 192 to 200 kHz, for detailed views of shallower waters. Learn to identify fish by species according to what you see on the screen. Search habitats like channels, banks, and sharp breaks in the bottom that project plankton and other food items to baitfish schools in a turbulent flow. Pay particular attention to abrupt, steep gradients in otherwise featureless areas of the seafloor. Check out known focal points for baitfish presence, and maintain a meticulous GPS waypoint library of these spots.

♦ *Once located, think about the most efficient way to catch them.* Should you drift, power-drift, or anchor? Are you spooking them with engine noise?

♦ *Try never to get between the sun and your quarry.* Shadows cast by you or the boat, especially superstructure or masts, and certainly by the airborne net, make fish nervous and give early warning at the time of the net throw. If you are in an anchored boat, and the lie of the vessel created by prevailing wind and current casts shadows over the chum slick, consider some combination of an anchor bridle and altered chum-bag placement to eliminate the problem. One possibility is to suspend the chum bag laterally with the aid of an outrigger.

♦ *Adjust your chum bag when the current runs into the prevailing wind.* Most of the times that you anchor and deploy a chum bag to attract bait, the chum slick flows cooperatively away from the transom, sometimes at an angle due to the resultant set of the boat in the prevailing wind and current. Thus, fish coming into the chum approach from the downwind side of the boat, allowing you to throw off of the wind. When the wind positions the boat so that the current runs transom to bow, you'll have to somehow position the chum bag upcurrent and far enough away from the boat to make a downwind throw. We usually fly a fishing kite out from the transom, tighten the release clip, and suspend the chum bag vertically from the kite-line clip at an appropriate distance. The fish swim *upcurrent* to the chum, tails to the boat, and in good position for a downwind throw.

Ballyhoo and Other Surface Dwellers

If the ballyhoo are not in any of your favorite spots, an efficient way to hunt for them is to climb to the highest safe vantage point on your vessel and cruise along at maximum speed. Wear polarized sunglasses and a billed cap, search with the sun at your back, and pierce the water with your eyes. The search image is a brief flash of slim, stick-like figures darting off rapidly in groups, occasionally with one or more individuals using their elongated lower caudal lobe to skitter and skip away over the water surface. Maintain speed, have your crew drop a chum bag lashed to a cleat overboard, and make a wide, fast circle encompassing the possible position of the fleeing fish. Reduce speed to idle, return to the approximate position of the last sighting, and anchor. If at all possible, try to position the transom over dark bottom, like a grass patch, since ballyhoo are reluctant to swim over bright sand and other light bottom where they provide strong silhouettes for hunting seabirds. Augment the chum bag with a dose of menhaden oil and a few sprinkles of oatmeal, stay in your perch, and wait for the telltale swirls and ripples of arriving ballyhoo.

Every day seems to be different for ballyhoo. Sometimes they come charging up to the transom en masse, literally eating out of the chum bag. Other times they hang way back, fearful of getting anywhere near the boat. This is the time to get out those little floats and hair hooks, and drift tiny squares of bait back on light spinning rods. Catch as many as you can this way. Try reeling a hooked individual in *very* slowly; this often induces the school to follow closely enough for a successful net throw.

On days when the current is negligible, ballyhoo tend to wander loosely and farther from the surface. Quite a few can be present, yet their scattered behavior reduces the number you can catch with a single throw; many times you only have a limited number of shots before repeated net throws scare the uncaptured school members out of range. In order to aggregate these ballyhoo in good position for a comfortable, full opening of the net, toss out a small handful of chum, ground fish, or rolled oats straight back and within easy throwing range.

Regardless of current and degree of shyness, the timing of your throw relative to the swimming behavior of the ballyhoo is usually critical. Don't throw the instant the first few individuals come within range; let the school get comfortable. They'll frequently develop a rhythmic pattern or circuit of swimming in relatively close as they work up the chum slick to the boat, and then circle back out again. Set up the net, then throw when their heads are pointed at you, rather than away from you. This means as the net becomes airborne, the ballyhoo must waste precious microseconds reversing direction before initiating flight, which can make all the difference between an empty net and one full of glittering fish.

One other ballyhoo trick I'll mention, lest it be lost to the past, comes from a grizzled veteran now long retired from the charter business. He would always have someone stomp loudly on the deck after the net was in the air. He swore this triggered the ballyhoo into wasting time and energy jumping up instead of out and away in their race to escape the flying net, resulting in a better catch. Whether or not you try this, always purse the net when you see the first ballyhoo flashing as the net sinks; this minimizes the mortality due to being gilled high up in the net, near the crown. Any time you purse, do it authoritatively with strong, overhand pulls.

Cigar Minnows and Other Patch Habitat Residents

Small *Decapterus* species and, at times, sardines, pilchards, and other clupeids, associate very specifically with small areas on the bottom—a patch of coral or other feature, perhaps surrounded by seagrass and perched near a steep sandy bank—for months at a time. These locations can provide consistent, daily sources of bait. It's often easiest to proceed to the spot, anchor, and put out a chum bag. At first, you may catch all you want by simply giving the bag a shake and letting the baitfish swarm up off the bottom into net range; however, this usually won't last long. The baitfish quickly become more wary, requiring more finesse to catch.

The critical element to continued success is proper use of beach sand. Keep plain sand in one container and mix up another with thawed or fresh chum (e.g., rolled oats, ground fish or invertebrates), as you did for reef-fishing, into a viscous mixture that packs like bread dough. Form six or so golfball-sized spheres of chum, and have the netter prepare to throw. Toss the chum balls in a tight pattern, just far enough out from the transom for a comfortable, easy, full net opening. Pause, wait for the baitfish to ascend and begin feeding heavily in the cloudy plume of chum and sand, then throw, centering the crown on the action. When the baitfish become even more wary, toss sprays of plain sand and unpacked sand/chum mix out over the sinking pattern of chum balls to form an opaque screen between the net and the fish. Unlike for ballyhoo, let the net sink all the way to the bottom as long as it's smooth sand, gravel, grass, or mud. If necessary, hook a gaff through the wrist loop of the net rope and lean overboard to extend the reach so that the brail lines do not purse from tension as the open net settles to the bottom; this results in maximum spread. When the rope goes slack, the circle of lead line is on the seafloor. You'll also feel the throbs of struggling fish through the line if your throw was successful. Purse quickly and strongly to minimize the number of escapees out the bottom of the net.

A few last tips: Don't purse the net prematurely—when the lead line hits the water, the school will momentarily spook out of the chum, then come darting back in *under* the falling net. And remember, *never* let a cast net settle onto hard coral or hard ground interspersed with soft corals. The only way to save it then is to dive down and gently pick it out of the substrate. Jerking hard on it from the boat could tear it badly under these circumstances.

Mackerel Scad: Most Popular Bait in the Tropics?

Decapterus macarellus occur worldwide and are highly prized baits throughout their circumtropical range. Mackerel scad are robust, active swimmers that wiggle and flash, and they may reach a length of at least 13 inches (33 cm). Pelagic, midwater, and bottom predator fish adore them. They work live or dead, stationary, drifted, or trolled.

These baitfish tend to hover in deeper midwater habitats, in lagoons, bays, and outer reef slopes to 650-foot (200 m) depths. They have great eyesight and are very fast. You will not cast-net them in daylight without using a few tricks. Anchor and put out the chum bag. Toss over some softball-sized chum spheres. If they're around, they tend to show themselves rapidly, rocketing up to the boat in large groups and feeding frantically between frequent plunges to the bottom. Form twelve more tightly packed baseball-sized chum spheres, have the netter get set to throw, and toss six balls overboard just as you did for the cigar minnows. This time, however, quickly throw the net over the chum balls, hesitate, and then toss six more balls *on top* of the sinking net.

The mackerel scad may disappear completely from view in response to the lead-line splash. After some delay, they'll consistently move deep and laterally into the first chum cloud, then ascend vertically while *under* the sinking umbrella formed by the net, toward the second set of chum balls that is descending from *above* the net. Purse the net hard and fast when you see the flashes of the fish hitting the net, before they can sound back down and out of the still-open bottom. Free-lined hair hooks and simple hand-lift nets with 1-inch (254 mm) stretch monofilament mesh and a stainless steel hoop of at least 48-inch-diameter (1.2 m) are also effective if you don't have a cast net.

Catching Baitfish at Night

You're probably thinking, hey, we see all of these planktivorous species swarming around our cruising boat at night, so what's with all of this searching and messy chumming? Very true, and just one more advantage of living aboard when it comes to fishing. You can often catch all the baitfish you could possibly want with a casual, clean throw from your boat, with no messy chum and no hassle, and no nasty, chum-filled net to clean afterward.

Generally speaking, cast-netting at night or in reduced light is far more effective than casting during the bright light of day. You can further concentrate baitfish before your net throw with a handful of chum or sand-chum mix if necessary. With or without the chum, the main trick is to switch all

lights off just before the thrower releases the net. The target fish can't see the silhouette of the net against the lights, no warning shadows are cast, and your catch will be much larger than if you left the lights on.

A Word on Mullet

Mullet comprise another worldwide coastal and estuarine fish family popular for food and bait. Most feed on detritus, plants, and microorganisms scraped and rooted from the seafloor, which means they generally could care less about chum. Thus for cast-netting, you'll be silently stalking them from a poled or drifting vessel or while wading stealthily in the shallows. They can sometimes be induced to take small hooks baited with bread balls or small pieces of fish.

Look for "muds"—areas of turbidity formed by rooting mullet schools. Scan the water surface for wakes and tail flips. Overcast conditions make for more difficult spotting but this works both ways, because the mullet can't see the net either. Try to determine swimming direction of the school. Just as with ballyhoo, time your throw to a moment when the fish are headed toward rather than away from you or, at the very least, are moving laterally to your position. Lead the school slightly with your throw. The ability to cast longer distances will help particularly with mullet, because they have good eyesight and they're very fast. Furthermore, they are accustomed to being hotly pursued by birds and a large variety of predator fish, which is not conducive to sedate, sleepy behavior.

Invertebrates

Fish aren't the only animals caught by cast nets. Squid, shrimp, and crabs become targets of this gear worldwide, particularly while moving along in groups or in reasonably high densities up off the bottom. Cast nets are also popular for use in turbid areas like estuaries, marshes, and lagoons. Provided the bottom is free of obstructions, working an area blind with repeated throws can accumulate reasonable catches. These may include invertebrates, particularly shrimp, which are partially buried in sediment and kick up into the net as the pursing lead line disturbs them.

Baitfish Conservation

Armed with effective baitfish-concentrating techniques and a good cast net, you have the capability to catch hundreds of fish or other organisms in a single throw. Do you have a high-volume live well (see chapter 8)? What is your goal—a few baits, one or two fish for dinner—or will you need enough to chum with handfuls of live baitfish at an offshore seamount, wreck, or reef? Do you wish to freeze or salt some bait for later use on an offshore passage or in locations where you do not anticipate plentiful baitfish?

Think about all of this in advance, before you throw the net. Part of your new life as a competent fisher is realizing and tempering the mortality inflicted by powerful fishing methods. *Never* take more than you need and *always*, if at all possible, release unused live bait on your way back in—preferably where you caught it, but at the very least in a similar depth and habitat. Fishing pressure is intense in many cruising destinations around the world, and all efforts to promote conservation will help these resources to be sustainable.

NET CARE

Finally you have returned from your fishing trip, having thrown your new net pretty well, caught some good bait, and realized a big difference in your fish-catching success. As the cast-net bucket comes out of the boat, you notice that it's no longer shiny and sweet-smelling. In fact, it has pieces of skin, bone, and meat from the chum, a couple of dead gilled pilchards, and it's been sitting in a sun-warmed compartment all day. You can no longer imagine draping it over your body, much less putting it in your mouth, in preparation for a throw. Don't do what many have done before you—attempt to rectify the situation by simply tossing in some of that soapy bleach water from the boat scrubbing bucket—because it will be the end of your net. Bleach in any reasonably strong concentration weakens and ruins the fabric.

Instead, stretch the net just as you did when you first got it out. Use the net-throwing line to tie a clove hitch just below the crown, the last part of the hitch with a loop of double line. Attach this to a davit hook or small block-and-tackle arrangement and raise the net to about 75 percent of its full height. If you're anchored out, use superstructure or sail halyards to raise the net. Spread the lead line in a circle, so the net is now in the shape of an inverted ice-cream cone. Spray the net thoroughly with a high-pressure hose if available, periodically grasping a handful of net and shaking vigorously to get as much of the chum and other material to fall out as possible. Hand pick the rest, respray, and leave the net suspended to dry. Occasionally, or if the net is particularly filthy, lower it back down into a bucket of freshwater with a shot of fabric softener and let it soak overnight; then resuspend and hose, shake, pick, and dry. There's nothing worse than having to floss yesterday's chum out of your teeth after throwing an improperly cleaned net.

Nets used to catch fish without chum will need much less attention. For cruising situations with limited deck space and freshwater, soak the net in a bucket with a weak solution of seawater and bleach-free laundry soap, rinse by dipping overboard by the crown, suspend it to dry, and stow. Stowing the net wet won't hurt it, but will promote odor. Don't store your net for extended periods in direct sunlight, which oxidizes and weakens monofilament mesh.

QUICK REPAIRS

The sight of all those flashing fish when you begin to purse your net frequently attracts the attention of predators. Sharks, barracuda, various other fish-eating predator fish, and occasionally sea turtles will snap and plow their way right through your net in pursuit of an easy meal. Occasionally, you will also accidentally net one of these larger fish, resulting in tears from sharp teeth, gill plates, or other body parts. Other net injuries may occur from snagging bottom or sharp corners, projections, and fasteners onboard your vessel.

You can get away with hand-sewing small holes and tears in the short term using a net needle, with uni-knots to start and rolling hitches to fasten and finish. Large holes require trimming the broken and mangled margins and sewing in a new piece of material. For this kind of repair, use slightly stronger monofilament (10 to 12 lb./4.5 to 5.4 kg test) than the strength of the monofilament mesh (usually 9 lb./4 kg test). You can get by with these "rough and dirty" repairs for quite a long time, especially if you exercise some caution regarding when and where you throw your net. You may wish to carry two nets—an old beater for higher risk situations and a fresh new net for clean, smooth bottom and low risk of predator attacks.

Eventually these improper repairs will deform your net enough to compel you to go over it more professionally. Near civilization, you may wish to employ the services of a professional netmaker. Most are so reasonable and fast that you can hardly afford not to take advantage of their services, especially for major damage. Longer-term cruisers, particularly those who spend considerable time in more remote areas, will want to learn how to make proper net repairs themselves. The same fundamental technique works for any kind of mesh net and, once mastered, will enable you to make your own hammocks, hanging baskets, and other items. It's really quite easy, so don't waste too much time messing around with improper technique.

Making and Repairing Nets

The art of net-making spans the history and diverse cultures of our species. The sheer number of different knots and weaving patterns could provide material for an extensive project in anthropology. The practice continues to play a strong role worldwide. Hand construction of entire nets is less common with widespread availability of reasonably priced, machine-made meshes of many kinds (most using either the weaver knot or any one of a number of knotless designs). However, the persistent need to mend and re-create sections of mesh keeps net-making skills very much alive, in both developed and less developed countries.

Watching an experienced fisher nimbly weaving and repairing a net, like watching someone create a basket from pandanus or palm fronds, is wonderful. Part of the motivation for cruising is often a return to a simpler, more basic lifestyle, where there's time

The Social Side of Net Repair Extends to Industrial Countries, Too

Take the example of an overcast, windy, late summer afternoon a decade and a half ago in St. John's, Newfoundland. The crew of the commercial swordfish vessel *Rush*, forced in for engine repairs from a tough two weeks of harpooning, longlining, and drift-netting offshore, had the big net spread out on the wharf. They were enjoying a few rums while they repaired the net and chatted with four local women, whom they were also plying with rum. One of the four was a previous acquaintance, and as the afternoon wore on and the rum flowed, her three friends also became quite smitten with the salty, rough, adventurous swordfishers. Inevitably, decision time arrived for the women; after considerable discussion and a split vote, some combination of virtue and health concerns narrowly tipped the balance in favor of a reluctant departure by the now decidedly drunk ladies. They had pulled the car in and parked over the net, and as they slowly and indecisively began to move forward, a drunk but fast-thinking crew member (no doubt purely motivated by highway safety concerns for the inebriated women), rushed to the hydraulic controls and engaged the net hauler. The car began to move slowly back toward the boat, a process that abruptly accelerated when a wad of net became hopelessly tangled and bound around the universal joint and rear axle of the vehicle. Screams and giggles came from inside the car, and mostly stunned silence prevailed outside the car, giving way to shouted instructions to the net hauler to shut it down before he dragged the car entirely off the wharf. This little excitement tipped everyone in favor of prolonging the social gathering until the next morning, despite the fact they could easily have called a taxi. By the time they'd cut the net out of the car's undercarriage the next morning, the status of both net and crew brain damage was far worse than before work had started the previous day. No one complained. It was nothing that a few hundred sheet bends wouldn't fix, and they'd made some good friends.

to do things like rediscover manual dexterity on a quiet beach. As with gathering, cooking, and other subsistence activities, net repair is customarily a social event, a time to relax, rest tired muscles, listen to music, and chat with family and friends. And, at least in the case of net repair, this approach is not limited to idyllic tropical islands.

ONLY ONE ELEMENTARY KNOT

Now that you're in the right mood, let's succinctly present a tiny slice of the vast world of net-making, just enough to teach you how to professionally repair your monofilament cast net or gill net. The first step is to acquire a net needle and to learn a single, fundamental knot for monofilament mesh creation: the modified sheet bend (fig. 7-10). This

knot can be used free hand or with a flat stick, shaped like a paint stirrer and called a paddle. The purpose of the paddle is to enable consistent, precise control over mesh size. Eye estimates are fine for most repairs.

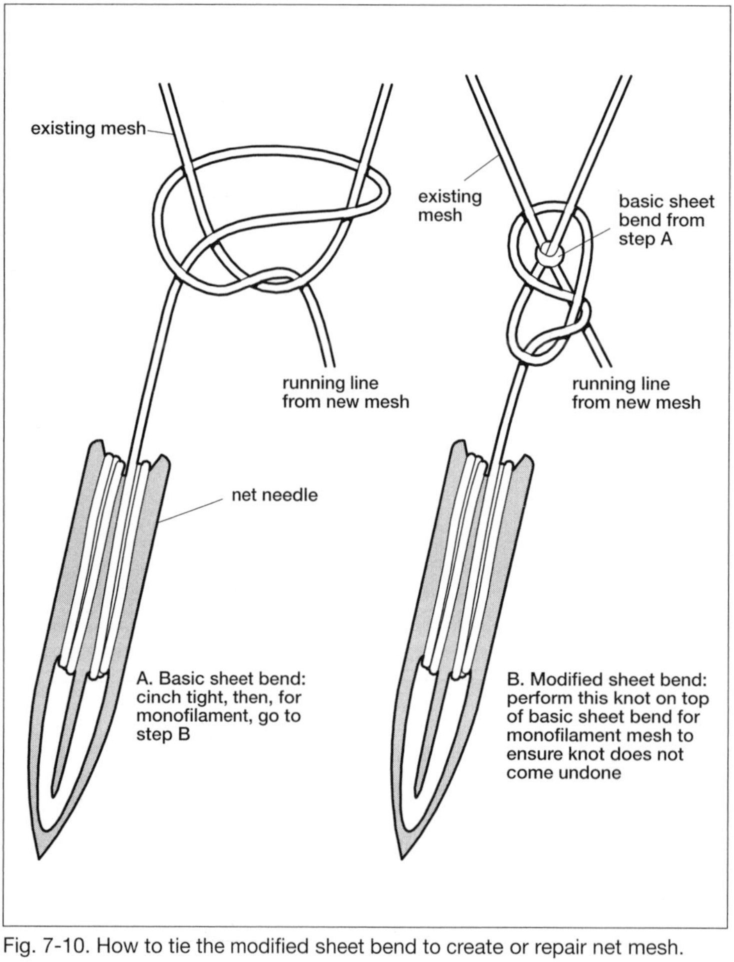

HOW TO ADD MONOFILAMENT MESH TO YOUR NET

The ability to create new mesh permits repairs and, with some additional materials, the making of an entire net. Load your net needle with 9-pound (4 kg) test monofilament (or other line size matching the size of your net's mesh). Hang the net so that the area requiring new material is accessible (e.g., over a horizontal tree limb, boom, or suspended by the crown) or spread it out neatly on a flat, hard surface. Trim any broken strands back to the mesh knot, so that you have a straight line of mesh corners analogous to the teeth of a saw (fig. 7-11). All you're going to do now is sequentially add a new row of teeth by fastening your needle line to each existing "tooth point" with a modified sheet bend, leaving *exactly* the same length of line between each knot (estimate by eye or use a paddle). The center of these "dips" between knots is where you'll fasten the next row of teeth as you head back in the opposite direction (fig. 7-12). Note that your new teeth form in the gaps between the old teeth. Eventually, as you form successive rows of mesh, you will come to the tooth points of the other side of the opening, so that on your last pass, you will tie a modified sheet bend to existing teeth points on either side to finish the repair.

Fig. 7-10. How to tie the modified sheet bend to create or repair net mesh.

existing mesh

existing mesh

basic sheet bend from step A

running line from new mesh

running line from new mesh

net needle

A. Basic sheet bend: cinch tight, then, for monofilament, go to step B

B. Modified sheet bend: perform this knot on top of basic sheet bend for monofilament mesh to ensure knot does not come undone

REPAIRING HOLES WITH PATCHES, AND SIMPLE TEARS

Figure 7-13 illustrates how to use this technique to insert a patch of

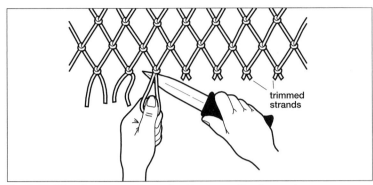

Fig. 7-11. Trimming torn sections of net in preparation for repair.

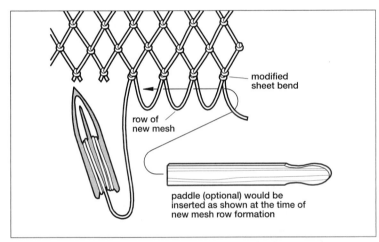

Fig. 7-12. How to add new mesh to properly prepared existing mesh.

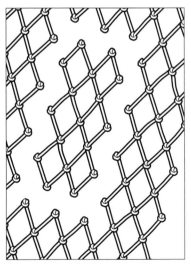

Fig. 7-13. Repairing a hole with a replacement patch of net material.

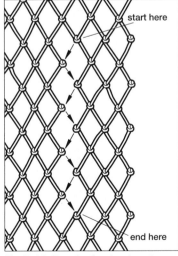

Fig. 7-14. Repair of a simple net tear.

net material into a hole. Again, trim broken ends and odd mesh until you form a square or rectangle. Trim the patch so that the perimeter is exactly one mesh smaller than an exact fit. Load your net needle and form the missing row of mesh with point-to-point modified sheet bends, continuing right around the gap between the patch perimeter and the surrounding net. Simple tears are even easier—trim off broken strands and make modified sheet bends in sequence from point to point (fig. 7-14).

What can possibly go wrong? Nothing, really, except possibly irregular new mesh size due to slight variations in eyeball estimates of the right distance to leave between modified sheet bends, which sometimes causes the repaired section to puff out a little from the surrounding net. Who cares? It will work just fine, and you'll become quite adept at creating near-perfect new mesh in short order. If it bothers you, and you have nothing better to do, you can always trim it out and try for a more aesthetically pleasing result. But wouldn't you rather be fishing?

OTHER APPLICATIONS OF NET-MAKING SKILLS

Constructing an entire net, hammock, or mesh basket from scratch requires a few more knots and techniques beyond the scope of this book. The use of twine in place of monofilament allows the use of a plain rather than a modified sheet bend (see fig. 7-10A); several tricks exist for shaping by widening and decreasing mesh sequences. Experienced net fishers also substitute additional knots for the careful trimming we described previously, permitting continuous weaving by eye and less laborious repair preparation—an important factor for professionals with many square yards (meters) of net to go over each day (see appendix 2 for references).

One common application is heavy twine mesh coverings for smooth-surfaced fishing floats. You may have thought these attractive adornments were solely the delicate renderings of lonely, idle commercial fishers whiling away peaceful hours offshore. They're actually purpose-built to interrupt the slick hydrodynamic flow of water over the floats, forcing them to skim along the air-water interface rather than getting sucked down under the surface when hauled speedily to the moving vessel, making retrieval much easier.

Gear Checklist

You could experience a highly successful fishing circumnavigation or shorter cruise without any of the gear presented in this chapter. Nevertheless, you would undoubtedly encounter repeated circum-stances where easily attainable, highly desirable seafood and bait would be beyond your means. We couldn't find trained cormorants or otters in any of the catalogs, although we found commercially produced versions of much of the other gear that might be appealing and practical for cruisers. For example, a few hand nets are worthy of consideration. You might also wish to purchase appropriate mesh and build a small invertebrate trap, which is really nice in a place like coastal Alaska or many other cold, biologically rich destinations; they quickly yield fresh shrimp, crabs, or lobsters for dinner in waters where diving is no casual affair. Simple hand spears and gigs, or larger harpoons, may provide excitement, food, and a chance to learn a skill that makes you feel like a Viking, although you'll likely be better off acquiring these skills locally in regions where this gear is still legal and in common use. You might have room for a small shrimp trawl or collapsible traps. Cast nets confer great fishing flexibility. Table 7-1 lists selected fishing gear readily available from sources given in appendix 1.

TABLE 7-1. GEAR CHECKLIST FOR HAND TOOLS, TRAPS, NETS, AND OTHER ASSORTED GEAR

Item	Specific Recommendation	Approximate Price
Snatch hooks	weighted, sizes 7/0 (1 oz./28 g), 10/0 (6 oz./170 g)	$1, $3
Shrimp dip net	18 ft. (5.5 m) 3-piece aluminum handle	$37
Bully net	22 in. (56 cm) bow, 12-ft. (3.7 m) handle	$23
Small shrimp trawl	5 x 3 ft. (1.5 x 0.9 m) PVC frame small boat net	$58 (net only)
Seine net	⅛ in. (3 mm) mesh, 4 ft. (122 cm) depth, complete	$5 per foot
Harpoon parts	bronze swordfish dart	$13
	matching harpoon shank	$30
Collapsible traps	galvanized, for lobsters, fish, eels	$11–$30
Danielson crab trap	for Pacific Northwest and similar environments	$31
CRB shrimp and crab traps	for Pacific Northwest and similar environments	$50–$64
Star traps	plastic coated mesh, for crabs	$7–$17
Trap bait cups	bait cup with lid	$1
Trap funnels	plastic, for lobsters or crabs	$1
Trap mesh	black plastic marine netting	Variable
Safety ties	black bar tie for trap construction	$9 per 100
Trap floats	round, 6 in. (15 cm)	$1
Cast net	12 ft. (3.7 m), 1 in. (254 mm) stretch mesh	$289
Net needle	sardine, 6½ by ½ in. (165 by 127 mm)	$.50

8

Modifying Your Vessel for Fishing

We'll make a bet with you. Regardless of your background, motivation for cruising, vessel type, previous lack of knowledge, or degree of prior interest in catching fish, you'll now do at least *something* to your cruising boat to make it a more convenient, powerful, efficient, and fun fishing platform. Even if you are a sailboat-racing-cruiser, with minimum windage, a spotless, highly organized deck layout dedicated solely to going fast with no motor, and you've never wet a fishing line, we'll get you. You've still got to eat, and the allure of all that fun you've been missing might tempt you to put out a trolling line or two. If you're really fast, think of the deadly high-speed lures you could pull for tasty, colorful, quick oceanic species. Inevitably you'll succeed, and it won't be long before a rod holder sprouts from a stanchion. Next you'll tire of crawling around on your hands and knees to clean your many catches, and a waist-high fish-cleaning table may appear somewhere aft. It's only natural to rinse steaks and fillets, and place them directly on a barbecue grill clamped conveniently nearby. Your purist friends will murmur and mutter about these adulterations, except when the aroma of fresh grilled seafood floats across the marina or anchorage and attacks their nostrils at cocktail hour. It won't be long before similar devices begin to sprout sheepishly from neighboring vessels.

The transition for many power cruisers may be more spontaneous. After all, some of the best designs are based on commercial fishing boats. You've got lots of space compared to most cruising sailboats, and since the engine will be running any time you make a move, you can afford to run more electrically powered devices . . . live wells, fish-finders, plotters. Flying bridges and upper decks lend themselves to numerous modifications helpful to fishing. Spacious cockpits make great work areas for all kinds of fishing and diving activities, and easily accommodate built-in fish boxes and other conveniences. Large flat transoms can handle add-on live wells and full-size dive platforms.

The encroachment of fishing into the world of cruising is only natural. It's slowly, subtly occurring as you read these words—quietly, inexorably permeating the very fabric of this lifestyle. Each cruiser will find a level of immersion commensurate to personal circumstances, but few will remain completely uninfected. So don't fight it. Check out the ideas and instructions in this chapter and select those that suit you. Start small; you can always get more elaborate later. We begin with the simplest, most basic modifications, those that apply to the greatest number of cruisers, and get progressively more advanced as we move along. Each time you reach a plateau in your fishing career and wish to advance further or try something new, refer to the point at which you left off. Hopefully, you'll stop yourself before you end up at the helm of a high-seas commercial fishing vessel that takes you away from cruising! We're supposed to be relaxing and enjoying ourselves, remember?

Clamps, Mounts, and Lanyards for Line Dispensers

Whether you purchased a revolving-spool fishing reel, with or without a fishing rod, or a commercial deck winch, you need to secure it firmly to the vessel.

The simplest scenario is to use the clamp built into or supplied with the device, find a section of railing pointing aft, and affix it so that the line can run off into the wake and be retrieved directly onto the spool unimpeded. Nevertheless, several alternatives are possible for those lacking an appropriate section of railing or for whom this mounting position interferes with other gear or activity.

One approach is to mount the reel in another convenient location and orientation, even if it means that the spool end faces aft. Attach a small block capable of handling the strain of a hooked fish anywhere near the back of your vessel, then lead the line from the spool out through the block and into the water. If the reason you can't clamp your reel is *lack* of railing, consider using some form of rod-holder arrangement. This is easy if you have a stand-up or other style of fishing rod but, if not, devise your own butt section of appropriate strength and diameter, clamp on the reel, and place this short, stumpy, rodless arrangement in a rod holder. Make sure that the line coming off the spool can't contact the end of the homemade butt during the action.

Commercial deck winches may have alternative mounts available for different afterdeck configurations. Here again, if you lack railing or choose not to use it, order a spigot-type mount rather than a G-clamp. Spigot mounts are essentially a form of rod holder. Bolt, clamp, or mount the female receptacle to a flat vertical or horizontal surface, stanchion, or piece of superstructure. The male end of the deck winch then inserts neatly, providing a firm, swiveling attachment that permits easy removal for storage when not fishing (see photo on page 33).

Regardless of mount type or choice of line dispenser, fabricate a lanyard for each device. Don't go through the labor and expense of setting everything up and then get lazy on this last detail. Fishing-supply catalogs offer these ready-made. Many choose to save the money and make their own. Splice three-strand nylon to a size of brass swivel snap that attaches to a strong, out of the way, handy part of the reel (many reels now feature a lanyard attachment ring). Alternatively, form lanyard connections with crimps using any flexible strong line or cable. *Important: make each lanyard length sufficient to move around the afterdeck with the device if necessary.* This is partic-

ularly true for rod and reel as opposed to fixed-station arrangements—when the fish hits, you have many more important things to do than fumble around with a lanyard snap. Furthermore, while you're running about or handling the device outside of rigging, superstructure, or other fishing rods and lines to keep the hooked fish tangle-free, you *want* the lanyard to be attached. These are the easiest circumstances to lose valuable equipment, so be sure the lanyard is long enough to do its job.

Rod Holders
We discussed dinghy-rod-holder installation in chapter 5. The principle for your cruising vessel is the same. Rod holders are like extra crew. They stand faithfully in position, tirelessly waiting for strikes, or they patiently hold arrays of fishing rods, gaffs, nets, flags, and scrub brushes until you need them, with nary a complaint. A sufficient number of rod holders, thoughtfully positioned for fishing and storage, adds immensely to fishing fun and efficiency.

Reasonably priced, individual commercial rod holders include designs with every conceivable mounting configuration.

- Flush mount for insertion into a hole drilled or cut in a horizontal surface, such as a cockpit covering board.
- Side mount for bolting to a vertical flat surface, perhaps at the transom or on the side on any console.
- Clamp-on for attachment to stanchions, superstructure, railing, or any other form of well-secured piping.

These rod holders are perfect for mounting possibilities available on a variety of afterdeck configurations. If you already have or, perhaps after reading this chapter, plan to add superstructure such as an arch, it's hard to beat custom-welded rod holders placed exactly how you want them. Some holders function mainly for accommodating trolling rods, others act mainly as vertical storage racks for weapons on standby, like spinning rods all rigged and ready to toss a bait or lure to fish you see near the boat. Follow these simple guidelines and these holders will last the life of your boat or longer.

♦ *Material.* Match the pipe material to that of the superstructure, usually either 316 stainless steel or 5086 marine-grade aluminum (or other 5000-series grade, depending on what country you're in). PVC pipe *can* work for light-duty spinning rod holders and for storage racks, but will not take the strain of heavier tackle or be convenient to attach to metal superstructure.

♦ *I.D.* Sufficient to accommodate your largest rod and gaff butts. An I.D. of at least 1⅝ inches (41 mm) is usually adequate; go bigger if in doubt.

♦ *Length.* Not less than 9 inches (229 mm) for appropriate support; longer is OK.

♦ *Support.* Weld upper and lower horizontal supports or struts between the rod holder and superstructure pipe. This takes the torque exerted by the sudden twisting loads of fish strikes. Make at least two welding passes at each attachment for aluminum. Don't let your welder talk you out of this—one pass just doesn't get it and will eventually crack under heavy-duty conditions. Another tip: if your welder shows up with a MIG (metal inert gas) outfit for this job, do not proceed—the control and maneuverability of a TIG (tungsten inert gas) unit is essential for this work.

♦ *Gimbal.* Always construct gimbals to prevent rotation of rod butts in the holder. Use hex-head ¼-inch (6.4 mm) 316 stainless steel bolts oriented at a right angle to intended rod orientation. Refer to figure 5-1 for galvanic isolation tips and other construction details.

Rod-holder arrays—units designed to compactly deploy sets of say four fishing rods in one spot—were exclusively custom-made until relatively recently. Now you can buy ready-made "rocket launchers" and similar specialty devices. All have the same concept: rather than spread fishing rods around the aft part of the vessel, forcing fishers to run around to deal with multiple strikes or other situations, why not locate them at a single handy position and create distance between baits by running the lines to various release clips? This mode is particularly popular for cockpits free of rigging and other obstructions.

Modified forms of multiple rod holders work well for any sort of afterdeck arrangement. For example, one commercial product consists of a stainless steel "tree" of three angled rod holders mounted on a horizontal support, the base of which is a single gimbaled butt that fits neatly into a standard individual rod holder. The idea is to enable fishing two rods from a kite, with both fishing rods and the kite rod mounted in a single console. The fisher has only to stand at this station for adjustments to the kite or either bait.

Rod-holder arrays for storage can go anywhere. Ready-made racks of PVC holders mounted on teak frames are widely available and bolt to any flat vertical surface. Horizontal rows of rod holders bristle from flying-bridge railing and upper-arch crossbeams. Vertical rod-holder rows ascend the legs of minitowers, arches, and full-sized tuna towers such as those on sportfishing charter boats. These usually store a variety of specialty rods prerigged for different purposes, but they may be used for trolling-line deployment, for example, to enhance the action of lures that skitter and skate more seductively when suspended from higher angles. To avoid tangling fishing lines around inactive rods, install such storage racks *forward* of wherever you normally set trolling lines.

Securing Downriggers, Upriggers, and Outriggers

Think of downriggers, upriggers (i.e., center riggers and fishing kites), and outriggers as equipment intended to extend the reach of fishing rods in order to place offerings where you'd like, relative to your vessel and to each other. It should be no surprise that rod-holder-like devices often secure them. Your downrigger *and* uprigger dispenser might simply be a commercial deck winch. Dedicated units built and marketed for exclusive downrigger service frequently come with a swivel base intended for bolting on a flat, horizontal surface. Others feature a gimbaled butt that mounts in a standard rod holder.

Center riggers—identical to outriggers except usually shorter, pointing straight aft, located on the midline of the vessel (usually on the aft railing of the flying bridge or pilothouse roof), and set at a 45-degree angle relative to the ocean surface—normally fit into a female receptacle similar to a rod holder. Smaller, lighter outriggers most appropriate for sailboats and more petite powerboats come with flush mounts intended for attachment to a flat horizontal surface. Stanchion mounts usually consist of makeshift clamp-on rod holders, fixed firmly and angled appropriately for outrigger use. This is the normal sailboat scenario (see photos page 214).

Important points about stanchion outrigger installations are as follows.

- *Ensure a snug fit of the outrigger butt into the holder.* Most center riggers and outriggers in this range have a smaller diameter than standard rod holders, requiring insertion of a sleeve to reduce the holder I.D. PVC is excellent for this because it's easy to bore out slightly for a perfect fit and it provides galvanic isolation. You might get lucky with the right size metal pipe. Installing gimbals will fix the sleeve in place.
- *Install a forestay to prevent rotation of the clamp-on holder on the stanchion.* The best clamp-on rod holders cannot normally apply sufficient pressure to resist the leverage exerted by a 15-foot (4.6 m) outrigger under the sudden pressure of a fish strike on tight release-clip settings. Without a forestay, they snap aft as they rotate forcefully on the stanchion, delaying or preventing the release of the trolling line from the clip. This frequently causes failure to hook up because the fish feels clumsy, indistinct resistance rather than the sharp sudden load that would drive a hook through the jaw. Affix a ¼- to ⅜-inch (6 to 9.5 mm) line 1 to 2 yards (meters) from the base of the outrigger with a rolling hitch and run it forward to an amidships cleat or other solid fixing point (see fig. 3-16). Maintain reasonable forestay tension while using the outrigger.

Larger outriggers, intended to maximize lure spread on fishing vessels over 25 feet (7.6 m), normally assume installation on the vertical flat surface of the pilothouse. Sliding support arms that pivot outboard and lock into place are a common feature. Fancy models gain further support from spreaders and stays fixed at intervals out the length of the outrigger. These are fine pieces of equipment, although completely unnecessary for fishing success.

Most cruisers will want to select relatively inexpensive, easy-to-stow outrigger models such as the telescoping type recommended in table 8-1. Less expensive models that come apart in sections are fine too. Homemade models work great—trim a stout length of bamboo or an appropriate length of wood. Use a downwind pole. Considering the low price of 15- to 18-foot (4.6 to 5.5 m) outriggers, ease of installation, the fishing efficiency they confer, and the number of hours spent trolling, however, we doubt you'll ever look back from buying a commercially produced set.

Superstructure

Raising the center of gravity of your cruising vessel is not to be undertaken lightly. Weight aloft increases the tendency to roll and can decrease your boat's righting moment. Modifying commercial fishing vessels without proper regard for these factors has killed many people. Coastal vessels with reasonable speed and normal operations near port get away with lofty tuna towers and other structures that would be dangerous in severe conditions. If the weather looks bad, they can cancel their trip or hustle into port. Slower cruising vessels that travel longer distances, however, must be prepared to face occasionally strong conditions impossible to outrun. Part of the challenge is more careful attention to loading, stability, and any act whatsoever that puts weight higher.

Superstructure installations *can* be safely accomplished. Know exactly how much your installation will weigh. Seek the services of a certified naval architect to compute expected impact on the stability of your vessel. Before you make structural additions, have the consultant empirically compute the righting moment by placing a standard weight off the centerline, measuring the angle of heel, and applying this data to stability formulas. Repeat the process after the installation. Counterbalance by adding ballast. If your motivation for adding superstructure is fishing, stowing the rest of your fishing gear low and near the centerline will likely provide the necessary compensation, *but put a pencil to it.*

Obviously, the less your modification weighs, the smaller the influence on stability. Calculate the difference between using aluminum and stainless steel. Despite the fact that you must use thicker grades of aluminum pipe for the same strength, you'll find that it's the lighter, more sensible choice from a stability standpoint. The slight difference in windage between more slender stainless steel pipe and aluminum is much less important. This is why many modern high-seas steel commercial vessels have aluminum deckhouses, and stainless steel tuna towers of any size essentially don't exist—they're aluminum. Seen any stainless steel sailboat masts or sport-fishing outriggers lately?

Now that we've got you thinking in terms of Schedule 40, Grade 5086 aluminum pipe and vessel stability precautions, let's take a look at what superstructure can do for you. Powerboats designed for pleasure have long featured towers of various descriptions designed to elevate and therefore improve the vision of the boat driver. Many incorporate built-in rod holders, outriggers, a center rigger, convenient railing, and frames for protective canvas or PVC sunshades and weathershields. Sailboats lagged far behind in this department, usually settling for folding Bimini tops as opposed to more permanent structures, and haphazardly mounting various antennas, wind generators, radar stands, and other paraphernalia on independent stands, generally in an obstructive clutter.

Dodge Morgan's record-setting circumnavigation aboard *American Promise* exerted a revolutionary change in the afterdeck clutter found on a decreasing number of sailboats today, all because of a single, elegant structure mounted over the transom: the arch. If this wasn't the first one, it was certainly the first to gain the immediate, widespread attention of cruising sailors around the world. Fishing aside, this is the perfect solution for clearing and reclaiming for practical use that most important area of the boat, the transom. The same structure quickly sprouted up amidships on fast powerboats for the same reasons—ridding the center console and gunwales of clutter, not to mention elevating dangerous radar-scanner output above the crew. Still more arches found their way onto the flying bridges of all kinds of power cruisers. Arches also provide an excellent vantage point for deck and spotlights, solar-panel mounts, and elevated places to sit, with legs and railing suitable for multiple rod holders, and they're a good place to terminate transom railing . . . little wonder they've become so widespread on cruising boats during the last fifteen years.

The photos on the next two pages illustrate the arch aboard *Élan*. I had an exciting quagmire of ideas, but my friend, master welder, and shipwright Jimmy Doll gets sole credit for its creation. Jimmy's arch continues to captivate the interest of sailors, fishers, and welders. Some sailors, offended by the thinly disguised fishing-trawler look, hate it. One guy in Fort Lauderdale started to hyperventilate and asked me why I didn't just buy a fishing boat. When I replied that I already owned two that I was selling so that I could afford to attempt a circumnavigation on a safer, more efficient platform, he stopped glowing red and sputtering long enough to say "Oh" and then walked away. Most cruisers love it. People sketch it all the time. Adults and kids like to climb on it, sit on it, dive off it, spot fish from it, and deploy trolling rods from its multiple rod holders. Many folks claim their next big project is to add one; at least three similar renditions have appeared on friends' sailboats. The wildest one is Frank Jensen's, a near replica mounted aft on his classic fiberglass sloop *Jubilation*, which features not only rod holders, but also a swiveling miniature armchair complete with gimbaled drinkholder. Now that's style.

I'd owned and sailed *Élan* for nine years before I put all the stuff on it that you see in the photos on the next few pages. The boat has never been and never will be anything other than a rugged, long-distance, live-aboard workboat. Despite careful planning, I was very worried about whether the superstructure would be any good or not. The nice thing about aluminum is I could always saw it off and throw it overboard if I didn't like it. However, six years, 15,000 NM, and half a planet later, neither of us would have it any other way. We enjoy it on a daily basis—it facilitates visibility, night lighting, trolling, and harness safety, and it keeps an array of electronic devices clear of the afterdeck. It has provided the opportunity to enjoy a countless number of memorable moments that would not have occurred without it. It's solid; it doesn't shake or move.

Schedule 40 anodized aluminum arch, integrally welded to the transom and afterdeck area of *Élan*, connecting to a permanent Bimini top/solar panel mount featuring a fold-down sunshade.

The permanent, fixed Bimini top with folding shade and solar panel (above right) helps arch stability via the diagonal support between the two structures. Height and configuration permit easy operation of halyard winches and clearance for the boom during tacks. It doubles as a solid handhold for standing aft and peering forward while steering the tiller by foot. It's also an effective rain catcher and an excellent leaning post while fighting big fish from near the cockpit.

The crow's nest is a simple design of Jimmy's, through-bolted to the mast. It's a great fish-spotting platform. It also takes all the pressure off navigation in coral-strewn, poorly charted shallows. One of us lounges in the crow's nest with a portable VHF and quietly speaks the course to the cockpit VHF, on low power and a conversation channel, to the person steering. No frantic signaling, loud voices, stress, or close calls. The elevation permits moves in low sunlight conditions that would be dangerous from lower spotting locations. It's the best seat in the house in calm conditions offshore.

Afterdeck, Bowguard, and Rubrails

The guy in Fort Lauderdale who hated *Élan* so much *did* make a good point. Fishing-boat experience planted the seeds of many of our sailboat-modification schemes. Power cruisers often already have features that perform the tasks intended for these alterations. The afterdeck of *Élan* is a good example of a cruising sailboat addition in this category (bottom photo page 216). It started as a guard for the Aries wind vane, which took frequent hits from commercial fishing boats and other friends that often tied off to us for social occasions in the Bahamas. It was part of a scheme that included aluminum rubrails welded the length of the hull and a Schedule 80 bowguard (top photo page 216). The design confers the ability to comfortably leverage the boat from seawalls, pilings, and marina slips, regardless of wind direction, using a single diesel—just like a workboat and requiring no other crew. Shouting orders to six individuals running around with fenders is unappealing.

One thing led to another and the aft wind-vane guard got railing, a thin bolt-on fiberglass deck supported by additional framing, fish-cleaning table, barbecue grill, scuba-tank racks, and dive ladder. It became the focus of all fish-butchering activity, taking the blood and guts out over the water and away from the rest of the boat. It has supported the final stages of many an epic fish battle and facilitates gaffing, landing, tagging, and releasing. Modern cut-away sailboat transoms offer better and easier water access than this afterdeck, as do the cockpit and transom configurations of most power cruisers. Also, non-metal sailboat transoms frequently do not have the structural integrity or strength to consider a similar modification.

Fish-Cleaning Tables

Backs and knees hate bending over to butcher fish lying on a deck, especially in any kind of seaway. It's messy, inconvenient, awkward, not good for you, and takes the luster off a nice catch. Cruisers need fish-cleaning tables that fulfill as many of the following conditions as possible.

♦ *Nonskid, knife-friendly cutting surface.* You can't beat white nylon block material, readily available from plastics suppliers in a thickness of 1 inch (25 mm) in up to 4- by 8-foot (1.2 by 2.4 m) sheets. Get a large piece to make a galley cutting board and fish-cleaning table. It cleans well and provides an excellent

Crow's nest's view of *Élan* underway in the lagoon of Fakarava, Tuamotus, French Polynesia.

Rubrail and bowguard (*top*) and afterdeck (*bottom*) of *Élan*. Note barbecue, scuba-tank racks, fish-cleaning table with knife rack, and dive ladder on the afterdeck. Fish-cleaning-table washdown pump is a foot-operated Whale Gusher MK III, with 90° PVC elbow inlet hose-clamped to a trolling planer, attached to the end of a section of flexible water hose. When this arrangement is dropped overboard while underway, the trolling planer digs in, holding the inlet underwater and allowing us to use this simple washdown even if we're at 8 knots (see trolling planer fig. 3-18, table 8-1).

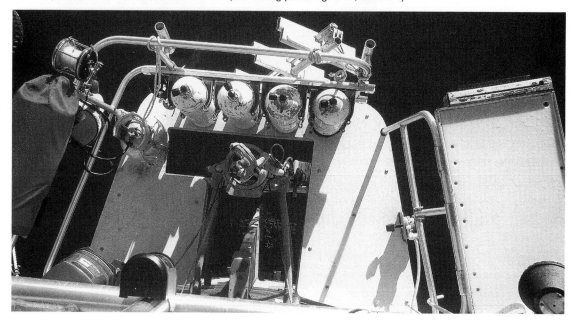

cutting surface, and it's very easy to cut, drill, and shape.

- *Make it big enough.* Try not to go less than 20 by 34 inch (51 by 86 cm). You're going to be catching some sizeable fish on a regular basis, and you'll need room to lay 'em out and create those nice steaks, fillets, and soup parts.
- *Make it a comfortable working height.* Belly-button high is perfect.
- *Form a retaining lip on the three sides other than the one at your belly.* This helps keep fish and fish meat from sliding off the table. You need a flush surface nearest you to lay your knife flat for skinning, filleting, and other operations—a lip here will force you to angle the blade, causing you to miss meat.
- *Build drains in the two corners farthest from where you'll stand.* This keeps blood, pieces of entrails, and rinse water flowing off the table and away from you. You may wish to wear a waterproof fish-cleaner's apron anyway.
- *Install a knife rack.* Bolt a long narrow rectangle of wood, nylon block, or other material to the end of the table, with a lengthy longitudinal slot for knives and your cleaver. This speeds up processing by keeping your array of fish-cleaning tools handy.

Commercial models mount in standard rod holders. Ours is permanently fixed on an afterdeck rail and may be folded down vertically or propped out to a horizontal working position. We welded the aluminum frame to two short sections of pipe fitted onto the rail for the hinge. Lacking an overhanging afterdeck, consider a short, waist-high section of railing run forward from your arch that would be a suitable fish-cleaning table and solar-panel mount frame. Folded vertically, either could double as impervious spray guards for the cockpit and provide windage where you want it, aft.

Small Conveniences That Make a Big Difference

Step aboard any top professional fisher's vessel—commercial, charter, or recreational—and some of the first things to catch your eye will be small conveniences that make fishing easier and more efficient.

Born of hard experience, these play a strong role in the poetry of movement on the work deck. These folks don't fumble around in confusion looking for something they need at the sudden appearance of fish or other fleeting opportunities—they glide quickly, often without taking their eyes off the water, and that fish has a bait in its face before it knows what happened.

Most of these conveniences place tackle or tools close at hand or position baits optimally, for example, by running trolling or drift lines to strategically placed roller-guide release clips on short lanyards. Racks and holders store knives safely in handy positions. Dehookers, gaffs, and nets should stow neatly in racks mounted on vertical surfaces or, in some cases, on horizontal overheads, discussed in more detail following. Carefully positioned plastic leader racks dispense rigged lures and hooks quickly and provide a fast, organized place to retire those coming out of the water. A mounted length of wood or aluminum dowel run through plastic spools of various strengths of monofilament makes a very handy line dispenser (to avoid line oxidation, don't install this in direct sunlight). Convenient tackle drawers and cabinets—with built-in dividers or containing flat, sectioned storage boxes—provide fast access to swivels, sinkers, hooks, rigging and leader wire, lures, small tools like wire straighteners, sharpening stones, hook files, spare reel parts, binoculars, clean polarized sunglasses, towels and rags, spray cans of light oil . . . everything you need. Fill hook bins with baby powder or talc to discourage corrosion.

Power-cruiser cockpits may have room for a small counter or workstation consolidating some of these features. With all components close at hand, rigging baits, lures, and leaders becomes a snap. Changes in fishing conditions, strategy, or target species pose no problem. Inevitable glitches like line tangles and chafed leaders become minor, ephemeral events. Fishing becomes less laborious and more fun.

That All-Important Barbecue

A commercial propane barbecue grill, fabricated from quality stainless steel and designed for installation on cruising boats, provides an invaluable outdoor cooking system independent of the galley. Price, parts availability, and convenience tip the balance in favor of this route as opposed to custom or home-made affairs for most cruisers. The 9- by 17-inch (23 by 43 cm) grill size of the largest barbecue currently offered in this market is *barely* adequate for dealing with any significant volume of seafood; even then, it often requires two or more rounds of cooking. As an active, competent fisher, you will likely be unsatisfied with anything smaller.

Mount the unit somewhere aft on railing, positioned to minimize messy drips on deck. Alternative mounting systems, including rod-holder types, are available. Few cruisers go the straight charcoal route, which normally engenders carrying voluminous, hard-to-store quantities of briquettes. Affix the propane tank outside near the grill where good ventilation prevents accumulation of heavier-than-air fumes in enclosed spaces.

This system is great in the tropics because it avoids galley heat generation inside the deckhouse or below-decks living areas. It has a way of leading to other things—it gets the chef outside in the fresh air to enjoy the sunset and the dazzling array of sea life attracted to the glow of deck lights after dark. One clear, calm, starry night anchored off the tiny, remote island of Maninita, Tonga, a large humpback whale surfaced scant yards (meters) from the after-deck of *Élan*, loudly expelling a cloud of steamy whale breath that drifted vaporously across the halo of the arch light. What prompted the visit—the pulse of reggae into the water through the hull, the underwater glow of the lights, or the dubious idea we might be fixing enough Antarctic krill to share with a guest? Whatever the reason, I'd have missed the memorable encounter had I not been outside grilling fresh marinated red snapper steaks.

Dive Tanks

As I spun around in surprise that night at Maninita, my leg brushed the row of scuba tanks stowed neatly and out of the way across the afterdeck railing. If you choose to carry this form of dive equipment, tank storage will require some consideration. Scuba tanks are heavy, bulky, and rounded. They can tip over and roll around dangerously if they get loose. A rolling scuba tank with a good head of steam is a formidable object.

Cruisers commonly stash scuba tanks in the lazarette or cockpit lockers. Smaller sailboat cruisers lash them on deck. Cockpit systems consisting of loops of bungee cord—one small enough to fit tightly over the tank valve base, another larger loop to secure the midsection, aided by crescent-shaped cutouts in wood planks—are common on commercial dive boats. Six years ago, we decided to try an advancement of this idea in the form of a then-new product (the Roll Control System), which featured hinged composite racks that mount on railings or vertical flat surfaces (see bottom photo page 216). Tanks snap tightly into the two jaws of the rack, one high, the other low (contact V-Jay Distributors in Florida or K.T.O. Enterprises in New Zealand; see appendix 1). Crimp loops of heavy steel cable around the tank valve bases to run a single lockable length of cable through all the tanks. Secure with a lashing for heavy weather and offshore passages. This system applies equally to power and sailboat cruisers. It can serve as temporary or permanent storage, either above or below decks.

Another approach that tends to occupy more space is horizontal tank racks. Commercial versions are available in foam, metal, and plastic materials. Tanks rest on their sides in semicircular-shaped supports. This is nearly always a temporary arrangement for the purpose of a dive trip.

(Mostly) Horizontal Racks and Holders

A variety of racks, clamps, and other devices secure fishing rods, spearguns, PVC tubes of spear shafts, gaffs, nets, tagging sticks, dive flags, harpoons—virtually any elongated piece of gear you might need for fishing. Most mount on either horizontal or vertical flat surfaces and orient the gear parallel to the water surface. This provides an opportunity to stow items out of the way, on the sides of the hull below the gunwales, or to indoor or outdoor overhead surfaces. Beware of stowing fishing rods below the gunwales because they are more vulnerable to damage from flopping fish and angler movements. Save these spots for gaffs and other more rugged gear that can take the pounding. Be sure to place a short length of tight-fitting hose over all gaff points—you'll never forget the experience of impaling yourself in the shin or calf with a gaff hook. I admit to accidentally trying this twice, and it wasn't any better the second time . . . it sends an incredibly strong, jolting shiver straight up your spine, and leaves a gaping, nasty hole in your leg.

One of the best recent innovations in horizontal rod racks is a brand-specific, spring-loaded device that firmly suspends revolving-spool reels by two stainless steel buttons that pop into the harness lugs. A second clamp secures the fishing rod with a rotating nylon insert. This system neatly and firmly secures your heaviest stand-up and other tackle overhead and out of the way—no more rattling, sliding, and rocking around.

Store the fishing rods you may need quickly in the vertical-pipe-style rod holders described previously, clamped to stanchions, mounted flush in covering boards, or welded to railing or arch and tower legs. These are faster to access than horizontal racks.

Spring-loaded pins mount revolving-spool reels neatly to overhead clamps.

Fish Boxes and Bags

The space limitation of sailboats relative to power cruisers creates a fairly distinct split here, with the latter often having space for a convenient built-in or movable, rigid fish box. The advent of insulated "body bags," discussed for dinghy use in chapter 5, came to the rescue of sailors.

Frankly, you can't beat a nice rigid fish box. Gaffing the fish, swinging it aboard, and depositing it quickly in a solid enclosure half-full of freezing seawater mixed with crushed ice, then slamming the lid shut, takes care of many things at once. The temperature shock quickly and humanely stuns most fish into an immobile state, chills the body rapidly and preserves attractive, fresh skin color, producing a firm, top-quality, easy-to-dress outcome. It also sharply reduces the danger from fish slashing and struggling on deck.

Alas, lack of large amounts of ice and, in the case of sailboats, space curtail this option for many cruisers. If you have a holding plate or other freezer of any size aboard, maintaining frozen jugs of water at all times will help keep the unit cold and also provide a way to chill fresh catches whether in a fish box or bag. Adding seawater helps distribute the chill by increased contact area around the body of the fish. With the help of seawater and ice jugs, insulated fish bags lash neatly on deck and do a great job of keeping your catch cold—even in harsh, direct tropical sun—until you can get free to clean it.

Interior Storage

All cruisers pay close attention to storage below decks. Those on extended trips are carrying *everything* they may need: provisions, tools, toys, books, parts, fuel, and water. They also must *live* among all of these things and, therefore, seek to minimize the tendency for a flea-market-like atmosphere. Stuff has to be compact. It must disappear from view and be secure from inevitable bumpy weather. The transition from land to water involves numerous difficult decisions over what and what not to bring.

If you had *just* finished this process prior to picking up this book, the excitement of your new life as an expert roaming fisher might somewhere have been tempered by the realization that this means finding a place for at least *some* additional gear. Fear not! Here are some pointers for efficient stowage of fishing gear. You'll hardly know it's there, and the things it can do to enhance the pleasure of your cruise will more than justify taking it along.

ROD RACKS AND LINE DISPENSERS REVISITED

We can pack half a charter-fishing business worth of rods and reels securely into overhead rod racks in the forepeak of *Élan*. Chances are you'll want to carry only a fraction of this array. Save space by orienting racks head to toe so that bulky reels alternate fore and aft. Premeasure the section of overhead you'd like to use and choose rod lengths that fit, purchasing two-piece rods where necessary. Squeeze in racks for nets, gaffs, and other gear, again making purchases that fit your space.

If you have no room or only limited space for a dowel-rod line dispenser above decks, consider installing one in your below-decks work area. The

photo below depicts a double-rack design made from aluminum rods mounted in standard rod racks. The location is less convenient to the outside work area, but the line suffers no oxidation from exposure to direct sunlight.

DEALING WITH TERMINAL TACKLE AND SUPPLIES

Plastic storage boxes with different-sized compartments and in a wide variety of sizes, shapes, and thicknesses are available from tool, hardware, household, and fishing-supply outlets. Measure your interior drawers, lockers, shelves, cabinets, and cubbyholes. Think about your fishing-gear budget and interests—what slice would you most like to pursue? Make a tentative list of intended purchases, right down to hooks, lures, swivels, and other supplies. Note that many items come packaged in handy divider boxes that may fit well into your boat's storage spaces. Take a good look at catalogs and in local stores before you buy additional divider boxes, and select those perfectly suited to your situation. If you have a cabinet drawer or two available, or you can

Two fishing-line dispensers or spool racks conveniently store various strengths of monofilament in the forepeak of *Élan*. Both the stacked, compact divider boxes (left compartment) and the mesh dive bag with gear in clear, labeled, resealable plastic bags (right compartment) keep items organized.

figure out a place to fit some in, consider divider boxes that match the drawers. This way you firmly enclose lots of tiny objects you don't want to end up in the bilge—yet, open the drawer, pop the lid open, and everything is at your finger tips.

Canvas bags store much better than rigid cases on boats. Big, blocky tackle boxes with multiple layers of fold-out trays, like you might spot on a bass-fishing TV show, don't store well on most cruising boats. Even if you lack dedicated cabinets or drawers for terminal tackle and the many other small items associated with fishing, you can easily store numerous divider boxes in zip-top canvas carry-alls or mesh dive bags placed in variously shaped storage spaces. Many fishing items (e.g., floats, plastic bait bodies, replacement lure skirts, unrigged trolling lures of all descriptions) fit well in zippered plastic bags, which then consolidate into the same type of larger canvas and mesh bags that can store divider boxes. Label all divider boxes and plastic bags. Pack them according to fishing theme into the larger bags, and label these accordingly (see photo page 220). Commercially marketed, compartmentalized lure satchels with Velcro latches are also popular for storing sets of offshore trolling lures.

The Wide World of Live Bait Wells

No matter where you are, there's usually no greater fish-attracting power than live bait. It's so deadly that some sport fisheries and fishing tournaments forbid it. In the presence of live baitfish, you can unglue fish that have lockjaw. For example, I pulled into Indian Key, near Islamorada, Florida, one evening on a tarpon *(Megalops atlanticus)* charter with my 20-foot (6.1 m) fishing skiff. My customer and I had worked hard to locate, chum up, and cast-net several hundred pilchards *(Harengula jaguana)*, which were now friskily plying the brisk current in the circular, on-deck live well. Numerous boats were anchored or drifting this popular location, fishing with live mullet suspended from corks.

Tarpon from 50 to 120 pounds (23 to 54 kg) were rolling on the surface and cruising slowly over the variegated sand and turtle grass patches, easily visible in the 12-foot (3.7 m) deep, crystal-clear water, completely ignoring the earnest offerings of the crowd of sportfishers. We anchored away from the crowd and, with fishing rods stowed, began pitching handfuls of live pilchards out behind the boat, squeezing or banging some against the hull to stun them. Soon tiny ripples and swirls broke the glassy sea surface all around us as disoriented packs of the frightened baitfish swam erratically, interspersed with stunned individuals twirling frantically in circles.

Huge, quiet boils quickly appeared as agitated tarpon made increasingly intense inspections and passes at the free-swimming baits. A 75-pounder (34 kg) noisily slurped a wounded pilchard at the surface not 15 feet (4.6 m) from the transom, several long silver flashes signaled subsurface takes, followed by a round of hard, rifle-shot explosions as burly, hyper-excited tarpon nailed surface-swimming pilchards. The tranquility of the quiet tropical evening was deteriorating fast. "OK, Dave, let's bait that rig, pitch it out 25 feet (7.6 m), and get ready to dip the rod tip and then set the hook." I chucked out another round of live chum, right on top of David's cork float just after it hit the water. It bobbed briefly and then was sucked under the surface amid a powerful, foaming swirl of seawater. Dave set the hook, a 100-pound (45 kg) mass of silver-scaled tarpon came crashing out of the water, and any semblance of serenity was long gone. The drag screamed and Dave whooped as the tarpon came out of the water again before speeding off for the horizon. After a wild hour-and-a-half battle that ended a mile from where we'd hooked up, I got photos of Dave gently reviving and releasing the fish to fight another day (see photo page 334).

A live well full of the same bait species made the day for Palmer (my dad) on a recent family trip to a spot some 12 NM distant from Indian Key, a seamount jutting up into the Gulf Stream called the Islamorada Hump. Palmer spun the wheel of his 18-foot (5.5 m) skiff to set up the power-drift. I scooped a dip net full of pilchards from his live well, hooked four to a 50-pound (23 kg) test monofilament teaser line (made with 5/0 Mustad 94150 hooks suspended from the main line by dropper loops), and sent them out behind the boat. Palmer kept the bow southwest into the current, idling gently in forward gear as the four terrified baits darted around 30 feet (9 m) back from the transom. I tossed a second scoop of pilchards on top of them. The free swimmers clustered in a ball around the teaser—a distinct ball of bait creating an irresistible silhouette for bruiser blackfin tuna *(Thunnus atlanticus)* cruising 20 to 80 feet (6 to 24 m) below.

Suddenly, a dense explosion of foaming seawater and pilchards jolted us like an electric shock. A pack of blackfins rocketed vertically through our living chum ball, crashing the calm sea surface to produce a 5-foot-high (1.5 m) spray of pilchards and white flecks of seawater. Palmer released the helm and flipped his bait into the middle of the melee, and loose coils of 20-pound (9 kg) test monofilament immediately began ripping loudly off the spool of his spinning reel. He allowed a three-second drop-back, flipped the bail closed, began winding the reel handle like a madman, and lifted the rod tip sharply when he felt resistance. The rod doubled abruptly, and the drag sang as the tuna flashed for the depths. Twenty-five minutes later, I lowered the tired 28-pound (13 kg) fish into the freezing slush in the fish cooler.

Chumming with live bait works equally for fishing reefs, wrecks, grass beds, holes and banks in channels and rivers—start sprinkling out favorite live food items and fish come rocketing off the bottom or away from structure, throwing caution to the wind.

Large quantities of precisely deployed live baitfish seduced both Dave's tarpon and Palmer's blackfin tuna to strike. You learned how to throw a big cast net and how to find and attract live bait into throwing range in the last chapter; all you need now to have experiences similar to those of Dave and Palmer is a decent live-bait well.

Live wells double as onboard aquariums for temporarily maintaining various forms of sea life collected for close observation by your children. *Warning: Kids love live wells, and you won't believe the variety of organisms you will be temporarily hosting. If you do not want them to become avid students of marine biology, don't get one!*

NATURALLY ASPIRATED LIVE WELLS
You've got plenty of DC power demands already, right? The idea of funding a 6- to 8-ampere continuous live-well pump probably wreaks havoc with the electrical budget. No problem . . . enclosures that use boat movement to circulate oxygenated seawater can work perfectly well.

Floating Buckets and Cages
Perforated floating containers—purpose-designed bait buckets; any size plastic garbage can with a tight-fitting lid with lanyard, peppered with holes and with Styrofoam floats lashed at intervals around the circumference; PVC pipe frames with floats and soft, knotless nylon mesh—anything that maximizes water exchange with openings small enough to prevent escape can work. Often such arrangements become temporary holding pens for large quantities of bait awaiting transfer to shipboard live wells for transport to fishing areas, or for leftover bait destined for use the next day. For example, if you worked hard to catch a large batch of shrimp or crabs for bait, you might want to house them overnight for use early the next day. Tie off your floating well to a transom cleat and they should be fine. The many functions of the dinghy shown in figure 5-2 include use as a floating live well.

Pay close attention to overloading and get a feel for ambient oxygen levels at your anchorage or marina. Areas with poor circulation support less bait. Also, oxygen and water-quality requirements vary considerably among the different species of fish and invertebrates you might wish to store. Toss a fresh-caught small tuna or squid into a small floating bucket and it will die in minutes. Hardy inshore bait species like octopus, pinfish *(Lagodon rhomboides)*, penaeid shrimp, or portunid crabs might live happily in the same container for weeks.

Submerged cages can be successful bait pens. Rigid plastic or plastic-coated mesh tends to maximize passage of water. Net, hair-hook, or otherwise catch your bait, place it in an appropriate-sized cage, and either suspend it from your boat or drop it to the bottom on a line with a marker float (any sealed plastic bottle will do for a marker). The latter strategy is superior if your boat is rolling in the anchorage, which may throw the bait against the sides of the cage, abrading fins, nose, and other areas, which leads to rapid bacterial infections and death.

Another variation on this theme is to let your

cage catch your bait for you. Refer to figure 7-4, choose a design, buy or construct a trap targeting the desired bait species, and you're set.

Transom Boxes

Perforated square or rectangular boxes of different sizes bolted, fiberglassed, or welded to the transom of all-sized boats serve as convenient bait wells. Placement submerges the bottom half or so below the water line. Advantages include ready access and complete separation from the inner hull. Disadvantages are normally lack of ability to empty these of water, adding constant weight to your vessel, and the existence of corners as opposed to a round shape, which does not suit many faster-swimming, more delicate bait species that tend to bump into the corners repeatedly until they die.

Many fishing vessels have more than one live well in order to separately maintain different bait populations. Thus, a transom well might house hardier fish or invertebrates long term, or some moderately delicate species of baitfish (e.g., mullet, ballyhoo, pilchards, thread herring, cigar minnows, other small jacks, and trevallys) for the duration of a day or night fishing trip. This can free up space and reduce oxygen demand in other live wells, permitting specialty use for selected bait types. Separate multiple live wells also solve the problem of species intolerant of each other; for example, the tendency of loose scales and slime shed by a large number of pilchards clogging the gills of ballyhoo kept in the same well, which results in their rapid deterioration.

Ram Jet Transom Wells

Why do tuna and some other fish species typically die so quickly when tossed into relatively spacious, naturally aspirated live wells of most designs? The major reason is their dependence on ram ventilation to breathe. If you closely examine fish in an aquarium, you'll see them rhythmically opening and closing their gills to pump water by the gill filaments, just as a human diaphragm expands and contracts to pump air through our lungs. Species like skipjack tuna don't do this—they depend on swimming fast with their mouths partly open to force water through the gill chambers. If you prevent the abil-

ity to swim rapidly and constantly, suffocation occurs quickly.

Innovative sport billfishers came up with a way to do this *for* them. They discovered that placing skipjack tuna and other ram-jet breathers head first into short sections of near-vertical pipe and delivering a strong flow of seawater through the apparatus keeps them very much alive, despite the fact that they're immobile. Pipe diameter is sufficient for a relatively close fit around the fish's body. Water delivery can be from a forward-facing scoop. Water exits out the top of the pipe and spills back into the sea, often aided by angling the water-exit end of the pipe mouth slightly aft of vertical. This permits catching one or more tunas on trolling feathers, placing them in ram-jet wells, proceeding to the chosen marlin fishing spot, and putting out the fresh, frisky baits.

Built-In Live Wells

Integral hull compartments for holding live bait have the advantage of enhancing vessel stability and optimizing fuel consumption by placing the added weight of the water in better places, namely low and near the centerline. Figure 5-2 illustrates a common form of built-in live well depending on multiple forward- and aft-angled holes for water flow. A relatively low number of holes allows insertion of plugs and then bailing or pumping out the water when the well is inactive, which can serve as a semidry storage area for gear items.

Multiple perforations provide excellent circulation but make it harder to stop water ingress for whatever reason. This motivated the development of scoops featuring forward- and aft-facing mouths to feed and suck out water from the compartment as the boat moves, and to provide lower-volume communication with the sea at rest (fig. 8-1). Therefore, these wells do not deliver nearly as much fresh seawater at rest as multiple perforations, but do generate considerable exchange underway, and do not require an electric water pump to operate.

POWER LIVE WELLS

The ability to pump large volumes of water through bait-holding compartments vastly increases their capacity and the number of potential species they

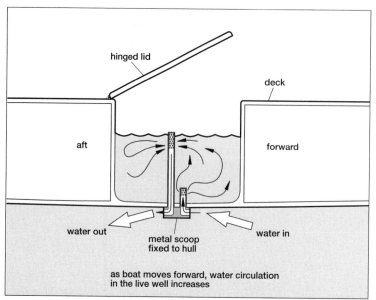

Fig. 8-1. Naturally aspirated below-deck live well using a scoop to enhance circulation while underway. Inlet and outlet fittings can be removed and caps screwed in their place when well is not in use, creating a semi-dry storage box.

can support. Combine high exchange with proper well configuration and you can keep almost any species alive long enough for a fishing expedition. Even the most budget-conscious cruisers may encounter situations that justify such a system.

General Principles

If you're going to install a power live well, there's no sense in going about it in a half-hearted manner. Figure out where you'll put it, compute the maximum sustainable amp draw your electrical system can reasonably tolerate relative to intended live well usage, buy the highest volume pump this allows, and plumb and configure your system using the following guidelines.

♦ *Maximize the rate of water flow.* Have you already been snooping through a catalog, possibly using the index to find "live-bait pumps"? If so, ignore this section—for some reason, manufacturers and marketers haven't caught on to the fact that 400 gallons per hour (gph) (1,514 L per hour) or less is generally insufficient for maintaining anything more than minimal numbers of hardy species. Head down to the docks,

ask your local professional fishers—their pumps start at 800 gph (3,028 L per hour) and go up to 3,700 gph (14,006 L per hour) and more; these include many small circular wells suitable for more casual cruising applications.

♦ *Buy or construct a circular live well tank.* Many marine bait organisms, particularly active swimming species, survive much better when they're not banging into corners.

♦ *Direct the pump flow into the bottom of the well.* You'll want to locate exhaust ports, either perforated standpipes or through-hull fittings, at the intended tank-water level. Therefore, if you direct the *inflow* high in the water column, much of the exhaust water is relatively fresh and high in oxygen; the volume low in the tank tends to become oxygen-poor. Freshwater ingress from the *bottom* of the tank, on the other hand, maximizes the opportunity for oxygen utilization by your guests before it spirals up the water column and out the exhaust port.

♦ *Orient the inlet fitting to create a circular flow.* Most bait species swim head first into the current. Circular flow patterns are less turbulent, more stable, and induce the organisms to move in a manner that minimizes contact with the tank walls.

♦ *Minimize 90-degree elbows in the plumbing.* Help your pump deliver maximum volume by omitting flow-resistant fittings other than the 90-degree elbow convenient for creating circular flow at the tank inlet.

♦ *Double the inlet plumbing I.D. for the correct-sized exhaust outlet and plumbing.* This general rule of thumb prevents a tank from chronically overflowing due to actively pumped inflow overwhelming passive exhaust. For example, if the pump outlet line and tank inlet elbow I.D.

is ¾ inch (19 mm), the tank exhaust outlet I.D. should be 1½ inches (381 mm). Total area of central standpipe perforations should also be double the inlet I.D. Precalculate or do it empirically by building your system, firing it up, and then successively peppering the top of the standpipe with holes until it can effectively handle the inflow.

♦ *Install screening across exhaust ports.* You don't want bait and debris running out the exhaust system; adjust screen size accordingly. Note that some screens, particularly round holes in stainless steel sink drains, tend to snag bally-hoo beaks as they swim by the opening. If this happens to you, tie finer screen to the permanent screen for ballyhoo use. Square, black plastic screening with ⅛-inch (3 mm) squares is usually good; go smaller if necessary.

♦ *Paint or tape a horizontal black circle around the inside circumference of the tank 60 to 75 percent of the distance from bottom to water surface.*

Research indicates this assists the ability of occupants to orient to the tank configuration and vastly increases survival of some species. One more secret: extend closely spaced bars from this circle to the tank bottom at a 45-degree angle, and you'll get even better results.

What in the heck does all of this look like? It's quite simple, as you can see from a sample of configurations shown in figure 8-2. Direct exhaust below decks and out of a through-hull, the normal motivation for a central standpipe, or out the side of the tank and overboard via a hose that can dangle overboard, run to a scupper, or connect to a through-hull located anywhere at or below the surface level of the live-well tank.

Whatever manufacturers lack in pump knowledge, they certainly compensate with a huge variety of truly wonderful, reasonably priced circular and oval plastic live wells in all sizes. The lid diameters are

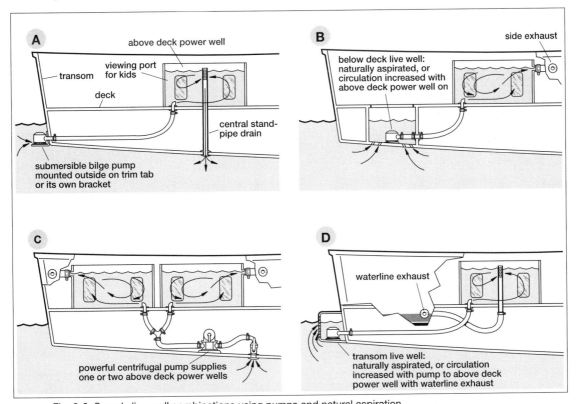

Fig. 8-2. Sample live-well combinations using pumps and natural aspiration.

only 60 or 70 percent of the tank top diameter, reducing sloppy splash potential. Semicircular braces attach to the deck, preventing tank movement in a seaway. Some highly effective models feature a donut-type circular tank that fits around any pedestal, so the fish swim around in an enclosed channel. Small tuna and bonito live in these for hours with sufficient pump capacity and tank-orientation markings.

Would you like to entertain your kids for hours at a time? Buy a piece of ⅛-inch-thick (3 mm) clear Plexiglas (also called Perspex), cut out a narrow rectangular shape, cut a slightly smaller vertical opening in the live well, and install the viewing port on the inside using a strong adhesive sealant (e.g., 5200 by 3M or Sika-Flex). You might reduce arguments by installing one for each kid, well spaced around the tank. Who says cruisers can't have an aquarium?

Hybrid and Combined Systems

Let's look at a few Cadillac live-bait well configurations. Now, before you snort disbelievingly or laugh out loud, bear in mind that the first time you saw many of the items in this book, you thought, "That's too much" or "Never me." Remember where all of us started, with nothing, or maybe with an old chafed handline of unknown strength that caught one fish every three years. Each will find a level of comfort and satisfaction but, rest assured, you maniacs out there who go all the way will lead significantly altered, much wilder fishing lives than the more sedate among you.

Submersible pumps give you more bang for the buck (and per-unit amperage) than in-line suction pumps. They don't have to work as hard. These must mount somewhere below sea level, of course, preferably in locations minimizing resistance to boat movement and other forceful turbulence. The ultimate such location is inside a naturally aspirated live well built into the hull or attached to the transom. Fishers are also attaching them to trim tabs and low on the transom with good success.

Submersible pumps mounted in live wells vastly increase bait-carrying capacity and flexibility. They enhance flow through the lower well as they pump seawater to the upper well. They're more accessible to clear, check, and maintain, and they afford the ability to separate bait species. Drawbacks are the tendency to suck debris and lower well bait up against the inlet screen, transfer slime and scales from lower to upper well, and the fact that you are pumping somewhat oxygen-depleted water to the upper well. If you don't think this matters, compare upper-well bait capacity and longevity with the lower well full and empty of bait.

The next logical step is to feed the lower and upper wells from separate sources. Attach your high-capacity pump on the transom and plumb it to your circular on-deck well. Enhance the natural aspiration of the lower well with an in-line, low-capacity bait pump mounted in the bilge and by assisting egress with a high-mounted automatic bilge pump switch or one of the new solid-state submersible bilge pumps that activate periodically at set time intervals. Sound over-complicated? I designed and installed a system like this on Palmer's fishing skiff before we sailed away from Florida; frankly, I think he hated it for a while, especially when he felt that the two full live wells threatened to sink his boat on several occasions (since attributed to lower-outlet-pump malfunction). However, the design was instrumental in creating the blackfin tuna episode at the beginning of this section. You should probably ask him (see contact information in appendix 2).

Yet another possibility is to have two independent power live wells, fed either by a single very-high-capacity pump (fig. 8-2C) with precise flow control to the tanks via a combination of adjustable in-line ball valves and a 45-degree Y-valve (fig. 8-3, upper right). This allows complete separation of bait species and the ability to adjust flow to the oxygen demands of each. The disadvantage is that you are always running a high amperage pump, even for small amounts of bait. It's all or nothing and requires appropriate electrical generation. Supplying the separate tanks with lower-capacity individual pumps permits cutting amp consumption by running only one, and gives you a back-up system in the event of pump failure. Figure 8-3 shows hybrid and combined power-assisted live-well systems.

I've had excellent success with every system described here on one fishing boat or another. You can see that the only limit, once you have a set of

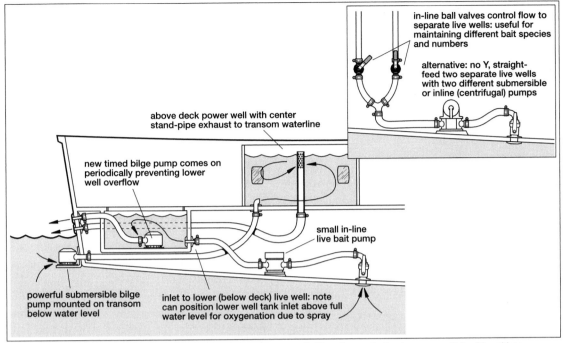

in-line ball valves control flow to separate live wells: useful for maintaining different bait species and numbers

alternative: no Y, straight-feed two separate live wells with two different submersible or inline (centrifugal) pumps

above deck power well with center stand-pipe exhaust to transom waterline

new timed bilge pump comes on periodically preventing lower well overflow

small in-line live bait pump

powerful submersible bilge pump mounted on transom below water level

inlet to lower (below deck) live well: note can position lower well tank inlet above full water level for oxygenation due to spray

Fig. 8-3. Mix and match live-well designs to suit your activities. Separate feeds, accomplished by either one or two pumps, maximize oxygen to different wells.

design guidelines, is your own imagination. When you decide to get serious, follow the tips for maximizing your ability to carry live bait. You will be able to "black out" the well; that is, load it with an extreme density of pilchards or similar bait that will live perfectly for hours, giving you enough time to get to the fishing spot and use them as live chum and bait.

Cold Storage for the Avid Fishing Cruiser

Intermittent power usage and availability, regardless of vessel type, almost always makes a holding-plate cold-storage system the right choice for cruisers. Luxury yachts and commercial fishing vessels that run an AC-generating plant around the clock have other options, and one could effect refrigeration by periodic offshore ice production, but none of these logically apply to most of our situations. They require too many crew members and too much money, weight, and space for most noncommercial operations.

Holding plates are liquid-containing stainless steel boxes that constitute refreezable ice blocks.

They maintain refrigeration temperatures of 33 to 45°F (0.5 to 7.2°C) and freezer temperatures of 10 to 20°F (−12 to −7°C) for twelve to thirty-six hours between system run times. Pumping refrigerant through coils of copper pipes inside the holding plates refreezes them, effecting removal and eventual transport of heat from inside the insulated cold-storage box to outside air or seawater. Number and size of holding plates and cold-storage boxes, and specific liquid mixture inside the holding plates, are highly flexible and easy to adapt to any boat interior and a range of budgets.

Effecting the refrigeration cycle requires various components, but the major consideration is the size, pumping power, and source of power for the compressor that moves the refrigerant around the system. The three most common choices available to cruisers are engine-driven, DC-electrical, and AC-electrical compressors. Compressors driven by belts from the power takeoff of the main engine are by far the most efficient, but obligate the operator to run the engine daily, or subject cold-storage items to warming temperatures. Twelve-volt systems are the least efficient, drain excessive amps for all but the tiniest boxes, often compelling operators to run the engine at least as much *or more* to keep the batteries charged as they would to keep holding plates frozen with an engine-driven compressor. Wind and solar electrical generators can help supply the amps necessary for a 12-volt system, and trouble-free, constant box temperature is highly advantageous (note the deleterious effect of temperature cycling on cold-stored seafood discussed in the next chapter). Also, it's quiet if you have enough wind and sun to keep pace with the amp draw. AC compressors, either 110- or 220-volt, are great if you spend much time dockside with access to commercial power or regularly run an onboard AC generation plant for significant periods.

A few practical facts can assist your thinking, now that you may want to retain for consumption big, tasty tuna and a myriad of other fish and invertebrate species. A holding-plate freezer and refrigerator system of sufficient size to handle the occasional 100-pound-plus (45 kg) fish will likely require the power and efficiency of an engine-driven compressor. Scale down your fishing targets, beef up your non-engine 12-volt-generation capability, and a 12-volt compressor might fit into your electrical budget. First calculate total daily DC electrical demands carefully, because it'll likely be your greediest component.

What's the upshot? Just like the common cruising-boat buying axiom, if you expect fishing for your own seafood to become an important part of your voyaging life, get the biggest refrigeration system you can fit and afford. We ripped an amidships bunk out of our 41-foot (12.25 m) sloop and installed a large freezer with two big holding plates that can hold 300 pounds (136 kg) of seafood. Our refrigerator, located in the galley, has a volume of 10 cubic feet (0.3 cubic m). The system is dual and can run off either a 5 hp engine-driven or a ⅓ hp 110-volt AC compressor. We have no AC generator, although in case of engine-driven system failure, we can run the AC compressor via an inverter while the main engine is running. However, this is very inefficient, practically good only for holding established cold-storage temperatures—although a 36-hour run time would in fact

freeze all plates starting from ambient temperature. Total cost was close to $7,000 in 1993 for self-installing a system custom designed by and purchased from Rich Beers Marine, Inc., in Fort Lauderdale, Florida. The system has performed flawlessly now for six years, requiring only routine maintenance. We have stored thousands of pounds (many hundreds of kg) of seafood and other frozen provisions worth far more than the initial cost, some of which was recovered during commercial fishing activities in Florida before we embarked on our long-term cruise.

A very high percentage of cruisers we meet wish they'd installed larger, engine-driven cold-storage systems. On the other hand, we must run our engine for forty-five to seventy-five minutes daily to keep everything at constant temperature. Smaller 12-volt systems are available for a fraction of what we paid—and self-installed auto air conditioner compressors from the junkyard will freeze holding plates too. We also muse over the attraction of having a third imbedded 12-volt capacity when we're watching our wind generator crank out far more amps than we use in stiff trade winds. From a simpler viewpoint, I did Bahamas charters and other voyaging happily for nine years before the big installation with no refrigeration, only a built-in galley-counter icebox. Whatever your situation, examination of figure 8-4, a diagram of the basic layout of a refrigerator-freezer holding-plate system, may prove helpful. You choose the capacity, box shapes and locations, compressor type, and consequent cost. Don't forget to factor into your cost-benefit analysis the cumulative future savings from additional seafood protein made possible by cold-storage versus store-bought meat.

Fishing Electronics

The advent of affordable Loran-C units in the early 1980s and affordable GPS units ten years later forever changed the world of fishing. No longer is relocation of deep-water structure a hit-or-miss adventure in dead reckoning or dependent on precise visual alignment of obscure coastal ranges. Over a very short period, average small-boat owners needed only to push a few buttons and a machine would steer them precisely to the spot. Powerful, inexpensive color depth-sounders show every detail

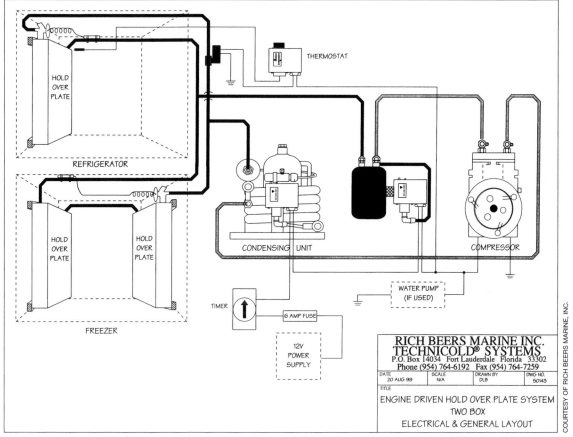

Fig. 8-4. Electrical and general layout for a two-box refrigerator/freezer, engine-driven holding-plate system.

of the bottom, and precise information about everything that swims between the hull and the seafloor. With the push of a button, chartplotters indicate and store events like billfish strikes, enabling precise return passes across the same productive patch of water. Radar allows safe passage in weather that might previously have kept amateur vessels at the dock.

Despite the quantum leaps in fishing power these electronic aids confer, full utilization of their capabilities still requires skill that comes only through practice. You surely have at least some of these capabilities on board for safety and navigation—how can you use them to influence fishing success? Should you consider purchasing any additional electronics for fishing?

RADAR

Reasonably priced, compact models targeting various small-boat markets make radar scanners a common sight on the majority of cruising vessels. Most operators feel they can hardly afford not to avail themselves of the safety and navigational information provided by an electronic eye that can see through rain, fog, darkness, and storm clouds and over the visible horizon.

You might be wondering, given the fact that radar scanners look above the water surface while fish swim below it, how they help with fishing. In addition to enhancing the safety and accuracy of passage to and from the fishing grounds, here's a trick that uses radar to find fish you might never see otherwise. The next time you spot a flock of seabirds hovering over a school of fish, flick on your radar. Compare returns on the screen to what you can see with the naked eye or the aid of binoculars. Tune the unit for maximum detail and record these settings.

The next time things are quiet offshore—you're not seeing any signs of life, nothing's biting—turn on the radar, tune for birds, and you have just radically increased your effective search area. That small flock of terns or single frigate bird you find with the radar could make your entire fishing day, and be the difference between getting skunked and boating a really nice catch.

GPS and Chart-Plotters

Most fishers focus on using GPS and chart-plotters to guide them to waypoints marking specific locations on the seafloor. Certainly this is of critical importance for catching resident or migratory fish that strongly associate with reefs, wrecks, rocky outcrops, ledges, holes, seamounts, and other bottom structure frequently invisible from the surface. Experts, however, use these tools for a much broader range of applications.

These might include the relocation, either later in the day or over a period of several days, of persistent conditions that concentrate target fish species. Eddies, current shears, oceanic temperature fronts, upwelling zones, meandering or undulating currents that frequently change paths, plankton blooms, and other factors heavily influence fish distribution, often where no distinct bottom feature, visible landmark, or other orientation clue exists. Recording these discoveries as a series of waypoints confers invaluable information on shape, magnitude, and position of the oceanic feature, allowing near-future returns to the strike zone.

Sometimes, however, not even the subtle changes in water color, surface patterns, and temperature zones typical of oceanic features are present, and yet some unidentified variable consistently concentrates open-water fish species in a restricted piece of ocean. We stumble over these areas occasionally, and suddenly the rods bend and the drags scream. If it happens again—hours, days, or months later—we may suspect a pattern. Now, the only way you'll *know*

about the pattern is if you're recording the waypoints of the strikes—even if it's a year later, something rings a bell, you look at the chart-plotter, and, sure enough, there's an icon on or near this same spot. Perhaps on another occasion, you'd like a billfish, wahoo, or tuna, so you give that same place a try and you get a third strike. At this point, you *know* you're onto something. Who cares if you lack an explanation for why the fish show at this place? At least you're catching them. Little things like this characterize experienced fishers and are one subset of the many small factors that contribute to highly consistent fishing success.

Depth-Sounders

It wasn't long ago that fishers depended on a belt-driven stylus to burn marks on rotating rolls of fairly expensive paper to view fish and bottom structure. This discouraged leaving the units on all the time, so that fishers frequently drove blindly over productive features and fish aggregations while underway or trolling for other target species. These machines also gave much less detailed information about bottom type and fish sizes, numbers, and species.

The development of affordable, water-resistant LCD (liquid crystal display) and CRT (cathode ray tube) depth-sounder viewing screens took the fishing world by storm. While both permit more detailed depiction of relative sonar return strengths, LCDs can't touch the ability of full-color, TV-like CRT screens. LCD technology does permit less expensive, far more compact units that may tell you all you need to know. The depth of a CRT unit must roughly equal the diagonal measurement of the screen, so it requires more space. Current CRT prices start below $500. If you can find the money and space, buy a CRT depth-sounder.

Both kinds of sounder, depending on specific model, may have the following capabilities.

♦ *Multiple frequencies.* Higher-frequency sonar (usually 192 to 200 kHz) typically conveys more detail in shallower depths; lower-frequency sonar (50 kHz) provides more accurate signals from deeper bottom (over about 150 ft./46 m). Units with both frequencies are highly desirable for many fishing activities, but they cost more.

♦ *Temperature display.* Changes in surface temperature can indicate current edges and other productive oceanic features. Most units have this ability.

♦ *Bottom hardness.* Special functions cause the display of the seafloor as a thin line, with a variable-width underlying band enabling differentiation of bottom composition. This display also permits separation of bottom-dwelling fish targets from the seafloor.

♦ *Zoom.* This function displays an enlarged, user-defined depth band on the screen. For this to be of any real value, be sure the unit shows increased resolution along with the magnification—many don't.

♦ *Bottom lock.* Displays from seafloor to user-specified depth, regardless of total depth. Effective for hunting demersal fish species like tilefish (Family Malacanthidae), cod (Family Gadidae), halibut (Family Pleuronectidae), and many other bottom-huggers.

♦ *Integration and display.* Most depth-sounders will talk to your GPS and other navigational gear and display information like current position and speed/distance.

The following tips will help you get the most from whatever model depth-sounder you choose.

♦ *Leave the unit on while underway fishing.* Record all interesting bottom features you cross for later reference. Starting this practice in my first year of charter operation while regularly trolling for mahi mahi resulted in the accumulation of a huge library of productive deep-drop spots that came in handy when surface- and reef-fishing was slow. You'll quickly develop a habit of scanning for surface activity while keeping half an eye on the depth-sounder.

♦ *Use shape, color, and distinctness of signals to identify fish species.* Start by examining the marks of fish of known identity; for example, schools of baitfish or target species visible in the water

column swimming under the boat. Graduate to confirming signal identity by sampling. For instance, you see a thin blue haze on relatively flat bottom at a depth of 495 feet (151 m) offshore of the southeastern United States; fire down a deep-drop rig, and catch blueline tilefish *(Caulolatilus microps)*. Your drift continues over a bumpy ledge covered with many distinct yellow blotches, a few with hazy borders and red cores, and you catch a bunch of pink porgies *(Pagrus pagrus)* and a couple of snowy groupers *(Epinephelus niveatus)* . . . and so on. Do this no matter the depth and you'll soon become an expert at accurately interpreting data from your machine.

♦ *Look around before anchoring or drift-fishing over bottom structure.* You'll often discover loose groups of fish that can be targeted by slow trolling or otherwise presenting offerings at precise depths, or accumulated into a chum slick by riding around and bombing them with heavy chum balls to get their attention prior to anchoring.

♦ *Gauge fish responses to your techniques when conditions allow.* Some conditions force you to work extra hard for each strike. Take the example of tuna hanging around a FAD or seamount. You can chum with live or dead bait material, run teasers, or fly a kite . . . your depth-sounder will show the fish rising to different degrees in the water column as you go through your bag of tricks, although you can't see a thing from looking out at the surface. How does this help? If you get a response to a three-bait teaser and toss out twenty free-swimming baitfish for chum but no strikes, put out a five-bait teaser and toss out thirty or forty free baits on the next drift. This may push them over the edge and induce the maximum number of strikes for the minimum expenditure of live chum.

♦ *Actively hunt for specific bottom types.* Let's say you're new to an area, but you have an idea of the species you might encounter and you know something about the particular seafloor profiles and depth most likely to attract them. A meticulous search of the correct depth contour can net you a fine day's catch.

♦ *Note water-column-density demarcations and vertical movements of the DSL.* Recall our chapter 4 description of the DSL: dense strata of zooplankton and associated predators that migrate vertically each night from great depths to near the ocean surface. You can watch this fascinating phenomenon on your CRT color depth-sounder and adjust fishing baits accordingly. Zooplankton densities often peak at boundary layers (e.g., discontinuities in salinity), which will by themselves show as a hazy bluish horizontal band on your screen. These frequently indicate the bottom edge of ocean surface currents, below which colder countercurrents regularly flow in the opposite direction. Such boundaries are often veritable highways for patrolling predator fish.

SCANNING SONAR

No, we haven't flipped our lids. The ability to electronically scan forward, side to side, and aft by aiming the sonar beam of the transducer is no longer strictly gear for research vessels, high-seas commercial fishing boats, and unlimited recreational budgets. This technology is currently available for under $800 and can double as a simultaneous vertical depth-sounder.

Why might you consider this device? Combinations of shallow depth and noise sensitivity can make many fish species reluctant to pass directly under your vessel. If you look only straight down, you'll never see them. This can be particularly useful for finding schools of midwater baitfish in the shallows. Likewise, if you are anchored in any current and producing a chum slick, your targets are usually positioned *behind* you in the water column. How far back and how deep are they? How many? Your scanning sonar can answer these questions and allow you to adjust the depth of baits accordingly.

Suppose you're anchored fishing a reef or wreck for midwater snappers and they suddenly quit biting. Why? Look around with the sonar—if you

mark a large, solid object moving about in the chum slick, a shark, maybe a large barracuda, or a member of the jack family has shown up and is spooking the schools of midwater fish you'd like to continue catching. This knowledge allows you to deploy an appropriate big bait to catch and release the predator, an entertaining way to encourage the big fish to leave the immediate area. The midwater fish now rise back into the water column and resume feeding.

Scanning under debris offshore can yield valuable information. Perhaps you've found an old pallet covered with gooseneck barnacles and surrounded by baitfish, obviously accumulated during a lengthy time adrift. You try standard mahi mahi baits and lures, but see nothing. Then you note an elevated ocean surface temperature, flick on the scanning sonar, and look deep below the debris. *There they are*, a cluster of blobs at 75 feet (23 m), with several more distinct dots below. A small group of mahi mahi, with wahoo underneath, is orienting to the pallet while seeking the cooler ambient temperatures of the greater depth. Now you know it's worth the time and effort to send presentations deep and catch fresh fish for dinner.

BALANCING NECESSITY AND DESIRE

Where does it all end, you wonder? You have probably already guessed . . . it really doesn't. The only effective limits are space, money, and enough common sense to adjust your fishing equipment purchases to the reality of what you're trying to accomplish. What do you *need* versus what do you *want*? We haven't discussed remote video cameras; miniature submarine-like devices that record temperatures to hundredths of a degree; or huge CRT units that show three-dimensional pictures of bottom features and sea life or incredibly detailed current, salinity, and temperature data from user-defined slices of the water column—yet commercial fishers and researchers are using them all. It should be some comfort to know that many of the greatest fishers in the world still operate from dugout canoes on remote coastlines, relying on sharp eyes and intimate knowledge of marine biology to feed their families on extremely low budgets.

Gear Checklist

Table 8-1 lists recommended commercial renditions of boat-modification hardware. Live wells, refrigeration systems, and fishing electronics vary widely according to vessel size, type, and budget, defying a simple tabulation of use to many readers. Instead, use the principles and diagrams in the text to guide your review of equipment in catalogs and boat shows as you make decisions appropriate for your personal circumstances (see appendix 1 for sources).

TABLE 8-1. **CHECKLIST OF BOAT-MODIFYING HARDWARE RELATED TO FISHING**

Item	Specific Recommendation	Approximate Price
Outriggers	SOS Tele-Outriggers	$300
Downrigger	Alvey 1225 RM Reef Master Reel	$350
Weighted planer	HS 8 Sea Striker	$20
Release clips	Aftco Roller Troller, outrigger style	$33
Rod holders	Lee's aluminum clamp-on	$73–$75
	Perko stainless steel clamp-on	$30
	flush mount—various brands	$20–$64
Multiple rod holder	SOS So-Lo Cluster Holder	$340
Overhead rod racks	Lee's locking ring and spring clamp	$11–$30
Assorted rod racks	Large suitable variety—see catalogs	
Knife and plier holder	Fentress	$16
Drink holders	Fentress	$14–$22
Fish-cleaning tables	Magma	$29–$70
Barbecue	Force 10 large	$180

9

Processing Your Catch

Sport anglers from developed economies may seldom process their catch. Fishing at this end of the spectrum, purely catch and release, is akin to playing golf—the aesthetics, athleticism, and intellectual analysis necessary for success, as defined by the participant, become the goal. Subsistence fishing, on the other hand, engenders similar challenges, except that the objective is to acquire protein for survival. Commercial fishers, including sport charter captains, comprise yet another category. They seek to procure protein (sometimes very temporarily) in exchange for money. Scientists capture some of the same fish and invertebrates sought by all of these fishers in attempts to answer research questions.

Where do cruisers fall in this spectrum? Like this book, they may cut across all lines and categories of the world of fishing at one time or another, but the motivation of most, at least initially, will be subsistence. At the same time, however, lack of suitable storage, small number of crew, inability to consume large quantities of fish in a timely manner, and a lifestyle conducive to frequent fishing success compels cruisers to release many of their catches unharmed, similar to sport-release fisheries and some scientific activities. Otherwise, cruisers will want to process that beautiful fresh fish or invertebrate for immediate or future consumption.

Think about the investment of time, money, and effort behind most catches. Also, consider for a moment the extreme amount of pressure humans place on populations of maritime food organisms worldwide. In many locations, a fat tuna like the one gleaming at your feet would fetch a huge price, befit

presentation to a dignitary or king, or represent an incomprehensibly rich culinary treat for a family or small village. Is this something to treat lightly, to waste through ignorance of proper tools, materials, and techniques for optimum handling, butchering, body-part utilization, and storage? Certainly not.

This chapter endeavors to make you competent in aspects of seafood-processing technology relating to the cruising lifestyle. Like your transformation into an accomplished, versatile, and flexible fisher, part of the task will be opening your mind to unfamiliar ideas, often gifts from native cultures. You can choose those that suit your personal taste, geographical location, and preferred fishing activities, and—just as with exposure to various fishing methods—you'll want to keep some in mind for survival situations. Once more, health and safety issues are as important for processing as they are for fishing practices, particularly for those who may wander far from medical care in relatively slow-moving vessels.

The Biochemistry of Seafood Quality

Proper treatment of your catch begins before the point of the gaff contacts the body of a fish, and comparably early for other modes of seafood capture. In fact, biochemical changes in the muscle tissue of target animals begin to occur very early in the capture process; for example, shortly after hookup. Before we get into sequential instructions regarding handling of live and dead animals for optimum quality, let's learn about aspects of marine food organisms that influence not only capture and handling, but also decisions concerning what species to target in the first place.

DIFFERENT KINDS OF FISH MEAT

We can classify fish muscle fiber, or meat, in one of three categories. Each has different characteristics.

- ◆ *Red muscle fiber.* Concentrated around the spine in most fish, and more pervasive in wide-ranging species like tunas, red muscle is adapted for low-level, low-power, nonfatiguing, sustained routine swimming activity. It is highly vascularized, high in myoglobin, and contains both lipid and glycogen energy stores. Fiber action is slow and aerobic, and features oxidative enzymes. The "blood line" visible in almost any untrimmed fish fillet is red muscle fiber.
- ◆ *White muscle fiber.* Often prevalent in more sedentary fishes that depend on rapid bursts of speed for feeding and survival; for example, cod. White muscle facilitates fast, powerful, short-lived activity, is less vascularized, stores energy mostly in the form of glycogen, and fiber action is anaerobic (i.e., doesn't require direct oxygen, but results in fatigue after a relatively brief time).
- ◆ *Pink muscle fiber.* Physically and metabolically intermediate between white and red muscle, pink muscle operation is fast although oxidative.

These distinctive muscle types are readily identifiable by color as you make incisions in fish. Red meat tends to have a stronger taste than white meat, particularly with time, causing some people to shy away from consuming it, or even from retaining fish with a large amount of it. This is particularly true of people from societies conditioned to consuming lighter-colored fish meat. Flesh carotenoid content is the other influence on fish meat color; for example, the characteristic orange hue of salmonids (trout and salmon) under certain conditions. The presence of carotenoids has little direct relationship to quality, although it may influence consumer behavior toward some species.

Another fish-meat dichotomy that transcends meat color involves general degree of oiliness, or high lipid content, which consumers also associate with stronger taste over time. This "fishy" taste derives from biochemical changes to the lipids, the same class of compounds also prevalent in red meat. Salmon, mackerel, herring, swordfish, tuna, and flying fish all have lipid-rich meat; cod, grouper, and snapper tend to store a higher proportion of these essential, concentrated energy compounds in the liver rather than the flesh. Oiliness may also vary cyclically according to spawning season due to deposition of lipids during feeding periods, followed by depletion during reproductive activities.

There's nothing wrong with oiliness; in fact, it's unquestionably very good for you. Numerous recent definitive research studies document the health benefits of consuming fish rich in omega-3 polyunsaturated fatty acids, a specific class of lipids prevalent in fish oil. They offer significant protection against cardiovascular disease by lowering plasma triglycerides (fat), discouraging atherosclerosis, reducing blood pressure in mild cases of hypertension, and enriching heart-tissue lipids, thus reducing risk of death from either a first heart attack or secondary myocardial infarcts for those who have experienced previous heart failure. Heart attacks are virtually unknown in Eskimo and Japanese populations with high-fish-oil diets. Further evidence indicates potential benefits for inflammatory disorders, such as rheumatoid arthritis and psoriasis of the skin, and even alleviation of cancer.

So why choke down a nasty spoonful of cod-liver oil when you can eat a nicely baked mackerel fillet or swordfish steak? And are you really so sure now about turning your nose up, as many fishers do, at eating bluefish (*Pomatomus saltatrix*, commonly caught in the temperate and subtropical Atlantic and Indian oceans) or kahawai (*Arripis trutta*, a popular sport fish in New Zealand and Australia)? Consider cooking them fresh; you may be surprised at how good they taste.

The consumer popularity problem with more oily fish comes from development of rancidity when frozen, following postcapture treatment that might not affect the taste of other species. Allowing captured fish to warm up and sit around, even for a brief time, further magnifies the problem. This off-flavor is the result of atmospheric oxidation of the unsaturated phospholipids. We explain later in the chapter how to mitigate this tendency with a little extra attention during processing.

Besides meat color and oiliness, fishers also worry about the "ammonia content" of sharks and rays. All marine fishes must deal with the facts that they are submerged in a salty solution, gill membranes and probably skin is permeable, and therefore the surrounding ocean would exert osmotic pressure and suck out their body fluids if they didn't do something about it. Bony fishes developed a fancy combination of ingesting seawater and then actively ejecting salts, mostly out of the gill filaments. Sharks and rays hit on the solution of retaining nitrogenous waste in the blood, primarily in the form of urea, in order to equalize dissolved body-salt concentration with seawater, thereby obviating dehydration problems. Like oiliness, urea-rich blood can result in a taste unpleasant to most people unless proper measures are taken after capture; however, the meat is otherwise highly palatable.

THE RELATIONSHIP BETWEEN pH AND FISH QUALITY

Glycogen in fish muscles is the main fuel for strenuous swimming, jumping, and thrashing around, the normal reaction to most capture methods. It is converted to lactic acid during such stressful physical exertion, and to some extent after death, which then remains in the muscle. This lowers the pH of the meat, although after twenty-four hours, post-mortem white muscle pH is a function of the total carbohydrate reserves of the individual just prior to capture. Excessively low pH makes fish tough; high pH can produce soft, mushy meat.

This impacts one paradigm often applied to fish and other seafood, that larger individuals are tougher. In fact, researchers have documented a small correlation between body size and toughness due to more contractile protein in the flesh of larger individuals, but also because of the mass effect of more carbohydrates equilibrating to lower pH per unit flesh in bigger fish. Although rate varies widely by species, frozen fish meat also toughens with time, which can firm up initially sloppy meat or eventually transform pleasantly firm flesh into a less desirable form.

Another measure of fish-meat condition influenced by pH is "gaping," the appearance of wide fissures and gaps in fillets due to ruptured connective tissue. Low pH and a number of other factors exacerbate this problem, including allowing whole fish to enter rigor mortis at ambient or raised temperatures, mechanical damage from contorting fish in rigor mortis, increasing the time between death and initiation of freezing, freezing whole (particularly ungutted) individuals, and taking an extended time to freeze the fish. Thawing method and length of time spent frozen don't affect gaping.

Generally, well-conditioned, vigorous individual fish have carbohydrate reserves, particularly amounts of muscle glycogen, which translate into a pH range associated with reasonable texture and elasticity. Less palatable meat results from pH values outside this range in either direction.

FLAVOR AND MINERAL CONTENT

As your cruise takes you "down island," you'll invariably (regardless of the culture or language) hear the refrain "Mon, dat fish is *sweet!*" If really fresh seafood was not a part of your life before cruising, take a moment to reflect on this statement. What *is* it about freshly procured, cooked seafood that so appeals to our senses? Perhaps the most identifiable distinguishing characteristic *is* in fact this quality of sweetness, which is not your imagination. It derives almost entirely from the amino acid glycine. Glucose, a result of posthumous muscle glycogen conversion less important than lactic acid, makes a smaller contribution. Maximum sweetness in nonfatty (white meat) fish occurs two to four days after death and disappears in seven to ten days, after which the taste of spoilage begins to develop due to the formation of trimethylamine.

The diet of the fish you capture can also have a distinctive effect on flavor, characteristic either of entire groups of fishes based on selective feeding regardless of location, or quite specific area effects between individuals of a group or species due to local availability of particular food items. For example, the flesh of parrotfishes (Family Scaridae) has a seaweed- or algae-like quality over widespread areas; the flesh of grunts and sweetlips (Family Haemulidae) frequently tastes mildly of iodine due to the invertebrates they habitually ingest. Many cultures customarily maintain and selectively feed fish, crabs, and other organisms to produce more desirable flavor before consumption.

Mineral content of fish flesh is generally low, another quality recommending it to those with heart trouble. It can vary sharply within the body of the fish, however, and also change significantly as a function of handling after capture. Sodium content of connective tissue, for instance, far exceeds that of contractile tissue, increasing the amount of this ion in areas featuring highest connective-tissue densities (e.g., tail-section musculature). Another study showed fast rates of sodium loss from the flesh of gutted cod resting in melting ice, and growing rates of potassium loss over time.

From Ocean to Cleaning Table

Let's use a widespread, highly desirable species caught around the globe to demonstrate proper handling techniques, the first step in fish processing. Your long dreamed-of cruise is underway, the weather is beautiful, and your investment of time, effort, and money has resulted in a big strike. The atmosphere aboard crackles and sparks with excitement and cautious jubilation as you handline the leader, steadily pressuring the strong fish from the azure depths, causing it to turn sideways, flashing silver and showing distinctly lemon-yellow fins . . . it's a yellowfin tuna that'll go 45 pounds (20 kg). Moments later, leader in one hand, gaff in the other, you lean out to secure your catch, now throbbing tiredly at the surface. As described in chapter 3, aim for the head—both for best gaff-holding and to avoid damaging the meat—stroke inward, and lift the fish over the rail or lifeline. Try not to gaff fish in the heart, located on the body centerline between the gill covers, because its continued function later assists thorough bleeding of the carcass. Stun the fish with blows to the top center of the head.

Kill the tuna by first pressing your thumb around this area of the head until you locate a soft spot midway between and slightly aft of the eyes. Insert an ice pick or other spike at a 45-degree angle into this soft spot. If the first dorsal flexes erect, the jaw falls open, and the fish becomes motionless after a last spasm, you had a successful hit; if not, try again.

Digging around with the inserted spike can also effectively destroy the brain. Duplicate this approximate target area for other species.

The biochemical clock has been ticking since the hook-up. Your next actions will substantially influence the ultimate quality of the catch. Pithing is optional, but it takes little time and will produce top sushi-grade fish. The idea is to stop biochemical reactions originating from the intact spinal cord by completely destroying it. Do this by first cutting an L-shaped wedge of flesh from the head to expose the brain, and then inserting a length of 300-pound (136 kg) test monofilament through the remains of the brain and into the entrance to the neural canal (fig. 9-1). This is the long hollow tunnel inside the backbone that houses the spinal cord. Run the monofilament as far into the neural canal as possible, which should induce one last shudder. This is called the Tanaguchi method. Commercial fishers trim the end of the monofilament and leave it protruding to prove to buyers that the fish was killed by this method, but cruisers can pull the line back out—it's done its job.

Next, bleed the fish. This removes large amounts of the lactic acid built up in the flesh during the fight, which can otherwise lower the pH enough to transform firm meat into a soft, even jelly-like consistency. In the case of endothermic (i.e., partially warm-blooded) species like tuna, swordfish, and billfish, bleeding also cools the body by releasing blood that may have heated to as much as 95°F (35°C) in the struggle to escape. Commercial fishers term this combination of heat and acidity "burn-up." In the case of sharks and rays, bleeding also releases urea from the flesh, the cause of ammonia-like odor and taste. For best results, make the following cuts quickly, while the heart is still beating.

◆ *Postpectoral cuts.* For tuna, make a short (1 in./ 2.5 cm) vertical ¾-inch-deep (2 cm) incision, 2 to 4 inches (5 to 10 cm) aft and in a line with the pectoral fin. This position traverses the pectoral fin recess and should sever the major blood vessel running longitudinally just under the skin (fig. 9-2). Repeat for the other side. Make similar cuts for other fishes. If blood doesn't emit freely from these cuts, try again.

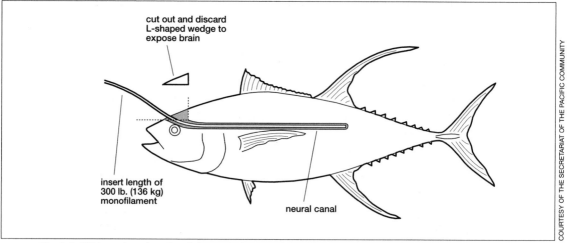

Fig. 9-1. Pithing a tuna (or other fish species) arrests biochemical reactions deleterious to meat quality. (Adapted from Blanc 1996)

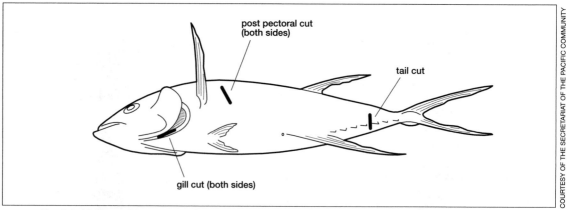

Fig. 9-2. Make precision cuts to bleed your catch properly. This enhances meat quality, particularly for tuna. (Adapted from Blanc 1996)

◆ *Gill cuts.* Slice into the whitish membrane between the red gill filaments and the gill collar of bony fishes two-thirds of the way to the throat (fig. 9-2). For sharks, make a horizontal cut straight through the middle of the gill slits. Repeat for both sides. Again, blood should issue freely from these cuts if you have successfully severed the arteries carrying blood to the gills.

◆ *Tail cuts.* These tend to be inefficient although still commonly practiced. Count back from the tail base to a spot between the third and fourth tail finlet of your tuna and make an incision like the postpectoral cut on either side of the body (fig. 9-2). Some fishers make a transverse ventral cut in this region. Don't sever the spine.

Now tail-rope or gill-rope the fish and suspend it overboard, at least partially submerged in the absence of sharks or other predators. Alternatively, if you have a seawater pump and deck hose, insert the hose into the mouth of the fish. Either way, allow the fish to bleed and flush for ten minutes.

Meat unblemished by discoloration or the presence of tiny dark vein networks results from properly bled fish. Bleeding optimizes texture and flavor in addition to visual appeal. If you have someone aboard who is new to fresh seafood, this may be the difference between acceptance and refusal. Those of you who become sushi connoisseurs will also grow to appreciate the delicacy of top-grade fish.

General Handling

Never toss or bang fish roughly around the deck. This damages the muscle tissues. Don't let them rest on a hot deck or lie exposed to the sun. The best thing you can do for your catch is to gut and gill the fish immediately, and then begin to chill it down. If the sea is too rough or you have your hands full with other matters, place the fish in a cooler or fish box containing a slush of block or crushed ice and seawater—this freezes the fresh skin color, retards bacterial spread, and makes the fish very cool and firm, and,

therefore, much easier to butcher later. Brace the fish inside the cool box in bumpy seas, using buckets or other space-fillers, to prevent excessive sloshing around and damage to skin and flesh. Sailboaters lacking the luxury of a fish box can do just fine with an insulated fish bag containing a plastic container or two of frozen water to cool the seawater. Otherwise, keep fish shaded, covered with wet towels or burlap, and doused occasionally with fresh seawater.

Tools of the Trade: Get 'Em and Keep 'Em Sharp

Arm yourself with the right tools. The photo below illustrates a fairly complete array. First purchase what you need to get started for expected catches

Tools of the seafood-processing trade; see table 9-1 for a complete checklist. **(a)** Heavy-duty cleaver (8 in./203 mm); **(b)** large (12 in./305 mm) cimeter or steaking knife; **(c)** medium (10 in./254 mm) cimeter; **(d)** breaking knife (8 in./203 mm); **(e)** curved fillet knife (6 in./152 mm); **(f)** straight fillet knife (6 in./152 mm); **(g)** sliming knife (4¼ in./108 mm); **(h)** bait knife (3½ in./89 mm); **(i)** fish scaler; **(j)** ice pick; **(k)** sharpening stone.

in your cruising area, and add to the collection as your fishing activities and cruising range expand. Refer to table 9-1 for specific recommendations. Circumnavigators might consider bringing everything pictured.

The second key to successful processing eludes a very high percentage of amateur fishers: how to sharpen and maintain the edge on a knife. We cannot overemphasize the importance of this skill. It's one of those things that is *very easy to do* if you get the right instruction, like many other aspects of fishing. One source of confusion is the presence of numerous approaches—you've seen the cylindrical sharpeners, the Japanese-restaurant grill chefs putting on a show sharpening knives on each other, the variety of little tools that you supposedly slide the knife through once or twice for perfect results, AC electrical devices . . . it goes on and on. All of that stuff may work under some conditions and for certain knives, but figure 9-3 illustrates a simple,

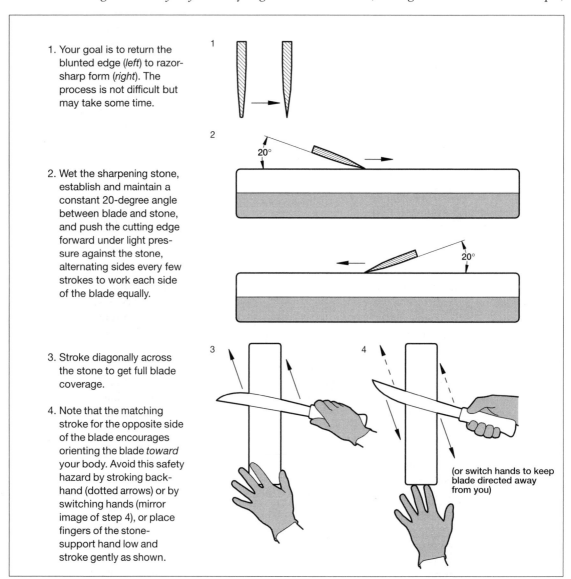

1. Your goal is to return the blunted edge (*left*) to razor-sharp form (*right*). The process is not difficult but may take some time.

2. Wet the sharpening stone, establish and maintain a constant 20-degree angle between blade and stone, and push the cutting edge forward under light pressure against the stone, alternating sides every few strokes to work each side of the blade equally.

3. Stroke diagonally across the stone to get full blade coverage.

4. Note that the matching stroke for the opposite side of the blade encourages orienting the blade *toward* your body. Avoid this safety hazard by stroking backhand (dotted arrows) or by switching hands (mirror image of step 4), or place fingers of the stone-support hand low and stroke gently as shown.

(or switch hands to keep blade directed away from you)

Fig. 9-3. Keeping fish-processing knives sharp.

highly effective way of creating and maintaining *razor-sharp* knife edges using one very basic tool: the sharpening stone (see photo page 239).

When are you finished? Hold out your thumb, orient the knife blade vertical to your thumbnail, make contact, and push gently toward the end of your thumb with no appreciable downward pressure (just the weight of the blade), in an outward scraping motion. A razor-sharp knife will not scrape—it sticks in place, stopped cold by the fine taper of the blade edge. A knife edge that's almost sharp slides reluctantly, possibly leaving a tiny white scrape. A dull knife slides and slips readily right off the end of your thumbnail. This is a very accurate gauge. Be patient, don't settle for less-than-perfect results. Remember, *it's the dull knife that often cuts you* because it encourages you to apply excessive pressure; sooner or later, you'll slip. Dull knives also cause enormous wastage and sloppy results.

Sharp knives, on the other hand, slice effortlessly, allowing you to excise meat neatly from skin and bone with precise control. If your blade begins to drag as you are cleaning your catch, stop, whip out your stone, and touch it up. Keep the following tips in mind.

♦ Meticulously maintain that 20-degree angle as you work through sharpening procedures.
♦ If the cutting edge does not respond to light stroking on the fine side of the sharpening stone, turn it over and repeat the procedure on the coarse side.
♦ For very dull, damaged, or unresponsive blades, rub the length of the blade in a circular motion, pressing the blade to the stone by placing your other hand against the flat blade surface; repeat for the other side of the blade. Return to normal stroking technique as the cutting edge begins to reestablish, as judged by the thumbnail test.
♦ Don't give up—many people become frustrated and quit too soon, assuming "I must be doing something wrong." You're not! Keep at it, maintain that angle, and you *will* prevail.
♦ Near the end of the process, increase the angle (make it steeper) by just a couple of degrees for the last few strokes on each side of the blade for a razor-like finish.

Observing the following rules will make it easy to keep your good knives sharp, and thus make seafood processing as easy as possible.

♦ Try to reserve your fish knives only for seafood-processing—don't allow yourself or the crew to use them for any other purpose. Abused knife blades take a lot of work to restore.
♦ Attempt always to use a proper cutting background, preferably untreated wood, nylon, or other suitable material; never metal, ceramic, porcelain, or soft paper material. Nothing dulls a knife faster, for example, than using a piece of cardboard for a cutting board (analogous to the dulling effect of paper on scissors).
♦ Use specific knives for particular purposes. For instance, don't trash the fine blade of a fillet knife attempting to saw or chop through thick ribs or backbones; sever them with a cleaver or heavy breaking knife.
♦ Keep an older or cheaper knife around for tasks like severing conch adductor muscle from the inner-shell spiral and other rough tasks, thus avoiding damage to more specialized blades.

Gutting and Gilling Fish

OK, now you've got a collection of sharp, high-quality processing tools and an older knife or two for rough work. Let's continue with specific top-grade preparation of that yellowfin tuna you just landed, and make comments specific to other species groups as we go along.

♦ *Make the gut incision.* For your tuna, insert your knife through the abdominal wall 6 inches (15 cm) forward of the anus, cut longitudinally aft to the anus, and then in a tight circle around the anus (do the same for swordfish, but start closer to the pelvic fins) (fig. 9-4).
♦ *Disconnect the digestive tube and gonads.* Insert your fingers into the abdominal cavity at the aft end of the incision, hook and then extract the aft end of the digestive tube and gonads. You shouldn't need to sever these organs, just pop them out of the cut. This helps prevent the transfer of bacteria around the abdominal cavity.

♦ *Cut the gill cover.* Hold the knife vertical to the body line, insert it into the upper gill-cover termination, and slice forward about 4 to 6 inches (10 to 15 cm) depending on the size of the fish. Repeat for the other side of the head (fig. 9-5). This enhances access for the gilling procedure.

♦ *Sever all gill connections to the body.* Cut the connection to the lower jaw (fig. 9-6a), slice in a crescent through the whitish membrane between the gill filaments and gill collar on both sides of the body (fig. 9-6b), then cut the connection between the gill apparatus and the skull base (fig. 9-6c) (leave attached for sword-fish and other species from which the head will be removed).

♦ *"Slime" the abdominal wall.* Using your razor-sharp sliming knife, start at the gut incision and progressively scrape downward toward the spine on both sides of the abdominal cavity without nicking or penetrating the integrity of the wall. Grasp the aft end of the membrane, place the end of the sliming knife on the spinal cord, and work aft to forward to detach the bloodline. Reach in and scrape the area in the enclosed space between the forward end of the gut incision and the gills, starting high under

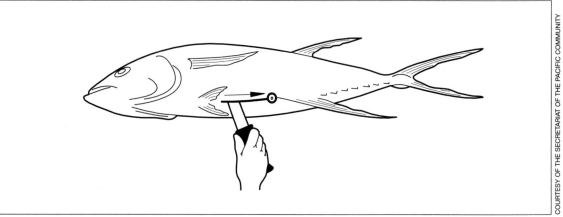

Fig. 9-4. Performing a correct gut incision on a tuna. For smaller fish, start at the anus and cut forward to the lower jaw, laying the belly open for gill and gut removal. (Adapted from Blanc 1996)

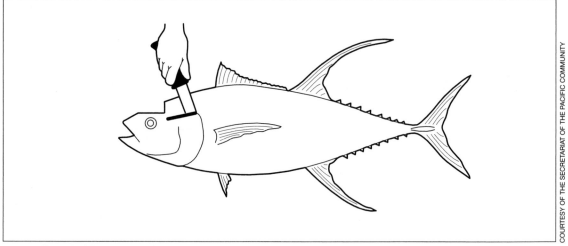

Fig. 9-5. Gill-cover cuts facilitate head access and removal on tuna, swordfish, and other large fishes. (Adapted from Blanc 1996)

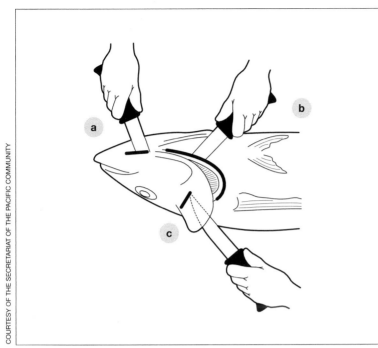

Fig. 9-6. Disconnecting the gill cage from the body involves several cuts on larger fishes. (Adapted from Blanc 1996)

the pectoral fins and working down each side to the backbone. This step detaches the membranes connecting various organs to the abdominal wall.

♦ *Remove the guts, slime, and gills in one piece.* For tuna and other species on which the head remains, firmly grasp the gill apparatus and pull it out of the gill opening. Gills, heart, digestive tract, and all other organs should come out in one unit. Where head removal is desired (as with swordfish), make a transverse cut connecting the two gill cover cuts, firmly grasp the bill or jaw of the fish, snap forcefully upward to break the spine, and remove the head with gills and guts attached.

The procedure takes less time than it sounds like it would. Top swordfishers complete everything to this point in well under five minutes. For smaller fish, such as reef fish, bottom fish, mackerel, and others, gutting and gilling is a fast simple matter of slicing from anus through the throat, quickly severing gills and guts from the body, and pulling it all out

by a firm grasp on the base of the gills. Scrub any blood and remnants out of the gut cavity, rinse or dip to flush, and your fish is ready for cold storage. Cut off caudal lobes and other fins as needed for fitting into your storage unit.

Cleaning Fish

Species, size, and intended modes and timing of consumption all affect preparations beyond or other than production of whole gutted carcasses for chilling and freezing. Many of these procedures apply to such carcasses after removal from storage.

PREPARATION FOR CONSUMPTION WHOLE

One of the most wonderful ways to prepare a fish for dinner is baking it whole. You can also fry, stew, broil, and roast whole individuals. In some cases, there's *no* preparation. Remember the story about bailing frantically to get home after catching flying fish with Hollis John in Tobago (see page 124)? After driving his severely overloaded pickup to the processing plant near Scarborough, we pulled into the darkened parking lot, which abuts the public bus maintenance depot. Two nightshift mechanics popped their heads out a side door. Hollis shouted gaily, "Stahht de fiah!" We finished offloading and packing just as the coals settled to a perfect glow; he tossed a handful of flying fish into a bucket and motioned me through a hole in the chain-link fence. Hollis dropped the fish casually around the margins of the bed of embers and turned them occasionally with a stick. The four of us passed around a flask of rum that appeared from the pocket of one mechanic's coveralls. Moments later, we squatted around the fire to munch on delicious, fresh roasted flying fish. We nibbled the moist, perfectly cooked meat off the back of the charred skin, plucked gently from the bone, as the melody of Bob Marley's "Stir It Up" drifted out the door from a radio inside the mechanical shop.

Preparation for more conventional procedures isn't much more trouble. The key here is to thoroughly remove the scales from your catch, a task made easy with the help of a cheap but effective scaling tool (see photo page 239) and by doing the scraping *before* you gut and gill. Work the scraper from tail to head, *against* the lie of the scales, and don't miss areas around the belly, throat, and head. Rinse thoroughly. Now make the gut and gill cuts, remove, and it's ready for the oven or pan.

FILLETING AND SOUP PARTS

Under the best of circumstances, filleting is the most wasteful cleaning procedure we discuss. Popular for developed-country markets, this processing method sees much less use in developing countries and anywhere else people are culturally averse to seafood improvidence. Many far-flung island cultures make jokes about how rich tourists and visitors don't want any bone in their fish, while they most dearly treasure eating fish *off the bone*. The head of a big tuna or marlin, for example, would be the part of a fish most appropriate to present a village chief in Fiji or the Kingdom of Tonga. In the Western Hemisphere, Bahamians have a ritualized method of processing groupers called "quarter fish." They painstakingly skin whole gutted fish, split the head, trim meat carefully from precisely half the length of the spine, cut through the spine, and then trim the muscle neatly from the second half of the spine, resulting in two perfectly intact fish halves. Why? So each half has an equivalent amount of bone . . . no Bahamian wants to be cheated out of any bone!

A Trinidadian restaurant owner—an intense Indian fellow—really drove this lesson home to me one evening several years ago. After a meeting in Port of Spain, I was finishing dinner with a group of mostly American scientists, several of whom had ordered the whole snapper special. The owner's face was deeply clouded as he cleared the dishes. When he reached for my plate, I quietly asked him what was wrong, and he said we'd wasted a great deal of delicious fish. Being a dumb white guy, I glanced at the bare skeletons, and then back at the owner. "What do you mean?" Disgusted, he exclaimed, *"You got to suck de bone!"* I still didn't get it . . . the backbones were reasonably bare. When I pointed this out, he realized my desire to learn something, so he smiled, sat down, and carefully showed me how, literally, to suck the choice meat off the head and throat of my snapper. I looked around the place and saw that all the natives were doing it. He was right; our table had wasted a lot of great fish.

Therefore, if you pull in to many native ports, drop the hook, start filleting fish, and toss the carcasses with heads, throats, and other meaty parts overboard, you will appear incredibly decadent to any local observers. And they have a good point. Strongly consider saving the carcass for soup parts or, once you get to know the local social intricacies, possible gifts to native friends. Be careful about the appearance of greed from giving only part of a fish. Feel people out first, let them know you've already processed the fish, but that you have some extra throats and heads you were planning to use but that you'd happily share. You'll make many people very happy and, of course, you can always give whole fish as well.

Figure 9-7 demonstrates the proper way to fillet, skin, and debone a fish, and then prepare soup parts from the carcass. The difference in using a good sharp knife will be apparent. Leave only a thin film of meat between the spines, so little you could just about read a newspaper through it!

STEAKING

Cutting fish into steaks wastes little or nothing, at least in the body zone appropriate for this procedure. Consequently, this processing method is far more popular around the world than filleting. It works particularly well for meaty, cylindrical, small-scaled species like wahoo, larger mackerel, tuna, swordfish, shark, amberjack, California and southern yellowtail, and larger rainbow runners. The steaking knife frequently appears for mahi mahi and various reef and bottom fish as well. Steaking is less convenient for species with an armor of large, heavy scales unless they are first removed.

Figure 9-8 demonstrates the procedure for steaking a whole gutted, gilled, and cleaned fish. Try not to exceed a 1-inch (2.5 cm) or so thickness for most efficient cooking results, and be consistent on this thickness as you move successively down the body of the fish. Space the successive transverse cuts

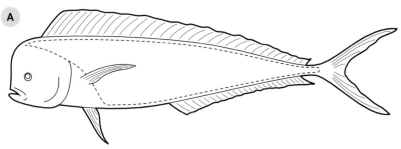

Place the whole, untreated fish flat on the cleaning table. Use a razor-sharp knife to make the illustrated incision, shallow (¼ in./6 mm) everywhere but the diagonal cut from upper head to belly region.

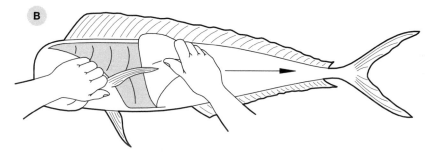

The skin of some species, notably mahi mahi, will peel off with firm hand pressure. For all other fish species, leave the skin on at this stage.

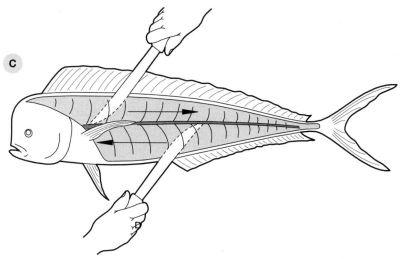

Spread the meat from the bone with one hand, and gently slice the meat from the spines in lengthy, longitudinal strokes, sequentially getting progressively deeper, until you reach the spine; then repeat for the lower half of the fillet.

Fig. 9-7. Filleting, skinning, and deboning a fish, and preparing soup parts from the carcass. *(continues next page)*

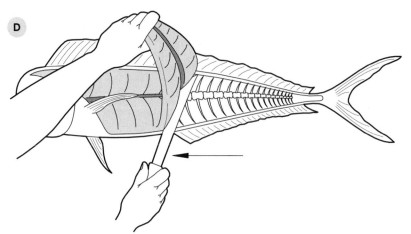

The fillet is now barely connected from tail to rib cage—start at the tail, lift the fillet by hand, and neatly trim from the backbone. When you reach the ribs, slice through them and lift the fillet free from the body of the fish. Note that, particularly for smaller panfish, it may be easier to start from the head and slice back to the tail, omitting the preincision and trimming steps, but you will waste meat doing this quick-and-easy method on larger fish. If you still need to skin the fillet, see figure 9-7G before continuing.

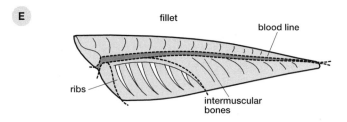

Debone and debloodline your fillet using the cuts shown. Keep the rib cage cut to a shallow arc *just* behind the ribs to avoid losing meat. Note that this leaves you with two boneless, clean pieces of meat, with the ventral portion about 60 percent the size of the dorsal portion.

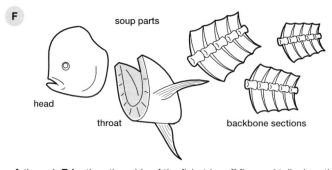

Repeat steps **A** through **E** for the other side of the fish, trim off fins and tail, chop the backbone into sections, and separate the throat and the head for soup parts. Note that heads, throats, and other meat adjacent to the viscera can be particularly ciguatoxic parts on reef fish—consult chapter 10 for guidelines. Chapter 13 describes how to make soup from these fish sections.

Fig. 9-7. Filleting, skinning, and deboning a fish, and preparing soup parts from the carcass. *(continued)*

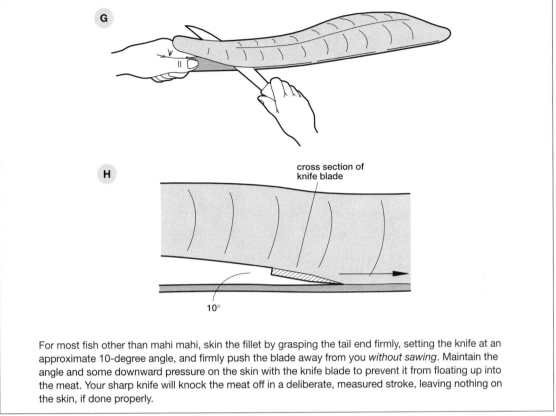

For most fish other than mahi mahi, skin the fillet by grasping the tail end firmly, setting the knife at an approximate 10-degree angle, and firmly push the blade away from you *without sawing*. Maintain the angle and some downward pressure on the skin with the knife blade to prevent it from floating up into the meat. Your sharp knife will knock the meat off in a deliberate, measured stroke, leaving nothing on the skin, if done properly.

Fig. 9-7. Filleting, skinning, and deboning a fish, and preparing soup parts from the carcass. *(continued)*

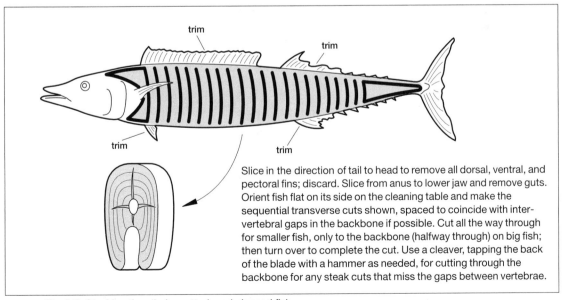

Slice in the direction of tail to head to remove all dorsal, ventral, and pectoral fins; discard. Slice from anus to lower jaw and remove guts. Orient fish flat on its side on the cleaning table and make the sequential transverse cuts shown, spaced to coincide with inter-vertebral gaps in the backbone if possible. Cut all the way through for smaller fish, only to the backbone (halfway through) on big fish; then turn over to complete the cut. Use a cleaver, tapping the back of the blade with a hammer as needed, for cutting through the backbone for any steak cuts that miss the gaps between vertebrae.

Fig. 9-8. Steaking the whole, gutted, and cleaned fish.

so they pass easily through the soft area between individual vertebrae along the spinal column. This saves extra work, especially on larger individuals. Otherwise, use the cleaver to chop through the spine. Leave the skin on.

SPECIALTY CUTS

Specific recipes and preparations may call for specialty cuts of fish meat. Often these are hybrids of filleting and steaking, or cuts made after these procedures. Figure 9-9 demonstrates the creation of boneless quarter or cutlet steaks that exclude the red meat of the bloodline, "logs" for searing recipes (see chapter 13), longitudinal general-purpose block cuts, cubes, and slices suitable for sushi and sashimi preparations.

The thin layer of belly meat overlying the abdominal wall can be particularly tender and succulent. Obviously, sampling this cut requires a relatively large fish, but don't miss it. Remove the belly and scrub the abdominal wall well. Slice the meat, transverse to the bodyline, into ½-inch-wide (13 mm) strips and sauté.

Once again, don't ignore those bony parts. First remove any scales and skin slime. The most efficient way to extract cheek, throat, head, and backbone meat is to boil the parts very briefly, then pick off these very tender pieces of boneless meat, suitable for numerous preparations.

The last item, processing rays, is a permutation of the filleting procedure. These dorso-ventrally flattened shark relatives have a delicate flavor, influenced by diets of mollusks and crustaceans. Lay the animal flat on the cleaning surface, and fillet from just off the dorsal body midline to the wing tip, running the knife neatly along the cartilaginous spines that splay laterally through the middle of the wing. Repeat for the other side, then flip the ray over and similarly fillet the bottoms of the two wings. Skin the four fillets and specialty-slice the boneless meat as you wish.

DEALING WITH PARASITES

Parasites in marine fishes are generally not a health concern for mammalian consumers. Their physiology and life cycles don't mix with our internal chemistry, and few visible individuals ever make it to the din-

ner plate anyway. Various classes are present in the guts of most species. If you don't believe this, place the entrails from your next mahi mahi in a bucket and leave them in the sun for a short time so that they become heated and anoxic. You'll see swarms of tiny nematodes (roundworms) wiggling all over the place, species of no consequence to humans.

Other fish species are well known for harboring flesh parasites, usually cestodes (tapeworms) and trematodes (flatworms), with concentrations varying by geographical location and age and body area of the fish. The ecology of these parasites is interesting. For instance, a high percentage of amberjacks caught off the Florida Keys have huge densities of large, white, pasta-like cestodes in the meat. Similar to most fish-flesh parasites, the amberjack is an intermediate host in the life cycle of this particular species of cestode, which depends on ingestion by large sharks to complete its life cycle. The density of these parasites nearly always peaks in the meat near the tail. Why? This is often the first place predatory sharks bite large fast-swimming prey such as amberjacks in order to immobilize them, so this is the place for worms to maximize the chance of being ingested by the shark.

Wahoo very often have a highly specific trematode in their belly meat—you'll see these stout, dark-colored, worm- or leech-like animals as you steak or otherwise slice the belly. Groupers commonly have smaller trematodes in various parts of the fillet, as do a host of other species. These appear as dark teardrops in the meat. Cestodes regularly pervade the flesh of various drums (Family Sciaenidae), particularly the sea trout *Cynoscion nebulosus*.

The solution? Most people don't appreciate this particular little extra source of protein, but they're easy to see, so just cut them out. If you fish an area enough to know that certain species and sizes tend to have large concentrations of parasites in the meat—possibly to the extent that what's left after excising them isn't worth killing the fish to obtain—then release suspect individuals unharmed.

THE CASE OF THE COOKIE-CUTTER SHARK

What if you catch an otherwise healthy, robust tuna, mahi mahi, or some other pelagic fish and notice one or more circular lesion-like wounds? Is this

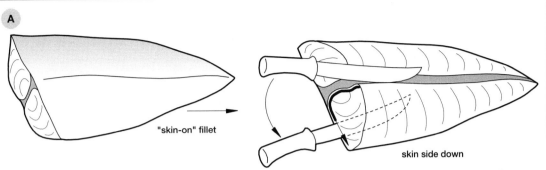

Start with a fat, untrimmed, skin-on fillet, say from a tuna, wahoo, amberjack, cobia, or any number of other fish species. Orient the knife lengthwise beside the bloodline, slice down, and then curve out as you reach the skin. Then keep the blade at a 10-degree angle and give it some downward pressure on the skin as you stroke out away from the bloodline. Repeat for the length of the fillet and again for the other half of the fillet. Trim the rib cage from the ventral portion.

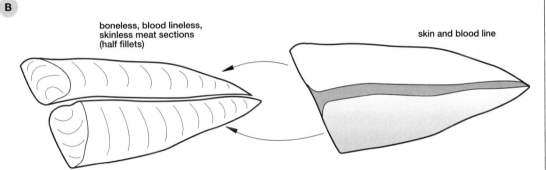

The result is dorsal and ventral portions lacking bone and bloodline, either of which is suitable for a variety of specialty cuts.

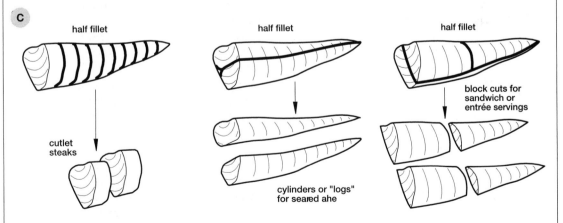

Make the illustrated incisions to form cutlet steaks, cylinders, or block cuts of the dimensions best suited to your recipes of the day. Note that simple cubing is excellent for soups, and thin slices find favor with sushi and sashimi chefs.

Fig. 9-9. Creating boneless quarter or cutlet steaks, cylinders, and uniform block cuts.

something dangerous to the consumer? Absolutely not. Your fish had a run-in with a cookie-cutter shark (*Isistius brasiliensis*, less commonly known as the Brazilian or cigar shark, a member of Family Dalatiidae). This strange-looking little open-sea relative of the spiny dogfish has fang-like upper teeth and overlapping triangular lower teeth that form a cutting edge. These small sharks are luminescent, emitting a greenish light from the belly area thought to draw the attention of larger fish. As the inquisitive fish turns away, the cookie-cutter dashes in—jaw distended—bites, twists, and excises a circular lump of flesh. Sci-

entists believe such treats only supplement a primary diet of squid. This species occurs worldwide in tropical and subtropical seas.

Processing Invertebrates

Invertebrate morphology varies more than that of fish. They might wear an exoskeleton, secrete a shell, or find protection in thickened skin with horns or spikes, or their body might be smooth and soft, depending on speed and illusion to avoid harm. Consequently, processing techniques vary sharply according to invertebrate category.

JANE GREENBLAT AND ANNE GREENBLAT

Typical cookie-cutter shark wound midships on 67 lb. (30.4 kg) bull mahi mahi caught sight-casting a whole squid on 20 lb. (9 kg) spinning tackle by Ken Hurtak *(middle)* offshore of Islamorada, Florida Keys (Steve McKenny, *right*).

CONCH

We discussed the presence and capture of different species of conch worldwide in chapter 6. Conch fritters, cracked conch, conch chowder, conch salad . . . delicious, firm white meat with wide appeal, consumed with relish even by folks who are squeamish about fish. But we're all faced with the same questions upon our tropical cruising debut: how in the heck do you get 'em out of the shell? Furthermore, how do you transform that slimy, dark-colored, thick-skinned beast into the lovely white meat that made these animals so famous?

♦ *Remove the animal from the shell.* With its opening oriented down just as you found it on the seafloor, rest the conch on a firm flat surface. Note the concentric whorls of the spire, each capped by knobs and spikes, emanating aft from the point or apex of the shell. Counting from the row farthest from this point, mark a spot midway between the second and third whorls, on *top* of the spire, and knock a hole in the shell (fig. 9-10). Peer inside—you may see the thin, whitish sheet of the adductor muscle attachment to the internal, tapered cone called the columella. Push a sharp knife through the hole and pressure the blade point along the surface of the columella. You'll feel resistance as the blade encounters the sheet of muscle. Press forward, then across, severing the muscle from the columella in a scraping action. Now turn the conch over, reach inside, grasp the operculum, and pull the animal out of the shell. If it won't budge, you haven't completely severed the adductor muscle—turn the conch back over and try again.

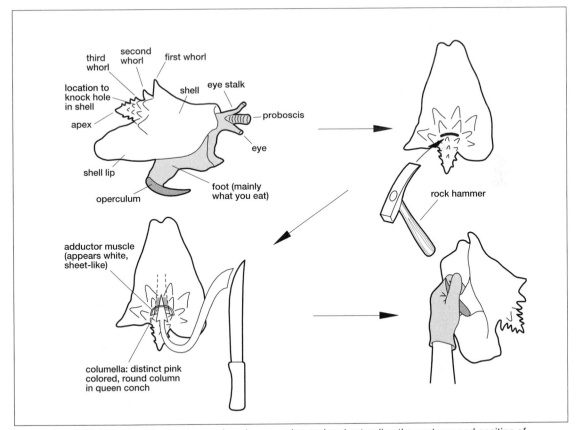

Fig. 9-10. Knowing exactly where to knock an opening and understanding the anatomy and position of the adductor muscle makes removing conch from the shell a simple matter.

♦ *Trimming and gutting.* Cut off the eye stalks, proboscis, penis (if present), and the mass of dark, loose material farthest from the operculum. Trim the enlarged, slack area of the translucent orange mantle lip, but retain the rest. Make an incision along the darkened area from proboscis aft, and scrape out the digestive tract with your thumb (fig. 9-11). Sometime during this process, you'll note the appearance of a transparent, noodle-like unit called the crystalline style—*don't discard it!*

♦ *Consume the crystalline style.* Like discarding fish heads, throwing away the crystalline style is sacrilegious to native conch lovers. They suck this spaghetti-like device right out of the meat the moment it emerges from the gut, claiming it confers all manner of energy and libido. The organ is actually a compact protein matrix full of starches that rotates and aids digestion in conch, other gastropods, and bivalves. It has a pleasant, delicately salty flavor. If you nonchalantly turn toward unsuspecting observers with the thing dangling from your lips, and slurp it in with suction like drinking from a straw, it will wiggle and whip around on the way in, eliciting strong reactions and interesting cultural discussion.

♦ *Skinning.* Make the incisions shown in figure 9-12 and remove the skin in two halves. Two main methods are popular. One is to use thumb pressure to press the skin firmly to the side of a relatively dull knife blade and peel the skin off. My favorite, taught to me by Bahamian Scrap Lightbourne, is called barking. Grasp the leading skin edge firmly in your teeth, hold the conch firmly on either side of your mouth, and forcefully rotate the body; the skin separates right off from the meat. Repeat for the other side. Scrap did warn me not to be seen doing this around Nassau, due to an uproar caused by the impromptu discovery by a visiting tourist of an old, yellow-stained fisher's tooth in a conch steak, which led to passage of a law making it a misdemeanor to bark conch. This is why all the guys in the public market now use knives, while barking remains popular in the out islands. *Warning: If you've already sucked down the crystalline style in front of most developed-country crew or visitors, barking the conch will further tarnish, perhaps irreparably, any semblance of "normality" or "civility" in their eyes as you pause to wipe stray strands of dangling mucus from your chin. Expect an annoying chorus of "Just one!" at your next*

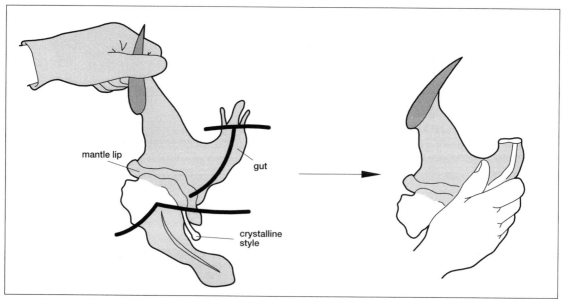

Fig. 9-11. Trim and gut the conch, and try consuming the crystalline style or "pistol," said to have properties that put Viagra to shame.

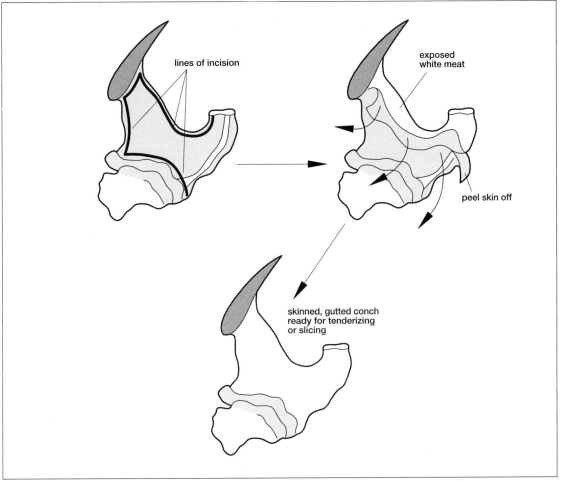

lines of incision

exposed
white meat

peel skin off

skinned, gutted conch
ready for tenderizing
or slicing

Fig. 9-12. Make shallow (⅛ in./3 mm or less) cuts as shown, and peel off the skin with thumb pressure against a dull knife surface or with your teeth.

port of entry when the customs official inquires if there are any animals aboard.

♦ *Preparation of the meat.* You've arrived. You're now holding a nice white chunk of meat by the operculum. Leave the operculum attached for a handle. Slice it thinly and dice it for conch salad. Consume raw—it's delicate and wonderful this way. For conch steak or any other application, you must tenderize the meat to produce what natives term *bruise conch*. This is an excellent description of what you should do for best results. *Many* folks use a small metal mallet with pyramid-shaped spikes on the face to beat the meat into a broad, thin patty. This is OK, but it macerates more than it tenderizes. You can't beat (no pun intended) a properly bruised conch, produced by holding the operculum firmly and whacking the meat with well-placed blows of an untreated section of 2 by 2 inch (5 by 5 cm) lumber. This also creates a broad, flattened patty, but with thoroughly broken down muscle fiber that remains extremely tender when cooked.

OTHER GASTROPODS, ABALONE, AND CHITONS

All of that finesse you learned for extricating conch from the shell usually goes out the window for top shells, whelks, and a variety of smaller marine gastropods. One controlled whap with a 4-pound (1.8 kg) hand sledge and it's all over. Trim, gut, and tenderize those large enough to permit it.

The meat of abalone and chitons is already exposed by virtue of their removal from the substrate. Extraction is a simple matter of a scraping-style severance with an appropriate knife, again followed by gutting, trimming, and whatever final cutting and tenderizing activities suit the chef.

BIVALVES

Locked tightly between two strong shell halves by a strong adductor muscle, mussels, oysters, clams, cockles, and the like are a little tougher to crack. Cooking, often steaming or on an open grill, relaxes the grip of the adductor muscle, and the shell begins to open. This signals removal time—the cooking's done. Consume "as is," or scrape the animals out of the shell for use in soups, chowders, sandwiches, and other dishes.

The other approach is removal uncooked using brute force, sometimes termed *shucking*. In this case, fishers insert a short stout knife between the shell halves and powerfully rotate the shell against the blade to sever and pry the shell halves apart. This is a popular process for scallops so that the distinct lump of white meat can be delicately prepared in light sauces without precooking, and also for oysters.

LOBSTERS AND LARGE SHRIMP

Both lobsters and larger shrimp (also prawns and crayfish) cook well whole, with no processing, often by brief boiling or steaming in seasoned water. Some preparers remove the tail from the head, which makes it easy to remove the intestinal tract from the tail meat. It *can* introduce flavor under some circumstances, but removal is probably mostly aesthetic for fresh product destined for immediate consumption. For spiny lobsters, break off an antenna a comfortable distance from the stout base, then break off the flexible tip at the other end. Insert this spiky small end into the anus, and rotate it as you push it in approximately one-third of the way up the tail. This entrains and binds the intestine. Keep twisting as you pull it back out; the entire intestine will pull out

with it. For shrimp, buy a commercially produced deveiner for about $1 and push the intestine right out of its dorsally located groove.

An alternative to cooking whole is to use your largest fish-steaking knife or a cleaver to split raw lobsters lengthwise down the middle for the grill. Place the lobster either belly up or belly down for the splitting process. The underside of the exoskeleton is thinner, yielding an easier start when belly up; however, we find it more efficient to blast through from the back. Whichever you choose, don't chop. Start by carefully placing your tool on the midline, then press firmly and decisively with the palm of your hand on the back of the blade (lean over and put some weight into this) or strike it sharply with a heavy hammer.

CRABS

Crabs are almost always cooked whole prior to processing. Consumers then crack the exoskeleton to access the meat, which falls away nicely from inside the hard shell after cooking. This is probably the most practical approach for cruisers. Pure meat derives from meticulous, labor-intensive picking from sections of cooked exoskeleton, using a variety of pointy, hooked instruments and specialized crabmeat knives. Commercial centrifuge processes also exist for separating cooked meat from the exoskeleton.

Another variation especially popular for portunid crabs is whole consumption of newly molted individuals. As crustaceans grow, they become too large for their exoskeleton, and it gets too tight. The new, soft exoskeleton forms underneath, and they work themselves out of the old shell. They usually attempt to do this in great privacy, because other crustaceans, including their own species, love to eat the soft, temporarily defenseless individuals. They hide until the new armor hardens, then resume normal activity. Humans maintain crabs and wait for them to molt, or provide natural habitats to induce entry of those ready to molt (for example, submerged brush in the marshes and bayous of Louisiana, United States). "Soft-shell crabs" are then steamed or boiled whole and consumed, exoskeleton and all.

We alluded in chapter 6 to some interesting geographical variations in specific land-crab preparations. Eastern Caribbean consumers utilize land

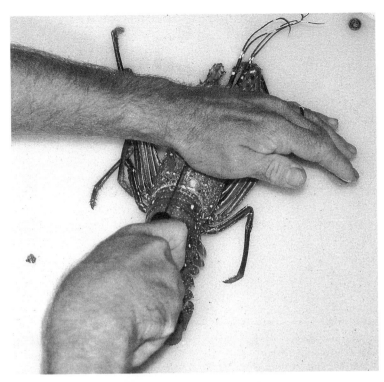

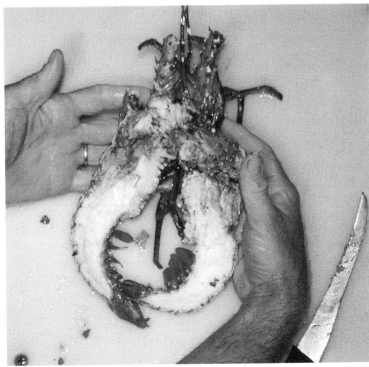

Splitting a whole (in this case cooked) spiny lobster.

crabs in the standard manner, cooking and extracting claw, body, and leg meat. In the Bahamas, however, you will notice stacks of legless, clawless land-crab bodies at certain times in the market. Upon closer inspection, you'll note eye movements—these crabs are maintained *alive* in this state for fresh-cooked use in traditional crab and rice dishes. The purchaser boils the bodies, then quarters them and allows the enlarged, rich brown hepatopancreas—a storage depot for glycogen, fat, and calcium—to cook down, permeate, and thus flavor and color the rice. It's delicious.

SQUID AND OCTOPUS

These highly evolved mollusks have become essentially "all mantle, hardly any shell," which makes for high and accessible meat yield. Split these animals lengthwise and remove the internal organs, transparent shell remnant, and hard beak-like mouth apparatus. The mantle and tentacles are good eating. Thin slices and smaller chopped sections of tentacles make the best end-products because the flesh toughens during cooking. Squid (calamari) rings, formed by cross-sectioning whole squid mantles like steaking a fish, have become mainstream items recently, although they're nothing new in many parts of the world.

ECHINODERMS

Consumption of sea urchins and sea cucumbers hasn't really caught on in many parts of the world the way it has, for example, in Asia, but there's something to be learned here. Sea urchins are easy to process—break open the shell with a knife long enough to keep your hands away from the spines. The key is collecting the right species at the right time of year and moon phase so that when you do this, you'll be greeted by large, ripe eggs that are delicious raw. This varies by specific location. The taste seems to appeal even to people unaccustomed to seafood, if they're willing to give it a try. Many indigenous maritime cultures exploit sea urchins to some extent (see chapter 12 on potential toxicity).

The epicenter of sea-cucumber usage and consumption is probably China, although many other areas now either exploit this resource for export profit or have long used holothurians for various purposes on a smaller scale. Processed sea-cucumber products include beche-de-mer or trepang, soaps, lotions, water, toothpaste, tablets, and cosmetics. Water-soluble extracts of one species of *Stichopus* produce mammalian pain-killing properties more effective than aspirin or morphine. An oil-soluble extract proved effective for treating and healing wounds, leading to medications still on trial in the form of syrup, ointment, cream, and tablets. Although the practice is now mostly outlawed because of the ecological impact, one traditional Fijian practice is to rub *Holothuria atra* in sand to collect nerve toxin–containing reddish-purple fluids that stupefy fish and chase octopuses out of holes in the reef. Indonesians seek small species that bury in the sand for "hard-times food," processing them prior to raw consumption. They start by scraping the outer tegument to remove the spicules (akin to peeling a carrot). They slice it lengthwise and remove the entrails, rinse the tegument in seawater, and finally cut it into pieces said to have the texture and flavor of oyster-flavored chewing gum.

The more standard commercial product (trepang) is boiled, dried tegument of various species, a prized flavor addition to soups and other seafood dishes. A representative process used in Mozambique is to make a lengthwise ventral incision, boil it for 1½ hours in seawater, bury it in sand or a box overnight, press to remove skin and entrails, clean, boil again, and then sun dry.

Preparing for Cold Storage

Let's forget for a moment exactly what it is you've just caught and cleaned. You have a fresh, rinsed product in hand, and time is of the essence. Maybe you've done well, catching a big fish or a bunch of lobsters, too much to consume in one sitting. A cold-storage facility enables you and your crew to enjoy this success for weeks or months, and it will taste *almost* as good as it did fresh, if handled properly.

Assume the units of fresh-rinsed seafood product at hand have three time-dependent destinations: immediate consumption, refrigeration, and freezing. Some of the meat can go straight into someone's mouth, onto the grill, or into a pan of hot seasoned oil, the oven, or the microwave. There's lots to be said for fresh, fast-cooked seafood unadulterated by any accoutrements whatsoever. Try it, you'll like it. Otherwise, you may wish to stack some meat in a plastic container half-full of one of your secret marinades to let it infuse for a few hours in the refrigerator—the same procedure for dishes to be "cooked" cold with lime- or lemon-juice-based solutions (see pages 360 and 362).

Refrigerate the remainder packaged in individual units or small groups; sealed plastic bags in different sizes work perfectly for this. Place the meat in flat (not rolled or bunched), squeeze the air out, and seal tightly to reduce atmospheric oxidation. Put them up against the holding plates or other cold surface in your box, or surround or bury them completely in crushed ice. The idea is to chill the entire unit as quickly as possible, en masse, avoiding a warmer internal core suitable for bacterial growth. Never stuff a big wad of steaks or fillets, for example, into a large bag or other container and throw it in a cooler or refrigerator; you'll likely ruin a lot of hard work. Chill whole gutted and cleaned fish or headless cores by packing them carefully in crushed ice. Fill the body cavity with ice prior to burying the entire fish. If you have a holding-plate system, keep sealed water bottles (refrigerated or frozen) on hand for placement inside the fish body. Place the fish in large, heavy plastic bags, and put more cold water bottles on the side of the carcass that isn't up against the holding plate, the equivalent of packing in ice but without the mess. Follow this same whole-fish procedure for refrigerating or freezing.

For smaller meat units bound for the freezer, place the meat flat in the sealable plastic bag, add a small quantity of drinking-grade fresh water, squeeze out air and excess water, and seal the bag. The water will form a protective glaze around the product, which greatly reduces dehydration (freezer burn) and atmospheric oxidation, as well as the attendant discoloration, toughening, and off-flavor, adding considerable time to the viable freezer life of your catch.

Work especially fast with invertebrates. Most species tend to "kick off" quite rapidly. Microbial action undetected by your nostrils will continue for some time in cold storage, sometimes enough to really clear your sinuses and alter dinner plans upon removal a few days later. Rapid discoloration of shrimp and lobster tails, although not directly indicative of microbial action, happens so fast that commercial operations sprinkle them liberally with sodium bisulfite to make them white for marketing purposes.

Chilling, Freezing, and Thawing

More knowledge of flesh biochemistry and other events will help you produce the best possible seafood on your cruise. Two processes cause loss of quality in cold storage. Autolytic spoilage occurs from the action of enzymes present in the gut and flesh. Microbial spoilage begins soon after, starting with the growth of microorganisms on the surface of the product, evident in the formation of slime, and continuing with the tissue breakdown and general deterioration associated with the invasion of bacteria into the flesh.

What is the storage life of chilled, unfrozen fish? This varies widely by species, latitude, and storage system. Properly cleaned whole fish and cores, maintained and repacked in ice as needed, *can* last up to a month or more at sea. Super-chilled commercial brine spray systems permit the precise maintenance of temperatures *just* above freezing so that fish might last forty days and still be adequate for sale as high-priced fresh product. Interestingly, chilled storage life of fish caught in tropical waters exceeds that of fish captured in cooler temperate seas. The condition of the fish upon entry to cold storage has a huge effect on storage life, as does temperature during storage. Count on a week or so in your cruising-boat refrigerator for properly packed, fresh-caught seafood, less if the fish sat around in a hot dinghy or on deck before you got around to processing it. If you have holding plates cooled by an engine-driven refrigeration compressor, and cyclic warming occurs due to irregularities in running the engine, you'll significantly cut the storage life of chilled seafood.

The goal of freezing rather than chilling is to further lower temperature, retarding or completely halting spoilage, and be able to thaw a product much later that bears some resemblance to fresh seafood. What happens to the meat when it freezes? Fish is about 75 percent water which, due to salt content, converts to ice at a temperature somewhat below that of freezing. This freezing action preserves through a combination of two bacterial-growth-suppression mechanisms, temperature reduction, and lowering what technologists term the *water activity* of the product—water molecules bound by the freezing process are no longer available to bacteria.

Quality loss will nevertheless occur in frozen seafood. The biggest culprit is dehydration, a process vastly enhanced by even small variations or cycles in freezer temperature. Other factors include drip loss and development of cold-store odor. Enzymatic oxidation accounts for a yellowish form of unsightly color. Severely freezer-burned product will be very dehydrated, yellow or brown in color and, upon thawing, will be dry and spongy due to protein denaturation. Vacuum-packing can help, but the simple cruiser's solution of sealed zippered plastic bags and water glaze is adequate.

How you thaw seafood can also affect quality. The main conditions to avoid are excessive drip loss and dehydration, bacterial growth, and localized overheating, which can cause protein denaturation. The best method for cruisers is to immerse the packaged product in ambient-temperature water. Exposed air-thawing engenders bacteria, flies, and less than ideal temperatures in many top cruising destinations. Removing the meat from the package prior to water-thawing causes loss of flavor and promotes unsightly appearance. Microwave-thawing inevitably overheats some areas relative to others, and usually surface-cooks exterior regions. So stick to the bag-and-water routine.

Do not necessarily be disheartened by discolored exterior meat and a little odor when you remove the thawed meat from the plastic bag. When you trim off the outside layer, you will be pleasantly surprised at the quality of the interior. For this reason, we usually create thicker blocks of skinned and deboned meat for freezing and freeze whole gutted fish. Yes, fillets from whole-frozen fish exhibit some gaping, but general quality is fairly good.

Canning

Canning is very serious business. Your life depends on scrupulously following strict procedures. Contents of cans are ideal habitats for the growth of a multitude of anaerobic microorganisms, and herein lies the real danger. The infected contents can become toxic before we notice any signs of what will probably be unfamiliar or virtually undetectable spoilage. Ingestion can easily be fatal. This phenomenon is so deadly that purposeful inoculations comprise an entire, carefully outlined procedure in at least one military "black bag" manual designed to cause multiple deaths in enemy camps.

Three factors are paramount to canning safety.

♦ *The use of proper containers with excellent seal integrity.* For cruisers, this means a glass jar with a metal lid, the center of which is separate from the threaded collar and features a rubber seal. An improper seal causes the vacuum in the jar to recontaminate initially sterile contents by sucking in microbe-containing moisture.

♦ *Heating temperature and duration lethal to the most dangerous microbes.* Unfortunately, some of the most dangerous pathogens are also very heat-resistant. Most canning procedures target perhaps the worst of these, *Clostridium botulinum*, a common inhabitant of a wide variety of marine and terrestrial environments. These protocols calibrate heating time to the equivalent time spent by the center of the contents at 250°F (121.1°C)—time compensates the fact that actual temperature rarely reaches this value.

♦ *Meticulous attention to hygiene during cool-down.* Hot, wet jars are the most vulnerable to seal leakage and, therefore, should never be handled until cool and dry.

One practical cruiser protocol, used with good success, is to prepare a container of raw processed seafood in a liquid medium (e.g., boneless pieces or sections of fish, lobster, conch, squid, scallops, shrimp-tail meat, you name it). The liquid can be oil, water, or a light brine solution, but you'll probably find that a sauce or marinade produces a more satisfying result. The liquid serves as a space-filler. Place your largest pressure cooker on the stove, add drinking-quality water to a depth of 2 inches (5 cm), and arrange clean empty pint jars upright in the pot. Fill each jar with seafood and liquid medium, leaving a small space at the top. Make sure the sealing surfaces of the jar top and lid are clean and free of visible debris, place the lid center on top of the jar, and then screw down the threaded ring one or two turns, not enough to exert pressure on the seal. Put the lid on the pressure cooker, tighten securely, adjust the stove burner to produce a steady pressure of 10 pounds per square inch (psi) on the gauge, with steam issuing from the pressure-release vent at a constant rate. Maintain this equilibrium, adjusting the burner if necessary.

Exactly how much time should you allow? Precise times depend on the size and number of your jars, and the size and configuration of the seafood packed in the jars. A good 120 minutes or so of steaming will overcook your seafood but would, under most conditions, be a conservative rule-of-thumb for canning safety. Turn off the stove burner, leaving everything untouched and in place. Go take a nap or a swim, read a book. As the inside of the pressure cooker and the jars slowly cool, the hot, expanded contents of each jar compresses, creating a vacuum that sucks the lid seal tight. When everything cools down, open the pressure cooker. The lid and jar surfaces should be dry, and the lids should be centered and firmly sealed. Screw the outer lid collars down firmly.

This procedure works for other food types as well, some of which you'll want to precook and add hot. Relatively brief normal cooking times usually make this unnecessary for seafood. Canning results in long shelf life, but you should always examine jars carefully before consumption. Check for any swelling of the metal lid, leakage, discoloration of contents, odor, or any evidence that the seal has been disturbed, including dents. If in any doubt whatsoever, reject the food rather than risk your life by eating it.

Curing Seafood by Drying, Salting, and Smoking

Canning preserves by destroying microbes and their spores. Curing uses a different approach; it preserves by rendering seafood unsuitable for growth and reproduction of microorganisms. Various procedures depend on removing water (drying), diffusing solutes into the meat (salting), or by depositing bacteriostatic chemicals (smoking). Curing practices often combine more than one of these processes.

DRYING AND SALTING

Like freezing, curing by drying and salting works by eliminating and tying up water molecules, reducing the water activity of the meat. Ionic forces of infused solutes bind the water, again rendering it unavailable to microbes, and they also dehydrate by wresting water molecules from these tiny organisms, causing them to become dormant or die. Salt performs this task far more effectively than sugar.

The Dehydration Process

Curing purely by drying is possible. The time involved to attain dehydration sufficient for long-term preservation exceeds that of any other common method, and some environments with excessive humidity, precipitation, and heat may make success difficult or impossible via natural means. It's a race to prevent the seafood from spoiling due to microbial growth and reproduction in the interior before adequate curing renders this impossible. Bacterial spoilage causes significant decomposition of the meat and—of critical importance to cruisers—poses a health hazard.

Enhance dehydration rate by increasing the surface area of your product. Reduce the distance water molecules must travel as they diffuse outward from the center to the exterior. Cut the meat into thin slices or strips rather than fatter blocks; consider mincing. Buy more time, if possible, by reducing the ambient temperature of the drying process, which suppresses bacterial growth and reproduction rates. On a cruising boat or in a survival situation, however, the dehydration power of direct sun usually proves more important than a small difference in ambient temperature—nevertheless, break up the batch and try some strung up in cool breezes under an awning, some in the direct sun.

Recall that fresh seafood is about 75 percent water. Reducing water content below 25 percent halts bacterial spoilage. Below 15 percent, molds can no longer grow. This action may occur by a number of modes, depending on specific conditions of the drying environment, including capillary flow, liquid diffusion according to concentration gradients and in liquid layers absorbed at the solid interface, and diffusion of vapor due to partial pressure gradients. Various food material structures, such as amorphous, crystalline, fibrous, or gel-like, also influence relative dominance of these processes.

Cruisers, like coastal natives, employ air-drying rather than complex industrial vacuum- and freeze-drying methods. Sun transfers heat to the seafood, causing water to evaporate, and open air carries the water molecules away. Think of hanging a wet sponge on a laundry line. The surface remains moist only briefly, soon becoming dry as movement of water from the interior by diffusion can no longer keep up with the rate of evaporation at the surface. The dehydration rate now depends on how fast water vapor travels the increasing distance from the constantly receding wet interface inside the sponge to the exterior, where the breeze carries it away.

As your seafood dries, it shrinks. If ambient temperature is too high, or the flow of air across the product is too strong, the layers of low permeability formed by shrinkage may suppress water-escape rates enough to cause spoilage. The more extreme cases are analogous to the process of searing meat on a grill or very hot pan—high temperature seals the surface, preventing water loss while the center heats to the desired degree. In fish drying, when some combination of hot sun and strong breeze seals or "case-hardens" the surface, the moist interior spoils fast. Overdrying, like freezer burn, results in yellow patches of discoloration that do not rehydrate well and so remain chewy and tough.

Obviously, we can't control many of these environmental factors, which introduces an element of chance to each drying episode. Time your seafood collection for drying to anticipated weather patterns or arrival at locations with consistent, favorable conditions. Remember that things could be proceeding well, only to be thwarted by a day or two of rain or elevated wind.

Speeding Things Up with Salt

The diffusion of salt inward from the surface of your curing seafood sharply accelerates the critical process of lowering the water activity of the product. Penetration to the center, as with pure drying, is the key to attaining a stable result that will store in the long term. The process is complete when salt concentration in the curing flesh equals that of the surrounding salt solution. The theoretical maximum is about 26 percent, actually lower because other solutes already exist in the meat. This is particularly true of oily, high-protein fish flesh where osmotic equilibrium occurs long before the concentration of salt in the flesh approaches that of the surrounding solution. Oiliness also retards the movements of water and salt, which means you'll do better air curing white meat species like mahi mahi, cod, shark, grouper, or snapper rather than tuna, mackerel, flying fish, or swordfish.

Salting allows curing of larger units than pure drying under equivalent conditions, or speeds the process greatly for thin slices and strips. Salt can tip the balance in favor of feasibility of air curing in a given environment. It works by simultaneously diffusing inward according to a dialysis mechanism, and encouraging water diffusion out from exerting osmotic pressure between exterior salt and less concentrated fluids in the flesh.

Sprinkle table-salt crystals on seafood prior to stringing it up to dry, or first soak it in a strong brine solution overnight in the refrigerator. Pickling permanently in concentrated brine is a popular method for preserving fatty fish because it reduces oxygen available for rancidity reactions; the amount that does occur is deemed favorable for development of traditional flavor. Note that skin is a barrier to salt penetration, which doesn't mean you have to remove it all, but certainly limits the size of fish that could be salted whole without gutting (only small anchovies, herring, and the like). Fillets, steaks, slices, and strips take up salt much faster than other configurations, although gutting, splitting, and surface-scoring can assist penetration. Brining, even briefly, is initially quicker than dry-salting by virtue of better contact between exterior solutes and the flesh.

How long does it take to air cure salted seafood on a cruising boat? It depends largely on prevailing environmental conditions. You're starting with fresh fish containing 75 percent or so water and 0.1 percent salt; ideally, you need to finish with a dry, biscuit-like result containing 25 percent water and 25 percent salt. Two weeks is not unreasonable.

Storage and Spoilage

Product with these specifications can last months or years if humidity is low and temperature stays under 50°F (10°C). Dipping it in vegetable oil can mitigate water uptake in humid environments. Storage time decreases in warmer, more humid conditions. Don't store dry-cured product in sealed plastic bags, which become humidors for moisture trapped in the air mass enclosed in the bag.

How do you know when it's spoiling? The first sign is usually a subtle pinkish hue on the surface indicating colonies of nontoxic, nonpathogenic "pink bacteria" (e.g., *Halobacterium salinaria, H. cutirubum, Sarcina morrhuae,* and *S. litoralis*). Rub these off as soon as you see them and dip the seafood in a solution of sodium bisulfite to prevent their return. The appearance of pink bacteria *does* indicate the product has rehydrated slightly; anything more than this initial sheen may indicate water activity sufficient to support food poisoning bacteria like *Staphylococcus aureus.* Throw it away.

Molds may appear any time relative humidity is 75 percent or more and temperature climbs above 50°F (10°C). The species common to cured seafood products often appear as brown areas and don't decompose flesh. Wipe them off, rebaste lightly with vegetable oil, and attempt to rectify storage conditions.

Salting as a Component of Other Curing Methods

It's obvious that storage time for dried and salted seafood is briefer in the balmy climates preferred by many cruisers. What measures do the inhabitants in these latitudes take to prolong storage? As with other aspects of seafood utilization, the amount of trouble they go to depends on relative scarcity, greatest where there are the most people. It should be no surprise that places like Southeast Asia and Indonesia lead the way.

Open-pan salt boiling in concentrated brine inactivates flesh enzymes and kills most non-spore-forming microbes. Boil until no free water remains in the pan, coat the product heavily with salt, place it in a jar, add a heavy layer of salt, and firmly secure the rubber-sealed lid. This prevents spoilage due to creating an environment unsuitable for outgrowth of bacterial spores, and can extend product life to nine months in the tropics. This is the basis of the popular Indonesian pindang; however, make your own rather than risk illness or death by purchasing local product. Problems persist with insufficient cooking time and salt, as well as possible lead and zinc poisoning from ceramic pots.

Other products with much longer storage lives are more widely popular. Dried fish and invertebrate products (e.g., small shrimp) result from laborious processes using combinations of repeated boiling, drying, pressing, reboiling, and smoking to produce barely or unrecognizable renditions of the fresh substance. People package and store these at ambient temperature until they're ready to add in small whole units or grate and sprinkle on rice or other starchy dishes or soups.

SMOKING

Twenty years ago, on a sunny afternoon in Miami, Florida, I grabbed the ringing phone on my way out the door. "Hello?" "I was driving along, saw an old chest of drawers lying in a ditch, and I had a vision." Utterances such as these were normal for John Malloy. How do you respond? He continued, "I knocked the drawer bottoms out and replaced them with screens. Cancel your plans for the afternoon because I'm going to teach you how to smoke fish. See you in thirty minutes."

It turns out that all you need is any enclosed space with an air vent and damper (i.e., means of air entry from down low) with stackable, removable racks, some sawdust or wood chips, and a heat source. Marinate fresh seafood in brine solution or seasoned sauce; place it on the racks; and set the heat

source, damper, and air vents to produce a smoldering action from wet wood chips. Rotate the racks so that each gets equal time low near the heat source and high in the cooler, more humid, less smoky (due to product uptake) upper layers. Rebaste the seafood at these times to promote smoke chemical deposition and uptake. John used hickory chips on a cheap electric hot plate and wrapped an old canvas sail around the dresser to reduce oxygen. Sufficient air entered the bottom and exited the drawers through the loose wraps of the cover. The thing occasionally caught on fire when we removed the canvas to refresh the supply of wood chips, but it produced many batches of smoked seafood over a period of about three years, prior to its final collapse from fire damage.

Smoke-curing of seafood appears to be an accidental discovery. Fishers attempting to cook their catch in damp, rainy conditions on the shore covered smoldering fires and tried to compensate lack of heat with time. Only later did they grow to fully appreciate the resulting preservation and taste. This remains the primary objective of smoking, although motives now also include fulfilling a market for smoked flavor and camouflaging or prolonging the useful life of aging product.

Smoking preserves with the aid of salting when brine dips are used, by dehydration, by the deposition of phenolic antioxidants that delay oxidation of unsaturated fish lipids, and by deposition of antimicrobial substances such as nitrites, phenols, and formaldehyde. Sound kind of toxic? Depositions can include known carcinogens, such as the high amounts of benzopyrene and other polynuclear aromatic hydrocarbons identified in wood smoke. Such compounds are most likely in hot-smoked fish, fish cold-smoked for excessive periods, and where direct gas or oil flames dried the product. Also, the nitroso-containing substances that give smoked fish a characteristic pink hue probably react with amines to form cancer-causing N-nitrosamines.

Reduce the potential for hazardous depositions by keeping temperature as low as possible. True cold-smoking temperatures never exceed 86°F (30°C). Achieve this by oxygen deprivation, encouraging wood particles to smolder rather than burn. Keep the seafood farther from the heat source. You must still counterpoise air vents with the damper to control fire and smoke intensity. Fully open air vents decrease the draw through the damper, increase dilution of smoke with air, and retard the fire. A fully closed position maximizes air draw through the damper and, therefore, fire intensity. High initial smoke density in this case tapers quickly as intense heat oxidizes smoke chemicals into carbon dioxide and water, which means you are no longer smoking. Seek balance.

Leave the skin on fillets and other slabs of fish. Whole split fish, carefully scrubbed of all gut and gill remnants, are also popular. Brine presoak solutions should be 70 to 80 percent because full saturation leaves white deposits. Any of your favorite marinades will do (see chapter 13 for more details). Use of fresh material, unbruised and tear-free, yields a superior product. As with drying, excessive heat and air flow may case-harden the meat and lead to inside-out spoilage from the moist, sealed-off interior. Cut smoking time when the goal is an alternative cooking method rather than long storage time. For instance, as little as two hours of smoking produced delectable, fully cooked results from 6 by 3 by 2 inch (15 by 8 by 5 cm) slabs of fish, as opposed to six hours necessary for longer-lasting products using the same material in John's dresser.

Smoking takes time and space. An assembled smoker of any size won't fit well on smaller cruising vessels, particularly sailboats. Easy-to-assemble kiln components that double as hull-patch material could work, as well as construction of a temporary kiln on shore. Flammable material is OK wrapped in a cover. Do not use chips or construct kilns from pressure-treated or other chemically infused lumber. Smoking constitutes a good group effort, where crews from several boats team up to collect seafood, construct the kiln, tend the smoker and, of course, share the results.

Alternative Seafood Processing

Several other approaches to seafood preparation in general require considerable time and effort, and

you've probably already guessed where they're most prevalent . . . Japan and Southeast Asia. At least one ingenious method has recently become a highly successful approach all over the world, one that you've no doubt sampled at one time or another. We briefly highlight this one—surimi—as well as production of fish mince and lactic-acid fermentation products.

FISH MINCE

Fish mince is by far the easiest of these alternative methods. It's just what it says—finely minced fish and other seafood. Mince may be consumed "as is," usually with sauce, or transformed into fillet-like products, and is commonly used as a base in soups and chowders. Its simplicity stems from lack of effort to separate chemical components like enzymes, lipids, and pigments that lead to degradation and rancidity. This also enhances protein denaturation during freezing; therefore, most commercial processes utilize microwave precooking before freezing in an effort to stabilize the mince.

The philosophy behind fish mince is primarily to create a palatable substance from organisms not considered prime commercial targets in their own right. One good example is the use of extremely bony but easily caught ladyfish (*Elops saurus*, Family Elopidae) by Chinese-Jamaicans. They suspend the silvery, well-armored fish and beat the sides thoroughly with a stick, without breaking the skin, into a mushy consistency. This creates mince, which then separates easily from the bone upon slitting open the skin. They press the fresh, boneless mince into compact balls and fast-fry them in hot seasoned oil, completing the transformation of an underutilized species into a very tasty delicacy.

SURIMI

Surimi means actomyosin gel, formed by separating or recovering, concentrating, and protecting a purified mix of the proteins actin and myosin. Surimi is an intermediate product, used to produce a growing range of imitation crab, lobster, and shrimp; sauces; dips; spreads; loaves; soups and chowders; pies; sausages; even desserts. Once more, depleted populations of the real thing partially fuel the popularity, made all the easier by the high palatability of the product—its pure, clean, nonfishy taste appeals to many people.

We're probably typical of Westerners who would assume this is a new invention; in fact, it's an old tradition in Asian circles. The recent boom and geographical expansion is due to the advent of substances called cryoprotectants, such as sucrose, sorbital, and polyphosphates, which preserve the protein gel during cold storage. Before that, surimi deteriorated quickly, which made it a traditional daily labor in Japanese households. Current large-scale manufacturing practices, however, mimic in large part the simple home process.

You *must* start with fresh material. Begin by separating white meat from red meat, bones, and skin. Mince the white meat. Wash three times using a solution of three parts water to one part mince, ten minutes contact each at a temperature from 41 to 50°F (5 to 10°C) or slightly higher for tropical species. Refine or strain to remove any residual skin, bone fragments, or bits of dark meat. Press until water content is about 80 percent (close to the natural moisture content of seafood). Chop, grind, and add salt and spices to taste. Use your imagination to shape your surimi, and then steam it. The correct Japanese term for this class of surimi product is *kamaboko*.

Traditionally, the raw material is fairly lean, light-meat fish species. Shark meat works very well. The number of species used is growing, but fatty fish are generally the worst candidates.

LACTIC-ACID FERMENTATIONS

The process of lactic-acid fermentation—controlled, purposeful growth in food of specific bacteria species such as *Lactobacillus*—is an ancient strategy for preservation still widely used for meat, vegetables, dairy products, and seafood. Scandinavians continue to produce traditional fermented fish, and Polynesians apply the method to fruits and seafood, but the procedure can fairly be described as waning in these and other areas of the world. Southeast Asia is another story.

It goes by many different names. The smell of "nuoc-mam" gave away more than one ambush in Vietnam. Similar sauces also remain extremely popular in Cambodia, Thailand, Malaysia, and the Philippines. Whole fish mixed with 25 percent salt sit for two days, half of the liquid is drawn off, the fish ferment for six months. Then bones and undigested skin are removed, six to twelve more months go by, the liquid removed on the second day is re-added, and several more months pass. Manufacturers may then repeat the protocol a few more times with brine prior to mixing several together to sell as quality fish sauce. Pastes are equally popular.

Others seeking prolonged storage life subject seafood to much shorter-term, partial fermentation. The practice is alive in remote areas of the tropical South Pacific and other regions. Many such preservations that began prior to cold storage, worldwide, continue to satisfy acquired tastes. I once tried two big helpings of partially fermented reef fish on rice while coinhabiting an isolated remote atoll with a group of Polynesian fishers. The preparation consisted of light salting, covering with burlap, and leaving shaded for two days. It smelled and tasted rotten. I noticed only three of the six guys went for it. I later asked one of the abstainers why, and he said that only his mother could make it the way he liked it. I downed it all, lasted through a short sail the next day to another atoll, and then became violently ill for a day. Perhaps the uninitiated should take it a little slower, at the expense of only a small amount of diplomacy.

We realize that lactic-acid fermentation of seafood is not likely to sweep the general cruising community for a number of reasons. Anything that works for hundreds of millions of people, however, must have something to it.

Gear Checklist

Table 9-1 lists fundamental seafood-processing tools that will greatly assist your ability to produce professional results, and get the most out of that hard-earned catch. Dexter/Russell and Forschner are the leading knife brands used by the pros—you can't go wrong with either brand (see appendix 1, for sources).

TABLE 9-1. **CHECKLIST OF SEAFOOD-PROCESSING TOOLS**

Item	Specific Recommendation	Approximate Price
Sharpening stone	#10 aluminum oxide (8 x 2 x 1 in.), coarse/fine	$4
Breaking knife	10 in. (25 cm) blade	$25
Fillet knife	8 in. (20 cm) blade	$18
Cimeter (steaking knife)	12 in. (30 cm) blade	$37
Cleaver	6¼ in. (16 cm) blade, 1½ lbs. (0.7 kg)	$27
Fish scaler	stainless steel, 9½ in. (24 cm)	$6
Crabmeat knife	2¼ in. (6 cm) blade	$14
Oyster knife	4 in. (10 cm) blade	$10
Clam knife	tapered, 3 in. (8 cm) blade	$7
Scallop knife	2 in. (5 cm) blade	$9
Shrimp deveiner	plastic	$1
Conch hammer	14 in. (36 cm), 1 lb. (0.45 kg)	$10
Apron	vinyl, 8 mm	$3

10

Medical Considerations for the Cruising Fisher

Commercial fishing ranks among the most dangerous occupations in the United States and elsewhere. Increased competition and the resultant pressure on fish stocks encourage vessels to brave worse weather and work longer hours than ever. Management by quota systems, whereby regulators promptly shut down access to the fishery at a fixed total catch, compel extreme, make-or-break behavior in some fishing fleets. Fortunes can be made or lost in a few days of fishing. Heavy winches, large hydraulic reels, massive traps, and other gear create constant high strains around the work deck. When something breaks, or if you stumble, make the wrong move, or become entangled, death or serious injury can be instantaneous.

Cruisers have far more control over how, when, and where they choose to fish than commercial fishing crews, and they use lighter, safer gear. Safety, not profits, comes first. Therefore, we don't get washed overboard or sink and drown *quite* as often as commercial fishers working in dangerous areas. But we do share the potential for more routine physical injuries, including minor cuts, punctures, and embedded hooks.

Furthermore, some of us travel widely to cruising waters that harbor exotic marine organisms posing special hazards. We must constantly guard against harmful physical contacts and consumption of toxic seafood. Our best defense is knowledge. We should understand a few fundamental biological principles that apply worldwide, shape our general safety protocol accordingly, emphasize correct identification of marine life, and always seek out local expertise.

Common (and Not So Common) Fishing Injuries

If you wear proper protective gear and use good techniques, fishing can be fairly safe. Nevertheless, rough seas, fatigue, heavy gear, and fast, large, strong, or toothy target species can shake things up on a cruising boat. You'll suffer a few minor dings regardless of conditions. Here's what to expect, and what you can do to prevent and treat small mishaps.

LINE CUTS

Line cuts can occur as you haul in a fish on a handline. Perhaps the fish struggles and attempts a run back to the depths, and the fishing line slips across your palms or fingers under pressure. Perhaps you're handling a leader to guide a subdued fish to net or gaff when the fish finds a burst of strength and races off, tugging the leader wire or monofilament rapidly through your hand and opening a "slice" wound.

Treatment for such injuries is straightforward. Stop the bleeding with direct pressure. Cleanse the wound with antibacterial soap. If necessary, close the cut with butterfly bandages, apply an antibiotic ointment such as Bacitracin, Triple-D, or Neosporin, and cover the wound with a sterile bandage.

Prevent line cuts by taking a moment to don gloves before handling or leadering fish. It sounds simple, but in the heat of the moment, it's easy to forget. Recall the discussion of proper handling and leadering technique from chapter 3. In particular, take line pressure *across the middle of your palms* rather than the creases of your finger joints.

FISHHOOK EMBEDDED IN FLESH

Fortunately, a little vigilance can make embedded fishhooks a rare cruiser injury. Unlucky or momentarily careless fishers, however, do sometimes find themselves pierced with a sharp fishing hook, the barb embedded in underlying tissue. Immediately cut the line attached to the embedded hook. Get the victim as calm and comfortable as possible. If the barb is embedded securely in the flesh, you will not be able to reverse the route of the hook without causing considerable damage. In this case, you must push the hook the rest of the way through the skin until the barb is exposed. Clip, file, or squeeze the barb closed with your fishing pliers or your hook file, or cut it off completely. Once the barb is shut or removed, you can easily remove the offending hook.

Treat the resulting wound by stopping the bleeding with direct pressure, soaking it in a solution made from hot water, Betadine, and Epsom salts. Apply antibiotic ointment and cover with a sterile dressing.

Always secure inactive hooks in the bridge of a fishing-rod guide, in a leader rack, or hooked firmly in the rim of handline yo-yos. Keep ample slack in fishing lines attached to hooks you are baiting, rigging, or tying. Make crew holding the rod or line aware that you have the hook in your fingers, and demand their attention. Instruct them to open the bail of a spinning reel or flip revolving-spool reels into free spool. Hold hooks and lures such that, should an accidental tug occur, the chance of impalement is minimal. Keep all loose hooks off the deck and other surfaces. Wear shoes.

Exercise extreme care when removing hooks from captured fish, particularly multiple or treble hooks. If you plan to retain the fish for food, kill it first, or cut the leader, place the fish in cold storage, and remove the hook later when you are processing your catch. With a fresh, lively fish you intend to release unharmed, *keep your hands away from the hook or hooks by using a dehooking tool*. This is the situation that causes the most accidents, due to the fish's strong, unexpected head shakes or other moves. If a hook or lure embedded in the jaw of a fish impales your hand or arm, immediately throw a towel over the fish's head. Covering the eyes suppresses movement. You may be able to clip through the shank, bend, or attachment point of light hooks with your fishing pliers, separating you from the fish. If not, grasp the shank of the hook firmly with a hinged jaw dehooker or other tool to immobilize it and reduce the damage inflicted by fish motion. Kill the fish with an ice pick, then extricate yourself.

If you imagine this situation with a big marlin or other large, strong, energetic fish, you should *never* be tempted to take chances. If this ever happens, hang onto the boat at all costs and sacrifice your hand, because if the fish gets loose with you attached and then sounds, your life will be in danger.

FISHHOOK EMBEDDED IN THE EYE

You Coast Guard–licensed operators out there probably remember this situation from your captain's test. Several days after I took mine, I was working on the deck of a partyboat in the Florida Keys, and it happened—one guy leaned his rod up against the rail to go get a fresh bait and forgot to secure the empty hook to a rod guide. The boat rolled gently, the hook swung in an arc, and went straight into the eye of the elderly gentleman fishing in the next rail position. I saw the whole thing happen, I just couldn't get there in time. The procedures from my recent test studies took over—I quickly grabbed the rod before it could fall and yank the hook. Then I cut the line, took off my shirt and wrapped it around poor Bill's head to blindfold him and reduce inadvertent eye movements, and instructed him to stay calm, relax, and focus on keeping his eyes absolutely still. We got everyone to reel up, upped anchor, and radioed for an ambulance. Bill was very lucky. The hook had entered gently between the surface of the eyeball and the eyelid, with the barb pointed away from his eye. The emergency-room doctor deftly removed the hook, and Bill was out fishing again the next day.

The recommended procedure states: Cut the line, gently place a clean gauze pad over the hook and eye, and wrap a clean bandage, T-shirt, or towel around the head and over both eyes to immobilize them (I should have used something cleaner than my T-shirt). Make the victim comfortable, and do everything possible to calm and reassure him or her. Seek professional medical help as soon as possible.

Religiously wearing sunglasses and a billed cap

Getting Hooked Is No Fun

A few anecdotes might stay in your mind and help reinforce caution around hooks. After a chance meeting, I once ended up replacing a swordfish longliner crewman who'd headed offshore with a bullet still imbedded in his stomach from a barroom altercation. He also had another older injury. When he exposed his belly to show me the infected bullet hole, I couldn't help but notice a nasty, perfectly straight pink scar that began at his lower abdomen and ran up the midline of his body to the collarbone. He'd been really lucky on that one, he said. Years ago, while he was operating a high-speed hydraulic cart to retrieve longline leaders, a hook had flopped around, penetrated his lower belly, ripped straight up, and popped out high in his chest. Miraculously— although it took many stitches to close the wound— the hook did not plunge through to muscle, bone, or internal organs, and the wound healed fairly quickly.

Several months later, a large boarding sea slammed me forcibly up against this same device, depressing the control lever. The spool of the leader cart accelerated, embedding a hook in the top of my left hand. I managed to backhand the lever to the off position halfway through my first whipping, bodily rotation around the spool, and then slash through the monofilament with a knife. A crew member severed the hook shank with heavy cutters and pushed it the rest of the way through. Incredibly, despite yawning tears showing muscle, veins, and bone, no critical damage occurred. Hot soaks, antibiotic ointment, and sterile gauze wrapped securely in duct tape permitted rapid healing and no work interruption. But what if it had been a carotid artery?

This incident prompted a number of hook-injury horror stories from my crewmates. I had later opportunities to corroborate two of the more infamous, in one of which a hook impaled the hand of a crewman who was baiting outgoing longline hooks. He quickly jumped overboard to save his hand, and they were able to stop the boat in time to rescue him from hypothermia in the cold waters of the North Atlantic. A less fortunate outcome followed the sudden dehooking of a large, powerful fish on the surface not far out of gaff range. A crewman's efforts to bring the fish into gaffing range accidentally became excessive as a big sea rolled under the boat. The hook flew out like a rifle shot, not an uncommon occurrence—you hit the deck as quickly as possible when this happens, but this was too close and too fast. On its way across the deck, the hook blew by the side of his face and snatched an eye from its socket. A heroic U.S. Coast Guard helicopter crew evacuated the stricken man, snatching the rescue basket through the pitching, rolling rigging of the fishing boat in high winds and mountainous seas.

while fishing will protect your eyes. If it's dark and cloudy, consider wearing safety glasses. Train yourself, and strictly instill in your children, *never* to leave a fishing rod with a free-swinging hook for even a moment. Remember that as you handline or leader a fish to the boat, the hook could come out. Don't hold the line in front of your face—try to maintain at least a slight angle in any direction away from your head. You can't afford a hook in the eye when you are far from medical care.

FISH AND LOBSTER SPINES

Most fish and lobster species have sharp spines. Puncture wounds can occur while handling lively specimens, but don't underestimate the potential for spike wounds inflicted by contact with dead individuals on the deck or cleaning table. These injuries always make you feel stupid. I believe I hold the record for the all-time dumbest fishing puncture wound. I was cleaning a set of jaws removed from a mako shark on a commercial fishing boat in rough seas. It kept sliding around as I carefully excised the flesh from between the teeth. I was nearly finished when the boat pitched violently, and I instinctively let go of the upper jaw to brace myself, causing it to fall heavily on my other hand and driving the many fangs deep into my palm. I had ample opportunity for self-recrimination because this occurred on the second day of a monthlong, labor-intensive trip.

Introduction of bacteria-rich slime deep into the cozy, moist confines of your flesh sharply enhances infection from this category of puncture wounds. Thinking back to the principles of curing fish flesh (see chapter 9) will help you understand effective treatment. The goal is the same: to create an environment unsuitable for bacterial growth and reproduction. Submerging puncture wounds in a soak solution made from hot water, Betadine, hydrogen peroxide, and Epsom salts exerts osmotic pressure to draw bacteria-containing fluids out, and infuses the antiseptic inward. Carefully examine the wound to ascertain whether the spine has broken off within. If so, you may be able to avoid more aggressive measures by enticing it out with the osmotic pressure of repeated applications of black drawing salve (Ichthammol is excellent) under a bandage. Failing this, invade the wound with a sterilized pin, needle, or fine tweezers, or make small incisions with a scalpel to remove the spine.

Pack spine-free wounds with an antibiotic ointment and bandage. Wash any nicks or cuts from handling fish or lobsters with antibiotic soap and coat with antibiotic ointment. If redness and soreness develop, treat repeatedly in the hottest soak solution you can stand. Dip the affected area first, and then, as soon as you can tolerate it, hold it submerged for ten to fifteen minutes. Do this several times a day, and apply black drawing salve and bandaging between soaks. If the condition worsens or shows no improvement in a day or two, begin a regimen of oral *Staphylococcus*-sensitive antibiotic (e.g., Augmentin, which is amoxacillin and clavulinic acid, or Keftab, which is cephalexin). Never ignore an infection, and never risk allowing one to get out of control. Take the time and trouble to treat it aggressively because serious injury or death can occur. Two cruisers have required emergency airlifts from remote Pacific locations in recent years because of such infections.

Avoid fish- or lobster-spine injuries by wearing gloves and by careful handling. Protect your feet with shoes. Wear gloves while scaling, gutting, steaking, and filleting fish, and pay close attention. Experienced fishers soak their hands in a weak solution of bleach at the end of each day as an effective preventive measure, whether or not they can see any injuries.

KNIFE CUTS

Careless handling of fish knives, attempting to clean fish in rough sea conditions, exerting excessive pressure with dull knives, and mistakes with sharp knives all can cause cuts, possibly serious. These can also occur from trying to clean fish while they are still alive. The fish jerks, the knife slips.

Apply the familiar first-aid protocol: Stop bleeding with direct pressure, clean the wound with antibacterial soap, close the wound with butterfly bandages, suture if necessary. Apply antibiotic ointment and cover the wound with a sterile dressing and bandage.

Knife-cut prevention starts with attitude. Inexperienced operators, particularly young and overconfident fishers, inevitably cut themselves fairly seriously before they develop the proper respect for a sharp knife. Try to eliminate this step. *Always cut away from your holding hand and body.* Similarly, push the blade away from you when sharpening. Keep your knives razor-sharp, touching them up the moment they begin to drag. Wearing gloves is the single-most effective protection after proper technique, particularly when you're forced to process in rough seas. Avoid this where possible, or minimize it by gutting and chilling your catch whole, leaving the finer work for calmer waters.

Other Ailments Caused by Fishing

Fishing tends to draw people outside their habitual comfort zone. This is mostly positive, but a little awareness can go a long way toward preventing unnecessary or even dangerous discomforts.

SEASICKNESS

Cruisers need little introduction to *mal de mer*, but a quick review based on our experience with thousands of customers in the charter-fishing business might give you a new idea. Boat motion disturbs the balance mechanism in the inner ear, and diesel fumes seldom help the nausea. Thwart mild cases by keeping victims off the bridge and superstructure, thereby reducing *their* boat motion, and in fresh air. You can prevent or greatly ease symptoms by becoming adept at observing and predicting possible victims. Watch for early signs such as changes in speech patterns and eye movements, particularly any combination of prolonged silence, distant gazes, or reluctance to make eye contact. If you see a pronounced swallow and skin pallor, it's coming on fast.

Compassionately confront the person, explain that it's the luck of the draw and has nothing to do with personal toughness or fortitude. Ask what measures have been taken. Immediate application of wristbands with acupuncture pressure-point beads, scopolamine back-of-the-ear patches and, less often, belated oral doses of motion-sickness medication can save the day. Don't let them feel embarrassed about vomiting, and *be sure* they're downwind and on deck, not below in the head. The latter obviously creates a mess, but more important, the odor and reduced air circulation greatly exacerbates their condition.

The best preventive is proper counseling before they ever step aboard. Have them select and purchase their own medication well before the trip. Several brands of motion-sickness tablets are available over the counter at any pharmacy. Follow the directions on the container for the appropriate dose and, for maximum effectiveness, start medication the night before going to sea. Taking a preventive dose at the onset of rough conditions may suffice for those less sensitive to motion sickness or for those concerned about becoming ill. Scopolamine patches, applied either before embarking or at the first sign of rough weather, seem to be more effective than any other treatment for the majority of people. All such medications can have varying side effects, including drowsiness, and therefore should be tested ashore before putting to sea.

Advanced, persistent cases are no laughing matter, particularly if the victim is old or suffers from a heart condition. Dehydration can be severe, augmenting physical and mental anguish. Keep the victim as comfortable as possible and under close observation. Get them to calmer conditions or ashore as soon as possible.

Here are a few last tricks to keep in mind. (Unscrupulous charter skippers are infamous for abusing them to shorten the fishing day.) If your crew is getting queasy, consider keeping the seas off the beam. Will your cruise plan accommodate a more comfortable heading for a while? Coasting downsea is the smoothest ride, but if you're running the engine, exhaust fumes billowing over the transom might wipe out the motion advantage. Can you quarter downsea and direct the fumes off to the side? What about laying-to for a while on a sea anchor? Reducing boat motion by these measures can have a pronounced impact on stricken crew and guests.

HEAT EXHAUSTION AND HEAT STROKE

Fishing not only tempts people into rough seas, it also may induce them to spend long hours exposed to hot, direct sunlight. In a hot environment, blood circulation to the skin helps release heat and keep the body cool. Heart output and circulation may be unable to keep up with the need for increased skin respiration. If this becomes severe, the sweating mechanism may shut down, causing heat exhaustion to advance to heat stroke.

Victims of heat exhaustion may feel dizzy and experience nausea and headache. Heart rate will be elevated, skin will be hot and dry to the touch. They will not be sweating, and may collapse and lose consciousness (i.e., heat stroke).

Get suspected victims to a shaded area. Lie them down and elevate their feet. If they are conscious, give them cool but not iced liquids, such as water with a pinch of salt and a spoonful of baking soda or a sports drink containing electrolytes. Bring down their body temperature with cool-water baths. Cover the victim in a sheet or towel that has been soaked in cool or iced water. In the case of heat stroke, the body temperature of the victim must be reduced as quickly as possible before brain damage results. Submerge the victim in an ice bath or place ice packs in the armpits and groin area. Seek professional help as soon as possible.

Prevent heat exhaustion by wearing cool, loose-fitting clothing on hot days. Stay out of the sun as much as possible and don't overexert. If you must be in the sun, wear a hat or wrap an iced bandanna around your head. A broad-brimmed straw hat is the most effective—tie it with a chin string to prevent it from blowing off. Drink plenty of water or non-alcoholic beverages.

Review of General Fishing-Tool Safety Measures

At the risk of overlap and repetition, let's summarize simple measures to prevent mishap. The basic themes are consistent habits, safe storage, protective coverings, and sound technique.

♦ *Rod harnesses and belts.* Make sure that they are properly adjusted to prevent back injuries. Check that the rod butt is properly fitted into the rod-belt gimbal to avoid nasty rod-butt bruises.

♦ *Gaffs.* Secure all gaffs with hooks facing outboard or down and tips covered with plastic tubing when not in use. Use proper gaffing techniques: controlled overhand strokes, no wild golf swings. Be wary of the exposed point when subduing a lively fish brought on deck with the gaff. Secure the gaff immediately after use.

♦ *Knives.* Keep knives secure in racks, holders, and drawers, never lying around loose on the fish-cleaning table, deck, or galley, especially at sea. Cover knife blades with a case or plastic sheath when not in use. Keep your knives properly sharpened.

♦ *Gloves.* Keep pairs of gloves handy at different workstations. Always wear gloves when handlining or leadering fish. Don gloves or use a towel when removing hooks from fish. Wear a glove at least on the hand opposite the knife when cleaning or filleting fish.

♦ *Sunglasses or safety glasses.* Always wear sunglasses or safety glasses when working around active fishing gear. Wear polarized sunglasses and a billed cap for physical and ultraviolet eye protection on bright days.

♦ *Fishhooks.* Keep fishhooks out of the reach of children, and closely supervise their fishing activities. Secure hooks on the bridge of fishing-rod guides when they are not in the water, or while you are fetching bait or other gear. Keep all hooks off the deck. Keep loose hooks in a tackle or gear box.

♦ *Foot protection.* While fishing, wear shoes with a thick rubber sole and canvas or leather uppers.

Diving-Related and Other Injuries

Free-diving is a challenging and fun way to collect seafood. Diving with the aid of scuba and other breathing apparatuses is more complex and generally involves higher risks. Cruisers should be fully aware of potential hazards, because slow boats and remote locations do not lend themselves to prompt medical care. Diving-related injuries include both physical injuries and those from hazardous and venomous marine life. Contact Divers Alert Network at 800-684-8111 (U.S.) for emergency and other diving medical advice. Some diving-injury conditions match those sustained from other activities (e.g., shock).

PHYSICAL PROBLEMS

Various physical problems can occur while diving or during other fishing activities. Trained divers and fishers avoid most of these by practicing sound technique and using common sense. You will undoubtedly face at least some of the minor physical phenomena discussed here, but knowledge and training greatly reduces the chance that you will experience the more serious problems. Unfortunately, most continue to occur with disturbing regularity.

Air Embolism

An air embolism occurs when the lung overexpands because of too much air pressure. Lung tissue tears, and air leaks into the bloodstream or into tissues such as those beneath the skin, surrounding the heart, or between the lung and the wall of the chest cavity. Holding your breath upon ascent *after breathing at depth* causes air embolisms and related problems. Thus, rising from the bottom while holding air inhaled at the surface, as when free-diving, is no problem. But if you inhale from a scuba tank or by any other means at depth and then ascend holding your breath, you'll have very big problems. This can occur in shallow water, as little as 3 feet (0.9 m), as well as in deeper water. Can you experience air embolism if you free-dive down to a scuba diver, buddy-breathe briefly, and then ascend? *Yes.* What about if you were to free-dive to a submerged vehicle that had an air pocket, breathe from the air pocket, and then return to the surface? *Yes.* Remember, *any* time you breathe air at depth, you're vulnerable.

A person suffering from air embolism may experience dizziness, visual disturbances, and chest pains. Breathing may be rapid and shallow; blood or froth may be visible in or around the mouth. The condition might progress to convulsions and unconscious-

The Hazards of "Overpressurizing"

Air embolism involves movement of air bubbles within veins and arteries to the heart, neck, and brain. Excessive pressure can also drive air into other areas.

- *Mediastinal emphysema.* Air exits the alveoli and enters the space between the lungs and heart (called the mediastinum), exerting pressure on the heart; this causes breathing difficulty, faintness, and chest pain.
- *Subcutaneous emphysema.* Air bubbles move out of the mediastinum and travel under the skin in the upper chest and neck, causing swelling, breathing difficulty, and possibly voice changes.
- *Pneumothorax.* Air moves out of the alveoli and into the pleural lining (i.e., the membrane between the lungs and rib cage), causing chest pain, breathing difficulty and, in the most severe cases, lung collapse and pressure on the heart that thwarts blood circulation.

ness. Recompression is the only treatment for air embolism and other "overpressure" problems. Artificial respiration and cardiopulmonary resuscitation (CPR) may be necessary en route to the recompression chamber.

Prevent air embolism by *never* holding air breathed at depth upon ascent. You must ascend slowly, no more than 60 feet (18.3 m) per minute (if you rise no faster than the tiniest visible pinhead-sized bubbles, you will stay below this rate). If you have an underwater air source, breathe slowly and regularly, emphasizing the exhalation. Lacking an air source, you are making what is known as an emergency ascent, and it is absolutely critical that a steady, strong bubble stream issues from your lips. Form a circle with your lips, and pretend you are whistling a song or gently blowing out birthday candles. You'll feel like you're going to run out of air, but you won't because the air space in your lungs continues to expand as you rise in the water.

If you choose to scuba dive to appreciable depths, keep in mind that you could have to make an emergency ascent. Try never to exert yourself at

depth to the point where you are huffing and puffing—if you experience an air-supply problem, your ascent will be extremely uncomfortable and require an iron will. If this happens, your eyes will water and your body will ache—think only of whistling out steadily and matching the speed of the tiniest pinhead bubbles.

Anoxia (Oxygen Deficiency) and Carbon-Dioxide Poisoning

Carbon dioxide builds up in the body because of breath-holding, strenuous exercise, hyperventilation followed by exertion, or breathing from a contaminated air source. Carbon dioxide levels eventually reach a poisonous quantity in the respiratory cells, causing them to stop functioning. Respiration ceases.

You may be in danger of carbon-dioxide poisoning if you are hyperventilating excessively before free-diving and pushing your breath-holding limits, or if you have repeatedly overexerted on dives with insufficient rest between plunges to the depths. Carbon-dioxide poisoning may also result from breathing air trapped in an underwater pocket or cave.

Divers suffering from carbon-dioxide poisoning may have a fogged mask. They'll definitely have a blueness of the lips and nail beds (cyanosis). They may report spots before their eyes and exhibit slowed, drunken responses and increased breathing rate, possibly followed by cessation of breathing. Sudden blackout is a sign of carbon-dioxide poisoning and can be fatal if this occurs while the diver is in the water. Recall that shallow-water blackout, discussed in chapter 6, is caused by *decreasing* the amount of carbon dioxide by pre-dive hyperventilation so that it does not rise enough to stimulate respiration, leading to anoxia.

In any case, bring the submerged victim (whether conscious or not) to the surface at the rate of 60 feet (18.3 m) per minute to reduce the chances of air embolism. Once on the surface, quickly remove the person from the water. The person might regain consciousness or might black out at any time. Lie the victim down and elevate the feet in an area with plenty of fresh air. Monitor breathing; administer oxygen or artificial respiration and CPR if necessary. Resting and breathing fresh air rectifies less severe cases.

Avoid carbon-dioxide poisoning and anoxia by not pushing your limits on breath-holding. When doing repetitive free dives, rest between dives when you get out of breath and avoid getting overexerted. Pay attention to signs of oxygen debt, such as a burning sensation in the thigh muscles from lactic-acid buildup. Breathe deeply and regularly. Never take a breath out of a trapped underwater air pocket. Be careful of air quality when filling scuba tanks.

Carbon-Monoxide Poisoning

Contaminated air supplies, from either problems with the compressor used to fill your scuba tanks or adverse confluences of wind and tide causing hookah-unit exhaust fumes to enter the air inlet, cause carbon-monoxide poisoning. This innocuous gas combines with red blood cells many times faster than oxygen molecules, effectively suffocating the victim. Possible early warning signs include vertigo, headache, irritability, inability to think clearly, and forgetfulness, which progress to nausea, vomiting, breathing difficulty, and weakening pulse. Victims may become flushed or cyanotic, lose consciousness, and die. Get suspected victims off the breathing apparatus and into fresh air, administer CPR if necessary, and pure oxygen. Seek professional assistance, which may include hyperbaric treatment.

Ear Squeezes and Eardrum Ruptures

Ear squeeze and possible subsequent eardrum rupture is caused by the failure to adjust the external pressure exerted at increasing depth and the internal counter pressure of the air in the middle ear. As the diver descends, the air in the ear compresses and the pressure differential between this air and the outside water must equalize. And guess when else it must equalize? On the way back up! If your internal air passages clog during your dive, you can experience a reverse block or difficulty clearing your ears upon ascent.

You'll feel it if your ears don't clear whether on the way down or up. You must halt, reverse direction, and attempt to equalize the pressure by yawning or by holding your nose and snorting very gently. It's one thing to slow or reverse a descent, and even go back to the boat if you can't clear your ears. What if it happens on an ascent from a deep free dive? This

is not good. Pause, sink a little, and try to get your ear to pop. If it won't, you must obviously surface anyway. Your eardrum might rupture, but it's better than drowning. A strong reverse block forced me to do this once while deep free-diving for conch during a research project, resulting in perforation of my left eardrum. Approximately 50 percent of such injuries heal on their own, the rest require surgery. Hearing will be impaired during the healing process for months and possibly indefinitely. You may hear a high-pitched, hearing-test–like ring for up to six months. Test progress by rubbing your forefinger and thumb briskly beside first your good ear and then your injured ear and comparing detection of the whispery sound, also a good test for how badly you traumatized it in the first place. Inner-ear tissues may suffer damage as well, resulting in dizziness or permanent hearing loss.

My case was relatively minor. I experienced ear-squeeze pain, climaxing in a sharp piercing sensation upon pinhole rupture. Worse ruptures produce dizziness and nausea as large amounts of seawater rush into the middle ear. Test for hearing loss and look for bleeding from the injured ear. If you suspect eardrum rupture, close off the ear passage with cotton. *Do not attempt to treat by placing anything inside the ear, such as ear drops, other medicines, or cleaning solutions.* Seek professional help as soon as possible; if it is not available, administer the following regimen: decongestant to reduce painful swelling of damaged middle-ear tissue, oral antibiotics to fight infection, and pain-relief tablets to make sleep possible the first night. Unlike certain of my colleagues, you might consider refraining from obvious jokes, like silently moving your lips to make the victim think it's worse than it really is.

Prevention upon descent is easy. Swallow, yawn, and blow gently into your nose after ascending slightly. Try this a few times. If you fail to equalize, quit diving for the day. You can also avoid a reverse block by heeding small signs, such as increasing difficulty clearing one ear or the other on the way up or down during repeated free dives. You may cause just enough pressure to induce a small amount of swelling that will eventually prevent equalization. Stop diving before you get caught. Don't run back to the boat, gobble decongestants, and hustle back out.

You're a cruiser, remember? Back off for the day, try again tomorrow. As they say in the Bahamas when something doesn't work out, "Next time, mon."

Ear Infections

Ear infections sometimes result from routine, uneventful diving. Residual, bacteria-containing moisture from seawater contaminates the outer auditory canal, causing soreness and inflammation that can become acute. More often, painful ear infections follow barotrauma (i.e., equalization problems). That same ear that cleared only with difficulty on repeated dives or depth changes keeps throbbing well after the conclusion of the dive and can *really* take off if you don't do something about it right away.

As soon as you notice even minor characteristic soreness (e.g., when you touch your ear), irrigate your ear with a solution of half-strength white vinegar solution, hydrogen peroxide, or isopropyl alcohol. (Acetic acid prescription eardrops are 2 percent, undiluted vinegar is 5 percent acetic acid, so a 1:1 vinegar to clean freshwater solution approximates this type of eardrop.) Lie on your stomach with your head turned and infected ear up, and let the rinse soak for five minutes. Hold a towel to your ear, sit up, tilt your head to cock the ear opening down, and catch the liquid in the towel. Now add one or two prescription eardrops, and repeat every three to four hours. Severe cases may benefit from decongestants to ease painful tissue swelling, and don't feel guilty about taking an over-the-counter pain tablet or two to sleep the first night. Really bad infections may dictate oral antibiotics.

Some divers are susceptible to more frequent ear infections than others. To suppress chronic problems after dives, physicians recommend regular irrigation with 1:1 white vinegar to isopropyl alcohol, or 1:1:1 vinegar to isopropyl alcohol to water. This practice won't hurt anyone and also applies to kids with the same tendency for ear problems, regardless of whether they dive.

Sinus Squeeze

The same advice applies for ear and sinus problems: if your sinuses are blocked or if you are have congestion, the safest course is not to dive. Like the middle ear, pressures must equalize between sinus passages and the sea around you. If you dive when congested, you may experience increasing pain in the sinuses during descent and ascent; in advanced cases, you may bleed or discharge mucus from your nose into your mask upon ascent. If you take decongestants and then dive, be sure the dosage does not wear off at depth. Otherwise, when the compressed air in the sinus needs to expand as you ascend, the mucus formed as the medication weakened will likely block it (another form of reverse block). The air pushes and strains against the delicate membranes, tissues may rupture and tear, and your nerve endings will tell you all about it. Bleeding and mucus discharge from the nose may add Christmas colors to the inside of your mask. Seek professional help for suspected sinus damage as soon as possible.

What if you haven't been in the water yet, you're a little congested, and you *really* want to dive? Judicious use of decongestants before diving *can* be OK. Use oral decongestants such as Sudafed (pseudoephedrine) in doses that last from four to twelve hours. Topical decongestants sprayed into the nose thirty minutes before diving act the fastest. Afrin (oxymetazoline) spray lasts twelve hours, providing a larger safety margin than neosynephrine spray, which lasts a few hours. Antihistamines are not recommended because they dry the mucous membranes and thicken mucous, as well as cause drowsiness.

Face Mask and Tooth Squeezes

We've seen that any failure to equalize the pressure differential between an air space and the sea as depths change causes trouble. In the case of the air pocket inside your face mask, the descending diver feels a sucking sensation. Stop or slow down and snort a little air into the mask to relieve the pressure buildup. Clear your mask of any water that leaks in and continue. Otherwise, you could end up with facial bruises and red in the whites of your eyes, which require cold packs and medications such as ascetominaphen to ease pain and reduce swelling (avoid aspirin in this case because it aggravates bleeding).

Tooth squeezes aren't so easy to solve. A deep cavity or any other trapped air pocket in a tooth can be very painful as it contracts and expands in response to ambient pressure. In this case, you should determine which tooth is causing the pain and find a dentist to relieve the problem.

Nitrogen Narcosis

Suppose you're using scuba or hookah to breathe perfectly good air, and you manage to descend without painful squeezes. You may begin to feel slightly inebriated, almost certainly by the time you reach a depth of 100 feet (30.5 m). At 150 feet (46 m), you might feel dizzy and, if you were to go deeper, eventually become incapable of lucid thought and motor skills. By 250 feet (76 m), an average diver is seriously impaired and at great risk. Why? Because breathing nitrogen under pressure intoxicates us. Many diving accidents begin with bad decisions induced by nitrogen narcosis.

Be aware of this effect and heed your certification training and safe depth-limit guidelines. Inexperience, sedatives or alcohol in the bloodstream (even a hangover), fatigue, excessive carbon dioxide, cold water, and a fast descent can lower your resistance. Increase your diving depths gradually, and try to first accumulate bottom time in the company of experienced divers. Never push decompression limits. Never dive deep unless you feel perfect and are completely unimpaired.

Decompression Sickness (Bends, Compressed Air Illness)

Decompression sickness results from dissolved nitrogen loading up in the bloodstream at depth, and coming out of solution in the form of tiny bubbles when it experiences overly rapid decreases in ambient pressure relative to the dissolved concentration in the blood. The origin of the nitrogen is the air you breathe at depth, whether from a scuba tank, hookah rig, or other source. Remember, normal air is 78 percent nitrogen and 21 percent oxygen; the longer you stay down and the deeper you go, the more nitrogen gas dissolves into the bloodstream. It will slowly and safely diffuse back out via the lungs, but not if you come up too fast after going too deep or staying too long. Published tables and fancy wrist computers can tell you these limits.

Exceed the limits and you have serious trouble. The nitrogen bubbles formed in the bloodstream interfere with circulation. The victim may experience an itching or prickling sensation, numbness, joint pain, skin rash, shortness of breath, and dizziness, followed by loss of consciousness. Victims may suffer stroke-like blood deprivation, paralysis, and death. Top free-divers are not immune if they spend enough time deep over the course of a day, particularly if they catch an afternoon airplane flight home; however, the cases I know of were mild.

If you suspect decompression sickness (e.g., someone's watch stopped, a diver grossly exceeded time and depth limits for whatever reason), the affected diver must go to the nearest recompression chamber as soon as possible, because the nitrogen bubbles will be traveling around in their tissues causing damage. Contact the U.S. Coast Guard, Divers Alert Network, local port captain, or other maritime authorities for information on the nearest recompression chamber. Administer artificial respiration and CPR immediately if needed and continue to the chamber if necessary. The victim should be treated for shock if it doesn't interfere with lifesaving measures.

Avoiding decompression sickness is simple, yet it afflicts large numbers of divers annually around the world. Dive in strict accordance with decompression tables, or control dive time and depths using a reliable dive computer programmed to show decompression times. Take a three-minute safety stop at 12 feet (3.66 m) en route to the surface from scuba or hookah dives. *Never* push the dive tables regarding depth, dive times, or decompression stops and limits. Many cruises take people far from the nearest recompression chamber—no place to risk a problem like the bends.

Drowning

A person drowns when water enters the lungs and they can no longer function. The victim then suffocates and loses consciousness, and the heart ceases to function. Combinations of equipment failure, rough sea conditions on the surface, the flooding of a face mask and mouthpiece, overexertion, or a mishap in the water followed by panic and improper emergency procedures usually predicate drowning.

Drowned persons will be unconscious with a blue tinge (cyanosis), and their breathing and heart will be stopped. Victims require immediate artificial respiration and CPR, and possibly recompression if they drowned at depth.

Avoid circumstances that could lead to drowning. Always carefully check your equipment before diving. If you are uncomfortable with the sea condition, don't go. Always dive with a competent buddy, and only dive in conditions within your personal degree of confidence, competence, and qualification. Plan your dive and stick to the plan. If you are uncomfortable with a dive plan, modify it to suit your level of experience or don't go. Try to remain calm and think clearly at all times while diving. Take everything slowly, deliberately. Stay cool. Follow proper emergency procedures if an accident occurs.

Attention, All Those on Medication!

Extremely important: if you are taking a beta-blocker type of blood-pressure-control medication, DO NOT DIVE! These medications may reduce the heart's ability to respond to the demands of diving. This creates back pressure on the blood-vessel network in the lungs, forcing fluid out into the lung cavities, particularly when diving in cooler waters. The victim essentially begins to drown in his or her own body fluids in a condition called *pulmonary edema.* Lack of ability to breathe at depth may cause panic, leading to rapid ascent and air embolism. The typical victim age is mid- to late fifties and older. The victim will be cyanotic (i.e., blue lips, earlobes, fingernails, and toenails) and may have brownish foam in the mouth. Distress and discomfort may develop at depth. It is imperative to control the ascent as much as possible. At the surface, inflate the buoyancy compensator, drop the weight belt, and transport the victim rapidly to the boat. Meanwhile, reassure the victim, who will be very far behind on oxygen and extremely distressed. Treat with oxygen administered by mask. Seek professional attention as soon as possible.

The previous information is a newly published discovery based on several documented cases in different areas, including Israel and New Zealand. One of the (fully recovered) cases was my mother, Betty Ann. Your physician may not know about this. Other medications can control blood pressure and pose no threat to divers. For further information, contact Dr. Simon Mitchell (see page 389, and Grindlay and Mitchell in appendix 5).

If you take any medication routinely, consult your physician before diving.

Muscle Cramps

Cramps are an involuntary contraction of a muscle group. Overexertion or extreme water temperatures (hot or cold) can cause this condition. A diver with cramps experiences pain and a tight bunching of a muscle group. Apply firm pressure and gentle massage to relieve cramps while in the water. For calf-muscle cramps, place the heel of your good foot under the toes of the cramped leg; with this leg straight, pressure the toes so that they angle up toward the knee, "unlocking" the calf muscle. If this fails, exit the water and apply heat to cramps developed in cold water, cool compresses to those induced by heat exposure. Ingest potassium-rich sport beverages or bananas. Avoid cramps by working up gradually to desired conditioning levels, and by not pushing beyond your limits. Suit up appropriately for the water temperature.

Sea Creature Attacks

Attacks from denizens large or small—bites from eels, barracudas, sharks, or other creatures—usually require fast action. Get the victim out of the water as quickly as possible. Stop the bleeding with a compress. Tourniquets are dangerous and may only be necessary in the case of a severed limb. If you must place a tourniquet between the wound and the heart, release it for ninety seconds every ten minutes. Treat the victim for shock. If the bite is severe, seek professional medical help quickly. Minor bites may only need to be cleansed thoroughly with an antibacterial soap, followed by application of an antibiotic ointment and covered with a sterile bandage.

Shock

Shock occurs with loss of blood pressure and oxygen deprivation of tissues. This can result from an injury involving loss of blood or body fluids. A person in shock will have a weak, rapid pulse, blueness around the lips and fingernails (cyanosis), dizziness, and shallow breathing. The victim may be unconscious.

The first step is to stop any bleeding. Lie the victim down with the head lower than the limbs. Keep the patient warm (a light blanket is excellent) and calm; reassure them. If they are able to drink, give them water with a pinch of salt and a teaspoon of baking soda or an electrolyte-rich sports drink. Seek professional medical help for the victim. Shock can result even from a moderate injury and can be life-threatening.

CONTACT WITH VENOMOUS MARINE LIFE

The sea closes over your head, and you enter a different world, floating gently downward, suspended among myriad creatures unlike those above the surface. The supporting density of water enables animals shaped as spheres, stars, pincushions, rhomboids, blocks, and missiles to float passively, swim actively, or slip, slide, glide, and crawl. Many are venomous, to at least some degree, as a defense against predators or to assist their own feeding activities. Some afflictions barely get our attention, others cause mild irritation, and a number pack enough wallop in stinging cells, spines, spikes, or fangs to inflict injury and even death.

Fan-shaped colony of the fire coral (*Millepora complanata*, center of photo, Florida Keys).

The specifics vary considerably between regions. Staying safe requires detailed knowledge of local sea life and the ability to differentiate between species and groups. Degree of diversity and deadliness peaks in the Indo-Pacific region. Use this section as a guide to familiarize yourself with hazardous marine life forms, and avail yourself of the most detailed possible information for your intended destinations (see appendix 5 for references and appendix 2 for further reading and upcoming publications). Some underwater denizens are beautiful to behold but deadly to handle. One rule applies no matter where you visit: If you're not sure, *don't touch it!*

Cnidarians

Phylum Cnidaria contains radially symmetrical invertebrates with a circle of tentacles. Some float freely, like jellyfish, and others live fixed to the bottom, like sea anemones and corals. All have interesting little cells called *cnidocytes*, which contain nasty stinging structures termed *nematocysts*. Nematocysts come in various shapes and designs. All contain protein toxins, and all forms encourage discharge of toxin into tissues of other animals following release of the nematocyst by the cnidocyte. Potency varies for humans, from undetectable to excruciating.

Hydrozoans (Class Hydrozoa)

Hydrozoans include stinging corals, false corals, and fire corals and the tiny free-swimming medusae that bud from the sedentary forms. All three attach to the substrate in shallow waters (3,250 ft./1,000 m or less). Feeding tentacles contain the nematocysts, which sting and stun prey, allowing ingestion. These stinging corals reproduce by budding—that is, releasing immense numbers of tiny free-swimming medusae into the ocean currents—which *also* contain stinging cells in their tentacles.

Sting intensity from these hydrozoans varies from mild to extremely painful, ranging from a mild prickling sensation to an intense, searing experience. Results may resemble a red bite similar to that of an insect or a red rash of bites. Pustules may form in severe cases. Victims can experience abdominal pain, chills, fever, and diarrhea.

Treat hydrozoan stings by applying meat tenderizer, vinegar, lemon juice, or sodium bicarbonate to the affected area. Aluminum-sulfate creams can be effective. The latest development on this front is a medicated pad called Wipeout!, which offers significant pain relief (see appendix 1 for contact information). Topical or oral cortisone preparations or antihistamines (e.g., Benadryl) may reduce the itching and stinging. Severe attacks may require doses of epinephrine.

Avoid many hydrozoan (and similar) stings by wearing a thin dive skin or wetsuit to protect against contact with stinging colonies on the reef, *regardless of how warm the water is.* Exit the water if you find yourself in a bloom of free-swimming hydrozoans (you may not see them, but you will feel a multitude of stings, particularly on your scalp and around your neck). Use a freshwater rinse immediately after exiting seawater, concentrating on the hair, neck, bathing-suit areas, underarms, and groin area. The specific gravity of the freshwater implodes the animals and greatly helps to negate the stinging action of cells caught in these body areas, as well as to rinse them away before they can continue stinging.

We performed an unwitting experiment during one diving expedition. We both felt the stings; Wendy exited the sea and applied freshwater, and I stayed slightly longer and used no freshwater upon emerging ("I don't need that, honey." "You'll be sorry." "Naw, I never use that stuff."). Wendy had a small number of barely visible red spots; I wore a collar of huge, angry, extremely uncomfortable welts for almost ten days (likely culprits: ctenophores).

The most dangerous hydrozoan is the free-floating, jellyfish-like Portuguese man-o-war *(Physalia physalia)*, found seasonally in scattered waters worldwide, and often most abundant during local springtime. Long, stringy, transparent or bluish contractile tentacles may trail far below the bubble-like float on the surface. Nematocysts from these tentacles deliver a severe, burning sting, potentially fatal in large doses.

Be wary of tentacle fragments dangling from trolling lines you retrieve. Exercise extreme vigilance when surfacing from dives, particularly if you have been seeing these organisms in the area—inadvertently thrusting one's head into a Portuguese man-o-war is a major event. Caution your children not to touch any of the individuals washed up on beaches, sometimes in large numbers at certain times of the

Portuguese man-o-war; note man-o-war fish *(Nomeus gronovii)* living among tentacles (Florida Keys).

year. Treatment for man-o-war stings is identical to that for treatment of dangerous stinging jellyfish—the critical first step is rapid removal of the tentacles adhering to the skin.

Jellyfish (Class Scyphozoa)

Jellyfish come in a wide range of sizes, shapes, and colors. Most consist of a bell-like medusa structure with tentacles underneath the bell. Here again, the tentacles contain the stinging cells. With the exception of deadly sea wasps (most prominently, *Chironex fleckeri*), jellyfish stings generally can range from mild to severe and may cause intense pain followed by numbness in the area of the sting. The skin affected by the sting will be raised and may blister. The victim may experience muscular cramping, respiratory distress, and chest constriction.

Treat jellyfish stings by first removing any tentacles adhering to the skin. *Do this immediately because any tentacles remaining on the skin continue to discharge venom into the victim.* Remove the tentacles by scrubbing the area vigorously with sand, towels, or clothing. Apply alcohol, oils, or suntan lotion to the wheals (i.e., raised skin) to further inhibit stinging-cell activity. For mild stings, apply household topical remedies (e.g., Wipeout!, meat tenderizer, lemon juice, vinegar, or sodium bicarbonate) to the affected area. Topical or oral cortisone and antihistamines may help with the itching and stinging sensation. Victims may require pain relief, adjusted to sting severity. Serious stings may dictate epinephrine doses. Treat the victim for shock when indicated.

Sea wasps or cubomedusae can cause a much worse horror story. They include some of the most venomous marine organisms in the world. Indo-Pacific species of *Chironex* and *Chiropsalmus* deliver the most dangerous stings. Fatal incidents involve excruciating deaths that may take from thirty seconds to three hours, but the norm is less than fif-

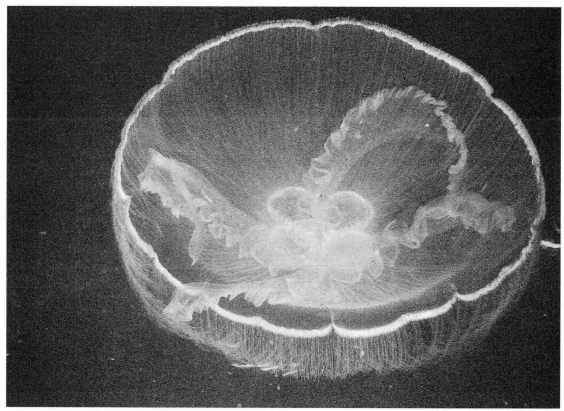

Moon jellyfish *(Aurelia aurita)* occur worldwide. The fringe of tentacles delivers a mild sting (Florida Keys).

teen minutes. The more fortunate survive with severe stings. Two prime culprits of fatalities are *Chironex fleckeri* in northern Australian waters and *Chiropsalmus quadrigatus* in the Philippines.

A sea wasp consists of a translucent, box-like bell with tentacles attached to each of the four corners. Stings cause intense pain and whealing at the site of tentacle contact. The victim experiences headache, chills, fever, nausea, muscular cramps, shock, and collapse. Evidence of the sting is excruciating pain with a whip-like skin lesion. Victims of the sea wasp quickly graduate to painful musculature spasms, respiratory distress, a weak but rapid pulse, pulmonary edema, and respiratory failure. Death from the *Chironex fleckeri* may take less than ten seconds. Commonwealth Serum Laboratories in Victoria, Australia, produces sea-wasp antivenin (see appendix 1 for contact information).

Prevent jellyfish stings by taking measures to avoid contact with them. Severity of these precautions should be commensurate with the danger of the species present. For example, many people in parts of northern Australia do not enter the sea for any reason at specific times of the year. Cruisers should heed local knowledge when choosing dive sites, and remember that jellyfish tentacles may have a wide reach. The use of a dive skin or wetsuit, boots, gloves, and hood may be enough to save a diver from jellyfish by minimizing uncovered skin area, but *any* exposed skin is still vulnerable. If you experience a significant jellyfish sting and severe symptoms occur, exit the water as soon as possible to avoid drowning.

Sea Anemones (Class Anthozoa)

Sea anemones have a short cylindrical body with a number of nematocyst-containing tentacles surrounding their slit-like mouth. A foot attaches them to various substrata. Contact with the tentacles may result in a localized sting. In mild cases, the victim may experience an itching or burning sensation. More severe stings may cause ulceration and necrosis of affected tissue, fever, chills, abdominal pain, vomiting, sweating, and extreme thirst. Follow identical treatment to that described for hydrozoan stings. Avoid touching without gloves and brushing bare skin against the tentacles while observing or photographing these lovely creatures.

The giant anemone *(Condylactis gigantea)* may produce only mild skin irritation from contact (Bonaire, Netherlands Antilles).

More on Anthozoans:
Cuts and Stings from True Corals

True corals are colonies consisting of countless miniature, anemone-like polyps with internal organs residing in individual columns or stony cups. Both tentacles and the body wall contain nematocysts. Coral cuts or stings can cause pain ranging from a mild, prickly itch to a more severe burning sensation. Whealing and weeping may occur at the lesion. Untreated coral cuts can lead to ulceration, enlargement of the lymph glands, and fever; pain may seem out of proportion to physical signs; therefore, even minor coral abrasions should be treated to avoid further complications.

Clean the wound first with antibacterial soap. Remove any foreign matter. Apply an antiseptic solution such as 2 percent tincture of iodine to the cut. Topical and oral cortisones and antihistamines

True coral colonies—lettuce coral (*Agaricia tenuifolia*, foreground) and elkhorn coral (*Acropora palmata*). (Belize)

may help reduce the itching and pain. If the coral cuts are severe (as in the case of being washed against coral heads by strong current or breaking surf), the patient may require bed rest. Kaolin poultices may help to lessen the pain of severe lesions. Antibiotics may be necessary in extreme cases. Wearing a wetsuit, boots, and gloves, as well as maintaining some space between you and the coral, greatly reduces exposure to this hazard.

Echinoderms

Phylum Echinodermata includes familiar sea life such as starfish and sand dollars, as well as sea cucumbers, sea urchins, sea biscuits, and feather stars. All echinoderms have pentamerous radial symmetry; that is, the body consists of five sections around a central axis. In addition, all feature an internal skeleton with spiky projections in various lengths. Many echinoderms are toxic or venomous to some degree, which is a common survival strategy for slow, obvious animals . . . touch me or eat me if you dare!

Crown-of-Thorns Starfish

The crown-of-thorns starfish *(Acanthaster planci)* occurs only in the Indo-Pacific, from Polynesia to the Red Sea, usually around corals. They're large, ball-like, covered with thorns, and obvious; color may range from gray or brown to deep red. The skin covering the thorns produces venom. Contact with these venomous protrusions may cause extreme pain, swelling, redness, nausea, and vomiting. Wash the wound with antibacterial soap; treat pain with analgesics like acetaminophen or codeine commensurate with severity. Coat the wound with drawing salve (e.g., Ichthymall) or a kaolin poultice, and cover it with a sterile bandage. If the reaction is severe, treat the victim for shock.

Divers get into trouble by attempting to pick up these animals in misguided efforts to "save the reef," since the primary food source for these starfish is coral polyps. Occasional population booms recently triggered panic, but research indicated these were probably within the bounds of ongoing, normal reef-ecosystem dynamics. Don't touch or disturb crown-of-thorns starfish, because even most dive gloves won't stop the sharp spines from penetrating.

Crown-of-thorns starfish *(Acanthaster planci)* (Cocos Island, Costa Rica).

Sea Urchins (Class Echinoidea)

Sea urchins have a ball-like or egg-shaped body with many, often lengthy spikes. Most have solid blunt spines with rounded tips, but some have long, slender, hollow, sharp spines that can easily penetrate skin through leather. These spines are very brittle and break off easily; some are venomous.

Treatment for sea-urchin spines is similar to that of other stings. If possible, halt intrusion of additional venom by immediately removing any spines embedded in the skin. Brittleness often creates mechanical problems with this process. If this is the case, get out what you can and leave broken-off, embedded pieces alone. Our bodies can efficiently dissolve many of these types of spines. Pain usually subsides after one to two hours. If spine particles fail to dissolve in a few days, you may successfully tease them out with drawing salve (e.g., Ichthammol).

Severe penetration of the long spines from *Diadema* species may warrant surgical removal. Never handle or contact sea urchins with long, needlelike spines—leather or canvas gloves and shoes won't save you. Handle only short-spine urchins and use heavy gloves. Don't reach blindly into holes and crevices as you seek lobsters.

Sea Cucumbers (Class Holothuroidea)

Sea cucumbers resemble thick, warty-skinned, worm-like slugs. They lack arms. Tentacles surround the mouth, which is located on one end of the body. Some can eject a liquid poison that causes blindness if it directly contacts the eyes, or local skin dermatitis. Wash affected skin areas with antibacterial soap and apply soothing lotion or cortisone cream. If poison contacts the eyes, flush them immediately with plenty of clean water. Local knowledge is the best protection—learn which species are safe to handle.

Molluskan Dangers

On a percentage basis, relatively few mollusks bother humans with venom. Deadly cone-shell species are limited to the Indo-Pacific. Potentially harmful octopus bites could happen almost anywhere, especially if you try Wayne's method of dispatching them.

Cone Shells (Class Gastropoda, Family Conidae)

More than four hundred different species of cone shells inhabit world oceans. Venomous cone shells occur in Australia, Indonesia, East Africa, the Philippines, and on Pacific islands. Preferred habitat is sand or rubble bottom in shallow tropical and subtropical waters. Shell sizes, colors, patterns, and shapes vary widely. They can inject venom into prey or the unwary diver with a detachable, dart-like tooth.

Cone-shell stings produce a puncture wound with localized numbness or sharp stinging and burning sensations of varying intensity. Swelling and numbness may travel to the lips and mouth. Severe cases may develop musculature paralysis, blurred vision, and nausea. Coma followed by death occurs in extreme cases. Recovery from cone-shell injuries can take from a few hours to weeks. Clean the wound as well as possible with antibacterial soap, administer analgesics for pain and swelling, coat the wound with a drawing salve, and cover it with a sterile bandage. Treat for shock if indicated. In extreme cases, seek professional medical help.

Many cone-shell stings occur from waders and divers noting an attractive individual, lifting it from the substrate, and placing it on the palm of a hand to examine it. Dangerous species are easy to identify by shell pattern and are well documented in texts. Learn your cone shells and confirm book knowledge with locals. Wear reef walkers or dive boots when walking or wading in sand or rubble areas. Only handle cone shells with heavy gloves and never carry a seemingly empty cone shell in your pocket.

Octopus Bites

Octopuses have two sharp, parrot-like jaws located in the central undersurface of the body web, the base from which the tentacles extend. The bulbous head and body crown the web. A single bite inflicted by these nasty little jaws consists of two small puncture wounds. Recall the description in chapter 6 of how venom drains into the bite to immobilize prey. If one bites you, expect immediate pain ranging from a burning to a stinging sensation, and a tingling or pulse-like feeling around the wound. Swelling, redness, and heat may develop, and the punctures usually bleed.

Octopus bites usually heal well if you cleanse the wound with antibacterial soap, apply antibiotic ointment, and cover it with a sterile dressing. Handle octopuses carefully and avoid any contact with the beak. Never place the octopus on your arm or allow it to crawl anywhere against bare skin. In particular, don't let them near your chest, back, or neck—octopus bites in these areas can be dangerous.

Fish with Venomous Spines

Numerous fish, including sharks and rays as well as bony fishes, have venomous spines; some are deadly. Summaries of important, widespread examples should help head off unnecessary cruising accidents. General treatment includes a standard regimen: treatment for shock if indicated, irrigation, limb elevation, oral analgesics for pain, soaking in a hot solution of Betadine, heavy concentration of Epsom salts and hydrogen peroxide, and oral antibiotics if secondary infection occurs. Confirm that the victim has a current tetanus shot. The best prevention: when in doubt, never permit contact with dorsal, pectoral, anal, or tail-base projections of fish.

Spiny Dogfish

Squalus acanthias is a common, good-eating small shark caught bottom-fishing from off the beach out to 600-foot (180 m) depths in temperate and cold waters all over the world. Spiny dogfish, however, have stout, sharp spines immediately in front of each dorsal fin, each covered with venom-cell-impregnated skin. Puncture wounds from these spines produce intense stabbing pain and swelling, and nearly always occur while removing the shark from a fishing hook or spear. Grasp dogfish with a heavy towel between your gloved hand and the body of the fish.

Stingrays and Skates

Stingrays and skates possess serrated daggers near the tail base, which are capable of secreting venom

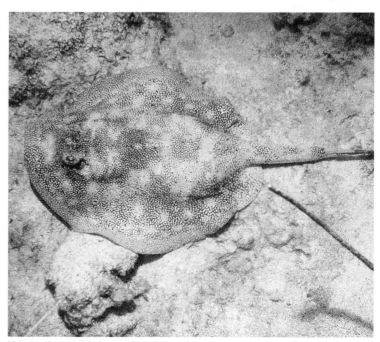

Yellow stingray *(Urolophus jamaicensis)*, common in shallows from Florida to Central America (Florida Keys).

as a defense against predators like sharks and fishers. Pain from an encounter with one of these spines will be immediate or occur within ten minutes. The pain may start slowly, increase to severe levels, and radiate up the limb in a sharp, shooting, and throbbing sensation, leading to primary shock if excruciating. The victim experiences a decrease in blood pressure, possible nausea and vomiting, sweating, musculature paralysis, sometimes death. The wound can be a laceration or a puncture.

Use cool salt water to immediately irrigate the wound. This will help flush away venom, and the cool water acts as a vasoconstrictor to retard poison absorption. Explore the wound for the barb and remove any foreign matter. Soak it for at least thirty to ninety minutes, maintaining hot solution temperature. Close the wound with butterfly bandages if necessary. To control severe pain, opiates may need to be administered.

Stingrays and skates provide a hazard for wading. The main danger is stepping on a buried ray. Remember, shuffle your feet along the bottom to roust rays and avoid pinning down the body with your foot, a position that allows the ray to strike with its tail. Probe the bottom with a stick in your projected path. Take extreme care when removing a hook or untangling fishing line from a captured ray.

Catfishes
(Suborder Siluroidei, Numerous Families)

Saltwater catfishes with hazardous dorsal and pectoral spines come in a variety of shapes and sizes worldwide. Wounds cause a stinging or throbbing sensation that may radiate up the limb of the injured person. Skin may appear pale at first, followed by redness and swelling. The victim may go into primary shock and experience weakness, decreased blood pressure, and respiratory distress.

Handle smaller catfish with pliers or dehookers. Wear heavy gloves and grasp larger catfish between the dorsal and pectoral fins using the number of fingers the space permits. If you doubt your ability to do this safely, cut the leader close to the hook and drop the fish back into the water.

Weeverfishes
(Family Trachinidae, Genus *Trachinus*)

Weeverfish are small (not over 18 in./46 cm), elongated fish that look like a cross between a cod and a sand perch. They inhabit flat, open, sandy or muddy bays in the North Sea from Norway south along the coasts of Europe, the Mediterranean, and the Atlantic coast of North and West Africa. Feeding strategy consists of burying in sediment with only part of the head exposed to ambush squid, marine worms, shrimp and other crustaceans, and sometimes small fish in a sudden rush. Weevers are not a significant commercial fishery target, but they are a delicacy in France, and have long terrorized fishers working the sandy shallows where they lie concealed.

Weevers sport seven venomous stingers, five dorsal spines, and two spines on the sides of the head (opercular spines), which inflict punctures causing instant, intense, burning, stabbing pain that quickly radiates outward from the wound. Most victims reportedly scream in agony and then lose consciousness. Swelling will be progressive, involving the entire wound, and persist for ten or more days. The victim may go into shock. Secondary infection is common from weeverfish spine wounds.

Alarmed weevers erect the dorsal spines and flare the gills to project the opercular spines. They may

---

Stingray Payback

I had a wayward roommate long ago who decided to bangstick a large stingray in a 140-foot (43 m) depth during a scuba dive near shore at Boca Raton, Florida. His reprehensible purpose was to secure the sizable stinger for a trophy. The blast instantly killed the large, motionless animal. George sliced off the stinger and placed it in a wetsuit sleeve pocket. Moments later he bent his arm forcibly to do something, driving the serrated stinger deep into his upper arm. He later described the pain as intensely agonizing. He somehow managed to ascend just in time for his dive buddy (who had surfaced previously, another error) to see his distress and drag him aboard the small anchored boat just as he lost consciousness. A trip to the hospital for surgery and treatment resulted in complete healing, leaving only an ugly scar and a remorseful, searing memory.

also use the latter as an accurate offensive weapon to stun prey. Take extreme care when releasing these fish from fishing gear. Note also that weevers are tenacious and hardy, clinging to life long after removal from the water, so watch out for stings from seemingly dead fish. Do not dive or swim close to sandy bottoms in weeverfish territory. Wear thick-soled shoes when wading in any area that may harbor these fish.

Scorpionfish, Stonefish, and Lionfish (Family Scorpaenidae)

Scorpaenids inhabit nearly all marine waters, from the equator to cold temperate latitudes. All have a bony plate extending across the cheek from eye to gill cover. They are highly camouflaged bottom fishes, typically resting motionless in rocky rubble and coral areas for long periods, awaiting the arrival of hapless prey items. Venomous dorsal, anal, and pelvic spines create a potential hazard of varying species-specific intensity to waders, divers, and fishers removing them from gear.

Dorsal spines inflict the greatest number of injuries. Some species are aggressive and will strike out if one reaches a hand or other body part within striking range. More passive species erect and orient venomous spines toward sources of alarm. A stung person feels immediate, sharp, violent pain that radiates from the wound. The wound area will be red, swollen, and hot to touch. The victim may experience profuse perspiration, restlessness, nausea, vomiting, and loss of consciousness. Tissue may slough off. The victim may suffer primary shock. Severe cases may include constriction of the chest, convulsions, respiratory distress, and death.

The deadliest scorpaenid and, indeed, probably the most venomous fish in the world, is the Indo-Pacific stonefish *(Synanceia verrucosa)*. They cause many severe injuries and occasional fatalities, nearly always from unwitting waders stepping on them or from inadvertent contact with the groping hands of a wader or diver. The stout spines easily penetrate even thick rubber soles; gloves are a joke. If stonefish didn't have the habit of resting under or up against rocks, decreasing the likelihood of being stepped on, surely even more incidents would occur.

Stonefish do not exceed 14 inches (35 cm) in length. They prefer the sand and rubble shallows of lagoons and reef flats from the Red Sea through eastern Polynesia. They may partially bury themselves,

Spotted scorpionfish *(Scorpaena plumieri)* inhabit Atlantic and eastern Pacific waters and can inflict painful, nonfatal wounds with their poisonous spines (Florida Keys).

which presents a nearly invisible menace in habitats highly attractive for cruiser seafood collection. Modify your behavior to reduce the chances of contact—avoid forceful, blind hand thrusts, wear protective footwear to at least reduce or slow spine penetration, and develop a sharp eye for the subtle profile. Form a search image by viewing good underwater photographs of this species (see appendix 2 for sources).

Another Indo-Pacific group of scorpaenids, the lionfishes (Subfamily Pteroinae), can cause painful injury and sometimes death. They are a very common sight in tropical reef areas, as well as from the Red Sea to eastern Polynesia. In contrast to stonefish, lionfish are usually obvious and dazzling in appearance, hovering in holes and crevices by day and venturing forth to forage at night. They are popular aquarium fish. *Never* harass or touch one—they'll stand their ground, flaring pectoral, dorsal, and anal spines that can easily penetrate gloves.

Follow the standard venomous-fish-spine regimen, aimed at controlling shock, alleviating pain, decreasing effects of the venom, and preventing secondary infection. Stonefish and some lionfish victims require immediate hospitalization, usually in intensive care. Commonwealth Serum Laboratories sells stonefish antivenin (see appendix 1 for contact information).

You are not safe from scorpaenid stings in cooler waters because these fish are common hook-and-line catches. Other scorpionfish spines, although less deadly, can easily penetrate gloves and give you a jolt if you handle them carelessly or inadvertently bump into them while diving.

Toadfish (Family Batrachoididae)

Toadfishes are small and bony, and thus not likely to be targets of cruisers looking for a meal (although natives do eat them in some areas, and the meat is firm, white, and tasty). Nevertheless, contact is highly probable when fishing in warm to temperate, often turbid coastal estuarine shallows and river mouths of every continent. Toadfish have big mouths and a propensity to pounce on offerings that are large compared to their body size. Their habit of lying partially buried makes contact with waders and divers a possibility. Trawls and seine nets sometimes load up with them.

Toadfish are incredibly hardy and can survive considerable exposure and trauma. Otherwise, my first day collecting toadfish from a commercial shrimp boat for physiology research as a University of Miami sophomore would have been a disaster. Unfortunate traffic-light timing caught me speeding back to the lab; I hit the brakes hard, and buckets of toadfish and seawater went flying. I opened the door and a waterfall of wiggling, thrashing toadfish cascaded out onto the hot pavement. Traffic stopped and drivers stared as I frantically ran around picking up imperiled, flopping specimens, tossing them roughly into near-empty buckets. A large depression in the van console held some spilled seawater, so I dumped one load there. Horns blared as I crawled under the van to sweep the last few into a hand net, jumped back in, and hit the gas. Total mortality? Zero. The upshot? If you think a toadfish suspended in a net or lying on deck is dead, you're probably wrong.

The key is to avoid the dorsal and opercular (i.e., head side) spines, which consist of unique, highly developed, defensive venom organs. Human victims experience stings akin to those of nonlethal scorpionfish, and treatment is identical. Toadfish antivenin is neither available nor known.

Surgeonfishes and Tangs (Family Acanthuridae)

These fish get their name from the sharp, lance-like, moveable spine on either side of their tail base (i.e., caudal peduncle) that resembles a scalpel. Worldwide in warm seas, these fish swarm in surge channels and over and around coral reefs. Wounds usually occur when handling fish captured by hook and line, net, or spears. *However*, believe it or not, surgeonfish schools *may* defensively lash out and slash en masse at the legs of waders who corner them in confined areas. These slashes cause intense pain followed by swelling of the affected tissue.

Queenfish, Leatherbacks, and Leatherjackets (Family Carangidae, Genera *Scomberoides* and *Oligoplites*)

Cruisers frequently catch these good-eating fish on small lures and light tackle near shore in the tropics from the Pacific coast of Central America to the Red Sea. Smaller, bright-silver versions with yellow dots called leatherjackets *(Oligoplites saurus)* may turn up in cast nets in tropical western Atlantic and Caribbean coastal areas. Be careful not to touch the venomous dorsal or anal spines, or you may suffer a painful sting.

Sea Snakes (Phylum Chordata, Class Reptilia, Family Hydrophiidae)

Sea snakes inhabit tropical, some subtropical, and even temperate waters of the Pacific and Indian oceans. Species ranges and abundance peak in the tropics between the Samoas and East Africa. Sheltered coastal waters and river mouths are prime habitat. You may encounter them ashore, especially in washed out hollows under and around tree roots, in rocky or coralline crevices and ledges, and similar habitats.

The general rap on sea snakes is that they tend to be easygoing and nonaggressive, and that the small, recessed fangs make successful penetration less likely. You may see natives handling them. Other accounts document aggressive behavior for certain species and at specific times, possibly correlated to breeding season. Most agree that provoked, harassed, or alarmed sea snakes will attack and bite viciously.

Sea snakes, similar to terrestrial poisonous snakes, deliver venom squeezed from a sac to the fang, where it drains out via a groove. The venom is extremely potent. Bites usually occur by accidentally stepping on the snakes, by fishers handling nets, or when wading or swimming in sea-snake-infested waters. Trolling lures occasionally snag sea snakes, and sometimes they take hook-and-line offerings. Bite symptoms can occur within five minutes, after no initial pain or other reaction at the wound. No symptoms after eight hours indicate that you dodged a bullet, and no venom was injected. Symptoms begin mildly and progress, starting with a general tongue-thickening, then aching and stiffening muscles, followed by motor weakness and paralysis. The victim may become nauseous and vomit. Telltale signs of a sea-snake bite are the limbs becoming extremely painful to flex and the victim's urine going from a dusky yellow to a reddish-brown color. The pulse will be weak and irregular; the pupils will be dilated. Failing vision is considered a terminal sign. Respiratory paralysis leads to death. If the victim survives the first week, he or she will most likely recover; however, full recovery can take months.

A sea-snake bite constitutes a medical emergency that requires immediate action. But what if you're not sure you were bitten or if the fangs got enough penetration to inject venom? Did your activities place you into possible contact with a sea snake (e.g., a blind reach into a hole or crevice)? Look very closely for characteristic bite marks: multiple pin-sized circular dots, including from one to four larger fang marks, and three to twenty posterior jaw marks. Fangs and teeth may break off in the skin. Drawing a hair over the site may extract the teeth. Try to get a positive identification on the snake, and sever the head and keep it for identification purposes if at all possible. Symptoms usually develop within one hour.

Absorption of sea-snake venom is rapid, so suction should be applied only within the first few minutes following the bite. If you miss this brief window, leave the bite undisturbed. Allow the victim no exertion, lie the person down, immobilize the limb in a position below the level of the heart, and get to a hospital fast. Administer antivenin at the onset of symptoms *in strict accordance with printed instructions* (currently available from Commonwealth Serum Laboratories; see appendix 1). Avoid swimming or wading in turbid waters and river mouths in sea-snake-infested areas. Use extreme care when unloading or hauling fishing nets. If you catch one on hook and line, do not attempt to remove the hook and do not handle the snake. Cut the line over the water and drop the snake back into the sea.

Freshwater Wading Hazards

If you venture inland, particularly in the warmer latitudes, in search of prawns or other additions to your diet that inhabit freshwater streams, rivers, ponds, or lakes, be aware of possible exposure to a variety of parasitic infections. Generally, these consist of worm-like organisms that can enter the body through the skin or various orifices. Still or slow-moving water bodies present the greatest hazards.

The most famous of these infections is probably schistosomiasis. A small blood fluke that uses freshwater snails as an intermediate host hatches and passes through human skin to the lungs and liver, causing inflammation, necrosis, and fibrosis, depending on the numbers present as they undergo development. The condition can be debilitating and fatal if untreated. Blood in urine or feces is the most important warning sign. Praziquantel kills all offending species. Consult medical references or a health professional for dosage and other critical details (see appendices 2 and 5).

Many other infestations, found predominantly in the tropics, are possible. Seek the advice and information available from local health officials or physicians before you go plunging inland into quieter freshwater habitats. In some cases, a single dose of prophylactic medication will save you from a medical ordeal (see appendix 2 for contact information for the International Association for Medical Assistance to Travelers).

Galley Injuries and Ailments

Cruisers might dodge the minefield of fishing hazards, process their catch, and think they can retire safely to the inner sanctum of the galley for restoration. Don't let your guard down yet! Physical injuries in the galley occur from boat motion in a seaway or from plain carelessness. Avoid these, and you could still get into trouble by ingesting a substantial array of toxic or contaminated seafood that cooking doesn't negate. Arm yourself with knowledge and follow safe protocols, and you should have no problem . . . you and your crew can finally kick back and relax after another great day on the water.

PHYSICAL TRAUMA

It's easy enough to slip with a knife on flat, immobile surfaces, and much easier in rough seas. Hot liquids can fly off the stove or you may inadvertently grab or contact a hot pot or pan. Take your time when cooking, and pay special attention when cooking or processing seafood in rough conditions. Make sure all pots containing hot liquids or foods are secure, unable to flip off the stove on a particularly violent pitch or roll. If you feel conditions are unsafe for using burners, consider microwave cooking, cold cooking with lime and lemon marinades, or waiting until conditions settle or the boat is on a more comfortable heading. Similarly, avoid processing if the degree of motion exceeds your confidence in processing safety. Don't be too proud to ask for help or to change galley plans.

Deep Cuts

First aid for deep cuts begins with applying direct pressure with a wad of clean cloth to stop the bleeding. Fast application is especially important if you note the characteristic bright red pulsing or squirting of arterial bleeding. Once the bleeding stops, clean the wound with antibacterial soap; close gaping wounds with butterfly bandages or sutures. Apply antibiotic ointment and cover the cut with a sterile dressing and bandage.

Burns

For first-degree burns or small second-degree burns, run cool water over the burned area or soak the injury in ice water. Coat the burn with Silvadene cream (i.e., silver sulfadiazine) and cover the injury with a sterile dressing and bandage. Relieve pain with analgesics such as acetaminophen or codeine. In case of a major burn (i.e., a large second-degree burn or a third-degree burn), seek professional medical help. With help days away, your main enemy is infection. Take prudent measures to reduce exposure to bacteria (i.e., keep the burn covered with an antibiotic-impregnated sterile dressing, avoid exposure to sea spray, and pour hydrogen peroxide onto the area in between dressing changes).

INGESTION OF TOXIC SEAFOOD

Fish or invertebrates may be toxic to eat due to accumulation of natural substances or pathogens and various contaminants of human origin in the flesh during the course of feeding and respiration. Some poisons are metabolic by-products of bacteria that grow in seafood flesh after the death of the organism. Still others are produced by the organism in order to inject prey. Toxicity from food-chain accumulation can be ephemeral or chronic; in most cases, it correlates strongly to a specific area, time of year, or environmental condition. Understanding the processes involved in seafood toxicity, categories of possibilities, and representative animal groups will get you asking the right questions of local inhabitants and avoiding risks in the absence of local knowledge. Mistakes can cause mild discomfort, debilitating illness, or death. When in a new area or in doubt, check with the locals before eating captured seafood. Eat only fresh or well-preserved seafood.

Mollusks (Shellfish) Contaminated with Pathogens

Pathogenic bacteria and viruses sometimes contaminate shellfish, although the mechanism is not always clear. These pathogens may enter the digestive tract from ambient seawater. Shellfish digest bacteria as food or excrete them, yet harvesting them when substantial amounts of bacteria are present may inoculate the product. Viruses, on the other hand, may actually invade the flesh of the shellfish through the wall of the digestive tract after entry in seawater, causing human consumers serious problems. Alternatively, both bacteria and viruses may invade otherwise good shellfish meat after harvest somewhere along the line during handling and processing. Whether from handling or the sea, both forms of pathogen often correlate with the presence of sewage and other sources of fecal matter.

Bacteria must usually be present in significant numbers to cause harm. *Escherichia coli* is a large coliform bacterium that includes some extremely virulent strains, but even the occurrence of relatively harmless forms indicates that other fecal pathogens are likely to be present. Many of the worst of such bacteria belong to the genus *Vibrio*, which includes those responsible for various forms of cholera, as well as less severe gastroenteritis. Most forms of gastrointestinal shellfish problems involve an incubation period of ten to twelve hours, nausea, vomiting, diarrhea, and abdominal pain; recovery time is reasonably brief, with plenty of fluids and rest.

Vibrio species prefer and multiply rapidly in warm temperatures. Some are widespread inhabitants of seawater. The primary danger is from uncooked seafood and from recontamination of cooked seafood by contact with *anything* (your hands, utensils, or containers) that has touched raw seafood, particularly crustaceans and mollusks. Diarrhea is the first sign that you may have a *Vibrio* infestation, which can range from mild to fatal. People with liver damage or other immune-system problems are most susceptible. One warm-season coastal species found predominantly in oysters, *Vibrio vulnificus*, causes potentially fatal blood poisoning (i.e., septicemia), but it is rare in cooler regions of the world.

Salmonella bacteria, unlike *Vibrio*, do not normally occur in marine environments. Therefore, poisoning from this source virtually always comes from unsanitary processing and handling techniques, and often fecal origins. This form of gastric disturbance can be violent and serious.

Another common group of bacteria, *Listeria*, causes occasional problems that were initially more apparent in the Southern Hemisphere. Unsanitary handling introduces these bacteria from fecal and other sources to shellfish. Mussels are prime carriers in New Zealand, while the majority of U.S. cases result from oyster consumption. Heating to 177°F (77°C) destroys *Listeria*; however, light cooking frequently does not achieve this temperature. Consumption may produce mild flu-like symptoms and even vomiting in healthy individuals, and fatal blood poisoning in AIDS patients. Listeriosis is dangerous to unborn fetuses, and pregnant women are far more susceptible to infection.

In contrast to bacteria, viruses may be present only in small numbers and induce illness, and cannot be treated with antibiotics. Like bacteria, the most harmful forms come from sewage, borne by seawater or unsanitary handling after capture, and most viruses afflict those with weakened immune systems. Two examples of viral disease contracted by shellfish consumption are Hepatitis A and Norwalk virus.

Most pathogenic shellfish contamination occurs near human populations. Risk is proportional to the size of the population and local sewage treatment practices. Open sewers and raw discharge into the ocean are common worldwide and may be exacerbated during periods of heavy rainfall. Don't take any chances collecting shellfish anywhere near these areas or purchasing shellfish from vendors not operating in scrupulously sanitary venues (and never from a mixed counter display of raw and cooked products); be sure to cook shellfish in piping hot conditions before consumption.

Mollusks Contaminated with Biotoxins

Shellfish contamination from biotoxins comes from filter feeding in seawater containing significant densities of microscopic dinoflagellates, diatoms and, in some cases, bacteria. Certain species of these tiny planktonic life forms contain chemicals poisonous to humans. Unpredictable blooms can be intense enough to discolor the sea (i.e., red tides). Other population pulses sufficient to contaminate mussels, oysters, clams, and scallops cause no gross visible changes in the appearance of coastal waters.

Cooking won't help in the case of biotoxin contamination. Known for centuries, new poisons and different forms of outbreaks nevertheless continue to arise with world population growth and development. The toxins don't seem to affect the shellfish themselves, and dangerous individuals don't look or smell any different from harmless ones. Planktonic dinoflagellates and diatoms produce most biotoxins, although the bacteria genus *Corynebacterium* produces surugatoxin.

Paralytic Shellfish Poisoning

Paralytic shellfish poisoning (PSP) has been around a long time. PSP plays a role in North American Indian folklore. Captain George Vancouver appears to have lost several crewmembers to PSP in 1793 while exploring what is now Canada's British Columbia coastline. Europe, Japan, and recently the Philippines have all experienced outbreaks. Culprits include at least eighteen various related toxins (saxitoxin and derivatives) produced by numerous area-specific dinoflagellate species, the details of which are academic because no treatment yet exists for any of them.

PSP is the most severe form of shellfish poisoning. The onset of symptoms is usually within thirty minutes. The victim experiences a tingling or burning sensation of the lips and tongue, progressing to the neck, arm, fingertips, legs, and toes. This sensation changes to numbness, making voluntary movements difficult. In severe cases, there will be motor uncoordination and the feeling of a constricted throat. The patient will feel weak, dizzy, and intensely thirsty. Gastrointestinal symptoms, however, are not common with PSP. In the terminal stage, death occurs by respiratory paralysis. The prognosis is good if the patient survives the first twelve hours. Susceptibility varies from person to person. Despite the absence of known antidotes, seeking professional medical help can still save the life of the victim. Providing artificial respiration to overcome respiratory failure may allow sufficient time for toxin dissipation.

Developed nations monitor PSP toxins in shellfish populations and close dangerous areas to har-

vesting. Taking shellfish from unmonitored or closed areas is dangerous, despite the apparent absence of red tides. For this reason, large shellfish resources continue to go unharvested in Alaska, for example, due to the inability to adequately monitor this extensive coastline.

Amnesic and Other Neurotoxic Shellfish Poisoning

Amnesic shellfish poisoning (ASP) is perhaps the newest problem, highlighted by a late 1987 outbreak in eastern Canada. The culprit is domoic acid, a potent neurotoxin produced by the cold-water diatom *Nitzschia pungens*. These diatoms may bloom in *winter* rather than the warmer conditions favored by many dinoflagellates. Victims experience short-term memory loss among other severe neurological symptoms. Some cases are fatal.

Other known neurotoxic shellfish poisoning (NSP) originates from a class of compounds called brevetoxins, produced by the warm-water dinoflagellate *Gymnodinium breve*. Documented blooms in the Gulf of Mexico, especially along the Florida coast, cause fish kills and frequent closure of shellfish grounds. NSP is milder than ASP, with no deaths recorded.

Diarrhetic Shellfish Poisoning

Compounds derived from okadaic acid cause diarrhetic shellfish poisoning (DSP), discovered in 1976 from a mussel-poisoning case in Japan. Dinoflagellates of the genus *Dinophysis*, which inhabit cool temperate coastal seas, produce them. DSP outbreaks occur around the North Sea area of Europe, northern Japan, and similar areas. Records indicate no fatal cases. Victims vomit and have diarrhea.

Venerupin Poisoning

Venerupin-poisoning (VP) outbreaks appear to result primarily from consuming oysters and clams in restricted areas of Japan at specific times of the year. Venerupin-producing plankton abundance peaks in late winter, and culprit species occur elsewhere in the world (e.g., off Portugal). The illness can cause rupture of the liver and kills about one-third of its victims.

Neosurugatoxin and Prosurugatoxin Poisoning

These toxins appear to originate from a bacterium, with research focus emanating from poisoning cases due to ingestion of the ivory shell *Babylonia japonica*, a popular seafood item in Japan. Symptoms include constipation, thirst, visual defects, lip numbness, and speech difficulties.

Macroalgae Poisoning

Ingestion of red algae can cause serious to fatal poisoning. In 1991, Guam experienced thirteen cases from ingestion of *Polycavernosa tsudai*, and three of the people died. Eating *Gracilaria chorda* and *G. verrucosa* caused previous episodes. Another toxin isolated from the blue-green algae *Lyngbya majuscula* causes severe dermatitis upon contact, known from incidents involving swimmers in Okinawa and Hawaii.

Group-Specific Shellfish Poisoning

Variability in the distribution of biotoxins within the bodies of different shellfish creates some preventive opportunities, just as it does for fish. Avoid consuming the viscera of mollusks and you should not encounter any problems from this source. Abalone poison people in Japan who habitually consume the entire animal, rather than only the foot. Symptoms include sudden burning and stinging of the entire body, followed by itching, swelling, and possible skin ulceration where it is exposed to sunlight. Treat with antihistamines and cold showers to ease itching and burning, stay out of direct sunlight, take plenty of fluids, and rest. It's much easier to restrict oneself to the meat.

Giant clams *(Tridacna)* may also concentrate biotoxins in the viscera. Cruisers shouldn't be collecting these overexploited, threatened populations anyway, but in case you are in a survival situation, be sure to consume only the meat. Otherwise, you could end up with symptoms similar to ciguatera fish poisoning.

Poisonous Mollusks

Certain mollusks can be toxic due to poisons they manufacture and store to stun prey or as a defense against predators. Problems from consuming this category of mollusks are usually minimal and not of major concern to cruisers. For example, large, slow-moving, slug-like marine gastropods called sea hares (Family Aplysiidae) contain several toxic glands used mostly for defense, but people usually avoid eating them anyway. Literature claiming toxicity to humans, or claiming that anyone consumes them, is quite dated.

Several predatory gastropods concentrate poison in glands in order to inject into prey to stun them for consumption. *Murex* provides one example, but many islanders eat these without apparent effects, despite at least one dated report that they can be toxic. Whelks (Family Buccinidae) are cause for more caution, because they concentrate poison in salivary glands, the consumption of which has caused headaches, dizziness, nausea, and vomiting in Japan. Other species, however, form the basis of commercial fisheries in Europe. Cruisers should carefully separate organs from meat and consume only the latter.

Octopuses also appear to have caused incidents in Japan relating to poison-gland consumption, but this is not considered a significant problem. Avoid eating the viscera.

Allergic Reactions to Seafood

Some people can experience hypersensitivity to specific marine organism groups, including most commonly crustaceans, but also mollusks and even some fish. Ingestion triggers an immunological response, usually to specific glycoproteins present in the flesh of particular animals. Substances that trigger allergic reactions are called food antigens. They may occur in fresh seafood or may, in some cases, be enhanced by inadequate preservation. Some food preparations alter them into nonallergenic form, but most resist heat and enzymes.

Such reactions typically occur quickly, after consuming only small amounts of the seafood. Time before onset may relate to simultaneous ingestion of other foods, treatment of the allergenic food before consumption (e.g., whether cooked or raw), and the amount consumed. Symptoms are typical of allergic reactions: diffuse swelling of the face and neck, possibly affecting the entire body. The victim may have a headache, dry throat, and swollen tongue. Usually the patient recovers completely in a few days. Antihistamines such as oral or injectable Benadryl can help with recovery. In fact, physicians recommend immediate self-administration of epinephrine at the first sign of symptoms, although severe cases demand professional medical assistance.

The chief defense is acute awareness and vigilance to prevent ingestion of food antigens. Sensitive individuals can even react to safe (nonallergenic) foods cooked in communal oil used for allergenic seafood. Cruisers with known seafood intolerance should carry epinephrine with them when eating ashore, and be aware of all ingredients in various dishes before consumption.

Potential Hazards of Eating Fish

The majority of tropical cruising grounds are rife with opportunity to poison oneself from eating fish. Some possibilities exist in cooler latitudes. Fortunately, following a few basic guidelines, sharpening fish identification skills, and religious adherence to local knowledge should completely shield you from these problems.

Ciguatera

Ciguatera occurs worldwide in mostly subtropical and tropical marine fishes, usually reef-associated predators with a preference for fish prey (piscivores), and some herbivores, that spend significant amounts of time foraging in less than 325-foot (100 m) depths. The source of ciguatoxin is highly area-specific populations of benthic dinoflagellates. *Gambierdiscus toxicus* appears to be the main culprit, although researchers believe other species may also contribute ciguatoxin to the food chain. These dinoflagellates comprise predominant, stable segments of the normal microscopic fauna, contributing to chronic, persistent incidence of ciguatera in resident reef fishes. Others appear to colonize substrate that has recently been disturbed in some way—for example, by ships running aground on reefs, dredging and blasting excavations for construction projects, earthquakes, and hurricanes—leading to increased numbers and species of ciguatoxic fishes in specific locations.

Nevertheless, the dinoflagellates responsible for ciguatera tend generally to exhibit relatively stable population dynamics rather than the sudden blooms of the planktonic species underlying shellfish biotoxins. Thus, ciguatera trends remain reasonably steady over time. If big amberjacks and groupers tend to be poisonous at a given island, you can return ten years later and the same sizes and species are likely to pose the same risk.

Ciguatoxin is a general term that describes at least twenty-four different molecules of varying toxicity. It gets magnified up the food chain, beginning with ingestion of the toxic dinoflagellates by algae eaters, coral scrapers, and planktivores. For some reason, fish appear not to physiologically rid themselves of the toxin, which thus accumulates gradually in the flesh with age. Primary-level dinoflagellate consumers frequently do not concentrate enough toxin to poison humans, although some parrotfishes (Family Scaridae), surgeonfishes (Family Acanthuridae), wrasses (Family Labridae), mullet (Family Mugilidae) and others, particularly larger, older individuals, can be highly ciguatoxic in some locations. More commonly, however, it takes years of eating numerous little packets of toxin, in the form of fish prey, to develop flesh concentrations that cause problems for human consumers, which is why large, older individuals belonging to highly predatory species inevitably pose the greatest risk.

This course of events can be so predictable that locals know exactly the safe maximum eating size of selected species, and refuse for consumption all larger individuals. They also know the precise horizontal and vertical boundaries for safe individuals of each resident species. Why can't you get such information from a book? It would have to be huge and would require several lifetimes of research. Why? Because no one species is ciguatoxic everywhere, and toxic patterns may vary significantly on a very small scale—such as along the shoreline of a single small island—and involve precise ranges of size and vertical distribution on the outer reef slope. Sometimes even the locals get caught out by occasional exceptions to their general rules.

For example, the ubiquitous tropical Indo-Pacific red snapper *(Lutjanus bohar)* is notoriously ciguatoxic in most areas, yet in the Marquesas Islands (French Polynesia), individuals captured outside a specific depth are usually safe, while virtually all individuals of this species are nontoxic in Tonga's

Vava'u Group. Fishers from Florida, the Bahamas, and the Eastern Caribbean consume great barracuda *(Sphyraena barracuda)* less than 30 inches (76 cm) or so total length without hesitation, but usually balk at eating larger individuals. People on the western side of the Caribbean, however—specifically in southern Belize—eat any size great barracuda with impunity and no ill effects.

Herein lies the general cruiser's solution: *always* seek the detailed knowledge of local residents before you decide to keep and consume *any* fish caught on or near the reef. If you are in a remote area, avoid all medium to large piscivorous reef fish, as well as coral scrapers and algae feeders. *Never eat tropical moray eels* because they are often markedly ciguatoxic. Stick to smaller individuals and fish species with invertebrate diets. Another strategy, in the unlikely event that you have an expendable mammal, is to feed it some fish first; alternatively, eat a very small amount yourself the first day and see if you experience any mild symptoms. Another choice involves a recently available chemical test kit.

You'll hear many native claims about tests allowing consumption of the wrong species and size. These consist mostly of observations relating to behavior of flies near the meat, visual characteristics of the meat, color changes of coins placed on the meat, and so on, but a mammalian test organism was until recently the only reliable field indicator for questionable selections. It's much better to avoid such fish. If in doubt, turn it loose. Don't get caught taking chances on any fish outside the species-size-area safety zone.

One Bahamian story involves an avid fisher and estate owner who for years would "generously" donate a portion of his catch to the gardener, who always thanked him profusely and returned bright and early, and in glowing health, for work the next day. The boss would then order a meal of his previous day's catch and consume it without fear, until one occasion when he became extremely ill. The gardener showed up for work the next morning in perfect health, causing the boss to exclaim, "I can't believe that fish didn't get you!" The gardener replied with a laugh, "Mon, you tink I *dat* stupid? All a dees yeahs, I nevah eat no fish 'til *afta* you, boss!" He strolled off, whistling happily, in the direction of the garden.

A few other facts will also help. Severity of ciguatera poisoning varies widely among people, and is a function of fish toxicity, amount consumed, and individual sensitivity. Humans appear also to accumulate toxins, so that habitual ingestion of mildly, undetectably ciguatoxic reef fish over time will gradually increase one's proclivity to experience symptoms. Also, remember this very important point: toxicity of fish parts, in descending order, is liver, intestines, testes, ovaries, and flesh. Soups involving viscera and heads of reef fish are frequent causes of ciguatera poisoning, even in cases where fillets of the same fish caused no symptoms. Avoid consuming reef-fish viscera.

What if you somehow come down with ciguatera? I've had it twice, once through the pure idiocy of spearing and consuming a 45-pound (20 kg) black grouper *(Mycteroperca bonaci)* at Norman's Cay, Exuma Islands, Bahamas. Had I checked local knowledge, I'd have learned that natives tend to avoid individual black groupers of *any* size throughout the Exumas, especially a big one. The captain of the vessel and I paid for this with ten days of aching joints and burning muscles—very mild cases. The second case followed consumption of a freshly caught 3-pound (1.4 kg) cero mackerel *(Scomberomorus regalis)* in Antigua, West Indies, resulting in twenty-four hours of nausea and diarrhea.

The following symptoms would constitute a mild case: onset of abdominal pain, nausea, vomiting, watery diarrhea, numbness, and tingling of the mouth and limbs within three to five hours. Acute symptoms lessen over eight to ten hours, and largely disappear within twenty-four hours. Weakness, numbness, and tingling might persist for one week. Severe cases commence with pronounced symptoms common to mild cases, starting anytime from immediately to within six hours, and followed by various combinations of debilitating problems, including profound exhaustion, muscle pain, feelings of loose and painful teeth, visual disturbances, dilated pupils, slow reflexes, skin disorders on hands and feet, loss of hair and nails, reversal of cold and hot sensations, muscular paralysis, coma, and death from respiratory paralysis. In nonfatal cases, recovery can take months, with some symptoms continuing for years.

No specific antidote exists. Attempt to eliminate as much of the toxin from the body as possible by repeated vomiting and drinking plenty of water. By far the most successful documented treatment, most effective within the first 48 to 72 hours, is infusion of mannitol, which completely reverses symptoms in the majority of patients. Make sure the patient rests quietly. Sedation may be necessary. Administer opiates to control severe pain. In later stages, cool showers may help to relieve the itching. Seek professional help for severe episodes.

Local remedies concocted by natives abound. Polynesians treat ciguatera by ingesting a tonic from crushed fruits of the Indian mulberry (*Morinda citrifolia*, a coffee-like shrub or small tree belonging to Family Rubiaceae and found from India to eastern Polynesia; variously called *nonu*, *noni*, or *nono*), which is also used to treat urinary-tract ailments, high blood pressure, diabetes, and various inflammations. They use it topically to treat infections and various marine organism stings as well. Recently, American interests "rediscovered" this herbal cure and are now importing it from the South Pacific and marketing it widely in health food stores.

Like other biotoxins, contaminated fish don't look, smell, or taste any different than nontoxic individuals, and cooking will not effect toxicity. If you are in a survival situation, attempt to capture a rat or other small mammal to maintain it for testing purposes. Strictly adhere to the fundamental rules of avoiding morays; larger coral scrapers and herbivores such as parrotfish and surgeonfish; fish-eating predators like barracudas, jacks, trevallys, snappers, and groupers; and all reef-fish viscera.

After much research and some false starts over the years, a simple chemical test kit for ciguatoxic fish became available in October 1997. Cigua-Check contains vials and test strips for five tests. Each begins by placing a rice-grain-sized piece of fish flesh into a vial containing alcohol for twenty minutes of toxin extraction, followed by insertion of a test strip. Any lipid-based toxins adhere to a membrane on the test strip. Remove the strip, allow it to dry for twenty minutes, then insert it into a vial of antibody-coated purple polystyrene, which in turn adheres to the ciguatoxins already stuck to the strip. Thus, the darker the shade of purple on the test strip, the greater the toxicity of your fish. The kit retails for under $30 plus shipping, is guaranteed to remain viable for six months, and can be ordered directly from Oceanit Test Systems Inc. (see appendix 1 for contact information). No false positive results are known. However, at least two fish that tested clear for ciguatera caused severe illness. Why? Unfortunately, other toxins also occur in tropical reef fishes.

Hallucinogenic Fish Poisoning

Hallucinogenic fish poisoning (HFP) is another reef-fish malady, reported to date only from Indo-Pacific regions. The poison is present in the flesh, most highly concentrated in the head, unaffected by cooking, and contaminated fish are indistinguishable from unaffected fish. Unlike ciguatera, HFP seems to have no clear patterns. Reported culprits include rabbitfish (Family Siganidae), chubs (Family Kyphosidae), small groupers (Family Serranidae), mullet (Family Mugilidae), goatfishes (Family Mullidae), surgeonfishes (Family Acanthuridae), and even small damselfish called sergeant majors (Family Pomacentridae).

The sporadic, less predictable occurrence of HFP dictates refraining from reef-fish head consumption in the Indo-Pacific (sorry, soup and stew lovers: use fillet meat instead). Affirmation of safety by locals might make it OK, but not as foolproof as for cigua-tera. This poison acts on the central nervous system within minutes of eating the fish and lasts up to twenty-four hours. It doesn't sound like fun—dizziness, loss of equilibrium and coordination, hallucinations, mental depression, and the sensation of chest constriction. Encourage vomiting, and keep the victim under close observation, calm, and resting.

Shark Poisoning

Poison is generally concentrated in the liver of the shark, but may be more commonly present in the musculature of medium to large tropical sharks. Tropical sharks are risky to eat, particularly in the Indo-Pacific, although the fresh flesh of at least one species common in Arctic and cold temperate seas is frequently toxic (i.e., the Greenland shark, *Somniosis microcephalus*). Symptoms of toxic shark poisoning are generally mild, including abdominal pain and diarrhea. However, toxic shark-liver poisoning can be severe, with symptoms developing within thirty minutes. The more acute cases experience nausea, vomiting, diarrhea, abdominal pain, headache, burning sensation of the tongue, weakness, muscular cramping, and a heaviness of the limbs. Victims may experience visual disturbances, delirium, respiratory distress, coma, and death. No antidotes are known. Give the patient plenty of liquids and bed rest. If symptoms are severe, seek professional medical help. Prevent this type of poisoning by not eating the liver or fresh flesh of medium to large tropical sharks, unless positively identified by the local inhabitants as safe to eat. Ordinary cooking temperatures do not destroy the poison, although elimination is possible by drying shark-meat strips, allowing juices to drip free, and then freezing the dried strips. Poorly dried shark meat may be more toxic than fresh meat.

Don't let this scare you away from consuming all sharks. They're generally excellent eating. Avoid gray reef sharks *(Carcharhinus amblyrhynchos)* and blacktip reef sharks *(Carcharhinus melanopterus)*, two very common Indo-Pacific reef species that have caused poisoning problems. Scratch great white sharks *(Carcharodon carcharias)*, blue sharks *(Prionace glauca)*, soupfin sharks *(Galeorhinus galeus)*, and oddballs like Greenland sharks (Family Dalatiidae), six-gilled sharks (Family Hexanchidae), and cat sharks (Family Scyliorhinidae) from your menu. Don't eat large individuals of tropical species, especially those caught near reefs, because fish-eating sharks, like bony fishes, accumulate ciguatoxin. This leaves you with many delicious options both inshore and offshore that are widely and safely consumed with relish—mako sharks *(Isurus)*, silky sharks *(Carcharhinus falciformes)*, blacktip sharks *(Carcharhinus limbatus)*, and spiny dogfish *(Squalus acanthias)*, to name just a few. Juveniles of many species caught inshore, particularly outside the tropical Indo-Pacific, should be safe, as records indicate no poisoning cases despite culinary popularity.

Puffer Fishes: Most Poisonous of All?
Do not, under any circumstances, eat any kind of puffer, porcupine fish, or ocean sunfish, no matter where you are.

We cannot emphasize this strongly enough. Our Japanese friends who relish traditional fugu might argue with this, but even they should take great care to partake of this dish only at a first-class establishment featuring a licensed puffer chef, and may wish to say a special prayer before dinner. Puffer poisoning rivals the most acute possible marine seafood intoxication and has sent many people to their graves prematurely. What if you are fighting to survive, and puffers or an ocean sunfish *(Mola mola)* are all you seem to be able to catch? Eat only musculature, no skin or viscera, and cut the meat into small bits first, soak in seawater for a minimum of three to four hours, kneading constantly and changing the water frequently. Otherwise, strict abstinence is the only logical course for cruisers.

Exactly what fish are we talking about? Any species of fish belonging to Families Diodontidae (porcupine fishes), Canthigasteridae (sharp-nosed puffers), Tetraodontidae (puffers), Triodontidae (three-toothed puffers), and Molidae (ocean sunfishes), all of which belong to Order Tetraodontiformes. You might also wish to avoid closely related boxfishes (Ostraciidae), although natives consume some of these over broad areas of the tropics with only occasional incidences of ciguatera and no reported true puffer poisoning. Tetraodontiform fishes occur just about anywhere you could possibly go cruising, except in polar seas and some of the coldest regions of temperate waters. You'll see them inshore and around reefs, you'll catch them on hook and line and by other means, and perhaps be entertained by their interesting habit of inflating into a sphere when alarmed. Ocean sunfish *(Mola mola* and several related species) are generally unmistakable large to giant fishes noted near the sea surface, usually out away from the shoreline or outer reef slope, and frequently well offshore. One rule that would keep you out of trouble: Don't eat any bony fish species that lack scales.

Tetrodotoxic fish poisoning occurs from eating the flesh, skin, or viscera of toxic individuals, which look no different from nontoxic specimens. Some correlation is evident with reproductive seasons, but patterns of toxicity generally remain unclear (for one thing, many tropical reef fish spawn sporadically

The porcupine fish (*Allomycterus jaculiferus*, Family Diodontidae), typical of similar species found worldwide in warmer seas.

year-round). Thus, extreme variability in toxicity between individuals and species by location and time is the rule.

Symptoms of puffer poisoning are equally variable and inconsistent. They usually commence ten to forty-five minutes after eating with a tingling of the lips and tongue, dizziness, and skin pallor, graduating to numbness and spreading to the appendages, possibly accompanied by gastrointestinal disturbance. Further symptoms include sweating, extreme salivation, headache, plummeting blood pressure and a fast, weak pulse, and respiratory distress eventually followed by blue, blistered skin, muscular tremor and paralysis, and fixed glassy eyes. Cause of death is respiratory paralysis. Victims get to fully enjoy every stage because mental acuity typically lasts until the end. People who survive the first twenty-four hours have a good chance of survival. Puffer soup, anyone?

If a mistake occurs and you believe that you're affected, induce vomiting as quickly as possible with any routine emetic, and commence enemas or suppository laxatives to help rid yourself of the toxin. Rush to a health professional if possible, as you will need intravenous fluids and other assistance.

Ichthyootoxic Fish Poisoning

Whereas puffer poisoning bears a clouded correlation with spawning, the relationship between gonadal toxicity and spawning is unequivocal for ichthyootoxic fishes. The problem is that quite a variety of fish families and species seem to exhibit this tendency. Prominent among these are certain sturgeons (Family Acipenseridae), alligator gars (Family Lepisosteidae), pikes (Family Escoidae), carps (Family Cyprinidae), salmon and whitefish (Family Salmonidae), burbot (*Lota lota*, Family Gadidae), killifishes (Family Cyprinodontidae), sculpins (Family Cottidae), pricklebacks (Family Stichaeidae), and members of many catfish families (Order Siluroidei). Patterns? Nearly all are brackish or freshwater inhabitants of Europe, North America, and northern Asia, and tend to have definable spawning seasons. Never consume roe from any of these fish in the high-risk areas during times of elevated reproductive activity.

If you do, you may feel basically like a puffer-poisoning victim except that you might have more convulsions. There's no antidote, so try to vomit (this will probably be no problem). The good news is you should recover in three to five days.

Toxic Clupeiform and Elopiform Fishes

OK, all you smug cruisers hanging out in the West Indies, shaking your head at Indo-Pacific and other regional terrors, here's one for you: clupeotoxism. Yes, there's been tropical Pacific incidents, but most reported cases are from the tropical Atlantic and Caribbean. As the name implies, the culprits are almost always swarming, near-shore schools of tropical clupeids (herrings, pilchards, sardines, and the like) or engraulids (anchovies) that may feed on toxic dinoflagellates present in summertime blooms. Evidence suggests also that these smaller species, as well as other larger members of Order Elopiformes, like tarpon, can develop toxicity by feeding on seasonal spawning swarms of palolo worms.

Cubans and other islanders are fond of netting various small clupeids, gutting them with a poke of a finger, and roasting them on open fires. Another favorite dish consists of fried clumps of tiny whole engraulids. It's all quite tasty, and locals will likely have accurate knowledge of safe harvest locations and times. Problems might occur, however, for cruisers who become adept cast-netters, develop a taste for these dishes, and try to duplicate their experience at an unfamiliar island without local advice.

As usual, affected fish look normal, cooking doesn't help, viscera have the most toxin, and there's no antidote. A distinct sharp metallic taste immediately upon ingestion, followed by sudden violent vomiting and diarrhea, identifies this poisoning. Victim mortality rate is high and may occur in less than fifteen minutes following sharp drops in pulse and blood pressure, chills, cool clammy skin with a blue hue, nervousness (who wouldn't be), dilated pupils, violent muscle cramping, and respiratory distress descending into coma and death.

Avoid consuming these silvery schooling fishes at tropical islands during warmer times of the year, and definitely any fish caught around a plankton bloom or palolo-worm swarm. These swarms occur throughout the tropics on very specific moon phases at distinct locations, often commencing in the early morning darkness, eagerly anticipated and known in detail by native inhabitants. Tremendous numbers of tiny segmented marine worms back out of burrows or crevices in the seafloor and break off the gamete-filled aft section of their body, which then swims up into the water column to release eggs or sperm in a mass frenzy. Fish, people, and birds all turn out in droves to catch and eat the worm segments (epitokes). There's little chance you'll be the first to discover a swarm at inhabited locations, so you should have no problem avoiding consumption of fish caught around such aggregations.

Scombrotoxism: A Dark and Oily Meat Problem

Hang on a minute! I know this chapter has been a little depressing, and now you see a subtitle implicating the fish family that could easily win the nomination for Cruiser's Mainstay: Scombridae, which includes wahoo and all of those delicious tuna and mackerel. Don't worry—other than easily avoided ciguatoxic individuals, this group is generally safe *unless you permit the onset of meat spoilage through improper handling*. Why? Because histidine is more prevalent in red and oily fish meat, and the metabolic processes of bacteria munching on it produce toxic by-products. Process and chill these fishes quickly, and don't tolerate slight rancidity in the meat. Reject any meat with the sharp or peppery taste characteristic of these toxins, or that exhibits other signs of significant spoilage.

Symptoms will be nearly immediate: intense headache, dizziness, throbbing arteries, heart palpitation, rapid, weak pulse, mouth dryness, inability to swallow, facial swelling. Bronchospasms and general respiratory distress, shock, and possibly death can result from serious cases. Treat by evacuating the stomach and administering antihistamine drugs (i.e., epinephrine, cortisone, or intramuscular Benadryl). Get to a doctor if possible and start intravenous fluids to assist rehydration, if necessary.

Parasites

Parasitism describes a relationship where one organism gains sustenance from close association with another often larger organism. Ideally, the parasites would "like" to do this without killing the host. They usually accomplish this through life cycles using different hosts for various developmental stages, which generally require adaptations specific to the targeted host organisms. Ingestion of parasites or their eggs generally gets humans into trouble when the physiological makeup of the intended target host is sufficiently similar to our own. By and large, this is not the case for marine fish parasites (chapter 9); furthermore, sufficient cooking kills parasite eggs and organisms.

Thus, fish bodies may provide veritable hotels for internal flukes (trematodes), tapeworms (cestodes), and roundworms (nematodes), and might have crustaceans like isopods and amphipods anchored to or crawling around their exteriors—virtually none are of any significant consequence for human consumption. We describe common examples in chapter 9—cut out those found in the meat for aesthetic reasons, and most others will be discarded with the viscera. It *is* possible to have a problem from ingesting a tiny coiled worm *(Anisakis)* present in the raw flesh of marine fish that have ingested them in the course of feeding on specific crustaceans, because the intended primary hosts are marine mammals (particularly seals). Most marine fish flesh, however, particularly that of pelagic species, is safe to consume raw.

Freshwater fish are a different story because they serve as intermediate hosts for numerous deleterious parasites that target terrestrial mammalian systems, often after beginning life in freshwater snails. Many are trematodes that infect the lungs, bile ducts, pancreatic ducts, intestines, and other organs of mammals. The infamous Chinese liver fluke *(Opisthorchis sinensis)* enters humans in the form of cysts ingested from eating raw or poorly cooked freshwater fish. *Never* consume raw brackish or freshwater fish, nor freshwater invertebrates.

The safety of raw marine invertebrate consumption varies between major groups. Raw conch, oysters, clams, mussels, scallops, squid, and octopus—provided they're extremely fresh, uncontaminated by pathogens or biotoxins, and you avoid poisonous viscera—are generally safe. Risks increase for raw crustaceans due to the extreme variety of parasites that use these for intermediate hosts—generally this is a poor idea. Other than sea-urchin roe, scratch echinoderms from the raw bar on the basis of noxious chemical possibilities, except when following strict protocol in the presence of a native.

Is That All?

Ingesting the flesh or selected organs of a number of other marine organisms can poison or debilitate you, although we've covered many of the more likely possibilities. Additional examples include the following.

♦ *Tropical reef crabs.* Consult local knowledge before consuming unfamiliar tropical reef crabs. A number of Indo-Pacific species belonging to Family Xanthidae can be biotoxic in selected areas.

♦ *Oilfish.* Oilfish *(Ruvettus pretiosus)* occur worldwide in offshore tropical seas and are often caught at night while targeting swordfish. Eating the flesh will probably give you very loose bowels or diarrhea and the extremely oily meat tends to spoil quickly, although it is otherwise not harmful.

♦ *Sea turtles.* Several species of sea turtle have produced ciguatera-like poisoning in humans at different tropical locations around the world. This should be survival food only because these animals are endangered. Keep the precautions noted previously for ciguatera in mind.

♦ *Raw eel blood.* Avoid ingesting uncooked eel blood or body fluids for all freshwater and marine eels. Cooking, however, should detoxify this particular type of poison.

♦ *Fish livers.* Avoid eating fish livers in general, cooked or raw, as they are occasionally biotoxic in a scattering of species.

♦ *Marine mammals.* Relax . . . this is just an interesting fact with remote survival value. Ingesting the livers or kidneys of polar bears, and the livers and, in some cases, flesh or viscera of certain walruses, seals, whales, and porpoises can poison you enough to cause acute symptoms and possibly death. Eskimos and certain Asian populations have the most experience with this (see Halstead, appendix 5).

Keeping Everything in Perspective

One of the first things lecturers tell incoming medical students is that as they learn all about the staggering array of disorders, diseases, ailments, and other disasters that can befall the human body, they will experience a normal, although irrational, psychological reaction of paranoia. Nearly all will fear or be temporarily suspicious that they are experiencing symptoms of some highly unlikely horror.

Cruisers must guard against this same natural overreaction when reviewing all the bad things that could possibly happen in connection with fishing and ingesting seafood. Remember, you have a great deal of control over the chance that you or your crew will ever experience the more serious problems described in this chapter. All it takes to embark on a safe and happy lifetime fishing adventure is a modicum of knowledge, a dose of common sense, taking your development as a fisher and consumer slowly, one step at a time . . . always keeping your mind open to new thoughts, facts, and possibilities, and what you can learn from experience, yourself, and others . . . keeping a cool head when something doesn't go right.

11

Getting the Most from Your New Cruising Skill

ruisers thrive on newfound success following exposure to accurate information about fishing. They are an ingenious lot and tend to use their new foundation to experiment constantly with additional ideas and innovations. The best fishers stay mentally open and fresh, adding to their knowledge daily, never too good to learn another viewpoint or to comprehend and interpret an unfamiliar environmental sign. Many such learning episodes emanate from the enthusiasm and curiosity of the kids aboard.

The avid interest and observations of your children can carry over to their academic life. Fishing has provided the spark for many underachieving pupils, igniting analytical abilities and scientific thought processes in a way no classroom lecture or textbook could. Expert fishers are in effect advanced vertebrate and invertebrate ecologists, with a dash of behavioral psychology thrown in. Work this form of intellectual stimulation for everything it's worth. Augment correspondence courses with the fascinating window on oceanography and marine biology provided by fishing.

Fishing is also a universal language. You now have a strong common bond with natives of seafaring nations. The sight of your fishing outriggers and other telltale signs immediately place you in a different category in their eyes. It opens a new world of common interest and information to discuss and exchange, whether or not you speak the native dialect. And make no mistake—your gift of an effective lure previously unknown to an area might feed a family on repeated occasions, and local

knowledge you glean can expose you to new species and save you from life-threatening experiences with toxic organisms. These are profound issues, a far cry from "making conversation" or idle chatter.

Responsibility to both host country and to the environment comes with your new fishing power. You might have posed little threat to fish and invertebrate populations before you learned how to fish, but now you're armed and dangerous. Seriously, you will soon realize the transition from not being able to catch a fish in a barrel to the ability to overexploit fish. This can measurably hurt the ecosystem of your location, and it can land you in severe trouble with local authorities. In this chapter, we discuss information that will help you avoid potential legal, social, and environmental pitfalls.

Your new pursuit might induce you to subscribe to periodicals, join organizations, and draw closer to the political and social issues constantly debated among different groups. Each has an opinion and sometimes an axe to grind. Different enthusiasts emotionally argue their views. Fishery managers and scientists are often caught in the middle. Who's right? Who's wrong? What's best for the environment and for sustainable levels of exploitation?

A small percentage of cruisers might someday find themselves in a survival situation. Remember that goofy survival fishing kit you saw at the boat show? You now have the knowledge necessary to build yourself a real one. Knowing how to fish could save your life.

What about those of you who prefer the pure joy of cruising under power or sail to fishing? The better you are at fishing, the less time you'll need to put dinner on the table. Your gear will go in the water efficiently, often briefly, and far more successfully. Read the signs and fish only when you need to, then adjust to cruise rpm or pop open the spinnaker, pole it out, and relax—you won't have to stop unexpectedly for a fish because there's already one in the box and no lines are out!

Creating the smoothest, least thorny path for your entry into the world of expert-level fishing extends well beyond showing you the technology and gear, and how to apply it. Review of the relevant social, political, educational, environmental, and survival issues will help you get the most out of your new cruising skill.

Sink Everyone's Boat but Mine

The antithesis of cruising ethics is the rallying cry that thinly underlies most conflicts among commercial fishing groups, commercial and recreational fishers, and individuals trying to catch the same fish. In essence, "sink everyone's boat but mine." Why? Because populations of marine organisms overwhelmingly remain common-property resources. It's more often than not impossible to buy property, fence them in, guard the property line, and keep them all to yourself. Citizens of each nation usually have an equal opportunity to exploit most living marine resources within the internationally recognized 200-mile limit, or Exclusive Economic Zone (EEZ), of their country. Visitors may be granted restricted rights to do so following customs and immigration clearance, or according to special licenses and international treaties.

What happens? Different groups and individuals hotly pursue species highly regarded as food, aesthetic sporting objects, or both. These enthusiasts use all the different types of gear permitted by law, and sometimes gear that's not. Some want money, some seek food for personal consumption, and others are just out for a good time. They run into each other on the water from time to time. Deep down, each wishes they had it all to themselves. Sometimes they fight and argue, and grow to dislike each other. Fishing spots and other helpful information become big secrets. Espionage is a problem.

Sound funny? Childish, out of hand? Outlandish? Don't laugh, because as you get really good at fishing, you'll find that petty jealousy and more serious conflict are pervasive among competing individuals, vessels, and fisheries. Let's ignore the political posturing and positioning for the pursuit of big-money commercial livelihoods for a moment, and take a look at the interesting psychology behind the fishing behavior of individuals. It's analogous to behavior above critical levels of vehicle traffic—otherwise nice people do illogical things behind the wheel of a car, sometimes endangering themselves and others, often running roughshod over another person's right of way . . . for what, to save a few seconds of time? Fishing, like driving a car, involves using a common-property resource. It tweaks some primal nerve in a surprising number of people as they emerge from early timidity, gain experience, and develop "territorial imperative" . . . suddenly, it's *their* fishing spot and *their* fish.

Charter skippers and private boats cut each other off and ruin or reduce the chances of catching bait or target fish. Folks in boats or on foot jostle and scrap for position and territory, sometimes growling, barking, or whining at each other—occasionally even when there's plenty of room, alternative locations, or opportunities to use non-conflicting strategy. The behavior is usually out of proportion to the reality, but incidents occur when the quietest, easiest-going fishers become the victims of unreasonable actions that cause measurable interference. The infliction may come at the hands of nonfishers—the enmity between fishers and jet-skiers is one infamous example.

Once again, cruisers have a great advantage in that they often go where other people are scarce. Now that you've been forewarned, the chance of experiencing this little side effect of fishing fever is less. However, remain vigilant. We once anchored alone at a remote, mountainous volcanic island. Three other cruising boats subsequently arrived, one thing led to another, and they all learned to fish. Within a week, competitive tension was evident between the new arrivals as they sought—subtly at first—to outdo each other. Friendly acquaintances prior to acquiring fishing expertise, they parted barely on speaking terms. We thought this an isolated, silly aberration until we observed similar interactions at other locations. If you think a few professional fishers fighting over the radio at a seamount is funny, try occupants of two tiny inflatables who couldn't possibly adequately fish the location in a lifetime! Nowhere is safe!

Fish for yourself, never to impress somebody else. If you make a great catch, you have every reason to be proud and you should enjoy it to the hilt. *You know what you did and how you did it, and that's all that matters.* Carouse and lie all you want with close friends, but tread lightly around those you don't know well in terms of fishing stories. Project humility. Quickly changing the subject, rather than discussing another fisher in anything other than glowing terms, allows you to get along with everyone and avoid being drawn into any group or clique. The number of fine folks outnumbers those with petty tendencies in the worlds of cruising *and* fishing. Nevertheless, be aware that the better you are at fishing, the more you'll bring out the quirky behavior of certain individuals.

Respect and Conservation Revisited

Cruisers should be diplomats and conservationists. By nature, we stray from our homeport and visit foreign nations, as well as other parts of our own country. Our actions reflect on the town painted on our transom and the flag that waves above our deck. It's not such a big world anymore. The immense increases in human populations, and the speed and ease of communications among them, makes us far more accountable for our deeds. We're also, as a species, putting a measurable dent in populations of marine life on a global basis. Thus, the responsibility engendered by fishing prowess includes social and environmental issues.

PROTECTING THE ENVIRONMENT
Regardless of fishery regulations and our perceived likelihood of experiencing enforcement, cruisers particularly need their own code of exploitation ethics. We've chosen a lifestyle that immerses us uniquely in the ocean world. Although our numbers are increasing, the opportunity is exceedingly rare viewed as a percentage of total world population.

When we increase the intimacy of our immersion by fishing, we become members of the marine food web. This membership comes with important responsibilities.

Minimize the mortality you inflict on fellow food-web members. We're usually apex predators, located near the top, but other predators do consume us on occasion. The technology and weapons at our disposal make it easy to kill far more than we need for personal consumption. Never take more than you need. Don't waste what you take. Be especially sensitive to species dwindling to critically low numbers, possibly threatening their very existence, and to species critical to catch-and-release sport-fishing tourism. To this end, we urge you to place the organisms listed in table 11-1 off limits regardless of local and international law, except in extreme survival situations.

Cruisers can further protect the environment by not using the following gear and methods except for survival situations: bottom trawls, towed dredges, towed bottom-entangling devices, and any fish-stupefying methods whatsoever, including natural ichthyotoxins from plant, animal, or other origins; sodium hypochlorite (bleach); and dynamite or other explosives. Strongly consider not using drift nets and trammel nets, and only consider the use of small, highly selective gill nets in limited situations. Carry a powerhead primarily for protection, never for dispatching big individuals of large, slow-growing species of bottom fish, except under highly specialized circumstances.

RESPECTING LOCAL LAW AND CULTURE
One mistake that has cost some cruisers dearly is to arrive at a foreign port of entry in possession of fresh indigenous seafood. You are never entitled to fish in a foreign EEZ without clearing first and securing a fishing license if required. Customs officials tend to be fair, and this *generally* extends to small amounts of processed pelagic fish packages in cold storage from species that could have been caught en route, before passage into their EEZ. On the other hand, show up and apply for entry at Bimini, Bahamas, with a big fat yellowfin grouper in the cooler with gills still pumping, and you could lose your boat—*and they'd be justified in confiscating it.*

Poaching of fishery resources is a major global problem, from Antarctic seas to isolated tropical islands. Small countries, particularly scattered island nations with little means of enforcement and extensive EEZs, continue to be raped by industrialized fishing nations, pirate boats, and greedy individuals. They generally know what's going on, may be powerless to stop it, and are understandably full of impotent rage. You show up after having dipped into the cookie jar on the way into the port of entry, and they drop a load on you. The jealousy of individual fishers seems to magnify upon ascent to higher organizational levels, resulting in potentially severe penalties, including boat confiscation and imprisonment. Poachers steal simultaneously from every citizen and, as with most serious offenses, pleading ignorance is unlikely to help your case. No matter how distant the port of entry or how practical it may seem to "just get enough for dinner" on the way in, *don't do it.*

We previously touched on the subject of local culture and unwritten custom. You might follow the letter of the law, clear customs and immigration, purchase a fishing license to go with your cruising permit, meticulously observe the regulations, and still manage to enrage your hosts. For instance, individual villages along a coastline frequently consider their jurisdiction to extend to the reef or shelf, sometimes beyond. Forget about legalities concerning the high-tide mark. If you go diving or fishing in this area, you are taking something they feel is theirs. From their view, your actions are no different than strolling uninvited into their front yard and harvesting vegetables and fruits from their garden. They may be happy to share if you ask first. They may offer to take you out or you may invite them to accompany you. It's a great opportunity to make friends. Check all of this out before you embark on unilateral expeditions.

TABLE 11-1. **CRUISER'S VOLUNTARY LIST OF PROTECTED MARINE LIFE**
marine mammals
sea turtles and their eggs
sea birds and their eggs
coconut crabs
Tridacna clams
iguanas
alligators
crocodiles
caimans
jewfish and other giant groupers (all giant species of *Epinephelus*)
humphead wrasse (*Cheilinus undulatus*)
tarpon (*Megalops atlanticus*)
bonefish (*Albula vulpes* and other species)
manta rays (Family Mobulidae)
any type of coral or sponge
any organism subject to local cultural taboo
any sublegal-size organism
any threatened, endangered, or very scarce species

Another thing to watch out for is appearing to harass or purposefully kill an animal that has religious or cultural significance. Few of us are ignorant enough to go to India and slaughter a cow, but let's say you anchored in a remote Polynesian bay and ended up catching a shark for dinner . . . or maybe you simply catch one with a poly ball and set line, photograph, and release it. You'd never do this if you knew that the residents watching from the shore believed that the sharks were reincarnations of their ancestors and could be summoned for aid and protection. The sight of a stranger cutting Grandpa into pieces won't endear you to many. Besides, there's surely something else to catch and consume.

Replenishing the Cruising Kitty

You love to fish. You selected professional-grade fishing gear, modified your cruising boat here and there, got some quality electronics, and built in spacious cold storage. Cruising and fishing are the perfect marriage—you'd rather catch fish than fry hamburgers, and you're becoming extremely success-ful at fishing . . . so why not fish to support the cruise and cruise to fish? Perfect, right?

We're all thinking of ways to make it last longer. We *know* how much our catches are worth if we could sell them at the right time and place, and we fully realize the magnitude of modest financial shots in the arm when we're on a cruising budget. If you think the boom can lower fast when you attempt to clear customs with fresh-caught indigenous fish, wait until you start selling fish locally. At first, every-thing will seem cool. There's always a tourist estab-lishment, or at least locals, that need fresh fish, and maybe your fishing technology, knowledge, and cold storage enables you to deliver a more consistent, higher-quality product than local fishers. Hey, you're in paradise, and now you've got a job doing what you love the most. *Do not fall into this trap, even for barter instead of money.*

Here's why. First, you are simultaneously break-ing a multitude of laws, including those governing commercial sale of seafood, and surely the provi-sions of your visitor's permit (you know, that ubiq-uitous stamp that says "Do not engage in gainful employment"). Second, you are competing with local fishers, literally taking money from their pocket and food from their family's table. Third, as a result, regardless of how happy your recipients might be, more than one local person will become justifiably angry with you, and you can be sure that things will deteriorate fast after this. Fourth, in the ensuing aftermath, where you somehow manage to avoid losing your boat or going to prison and are relieved to depart legally—if quickly and uncere-moniously—think of the legacy you leave behind. The next unlucky cruiser who arrives in your dirty wake, particularly if they are unfortunate enough to fly the same national flag and possibly possess a fishing rod, will bear the consequences. The repu-tation of cruisers has slowly struggled from the depths of infamous 1970s-era boat bums and spongers of native hospitality. Although you've surely heard about the odd black eye continuing to occur from time to time, native hosts in general are friendly and receptive. More cruisers are trying harder to give more than they get, and *this* is how you can do something very positive. Spread some

of that fish around, no strings attached, in a manner that does not interfere with local fish sales.

What if you can fill some unique charter or commercial fishing niche in the foreign island par-adise of your dreams? Great—be sure to secure unequivocally clear written licenses and immigra-tion status from the government. Involve locals as much as possible in your operation, try not to over-lap with local activities, keep your nose clean, and be extra good to everyone, so that no matter how things eventuate, your conscience is clear. Just like in your own country, if you struggle at the bottom of the heap, no one will notice, but as you realize success, expect a certain amount of potential for jealousy. Suddenly you may no longer be "one of the girls or boys," and your rights might receive less than stalwart protection. Most work through all of this, some are forced out. Keep it fun, don't jeopar-dize your life savings, and you will probably have a good experience.

Occasional opportunities to support your cruise by fishing may arise in a destination that happens to fall within the jurisdiction of your own nation. This certainly simplifies legal matters, although you need to remain sensitive to the same subjects as in a foreign situation, especially if local culture is signif-icantly different than that of your home port.

Survival Fishing

Fishing to earn an extra buck helps survival when you anchor near people, but your fishing skills could someday be the difference between life and death. All cruisers should give careful consideration to build-ing a serious fishing kit tailored to the possible envi-ronments they plan to traverse, and pack it carefully into the ditch bag or life raft canister, if not both. We examined several commercially produced versions, and it was obvious that whoever put them together had little knowledge of fishing. They were woefully inadequate for most situations we could imagine. It's easy to put together a kit that will really work, and you now have all the necessary knowledge.

Table 11-2 summarizes candidates for contents of a generalized fishing survival kit that will fit into a small space. Adjust what you include to your ditch-bag size, or do what we did—construct a sur-vival canister large enough to accommodate everything you think you might need. We purchased a 5-foot (152 cm) length of 6-inch (152 mm) I.D. PVC pipe with end caps, which we keep lashed to the wheelhouse roof (see photo page 215). We found a combined knife/ sheath/line cutter/sharp-ening stone/gripper unit called the Fisherman's Solution attractive for the first two items in table 11-2 (available from Cutco Cutlery Corporation; see appendix 1 for contact information).

TABLE 11-2. **POTENTIAL ITEMS FOR SURVIVAL FISHING KITS**

Item	Purpose
first-aid kit	treatment of cuts, punctures, motion sickness, etc. (see chapter 10)
fishing knife in sheath	dressing food fish and bait
sharpening stone	maintain fishing knife edge
fishing pliers in sheath	rigging and de-hooking
self-sheath ice pick	for killing food fish
barbless hand spear	primarily for repulsing and killing sharks by close-range spiking
pole spear with assorted attachments	for food fish capture
belt	to keep pliers and knife sheaths handy
gloves	hand protection
billed cap	sun protection
surfer shorts	fast drying protection
T-shirt	sun protection
sunscreen	sun protection
polarized glasses	eye protection and enhanced visibility
10 lb. (4.5 kg) monofilament	capture of bait and small food fish
gold hair hooks	capture of bait and small food fish
bait quills	capture of bait and small food fish
20 lb. (9 kg) monofilament	capture of small food fish
live bait/general-purpose hooks	capture of food fish
pork rinds, salmon eggs in sealed jars	for capture of bait and food fish
squid jigs	squid capture
bucktail jigs	food fish capture
jigs and plastic bait bodies	food fish capture
wire leader material	capture of fish with sharp teeth (#2, #5, #8, #12)
barrel swivels	for connecting wire leader to monofilament
toy-store balloons	fishing floats
telescoping spinning outfit	for fast lure retrieval and capture of smaller food fish
picker gaff	for gaffing small food fish
hand gaff with 4 in. (10 cm) hook	for gaffing larger fish
tail rope/noose	for capture and securing larger food fish
50 lb. (23 kg) monofilament	capture of medium food fish, stringing fish meat to dry cure
100 lb. (45 kg) monofilament	capture of medium-large food fish
300 lb. (136 kg) monofilament	capture of large food fish
stainless steel big-game hooks	variety of sizes for all the previous handlines
wood or plastic yo-yos	for line storage
rag	general-purpose wiping, hand protection
sponge	cleaning, wiping, bailing

Catch-and-Release and Light Versus Heavy Tackle

Aesthetic fishing and discussions of light versus heavy tackle lie at the opposite end of the spectrum from fishing to survive shipwrecks, sinkings, and other catastrophes, although light tackle can be highly useful in these situations. Sport fisheries tend to develop in countries where most of the population have sufficient protein, and usually after industrialized commercial fishing has supplanted widespread subsistence fishing. The final typical evolutionary stage is heavy regulation of commercial *and* recreational fishing, with gear limitations, marine sanctuaries, closed seasons, strict bag and size limits, and complete moratoriums to protect especially beleaguered or sport-designated species.

Yet people still love to fish, long after and far beyond the extent sufficient for personal consumption. Cruisers bitten by the fishing bug are no different in this respect from anyone else. Little wonder that the practice of catch and release, so completely foreign to subsistence and other native fishers in less-developed regions, has become so heavily promoted in recreational fishing circles. It's an excellent way to keep desirable fish populations at healthy levels so that everyone can get in on the fun, and it provides a wonderful opportunity for reaping scientific knowledge by tagging the fish prior to release, after measuring and weighing them.

Catch and release is not possible for deeper-water bottom fisheries. Rapidly reeling fish to the surface from depth causes fatal embolisms emanating mostly from the air bladder. A careful perforation with an ice pick just behind the pectoral fin can sufficiently relieve mild cases to enable survival (i.e., listen for the sound of escaping air, squeeze gently to evacuate, release). However, one normally would cease fishing at these depths after reaching the legal bag limit or, frequently in the case of cruisers, getting just enough for dinner and then quitting without catching the full limit.

Under the best of circumstances, some released fish die from exhaustion, inability to avoid predators, or injuries like ruptured gill filaments incurred during the battle. This brings up an interesting point about sportfishing, which has gravitated toward the use of increasingly light tackle. Early sportfishing enthusiasts admittedly had a habit of employing very heavy tackle almost across the board. They happily cranked sailfish, salmon, tarpon, and many other species to the boat in minutes (and then usually killed them just for photos and bragging rights). It didn't take people long to figure out that by using lighter line and whippy rods, they could prolong the pleasure of the central part of the fishing experience, doing battle with the hooked gladiator. The fish tended to leap and take runs instead of skipping across or under the water straight to the boat. Sometimes this allowed the fish to escape. People loved it and extolled the virtues of being "more sporting."

This trend continued with the invention of spinning tackle and fly tackle applicable to essentially every conceivable marine possibility, although the very largest and deepest targets still remain within the purview of conventional tackle. Stand-up outfits now permit the capture of increasingly large behemoths with the same revolving-spool reels utilized in more conventional gear. IGFA established line class and fly tippet category records, and soon folks were going after all kinds of fish with wispy monofilament line of as little as 2-pound (0.9 kg) test. Somehow the idea that this was more benevolent to the fish persisted, and not only was fish size important at cocktail hour, but also everyone had to tell what strength line they used (they still do).

This light-tackle trend is mostly positive stuff. It gives people more options and more ways to fish and goals to fish for, it helps involve more children, and it tends to be heavily associated with catch and release. The only problem is that those who believe they're doing fish a favor by playing them for excessive amounts of time on very light line are mistaken. Fish that can barely move by the time the hook comes out have excessive lactic-acid buildup in the muscle tissue that does not get moved to the liver for more rapid breakdown as it does in mammals; cardiac arrest may occur. It is possible to carefully revive the fish by holding it gently and using either the boat or hand motion to push the fish ahead, forcing water through its gill chamber, sometimes for up to thirty minutes before signs of life and the ability to swim return. A greater help would be to adjust line strength to a value that provides an enjoyable angling experience but permits relatively fast conclusions to

Fred Bannerot *(right)*, Scott's great-grandfather, with a big catch landed on heavy trolling gear April 21, 1919, off of Miami, Florida, United States. **(a)** Sailfish *(Istiophorus platypterus)*; **(b)** great barracuda *(Sphyraena barracuda)*; **(c)** bonito or little tunny *(Euthynnus alletteratus)*; **(d)** king mackerel *(Scomberomorus cavalla)*; **(e)** mahi mahi *(Coryphaena hippurus)*. Today's anglers use lighter tackle and release a high proportion of their catch.

the battle (except when seeking a specific IGFA line class record). "Safe battle times" differ widely, from a few minutes for some species of trout to hours for large marlin.

Sensible line strengths also prevent the number of incidents where fish either run all the line off the fishing reel, or take excessive runs and then break off, trailing many yards (meters) of monofilament behind them. There's nothing sporting about this from at least two standpoints. First, the probability of the fish surviving decreases. Second, regardless of survival outcome, you have just released a very long strand of nonbiodegradable material that can entangle, choke, maim, and kill a variety of wildlife. Cruising boats customarily don't maneuver as quickly as some other vessels to recover line being run off by a hooked fish, so we need to be more sensitive about line capacity and strength.

Social Facilitation

One year we needed to raise the waterline on *Élan* before departure from French Polynesia for the hurricane (cyclone)-free Line Islands, Republic of Kiribati. We hauled out on the island of Raiatea, and I set to work grinding, priming, and painting, working long hours because storm season had officially begun. The boatyard housed a mixture of cruising boats, private recreational boats, and a couple of local commercial bonito fishing boats. One evening after a long hard day, as I set down my tools and removed my hood and respirator, I was startled by a silent dark hand proffering a cold, sweating can of local Hinano beer. I recognized the young Polynesian as one of the crew working to recondition an aging bonito boat across from *Élan* in the yard.

We sat together on a board under twinkling stars in a clear night sky, fanned by a balmy breeze, and chatted in broken French, bits of Polynesian, and hand signals for an hour. Terii Loyat turned out to be the captain and owner—an innovative, ingenious, hardworking, and highly successful fisher who'd convinced a bank he was capable of managing his own operation. Topics for conversation are endless for intense fishers—comparing notes on analogous incidents, observations, and tendencies; asking questions to learn from each other's experience. We drifted over for a tour of his boat and a fresh grilled skipjack tuna steak from the makeshift barbecue back against the fence. I met his crew and we spent more time together in the ensuing week. Nine months later, Wendy and I finally entered the pass at Maupiti to accept his invitation to visit him at home. We remain close and correspond regularly.

Similar incidents occur from time to time wherever we go. Friendships born of mutual interest in fishing now span many years and locations: Hollis John, Tobago, West Indies; Kim Andersen, Christmas Island, Republic of Kiribati; Hogarth Lucas, Tahiti; Paul Mead, Tonga; Arthur Albury, Bahamas, to name a few—solid, honest, hard-working, good people I feel extremely privileged to know and count as friends. I guess it's like other professions and passions—it doesn't take long to realize that you share the same wavelengths and thought processes with someone. I asked Terii what made him approach me; he said it was the outriggers and afterdeck layout.

Welcome to the world of fishing. You can't hide it—your gear and boat modifications identify your pursuit. Wherever you go, expect the occasional approach of some very special people. You won't always speak their language, but this won't prevent you from communicating in the universal language of fishing. Share your thoughts. Show them your lures

Reviving a striped marlin *(Tetrapterus audax)* before release (between Tonga and New Zealand).

and those bill marks on the teaser from when that big marlin tried to pulverize it. Ask questions as best you can. Have them over for dinner. Accept invitations to their home and for fishing expeditions aboard their boat. The experiences will enrich your life in a manner quite beyond any words printed on a page.

Intellectual Stimulation

Actor Alan Alda once said, "Your assumptions are your windows on the world. Scrub them off once in a while to let the light come in." Fishing forces you to follow Alan's advice on a very frequent basis. Every time you think you know something, nature will put just a little different spin on the next episode. Each day is different. Sure, you figure out some patterns and develop a degree of consistency, but no single lifetime can scratch the surface of what there is to know. Little wonder that, unlike many other activities, fishing becomes a lifelong passion. How many people do you know have completely retired their fishing rods?

Cruisers are particularly fortunate because the breadth of potential fishing experiences constantly at their fingertips far exceeds that of almost anyone else on the planet. They can choose from an incredible smorgasbord. Variety is the key to the overwhelming success of fishing and associated activity in piquing the curiosity of everyone aboard; nowhere does this have a greater impact than on young, flexible, developing minds.

When you take a kid fishing, the range and number of questions will likely astonish you. And guess what? No matter how much you think you know, they'll stump you more than once, sometimes dozens of times a day. Following a chance meeting, I once took three underprivileged children—residents of a poor, drug-infested, violent, predominantly African-American neighborhood in Fort Myers, Florida—fishing when they were aged six, seven, and eight. The tradition continued from time to time through their high school years, and I'm not sure who got the better end of the deal—we learned a lot from each other and have continued mutual support and inspiration since. Fellas, you haven't been real good about writing since Wendy and I sailed off, but neither were we at your age. At last contact, Tony still had a 4.0 grade-point average on full scholarship at the University of Miami, Errick had begun a career in the U.S. Army, and Shannon was just finishing high school. Without going into details, let us state simply that the odds of this happening, given certain hardships involving their environment, weren't high. Congratulations, guys. We'd like to think that fishing played some small role in your success.

What Tony, Errick, and Shannon wouldn't have given to grow up on a cruising boat. OK, all you lucky boat kids, let's give you some material inspired over the years by questions from these three fine guys. Whether you're trolling offshore, drifting or anchored, fishing from the dinghy, or wading and diving, start thinking about your answers to the following questions. Don't rush. You'll need to research some of the references in appendix 2 and materials you locate yourself, and you'll find that the questions will focus your numerous field observations.

OFFSHORE PREDATOR FISH

You are about to see some rare, beautiful, and amazing images—feats of power, color, speed, and form that help incredible animals thrive in a challenging environment. As you gain your first close views of offshore predator fish, think about the following.

- *Hydrodynamics.* Many of the fish you capture have been clocked at swimming speeds in excess of 50 mph (80 km per hour). Examine the specialized slots and grooves for every fin, allowing appendages to fold neatly into a smooth, torpedo-like profile that offers little resistance to the water. Sailfish have a large dorsal groove that allows them to fold away their sail completely—they can make the whole thing disappear—when they need to accelerate (see photo of sailfish, page 306).

- *Internal and external anatomy.* Why is the lower lobe of a flying fish tail longer than the upper lobe? How do fins help fish stop, go, and steer? How do fish keep from sinking? How do they see so well in the dim-lit depths and at night? Do fish see color? Why do different species have different jaw structure and dentition, and how does this help them survive? How do they hear, smell, and taste?

- *Feeding ecology.* Carefully examine the stomach contents of the fish you clean. What was it eating and where do you think it was when it ingested these items—on the surface or down deep? Keep an eye out for prizes like juvenile billfish and preserve them in alcohol if you can—there's a reward for them offered by the U.S. National Marine Fisheries Service (see contact information in appendix 2).

- *Reproduction.* Does the fish have any eggs inside it? Is it a male or female? How do fish reproduce, and what stages are involved for a tiny fertilized egg to grow into, say, a 1,000-pound (454 kg) blue marlin? Do sharks reproduce differently than bony fishes?

- *Physiology.* Marine fishes live immersed in salt water, which would dehydrate and kill us. How do they regulate their body's salt and water? How do fish—for example, the mahi mahi—completely and instantly change their colors?

What allows highly migratory species like tuna to swim thousands of miles, night and day, without getting tired? Why is the inside of a tuna warmer than the surrounding ocean? Are they warm- or cold-blooded? Would you believe some polar fishes actually produce and circulate a natural antifreeze, similar to the kind used by cars and inboard boat engines?

♦ *Population biology.* Where did the marlin or other fish you brought in today come from, and how old is it? What are the geographic distribution ranges of the different species you have been catching during your travels? How fast do they grow, and how can you estimate their age?

♦ *How you can help.* Write to the U.S. National Marine Fisheries Service (see appendix 2) for tagging kits. Write to Dr. Eric Prince at the same address for instructions on what to do with baby billfish found inside stomachs of other fish. An information card must be filled out and sent in for each fish tagged and released; in return, you'll receive the annual tagging report full of interesting information about time at large and growth of recaptured fishes. In addition, if one of *your* tagged fish is recaptured, you'll be personally contacted with the information specific to that fish, and you'll receive a free hat or other token of the researcher's appreciation.

STATIONARY OCEANOGRAPHY

Drifting and anchoring provide a whole new level of visual detail unavailable while underway. You may have opportunities to observe at close range free-swimming fish that have appeared mostly as a rapid, indistinct blur behind a trolled bait or lure, as well as minute facets of the daytime and nocturnal environment in which they reside. Some of the fish that you can catch in stationary mode will be completely different than any you have observed so far. The reality that surrounds you, once you know how to see it, may seem far more improbable and exciting than science fiction.

♦ *Pelagic microcosms.* You can start your lesson very simply by scooping up a cup of seawater. Look closely with just your unaided eye. Note the tiny creatures collectively termed *plankton*. What's the difference between phytoplankton and zooplankton? What kinds of animals comprise zooplankton? Are they adults or babies that will grow larger? If you are fortunate enough to have any kind of microscope on board, prepare and examine a slide of seawater. Try to identify some of the many different life forms you see. Otherwise, use a magnifying glass to get a closer view. Do you realize that you are actually sailing along in a vast seafood soup? Now fashion your own plankton net out of a cone of fine cloth with a glass jar attached to the base, deploy it overboard on a line, and retrieve it after a while. What do you see?

♦ *Pelagic macrocosms.* Keep a lookout for a floating clump of yellowish-brown sargassum weed. When you drift close enough to one, scoop it up in a bucket. Don't touch it at first—examine it very closely, and try to see the many highly camouflaged animals residing among the branches. Now grasp the clump, raise it just above the water surface in the bucket, and give it a firm shake or two. Can you believe it? Most of these animals are specially adapted for a life of floating along in this brown algae. If you are lucky, you may find a bizarre sargassum fish *(Histrio histrio),* no larger than 4½ inches (11.4 cm)—note the many fleshy tabs and the bulb with filaments sprouting out of its forehead; this is actually a lure attached to a short pole, used to entice food items close enough to gulp down for dinner. You can find these fish worldwide in tropical and warm temperate seas. Debris other than sargassum weed also attracts a variety of sea life—gooseneck barnacles, various other crustaceans, and small fishes.

♦ *Squid.* Where do these invertebrates fall in the organizational scheme of the animal kingdom; that is, to which phylum and class do they belong? Did you know that squid have a very advanced and complex nervous system and great eyesight, and that much of what we know about the human nervous system is from research performed on squid axons? At night, watch the squid darting in and out of the glow from the lights of your boat—how do they change colors so fast? Carefully examine the tentacles and mouth of any squid you capture—how do they catch and eat their food? Think about your observations as you watch the live squid in the ocean around you. How do they propel themselves? Watch very closely—do you see behavioral interactions between any individuals, evidenced by their posture and color pattern?

♦ *Deepwater bottom fish.* What is the organ normally protruding from the mouth of fish brought up rapidly from the depths? Why does this occur, and why are the eyes bulging? What about eye size—aside from the bulging, why are they so big? Red is a dominant color theme—is there a reason for this? Are these fish capable of the swimming speeds possible for the pelagic species you have been catching by trolling? Examine the shape and size of the scales, fins, and body form—what are the differences? What do they eat? Is there any light where they live?

♦ *Sharks.* You will have a better chance of sighting or catching one of these magnificent animals drifting or anchored than while underway. Do they have bones and scales? Do they keep from sinking by using an air bladder like bony fishes? What is the purpose of the complex array of tiny pores especially visible on the underside of the snout? How does their digestive system differ from bony fishes? Are they more active by night or by day, and how is this reflected in the internal anatomy of their eyes? How long do scientists estimate that sharks have been on the planet? Do all sharks have the same kind of teeth?

COASTAL OCEANOGRAPHY AND MARINE BIOLOGY

Most cruisers spend more time at anchor than they do at sea. This creates ample opportunity for rich explorations of coastal sea life and the physical processes that shape its existence, and it gives the explorer more control over the circumstances into which she or he chooses to venture. Somewhat the opposite is true for inshore life forms; whereas the open-sea underwater environment is relatively constant over large areas in many respects (temperature,

salinity, current velocity), plants and animals along the coast are subjected to much greater, more rapidly changing extremes. These conditions mold the life forms, species diversity, and levels of biological productivity of the coastlines you visit. Fishing expeditions near shore will expose you to constantly changing surroundings that harbor an unparalleled profusion of fascinating marine life.

♦ *Tides.* Exactly what is a tide? Why do tides occur? How many tides occur each day, and how long does each tidal stage last? What is tidal range? Is the daily number of tides, tidal-stage duration, and tidal range the same everywhere in the world and each day of the year? Explain your answer. Now observe these aspects of the tide at your current location. How do fish and other animals use the tide to their advantage?

♦ *Flats fish.* What general themes apply to many of the fish you see and catch on the flats—color, speed capability, morphology, eyesight? What kind of food items do these fish search for and eat, and what special mechanisms do they possess for food procurement and processing? Take your face mask with you, lower yourself prone in the shallow water, and slowly drift along. Focus your eyes on every small creature you encounter, try to identify and mentally categorize what you are seeing—put yourself in the place of the fish. Make decisions—is this a prey item? Do you see any excavations where eagle rays or fish have been rooting? What were they eating? *Do not pick up venomous cone shells (Indo-Pacific), and be on the lookout for stonefish (Indo-Pacific), scorpionfish, and motionless, partially buried stingrays. Don't grab mantis shrimp (stomatopods).*

♦ *Juvenile sharks.* Small sharks are one of the most common sights in tropical near-shore shallows because these areas serve as nurseries. How many different species of sharks can you identify? Using light wire leaders longer than the body length of these sharks, cast a bait out in front of them, and hook and capture some on your light spinning rod. If you are old enough and have proper supervision, and the shark is 3 feet (91 cm) or less in length, play it gently into the landing net, lift it onto the deck or beach, grab it behind the head (quickly, carefully, and firmly), secure the tail with your other hand, and invert the shark to an upside-down, horizontal position—it will become immobile. Closely examine the teeth, eyes, nostrils, and snout; feel the rough skin. Is it a male or female? Tag the shark if you wish, carefully de-hook it, and then release.

♦ *Shallow inshore habitats.* How many different species of fish can you capture around the rocks, kelp, or coral in your area? Can you come up with the scientific name of the family, genus, and species for each? What areas of the world have the greatest number of inshore fish species, and what are the estimated pathways of fish colonization around the globe?

MORE UNDERSEA BIOLOGY AND PHYSIOLOGY

We got your face under water in the last section. Let's continue on the theme of intimate views and encounters possible while wading, and probable to certain depending on where you choose to go diving, with or without the help of a breathing apparatus.

♦ *Conch.* You've seen snails on land. The numerous species of conch throughout the world's subtropical and tropical seas are larger, ocean-going versions of the same fundamental animal. Locate the eyes, proboscis, and operculum. What and how do they eat? How do they move across the bottom? What are their natural predators? What do their egg masses look like—can you find any? After the eggs hatch, how long do the larvae float suspended in the water column before they settle to the seafloor and metamorphose into miniatures of the adult form? How does the shell form and grow? How long does it take for a queen conch *(Strombus gigas)* to reach the minimum legal size for consumption?

♦ *Spiny lobsters.* You can encounter these animals regardless of the tropical or warm temperate region of the world you are cruising. What are the primary species you are likely to encounter during your voyage? How do they differ from

one another in size, morphological detail, depth distribution, and activity patterns? How can you identify males and females? How do they achieve egg fertilization? How long do the hatched larvae remain at sea? How many and what morphological transitions do they experience during this time? Do they look like tiny adult lobsters, or something completely different? How far might they drift from hatching site to settling location? Does this have implications for lobster-stock management?

♦ *Diving physics.* Take a deep breath of air. What two gases form the majority of what is now in your lungs, and what is the approximate percentage of each? What happens to this pocket of gas that fuels your every movement and conscious thought, and without which you would soon perish as you descend beneath the sea surface? What atmospheric pressure in psi does your body experience at the sea surface, and as you dive to depths of 33, 66, and 99 feet (10, 20, and 30 m)? What effects does this pressure change have on that all-important pocket of gas in your lungs? How does diving affect the gas composition of your blood, and what implications does this have for your thought processes and physical safety and health? Practice free-diving and have someone time you. How long can you stay down? How deep did you go? What is the deepest known free dive by a human?

♦ *Marine mammals.* However well you did free-diving, you didn't come close to the performance of our marine cousins. Scientists have determined that dolphins can stay submerged for at least twelve minutes and achieve dive depths to 900 feet (274 m), seals up to seventy minutes and 1,800 feet (549 m), and whales to well over seventy-five minutes and more than 3,400 feet (1036 m). How are they able to accomplish these feats? If you guessed exceptional lung capacity, you were wrong. Their respiratory and vascular systems are modified for diving, although lung capacity and heart size, shape, and mass are comparable proportionally to yours. So, how do they do it? Start with anatomical modifications, and then study physiological adaptations involving oxygen capacity and blood distribution. While you're at it, how do they sleep without drowning, avoid dehydration, and how fast can they swim?

Your new intimacy with the sea around and under you will naturally spark your curiosity. Your cruising life uniquely exposes you to this most wonderful and stimulating classroom. Never stop asking yourself and others questions. Avail yourself of every opportunity to learn more, whether from periodicals, books, the Internet, your own observations, or others. Don't be shy—respectfully approach that old, weathered native fisher or diver. Don't worry if you can't speak the language—communicate the best you can, watch everything they do, meet their children. You can always learn something from others. They have a lifetime of experience for their area that you can never duplicate. Use all the knowledge you gain to abstract and generalize; this allows you to deduce new patterns based on familiar principles as you once again get underway and encounter different areas and species of plants and animals on the next phase of your voyage.

The Successful Cruiser-Fisher

The observations of any single boat crew, one tiny speck in the vast world of voyagers, are by definition anecdotal. Despite this, we ask, is a distinctly *fishy* trend developing in the worldwide cruising community? We'll forget, for the moment, the Aussie cutter that sailed into Neiafu in Tonga recently, fully rigged with outriggers and rocket-launcher rod rack loaded with offshore tackle . . . the roomy sailing catamaran with flying bridge, outriggers, and two fighting chairs doing fishing charters out of Bora Bora . . . the countless visits and inquiries instigated by *Élan*'s outriggers, afterdeck arrangement, and fishing activities . . . the widespread, eager embrace of all sorts of fishing endeavors—sometimes stunning successes—by cruisers of all ages, genders, backgrounds, and budgets . . . the existence of a sailboat division in an annual Jamaican blue-marlin fishing tournament. After all, we must strive for objectivity as we examine this hypothesis.

What deductive reasoning might support the contention? And, if it's true, what are the chances that you, as a cruiser, will be infected to at least some degree by this encroaching scourge? Pretty good, it seems. Why now and not before? Our guess would be the radical change in the average voyager's environment during the past twenty or so years.

♦ *Laborsaving devices.* Like roller furlers and GPS.
♦ *Onboard comforts.* The increase in amenities such as microwaves, TVs, and VCRs.
♦ *Better safety gear.* For example, 406 EPIRBs, satellite communications, series drogues, and improved sea anchors.
♦ *Increased affluence.* More people than ever before can afford to buy these items before departure.
♦ *Increasing popularity of cruising.* The rapidly growing number of people attracted to the voyaging lifestyle—sail or power, short term or long—means more company at sea and in various destinations.

All of this has one fundamental result: it removes a great deal of pressure and time constraints from many modern cruisers. Voyaging still takes competence, sound seamanship, energy, and constant vigilance, but we have more help now. We have the option to seek lonelier, more strenuous conditions, yet we travel more comfortably, experience less uncertainty and mental strain, and may, therefore, arrive better rested. We can explore more remote areas in greater safety. We have both additional time and a more suitable environment for extracurricular pursuits, few of which are more natural to a seafarer than fishing.

Can the day be far off when cruisers gathered at potlucks will have conversations like this:

"Hey, Charlie, how'd you do on those bait showers you were chasin' this afternoon?"

"Aw, OK, released a couple of 50-pounders 'cause the fridge is full, but Sherry and my daughter Sarah love the action and are really into tagging 'em. How'd you do the other morning, Donna?"

"'Bout the same . . . Ted was doing the laundry and cooking, I'd finished changing the engine oil, and we were just in his way, so I took the kids out for a little fun. Sure is nice to be around a place with good action."

"Yeah, sure is. Here, let me get this round. Well, when are you guys off and how'd your generator overhaul turn out?"

Or when we hear ham and single-sideband radio chats similar to the following:

" . . . we were all dived out and ready to get back offshore . . . just tacked off the rhumb line into the center of the high looking for a zone of no wind."

"Did you find it?"

"You bet, slick calm."

"You lucky dog."

"Yep, we're lovin' it. Got a 70-pound broadbill swordfish last night, now the awning's up and we're just lighting the grill."

"Gimme that position again?"

Who knows? Unless you actively resist, conditions like these could infect you, not to mention other boats in your anchorage or marina. Most of all, enjoy your fishing skills and the experiences they provide. Cruising boats may not have many of the amenities and assets of dedicated fishing boats, but the voyaging lifestyle often takes us far away from the harder-fished areas near civilization. Along with a little knowledge and the proper gear, this enables us to enjoy a quality of fishing many enthusiasts and professionals find difficult to imagine. Help others and increase your own pleasure by passing on the knowledge. *Give a person a fish, feed them for the day . . . teach someone to fish, and feed them for a lifetime.*

12

A Guide to Edible Fish and Invertebrates

Obviously, one could fill thousands of pages with this subject. We highlight representative bony fishes, sharks and rays, and invertebrates that cruisers could encounter, with comments on habitat, capture, and consumption.

Bony Fishes (Phylum Chordata, Class Osteichthyes)

Most fish sought by fishers fall into the bony-fish category, a class of Subphylum Vertebrata containing more living species than any other. Bony fishes inhabit nearly every aquatic habitat, from cold, clear, high altitude streams to low-lying swamps; from sun-drenched, wind and waved-tossed sea surface waters to the freezing cold, pitch-dark stillness of the greatest ocean depths.

MAHI MAHI (FAMILY CORYPHAENIDAE)

Widely known also as dolphin or dorado, these fish occur in schools of tens to hundreds as juveniles, and adopt a more solitary lifestyle after reaching a mass of 16 pounds (7.3 kg) or so. From this size they normally travel in small harems consisting of multiple females (cows) and one or two males (bulls). These fish attain sexual maturity in the first year of life. Bulls develop a distinctive high, blunt forehead and reach a larger maximum size (commonly more than 35 lbs./16 kg) than cows (more than 35 lbs./16 kg is rare).

Mahi mahi spend a lot of time feeding near the sea surface and associate strongly with floating debris and pelagic algae formations (e.g., sargassum weed). The predominant species is *Coryphaena hippurus*, although a smaller, slightly more rotund species might occasionally show up in the catch (*Coryphaena equisetis*, or pompano dolphin). They generally strike artificial and natural baits readily, and flash from their normal blue color to yellow, green, brown, and silver in various stages of excitement or stress. The meat is firm, white, highly acclaimed table fare, and bears almost no risk of ciguatera (a few claims of ciguatoxic mahi mahi exist in older literature, dating from 1817 to 1963). See chapters 3 and 4 for more specific details about the biology and capture of mahi mahi.

WAHOO, TUNAS, AND MACKERELS (FAMILY SCOMBRIDAE)

The meat of this large, diverse, fast-swimming family of fishes ranges from red to oily white, and includes some of the highest-priced fish flesh in the world when fresh. Most species may forage from surface to significant depths, with average vertical range below that of mahi mahi. Flashy, deep presentations and pink, red, purple, and black squid imitations work well, as do live and dead natural baits. The entire group has excellent eyesight; therefore, strike rates tend to be extremely sensitive to leader size, hook dimensions, and atmospheric conditions. If fishing is slow, despite the known presence of these fishes, first use lighter leader material, then try more subtle hook models and arrangements. See chapters 3, 4, and 5 for more details.

Scombrids are also famous for ephemeral feeding moods, biting aggressively for relatively brief periods, and then shutting down as abruptly as though someone switched off an electrical circuit. Feeding activity of no other fish group is more strongly tied to early morning and late afternoon, overcast conditions, specific tides and current conditions, wind direction and velocity, sea state, and barometric pressure.

Wahoo (Acanthocybium solanderi)

Long, cylindrical fish with elongated jaws tapering to a point, full of razor-sharp, same-sized small teeth, wahoo are instantly recognizable by a strong pattern of bands that appear light blue against the dark navy to purple dorsal surface when they're excited. They habitually rocket up from the depths to take lures and natural baits at high speed, although they'll bask lazily near the surface at times (see chapter 7) and calmly ingest drifted dead baits. Recall from chapter 3 that maximum size is about 183 pounds (83 kg), with average common catch size ranging from 15 to 65 pounds (7 to 27 kg). The meat is light and firm but sensitive to slight over-cooking, becoming dry and less tasty. See chapters 1 and 3 for more details about wahoo, and photo page 5.

Tunas and Bonitos

Members of this ubiquitous group feature a more truncated, fusiform shape than wahoo, come in all sizes, from species that might not reach 20 pounds (9 kg) to giant bluefin tuna as large as 1,500 pounds (680 kg). Tunas tend to have firm, high-quality pink to red meat. They strike all kinds of artificial and natural baits depending on the situation, and probably represent the most common type of fish available from near-shore to oceanic environments encountered by cruising vessels—from the equator to temperate latitudes depending on time of year. Nevertheless, they are often not the easiest to catch due to their sensitivity to noise and visual cues. If cruisers had to single out one group of fishes for special attention and effort, this would be it. Paying close attention to the many details regarding successful capture of these species in chapters 3, 4, and 5 will greatly alter your fish catch rates while cruising.

Mackerels

Mackerels, like wahoo, are long and cylindrical and, like tuna, feature a large number of species worldwide from the tropics to cool temperate seas, with the biggest (to more than 100 lbs./45 kg) found in tropical and subtropical latitudes (see photo page 121). Nearly all have sharp teeth and feed in a slashing manner similar to wahoo, dashing in and often cutting prey neatly into pieces, then returning to take the severed, slowly sinking remainder after the initial attack. The meat is usually an oily off-white, excellent when cooked fresh or used for ceviche (see recipe page 360).

Mackerels are distinct from tunas and wahoo in that they are coastal pelagics, generally not found far offshore in the open sea. Migrations follow shelf contours and features, and they associate strongly with specific depths, temperature regimes, and habitats such as steep drop-offs, shallow seamounts, wrecks, reef points, and other underwater promontories. They tend to feed heavily on silvery baitfish species and are therefore highly susceptible to flashy, erratic spoons, hard-wiggling swimming plugs, and live baitfish on delicate leaders and light, small hooks. They also take a variety of jigs, flies, plastic bait bodies, and other lure types, as well as drifted or trolled dead baits. Some species feed heavily on shrimp and other invertebrates flushed out over the reef on the outgoing tide, making a Captain Hank Brown's Hookup jig baited with a live or dead shrimp an excellent choice under these conditions.

MARLINS, SAILFISH, AND SPEARFISHES (FAMILY ISTIOPHORIDAE)

Almost everyone who fishes has a little Zane Grey, Ernest Hemingway, or Marsha Bierman spirit buried somewhere in his or her soul. Regardless of how humble the gear or budget, few would fail to be thrilled by an intimate billfish encounter of some kind. The tendency of these fish to gyrate, leap, and dash wildly across the sea surface at blinding speed creates an intense visual phenomenon rivaled by few others on the planet. The historic problem for the rank and file is that, because these fish are top-level predators, there aren't that many of them, which translates into many expensive hours of trolling in substantial seagoing boats for each strike. Most people can't justify the cost. But, once more, here's another area where cruising permits us to live like millionaires on a substantially lower budget. Our boats must be seaworthy anyway, we are already traversing the oceans for many consecutive hours at greatly reduced fuel consumption relative to most fishing vessels; now all we have to do is drag something appropriate on suitable gear.

Chapter 3 discusses this subject in detail, as well as information on sizes and ranges, for marlin, sailfish, and spearfish (see photos pages 6, 17, 80, and 306–7). All have oily, pink to gray meat of excellent eating quality, but most cruisers release them after photographs for several reasons. First, the size of many individuals overwhelms most cruising-boat cold-storage facilities. Second, worldwide fishing pressure from commercial operations exerts significant mortality rates on these species due to their association with tunas and other targets, and their susceptibility to longline gear and even purse seines intended for other fishes. Third, these fish generally represent a greater value to local tourist economies alive than as relatively low-priced dead flesh, whether or not the particular country you are visiting has yet fully developed billfishing tourism. Fourth, they're highly migratory, so wherever you catch one, killing it potentially hurts tourism for more than one country that desperately needs the cash.

BROADBILL SWORDFISH (FAMILY XIPHIIDAE)

Broadbill swordfish steaks have captured the palates of developed-country restaurant diners around the world. The meat is oily but normally almost white, very firm and tender, flaking nicely off the bone in moist chunks from the pressure of one's fork. Would we be hypocritical to promote retaining swordfish while encouraging release of other billfish? Certainly, there's nothing wrong with releasing these fish, particularly if you can't handle the size of a particular individual. If you do choose to keep one that your cold-storage facilities can handle, we'd argue that you aren't doing the same potential economic and ecological damage as when consistently killing other billfish.

First, although recent special innovations now permit limited daytime recreational fisheries, the widespread use of sport gear generally occurs at

night, well offshore. This practice experiences spurts of popularity among hard-core anglers, but hardly constitutes a generalized mainstay of national tourist economies. Furthermore, directed commercial fishing for swordfish is capital-intensive and only feasible for high-dollar markets, which can or do probably contribute more revenue than swordfish sportfishing for any given country (placing a lower economic premium on live versus dead individuals).

Last, broadbill swordfish are more widely distributed than any other billfish, which enhances resiliency to biological overfishing, a probability further reduced by infeasible high capture expense that forces cessation of fishing before extreme species-threatening scarcity (as opposed to the case of bluefin tuna). In other words, despite the hammering dealt swordfish populations by longliners, economic extinction could precede biological extinction by a comfortable margin for this species. Also, swordfish are somewhat less susceptible than other billfish to commercial fishing practices such as purse seining and, therefore, experience lower incidental catch rates. Thus, while tag and release of swordfish and all other species not needed for food is highly desirable, cruisers might choose to retain the occasional appropriate-sized broadbill for consumption without an overly guilty conscience.

Swordfishing is particularly well suited to cruising vessels adrift offshore. See chapter 4 for more details on their biology and capture (see photo page 115).

SNAKE MACKERELS (FAMILIES GEMPLYIDAE AND TRICHIURIDAE) (SUPERFAMILY TRICHIUROIDEA)

This large group of mesopelagic fish occurs from 160 feet (50 m) to over 4,875 feet (1,500 m), from the equator to cold temperate latitudes, rising to shallower depths at night—some species even leap aboard ships after being attracted to deck lighting. They are voracious predators and readily take natural baits drifting on longlines or other gear set at an appropriate depth range, often intended for swordfish. Otherwise, midwater commercial trawls account for much of the world harvest.

Perhaps the most common possibility for most cruisers is the oilfish *(Ruvettus pretiosus)*, which may attain 100 pounds (45 kg) and frequently takes swordfish baits. Like other members of this group, the flesh is very oily and soft, and it spoils quickly; however, it finds favor in some cultures. You might also catch or spot the bizarre, elongated snake mackerel *(Gempylus serpens)* in the glow of deck lights offshore, or ribbon-like cutlassfish *(Trichiurus lepturus)*. Cutlassfish sometimes enter shallow bays and passes, and readily strike small lures cast on light tackle in the vicinity of lights at night. Some captains rig these silvery, undulating fish to troll for blue marlin. Another possibility, particularly for coastal light-tackle anglers around New Zealand, is the snake mackerel *Thysrites atun*, locally called "barracouta."

POMFRETS (FAMILY BRAMIDAE)

Pomfrets are medium-sized (not more than 2 ft./60 cm) trevally or jack-like fish that inhabit the surface to midwater layers (to 1,500 ft./460 m) of tropical to temperate seas worldwide. The species *Brama brama* often strikes trolled tuna lures in the cooler parts of their range. The meat is good eating, although fairly soft.

BUTTERFISHES AND RUDDERFISHES (FAMILIES CENTROLOPHIDAE AND STROMATEIDAE)

This group of fishes inhabits coastal and oceanic habitats, typically midwater from 195 feet to more than 2,275 feet (60 to 700 m), and most are unfamiliar to hook-and-line fishers. General appearance, like the pomfrets, is similar to the more familiar trevallys or jacks. Many are small, reaching a size of about 12 inches (30 cm)—a few may attain 24 inches (60 cm)—with rudderfish *(Centrolophus niger)* and bluenose warehou *(Hyperoglyphe antarctica)* growing to

Blue warehou *(Seriolella brama*, Family Centrolophidae).

lengths of 4½ feet (140 cm). Larger species take baited hooks fished deep, and representatives occur worldwide from the tropics to cold temperate seas.

MOONFISH (OPAH) (FAMILY LAMPRIDAE)

Moonfish *(Lampris guttatus)* are a large (to 6 ft./180 cm, 225 lbs./102 kg), disc-shaped, offshore pelagic species that will take midwater baited hooks. They range from the equator to temperate latitudes and are a highly prized food fish in Europe, among Polynesians and French in Tahiti, and the Maori people of New Zealand. The flesh is firm, white, and delicately flavored. Some commercial longliners target this species in French Polynesia. Cruisers adrift offshore can easily target these unusual fish with deep-set lines.

TRIPLETAILS (FAMILY LOBOTIDAE)

These delicious sea-bass- or grouper-like fishes are most often seen drifting on their side near debris offshore, although they will also associate with crab trap floats and other similar objects in shallow inshore waters. They occur worldwide in tropical and subtropical latitudes, growing to 42 inches (107 cm). Tripletails readily take flies, small lures, and baited hooks cast near them, and sometimes boaters can drive closely by and scoop-net them. The meat is firm, white, and of high quality.

JACKS AND TREVALLYS (FAMILY CARANGIDAE)

Carangids consist of about 140 species worldwide, occurring from the tropics to warm temperate seas, ranging in size from 6 inches (15 cm) to 5 feet (152 cm) and 176 pounds (80 kg), and feeding on a variety of other fish and invertebrates. They tend to lack brilliant coloration, are silver on sides and belly, have deeply forked tails, and feature a strong-swimming, sleek morphology. Individual species habitats range from shallow estuaries, bays, beaches, and inshore reefs, to the outer reef slope, seamounts, wrecks and, in some cases, open offshore waters in the vicinity of debris. Rainbow runners *(Elegatis bipinnulata)*, for instance, commonly form groups around floating objects offshore and near outer-reef drop-offs, including anchored cruising vessels. Smaller planktivorous species swarm into the glow of night lights; larger carangids forage around the perimeter for unwary prey (see photos page 90).

Cruisers encounter members of this family wherever they go in warmer regions of the globe. Carangids readily strike a variety of spoons, plugs, flies, and jigs, either trolled, cast, or deep-jigged, as well as live and dead natural baits trolled, drifted, or fished deep on weighted rigs. They are renowned for great strength and durability after hook-up, attracting the attention of light-tackle anglers throughout their range. The flesh tends to be somewhat oily, ranges from white to gray, and is in general highly regarded table fare. Larger jacks and trevallys are frequently prime candidates for ciguatera. Chapters 1, 3, 4, and 5 contain information on capturing various species.

ROOSTERFISH (FAMILY NEMATISTIIDAE)

Roosterfish *(Nemastistius pectoralis)* look like a carangid, except for lengthy, plume-like dorsal rays that they raise when excited chasing bait or hooked on a fishing line. These are coastal fish inhabiting surf areas and sandy bottom only in the far eastern

Gregg "No Mercy" Homola with roosterfish *(Nemastistius pectoralis)* (Baja, Mexico).

Pacific, from the Gulf of California to Peru. Anglers and commercial fishers place great value on roosterfish—they reach a size of 114 pounds (52 kg), fight hard, and (unlike carangids) may leap and greyhound. They also have excellent tasting firm light meat. Their primary prey is small fishes and, although they take cast or trolled artificials and dead natural baits, by far the most effective method is drifting, anchoring, or slow trolling with live bait.

BLUEFISHES (FAMILY POMATOMIDAE)

The best known member of this family is the bluefish *(Pomatomus saltatrix)*, a migratory coastal fish that bears a general resemblance to some of the more elongated carangids and has prominent, very sharp, triangular teeth capable of inflicting a nasty wound or severing a finger. They reach at least 32 pounds (14 kg), usually swim in voracious feeding schools, and occur widely near landmasses in the subtropical and temperate Atlantic and Indian oceans, though usually not in the tropics. They strike artificial and natural baits aggressively. The meat is an oily gray, good fresh but subject to rapid spoilage.

Scombrops *(Scombrops oculatus)* are a lesser-known pomatomid with large, fang-like teeth and smaller maximum size than bluefish (to 2 ft./60 cm), caught by fishers deep-dropping in depths of 660 to 2,000 feet (200 to 610 m) in tropical regions around the world.

KAHAWAI (FAMILY ARRIPIDAE)

Kahawai *(Arripis trutta* and two other species) are ecologically and morphologically similar to bluefish, except for the sharp teeth, and occur throughout western and southern Australia, Tasmania, and New Zealand. Like bluefish, they swim in schools, may leap and thrash at the surface when hooked, reach 33 pounds (15 kg), have oily gray meat, and readily strike a variety of lures and natural baits. Juveniles sometimes occur in and around bays and estuaries.

COBIA (FAMILY RACHYCENTRIDAE)

Cobia *(Rachycentron canadum)* inhabit warmer waters nearly worldwide, migrating along coastlines, but are also found occasionally in the open ocean. They associate with stationary structures like floating navigational aids, various buoys, and oil

Kahawai *(Arripis trutta,* Family Arripidae).

rigs, and often swim around eating discarded by-catch from shrimp trawlers. Adults may be solitary or swim in schools, very often in association with large stingrays in coastal waters. Common sizes range from 10 to 50 pounds (4.5 to 23 kg) to individuals 6 feet (1.8 m) long and weighing 150 pounds (68 kg). Unpracticed eyes may mistake these large, brownish, sluggish-looking swimmers for sharks. Natural baits, particularly live fish, work better than lures for cobia, although they strike big jigs, flies, and plugs. The best live baits are relatively inactive small bottom species like the white grunt *(Haemulon plumieri).*

Cobia fishing in clearer coastal waters involves first searching for a large stingray from a high observation point on your boat, usually in spring time, and then sight-casting weighted live baits in front of the associated cobia school. Some fishers release a small cobia with a float attached on a line tied through the flesh to help them keep track of the school. Always keep your bow into the sun, staying between the stingray and the glare, to avoid losing sight of it. The action around a school of larger cobia is wild as multiple hook-ups surge strongly in all directions on heavy spinning gear. The meat is firm, white, and of the very highest quality.

DRUMS, CROAKERS, SEA TROUTS, AND CORVINA (FAMILY SCIAENIDAE)

This large, varied fish group tends to forage near the bottom in turbid waters near continents, often in estuarine systems, muddy bays, shallow banks, and the surf, with few species occurring in clear reef waters or near oceanic islands. Representatives occur from the equator to temperate latitudes, some

migrating seasonally. Many are panfish, others grow to moderate size, and some may exceed 100 pounds (45 kg). They feed on fish and invertebrates, sometimes in midwater and near the surface. Many will take lures aggressively—use white jigs that stand out in muddy water; tip them with a piece of shrimp or fish or use loud, splashy surface plugs in the shallows to get their attention. Gold spoons also work. More famous members include corvina *(Cynoscion xanthulus)* (far eastern Pacific); sea trout *(Cynoscion nebulosus),* weakfish *(Cynoscion regalis),* and redfish *(Sciaenops ocellatus)* (all three eastern United States); white sea bass *(Atractoscion nobilis)* (from Alaska to Chile in the eastern Pacific); and innumerable species of croakers found worldwide. Meat is mild, white, and generally high quality, although the flesh of some species tends to be soft.

PORGIES AND SEA BREAMS (FAMILY SPARIDAE)

Sparids constitute another extremely widespread and diverse family (about 120 species) of generally

Betty Ann and Palmer Bannerot with sea trout *(Cynoscion nebulosus,* Family Sciaenidae, Florida Keys).

small- to medium-sized bottom dwellers that inhabit a huge range of depths and bottom types around the world from the equator to temperate seas. Habitats include everything from sandy shallows to deep outcrops and outer reef slopes, but most species tend to associate with rocks, coral, and similar structure (see fish b page 107). The meat is firm, white, and delicious. Invertebrates figure prominently in the diet, and the best fishing method is usually live or dead natural bait fished near the bottom.

Africa has the largest number of species, but the abundance of smaller numbers of species causes sparids to play a prominent role in recreational and commercial fishing worldwide. Red and pink porgies *(Pagrus)* occur from near shore to deep regions of continental shelves; porgies and sea breams of numerous genera from pan-sized to 20 pounds (9 kg) are prized by anglers of every continent.

TEMPERATE BASSES (FAMILY PERCICHTHYIDAE)

Temperate basses occur in many of the same environments worldwide as sparids, but many grow larger and tend to occupy a higher trophic level in the food web, with fish comprising a relatively larger portion of the diet. Members of this group prefer cool temperate water and usually are found deep in subtropical portions of their ranges. The family includes highly sought Japanese sea bass (*Lateolabrax japonicus*, to 20 lbs./9 kg), striped bass (*Morone saxatilis*, to 125 lbs./57 kg), European bass (*Morone labrax*, to over 30 lbs./14 kg), and wreckfish (the Atlantic *Polyprion americanus*, to 106 lbs./49 kg, and the southern Australia/New Zealand *Polyprion oxygeneios*, to 220 lbs./100 kg), as well as a number of smaller cold-water basses caught

Wreckfish or hapuku (*Polyprion oxygeneios*, Family Percichthyidae).

bottom fishing off rocky temperate-zone coasts. All feature delicious firm, white meat and will strike lures and natural baits.

GROUPERS AND SEA BASSES (FAMILY SERRANIDAE)

Family Serranidae contains many tropical counterparts to temperate basses, although it also includes small, colorful, plankton-eating basslets that swarm over tropical reefs and 1,000-pound (455 kg) giants that lurk in caves and wrecks. Generally, fishing interests begin with small temperate species such as sea basses of the genus *Centropristis*, which range into the rocky shallows of cooler seas and normally don't exceed 8 pounds (3.6 kg), and a far larger number of reef-associated ecological equivalents worldwide from the subtropics to the equator (primarily smaller species of genera *Epinephelus* and *Cephalopholis*). These species tend to feed heavily on crustaceans but also take small fishes and cephalopods. Larger *Epinephelus*, such as the tropical Atlantic/Caribbean red grouper *(E. morio)* and Nassau grouper *(E. striatus)*, and the Indo-Pacific marbled grouper *(E. polyphekadion)* and blotchy grouper *(E. fuscoguttatus)*, attain weights of 20 to 50 pounds (13.6 to 22.7 kg). Fish play a larger role in the diet of these species, increasing the risk of ciguatera in some reef locations.

Other groupers, particularly genera *Mycteroperca*, *Plectropomus*, and *Variola*, consist of medium to larger species that feed more heavily on fish and therefore have a higher overall incidence of ciguatera (see photos pages 18 and 80). The largest individuals of the family all belong to the genus *Epinephelus*: jewfish (*E. itajara*, tropical western Atlantic, Caribbean, and eastern Pacific—to 1,000 lbs./455 kg), Warsaw grouper (*E. nigritus*, tropical western Atlantic—to 580 lbs./263 kg), misty grouper (*E. mystacinus*, Caribbean and western tropical Atlantic—to more than 200 lbs./91 kg), potato grouper (*E. tukula*, Indo-Pacific—to 245 lbs./111 kg), and giant grouper (*E. lanceolatus*, Indo-Pacific—to at least 880 lbs./400 kg). High risk of ciguatera and relative rarity of these spectacular giants should be ample reason to avoid killing them under any circumstances.

Most cruisers will come into frequent contact with groupers, very common residents of warm-water rocky shallows and reefs worldwide, prone to spearfishing and hook-and-line techniques of all kinds. They readily attack swimming plugs, jigs, spoons, plastic bait bodies, and live and dead natural baits fished near the bottom. They can rocket up a considerable distance (at least 40 ft./12 m in clear water) from the seafloor to take offerings. The meat is firm, white, and tasty, occasionally tempting seafarers to take consumption risks. Check *very carefully* with locals for highly specific information on species and sizes prone to ciguatera, and realize that misidentification can result in poisoning, and that trends vary over extremely small distances and between species with very similar appearances.

Nassau grouper *(Epinephelus striatus,* Family Serranidae), tropical Atlantic/Caribbean (Exuma Islands, Bahamas).

SNAPPERS (FAMILY LUTJANIDAE)

Snappers inhabit many of the same habitats as groupers, provide good targets for both spearfishing and hook and line, have delicious, firm, white meat, and thus comprise another large group (just over a hundred species) many cruisers encounter around the world, mostly in the subtropics and tropics. These fish primarily associate with reefs and other bottom structure, although they may range into shallow estuaries and channels, and deep on outer reef slopes. Many school near shelter by day and feed more actively at night. Invertebrates dominate the diet of a high number of snappers, though some larger species are piscivores known for ciguatoxic tendencies (e.g., dog snapper, *Lutjanus jocu,* and cubera snapper, *L. cyanopterus* in the tropical western Atlantic and Caribbean, and red snapper, *L. bohar,* among others, in the Indo-Pacific).

Many smaller species are pan- or medium-sized, with a maximum size of 125 pounds (57 kg) or so for the family. Some snappers feed primarily in midwater or can be induced from the bottom with chum and taken on drifted dead baits. They also take trolled and cast lures, particularly bucktail jigs,

Mangrove snappers *(Lutjanus griseus),* tropical Atlantic/Caribbean, and neighbors: **(a)** elkhorn coral *(Acropora palmata)*; **(b)** small mahogany snapper *(Lutjanus mahogani)*; **(c)** bluestriped grunt *(Haemulon sciurus)*; **(d)** slimy sea plumes *(Pseudopterogorgia americana),* Class Anthozoa, Subclass Octocoral-lia—octocorals or soft corals; **(e)** French grunt *(Haemulon flavolineatum)*; **(f)** sergeant major *(Abudefduf saxatilis,* near Key Largo, Florida).

plastic bait bodies, and swimming plugs (see photos pages 17 and 19, top). Live baits, both small fish and invertebrates like crabs and shrimp, are deadly.

GRUNTS AND SWEETLIPS (FAMILY HAEMULIDAE)

Haemulids are similar in shape and general appearance and to the smaller size range of snappers. Some Indo-Pacific species approach 33 inches (83 cm), whereas western Atlantic grunts do not exceed 24 inches (61 cm). They occur worldwide, mostly in tropical and subtropical near-shore waters, often grouping up by day near reefs and other structures, then dispersing at night over adjacent grass beds, sand, and mud at night to feed, primarily on invertebrates. Lack of canine grasping teeth and presence of pharyngeal crushing teeth (which they use to make the croaking sounds that give them their name) reflect this diet. Grunts and sweetlips tend to be less wary than snappers, and therefore among the easiest targets for spearfishers. They readily take hooks baited with cut pieces of fish or invertebrates

fished still near the bottom. The meat is firm and white, of generally good quality, although it sometimes has an iodine-like taint. Haemulids are less likely to be ciguatoxic than snappers, groupers, and other higher-level predators.

Harlequin sweetlips *(Plectorhincus chaetodonoides)*, west Pacific.

(a) Bluestriped grunts *(Haemulon sciurus)*; **(b)** Caesar grunts *(Haemulon carbonarium)*; **(c)** French angelfish *(Pomacanthus paru)*; **(d)** schoolmaster snappers *(Lutjanus apodus)*; **(e)** mangrove snappers *(Lutjanus griseus)*; **(f)** Bermuda chub *(Kyphosis sectatrix)*; **(g)** elkhorn coral *(Acropora palmata)*. Near Key Largo, Florida.

SQUIRRELFISHES AND SOLDIERFISHES (FAMILY HOLOCENTRIDAE)

Squirrelfishes and soldierfishes are common world-wide in the tropics around rocky and reef shallows. Their large eyes, reddish color, bony heads, prominent scales, small size (14 in./36 cm or less), and nocturnal habits are distinctive. They hide under overhangs and in or near the openings of caves and crevices by day, emerging to feed mostly on plankton and small benthic invertebrates at night. Holocentrids take small bottom-fished natural baits day or night, and Indo-Pacific islanders target them specifically by jigging tiny bait quills on cane poles in and near coral areas at night. The most popular preparation of the firm white meat is roasting the fish whole over an open fire.

EMPEROR FISHES AND LARGE-EYE BREAMS (FAMILY LETHRINIDAE)

Cruisers newly arriving to the tropical Pacific islands will soon catch or spot fish that look and act like, what, snappers? No, wait, maybe they're grunts or porgies. You might very well consult your fish identi-

Soldierfish *(Myripristis)*, worldwide tropics.

Dusky squirrelfish *(Sargocentron vexillarius)*, tropical Atlantic/Caribbean, photographed at Carrie Bow Cay, Belize, at night; **(a)** common sea fan *(Gorgonia ventalina)*; **(b)** long spine sea fan *(Muricea pinnata)*, Class Anthozoa, Subclass Octocorallia—soft corals.

fication book and discover that you're seeing members of the ecologically similar, largely Indo-Pacific Family Lethrinidae. These are coastal bottom fishes who feed largely on invertebrates, including mollusks and even sea urchins, although a few have long snouts and conical teeth enabling more fish in the diet. Most feed more actively at night than day, some species resting on reefs and foraging in adjacent areas, and others doing the reverse. They tend to be quite wary of divers, and you'll seldom get any but long, going-away spear shots. Size seldom exceeds 27 inches (69 cm), with most species averaging considerably less.

Hook and line is a different story. Lethrinids take baited hooks fished still near the bottom, live baits, and various lures, including bucktail jigs and plastic bait bodies, as well as small swimming plugs retrieved or trolled among coral heads with the dinghy. The meat is white, firm, and tasty, and less likely to be ciguatoxic than snappers or groupers.

THREADFIN, WHIPTAIL, AND CORAL BREAMS, AND SPINECHEEKS (FAMILY NEMIPTERIDAE)

Nemipterids are another fairly large group of small (usually less than 12 in./30 cm) snapper-like fishes, inhabiting open sand and mud bottoms along the coast and coral reef environments throughout the Indo-West Pacific, feeding by day mostly on invertebrates and some small fishes. Some species are important to both commercial and artisanal fisheries and are taken by a wide variety of methods, most importantly handline and bottom trawl. Cruisers should fish relatively small natural baits still near the bottom, although some rise in response to chum and take free-lined drift baits. Small artificial lures imitating worms, shrimp, and other invertebrate prey, deep-jigged or fished near the bottom, also work but not as well as natural bait.

PEARL PERCHES (FAMILY GLAUCOSOMATIDAE)

Pearl perches consist of only four large-eyed, snapper-like species that forage near the bottom around deeper reefs and rocky substrate, outcrops, and pinnacles in the Indo-West Pacific from warmer temperate Australia to the coasts of China and Japan. Maximum species sizes range from about 5½ pounds

(2.5 kg) to 58 pounds (26 kg). The best hook-and-line method is stationary baits fished deep (90 ft./27 m to over 390 ft./120 m), either crabs, lobsters, squid, or small whole split fish, with size adjusted to target species. The meat is highly prized, firm and white.

BOARFISHES (FAMILY PENTACEROTIDAE)

Boarfishes have prominent bony heads and protrusile mouths adapted for probing and sucking in invertebrate fare. They occur usually in pairs or small groups around deep reefs, rocky slopes, and seamounts in the Indo-Pacific, ranging up into depths frequented by divers mostly in temperate seas. Giant boarfish (*Paristiopterus labiosus*, to 33 in./85 cm) in particular tend to feed out on open mud and sand bottom similar to the tropical Atlantic hogfish (*Lachnolaimus maximus*, Family Labridae). The best fishing method: pieces of mollusk meat, crustacean parts, or whole smaller crustaceans fished on relatively small hooks, resting stationary on or close to the bottom. The meat is white and excellent.

Southern boarfish *(Pseudopentaceros richardsoni)*, temperate Southern Hemisphere.

KNIFEJAWS (FAMILY OPLEGNATHIDAE)

Knifejaws, like boarfishes, inhabit rock and coral Indo-Pacific areas primarily in warm temperate seas. They also feed almost exclusively on invertebrates, but occupy a different ecological niche, utilizing strong jaws and fused, beak-like teeth to break and eat barnacles and mollusks. Spotted knifejaws *(Oplegnathus punctatus)* and the African cape knifejaw *(O. conwayi)* attain the same size as the giant boarfish, 33 to 36 inches (85 to 91 cm), are susceptible to similar hook-and-line fishing methods and bait, and also have white, high-quality meat.

Dories (Family Zeidae)

Dories are laterally compressed—the bodies are thin in cross section, but exhibit a deep, disc-like profile. They live in midwater, from shore to deep continental-shelf areas worldwide in temperate seas, and feed largely on fish and, to some extent, invertebrates. Dories tend to float and hover along slowly until close enough to surprise food organisms, using a highly protrusive mouth to rapidly suck in prey swimming in the water column. These fish tend not to exceed 24 inches (61 cm) in length, and are often most abundant deep, from 650 to 2,600 feet (200 to 800 m). Nevertheless, several species range into cooler temperate shoreline shallows and are prized targets of hook-and-line anglers fishing mostly natural weighted or drifting baits well below the surface. Dories also take slow-retrieved lures and deep jigs. Meat is firm, white, and highly esteemed.

John dory *(Zeus faber)*, widespread in subtropical/temperate seas around the world.

Morwongs (Family Cheilodactylidae)

Morwongs are relatively slow, snapper-shaped invertebrate feeders filling an Indo-Pacific temperate and subtropical ecological role occupied by grunts and sweetlips in warmer waters. These fish may live near rocky areas and reefs, hiding in holes and crevices by night and emerging to forage by day, often on nearby open sand or soft sediment substrate, or survive in schools primarily out on open sandy seafloors to 650 feet (200 m) on temperate continental shelves. They represent fairly easy targets for spearfishers and take stationary bottom baits. Maximum sizes range from 12 to 24 inches (30 to 60 cm), and meat is firm, white, and tasty.

Porae *(Nemadactylus douglasii*, Family Cheilodactylidae*)*, subtropical/temperate eastern Australia and New Zealand.

Trumpeters (Family Latridae)

Trumpeters are similar to morwongs in appearance, mouth morphology, feeding habits, preferred bottom types, fishing-gear susceptibility, and meat quality, although they have a more restricted, colder temperate, Indo-Pacific range. Some species reach larger sizes, from 35 to 40 inches (90 to 100 cm), and are highly sought sport and commercial fishing targets in southern Australia and New Zealand, as far south as Stewart Island.

Trumpeter *(Latris lineata)*, subtropical/temperate Indo-Pacific (Stewart Island, New Zealand).

Roughys (Family Trachichthyidae)

Roughys (particularly the orange roughy, *Hoplostethus atlanticus*) burst onto the worldwide seafood market fairly recently, finding widespread favor due to their delicate firm white flesh. Representatives occur in most temperate seas around the world, and support commercial bottom-trawl fisheries in depths from 325 to over 1,600 feet (100 to 500 m) depth in the North Atlantic, and off of South Africa, Australia, and New Zealand. Roughys have enlarged bony heads, big eyes, laterally compressed bodies, and enlarged gill rakers to prevent the escape of their largely planktonic organism diet. They are a relatively small, deepwater species, seldom exceeding 16 inches (40 cm) in length. Cruising vessels adrift over temperate continental-shelf areas may wish to drop weighted vertical rigs with small, offset circle hooks and natural bait below 325 feet (100 m) to take a stab at a meal of fresh roughys, particularly if the depth sounder shows dense midwater readings.

Orange roughy *(Hoplostethus atlanticus)*, temperate Southern Hemisphere.

Cods, Pollocks, Haddocks, and Hakes (Family Gadidae), Other Gadiformes, and Cod-Like Odds and Ends

If the roughys aren't biting, you might drop your baited line down to the bottom, depth permitting, for a shot at gadids or some of the at least eight other families belonging to the Order Gadiformes. These fishes have long been the focus of intense commercial fishing effort—often in cold, rough seas at the cost of many lives—and the subject of international disputes over territorial fishing rights on continental shelves and offshore banks in temperate and polar seas. Family Gadidae consists of about fifty species,

with average sizes far below the maximum of 211 pounds (95 kg). Many inhabit continental-shelf waters around the North Atlantic and ranging along arctic coastlines, but also include some important Pacific representatives. Other gadiformes are abundant in the Southern Hemisphere, most often in temperate and Antarctic waters, but may also range into the tropics in very deep waters. Family Nototheniidae, for example, consists of a hundred or so species of Antarctic cods and icefishes that manufacture an antifreeze-like substance to circulate in blood and tissues to survive very low water temperatures.

Members of this large group of fishes can provide a mainstay for the increasing number of vessels cruising in temperate and polar latitudes in any hemisphere, particularly because they tend to move near shore during summer months after a retreat to greater depths in the harsh cold of winter. They even venture into areas of estuaries and freshwater runoff to forage over muddy bottom. The meat is firm and white, and ciguatera is never a problem. For best results, fish stationary natural baits on bottom rigs or deep-jig with heavy metal lures to keep warm.

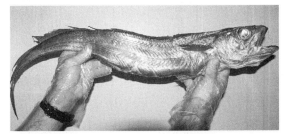

Hake *(Macruronus novaezelandi*, Family Merluccidae), temperate South Pacific.

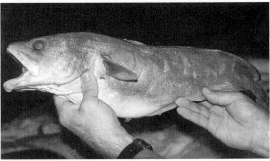

Red "cod" *(Pseudophycis bachus*, Family Moridae), temperate Indo-Pacific.

Commercial fisherman and Stewart Island legend John Leask with blue "cod" (*Parapercis colias*, Family Pinguipedidae)—this fish is endemic to New Zealand.

Sea perch *(Helicolenus percoides)*, a typical scorpaenid found in cool waters of southern Australia and New Zealand.

SCORPIONFISHES (FAMILY SCORPAENIDAE)

You might well catch a scorpionfish while fishing for cod or other gadiformes in temperate waters, or see one while diving or bottom-fishing around a tropical reef, because this large family of seafloor dwellers is widespread throughout the world, with the exception of polar waters. They are relatively small (seldom over 24 in./60 cm), well camouflaged, and some members possess certain of the more venomous spines known for fishes (see chapter 10), warranting great caution. The sea perches (e.g., *Helicolenus papillosus*) and redfishes *(Sebastes)* include sought-after cooler temperate latitude sport and commercial fishing targets and quality table fare. They sometimes occur on open sandy bottom well away from the rocky lairs preferred by many family members. Stationary, natural, live, or dead bottom baits work best.

SEAROBINS AND GURNARDS (FAMILY TRIGLIDAE)

Searobins and gurnards have the enlarged bony heads and bulging eyes typical of scorpionfishes, and also reach similar maximum sizes (about 18 in./46 cm); they respond to the same fishing method, but often have brightly colored, wing-like pectoral fins. Representatives are widespread in temperate to tropical regions worldwide. Fishers of many areas consider them to be a mere curiosity or nuisance, although in some cases, species are targeted and considered esteemed table fare. The red gurnard *(Chelidonichthys kumu)*, for example, is a popular food fish in Japan, New Zealand, southern Australia, and South Africa.

Red gurnard (*Chelidonichthys kumu*), cool seas of South Africa, Australia, and New Zealand, very similar to North Pacific counterpart.

FLOUNDERS, HALIBUTS, AND SOLES (FAMILIES BOTHIDAE, PLEURONECTIDAE, AND SOLEIDAE)

All of these flatfishes are grouped into Order Pleuronectiformes. The pelagic larvae exhibit conventional morphology for a while, but then one eye migrates across the head to join the other; this side of the fish develops darkened dorsal morphology and faces the sea surface. The underside is typically white and the body is, as the name implies, very horizontally flattened. Adults of some species fit in the palm of your hand, while the Pacific halibut reaches at least 459 pounds (208 kg) and is the focus of intensive commercial and recreational fishing. Flatfishes occur around the globe in a variety of cold temperate to tropical habitats, from estuarine shallows where fishers seek them day and night with gigs to at least 3,200 feet (970 m) in icy cold seas. They take bottom-fished artificials, although live and dead bottom baits are best. Fishers seek most any species large enough to eat because the meat is delicate and white, and features prominently on restaurant menus, especially in temperate latitudes.

Lemon sole (*Pelotretis flavilatus*, Family Pleuronectidae), New Zealand, typical of flatfish species found worldwide.

TILEFISHES (FAMILY MALACANTHIDAE)

Tilefishes are a small group (less than thirty species) of bottom dwellers that occur worldwide in tropical, subtropical, and, in at least one case, temperate latitudes. The most important commercial and recreational fishing and food species occur relatively deep, from 90 to 900 feet (27 to 275 m), often on relatively open sand or rubble bottom with occasional ledges and rocky outcrops. Two Atlantic species typify popular fishing targets: blueline tilefish (*Caulolatilus microps*, to 30 in./90 cm) and golden tilefish (*Lopholatilus chamaeleonticeps*, to 42 in./107 cm and 50 lbs./23 kg). Commercial exploitation is usually by bottom longline or deep-dropping, and even recreational anglers resort to electric reels and wire line for best results. Chunks of fish or squid, fished on a weighted vertical array

of three to six offset circle hooks from a drifting or power-drifting vessel, work fine (see chapter 4 for information about deep-dropping, and chapter 8 for tips on reading fish finders to locate these and other species). The meat is top quality, firm and white, and tastes somewhat like lobster.

Smaller tilefish (particularly *Malacanthus*) construct burrows or live in the vicinity of shallow tropical and subtropical reefs throughout the Atlantic and Indo-Pacific regions. These species take small baits fished near the bottom; fall prey to accurate, fairly long-range spear shots; and usually represent a low ciguatera risk, although they're slender and meat yield is low.

WRASSES (FAMILY LABRIDAE)

Most of the large number of wrasse species are colorful, small members of tropical reef fish communities, but some inhabit cooler temperate climates, and several sizable species are highly desirable food fish sought by anglers and spearfishers. Prominent among these are tautogs (*Tautoga onitis*, to 24 lbs./11 kg), coastal inhabitants of temperate/subtropical Atlantic rocky shores, jetties, docks, and other structures; hogfish (*Lachnolaimus maximus*, to 20 lbs./9 kg, tropical western Atlantic; see photos pages 10 and 107), and giant Indo-Pacific humphead wrasses (*Cheilinus undulatus*, to at least 420 lbs./191 kg). Despite an exclusively invertebrate natural diet, large wrasses can be ciguatoxic, although they generally represent less risk than most piscivores.

Hogfish are common in reef shallows, particularly scattered coral heads interspersed with sand and seagrass beds in channels and reef shelf expanses inshore of the outer reef break (10 to 60 ft./3 to 18 m depth). They range out onto the open sand beyond shallow outer reef slopes from 60 to 120 feet (18 to 36 m) and deeper. They tend to be easy spearfishing targets unless they inhabit more heavily fished areas. The best hook-and-line bait is a lobster leg, highly attractive to hogfish and difficult to steal quickly by the swarms of haemulids and other fishes normally present.

Humphead wrasses, on the other hand, tend to be very wary of divers and represent more difficult spearing targets, which doesn't seem to dampen the enthusiasm of local divers in pursuing them. Strong handlines or rod and reels baited with crabs, lobsters, or mollusk meat fished near bottom or free-lined in light current are effective and, like all wrasses, the white, firm meat is considered a delicacy. Thus, large individuals are an increasingly rare sight on Indo-Pacific reefs. Cruisers should avoid killing individuals of this hard-pressed species except in survival situations.

Scarlet wrasse *(Pseudolabrus miles)*, a subtropical/temperate Pacific species that ranges south to the subantarctic convergence in New Zealand. (Stewart Island, New Zealand)

PARROTFISHES (FAMILY SCARIDAE)

Parrotfishes consist of many species of brilliantly colored tropical reef fish and occur worldwide in relatively shallow waters, although a number of more drab-color forms also exist. Most are small to medium size, with the largest being the Indo-Pacific bumphead parrotfish (*Bolbometopon muricatum*, to 51 in./130 cm) and the tropical Atlantic blue parrotfish (*Scarus coeruleus*, to 48 in./122 cm). They swim and look like many of the closely related wrasses, rowing along with the pectorals instead of wagging their tails. Most parrotfish use beak-like, fused teeth to scrape the thin film of algae from hard corals, although some pick at leafy macroalgae or seagrasses. Parrotfish, like other algae eaters, can be ciguatoxic.

Nevertheless, indigenous peoples of tropical islands worldwide consider parrotfish to be quality table fare, especially consumed fresh. Most are captured by spearing (go for a head shot; they tear off easily) or in gill nets, although they can occasionally be induced to take small baited hooks free-lined or fished near the bottom. The flesh tends to be soft and light-colored, sometimes with a slight greenish or gray cast, and the smell and appearance of the gravelly green gut contents dissuades some consumers. The meat, however, cooks up white and relatively firm and can sometimes pass for grouper fillet (one Bahamian friend jokingly calls it "blue grouper").

SURGEONFISHES (FAMILY ACANTHURIDAE)

Surgeonfishes derive their name from the sharp, switchblade-like apparatus near the tail, capable of inflicting a painful wound (see chapter 10). Members of this large family of fishes (about a hundred species) are one of the most common sights worldwide in tropical inshore shallows, swimming in schools over and near reefs, rubble zones, and adjacent grassy areas. Some are brilliantly colored, others are quite drab. They are generally small (6 to 12 in./15 to 30 cm, to 18 in./46 cm), disk-shaped, with little mouths and generally flattened teeth adapted to their almost exclusively herbivorous feeding habits. Fishers catch them on occasion with small baited hooks; more commonly, they end up in gill nets, and

Blue parrotfish *(Scarus coeruleus)*, tropical Atlantic/Caribbean. Most parrotfish secrete a mucous cocoon in which to sleep—this one has just been disturbed from sleep during a night dive (near Miami, Florida).

they sometimes fall prey to spears. They constitute an important food resource for local inhabitants of many tropical islands. The flesh is firm and off-white when fresh, becoming white when cooked. Whole fried surgeonfish are common fast-food items in the Caribbean and elsewhere. Nevertheless, the flesh of some species in specific locations can be highly ciguatoxic, and seafarers should exercise great discretion regarding consumption of any surgeonfish.

Ocean surgeonfish *(Acanthurus bahianus)*, tropical Atlantic/Caribbean (Bonaire, Netherlands, Antilles).

Make a positive species identification, seek several local opinions, and avoid eating them in the absence of information.

SEA CHUBS AND DRUMMERS (FAMILY KYPHOSIDAE)

Sea chubs and drummers consist of a relatively small number of species that occur worldwide in the tropics, with some subtropical species, often in groups around reefs or other bottom structure. Maximum sizes range from around 12 to 30 inches (30 to 75 cm). The body is laterally compressed and has an oval profile, with a small head and mouth. Flattened teeth serve well for their largely herbivorous feeding habits: mostly picking at algae attached to the substrate or other structures like docks and boat bottoms. The flesh tends to be soft and more distinctly grayish-green than parrotfish, making them somewhat less popular but nevertheless consumed in some areas. The meat can have a residual algae taste. Small, long-shank hooks baited with pasta or breadballs, drifted on light line with no weight, are usually best for capture.

Bermuda chubs *(Kyphosus sectatrix)*, tropical Atlantic/Caribbean. Elkhorn coral, *Acropora palmata*, is in the foreground (Little Whale Cay, Berry Islands, Bahamas).

SPADEFISHES AND BATFISHES (FAMILY EPHIPPIDAE)

Spadefishes and batfishes comprise a small family of highly compressed, angelfish-like species that don't exceed 36 inches (91 cm) total length. This family appears worldwide in warm coastal seas. They pick at algae like chubs and also consume invertebrates and fish, and readily take small baited hooks drifted in midwater or fished near the bottom. Large schools of the adult Atlantic spadefish *(Chaetodipterus faber)* may hang in midwater around wrecks, oil rigs, and deep outer reef walls. Conversely, adults of the similar-looking Indo-Pacific pinnate spadefish *(Platax pinnatus)* appear to prefer solitary habits under overhanging reef structure. Eating quality is good.

SICKLEFISHES (FAMILY DREPANIDAE)

Drab-colored sicklefishes are very similar in morphology and ecology to spadefishes. *Drepane longimanus* and *D. punctatus* forage for invertebrates in silty inshore shallows near rock piles and reefs in the Indo-West Pacific. They normally do not exceed 20 inches (50 cm) and may be taken on small baited hooks fished near the bottom.

STONEBREAMS (FAMILY SCORPIDAE)

Grouped by some ichthyologists under Family Kyphosidae, stonebreams are small to medium (16 in./40 cm or less) midwater planktivores that occur in large schools near shallow rocky structure, right up to the shoreline. They are common in warm temperate waters of New Zealand and southern Australia. Fishers take blue maomao *(Scorpis violaceus)* by free-lining or bottom-fishing small baited hooks, and laud the quality of the firm, light flesh. These are easy targets for cruisers, and good for children because the shimmering blue mass of the school provides a spectacular view from the surface and the action can be fast. These fish are not known to be ciguatoxic.

Blue maomao *(Scorpis violaceus,* Family Scorpidae*)*, warm temperate south Indo-Pacific (Poor Knights Islands, New Zealand).

Atlantic spadefish *(Chaetodipterus faber)*, equator to subtropical Atlantic/Caribbean (Puerto Rico, Greater Antilles).

TRIGGERFISHES (FAMILY BALISTIDAE)

Triggerfishes have a first dorsal spine that locks in the upright position, making extraction from holes and crevices difficult or impossible. They are widespread around the world from tropical to warm temperate waters, many inhabiting rocky areas and reefs from the shoreline to less than 145 feet (45 m) depth, with some species ranging deeper or living in midwater coastal or surface pelagic environments. Triggerfish species normally don't exceed 36 inches (91 cm), have long tapered heads with eyes set well back from the small terminal mouth, which features strong teeth and jaws well suited to picking at sea urchins and breaking apart shells and exoskeletons of various other invertebrates. Some islanders once used their thick, heavily armored skin as sandpaper. Cruisers commonly spot them while snorkeling, diving, and wading on shallow reef, sand, and grass flats.

Triggerfish readily take small baited hooks and present reasonable spearfishing targets, particularly because good penetration nearly anywhere in the body causes the spear to hold well in the firm flesh and tough skin. Be wary of bites from the strong jaws, particularly as you hold a speared individual close to your body (a large queen trigger, *Balistes vetula*, repaid me for spearing it with near-religious-level pain when it clamped onto my left nipple during ascent). The meat is firm, white, and tasty, although even small triggerfish species have been the cause of ciguatera poisoning (e.g., the diminutive Indo-Pacific pinktail trigger, *Melichthys vidua*).

Queen triggerfish *(Balistes vetula)*, equator to subtropical Atlantic/Caribbean (Andros Island, Bahamas).

FILEFISHES AND LEATHERJACKETS (FAMILY MONOCANTHIDAE)

Like triggerfishes, filefishes and leatherjackets have a laterally compressed body with a slightly elongated oval profile and a long tapered head, and consist of many small species, the largest possibly reaching 36 inches (91 cm). They feed by picking at soft invertebrate prey (e.g., various jellyfish, hydrozoans, soft corals, and sponges), yet they can be ciguatoxic. Most inhabit rocky and reef shallows worldwide from the equator to warm temperate seas, with some pelagic members associating with floating seaweed and debris offshore. Some are masters at changing colors to mimic different backgrounds. Filefishes have very small mouths and take tiny baits free-lined on little hooks or lightly weighted bottom baits.

Scrawled filefish *(Aluterus scriptus)*, worldwide temperate to tropical seas (near Key Largo, Florida).

GOATFISHES (FAMILY MULLIDAE)

Goatfishes are fairly slender and elongated, small- to medium-sized (not exceeding 20 in./50 cm), and very common sights around shallow reefs and rocky areas worldwide in clear seas from the equator to the subtropics (see photo page 107). Bright colors characterize many of the fifty or so known species, and all have distinct barbels under the chin used to probe the sediment for small fish and invertebrate prey. Goatfish are prized food items in many island areas, commonly taken on small baited hooks fished near the bottom. They also hit small artificials fished near the bottom—and we once even caught a large two-barred goatfish *(Parupeneus bifasciatus)* trolling a small swimming plug from the dinghy—but natural baits are best. Island spearfishers also target larger species. They consider the relatively soft white meat a delicacy.

Yellowsaddle goatfish *(Parupeneus cyclostomus)*, Indo-Pacific.

WHITINGS (FAMILY SILLAGINIDAE)

Whitings are often small to moderately sized (12 to 18 in./30 to 45 cm, occasionally larger) cylindrical bottom fish distributed over sand and silt continental-shelf shallows to deeper waters throughout the tropical and warm temperate Indo-West Pacific. They feed primarily on worms, crustaceans, and small fish, and can bury themselves in the sediment, which prompts seine fishers to wade along in between two nets to coax them back up into the water column. In addition to beach seines and cast net—and bottom trawls in deeper water—recreational and subsistence fishers harvest considerable amounts with small baits (often marine polychaete worms or soldier crabs) on the bottom in surf and estuarine areas. Cruisers visiting Australia, Southeast Asia, Japan, India, or eastern Africa will almost certainly encounter these fishes. The meat has extremely low oil content, making it very white, tender, and tasty.

MARINE CATFISHES (ORDER SILURIFORMES)

This large group of fishes consists of numerous families, many possessing venomous spines (see chapter 10), with few occupying the same food and sport fishing status as a bigger fraction of their freshwater counterparts, despite their worldwide distribution from the equator to temperate seas. They readily ingest natural bottom baits, usually in turbid coastal waters. One example of a good-eating species is the gafftopsail catfish (*Bagre marinus*, to 24 in./60 cm and 6 lbs./2.7 kg) of eastern North and South America.

MULLETS (FAMILY MUGILIDAE)

Mullets are ubiquitous around the world in coastal waters, throughout estuarine systems including far inland into fresh waters, in shallow muddy bays, off beaches and in the surf, and in clear tropical reef and associated environments. Many species make distinct mass migrations. Most don't exceed 20 inches (52 cm), but a few reach 36 inches (91 cm). They are cylindrical, silvery-sided, and have small mouths specialized for feeding on algae and bottom detritus, rooting en masse and creating highly visible mud clouds that disturb prey organisms for predatory fishes. Mullet themselves are preferred prey for many larger fish as well as for people. Fishers capture them primarily in nets (usually cast nets and gill nets), although they take small hooks baited with breadballs or tiny pieces of invertebrate or fish flesh. They also make great live bait for catching larger fish. The flesh tends to be an oily gray to off-white, best consumed fresh or smoked.

Striped or "gray" mullet *(Mugil cephalus)*, worldwide in warm seas.

MILKFISHES (FAMILY CHANIDAE)

Milkfishes are a silvery Indo-Pacific ecological analog to mullet that feed on benthic detritus, algae, and small associated invertebrates in more turbid inshore waters and, to a lesser degree, in midwater to surface tide and current lines in the vicinity of atoll passes and inside lagoons. *Chanos chanos* grows to 71 inches (180 cm) and is the dominant food fish in much of Southeast Asia. Milkfish are the subject of widespread aquaculture. Fishers catch wild individuals primarily in monofilament gill nets. They take small hooks baited with partially cooked pasta elbows and breadballs; well-known fly-fishing guide Rick Ruhoff has taken them on a drifted "algae fly" at Christmas Island (Republic of Kiribati). The meat is fatty and oily, best grilled fresh (but natives prepare it in numerous other ways).

LADYFISHES AND TARPONS (FAMILY ELOPIDAE)

Closely related to milkfish, ladyfish and tarpon are voracious generalized carnivores that feed on a variety of invertebrates and fish, and occur primarily in the subtropical and tropical Atlantic. Ladyfish *(Elops saurus)* do not exceed 36 inches (91 cm), occur in schools in shallow bays and mangrove environments commonly from North Carolina to Brazil, and readily take a variety of small artificials cast and retrieved on light spinning or fly tackle. The tarpon *Megalops atlanticus* attains a maximum size of 8 feet (2.4 m) and 300 pounds (136 kg), takes various lures and live and dead invertebrate or fish baits, and is revered by light-tackle sport anglers for great leaps, showy runs, and head shakes during battle. A smaller tarpon species *(Megalops*

cyprinoides, to 35 in./90 cm) occurs in the Indo-Pacific, primarily inshore in estuarine areas. None are highly esteemed food fish, and tropical Atlantic tarpon can be toxic (see chapter 10).

BONEFISHES (FAMILY ALBULIDAE)

Bonefishes belong to Order Elopiformes along with milkfishes, tarpons, and ladyfishes, and share their forked tail, silvery appearance, and muscular, cylindrical body form (see photo page 9). At least several similar species (genus *Albula*) are widely distributed around the world in the tropics and subtropics. They often swim in schools over inshore flats and shallows feeding on invertebrates and small fishes. Their mouths are located under the snout, which they use to root in the sediment for buried prey. Maximum size is 19 pounds (18.6 kg); average size is well under 10 pounds (4.5 kg). The meat is solid, white, and heavily infused with fine, branching bones. Eating is a chore unless the fish is specially cleaned in a manner that allows the flesh to bake off the skeleton

COURTESY DAVID PAUL

David Paul preparing to revive and release a tarpon caught on 20 lb. (9 kg) spinning tackle *(Megalops atlanticus)* in the Florida Keys using a live pilchard *(Harengula jaguana)* for bait.

(this practice is common in the Bahamian out islands). Like most billfish, however, bonefish are more valuable to local economies alive than dead, because they are extremely popular targets of a growing number of well-heeled saltwater fly fishers willing to pay top dollar for guides and accommodations. Thus, many small island and other nations blessed with appropriate habitats for stalking these fish in shallow, clear waters have been quick to discourage gill-netting and other activities deleterious to bonefish populations (e.g., Bahamas, Republic of Kiribati, Belize, Cayman Islands, Turks and Caicos, Venezuela, United States). See chapter 5 for tips on catching bonefish, and consider releasing them to help the local economy of your host country.

Snook *(Centropomus undecimalis)*, southeastern United States to Brazil, similar to congenerics in Pacific Central America and Africa, and other genera in the Indo-Pacific.

SNOOKS AND BARRAMUNDI (FAMILY CENTROPOMIDAE)

Snooks and barramundi play a role for fishers and seafood diners fulfilled by striped bass *(Morone saxatilis)* and European bass *(Morone labrax)* in the more temperate waters of North America and Europe. Centropomids occur in warm, estuary-associated coastal waters, including mangrove rivers, well into freshwater (barramundi, *Lates calcarifer*, mature here before moving downstream into brackish and salt water), and to nearby mudflats, bays, and beaches. The distribution of barramundi is Indo-Pacific, from subtropical Australia to southern China and the Philippines, to India and west to the Persian Gulf. Various species of snook *(Centropomus)* occur in the tropical eastern Pacific and both sides of the Atlantic; related genera occur in African lakes and elsewhere in the Indo-Pacific.

Centropomids are active predators with sharp gill plates, jutting lower jaws, and big mouths. They feed voraciously on invertebrates and fish, and some species can exceed 100 pounds (45 kg). Fishers actively seek them for food and sport, and they take all manner of cast and trolled artificial lures, as well as natural baits. Meat quality is solid, white, and excellent. Remove the skin before cooking because it can produce a noxious, soap-like substance.

BARRACUDAS (FAMILY SPHYRAENIDAE)

Barracudas consist of twenty species distributed worldwide in tropical to warm temperate waters.

They sport long jaws with pronounced canine and formidable shearing teeth. The smaller species may not exceed 18 inches (46 cm); the circumtropical great barracuda *(Sphyraena barracuda)* might reach 6½ feet (198 cm) and 106 pounds (48 kg) (see photo pages 107 and 306). Barracudas feed aggressively on other fish; they chop large specimens in half and then feed on the severed pieces. Records indicate attacks on humans, usually associated with spearfishing and swimming in murky water, particularly with bright jewelry, watches, and other adornments. Don't wear bright objects and treat aggressive displays observed while diving with caution (see chapter 6); otherwise, there's little cause for concern unless you are spearfishing.

These predators react strongly to flashing silver spoons adorned with fish strips, swimming and surface plugs, and long lures made of brightly colored surgical tubing, as well as just about any other trolling feather, bucktail, or jig or plastic bait body. They also strike glittery streamers and flies, and live or dead natural bait. Some feed primarily during daylight hours; others rest in large groups by day and then feed at night. The Indo-Pacific blackfin barracuda *(Sphyraena genie*, to 58 in./147 cm), for example, is a common catch trolling during darkness hours in the tropical Pacific islands.

The group has a wide habitat preference, from near-shore flats and shallows to estuaries, bays, channels, passes, patch reefs, outer reef slopes, seamounts, wrecks, and fairly deep open water over island and continental shelves. Larger barracuda can be highly ciguatoxic in numerous locations, causing fatal cases in the West Indies and Indo-Pacific. Part of the problem is that the delicate white, somewhat soft meat is good eating, tempting people to push size/location safety margins. Be sure to check these out carefully before you retain one for dinner.

Great barracuda *(Sphyraena barracuda)*, worldwide in the tropics (Florida Keys).

NEEDLEFISHES (FAMILY BELONIDAE)

Needlefishes occur around the globe from the equator to warm temperate zones. They are silvery, extremely long and cylindrical, and have long, thin, same-sized jaws studded with sharp teeth for grasping small fish. Most are fairly small; however, houndfish *(Tylosurus crocodilis)* reach 59 inches (150 cm) and 10 pounds (4.5 kg); pounce aggressively on small flashy swimming plugs, other artificial baits, and natural baits; and provide good light-tackle entertainment with fast runs and greyhounding leaps. The flesh is grayish white and of reasonable quality, although few consume it. It makes great strip baits for fishing lures.

Houndfish and other needlefish are favored prey items of some predators, including barracuda and sailfish, which swim over the reef crest and chase them, causing huge showers of airborne, panicked individuals splashing across the sea surface (see chapter 5 for how to fish these bait showers). They tend not to be hardy live bait species, swimming weakly and dying fairly fast when slow-trolled. Larger species are a nuisance to clear from monofilament cast nets and may tear the mesh entangled in their teeth, so try to avoid throwing a net on a section of a ballyhoo school with needlefish swimming over it.

Needlefish are also known for becoming confused in spotlights or other vessel lighting, jumping out of the sea in panic, and sometimes like missiles, directly aboard. Duck!

HALFBEAKS (BALLYHOO) (FAMILY HEMIRHAMPHIDAE)

Halfbeaks or ballyhoo are silvery, small (6 to 16 in./15 to 41 cm), and cylindrical; they occur worldwide in tropical and subtropical areas; and they have a long, stick-like, toothless lower beak. They are among the most famous baitfish species worldwide

Redfin needlefish *(Strongylura notata)*, tropical Atlantic/Caribbean (Exuma Islands, Bahamas).

with fishers for use live or dead, and with many predator fish species fond of flying fish or ballyhoo. Capture them with hair hooks or cast nets (see chapters 4 and 7), maintain them in live wells (chapter 8), and rig them for trolling (chapter 3) or casting (chapters 4 and 5).

Ballyhoo are common inshore in tropical reef areas, feeding near the surface on plankton. Cruisers frequently notice them hanging around in back of their anchored vessels, swimming back and forth in the mild turbulence of the tidal flow caused by the hull of the boat. The meat is grayish and oily, possibly slightly darker than that of flying fish. Islanders in some regions utilize them for food.

An even wider variety of predators than those seeking houndfish enthusiastically chase ballyhoo, including larger mackerels, snappers, groupers, barracuda, big jacks and trevallys, wahoo, yellowfin tuna, sailfish, and marlin. Cruisers anchored in sight of or traveling near reef drop-offs in the tropics often witness spectacular, undulating showers of silvery ballyhoo skipping airborne with the aid of their elongated lower caudal lobes, desperately fleeing their pursuers, usually near dawn and dusk (see chapter 5).

Ballyhoo *(Hyporhamphis ihi)* endemic to New Zealand but typical of family members found worldwide.

FLYING FISHES (FAMILY EXOCOETIDAE)

Few seafarers who have traversed subtropical and tropical latitudes anywhere in the world are unfamiliar with flying fish, generally small silvery species with bluish backs that glide out of the sea surface in long, arcing flights on enlarged, transparent pectoral fins. We previously discussed island commercial fisheries (see chapters 4 and 7) and rigging and using these for bait (see chapters 3, 4, and 5) or for food

(see chapters 4 and 9). Some species reach 18 inches (46 cm), although most seldom exceed 12 inches (30 cm). Flying-fish meat is grayish and oily, but delectable when fresh. Southeastern Caribbean processors quickly transform whole flying fish into boneless butterfly fillets, perfect for use in fast-food sandwiches or mixed as delicate chunks with rice and seasonings. Barbados is the capitol for flying-fish dishes—most eating establishments in Bridgetown offer delicious renditions. Go to the public market and request a flying-fish-processing lesson from one of the friendly gals there . . . they can do one in seconds, yielding one flat, boneless unit. Otherwise, refer to chapter 9 and scale them whole, then fillet each side but don't completely sever the skin of the belly. Debone and trim out the rib-cage sections, scrape off any entrails, and you've got it: a complete butterfly fillet of flying fish.

FUSILIERS (FAMILY CAESIONIDAE)

Fusiliers are small (less than 12 in./30 cm), cylindrical fishes that typically hover in large daytime schools in midwater, feeding on plankton near steep reef drop-offs and outer slopes only in the Indo-Pacific. Most are brightly colored. They support no industrialized commercial fisheries but are important to scattered artisanal trawl-and-net fisheries, most prominently in the Philippines. Fish traps set on the adjacent reef take advantage of their night time habit of seeking shelter there. Natives of some areas routinely capture them on small, light hook-and-line arrangements. Eating quality is good, and they command a respectable price in Sri Lanka, Thailand, and elsewhere. Try hair hooks, light monofilament, and tiny baits, or drop bait quills deep and then jig them in twitches to the surface.

SILVERSIDES (FAMILY ATHERINIDAE)

Silversides swim in glittering schools composed of a few to many hundreds of tiny (6 in./15 cm or less) individuals in the coastal shallows of tropical to subtropical coastlines worldwide, often in clear water coral reef habitats. Fishers catch them for bait and food with fine mesh seine and cast nets, particularly during periods of seasonal abundance in specific locations. Sold as frozen blocks labeled "glass minnows," they make excellent chum for midwater snappers and other reef fish and may be sprinkled into other chumming materials to "sweeten" the mix. Fishers toss a handful of thawed silversides out behind the boat, then gently cast a small, light hook threaded through the heads of a few individuals, and free-line it with the chum in the current flow. This method is deadly when anchored on bottom structure over a broad range of latitudes and different situations.

Islanders sometimes fry globs of silversides whole, similar to the European practice of preparing "whitebait" caught in temperate latitudes (see recipe page 376).

WHITEBAIT (FAMILY GALAXIIDAE)

The term whitebait applies to young clupeids in Europe. In cooler waters of New Zealand, Australia, and Chile, whitebait refers to huge masses of tiny elongated fishes (at least five species of *Galaxais*, averaging 1½ to 2 in./4.5 to 5.5 cm) caught in fine-mesh dip, push, seine, and other nets as they enter estuaries in springtime. The fish are delicate and soft, and require careful handling to avoid spoilage, relegating them mostly to local markets. The flavor is delicate, and even squeamish seafood eaters find it acceptable if they can forget they're eating whole fish.

ANCHOVIES (FAMILY ENGRAULIDAE)

Almost everyone is familiar with those salty, strong-tasting, dark little fish parts few people order on their pizza, members of a vast group of small schooling planktivores found worldwide from the equator to cool temperate seas, near coastlines and up into estuaries, and with some open-ocean species: the anchovies. Species identification is difficult, but if the fish you hold in your hand is small (6 in./15 cm or less), fairly elongated with scales that fall off easily, brilliant silver along the sides, and an underslung lower jaw (tip is behind the snout), it's probably an anchovy. They support large-scale commercial net fisheries, usually in regions with cheap labor, and are sold fresh for con-

Silversides (Family Atherinidae), worldwide from the equator to warm temperate seas (Florida Keys).

Anchovies (Family Engraulidae), worldwide from the equator to cool temperate seas (Bahamas).

sumption or as bait, canned, or turned into fish paste and other products. Several populations have experienced catastrophic collapses from combinations involving heavy fishing mortality (Peru and California) and climate fluctuations. Pole-and-line tuna fisheries use live anchovies for bait. Locals also use and prepare them similarly to silversides and whitebait. Southeastern U.S. "glass minnows" are, in fact, often small species of anchovy.

PILCHARDS, SARDINES, AND OTHER HERRING-LIKE FISHES (FAMILY CLUPEIDAE)

Clupeids belong to the same order as anchovies (Clupeiformes) and include a large number of species grouped by common names like sprat, shad, menhaden, herring, sardines, and pilchards. Most attain a maximum size well under 30 inches (76 cm). Like anchovies, their distribution is worldwide from the equator to cold temperate seas, they often occur in immense migratory schools, and they may ascend rivers and spend time in fresh water. The group has a long relationship with man and continues to support large-scale commercial net fisheries and even sport fisheries in some areas. They are entirely coastal and usually inhabit near-shore or reasonably

shallow water. The main difference between a clupeid and an anchovy is the terminal rather than underslung mouth. Large numbers of species also have a deeper, more laterally compressed body profile and heavier scales. Chapters 4 and 7 contain information on how best to capture these for bait and food, with notes on potential toxicity in chapter 10. They make excellent live and dead bait. The meat exhibits varying degrees of oiliness, is usually grayish in color, and is typically consumed fresh or smoked. Some especially oily species like the menhadens are processed into fish meal, chum, bait, and oil products, and seldom eaten by people.

SALMONS AND TROUTS (FAMILY SALMONIDAE)

Salmonids primarily consist of freshwater fishes that inhabit cold, clear, highly oxygenated water of extremely high quality; however, given the opportunity, they will exit rivers and spend considerable time at sea before returning to the river or stream of their origin to spawn. They occur throughout most of the Northern and Southern hemispheres, and have been successfully farmed and introduced to nonnative areas like New Zealand and Australia. The group includes salmon, trout, chars, and whitefishes.

The largest reach 100 pounds (45 kg), with much smaller averages for most species.

Even cruisers who dream mostly of tropical beaches and swaying palm trees should consider packing a couple of simple trout and salmon lures in their fishing kits. Why? Because some of the places you might visit to avoid hurricane season, not to mention many of the spectacular temperate cruising destinations, harbor salmonids.

Two basic lures work extremely well: for salmon, an elongated, diamond-shaped spoon called the Buzz-Bomb; for trout, small lures called spinners by Mepps and Panther Martin. Work the Buzz-Bomb in a deep jigging motion after you cast it out and let it sink below salmon visible near the surface, or down to the bottom. Sweep the rod upward in large arcs, then let the lure flutter downward (the lure should drop about 2 ft./61 cm in the water column). This technique is called *mooching*, and fishers also employ it using dead natural bait. Most strikes occur as the lure or bait is sinking, so be ready. Mepps and Panther Martins feature a little silver, gold, or painted round metal plate that rotates in a circle in front of a lightly dressed body. Cast or troll these near likely lairs and retrieve at a steady, moderate speed. These work with great success in a variety of situations and take little talent to use. You may have to replace treble with single hooks, and be sure never to venture into "fly-fishing only" areas with your spinning gear. Also, bear in mind that strict minimum sizes, bag limits, restricted areas, and closed seasons characterize most salmonid fisheries due to their high attraction.

Salmonid meat quality is usually excellent, except in specialized circumstances, such as atrophied fish involved in spawning rituals and trout whose natural diets taint the flesh with undesirable flavor. Brown trout *(Salmo trutta)* caught in sluggish water bodies with sediment bottoms, for instance, may acquire a "muddy" taste, as can rainbow trout *(Oncorhynchus mykiss)* that feed heavily on snails in thick lake vegetation. Both are popular

fresh and smoked, and a large amount of commercially caught salmon ends up in cans.

If you spend some time camping or cruising in a good trout area, you may soon observe your quarry feeding on various aquatic life that you will have difficulty duplicating with spinning tackle. This is yet one more excuse to consider fly-fishing (see appendix 3).

CATADROMOUS EELS (FAMILY ANGUILLIDAE)

In chapters 6 and 7 we discussed aspects of the biology and capture of anguillid eels in various parts of the world, and their habit of entering rivers as juveniles, spending a lifetime in fresh water, and then descending to migrate over immense sea distances for mysterious spawning rituals; we also discussed aspects of preferred preparation. These eels occur in all tropical and temperate areas of the world except the eastern Pacific. Remember from chapter 10 never to consume them raw, and carefully wash blood or fluids from your hands because of possible ichthyohemotoxic serum or blood, which is neutralized by cooking.

MORAY EELS (FAMILY MURAENIDAE)

Cruisers will very likely come into contact with moray eels if they venture below subtropic latitudes anywhere in the world and go bottom fishing with natural bait or diving. Morays may be brightly col-

Catadromous eels *(Anguilla).*

ored or drab, and most of the many species are well under 4 feet (122 cm), although some representatives attain 8 feet (244 cm). The majority hide in holes, crevices, and dens during the day, emerging at night to forage primarily for fish. They readily take natural bottom baits, and the smell of fish blood or sounds of struggle from a hooked or speared fish may arouse them from daytime rest. Morays can become agitated over such activities, and most certainly when brought to the surface after being hooked. They can deliver a debilitating bite with their strong jaws full of sharp teeth, and alternately ball up and uncurl with great strength. Hold them overboard and don't allow an eel to flip its body up and over an arm, which can provide enough leverage for it to move in for a bite. Dehook if you can; otherwise, cut the leader a safe distance from the mouth, apologize profusely, and drop it back into the water.

You should consider never having anything to do with retaining a moray for food under normal circumstances. They can have ichthyohemotoxic raw blood and serum, for starters, and they are notorious for concentrating ciguatoxin in their tissues, causing serious poisoning cases worldwide. That being said, if you have a chemical test kit or test mammal, and if you are for whatever reason desperate for protein, you could safely test an eel for toxin and then eat the firm white meat without concern if it passes (see chapter 10 for more information about ciguatera testing).

Sharks and Rays (Phylum Chordata, Class Chondrichthys)

Chondrichthyans represent a much smaller, evolutionarily older group than osteichthyans or bony fishes, with about 425 species of skates and rays, 340 sharks, and 30 in an odd-ball group called *chimaerids*. Their solutions to making a living in the ocean are quite different—cartilaginous rather than bony skeletons, completely different forms of scales and dentition, urea retention instead of active transport mechanisms to control salt and water balance, well developed, high-acuity electrosensory organs, penis-like claspers to effect internal fertilization, and an anatomically distinct approach to food digestion.

Snowflake moray eel *(Echidna nebulosa)* and sea urchins (Class Echinoidea), Indo-Pacific (reef flat, South Minerva Reef, Tonga).

The distribution of sharks and rays is pervasive, and they bear a significant relationship to cruisers: they are a potential source of food, natural wonder, and danger. Species size ranges from diminutive to 26-foot (8 m) great white sharks, 22-foot (7 m) manta rays, and 60-foot (18 m) whale sharks weighing thousands of pounds/kilograms. This chapter focuses on representative examples of those suitable for eating.

SHARKS (ORDERS LAMNIFORMES AND SQUALIFORMES)

Sharks generally provide a source of quality protein and some specialty items for specific cultures (e.g., shark-fin soup in Asia, jaws for display, teeth for jewelry and weapons). Chapter 10 discussed the potential danger of ingesting the meat of medium to large tropical and other sharks, and of consuming the liver or other viscera. Chapter 9 outlined processing techniques—importantly, keeping sharks fresh and bleeding them immediately to release urea from the flesh. Chapter 6 covered aspects of dealing with sharks underwater.

Despite some advisable restrictions on shark consumption, this group provides important sources of protein for indigenous people of nonindustrialized regions; traditional mainstays for Europeans, Americans, and inhabitants of other industrialized areas; and gourmet restaurant items for many cultures.

Spiny Dogfishes (Family Squalidae)

Spiny dogfishes, discussed in chapter 10, are generally small, with notable exceptions. They have small mouths and occur worldwide in the tropics but more commonly in warm to very cold temperate seas. The best-known food species is probably the spiny dogfish *Squalus acanthias*, of fish-and-chips fame, and also marketed as scallops. The meat is white and of good quality, and they're extremely abundant and easy to catch in numerous areas on bottom baits.

Nurse Sharks (Families Orectolobidae and Ginglymostomatidae)

Most nurse sharks are Indo-Pacific, with one common species (*Ginglymostoma cirratum*) in tropical Atlantic shallows and reef areas. All have small mouths with harmless, rounded teeth for feeding on

crustaceans and mollusks, and with two distinct nasal barbs nearby. They tend to be sluggish, lying motionless on the bottom for long periods. They can be aggressive when poked or disturbed, and they will bite. They readily ingest bottom baits and are a frequent by-catch in some areas. The meat is similar to that of other sharks. We found no data on toxicity and haven't tried it ourselves. One Bahamian diver claimed it was acceptable and tasted more like a crustacean than a fish.

Requiem Sharks (Family Carcharhinidae)

Requiem sharks include most of the formidable, potentially dangerous reef, coastal, and pelagic sharks with which cruisers and other people come into the most frequent contact around the world. They are usually easy to catch on natural live and dead bait, and they often take swimming plugs, other lures, and fish struggling on a hook or spear. Check local knowledge on toxicity. We have consumed lemon sharks (*Negaprion acutidens*), blacktip sharks (*Carcharhinus limbatus*), tiger sharks (*Galeocerdo cuvieri*), and several other species in Florida and the Bahamas without mishap, but this is anecdotal. Two Indo-Pacific reef dwellers—gray reef sharks (*Carcharhinus amblyrhynchos*) and blacktip reef sharks (*C. melanopterus*)—have been linked to poisoning cases, and tropical members of this family pose a risk. Between local knowledge and testing meat samples on an expendable mammal, however, you could utilize the high quality meat for food. See chapter 10 for further details.

Hammerhead Sharks (Family Sphyrnidae)

Various hammerheads occur in tropical to warm temperate seas around the world, including small inshore species and large coastal migratory and offshore members with elongated head lobes in the shape of a hammer. Hammerhead meat is firm and tastes fine, although poisoning from at least the smooth hammerhead (*Sphyrna zygaena*) is on record. Exercise precautions for large tropical sharks (see chapter 10).

Mackerel Sharks (Family Lamnidae)

Mackerel sharks include shortfin and longfin makos (*Isurus oxyrinchus* and *I. paucus*), porbeagle sharks

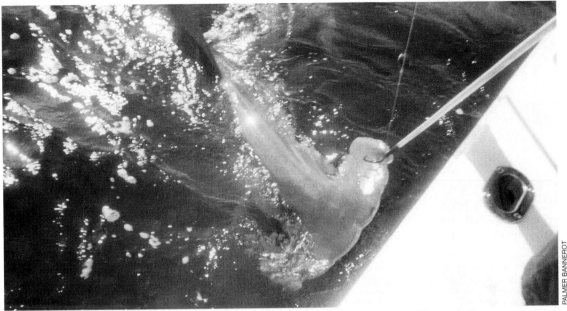

Scalloped hammerhead *(Sphyrna lewini)* about to be tagged and released at the Islamorada Hump, a seamount offshore of Islamorada, Florida Keys.

(Lamna nasus), and the infamous star of the movie *Jaws*, the great white shark *(Carcharodon carcharias)*. The latter reportedly has caused poisoning, but makos, particularly, are widely consumed with relish in the form of delicious broiled steaks. Lamnid sharks occur worldwide from the tropics to cold temperate seas and tend to be more abundant in the cooler portion of this range. The meat is mild, white, solid, and very tasty.

Thresher Sharks (Family Alopiidae)

Thresher sharks *(Alopias)* have a distinctive, greatly elongated upper caudal lobe, a pointed snout, and occur from the surface to 325 feet (100 m) worldwide from the equator to temperate latitudes, usually offshore in deep water. Commercial fishers target them in some areas, and the meat is first-rate and safe to eat.

SAWFISHES, SKATES, AND RAYS (ORDER RAJIFORMES)

Imagine placing a shark in an oversized waffle iron, pressing the lid down, and squishing the shoulder and back meat out into the pectoral fins, creating an enlarged, flattened disk. The ones you press hard

Thresher shark *(Alopias)* captured aboard a swordfish longline vessel in the Caribbean Sea.

come out nearly circular (like stingrays), less pressure results in a shape like two fused triangles (eagle and manta rays), and the lightest pressure results in a form that's part ray, part shark (guitarfishes and sawfish). The first form swims by undulating the outer disk margin like a flounder, the second by flapping the pointy-tipped wings like a bird, and the third swims shark-like by sweeping the tail back and forth. All have five gill slits, a mouth on the ventral surface, and eyes on the dorsal surface above and behind the mouth. Most have tightly packed, nurse-shark-like, flattened teeth or no teeth, indicative of feeding on bottom invertebrates or midwater plankton. The entire group is good eating, and the solid white flesh is not known to be poisonous.

Sawfishes (Family Pristidae)

Sawfishes are awe-inspiring creatures, some reaching 23 feet (7 m), including a long, stout, flattened snout that resembles a nontapered swordfish bill armed with pronounced, sharp-pointed lateral teeth (the "saw"). Four to seven species grouped in two genera occur worldwide in shallow, frequently murky tropical waters, usually bays, estuarine systems, and far up rivers. They use the saw to disable or dispense bottom-dwelling invertebrate and fish prey for consumption. They are not known to be aggressive toward humans, although inadvertent contact (mostly while clearing fishing gear) can result in grievous injury. Sawfish don't attract the attention of much directed subsistence or other fishing effort, although they readily take cut fish and other bottom baits and occasionally become tangled in shrimp trawls. Fishers occasionally dry the saws for sale to tourists. Handle sawfish with great care and release them alive if possible.

Stingrays (Family Dasyatidae)

Stingrays are sometimes large (to 6½ ft./2 m disk width and over 700 lbs./318 kg), highly diverse (at least 118 species), mostly bottom-dwelling inhabitants of subtropical and tropical shallows around the globe. A venomous defensive barb adorns the base of the fairly long, fleshy, tapered-tube tail (see chapters 6 and 10). They are common sights on clear tropical flats, sandy shallows, grass beds, and near reefs, and can be harpooned (see chapter 7), speared (see

chapter 6), or caught on hook and line using chopped or live fish and invertebrate bottom bait. If you hook up with something powerful that occasionally *stops*, and the bottom is free of obstructions, raise the rod, twang the line like a guitar string, and the stingray will "unstick" from the seafloor sediment and once again swim so you can tire and raise it to the boat. The meat is delicious (see chapter 9 for how to clean a ray) and usually ignored by humans, but not by sharks—stingrays are a favorite food.

Skates (Family Rajidae)

Skates are similar to stingrays in diversity (about a hundred species), general body form, barb possession, food quality, and willingness to take bottom baits. Their vertical and geographical distribution is far greater, with some living as deep as 6,500 feet (2,000 m), with abundant representatives from the tropics to extremely cold temperate seas worldwide. Although some species are large (to 5½ ft./172 cm disk width), a high percentage are well under 39 inches (1 m). Nearly all have a more pointed snout than stingrays, and all are bottom dwellers. Skates are more widely appreciated for human consumption than stingrays, with significant harvests in some areas of the world for food. Sometimes markets label them *scallops.*

Eagle Rays (Family Myliobatidae)

Eagle rays swim worldwide, from the equator to mostly warm temperate latitudes, like graceful undersea birds in midwater. Some species make lengthy seasonal migrations in huge groups. These rays feed on benthic invertebrates often rooted from soft sediment with blunt, elongated snouts. Wingspan exceeds disk-midline length, and they have a long, bony, whip-like tail that is sometimes dried and retained for a weapon (possession of an eagle-ray tail is illegal in Nassau, Bahamas). A stack of multiple venomous defensive barbs sits astride the tail base. *Aetobatus* eagle rays are not especially prone to take baited hooks. We once collected several large individuals (spotted eagle rays, *Aetobatus narinari*) for a conch predator research project in the Bahamas by chasing them with a skiff in sandy shallows and harpooning them swordfish-style. The largest weighed 250 pounds (113 kg) and the stomach contained forty-one clam and fourteen juvenile queen conch meats; only small fragments of shell were in the gut, the rest ejected or allowed to drop free of the mouth after crushing between two large, very hard, flat plates. The meat was delicious, tasting more like an invertebrate than a fish, and fed the small population of an out island. However, no one was happy to see one of these large, graceful animals die, and we would not pursue them for food unless we found ourselves in a survival situation.

Other eagle rays—for example, the Indo-Pacific *Myliobatis tenuicaudatus* and congeneric species— are like stingrays, often observed resting on sandy or muddy bottom, quite readily taking bottom baits, fighting strongly, and periodically sucking onto the sediment during the battle (unlike *Aetobatus*). Anglers in New Zealand and Australia seem to place some value on their capture and may retain them for food.

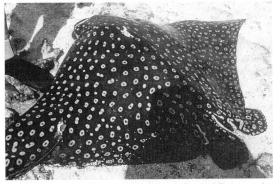

Spotted eagle ray *(Aetobatus narinari, Central Bahamas)*.

Manta Rays (Family Mobulidae)
Manta rays include monsters to a 22-foot (6.7 m) disk width and are entirely surface to midwater pelagic feeders on small fish and plankton, which are swept into the wide mouth and specialized gill filaments with the aid of two distinctive lobes that project forward from the head. They venture from the deep sea into the shallows, particularly those near steep oceanic drop-offs. Ranges are mostly tropical, worldwide, with some extension into the subtropical latitudes. Manta rays occasionally take longline baits offshore and can tangle miles of gear, particularly when several become hooked over a short distance of mainline. Historically, every so often

someone will harpoon one for a stunt and then suffer boat damage and other problems from the struggles of these potentially immense animals. Others become entangled in drift nets. Harvest is discouraged, taboo, or illegal in most places, as the spectacular sight and frequent tameness of these interesting animals around divers is far more valuable to the tourist economy than the dead meat. Cruisers should avoid killing them for obvious reasons.

Manta ray (Family Mobulidae, Tuamotus, French Polynesia).

Sea Turtles (Phylum Chordata, Class Reptilia, Family Chelonidae)
Sea turtles and their eggs constitute a traditional food source throughout the tropics worldwide. However, almost every sea turtle is on the threatened or endangered species list of the International Union for the Conservation of Nature and Natural Resources (IUCN), severely limiting commerce and encouraging sharply reduced or entirely illegal harvest of eggs or individuals. Compliance, voluntary and otherwise, is now encouragingly widespread and increasing with awareness campaigns, even by native fishers in remote areas with little chance of penalty.

Cruisers should never kill one except for survival. In this unlikely event, keep in mind that the posterior midline of the shell is somewhat softer than other areas, often allowing spear penetration. Natives chase turtles in the shallows and fall upon them, or free-dive down and grasp turtles firmly at the front lip of the shell, steering them upward to the surface (note that they frequently try to crank their head around and bite their assailant). Sea turtles may also blunder into gill, drift, and other nets, and females are extremely vulnerable when they make their way up sandy beaches at night to lay eggs. Butchering involves slicing the lower carapace from the upper carapace, evisceration, and excising the meat (and eggs if present). Ciguatera-like poisoning can occur from eating sea-turtle meat during specific times of the year, particularly at scattered Indo-West Pacific locations.

Invertebrate Seafood

Collecting most invertebrate seafood differs fundamentally from catching many fish, particularly on hook and line. Chapters 6 and 7 discuss the more typical methods associated with wading and diving, chapter 9 covers representative processing techniques, and chapter 10 describes potential physical and consumption dangers involving this class of creatures. This section is a guide to representative groups appropriate for cruisers to catch and eat, and fills in some identification, habitat, and capture details not given elsewhere.

MOLLUSKS (PHYLUM MOLLUSCA)

Quick: name the first invertebrate seafood that comes to mind! Chances are good you just rattled off either a crustacean or a mollusk. The latter includes many of the more noticeable marine invertebrates, a number of which play important roles in the diets of people around the world. Chapter 6 outlines much of the basic molluskan biology and systematics; here, we focus on identification and utilization.

Bivalves (Class Bivalvia)

Cruisers collect the majority of these by wading and diving, often with best success above the tropics. Carefully review bivalve poisoning information in chapter 10.

Mussels (Family Mytilidae)

Mussels occur usually in clumps attached to the substrate worldwide in coastal waters and have been farmed extensively for centuries. Most of the hundreds of species look fairly similar, with often dark- to medium-colored drab shells the shape of an elongated, asymmetrical oval. Europeans and Asians use mussels more extensively than North Americans. Mussels substitute or complement most clam and oyster recipes, and may be more abundant or less expensive to purchase locally. Process for consumption *only* live mussels, and don't remove the beards until immediately before cooking because doing so increases the chances they'll die. Reject any dead individuals.

Blue mussels *(Mytilus)* and green mussels *(Perna)* are the most widely used seafood groups, but you may find significant populations of the commonly underutilized, much larger horse mussel *(Modiolus)*. These meats are larger, usually reddish to orange, and may be tougher than the other species. Tenderize by beating (see conch-processing instructions in chapter 9) or use them "as is" in soups and chowders. Another large species, with more typical meat quality than that of horse mussels, is *Aulacomya ater* of Chile and Peru.

Oysters (Family Ostreidae)

Oyster shells are usually lighter colored than those of mussels, usually off-white or grayish, and the outer surface consists of a rougher-textured series of wavy fluted rows. The two dominant forms of commercially important oyster species are cupped oysters *(Saccostrea, Crassotrea)* and flat oysters *(Ostrea* and *Tiostrea)*, indigenous to Europe and other areas.

Green-lipped mussel *(Atria pectinata zelandica)*.

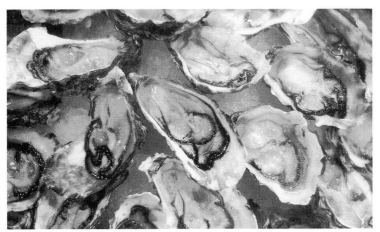

Pacific oyster *(Crassotrea gigas)*.

slip in the knife. Scrape the blade against either shell to sever the adductor muscle. Another trick is to gently microwave a few at a time until the shells *just* open, then take them out and cut the meat out before it cooks.

Clams, Cockles, and Ark Shells (Numerous Families)

Table 12-1 summarizes selected examples of important clam, cockle, and ark shell species most available to cruisers. These bivalves tend to be more round than mussels and oysters, thicker in cross section, and have smoother shell surfaces, with fine concentric lines or regular, low-profile ridges. For some intertidal species, tossing rocks or shells out on the mudflat ahead of you can elicit telltale squirts of water from startled clams suddenly retracting their siphons. The most efficient way to collect some subtidal species, like geoducks, is to dive for them. Capture of species that dwell in deep, cold offshore waters (e.g., ocean quahogs, *Arctica islandica*, and surf clams, *Spisula solidissima*) usually requires power dredges and is therefore beyond the means of most cruisers.

Oysters also occur worldwide, although a relatively small number of the more than two hundred species are used extensively by humans. They have also been farmed throughout recorded history.

Oyster stocks fluctuate radically from natural and human causes. Spawning success depends on specific confluences of shifting environmental conditions, and they are especially susceptible to natural pathogens, deleterious plankton blooms, and pollutants. Pry the shells open and remove the meats—it's easiest to break off a small piece of shell directly across from the hinge for a place to

TABLE 12-1. **SOME CLAMS, COCKLES, AND ARK SHELLS USED FOR FOOD AROUND THE WORLD**

Common Name	Scientific Name	Comments
geoduck	*Panopea abrupta*	huge (to 13 lbs./6 kg), buries deep (to 48 in./122 cm)
butter clam	*Saxidermis giganteus*	to 5 in./13 cm, lives off sheltered beaches
Japanese littleneck	*Tapes philippinarium*	tend to cook much faster than other littlenecks
Pacific littleneck	*Prototháca staminea*	better steamed than raw due to toughness
softshell clam	*Mya arenaria*	buried in shallow waters off beaches and estuaries
quahog	*Mercenaria mercenaria*	intertidal to subtidal zone off beaches
razor clam	*Siliqua* and *Ensis*	strong surf beaches, fast evasive burying ability
horse clam	*Tresus nuttalli*	bury deep (to 36 in./91 cm)
basket cockle	*Clinocardium nuttalli*	large for a cockle (to 5 in./13 cm)
common cockle	*Chione stutchburyi*	small, buries shallow in sand, New Zealand favorite
blood ark shell	*Anadara granosa*	cooked meat is red, abundant in Southeast Asia
European cockle	*Cardium edule*	on or just below sand, small (to 2.5 in./1 cm)
reef clam	*Tridacna*	overfished; best left alone by cruisers (Indo-Pacific)

Reticulate venus *(Periglypta reticulata)*, left, and common basket lucine *(Fimbria fimbriata)*, right, examples of delicious bivalves similar to those available worldwide from tropical to cold temperate environments.

Scallops (Family Pectinidae)

Good eating scallops are abundant worldwide from freezing cold temperate seas to the subtropics, from subtidal shallows to great depths, commonly living on or near the surface or sandy bottoms. The best seafood candidates come from colder waters, although significant tropical stocks *(Amusium)* exist in places like Thailand and the Philippines. Shell form among important food species belonging to genera *Pecten, Chlamys, Argopecten,* and *Patinopecten* is very similar, consisting of a broad, round disk tapering to a dull point framed by two distinct square corners at the hinge. Strong, regular ridges emanate from the hinge, like feathers in a displayed male turkey or peacock tail.

Because of their preferred depths mostly well beyond the range of waders, towed dredges account for most of the world scallop harvest. Recreational fishers and cruisers normally dive for scallops (see chapter 6 for details). The meat is white and usually in the form of a stout cylinder, delicate, and easy to overcook, which causes shrinkage and toughening. Most recipes involve gentle heat and mild sauces, often incorporating a dash of dry white wine (see chapter 13).

Gastropods (Class Gastropoda)

A lower percentage of the more than thirty-five thousand known species of gastropods constitute sought-after seafood items than is the case with

Scallops (Family Pectinidae).

bivalves. Nevertheless, selected gastropods comprise highly valued delicacies from the tropics to cold temperate climates.

Abalone and Limpets (Order Archaeogastropoda)

Abalone and limpets are flattened, one-sided shelled animals attaching strongly to hard substrate in cooler climates. Limpets are far less known and utilized than abalone, but larger species provide important sustenance to natives of scattered coasts around the world. The shells are low-profile cones with concentric patterns around an apex that may have a central siphon hole and, when undisturbed, a typical snail-like head with two tentacles protrudes from the anterior end.

Abalone *(Haliotis iris)*.

Abalone, on the other hand, are vaguely asymmetrical, oval, with a whorl of indistinct ridges and a well-defined row of neat, round perforations out near the shell margin. The genus *Haliotis* forms the basis of significant fisheries and seafood markets in North and South America, Europe, Australia and New Zealand, and Asia, particularly Japan. Most stocks are under heavy pressure; therefore, strict regulations typically control harvest, which is primarily by diving with prying tools (see chapter 6 for tips).

Conch (Family Strombidae)

Chapter 6 discusses important members of these unattached giant marine snails and how to collect them worldwide in the tropics and subtropics. Chapter 9 outlines extraction and cleaning procedures, and chapter 13 provides cooking recipes. Conch, like abalone, get a lot of attention in areas of traditional abundance, resulting in depleted population levels and attendant harvest restrictions. They are free of known toxins and pathogens, have delicious meat, and occur in both wading and shallow diving depths, making for easy capture. Natives often grind off the apex of the shell to form a "conch horn," which requires a pursed-lip, pressurized blowing technique similar to that used with a trumpet.

Collecting spider conch *(Lambis lambis)*, South Pacific.

Whelks (Order Neogastropoda)

Whelks take over the seafood status of conch for cooler waters, even ranging into polar seas. Their shape and morphology is somewhat similar to an elongated conch shell and, as with conch, humans consume the flesh of the thickened foot. Whelks are usually smaller than conch, and biologically different because they are carnivorous predators of other mollusks. The common practice for removing the meat from the shell is partial cooking. Channeled whelk *(Busycotypus canaliculatus)* and knobbed whelk *(Busycon carica)* are uniquely opposite of most seafood in that they require *hours* of cooking before they become tender and palatable. If you run out of stove fuel before this happens, take them out and beat them into submission with a mallet. Marinating can also help. Note that they give off a strong, foul odor the entire time they're cooking, so be ready. One reason they're typically used in heavy, tomato-based sauces is to mask the smell!

Another important representative, waved whelk *(Buccinum undatum)*, typifies a large family of similar species widespread in cooler temperate and polar seas. Cook these small (less than 6 in./15 cm) whelks in the shell, gently pry or pull the body free (it comes easily), discard the viscera, cut off the hard operculum, and add to soup, pasta sauce, or stews and chowders.

The carnivorous diet of whelks makes them susceptible to trapping, often a desirable alternative for less hardy divers unwilling to brave some of the cold waters these animals prefer. Most other whelk harvest is by trawls, including some specialized designs in northern Europe.

Topshells (Family Trochidae)

Occasionally you might hear a Bahamian or West Indian talking about "whelks," but they are actually referring to the next most important gastropod to conch in terms of regional seafood importance: the topshell *Cittarium pica.* Chapter 6 discusses capturing these largely intertidal marine snails, and chapter 9 describes their preparation for eating. Of the thousand or so additional trochid species, others are large enough to consume or have commercial importance for jewelry-making. The Indo-Pacific *Trochus niloticus* fulfills both of these criteria, for instance,

Whelk (Order Neogastropoda).

and is in great demand for the manufacture of pearly-looking shirt buttons and other items. These and similar species occur from the lower intertidal zone to 50 feet (15 m) or more depth, often near coral in lagoons and on the outer reef slope.

Nerites and Periwinkles
(Families Neritidae and Littorinidae)

Nerites and periwinkles are pervasive, ubiquitous tropical and temperate counterparts inhabiting intertidal zones of world shorelines. They're small and easily collected (often without getting wet) in large numbers. Cook them in the shell, remove the meat with a pin, discard the operculum, and don't worry about trying to separate the viscera—plop them whole into any seafood concoction. One reason these groups are so plentiful is that their small size renders commercial-scale extraction for marketing economically infeasible, and the time and labor involved discourages subsistence and recreational use where alternatives are abundant. On the other hand, they're quite popular in Europe. Cruisers on a leisurely schedule, as well as stranded shipwreck survivors, might also find them to be a pleasant, safe diet supplement. Send the kids out to collect them.

Chitons (Class Polyplacophora)

We describe chitons and their capture in chapter 6 and processing and consumption in chapter 9. Keep in mind that since they are not filter feeders and do not ingest toxic midwater plankton, they are more likely to be a safe potential seafood alternative where other shelled mollusks are questionable.

Cephalopods (Class Cephalopoda)

Cephalopods are highly valued worldwide for their culinary qualities and receive considerable coverage in many chapters of this book. They are safe to eat and widely available once you know how to find or attract and then capture them. Many cruisers choose to make cephalopods an important part of their new life as competent fishers. The three main groups of interest are cuttlefishes, squid, and octopuses. Oceanic cephalopods comprise an important component of the nightly vertical-migrating DSL. People consume the high-protein, low-fat flesh cooked or raw.

Cuttlefishes (Order Sepioidea)

Cuttlefishes usually resemble large (commonly 36 in./91 cm, although the smallest species reaches just over ½ in./13 mm), stout, thickened squid with nearly oval mantles and broad, fat arms. They are slower, more deliberate swimmers than squid and may rest on or be buried in the bottom by day, rising into the water column to actively forage during the night. Cruisers who dive near dawn or dusk will most likely encounter these animals hovering in the vicinity of an Indo-West Pacific reef, where they are highly prized targets of spearfishers. Fishers specifically target cuttlefish in the Mediterranean and elsewhere with seine nets, trawls, dredges, pots, and fishing lines with jigs.

Squid (Order Teuthoidea)

Fifteen families or so of squid are of potential interest to cruising seafarers, and they inhabit nearly every ocean environment the planet has to offer. Two common groups are the tropical arrow squids (Family Loliginidae), slender, fast animals that often appear in groups darting into the glow of night lights; and occasional open-ocean members of the larger, broader-bodied, frequently orange-hued Family Ommastrephidae. Chapters 4 and 7 provide information on dip-netting and jigging these and other squid, the two most practical techniques for small-boat voyagers. Spearing squid while diving typically requires great accuracy, and shooting one usually spooks the rest of the group away.

Octopuses (Order Octopoda)

The octopus species most important from a fisheries standpoint are bottom-associated, inhabiting near-shore waters suitable for diving or wading, and nearly all belong to the genus *Octopus*. Practical capture techniques for cruisers include spearing, gaffing from holes and crevices with a hand hook, and possibly traps (see chapters 6 and 7, and bite precautions in chapter 10). Octopuses are most active at night.

Reef squid *(Sepioteuthis sepioidea)*, tropical Atlantic/Caribbean.

CRUSTACEANS (PHYLUM ARTHROPODA, CLASS CRUSTACEA)

Crustaceans represent a massive group of animals (around twenty-six thousand known species) within a phylum containing the better part of one million species (that's about three-quarters of all known animal species!). Among these are animals that seafood lovers hold dearest to their hearts, reveling in the opportunity to collect and consume "free" while traveling around to beautiful areas of the world on cruising vessels. Chapters 6, 7, and 9 contain abundant information on these practices, for well-known representatives, and for other groups possibly not familiar to many people.

Lobsters (Section Macrura)

Three families of lobsters include species of greatest significance to fisheries, as a group inhabiting accessible depths in most ocean waters of the world. Most enter traps readily (see chapter 7). Diving is an effective means of capture, and some conditions permit

True or clawed lobsters (Family Nephronidae).

use of special long-handled nets and gigs (see chapters 6 and 7). Cook all lobsters fresh by boiling briefly whole or splitting longitudinally and grilling. One excellent method is to bring water to a boil, then remove it from the burner *just* before putting the lobsters in; immerse them for about ten minutes. This results in delicate, tender, perfectly cooked meat.

True (Clawed) Lobsters (Family Nephronidae)

The largest, best-known species are the cold-water American lobster *(Homarus americanus)* and European lobster *(Homarus gammarus)*, both armed with formidable claws and occurring from inshore shallows to beyond comfortable diving depths. Once caught primarily in bottom trawls, traps now account for most of the catch. Three smaller species with reduced, longer claws—the bright orange and yellow Norway lobster *(Nephrops norvegicus)*, Florida lobsterette *(Nephropsis aculeata)*, and Caribbean lobsterette *(Metanephrops binghami)*—occur too deep (often over 1,000 ft./305 m) for practical, noncommercial collection by the average voyager. Numerous *Nephrops* and *Metanephrops* also occur in deep Indo-Pacific waters.

Spiny Lobsters (Family Palinuridae)

Many species of spiny lobster inhabit rocks, reefs, mangrove shorelines, undercut banks and channels, seawalls, and wrecks. They forage on adjacent sand flats, seagrass and kelp beds, and hard ground interspersed with sponges and soft corals from the equator to the warm temperate latitudes worldwide. The only notable exception to this pattern is a range truncation from near the equator south on the western coast of South America caused by the strong cold influence of the Humboldt and Peru currents sweeping up from the Antarctic. Thus, spiny lobsters are by far the most important for cruisers, and they conveniently lack claws.

Traps, waders, and divers catch most spiny lobsters. Chapter 6 describes wading reef flats at night and diving tricks, and chapter 7 discusses traps, snares, tickler sticks and landing nets, and bully nets. The general strategy for locating those species that cluster in shallow-water dens during the day is to develop a keen eye for likely looking holes, undercuts, and ledges, and the image of thin, protruding antenna tips. Examples of such species are the Caribbean spiny lobster *(Panulirus argus)*, Indo-Pacific painted lobster *(Panulirus versicolor)*, and New Zealand rock lobster *(Jasus edwardsii)*, among numerous others. Repeatedly dive down and look up and under reef, rocks, ledges, and other cover.

Other species seek very deep cover during the day, requiring divers to search the far recesses of coral caverns (e.g., the spotted spiny lobster *Panulirus guttatus* of the Caribbean). Other Indo-Pacific species are rarely found in deep recesses of shallow-water dens by day, but nearly always migrate vertically to considerable depths, and only climb to reasonable diving or wading collection depths at night (e.g., *Panulirus penicillatus,* see photo page 10).

Slipper Lobsters (Family Scyllaridae)

Rather than being long and tapered as for spiny lobsters, the antennae of slipper lobsters are reduced to broad, flat, shovel-like plates, and the carapace is more flattened. Members of this family occur around shallow reefs, reef flats, and subtidal rocky shores, to relatively open bottom and depths of 1,500 feet (457 m), in tropical to warm temperate seas. Cruisers find representatives in deep, dark recesses of dens during daytime and out foraging in the open at night, sometimes in very shallow water on reef flats. Some species support commercial fisheries, particularly in the Indo-Pacific, including *Ibacus peronii, Parribacus antarcticus,* and *Thenus orientalis.* The slipper lobster *Scyllarides aequinoctialis* occasionally rewards diligent hunters in the Bahamas, Florida, and the Caribbean.

Slipper lobsters are excellent eating, claimed by many to be superior in taste and texture to spiny lobsters. Apparently low population densities and somewhat solitary habits, at least in the shallows, normally make them only an occasional treat.

Freshwater Crayfish (Section Macrura)

Freshwater crayfish are common in selected zones worldwide, in warm areas to very cold temperate creeks, ditches, canals, ponds, streams, rivers, and lakes—and entirely missing from many other areas (i.e., the African continent, most of South America, and Middle Asia). Chapter 6 discusses the capture of freshwater crayfish on baited lines. Other methods include baited nets and seine nets.

More than 240 species are indigenous to North America, with five *Pacifastacus* species (Family Astacidae) in the northwestern United States and the rest (all members of Family Cambaridae) inhabiting southern Canada, central and eastern United States, and Mexico. The most famous might be the Louisiana red crayfish *(Procambarus clarkii)* and white crayfish *(P. blandingi),* both of which are subjects of aquaculture.

Caribbean spiny lobster *(Panulirus argus)* marches out to inspect photographer briefly before retreating rapidly backwards to its den (near Miami, Florida).

Freshwater crayfish.

Most of Europe and a slice of western Asia harbor Family Astacidae *(Astacus* and *Austropotomobius),* and temperate eastern Asia has the single cambarid genus *Cambaroides*. Australia has many species (more than a hundred, in nine genera) all belonging to Family Parastacidae, and including the largest species in the world: the giant freshwater crayfish *Astacopsis gouldi* (old records indicate weights over 13 pounds/6 kg). Other prominent genera include *Euastacus* and *Cherax*. Freshwater crayfish inhabit Papua New Guinea and Madagascar, but not Southeast Asia, India, or the Middle East.

Freshwater Shrimp and Prawns (Family Palaemonidae)

Palaemonids occur in pantropical freshwater, brackish, and marine environments, in many places where freshwater crayfish are absent. *Macrobrachium* is the most important genus for fisheries and aquaculture activities, enthusiastically sought by local residents with seine nets, small spears, and other gear (see chapter 6). This type of activity is a daily ritual in rice paddies and ditches in Southeast Asia. The meat is white and tasty, but customarily softer than true marine shrimps. Other rock-pool, estuary, and commensal family members (i.e., *Palaemon, Palaemonetes,* and various pontoniine shrimp) are usually too small to attract much human attention.

Freshwater prawn *(Macrobrachium).*

Marine Shrimp and Prawns (Families Penaeidae, Aristeidae, Pandalidae, and Others)

Humans exploit numerous marine shrimp families. The families Penaeidae, Aristeidae, and Pandalidae comprise a representative spectrum of important food species. Penaeids are particularly widespread, with various species of *Penaeus* and *Metapenaeus* supporting important warmer water trawl fisheries worldwide. Cruisers can get in on the fun with a small homemade trawl or night light and dip net (see chapter 7). Some cold-water penaeids are significant; for example, the small red *Artemesia longinaris*, which co-occurs with the large red solenocerid *Hymenopenaeus muelleri* to 60-foot (18 m) depths off Argentina.

Other cold-water groups such as the pandalids (primarily *Pandalus* and *Heterocarpus*), aristeids (e.g., the giant red prawn *Aristaeomorpha foliacea*), and other solenocerids (e.g., the royal red shrimps *Hymenopenaeus sibogae* [Australia], and *H. robustus* [western Atlantic]) generally prefer depths beyond the scope of cruisers (580 to 2,275 ft./180 to 700 m). The willingness of assorted small species to enter traps set in cold-water anchorages—for example, in the Pacific

Marine shrimp (Family Pandalidae).

Northwest and Alaska—however, makes the practice worthwhile for traveling seafarers (see chapter 7).

The Wide World of Crabs

Crabs swim from surface to bottom in warm to freezing-cold seas, crawl on the seafloor to great depths, construct burrows in muddy and sandy intertidal zones, walk on exposed beaches and rocky shorelines, make homes on dry land, and sometimes climb tall trees. Humans grab, net, trap, and sometimes catch crabs on baited lines, then usually boil them whole and extract the meat by breaking the shell. They're a little more trouble to eat than lobsters, but this doesn't seem to dampen the enthusiasm people have for the sweet, succulent meat. (See chapters 6 and 7 for more capture details.)

Aquatic Marine Crabs

Many crabs live submerged in ocean waters, from subtidal to cold, darkened depths far from the grasp of the average seafarer. Cruisers can catch delicious species themselves at most latitudes, and some familiarity with less accessible commercial species may alert you to local purchasing opportunities from professional fishers.

Cold and temperate North Pacific and Indo-Pacific crabs. From Korea, arcing across the Bering Sea to British Columbia, live several species of the famous king crab (Family Lithodidae). The largest and hardest fished is *Paralithodes camtschatica* (averaging 10 lbs./4.5 kg and reaching 28 lbs./13 kg), caught in immense baited steel traps by hardy commercial fishers in deep continental-shelf waters. Two smaller species overlap the same range, *P. brevipes* and *P. platypus*. Farther south on both sides of the Pacific, spider crabs *(Chionoectes)* are commercial targets, including the tanner crabs *(C. bairdii* and *C. tanneri)* and snow crabs *(C. opilio* and *C. japonicus)*. The deep, cold-water Japanese spider crab *Macrocheira kaempferi* may have a claw spread of 10 feet (3 m). Moving down to the Pacific Northwest and northern California, the more modest sized (9 in./23 cm bodies) Dungeness crabs *(Cancer magister)* and congenerics become important. These crabs enter baited, round-shaped wire traps.

Australia's answer to the king crab is the giant southern crab *(Pseudocarcinus gigas,* Family Xanthidae), found only in Tasmania and southern Australia, which may grow to 35 pounds (16 kg). These animals live mostly between 325- and 650-foot (100 and 200 m) depths, but brave cruisers with thick wetsuits could challenge the odd individual that wanders into shallow waters, occasionally into the intertidal zone (movie stars for *Claws*?). A deeper dwelling, much smaller (7 in./18 cm carapace) snow crab, *Chaceon bicolor* (Family Geryonidae) that lives on gravel, sand, or mud bottom at 650 to 6,500 feet (200 to 2,000 m) shows commercial promise around the top half of Australia.

The cold-water southern spider crab (*Jacquinotia edwardsii*, Family Majidae) looks very similar to the Caribbean *Mithrax*, also occurs relatively shallow (65 to 325 ft./20 to 100 m), and is generating seafood industry interest in New Zealand. A more widely distributed Southern Hemisphere portunid, the common swimming crab *Ovalipes catharus*, frequents sandy inshore shallows in New Zealand and temperate Australia. This crab is a larger, good-eating, and easily accessible relative of the deeper-dwelling red swimming crabs (*Nectocarcinus*).

Atlantic crabs, from cold waters to the tropics. Some of the most commercially important cold-water Atlantic crabs began as accidental by-catch of the clawed-lobster (*Homarus*) trap fishery, includ-

ing the deep-sea red crab (*Geryon quinquedens*), Jonah crab (*Cancer borealis*), and congeneric rock crabs (*C. irroratus* in the western Atlantic; *C. pagurus* from Norway to Portugal). The most important inshore species, the blue crab (*Callinectes sapidus*, Family Portunidae) occurs from cool temperate waters into the tropics in many areas highly accessible to cruisers (see chapters 6 and 7). Small individuals also make prime hook-and-line bait, as does the temperate green crab (*Carcinus maenas*).

The claws of stone crabs (*Menippe mercenaria*, Family Menippidae) are revered seafood items with mostly Florida commercial origins. These crabs burrow from subtidal to shallow depths in muddy and sandy bottoms, or may take advantage of rock edges bordering sand for shelter. Trap fishers remove the claws and throw the crabs back alive to regenerate new ones. These crabs are large and sluggish, and can be collected by diving, although some of their most favored habitats are warm, murky bays with significant populations of dangerous sharks. Smaller reef-dwelling *Menippe* inhabit clearer water, taste good, and may make safer diving objectives. Don't kill the crab because the body has little meat. Stone-crab claws keep well frozen.

Several tropical spider crabs—for example, *Mithrax spinosissimus* (Family Majidae)—found

Alaskan king crab (*Paralithodes*).

inshore on seawalls and in reef caves, holes, and crevices to depths of 130 feet (40 m) are large enough (5 to 7 in./13 to 18 cm carapace, with long legs and claws) to have some food value. At least one Caribbean aquaculture attempt failed, and natural population densities tend to be low. Regardless, you can easily collect slow-moving individuals with a pole spear, Hawaiian sling, or gig and give them a try. Many areas where they occur do not have other abundant food species of aquatic crab.

Crabs from warmer Indo-Pacific waters. As we mention in chapter 10, one family containing very accessible, sometimes meaty, shallow reef-dwelling crabs (Xanthidae) has numerous toxic species, particularly west of the International Dateline. Eight highly toxic and four mildly toxic species are now known. In the Philippines, ingestion of the crab *Demania reynaudii* has killed people, and other members of this and the genus *Lophozozymus* are known to contain the same type of toxin (i.e., palytoxin). At least one parthenopid is also mildly toxic, but this is an oddball not as likely to tempt consumers.

Various reef and stone crabs of the Family Menippidae look like xanthids, are good to eat, and appear not to be toxic. They occur from the intertidal shallows to deep water. For instance, the spiny deepwater crab *Hypothalassia armata*, a common spiny lobster-trap by-catch in Australia, is eliciting commercial interest.

Numerous portunid crab species find favor with seafood procurers and consumers in the Indo-Pacific, just as they do in the rest of the world. The mud crab *Scylla serrata* can exceed an 8-inch (20 cm) carapace width, occurs widely in muddy brackish shallows, enthusiastically attacks baited lines and crawls into various baited traps, and is highly regarded for food. The sand crab *Portunus pelagicus* reaches the same size as the mud crab, occurs throughout shallow bays and estuaries and out to deeper offshore waters, supports extensive commercial and recreational fishing, and looks and tastes much like the Atlantic blue crab. The long-eyed swimming crab *Podophthalmus vigil* is another abundant, shallow-water estuarine crab popular for food in this part of the world.

Another highly accessible, good eating crab of this region, the odd-looking spanner crab (*Ranina ranina*, Family Raninidae), lives on sandy bottoms from the subtidal zone to 195-foot (60 m) depths. These crabs have a habit of burrowing backwards into the sand upon sensing danger, and their thick carapace can measure 6 by 5 inches (14 by 12 cm).

Crabs that Live (Mostly) on Land

Most of us lucky enough to have spent any time on a seashore as kids are probably guilty of having harassed shore crabs (Family Grapsidae) or ghost and fiddler crabs (Family Ocypodidae), those incredibly fast, small sprinters that almost always evaded our best efforts. We didn't *really* want to catch them, anyway, because the fun was in the chase. Yet many coastal inhabitants set out at night with lights to do just that, seeking the small quantities of incredibly sweet meat these small crabs offer (see chapter 6 and photo page 150). They also make excellent fishing bait.

Another familiar family, the hermit crabs (Family Coenobitidae), takes some of the kid pressure off of grapsids and ocypodids in subtropical and warmer latitudes by serving the dubious role of being their pets (see photo page 149). Their slow-moving ways, great

Purple spider crab (*Mithrax*, Staniel Cay, Exuma Islands, Bahamas).

abundance, habit of tucking "safely" inside the borrowed shell they call home, and willingness to eat junk food in captivity make this inevitable. Larger species, big enough to eat, abound but have so far mostly avoided becoming popular food items. The exception is the well-known, beleaguered, Indo-Pacific coconut crab *(Birgus latro)* discussed in chapter 6 (see photo page 150). Cruisers should cross this one off their list except under survival or other special circumstances due to its increasing scarcity.

Land crabs (Family Gecarcinidae) are a different story. They're widespread in tropical and subtropical zones, prolific, usually hard to catch, and underutilized in many areas. Therefore, populations are generally in reasonable shape, and neither local hosts nor native ecosystems are significantly harmed by your taking them. We describe capture techniques in chapter 6 and processing and preparation for eating them in chapter 9. The most important species for Western Hemisphere fisheries is the white land crab *(Cardisoma guanhumi)* avidly sought for claw meat and the fat-rich hepatopancreas in the Bahamas, Puerto Rico, the Lesser Antilles, and other areas, particularly during rainy periods that drive them from their burrows. The nearly identical *C. crassum* occurs from Baja California to Peru. Purple land crabs of the genus *Gecarcinus* large enough for consumption (e.g., *G. ruricola*) also have significant culinary status in regions where they flourish (the Caribbean, Africa, and Central America).

SEA URCHINS AND SEA CUCUMBERS (PHYLUM ECHINODERMATA)

"Echinoderm" means "spiny skin," aptly describing one unifying characteristic of this assemblage of more than fifty-three hundred species of sluggish, bottom-dwelling invertebrates, largely unfamiliar as mainstream seafood items in much of the world. Chapter 9 discusses processing of sea urchins (Class Echinoidea; see photo page 341) for the excellent-tasting roe, and the rather involved procedures used to force sea cucumber (Class Holothuroidea) flesh into some form of submission. Indo-Pacific peoples consume raw sea cucumber flesh and intestines in

some locations. Cruisers, however, should only try this in the company of locals (whom you're reasonably sure like you). Numerous sea cucumber species contain noxious and toxic substances that can squirt out and irritate your skin or, worse, blind you, and sea urchin eggs *can* be toxic to ingest. Most regional sea cucumber flesh preparation regimens involve repeated rinsing, perhaps because of the potential for toxic fluids emanating from the body cavity.

Toxins notwithstanding, sea cucumbers are highly prized seafood items starting in the Western Pacific and continuing all the way to Africa. Valued genera include *Stichopus, Holothuria,* and, to a lesser extent, *Thelenota* and *Actinopyga.* Mariculture- and fisheries-related research projects are active in the area, and countries both consume and export processed products to Asian and other markets. Remember that sea cucumber species identification is sometimes not easy, so if you develop a taste for one under local tutelage in a given location, tread carefully after you relocate to a new area, particularly in the absence of expert advice.

The same goes for sea urchins. Records of intoxication from egg ingestion include the West Indian sea egg *(Tripneustes ventricosus),* a common shallow-water inhabitant of grass beds and reefs in the Caribbean region; and the sea urchins *Paracentrotus lividus* and *Centrechinus antillarum.* Many other species don't appear to be a problem. The key is avoiding consumption during peak spawning times, which apparently correlate to greatest toxicity. For example, amateur and commercial fishers all around the coasts of New Zealand enthusiastically harvest the sea egg *Evechinus chloroticus* during the months leading up to the summertime spawning season, and consume the ripening gonads with relish. This species is most abundant from subtidal to 50 feet (15 m) and occasionally reaches very high densities (more than fifty per square yard/meter). Polynesian hosts treated us to delicious sea urchin roe in the Marquesas Islands. Checking carefully with your new friends before you partake should ensure yet another delightful and safe culinary experience.

13

More Seafood Recipes

These recipes represent a collection of favorites from our travels. Use your fresh catch for best results. Remove the bloodline (dark or red meat), particularly for oily fish (e.g., tuna, mackerel, trevally) when filleting unless you enjoy a stronger taste. Don't overcook! Also, be sure to review chapter 10 carefully, follow safety rules to avoid toxic seafood, and always check with local inhabitants about which organisms may be toxic to ingest or physically contact.

Our cooking is informal, throw-it-together island style, where nobody reads recipes, much less suffers through tedious ingredient measurements or precise serving sizes. We've left rigid cookbook directions behind in our wake, and we hope you'll join us for some happy, creative fun within a purposely semiorganized framework. Many of the following recipes don't give specific amounts for all ingredients but provide all you need to know. Read through each recipe, compare basic ingredients with your provisions, be flexible, and blast off. You'll get gourmet results, five-star dishes to delight your most discerning guests, and you'll find the more relaxed atmosphere thoroughly infectious.

Starters

Use starters to tantalize your crew and guests prior to the main course, as a tasty snack between regular meals, or as light fare.

Seared Ahe (Tuna)

fresh cylinders of tuna meat, 8 inches (20 cm) in length, 1 inch (2.5 cm) in diameter, cut from fillets	Cajun seasoning vegetable oil

Fillet tuna, slice boneless meat from the skin, leaving the bloodline attached to the skin (see fig. 9-9). Cut into cylinders and roll them in Cajun seasoning. Sear in hot oil, 12 to 15 seconds per side. Remove from heat and place in freezer (or next coolest place) for 1 hour. Slice thinly (⅛ in./3 mm), just as you would a loaf of bread or a sausage, and serve with sauce.

Seared Ahe Sauce

small jar of fruit jelly or jam ketchup soy sauce	Worcestershire sauce horseradish

Melt jelly or jam in microwave or on stove. Add 3 tablespoons ketchup, 3 tablespoons soy sauce, and 3 tablespoons Worcestershire sauce. Add horseradish to taste. Serve with seared ahe.

Sashimi

> fresh tuna, trevally,
>   jack, wahoo,
>   or other fish
> soy sauce
> wasabi

Fillet fish, remove bloodline, and chill. Slice thinly and serve with soy sauce and wasabi on the side.

Nori Rolls

> fresh tuna, trevally,   vegetable sticks
>   jack, wahoo,   (carrot, green
>   or other fish   pepper,
> nori seaweed sheets   cucumber, etc.)
> cooked rice (sticky)   vinegar

Cook rice with a little extra water for sticky texture, and spread thinly over one third of the nori sheet. Place thin strips of fish and vegetable on rice, close to the edge of the sheet. Roll sheet, starting with rice end. Use vinegar to moisten fingers and nori sheet. Slice roll into 1-inch (2.5 cm) sections. Serve with soy sauce and wasabi.

Ceviche

> fresh fish (grouper,   green, red, or
>   snapper,   yellow peppers
>   mackerel, and   tomato
>   other species)   lemon or lime juice
> onion

Chop equal amounts of fish and vegetables into small bits and place in a plastic container. Add enough lemon or lime juice to cover about one third of the mixture (sprinkle lightly with seasoning to taste if you wish). Shake vigorously to infuse marinade and refrigerate overnight. Serve cold; optionally add Tabasco sauce to taste.

Poisson Cru
(Raw Fish with Coconut Cream)

> fresh fish (tuna,   cucumber
>   trevally, jack,   tomato
>   wahoo, or   green, red, or
>   other fish)   yellow peppers
> onion   coconut cream
> garlic   lemon or lime

Chop fish into ½-inch (1.3 cm) cubes and vegetables into bits, using equal amounts of fish and vegetables. Add enough coconut cream to cover, then a small amount of lemon or lime juice—sprinkle in as you mix the concoction thoroughly with a wooden spoon or your (very well washed) hands. Refrigerate 2 to 3 hours. Serve cold.

Crab Dip

> fresh picked   garlic
>   (from boiled crab   green, red, and
>   bodies, legs, and   yellow peppers
>   claws) or canned   sour cream
>   crabmeat   chopped walnuts
> onion

Mix two parts crabmeat, one part chopped vegetables, and walnuts to taste with enough sour cream to moisten mixture thoroughly. Serve with crackers or chips.

Crab and Corn Fritters

> crabmeat   Old Bay seasoning
>   (fresh picked   baking powder
>   or canned)   cream
> corn   butter
> eggs   mixed herbs
> flour   cocktail or honey-
> salt and pepper   mustard sauce

Beat 3 eggs. Add 1 teaspoon baking powder; 1 tablespoon each Old Bay seasoning, mixed herbs, and pepper; and a dash of salt. Add 2 cups (500 mL) each crabmeat and grated corn. Add 2 tablespoons cream and mix well. Melt 4 tablespoons butter in skillet. Drop mixed batter by the spoonful into hot butter and brown on both sides. Serve with cocktail or honey-mustard sauce.

Smoked Fish Dip

> smoked fish (see chapter 9 for fish-smoking
>   instructions)
> onion
> green, red, or yellow
>   peppers
> cucumber
> tomato
> mayonnaise

Chop equal amounts of fish and vegetables into
bits. Mix well with enough mayonnaise to moisten.
Serve with crackers or chips.

Steamed Clams/Mussels

> clams or mussels   water
> beer   butter

Bring 1 cup (250 mL) water to boil in steaming pot,
and add 1 cup (250 mL) beer. Lower steamer containing clams or mussels into pot, and steam until
clams or mussels open. Squeeze lemon juice over
opened shells and serve with melted butter. *Do not*
force open any bivalves with shells that remain
closed after steaming—discard these, since they're
not safe to eat.

Clam or Mussel Casino

> clams or mussels   onion
> bacon   grated cheese
> green, red, or   of your choice
>   yellow peppers

Steam clams/mussels. Remove from shells.
Chop equal amounts of bivalve meat, bacon,
and vegetables into bits. Mix thoroughly, and
put a dollop of the concoction back into shells.
Sprinkle with grated cheese. Bake or broil until
cheese melts. Serve with a drop or two of
Tabasco if desired.

Conch Fritters

> conch meat   Cajun seasoning
> flour   vegetable oil
> egg
> onion
> green or red
>   peppers

Chop equal amounts of conch and vegetables into
small bits. Mix with enough beaten egg and flour to
form an adhesive blend. Add Cajun seasoning to
taste. Form batter mix into 2-inch (5 cm) balls.
Deep-fry in hot oil until brown.

Conch Salad

> conch meat   tomato
> onion   celery
> green or   lemon or lime
>   red peppers

Chop equal amounts of conch and vegetables
into bits and place in a plastic sealable container.
Add enough lemon or lime juice to cover bottom
quarter of mixture. Stir thoroughly and shake
vigorously to infuse with marinade. Refrigerate
from 1 hour to overnight. Add Tabasco sauce
to taste.

Lobster Salad

> cooked lobster meat   celery
>   (boiled and re-   tomato
>   moved from   mayonnaise
>   shell, carapace,   garlic
>   and appendages)   basil
> onion
> greeen, red, or
>   yellow peppers

Chop equal amounts of lobster and vegetable into
bits. Stir in enough mayonnaise to moisten. Season
with garlic and basil. Serve chilled.

Calamari (Squid) Rings

squid	vegetable oil
egg	tartar sauce or
flour	cocktail sauce

Lay squid out on flat surface. Slice thin (¼ in./6 mm) cross sections of the tube-like body (mantle) as though slicing a loaf of bread. Rinse the viscera from these rings of meat. Slice off the tentacles and use these, too. Make a batter with egg and flour. Dip squid pieces into batter and fry in hot oil. Serve with tartar or cocktail sauce.

Warm Calamari (Squid) Salad

squid	salad greens
olive oil	honey-mustard
ginger	salad dressing
sweet chili sauce	

Lay squid out on flat cutting surface. Make a slice the length of the body (mantle), eviscerate, and rinse. Slice off and retain tentacles. Cut mantle meat into ¼- by 3-inch (6 by 8 mm) strips. Place in a plastic sealed container. Stir in crushed garlic, grated ginger, and sweet chili sauce (approximately 1 tablespoon per individual serving). Marinate overnight in refrigerator. Add 2 tablespoons olive oil to pan, heat until a drop of water added to the pan sizzles in the oil. Sauté squid ribbons until just tender (this is a brief process—don't overcook). Serve over green salad tossed with honey-mustard dressing.

Sea Urchin

urchins (usually "pencil" urchins, those with stout, thick spines)
lemon or lime juice

Harvest near-ripe pencil urchins. Spawning usually occurs near the full moon, but check local knowledge or open a single urchin and check for presence of well-developed eggs. Process the urchins by chopping open the exoskeleton with a machete, long knife, or cleaver. Remove the abundant, enlarged golden eggs. Serve raw, with lemon or lime juice for dipping.

Marinated Octopus Salad

fresh octopus	salad greens
ginger root	oil and vinegar
lemon or lime juice	salad dressing

Split the body of the octopus, eviscerate, remove mouth parts and all associated material, and rinse thoroughly. Chop tentacles into ½-inch (13 mm) sections, and slice body into similar-sized pieces. Place in a plastic sealable container. Add one part thin-sliced ginger root to four parts octopus, and enough lemon or lime juice to cover the bottom quarter of the mixture. Stir thoroughly, seal the container, and shake vigorously; then marinate overnight in the refrigerator. Serve over green salad with oil and vinegar salad dressing.

Garlic-Marinated Raw Fish

fresh fish (tuna,	green and red
wahoo, jack,	peppers
trevally, mackerel,	tomato
or other fish)	garlic
onion	Tabasco sauce

Chop fish and vegetables into bits (two parts fish to one part vegetables). Mix in generous amounts chopped garlic and Tabasco sauce to taste. Marinate overnight in refrigerator. Serve cold.

Salmon Pate

canned red salmon	butter
cream cheese	basil
mayonnaise	salt and pepper
lemon or lime juice	

Drain canned salmon and add ½ cup (125 mL) each cream cheese and mayonnaise. Add 2 tablespoons each lemon or lime juice and melted butter. Add 1 teaspoon basil and salt and pepper to taste. Mix well and refrigerate 1 hour before serving.

Soups and Chowders

Serve soups and chowders as a main meal or as an appetizer. Complement them with bold slices of crusty fresh bread on the side. Sprinkle croutons over the surface just prior to serving.

Passage Fish Soup

fish	onion
water	mixed herbs
chicken or beef	curry powder
stock cubes	Tabasco sauce
any fresh or canned	
vegetables	
any combination of	
potatoes, pasta,	
rice, or dried beans	

Fill large pot half full of water. Add 4 to 5 stock cubes, mixed herbs, curry powder, chopped onion, and any combination of starch, until pot is two-thirds full. Simmer until starch is tender. Add various vegetables and simmer to desired tenderness (try crunchy, too). Add boneless fish chunks until pot is almost full. Simmer 5 to 10 minutes until fish is cooked. Serve with Tabasco sauce to taste.

Fish Stock

head, throat, and	celery or celery
backbone sections	powder
of one large	pepper
filleted fish	
water	
onion	

Chop 1 large onion and 2 stalks celery (or substitute 2 teaspoons celery powder) and add to large pot with fish soup parts (see fig. 9-7) and 12 cups (3 L) of water. Add pepper to taste. Simmer uncovered 20 to 30 minutes. Strain broth through muslin cloth. Refrigerate until needed; can be frozen. Skim stock before use.

Seafood Gumbo for a Small Army

fresh shrimp	thyme
scallops	oregano
mussels, scrubbed	paprika
and debearded	allspice
boneless white fish	crushed dried peppers
fillets cut into 1-in.	(chilies)
(2.5 cm) cubes	Cajun seasoning
onion	Worcestershire sauce
red pepper	fish stock
yellow pepper	canned tomatoes
celery	sugar
okra	olive oil
garlic	tomato paste

Heat 1 tablespoon olive oil in large pan. Chop 2 onions, 1 each of the peppers, and 2 stalks celery. Sauté vegetables and garlic in oil until onion is soft. Add 1 small can tomato paste, 1 tablespoon oregano, 2 teaspoons each of thyme, paprika, allspice, sugar, chilies, Cajun seasoning, and Worcestershire sauce. Also add 3 cups (750 mL) fish stock, 2 large cans tomatoes (including juice), and 15 chopped okra. Simmer uncovered 15 minutes. Add 2 dozen shrimp, 1 dozen mussels, 2 dozen scallops, and 2 pounds (1 kg) fish. Simmer uncovered 5 to 10 minutes. Serve with Tabasco sauce to taste.

Cajun Bouillabaisse

boneless white	tomato paste
fish fillets	(1 small can)
shrimp	canned tomatoes
scallops	(2 large cans)
olive oil	fish stock
Cajun seasoning	(6 cups/1.5 L)
onion	dry white wine
garlic	(½ cup/125 mL)
flour	

Cut fish into bite-sized pieces. Shell and devein the shrimp. Put 2 pounds (1 kg) fish, 2 dozen shrimp, and 2 dozen scallops (meat only) into a plastic sealable container. Add 2 tablespoons each olive oil and Cajun seasoning, mix well, and marinate 1 hour in refrigerator. Heat 3 tablespoons olive oil in a large pan. Chop 1 large onion and 4 to 5 cloves garlic; sauté in hot oil until soft. Add ½ cup (125 mL) flour, stirring until brown. Gradually add 6 cups (1.5 L) fish stock, stirring until mixture thickens and boils. Add 1 small can tomato paste, 2 large cans tomatoes (with liquid), and ½ cup (125 mL) dry white wine. Stir until mixture boils, then boil until mixture thickens. Sauté fish, shrimp, and scallops in separate pan until tender. Add to soup base just before serving. Serve with Tabasco sauce on the side.

Tomato Shellfish Soup

mussels, clams,	canned tomatoes
or oysters	tomato paste
olive oil	fish stock
garlic	dry white wine
onion	mixed herbs
zucchini squash	croutons
celery	
hot red peppers	
(chilies)	

Heat 3 tablespoons olive oil in large pan. Chop 1 large onion, 4 cloves garlic, 2 medium-sized zucchinis, 2 celery stalks, and hot red peppers (to taste). Sauté in oil until onion is clear. Add 1 cup (250mL) white wine, 2 cups (500 mL) fish stock, tomato paste, tomatoes (with liquid), and 1 table-

spoon mixed herbs. Simmer uncovered 30 minutes. Add 2 dozen shellfish and simmer uncovered until they open. Serve with croutons.

Easy Salmon Soup

canned salmon,	milk
drained and flaked	flour
butter	salt and pepper

Melt 4 tablespoons butter in a large pot. Add 8 cups (2 L) water. Add 2 cans salmon. Simmer 15 to 20 minutes. Add ¼ cup (63 mL) flour, stirring until soup thickens. Add salt and pepper to taste.

Pepper, Fish, and Lime Soup

boneless white	garlic
fish fillets	ginger
carrot	hot red peppers
celery	(chilies)
onion	lime juice
spinach	soy sauce
bean sprouts	fish stock
peanut oil	

Heat 1 tablespoon peanut oil in large pan. Chop 1 large onion, 3 cloves garlic, and red peppers to taste. Mix in 2 teaspoons grated ginger, and sauté until onions are clear. Add 2 tablespoons each soy sauce and lime juice, and 8 cups (2 L) fish stock. Simmer uncovered 30 minutes. Add thinly sliced carrot, 1 celery stalk, and 1 bunch shredded spinach. Cut 1 pound (455 g) fish into bite-sized pieces and add to soup. Simmer uncovered 5 minutes.

Oyster Chowder

oysters	milk
bacon	butter
potatoes	flour
onion	salt and pepper

Fry 8 slices of bacon until brown. Add 2 chopped potatoes, 2 onions, and 1 teaspoon each salt and pepper. Add boiling water to the pan until this mixture is covered. Simmer uncovered until vegetables are tender. Add 4 cups (1 L) milk, 1 tablespoon butter, and 2 tablespoons flour. Simmer, stirring until mixture thickens. Add 2 dozen oysters and oyster juice. Simmer uncovered 3 minutes. Serve with croutons or toast.

Crab and Corn Chowder

crabmeat,	potatoes
canned or fresh	tomatoes
corn	milk
celery, chopped	olive oil
onion	salt and pepper

Sauté celery and 2 chopped onions in 3 tablespoons hot olive oil. Add 2 cups (500 mL) each corn (fresh off the cob, canned, or frozen) and crabmeat and sauté 3 minutes. Add 2 finely chopped potatoes, 3 chopped tomatoes, and 1 cup (250 mL) water. Cover and cook on low heat 30 minutes. Add 2 cups (500 mL) whole milk and heat to boil. Sift in 3 tablespoons flour and stir until chowder thickens. Add salt and pepper to taste.

Leek, Potato, and Clam Chowder

chopped clams	milk
bacon	grated cheese
potatoes	butter
leeks (for onions)	parsley
garlic	salt and pepper
fish stock	

Chop 5 potatoes and boil in salted water until tender; drain and mash. Heat 1 tablespoon butter in large pan. Sauté 2 chopped leeks, crushed garlic, 6 slices bacon (cooked and crumbled), and 2 cups (500 mL) clams. Add 6 cups (1.5 L) fish stock and ¼ cup (63 mL) chopped parsley. Bring mixture to boil, then reduce heat and simmer uncovered 25 minutes. Add mashed potato and stir in 1 cup (250 mL) whole milk. Simmer 15 minutes. Stir in 1 cup (250 mL) grated cheese of your choice. Add salt and pepper to taste.

Easy Leftover Soup

fish stock or cubed chicken/beef stock	red, green, or yellow pepper
seafood (leftover cooked fish fillets, lobster tails, shrimp)	coriander
	mixed herbs
	croutons
ginger	
carrot	

Heat broth in pan. Divide and place a mixture of chopped vegetables, bite-sized seafood, grated ginger, coriander, and mixed herbs in serving bowls. Pour boiling broth over mixture in bowls. Serve with croutons and hot sauce on the side.

Island Fish Soup

fresh fish (boneless chunks of fillet,
    sections of backbone, throats,
    split heads—any meaty fish part)
water
vegetables
potatoes, rice, pasta, or any local starch
seasonings
hot sauce to taste (optional)
peppers to taste (optional)
olive oil

This one works for any kind of fish and is more than a personal favorite—it's a way of life, worldwide, particularly in less developed areas. It is a flexible, highly variable recipe, and can be shaped according to the spices, starches, and vegetables of the region you are visiting. It's delicious any time of day, actually improves with overnight refrigeration and with reheating, and you need not prepare anything else to accompany it. You can easily invite a dozen or more people to dinner and satisfy them all from one big pot. No dish better expresses the soul and imagination of the chef, nor is better appreciated by native guests from any shore. It's easy and *fun*, even therapeutic, to prepare. We would like to salute Arthur Albury (Nassau, Bahamas), Hollis John (Tobago, West Indies), Granny Bell (Antigua, West Indies), Patrick Rogers (St. Kitts, West Indies), and Franklin Thomas (Jamaica, West Indies) as influential masters of this approach, with whom we have had the good fortune to share many a pot over the years.

It's imperative to the end result to crank up your sound system a little and play music that is as soulful and bass-heavy as possible, with reggae, junkanoo, calypso, and soca being top choices. Brazilian and other Latin and Caribbean beats, bossa nova jazz, or New Orleans jazz also work. If you're at a complete loss, put on Kermit Ruffins and the Barbecue Swingers *Live* and play "What Is New Orleans?" very loud (available from Basin Street Records; see appendix 1).

Add water to your biggest pot, just over half full. Place on high heat. Chop onions and potatoes and dump them in. Add a dash of olive oil, and sprinkle in seasoning. Grab a large wooden stirring spoon and stir—the motion is critical: move yuh hips . . . wine yuh wais' to dah drum an' de bass . . . an' raise yuh (nonstirring) hand if ya' like it! The motion of your body is now stirring the pot.

OK, cool it for a moment and cut up the vegetables, adding the hard ones first (like carrots). Stir. Add softer vegetables (like green beans and chopped bell peppers) when the potato chunks are just done. Stir. Reduce the heat to medium-high.

Sprinkle in some seasoning. Add a dash of your favorite sauce, such as Jamaican Pick-a-Peppa, teriyaki, Worchestershire, local concoction, or a bit of tomato paste or sauce. Turn up the music slightly, sip a favorite wine, beer, rum, fruit juice, or herbal tea, and stir it all together with the same motion. Feel your soup, smell the aroma—add a dash of this or that. When the last vegetables are just cooked, turn the heat to low and add boneless fish chunks. Stir lightly and cover. Turn off the heat as the fish is just cooked and serve. Total time: about an hour and a half, less with a pressure cooker.

Additions:

Rice: Add just before vegetables are done.

Pasta: Add just after vegetables are done.

Limes: Slice, and squeeze in a little juice.

Any other starches and vegetables: Add at the times given for similar items.

Dumplings: Thicken flour with water and vegetable oil, form into golf balls, and add shortly before vegetables are done.

Variations:

White chowders: Overcook the onion/potato base, thicken with condensed milk or similar product, omit vegetables or add sparingly during the last third of the base cooking process.

Red chowders: Same as white, but add tomato sauce and diced stewed tomatoes instead of dairy product.

Use of bony fish parts: Put second pot on stove, half-fill with water, and bring to a boil. Chop fish to submersible size, grab with tongs, hold each piece in boiling water for two minutes, piling onto a large plate as they are done. Carefully pick the meat off each bony section and place on a second plate. Add as vegetables are done, turn off heat, stir in, serve. We realize that most coastal native folks drop the heads and other parts straight in just as they would a boneless chunk, and that eating it off the bone is great. However, accidental swallowing of a fish bone while far from medical care can actually be fatal if it ruptures the esophagus. It is quite easy to do, especially for kids, so we recommend boneless fish soup for voyaging sailors.

Main Courses

Just in case you elect not to immerse yourself totally in eating soup and assorted starters full time, we include recipes best suited for the main course of your meal.

Whole Marinated Snapper

> snapper, grouper, porgy
> (smaller fish with delicate,
> firm, white meat
> preferred)
> garlic
> shallots or spring onions
> ginger
> basil
> fresh hot red peppers (chilies)
> balsamic vinegar
> sugar
> soy sauce

Gut, gill, and scale fish (1 small- to medium-sized fish per person). Cut 3 to 4 deep slits on both sides of the fish. Mince 4 cloves garlic, 3 tablespoons grated ginger, chop 3 shallots, and dice 3 hot peppers. Combine these ingredients with 1 tablespoon basil, 1 tablespoon sugar, ⅓ cup (83 mL) balsamic vinegar, ¼ cup (63 mL) olive oil, 3 tablespoons of soy sauce, and 1/2 cup (125 mL) water. Mix all ingredients completely. Place fish individually in the marinade container. With your hands and fingers, rub the blend well over the exterior of the fish, into the slits on the sides of the body and the inside of the head and gut cavity. Pour the remaining marinade over fish until submerged, and refrigerate overnight. Place fish in a deep baking dish and thoroughly ladle the marinade over the fish, covering and barely submerging them. Bake uncovered in moderate oven until fish is just cooked to the bone—moist and tender. Remove fish and place on serving plate, ladle or spoon marinade over the fish before serving.

Baked Coconut Fish #1

boneless white fish fillets (enough for four adult servings)	coconut cream paprika rice or couscous
shallots or spring onions	
green, red, or yellow peppers	
zucchini squash	
mushrooms	

Place fish fillets in deep baking dish. Chop enough shallots, peppers, mushrooms, and zucchini to yield 2 cups (500 mL) mixed. Sprinkle chopped vegetables over fish. Pour 1 can unsweetened coconut cream over mixture. Sprinkle with paprika. Bake in moderate oven until fish is just cooked through, and parts gently in moist flakes (about 20 to 30 minutes for 1-in./25 mm thick fillets). Serve over rice or couscous.

Baked Coconut Fish #2

boneless white fish fillets (enough for four adult servings)	tomato onion flour salt and pepper
coconut cream	paprika
curry powder	olive oil

Rinse fillets, allow to drain, and pat dry with a clean, absorbent rag or paper towel. Roll in flour seasoned with salt, pepper, and paprika. Sauté fish 2 to 3 minutes on each side in 3 tablespoons hot olive oil. In a separate large pot, add 2 cups coconut cream, mix with 2 teaspoons curry powder and one large chopped onion. Bring to boil. Add fish and 2 quartered tomatoes. Boil 1 to 2 minutes. Serve over starch (e.g., rice, pasta, potatoes, or couscous).

Steamed Fish

grouper, snapper, hogfish or other wrasse, sea bass, porgy (any smaller firm, white meat fish)	salt ginger onion peanut oil soy sauce

Gut, gill, and scale fish. Wash in cold water. Drain and pat fish dry with a clean absorbent rag or paper towel. Make 3 to 4 diagonal slits down each side. Rub thoroughly by hand with a mixture of salt, grated ginger, and minced onion. Steam fish until just cooked to the bone, so translucent raw meat has barely turned white and will flake off bone (10 minutes or so for small fish with compressed bodies, 25 minutes for more cylindrical fish and individual fish exceeding about 2 pounds (1 kg). Pour ¼ cup (63 mL) *hot* peanut oil over fish. Serve with soy sauce.

Stuffed Mussels

mussels, scrubbed and debearded	tomatoes
	bread crumbs
bacon, cooked and crumbled	lemon or lime
	fresh Parmesan cheese
olive oil	string or twine
garlic	
shallots or spring onions	

Steam 2 dozen mussels; discard any that do not open. Heat 2 tablespoons olive oil in large skillet. Sauté 2 cloves chopped garlic and 1 bunch chopped spring onions. Add 2 to 3 minced tomatoes and ½ cup (125 mL) bread crumbs. Remove from heat and mix with juice from 1 lemon or lime, ¼ cup (63 ML) freshly grated Parmesan cheese, and salt and pepper to taste. Place 1 teaspoon of stuffing into each opened mussel. Close mussel, and tie with string or twine. Steam stuffed mussels 3 to 5 minutes. Serve with Tabasco sauce on the side.

Banana Leaf Lime Fish

banana leaves (can substitute aluminum foil)	olive oil
	onion
	fresh ginger root
boneless fish fillets (enough for 6 adult servings)	cayenne (hot chili) pepper
	bananas (or other fresh fruit, such as apricot or mango)
garlic	
lemon or lime	
saffron	

Cut fish and fruit (two parts fish to one part fruit) into bite-sized pieces and marinate with 3 cloves minced garlic, 2 tablespoons freshly grated ginger root, 1 teaspoon saffron, the juice of 1 lemon or lime, and cayenne (hot) pepper to taste. Refrigerate marinating mixture for at least 1 hour. Using a large skillet or wok, quickly fry fish mixture in 2 tablespoons of *hot* olive oil. Lay out banana leaves (or foil pieces) so they cover the bottom of a steamer. Put in fish-banana mixture and wrap in leaf or foil so no juices can escape. Steam 20 to 30 minutes. This goes very nicely with sweet potato (kumara).

Crabs, Prawns, or Shrimp in Coconut Milk

live crabs (almost any sufficiently large species works fine), prawns, or shrimp	fresh ginger root
	onion
	coconut cream
	butter
garlic	tomato sauce
fresh red chili peppers (optional)	turmeric
	saffron

Crabs: Steam live crabs in a large pot over boiling water. Remove from pot when bright red, open "key" underneath crab (start at point of V indentation) and lever off shell, remove guts and gills, and wash. Quarter body.

Shrimp or prawns: Sauté whole (unshelled) in olive oil until pink or red.

Combine ½ cup (125 mL) tomato sauce, 1 can coconut cream, 1 tablespoon butter, 4 cloves chopped garlic, 1 large chopped onion, 2 tablespoons freshly grated ginger root, 1 teaspoon each turmeric and saffron, chopped hot chili peppers to taste, and 1 cup (250 mL) water. Bring slowly to boil in a large pot. Add crab pieces, prawns, or shrimp and simmer covered 20 minutes. Serve over rice or couscous.

Maryland Steamed Crabs

live blue crabs (*Callinectes sapidus* or similar species)	Old Bay seasoning
	garlic
	vinegar

Bring equal parts water and vinegar to a vigorous boil in a large steamer pot. Add live crabs, whole garlic buds cut in half, and a generous amount of Old Bay seasoning. Steam crabs until they're bright red. Dump the crabs on an improvised picnic table—preferably on shore, perhaps on deck—and cover any valued surfaces with a drop cloth or newspapers. Hammer and crack away, breaking exoskeleton to get at the sweet seasoned meat in the body, legs, and claws. Most folks take care not to eat the gills.

Whole Ginger-Baked Fish

sea bream, snapper,	lemon or lime juice
sweetlips, small	soy sauce
grouper, mahi mahi	olive oil
(firm white fish	parsley
meat preferred)	dry white wine
ginger	sugar
garlic	

Gut, gill, and scale about 3 pounds (1.5 kg) fish. Rinse thoroughly, drain, pat dry with a clean rag or paper towel, and rub with a mix consisting of the juice from 1 lemon or lime and 3 tablespoons olive oil. Refrigerate 1 hour. Form ginger marinade by mixing 1 tablespoon crushed ginger, 2 cloves crushed garlic, ¼ cup (63 mL) soy sauce, and 1 cup (250 mL) white wine. Place fish in deep baking dish and pour ginger marinade over fish. Bake in moderate oven, basting frequently with marinade, 30 minutes. Sprinkle fish with 1 tablespoon sugar and broil (turn up heat in oven) briefly to glaze fish. Serve fish garnished with grated ginger, and serve the juices on the side.

Aluminum Foil Beach Bake

fish (any type)	any other fresh
onions	indigenous
potatoes, yams,	vegetables
sweet potato, or	lemon or lime
similar starchy	garlic
produce	mixed herbs
celery	olive oil
tomato	tinfoil
zucchini squash	

Spread aluminum foil out as an oversized plate. Gut, gill, scale, and slit the sides of the fish, then rub thoroughly with a mixture of crushed garlic, mixed herbs, and pepper. Place the fish on the foil. Chop vegetables and spread over fish. Drizzle 1 tablespoon olive oil and the juice of 1 to 2 lemons or limes over the vegetables. Wrap the foil securely up, over, and around the prepared fish so the juices cannot escape. Place the packet on or just beside hot cooking coals, turning occasionally. Remove when fish is done (white to the bone, moist chunks that separate easily from bone). Eat right out of the foil.

Fire-Roasted Beach Fish

flying fish, small jacks and other reef fish (e.g., soldierfish or squirrelfish, surgeonfish where safe from ciguatera)

Gut and gill fish; scaling is optional. Grill over open fire or place in or near embers from dying fire, turning with a stick. Remove the moment meat is done to the bone, and eat as finger food.

Barbecue Marinades for Fish

Marinades particularly enhance the flavor of fish bound for any sort of grill, barbecue, coal pot, or other outdoor cooking device. Like island fish soup, variations are endless, and it's more important to understand basic ingredients and how they work together than to measure anything or worry about precision. You can start with simple, prepackaged marinades such as various salad dressings (e.g., Italian, honey-mustard), barbecue, teriyaki, Jamaican jerk, plum, sweet chili, and all manner of other sauces, even the new canned Indian curry sauces (e.g., Tikka Marsala, Rosen Josh, Korma, Madras, and others). These all produce wonderful results when allowed to soak into fish steaks, fillets, or whole fish before grilling.

Many such mixes are simply a seasoned, flavored liquid based on oil, vinegar, and water. You can easily concoct your own delicious marinades. Graduate from store-bought blends to a few quick fixes based on stuff you probably have stashed somewhere on board, and then get as elaborate as you like.

Quick Marinade #1

soy sauce	ketchup
Worcestershire sauce	water
garlic	

Combine 1 cup (250 mL) soy sauce, ¼ cup (63 mL) Worcestershire sauce, 2 tablespoons minced garlic, 2 tablespoons ketchup, and 1 cup (250 mL) water. Mix well.

Quick Marinade #2

honey	mixed herbs
mustard	peanut oil
vinegar	water

Combine ½ cup (125 mL) honey, ½ cup (125 mL) mustard (spicy brown mustard is best), 1 cup (250 mL) wine vinegar, 2 tablespoons mixed herbs, 3 tablespoons peanut oil, and 1 cup (250 mL) water. Mix well.

Quick Marinade #3

teriyaki sauce	lemon pepper
lime	red wine
parsley	olive oil
thyme	

Mix 2 parts teriyaki sauce, 2 parts olive oil, 1 part lime juice, and 1 part red wine. Throw in hefty doses of parsley, thyme, and lemon pepper, and stir with feeling. While stirring, if you're feeling frisky, sneak in a little shot of your favorite yellow or red pepper sauce and taste; mellow with a shot of tomato paste or ketchup if it was too much.

Barbecued Fish

Tuna, wahoo, big snapper and grouper, shark, mahi mahi, swordfish and other billfish, mackerel, trevally and large jacks (California and southern yellowtail, almaco jacks, amberjacks), and any other firm-fleshed fishes, cut into steaks, slabs, or fillets, are wonderful candidates for the grill. Smaller, more delicate fishes should be gutted, gilled, scaled, and barbecued whole. Cut the bloodlines out of fillets to avoid a strong taste. Marinate fish at least 1 hour before barbecuing. Brush hot grill with oil (to prevent fish from sticking). Adjust heat to medium (if your grill has cold spots, you can attain the same effect by moving fish around). Place fish on the grill, basting occasionally. When upper side of fish begins to visibly change color, turn it. Baste and continue to cook 3 to 5 minutes, depending on thickness of fish.

Do not overcook, keeping in mind that fish will continue to cook after you've removed it from the source of heat. Slight pink coloration in the middle of a tuna steak or slab is cooked *perfectly* for maximum flavor and tenderness.

Grilled Lobster Tails

lobster tails, split lengthwise	butter
	garlic

Mince garlic and add to melted butter. Place lobster tails on hot grill, shell side down. Frequently baste tail meat with garlic butter (which infuses down and pools in the shell). Meat is done when the shells are red and meat is white and tender—about 5 to 10 minutes cooking time, depending on size.

Grilled Shellfish

clams, mussels, scallops, oysters (whole, in shell)	lemon or lime
	butter
	garlic (optional)

Scrub shells and remove beards from mussels. Place on hot grill, turning occasionally until they open. Mince garlic and add to melted butter. Squeeze lemon or lime juice over meat in opened shells. Serve with melted garlic butter for dipping.

Blackened Fish Fillets

boneless fish fillets (enough for four adult servings)	oregano
	chili powder
	garlic
Cajun seasoning	olive oil
onion salt or powder	
paprika	
ground black pepper	

Combine 1 tablespoon each Cajun seasoning, onion salt, paprika, pepper, oregano, chili powder, and minced garlic. Roll fish in spice mixture. Heat 3 tablespoons olive oil in a large skillet. Sear fillets briefly in very hot oil, flip, sear other side, and remove.

Crunchy Baked Fish Fillets

boneless white meat	butter
fish fillets	lemon or lime
corn flake breakfast	ground pepper
cereal	

Crush cereal into small bits (you'll need about ½ cup/125 mL crushed flakes per fillet), mix in pepper to taste, and set aside this container. Squeeze the juice from 1 lemon or lime into melted butter into a second container. Rinse, drain, and pat dry fish fillets. Dip fillets into melted butter-lime mixture. Roll in cereal mix until well coated. Place fillets on nonstick baking sheet. Bake in moderate oven until just cooked through and remove (usually about 20 to 30 minutes, depending on thickness).

Fruity Fish Sauté

fillet sections of	lemon or lime juice
firm fish meat	butter
(mahi mahi,	fish stock
snapper, grouper,	dry white wine
emperor, porgy,	flour
and the like)	paprika
mango, pineapple,	salt and pepper
banana, papaya—	
any medley of	
sweet, fresh	
fruit (use canned	
fruit if necessary)	

Select equal amounts of fish fillet and fruits. Rinse, drain, and pat dry the fillets. Skin and slice the fruit. Roll fish in flour seasoned with salt, pepper, and paprika. Heat 1 tablespoon butter in skillet and sauté fish 2 to 3 minutes per side, then remove from pan. Add 2 tablespoons butter, ½ cup (125 mL) white wine, and the juice from 1 lemon or lime to pan and reduce over medium heat. Add fruit and cook until fruit is heated throughout. Pour fruit mixture over fish and serve immediately.

Fruity Baked Fish

boneless white fish	papaya
fillets (enough for	lemon or lime
4 adult servings)	red and green peppers
onion	mixed herbs
mangos	paprika
pineapple	rice or couscous
bananas	

Rinse, drain, and dry fish fillets. Place in deep baking pan. Slice 2 cups of mixed fruit into bite-sized pieces and combine in separate bowl with thin strips of red and green pepper, chopped onion, 1 tablespoon mixed herbs, 1 teaspoon paprika, and 1 cup (250 mL) fruit juice. Mix well and pour enough into baking dish to cover fish 3 inches (8 cm) or so. Bake in moderate oven 20 to 30 minutes or until fish is perfectly cooked. Serve over rice or couscous.

Sweet & Sour Fish

boneless fish fillets	soy sauce
(enough for 4	wine vinegar
adult servings)	sugar
tomato sauce	flour
pineapple	salt and pepper
water chestnuts	mixed herbs
green and red peppers	vegetable oil
egg whites	corn flour
Worcestershire sauce	rice or couscous

Chop fish into bite-sized pieces. Soak in egg whites (enough to cover). Roll fish chunks in flour seasoned with salt, pepper, paprika, and mixed herbs. Deep-fry fish in hot vegetable oil. Mix ½ cup (125 mL) each tomato sauce, Worcestershire sauce, and soy sauce in large pot. Add 1 cup (250 mL) wine vinegar and ½ cup (125 mL) sugar, and slowly bring to boil. Add 2 cups (500 mL) pineapple chunks, 2 cups (500 mL) chopped green and red peppers, and water chestnuts. Return sauce to a gentle boil. Add fish chunks, reduce heat. If necessary, add corn flour to thicken. Serve over rice or couscous.

Thai Satay Tuna

tuna, wahoo, mahi mahi, trevally, or other firm fish (enough for 4 adult servings)	fresh ginger
	low-salt soy sauce
	peanut oil
	Tabasco sauce (or chili sauce or fresh hot peppers)
chunky peanut butter	
garlic	

Melt 4 tablespoons chunky peanut butter in a large skillet with 1 tablespoon peanut oil, 1 cup (250 mL) low-salt soy sauce, 1 tablespoon each minced garlic and fresh ginger root. Add Tabasco sauce or chopped hot peppers to taste. Bring sauce to gentle boil, stirring well. Rinse, drain, pat dry, remove bloodline, and cut fish fillets into serving-sized pieces. Add fish to boiling sauce, turning pieces in order to cover well with the sauce. Reduce to medium heat, cover, and simmer 10 minutes, occasionally basting with sauce. Remove from heat, turn fillets, and replace cover. Let sit 5 minutes. Fish will continue to cook and should be perfectly done. Serve over starch of your choice (rice, pasta, or couscous).

Curry Fish/Seafood

boneless fish fillets or any type of shelled, cleaned, viscera- and debris-free seafood flesh	celery
	curry powder
	coconut cream
	turmeric
	cumin
potatoes	coriander
bananas	chili powder
onion	olive oil
carrots	water
apple	fish or chicken stock
green beans	rice, couscous, or
sultanas/raisins	other starch
broccoli	
mushrooms	

Use a large skillet to heat 3 tablespoons olive oil, adding 2 finely chopped potatoes and 1 large onion; sauté until onion is clear. Add 1 teaspoon each coriander, turmeric, and cumin, then 3 tablespoons curry powder and hot chili powder to taste. Add 1 tablespoon each minced garlic and fresh grated ginger. Add enough water to make a thick paste. Add 4 cups (1 L) fish or chicken stock and 1 cup (250 mL) coconut cream. Simmer uncovered until potatoes are cooked. Add 1 to 2 cups (250 to 500 mL) various chopped vegetables. Rinse, dry, and cut fish/seafood into bite-sized pieces. Stir 2 to 3 cups (500 to 750 mL) seafood into skillet, simmering until seafood is just tender. Serve over rice, couscous, or another starch. Serves 4 to 6.

Sautéed Fish or Seafood with Chinese Cabbage

boneless fish fillets or any type of shelled, cleaned, viscera- and debris-free seafood flesh	green and red peppers
	soy sauce
	peanut oil
	Worcestershire sauce
	red curry paste
	mixed herbs
Chinese cabbage (can substitute regular cabbage)	cumin
garlic	
fresh ginger	
carrots	
celery	
zucchini squash	

Use a large skillet to heat 3 tablespoons peanut oil. Sauté 1 teaspoon of minced garlic and 1 tablespoon freshly grated ginger. Add 3 cups (750 mL) shredded cabbage, 2 grated carrots, 2 finely chopped stalks celery, and 2 chopped zucchini. Mix 2 cups (500 mL) soy sauce, 1 tablespoon red curry paste, 3 tablespoons Worcestershire sauce, and 1 teaspoon each mixed herbs and cumin. Pour this blend into skillet, mix well—thoroughly infusing vegetables—and simmer uncovered 20 minutes. Rinse, drain, pat dry, and chop 2 to 3 cups (500 to 750 mL) fish/seafood into bite-sized bits. Add seafood to skillet, stirring well. Cover and simmer 5 minutes or until seafood is tender. Serve over starch (rice, pasta, or couscous). Serves 4 to 6.

Fish Stuffed with Crab and Scallops

boneless white fish fillets (flounder, striped bass, sea bass, bream, snapper; 2 thin pan-sized fillets per serving)	scallops
	onion
	green and red peppers
	bread crumbs
	grated cheese
	egg
	butter
crabmeat, fresh or canned	paprika
	lemon or lime

Rinse, drain, and pat dry fillets (fillets need to be thin; if necessary, butterfly so that you have two thinner fillets). Spread smaller fillets, side to side, on bottom of shallow baking dish (one fillet deep). Use a separate bowl to mix 1 cup (250 mL) crab, 1 dozen scallops, 1 cup (250 mL) bread crumbs, 1 cup (250 mL) grated cheese, two beaten eggs, ¼ cup (63 mL) each minced onion and green and red peppers, and 1 tablespoon melted butter. Create small mounds, and place one atop each fillet in baking dish. Cover each fillet and crab mound with another, slightly larger fillet. Press edges of sandwiched fillets together. Brush top fillet with melted butter and sprinkle with paprika. Bake covered in moderate oven for 30 minutes or until fish is done. Serve with lemon or lime wedges.

Coconut and Spinach Fish/Seafood

boneless fish fillets or any type of shelled, cleaned, viscera- and debris-free seafood flesh	coconut cream
	olive oil
	garlic
	fresh ginger root
spinach (or substitute well-cooked taro leaves or silverbeet)	

Mix 1 tablespoon each minced garlic and fresh grated ginger in 2 tablespoons olive oil and sauté in a large skillet. Shred 3 to 4 cups (750 mL to 1 L) spinach and add to skillet. Pour 2 cups (500 mL) coconut cream into skillet and simmer uncovered 20 minutes. Chop 2 cups (500 mL) seafood into bite-sized bits and mix into spinach-coconut cream. Simmer covered 5 minutes or until seafood is tender. Serve over starch (rice, couscous, pasta). Serves 4.

Fish/Seafood in Spinach/Taro Leaf Parcels

boneless fish fillets or any type of shelled, cleaned, viscera- and debris-free seafood flesh	green and red pepper
	salt and pepper
	coconut cream
	string or twine
spinach or taro leaves	
onion	

Rinse, drain, pat dry, and cut fish or seafood into large bite-sized pieces. Wash and dry spinach or taro leaves, and arrange in a layered pattern on a flat surface with two lines of string intersecting at 90 degrees (forming a cross) underneath the leaves. Make one "leaf plate" per serving. Chop 1 onion, 1 green pepper, and 1 red pepper and combine in a separate bowl. Then add 1 cup (250 mL) fish/seafood per serving, 1 cup (250 mL) coconut cream, and salt and pepper to taste. Mix well. Place 1 cup (250 mL) seafood mixture in the center of each leaf plate, wrap leaves around to form parcel, and tie with string. Place each parcel in the baking dish and cover with coconut cream. Bake covered in moderate oven for 30 to 40 minutes (or cook underground in a Polynesian-style umu, see page 377; for umu cooking, wrap finished taro or spinach packet in banana leaves).

Seafood Enchiladas

boneless fish fillets or any type of shelled, cleaned, viscera- and debris-free seafood flesh	flour tortillas
	grated cheese
	mixed herbs
	coriander
	jalapeño peppers (optional)
onion	olive oil
canned minced tomatoes with juice	lettuce, tomato, guacamole
sour cream	

In a large skillet, sauté one chopped onion in 2 tablespoons hot olive oil. Cut seafood into bite-sized pieces (½ cup/125 mL per serving), and add 1 tablespoon each coriander and mixed herbs. Sauté until seafood is tender. In a separate bowl, mix one large can minced tomatoes (including juice), 1 cup (250 mL) of sour cream, and jalapeños to taste. Dip tortillas in this tomato mixture and allow to drain. Place ½ cup (125 mL) or so seafood mixture on tortilla and roll, folding in edges, and place (seam side down) in baking dish. Repeat with remaining tortillas/seafood (allow 1 to 2 enchiladas per person). Pour remaining tomato mixture over enchiladas and sprinkle with grated cheese. Bake in moderate oven for 30 to 40 minutes. Top with shredded lettuce, tomato, and guacamole.

Seafood Marinara for a Big Crew

mussels, scrubbed and debearded	onion
shrimp, shelled and deveined	red, green, and yellow peppers
squid, eviscerated, rinsed, cross-sectioned into rings, and sliced tentacles	garlic
	tomatoes (fresh or canned)
	basil
	oregano
scallops	olive oil
boneless white fish fillets	dry white wine

Add three cloves chopped garlic and 1 large onion, chopped, to 2 tablespoons olive oil in a large skillet

or wok and sauté. Add ½ cup (125 mL) dry white wine and 2 dozen mussels, cover and cook until mussels open (throw away any that don't open). Set mussels aside. Add 2 cups (500 mL) chopped peppers, 2 large cans tomatoes with liquid (or 4 cups/1 L fresh minced), and 1 tablespoon each basil and oregano. Sauté uncovered until juices reduce by half. Add 2 dozen shrimp, 1 dozen small squid, 2 dozen scallops, and 1¼ pounds (500 g) fillets, stir well, and sauté until seafood is tender. Serve over pasta.

Seafood Pesto Lasagna

boneless white fish fillets	ricotta cheese
	lasagna sheets
shrimp	pesto
pepperoni, sliced	grated cheese
spring onions	garlic
mushrooms (fresh or cooked)	olive oil
green, red, and yellow peppers	
cottage cheese	

Place chopped garlic, 2 pounds (1 kg) boneless white fish fillets, and 2 dozen shrimp (shelled and deveined), all cut into bite-sized pieces, in 2 table-spoons hot olive oil in a large skillet and sauté. Add 2 cups (500 mL) pesto and cook until seafood is tender. Chop spring onion, peppers, and mushroom; set aside. Spread small amount of seafood mixture in deep baking pan, then layer lasagna noodles, cottage cheese, ricotta cheese, seafood mixture, chopped vegetables, and pepperoni. Continue layering to fill baking pan, ending with a top layer of lasagna noodles. Spoon remaining seafood mixture on top, and sprinkle with grated cheese. Bake in moderate oven for 1 hour. Serves 6.

Seafood Quiche

pie pastry (follow instructions for easy "all-in-one" pastry in next recipe)	free seafood flesh chopped vegetables (broccoli, peppers, mushrooms)
eggs	milk
boneless fish fillets or any type of shelled, cleaned, viscera- and debris-	butter grated cheese mixed herbs

In a large bowl, beat 8 eggs and add ¼ cup (63 mL) milk, 1 tablespoon melted butter, 1 tablespoon mixed herbs, 1 cup (250 mL) chopped vegetables, and 1 cup (250 mL) seafood. Pour into pie crust. Bake in moderate oven 30 minutes or until eggs set. Sprinkle with grated cheese and bake until cheese melts.

Nancy's Easy "All-in-One" Pie-Plate Pastry

flour	vegetable oil
milk	salt

In a pie plate, combine 2 cups (500 mL) flour, 2 tablespoons cold milk, ½ cup (125 mL) vegetable oil, and a pinch salt. Mix and press into plate, bevel edges. Fill and bake. This pie crust works great for seafood, meat, and fruit pies, and its simplicity well suits life afloat.

Fish Pie

canned tuna, salmon, or smoked fish fillet	canned mixed vegetables butter
pie pastry (see previous recipe)	garlic onion
cooked mashed potatoes	milk mixed herbs
flour	

Heat 2 tablespoons butter in a skillet, and sauté 1 clove minced garlic and 1 small chopped onion. Stir in 1 tablespoon each flour, mixed herbs, and

milk. Add salt and pepper to taste. Gradually add 1 cup (250 mL) additional milk and bring to boil, stirring until sauce thickens. Add 1 can drained tuna or salmon or 1 pound (½ kg) minced smoked fish, and 1 can drained, mixed vegetables. Line bottom of pastry with ½ cup (125 mL) mashed potatoes, and pour fish-vegetable mixture over potatoes. Cover with another ½ cup (125 mL) or so mashed potatoes. Bake in moderate oven 30 minutes.

Fish/Seafood Cakes

cooked boneless fish or seafood (fish fillet, crab, clam, conch, shrimp, lobster)	red, green, or yellow peppers garlic eggs bread crumbs
mashed potatoes	peanut oil
onion	mixed herbs
	salt and pepper

Mix equal amounts chopped fish/seafood and mashed potatoes. Chop and add 1 medium onion and 1 cup (250 mL) chopped peppers. Add 1 cup (250 mL) bread crumbs, 1 to 2 beaten eggs, 1 tablespoon mixed herbs, and salt and pepper to taste. Form mixture into patties and fry in hot peanut oil. Drain on paper towels. Serve with cocktail or tartar sauce.

Seafood Coconut Rice

long-grain rice	coconut cream
seafood, cleaned, deboned, shelled, deveined, blood-line removed; fish or invertebrate	coconut flakes water chili powder

Add to a large pot with fitted lid 1 cup (250 mL) each rice, chopped or diced seafood, coconut cream, and water; 1 teaspoon chili powder; and 2 tablespoons flaked coconut. Cover pot and cook on high heat until mixture boils; *do not stir*. Reduce to low heat and cook covered until all liquid is absorbed. Remove from heat and let sit covered 5 minutes before serving. Serves 2 to 4.

Tuna Mac

canned tuna/salmon	milk
cooked macaroni	butter
or rice	eggs
garlic	mixed herbs
onion	paprika
grated cheese	flour

Melt 2 tablespoons butter in a large skillet, add 2 cloves of minced garlic and 1 medium chopped onion; sauté. Stir in 1 tablespoon flour, 1 cup (250 mL) milk, 1 teaspoon each mixed herbs and paprika and stir until mixture boils. Add 2 eggs and ½ cup (125 mL) grated cheese. Stir in drained can of tuna or salmon. In a deep baking dish, mix tuna sauce with 3 cups (750 mL) cooked pasta or rice. Bake in moderate oven 30 minutes. Serves 4.

Coconut Scallops

scallops	bread crumbs
coconut cream	lemon or lime
flaked coconut	

Rinse and dry scallops, dip into coconut cream, roll in mixture made of one part coconut flakes and one part bread crumbs. Place single layer of coated scallops on nonstick baking pan. Bake in moderate oven 30 minutes. Serve with lemon or lime wedges.

Cracked Conch

conch steaks	flour
eggs	salt and pepper
beer	

Beat conch steaks according to instructions in chapter 9, using a 2- by 2-inch (5 by 5 cm) piece of wood, a mallet, or a metal tenderizing hammer to beat methodically each steak into a crushed, flattened patty; proper pretreatment is the key to this dish. Roll in beaten eggs. Dip in batter made of ½ cup (125 mL) flour, ¼ cup (63 mL) beer, and salt and pepper to taste. Fry in hot vegetable oil. Serve with lemon or lime wedges.

Ginger-Baked Ray Wing

skate/stingray wing	paprika
fillet meat	turmeric
butter	garlic
spring onions/shallots	grated ginger
wine vinegar	

Grease shallow baking dish with a little butter. Rinse, drain, and dry fillet meat, cut into serving-sized pieces, and place in baking dish. Sprinkle meat with a blend of chopped spring onion, garlic, wine vinegar, 1 teaspoon each turmeric and paprika, and 2 tablespoons freshly grated ginger root. Bake in moderate oven 20 to 30 minutes or until flesh just cooks through the middle. Serve with lemon or lime wedges.

New Zealand Whitebait Fritters

whitebait, whole 1- to 2-inch (2.5 to 5 cm) slender translucent galaxiid fish in New Zealand, Chile, and Australia; usually juvenile clupeids or engraulids in Europe, the Caribbean, and elsewhere; can substitute thin short strips of boneless fish meat	flour (self-rising) egg milk vegetable oil

Mix 1 cup (250 mL) flour, ½ cup (125 mL) milk, 1 beaten egg, and salt and pepper to taste in a large bowl. Rinse, drain, and lay out on absorbent towel to dry 2 cups (500 mL) whitebait. Mix the whitebait and batter. Heat oil in a large skillet, form and drop in fritter-sized globs of battered white-bait, and fry until brown on both sides. Drain on absorbent cloth or paper towel. Serve with lemon or lime wedges.

Jenny Hart's Fish Mornay

boneless white	water
fish meat	butter
celery	flour
carrot	mayonnaise
salt and pepper	cheese
chicken stock	parsley

Cut 1 carrot and 1 celery stalk into strips and place in a flat-bottomed deep dish. Sprinkle with ½ teaspoon each pepper and chicken stock, add 1 cup (250 mL) water, cover, and microwave on high for 3 minutes. Slice 1 pound (450 g) fish fillet and spread evenly over the carrot-celery mixture, cover, and microwave for 2 minutes. Set aside. Microwave 3 tablespoons butter 30 seconds in a large cup; add 3 tablespoons flour. Drain liquid from fish, and gradually add this to the butter and flour mix. Put this concoction back into the microwave and cook on high heat 3 minutes, removing to stir after the first 1 ½ minutes. Stir in 1 tablespoon mayonnaise and ¾ cup (190 mL) cheese. Add salt and pepper to taste. Pour this finished sauce over the fish, top with ½ cup (125 mL) cheese, and sprinkle parsley on top. Microwave uncovered on high 3 minutes. Serves 2.

Construction and Use of an Umu, or Underground Oven

The umu, or underground oven, plays a central role in many Polynesian cultures. It represents an efficient, healthy way of cooking large quantities of seafood, meat, starches, and vegetables in a relatively short time. The sealed nature of the cooking site promotes tender, delicious results. Best of all, it's easy to do and is perfectly suited to widespread use by cruisers anchored near appropriate shorelines of any latitude.

1. Dig a hole 2 feet (60 cm) or so deep and 3 feet (1 m) across, piling the dirt carefully on a burlap bag, tarp, piece of old sail, or strong plastic sheet. Fill the bottom of the pit with baseball-sized rocks.

2. Place dry firewood over the rocks and light the fire, allowing it to burn until stones become heat-darkened and very hot.

3. While the fire burns, prepare your food for placement in the oven. Wash off cassava (manioc), potatoes, and similar starches. Collect and set aside breadfruit. Prepare packets of seafood and vegetables using taro or spinach leaves and banana leaves (see Fish/Seafood in Taro Leaves recipe, page 373).

4. Cut green saplings and collect broad green leaves from any nontoxic tree or bush (collect a pile of leaves with 4-inch/10 cm or bigger diameters).

5. Place cassava, breadfruit, potatoes, similar items, and seafood packets on the hot rocks.

6. Cover with cross-hatched layers of green saplings, then pile thoroughly and thickly with green leaves.

7. Lift the piece of covering material that has the dirt piled on it and place it over the pit. Spread dirt out to seal the pit completely. Step back— do you see any smoke escaping? Pile dirt on any such vents, no matter how small. Use more dirt from surrounding area if necessary. Occasionally glance over to see if any smoke vents appear, and if so, seal them.

8. *That's it!* Remove the seal in exactly one hour and the food will be perfect—the leaf packets in particular contain some of the most flavorful, succulent seafood you'll ever taste. Discard the outer banana-leaf wrapping but eat the taro inner wrapping. In the tropics, peel and skin cassava (manioc), scrape the skin from breadfruit with your fish scaler, slice, and serve.

Will you remain in this anchorage for a few days or longer? If so, as long as it doesn't offend any locals, leave your umu just as it is for repeated use over the course of your stay.

The Simple Approach

Wendy is the true chef aboard *Élan*. Her creations blend local dishes, seasonings, and techniques with conventional practices, and she is fast and efficient in the galley. She pleases locals, fellow seafarers, fishers, and the occasional professional chef with her creations. No compliment is greater than having a local inhabitant ask for a recipe that utilizes indigenous seafood and produce, or eliciting a sincere positive review and questions from a cooking professional.

Nevertheless, all chefs occasionally experience the need for a break. It's hard work to focus on managing all of the details involved with gourmet meal preparation. And that's precisely the time to employ a little down-island fisher's wisdom and recall that fresh seafood is intrinsically wonderful—and actually requires *very little or no help*.

Eating It Raw

What do I mean by "little or no help"? Well, the most obvious case is consumption raw, on the spot. For instance, the typical routine of a day aboard an off-shore charter-fishing boat in the Florida Keys ends with backing the boat into the marina slip, then offloading the catch for display and photos (unless it was a catch-and-release outing). Next, we process fish at the fish-cleaning table behind the slip while chatting with glowing customers and onlookers. Many clients first step up to the adjacent bar, purchase a cocktail, and sidle back to watch the work. During the course of filleting and steaking, one of my favorite practices was to slice a sizable piece of raw meat from the bone neatly and, without looking up or breaking stride, devour it.

Now, in the islands this wouldn't cause a blink of an eye . . . but folks accustomed to a more processed environment (like most of our customers) would usually choke and sputter something like, "Oh my God! Honey, did you see that!?" This was my cue to glance up innocently. "Excuse me?" By this time of the day, you have (hopefully) developed some credibility: your customers have watched carefully as you played the elements to put together (with a little luck) an exciting day of fishing action, and patiently and authoritatively answered many varied questions about sea life and the ocean (with a few "I don't know"s, too). Thus, while they consciously reject the act they just

witnessed, somewhere in the back of their mind a little voice is saying, "He's been right so far . . . this apparently repulsive practice must have some merit."

This logic nearly unfailingly struggles to the surface. "It won't make you sick? How does it taste?" The majority soon sally forth for a sample: "Just a sliver . . . yeah, real thin, like that." The delicate taste of fresh, firm tuna wins many converts. Sometimes I ask questions like, "Ever been to a sushi bar? How did it taste? How much do you think you'd pay for a piece this size in that place, for something a heck of a lot less fresh than this?"; this occasionally persuades a few more takers. Some folks really get into it and eat quite a bit, but even those who take a taste have made a large, open-minded stride relative to their normal culinary habits. Nearly all of these return customers arrive for the next fishing trip armed with sushi accoutrements, and fall upon the first hapless tuna of the day with relish.

Straight into the Cooker

Captaining a small longliner part-time with a West Indian crew in the Caribbean contrasted in many ways to serving on a much larger American high-seas longliner. Most of the U.S. guys relished store-bought steaks and other red meat, whereas my West Indian crew worshipped fresh seafood. Handlines with trolling feathers and strips would go out the moment we left the dock at Falmouth Harbour, Antigua, and we'd never get much past the cliffs of Shirley Heights by the time the first bonito *(Euthynnus alletteratus)* was aboard. An inch (2.5 cm) of hot seasoned oil by then crackled in the bottom of a deep pot on the gimbaled stove, rising to a crescendo as chunks of boneless, skinless bonito splashed in for brief stints, cooking in a flash. The savory, moist, steaming chunks then made the rounds as the F/V *Jenny B.* steamed eastward, away from the Caribbean sunset, into the long swells of the open Atlantic for a half-week of fishing.

Thanks guys, for teaching me how to work, eat, and cook at the same time, and for teaching me to appreciate the great taste of a species people don't eat in Florida and other "developed" coastlines. The oil stayed on the stove most of the trip, and the still-pulsing hearts of bigeye tuna, yellowfin tuna, and sword-fish took the place of the bonito chunks as we handlined and butchered each night's catch.

The hot-oil method seems to be generally well known among experienced working seafarers. I'll always remember my first exposure one windy, rough, overcast summer day departing West End, Grand Bahama Island, for Walker's Cay on S/V *Small Hope*. Cero mackerel *(Scomberomorus regalis)* were hitting small Clark spoons one after the other. We pulled the lines out soon, and salty old Freddy Austin, never one to be put off by a little rough weather—or to mince words—groused, "OK, *now* I'm gonna show you fellas the *best* way to eat fish." Ten minutes later the aroma from a plate of tasty, tender chunks of mackerel passing around among the crew filled the wheelhouse, and spirits were never higher.

Fast cooking in plain hot oil also works particularly well for fresh-caught squid. While anchored on offshore banks in the Gulf of Mexico aboard the University of Texas vessel R/V *Erin Leddy Jones*, night lighting—used to attract and dip-net live squid for medical research—provided a first taste. Inevitably, several of the dozens of live specimens in the holding tank would show signs of terminal stress and quickly end up eviscerated, cut into strips, and in the sizzling oil. Some of the crew seemed to *imagine* more than actually note signs of duress during the long night. The high correlation between lengthy time since the last snack and newly stressed squid was purely coincidental, I'm sure.

When power levels permit, it is sometimes better to take the same simple "plain, fast-cooked seafood" approach using the microwave rather than the hot-oil method, especially when it's *really* rough. I remembered the impact of Freddy's effort nearly five years later aboard *Small Hope* when we were caught in a sudden-developing tropical depression en route from St. Lucia to St. Croix in the Caribbean. We'd taken a large breaking wave over the transom that shifted the entire wheelhouse 6 inches (15 cm) and filled the hull with enough seawater to drown the engine. Freddy's nephew Bruce somehow got it going again after we evacuated the water with an emergency hand pump (all sails were blown out, and we were controlling our speed on the wave faces with the engine). We were OK, but the crew was tired, a little beat up, and hungry. A quick zap in the microwave of fresh mahi mahi fillets from the refrigerator, slapped between bread slices with a little mayonnaise, and you'd think they had just dined at a five-star restaurant—weariness and light gloom gave way to a mild party atmosphere.

You're Gonna Eat *That?*

With all due respect to more complex and strenuous seafood preparations, now that we've instilled the virtue of simplicity, let's take a brief look at the utilization of various fish and invertebrate species. You'd think that advanced communications, travel, and the generally increasing global nature of our planet would have made faster inroads into this area; however, expanded and more uniform appreciation of seafood is still occurring slowly.

Examples are numerous. To this day, you can stand in back of a charterboat slip in the Florida Keys and fillet or steak a fresh amberjack *(Seriola dumerili)*, and possibly garner a negative comment or deprecating glance from a local. Until recently, you could sometimes even show up at a charter dock early in the morning and see whole bloated amberjack carcasses tied off to a boat transom, awaiting a tow out the channel to be dumped (having provided a pull on the line and a dead fish photo for yesterday's tourist). Yet 300-plus miles (483 km) away in the "panhandle" of *the same state*, amberjack is a prized, popular entreé on most seafood-restaurant menus. Furthermore, amberjacks and other members of the genus *Seriola* (almaco jacks, California yellowtail, southern yellowtail) are highly revered for their food value along other U.S. coastlines and the rest of the world.

Less recently, southeastern Florida charter boats would make fine catches of blackfin tuna *(Thunnus atlanticus)* and toss them whole in the bait freezer, or sometimes discard them after photos, because they were "too bloody, no good to eat"! And do you know that these same boats *still* apply this lack of logic to skipjack tuna *(Katsuwonus pelamis)*? Skipjacks are one of the most popular eating fishes throughout Polynesia and much of the rest of the world. *Many* of the same people who reject the skipjacks they catch then go to the grocery store and buy canned tuna, much of which is . . . *you guessed it, skipjack tuna!* And that canned tuna got heavily stressed in a purse seine, dumped en masse on a hot deck in the tropics, and then slid roughly down a chute to spend up to three months frozen whole before processing! Go to the tuna canneries in Puerto Rico or American Samoa sometime for a tour, and compare the fish rolling down the assembly line to that sleek, fresh fish that wasn't good enough for you; then ask yourself if you're making any sense. Don't get me wrong, canned tuna is great, but few would argue that it's better than fresh-caught tuna.

In the early 1900s, spiny lobsters swarmed the reefs and shallows of southeastern Florida. No one ate them—they were "only good for bait." Sorry for so many hometown examples—more general trends include the increasingly widespread acceptance of squid and octopus dishes in the United States, long a staple in Europe, Asia, Latin America, and tropical islands around the world. High-grade sushi and similar raw marine fish products, once the purview particularly of Japan, are now high-class fare around the world. Serving fresh tuna and broiled swordfish steaks as relatively expensive, high-class restaurant offerings became widespread, mainly as the result of intensive industry marketing in the United States. Blackened redfish *(Sciaenops ocellatus)* was a less calculated, more sudden trend, causing a flurry of overfishing that only emergency regulations curtailed (many other species work fine in this recipe, see page 370).

The point is that, naturally, where you grow up, what you hear and observe from the people around you, and what your family tended to eat shapes your own prejudices and tastes. This frame of reference is seldom completely logical, usually involves a degree of ignorance, and sometimes suffers from location. For instance, many Americans who grew up in the inte-rior of the country don't particularly care for fish. Often this is due to memories of the mildly rancid aroma of long-frozen, relatively poor quality, bland groundfish—the only product reasonably available in the local grocery store—baking in the oven and then not tasting much different from the smell. Present these same people with delicious fresh snapper or various other species, and new seafood lovers are born. Meet new seafood the same way you treat a stranger—rather than make a judgment based on skin color, size, details of skeletal morphology, or exterior features, find out what's inside! Some beautiful, flashy, seductive seafood is dangerous and unreliable, while other humble, less familiar forms never let you down.

Will raw sea-urchin eggs ever attain the popularity of sushi? What undiscovered or undeveloped processes lie in the future, like the huge recent world-wide upsurge in the use of surimi products? Large-scale trends will always depend on availability and abundance of suitable raw material, and the price of catching, processing, and transporting it to the consumer. And therein lies the beauty of collecting and preparing your own seafood as you cruise the world's oceans: you don't need to wait for it to come to you. The occasional mass hysteria and inflated prices over a product that at least *someone* has known for years need not be a part of your life. Regardless of voyage duration or style, power or sail, you'll always be in a position to shape and expand your own horizons with a degree of independence and self-sufficiency that is rare in modern society.

Appendix 1

Sources for Fishing and Related Gear

Shopping from the convenience of your cruising vessel, whether for boat needs or fishing equipment, has never been easier, almost no matter where you are. This appendix can help you contact reliable suppliers for the specific gear recommended in this book. Our selection criteria were combinations of quality equipment selection, competitive prices, prompt international service, good customer service, and professional expertise. We've dealt with each recommended company, some extensively for more than twenty years, enough to know they'll deliver. The net total result is a "one-stop shop" capable of supplying your every need, regardless of particular fishing interest and current location.

Saltwater Fishing Specialists

We selected the majority of lures, hooks, terminal tackle, special accessories, and fishing rods and reels for hook-and-line fishing from the following two current leaders in saltwater sportfishing equipment supply:

Captain Harry's Fishing Supply
100 NE 11th Street
Miami, Florida 33132-1726
305-374-4661
Fax 305-374-3713
Order toll free: 800-327-4088 (from continental U.S., Canada, Hawaii,

Puerto Rico, and U.S. Virgin Islands)
E-mail: sales@captharry.com
http://www.captharry.com

Offshore Angler
2500 E. Kearny
Springfield, Missouri 65898
417-863-2499
Fax 417-873-5060
Order toll free: from continental U.S. only, 800-566-4600; from Australia 800-504-638 or fax 800-504-639; from New Zealand 0-800-445-909 or fax 0-800-445-911
http://www.basspro.com

Both suppliers also market competitive boat-modification equipment related to fishing, including outriggers, downriggers, fish-cleaning tables, rod racks and holders, and other general equipment.

Check out the following subsidiary of Offshore Angler for a full selection of Captain Hank Brown's Hookup Lures and an expanded line-up of saltwater fly-fishing gear, books, and videos:

World Wide Sportsman
P.O. Drawer 787
Islamorada, Florida 33036
305-664-4615
Fax 305-664-3692

Order toll free 800-327-2880 (U.S.)
http://www.outdoor-world.com

Major Boating-Supply Companies

The following major boating supply houses now market a growing amount of fishing gear (including some that overlaps Captain Harry's and Offshore Angler), several specialty items unavailable elsewhere, and a larger array of electronics and other selected boat gear applicable to fishing:

West Marine
P.O. Box 500700
Watsonville, California 95077-5070
408-728-4430
Fax 408-761-4421 (U.S. and Canada), 408-761-4020 (International)
Order toll free: from U.S. and Canada 800-262-8464; from New Zealand 0-800-445-635
E-mail: wmarinternat@earthlink.net
http://www.westmarine.com

Defender Industries, Inc.
42 Great Neck Road
Waterford, Connecticut 06385
Phone orders: 860-701-3400
Customer service: 860-701-3415
Fax 860-701-3424
Order toll free: from U.S. and Canada 800-628-8225; fax 800-654-1616

BOAT/U.S.
884 South Pickett Street
Alexandria, Virginia 22304
Fax 703-461-2883
Order toll free from U. S.:
    800-937-2628
International orders: 703-461-4750
http://www.boatus.com

Fisheries Supply Company
1900 Northlake Way
Seattle, Washington 98103
Phone 206-632-4462
Order toll free 800-426-6930 (U.S.)
Fax 206-634-4600

Commercial and Heavy-Duty Equipment Suppliers

Commercial fishing-supply companies have heavy-duty foul-weather gear, knives and other fish-processing tools and accessories, netting and net-repair supplies, and selected hook models and other useful gear not found elsewhere. They're old hands at international shipping and service.

Atlantic and Gulf Fishing Supply
7000 NW 74th Avenue
Miami, Florida 33166
305-888-9646
Fax 305-888-6027
Order toll free: 800-327-6167 (continental U.S., Alaska, Hawaii, Puerto Rico, and U.S. Virgin Islands)
E-mail: webmaster@atagulf.com
http://www.atagulf.com

Ocean Producers International
965 B North Nimitz Highway
Honolulu, Hawaii 96817
808-537-2905
Fax 808-536-3225
Order toll free: from Australia
    800-144-488
E-mail: tony@pop-hawaii.com
http://www.pop-hawaii.com

Captain Fred King
P.O. Box 485

Tavernier, Florida 33070
305-664-8422

Unique Hand-Operated Winches

Some cruisers may be interested in a single, relatively inexpensive, compact, and rugged line dispenser complete with adjustable drag, and capable of catching everything from large billfish while trolling to deepwater snappers from a 1,000-foot (305 m) depth, operated with a simple hand crank. Thus, no electrical draw or complication, or complex hydraulic drive system, is necessary. Other models can be used on casting rods or as lighter duty reels or rail winches.

Alvey Reels
2-6 Antimony Street
Carole Park
Queensland, 4300 Australia
61-7-3271-2844
Fax 61-7-3271-2451
E-mail: info@alvey.com.au

General Outfitters

Several catalogs market a massive variety of gear aimed at hunters, freshwater and saltwater sportfishers, and campers, some of which cannot be found in any of the other sources. These catalogs also feature a vast array of primarily light-tackle fishing lures applicable to assorted cruising situations, most notably a variety of salmon and trout gear.

Cabela's
812 13th Avenue
Sidney, Nebraska 69160
Order toll free: 800-237-4444 (U.S.)
http://www.cabelas.com

Bass Pro Shops Fishing Specialist Catalog, Red Head Hunting Specialists Catalog, and White River Fly Shop Catalog
Outdoor World
1935 S. Campbell
Springfield, Missouri 65898

Phone 417-887-7334
Order toll free 800-227-7776 (U.S.)
http://www.basspro.com

Diving and Spearfishing Supplies

As we discussed in chapter 6, it's best to fit some gear in person, but if you want to discuss aspects of dive gear, spearguns, and other equipment and make some purchases, contact

Austin's Diving Center
10525 South Dixie Highway
Miami, Florida 33156
305-665-0636
Fax 305-665-0789
E-mail: diving@austins.com
http://www.austins.com

Holiday Isle Dive Shop
84001 Overseas Highway
P.O. Box 482
Islamadora, Florida, 33036
305-664-3483
Fax 305-664-4145
E-mail: diveshop@divetheisle.com
http://www.divetheisle.com

If you want a custom New Zealand stainless steel lobster snare, talk to Lyndon Rea at

Coast Dive Centre
P.O. Box 550
673 Whangaparaoa Road
Whangaparaoa, New Zealand
64-9-424-8513
Fax 64-9-424-8540

For a look at the full range of commercial diving equipment, compressors, and other gear:

Amron International
759 West 4th Avenue
Escondido, California 92025-4089
760-746-3834
Fax 760-746-1508
E-mail: amron@connectnet.com

Roll Control scuba tank storage racks are available from

V-Jay Distributors
P.O. Box 10563
Pompano Beach, Florida 33061
954-941-8122

Cold-Storage Equipment and Installation

One company with a solid reputation among power cruisers, sailors, commercial boats, and commercial fish-processing facilities in the United States and Caribbean Basin is

Rich Beers Marine, Inc.
Technicold Refrigeration Systems
P.O. Box 14034
Fort Lauderdale, Florida 33302
407-764-6192
Fax 407-764-7259

Rich specializes in adapting chilling and freezing technology to a wide variety of power sources and configurations, primarily in marine power and sailing vessels.

Custom Marine-Metal Fabrication

Depending on how serious you get about fishing, you may be able to get by with off-the-shelf rod holders, rod racks, and similar efficiency-enhancing components. Many cruisers end up seeking the services of custom marine metal fabricators for arches, solar-panel mounting devices, davits, sunshades, crow's nests, railings, platforms and towers, and other structures. Consider an integrated approach, tying together components, and creating highly convenient and comfortable workstations and observation points. Be careful about the welder you select. Ask to see some of his other work, check out the shop. It should have state-of-the-art TIG (tungsten inert gas) and MIG (metal inert gas) welding machines, as well as

hydraulic-pipe and sheet-metal bending and shaping equipment. Discuss plans and drawings to the last detail, and do not agree to "time and materials"—request a written quote for the finished, installed product.

Obviously, you and your boat must be fairly near the metal fabricator; therefore, a specific shop recommendation will assist only a relatively small percentage of readers. Fortunately, you can find good specialty (shielded gas) welders in many ports, particularly in more developed countries. Europe, New Zealand, Australia, and the United States all have outstanding stainless steel and aluminum TIG artists. One example of an extremely imaginative fabricator who is an American Bureau of Shipping (ABS)–certified shipwright, designer, master welder, and creator of many of the tuna towers, arches, poling platforms, and other fishing-related superstructure in Southeast Florida is

Doll Marine Metal Fabrication, Inc.
250 South Dixie Highway East
Pompano Beach, Florida 33060
James S. Doll
954-941-5093
Fax 954-587-8571

We also got excellent results from

Peninsula Engineering Limited
611 Whangaparaoa Road
Whangaparaoa, New Zealand
Ken Kiddie
64-9-424-7255
Fax 64-9-424-7613

And If You Just Happen to Be Out in the Middle of the South Pacific . . .

There's a unique store you should know about, where you can purchase virtually any lure you could possibly need, reasonably priced commercial- and sport-grade fishing supplies, and all the *right* stuff; get expert advice on

rigging, knots, lure deployment; *and* have lessons on exactly how to do it . . . all at a remote, idyllic seafarer's paradise that nearly every Pacific cruiser passes through

Ikapuna Store
Fishing Gear Sales
P.O. Box 106
Neiafu, Vava'u, Kingdom of Tonga
Captain Paul and Alisi Mead
676-70-698 (store),
    676-70-416 (home)
Fax 676-70-174

Paul served as a master fisherman all over the tropical Pacific for the South Pacific Commission (now the Secretariat of the Pacific Community) for nearly twenty years before settling in Vava'u. He and his wife Alisi run a complete service, including fishing charters aboard his *Dora Malia*, in addition to a complete fishing supply outlet on the main street of Neiafu.

International Gear Sources by Country

The following contacts may be useful for world cruisers interested in fishing and related activities.

Australia (country code 61)

Aqua Sports & Dive
Sportsman's Paradise
32 Strathaird Road
Bundall, Queensland 4217, Australia
7-5538-2799
    Spearfishing equipment specialists.

Bias Boating Warehouse
400 Pacific Highway
Lane Cove, Sydney 2066, Australia
2-9428-3222
Fax 2-9418-7077
    Plus three other Sydney-area stores and stores in Perth, Newcastle, Belmont, Gosford West, and Tuggerah.

Boat Suppliers Pty Ltd.
7-9 Porter Street

Port Lincoln, SA 5606, Australia
8-86-823-122
Fax 8-86-826-976

Jack Erskine's Fishing Tackle Shop
P.O. Box 1145
51 Mulgrave Road
Cairns, North Queensland 4870,
    Australia
7-4051-6099
Fax 7-4052-1080
    An outstanding shop with
knowledgeable staff.

Got One Fishing Stores
8-8351-2322
Fax 8-8351-2789
    This large chain has fishing equip-
ment outlets throughout the country.
Contact the head office, located in the
territory of South Australia.

Outdoor World (Offshore Angler's
    Australian outlet)
P.O. Box 472
Chesterhill, NSW 2162, Australia
Order toll free: 800-504-638

Taylor Marine
123 Brisbane Road
Mooloolaba, Queensland 4557,
    Australia
7-5444-0800
Fax 7-5444-0468

New Zealand (country code 64)
Black Magic and Wasabi Tackle
P.O. Box 15170
New Lynn, Auckland, New Zealand
Fax 9-828-6009
http://www.blackmagic.co.nz

Burnsco Marine
P.O. Box 68
Whangaparaoa, New Zealand
9-424-1092
Fax 9-424-1097
    Outlets around the country.

Hooked on Fishing
741 Whangaparaoa Road

Whangaparaoa, New Zealand
Phone and Fax 9-424-2358

K.T.O. Enterprises, Ltd.
P.O. Box 38551
Howick, Auckland, New Zealand
9-534-8236
Fax 9-534-8239
E-mail: mcwatt@clear.net.nz

Mount Smart Marine
123 Beaumont Street
Westhaven
P.O. Box 91180
Auckland Mail Centre
Auckland, New Zealand
9-358-2850
Fax 9-358-1742

Outdoor World (Offshore Angler's
    New Zealand outlet)
P.O. Box 53037
Auckland Airport
Auckland, New Zealand
Order toll free: 0-800-445-909

Sailor's Corner Ltd.
Westhaven Drive, Westhaven
P.O. Box 543
Auckland, New Zealand
9-309-6153
Fax 9-379-4796

South Africa (country code 27)
A. Rutherford Marine, Ltd.
30 Farnia Road
Umbilo, Durban 4000
Republic of South Africa
31-206-2155
Fax 31-205-2013
E-mail: kiran@rutherford.co.za
http://www.rutherford.co.za
    Stores throughout the country.

Central Boating
85 Bree Street
Cape Town 8001
Republic of South Africa
21-424-8026
Fax 21-424-2564
E-mail: cboating@gem.co.za

Williamson Lures
33 Churchill Road
Durban 4001
Republic of South Africa
31-303-3250
Fax 31-303-3253
E-mail: lures@williamsonl.com
http://www.williamsonl.com

United Kingdom (country code 44)
Nautical World
Phone 1702-444-444
Fax 1702-461-669

    The following three large outlet
stores are now all owned by this company.

Telesonic Marine, Ltd.
60-62 Brunswick Centre
Marchmont Street
London WC1N 1AE, United
    Kingdom
171-713-0690

London Yacht Centre, Ltd.
13 Artillery Lane
London E1 7LP, United Kingdom
171-247-2047

Cruisermart
36-38 Eastern Esplanade
Southend-on-Sea
Essex SS1 2ES, United Kingdom
1702-444-4423

Pumpkin Marine
100 The Highway
London, E1 9BX
171-480-6630
Fax 171-481-8905
E-mail: Pumpkin@marine-world.
    com
http://www.pumpkinmarine.co.uk

Sources for Miscellaneous Products

For new jellyfish and hydrozoan sting
medication (chapter 10):

Wipe Out Company
P.O. Box 6246
Laguna Niguel, California 92607
949-362-0735
Fax 949-362-0128
E-mail: sales@wipeoutpad.com
http://www.wipeoutpad.com

For sea snake, stonefish, sea wasp antivenin (chapter 10):

Commonwealth Serum
  Laboratories
45 Poplar Road
Victoria 3052, Australia
61-39-389-1434
Fax 61-39-389-1911

For ciguatera test kit (chapter 10):

Oceanit Test Systems, Inc.
1100 Alakea Plaza
1100 Alakea Street, 31st Floor
Honolulu, Hawaii 96813
808-531-3017
Fax 808-531-3177
E-mail: oceanit@oceanit.com
http://www.cigua.com

For the Fisherman's Solution (chapter 11):

Cutco Cutlery Corporation
1116 East State Street
Olean, New York 14760
800-828-0448

For Kermit Ruffins and the Barbecue Swingers *Live* (chapter 13):

Basin Street Records
4151 Canal Street, Suite C
New Orleans, Louisiana 70119
504-483-0002
Fax 504-483-0033
E-mail: basinstrec@aol.com
http://www.basinstreetrecords.com

Appendix 2
Further Reading and Information

This appendix highlights some of the material from appendix 5 and selected periodicals most appropriate for those who want to go beyond the scope of this book in various subject areas.

Books

Good references are invaluable for the learning process, for detailed technical instructions, and for organism identification sometimes critical for health and safety. Yet space onboard most cruising vessels is limited; therefore, we seldom carry large personal libraries. We must review and abstract information from bulky tomes, perhaps choosing a few critical ones to bring along. Otherwise, we must select books with pervasive, rigorous coverage and the widest possible applicability, not high-gloss, low-information coffee-table items. We offer suggestions by category with these criteria in mind. (See appendix 5 for each reference cited.) Our first recommendation is an excellent general overview of the current state of selected marine resources on our planet, *Song for the Blue Ocean* (Safina 1997). This book provides perspective and strongly reinforces the conservation ethic so important to responsible exploitation of sea life.

FISH AND INVERTEBRATE IDENTIFICATION

You will probably want to augment for your area the fundamental information supplied by chapter 12, particularly if you are cruising in tropical areas featuring high species diversity. Focus on dense, scientifically accurate material with abundant, clear photographs, line drawings, and detailed biological keys that permit positive identification through logical, sequential examination of morphological features and markings.

The Food and Agriculture Organization of the United Nations (FAO) allocates significant resources to highly detailed species catalogs for fish and invertebrate families in the form of the FAO Species Catalog series (see listings in appendix 5) and even more detailed treatises by specific geographic area consisting of more than sixty volumes of FAO Species Identification Sheets for the world. The identification sheets are decidedly bulky, and few cruisers choose to take fisheries synopses, either, except possibly for organism families of specific interest.

Compact texts are more appropriate for most seafarers. Fish identification books of this nature greatly exceed the number of those available for invertebrates. Robins and Ray (1986), Lieske and Myers (1994), and Myers (1991) are stellar examples of books that fit in the palm of your hand yet enable accurate identification of thousands of fish species in the Atlantic and Indo-Pacific regions.

Myers (1991) has a particularly good underwater photo of the deadly stonefish *(Synanceia verrucosa)* that Indo-Pacific cruisers should view. Humann (1992, 1993) is rigorous and features excellent photographs, but for smaller regions.

Shell collectors' books for identification of various mollusks tend to be the most detailed of the invertebrate texts. Tomes like Abbott (1974) provide lots of information about North American species. Books like Romashko (1984) offer considerable geographical coverage in a smaller package, and most places you'll visit have books for the local area, such as Salvat and Rives (1984). Although reef coral identification has also received considerable attention, few authors similarly tackled crustaceans and other groups until recently, usually mentioning only selected species in general shoreline and other sea-life texts. Humann (1994) and Jones and Morgan (1994) are two wonderful examples of dense, information-packed invertebrate identification texts covering many crustaceans in a manner similar to groups of fish and mollusks.

MEDICAL GUIDES

This critical subject might tempt cruisers to carry a tome or two. We carry a relatively current *Physicians' Desk Reference* (MEDPC 1995) and Larson

(1990) and have had frequent occasion to be glad they were aboard. We also carry a handful of highly useful, more compact guides (Beilan 1985, Eastman 1987, Werner 1992, and Lippman and Bug 1989). All cruisers should at least have a look at Halstead (1988), an extremely detailed, worldwide review of poisonous and venomous marine life, and a major reference for parts of chapter 10. Watch for the upcoming arrival of a comprehensive series of field guides by Dr. Bruce Halstead; contact Darwin Press, Princeton, New Jersey, 609-737-1349, fax 609-737-0929, for more information.

TOPICS IN BIOLOGY AND OCEAN SCIENCE

A multitude of texts addresses these subjects. Let's look at it through the eyes of a young person aboard a cruising vessel, initially underwhelmed by correspondence-school coursework but ignited by fishing. You might first find interesting material in fish biology books like Bond (1979) and Bone and Baxter (1995), and may develop sufficient enthusiasm to tackle something highly technical, perhaps Evans (1993). For invertebrate life history, start with texts such as Bliss (1990) and graduate to more highly detailed discourses such as Barnes and Ruppert (1993).

Young people with enthusiasm leading first to knowledge about identification, then graduating to curiosity about the biology of the organism, usually seek further enrichment by ever-expanding ideas and analyses of broader questions and the variables that influence the answers. For example, how do species and populations survive, what influences their movements and distribution? This opens the door for books on every subject: ecology; and biological, chemical, geographical, physical, and meteorological oceanography—which engender fundamental disciplines like physics, chemistry, probability and statistics, mathemat-

ics, and language skills. Start down this path with texts similar to Davis (1977) and Levinton (1982) that emphasize fundamental principles applied to oceanic subjects, and see where it takes you.

Your activities will also bring you into contact with other animals, some of whose identification and behavior can yield important clues about fishing prospects. Frustrated with not knowing what species of seabird, whale, or dolphin you're looking at? Regardless of where you are in the world, Harrison (1983) will probably yield accurate seabird identification, as will Jefferson et al. (1993) for marine mammals. We highly recommend both of these compact books for inclusion aboard all cruising boats.

Allen and Steene (1996) tackle Indo-Pacific reef fish and invertebrates and marine reptiles, birds, and mammals with many excellent identification photos.

FISHING FUN AND METHODOLOGY

Von Brandt (1984) exhaustively reviews the many ways people go about catching fish all over the world, past and present. If you'd like more practical information on how to expand your net-making skills in order to construct hammocks, entire nets, or other mesh devices, see Dahlem (1968), a small softcover that fits aboard any boat. Last, everyone enjoys a good yarn, especially if it's true—the whole crew will enjoy Morey (1994) and his more recent compilation, *Incredible Fishing Stories for Kids.*

Periodicals

Magazines, newsletters, and other periodicals represent an attractive cruiser information option. The information is fresh and current, and the publications are lightweight, and can be reviewed and then passed along or relegated to land-based storage, saving clutter aboard your vessel.

SPORTFISHING

Sportfishing magazines offer news, fishery descriptions, technical information, destination reports, and information and updates on conservation and political issues affecting sportfishing.

The Big Game Fishing Journal
Offshore Informational
    Publications, Inc.
1800 Bay Avenue
Point Pleasant, New Jersey 08472
732-840-4900
Fax 732-223-2449
E-mail: bgfcaputi@aol.com

Features hard-core, highly detailed articles, mostly by professional fishing captains, on exactly how to catch primarily offshore fish species accessible to the coasts of U.S. territories and North, Central, and South America. Emphasizes techniques and advice.

Florida Sportsman
Wickstrom Publishers, Inc.
5901 SW 74th Street
Miami, Florida 33143
305-661-4222
Fax 305-284-0277
E-mail: editor@
    floridasportsman. com
http://www.floridasportsman.com

The primary focus is general saltwater angling of all kinds and in a full range of habitats in Florida, the Bahamas, and the Caribbean Basin. Also has some coverage of other outdoor activities, including diving for seafood. Space allocated to travel destinations, fishery descriptions, technical advice, and conservation news.

Marlin and *Sport Fishing*
World Publications, Inc.
330 West Canton Avenue
Winter Park, Florida 32789
407-628-4802
Fax 407-628-7061
E-mail: editor@marlin-mag.com,
    sportfish@worldzine.com
http://www.marlinmag.com
http://www.sportfishingmag.com

Marlin covers all aspects of sportfishing for billfish around the globe, with some treatment of other highly migratory pelagic species, including technical advice, biological information, and international destination reviews and analyses. *Sport Fishing* publishes similar information for general saltwater angling of all kinds and habitats, covering the United States, as well as international locations.

Salt Water Sportsman
263 Summer Street
Boston, Massachusetts 02210
617-790-5400
Fax 617-790-5455
E-mail: editor@saltwatersportsman.com
http://www.saltwatersportsman.com
Covers general saltwater angling of all types and habitats, with emphasis on U.S. and international travel destinations. Also features technical advice and news.

COMMERCIAL FISHING
One publication leads this category, covering fisheries everywhere in the United States, as well as international fishing activities related to or impacting domestic fishers. Featured information includes fishery descriptions and news, boat building and design, technical innovations, survival stories and losses, conservation issues, and political updates.

National Fisherman
121 Free Street
Portland, Maine 04112-7438
207-842-5608
Fax 207-842-5609
E-mail: bdudley@divcom.com
http://www.nationalfisherman.com

CRUISING
Popular U.S. publications featuring domestic and international coverage of cruising vessels and issues relating to

voyaging aboard them, including some direct fishing coverage at times, follow. Similar publications emanate from France, Germany, the United Kingdom, other European countries, Australia, New Zealand, South Africa, and other centers of power and sailboat cruising interest.

Cruising World
5 John Clarke Road
Newport, Rhode Island 02840-0992
401-847-1588
Fax 401-848-5048
E-mail: editor@cruisingworld.com
http://www.cruisingworld.com
Focuses on sailboats, every aspect relating to sailing, chartering, destinations, personal accounts, adventure stories, do-it-yourself maintenance, and all other tasks involved with succeeding at a cruising lifestyle. Occasional articles on seafood procurement and related issues.

Ocean Navigator
Navigator Publishing Corporation
18 Danforth Street
Portland, Maine 04101
207-772-2466
Fax 207-772-2879
E-mail: Editors@OceanNavigator.com
http://www.oceannavigator.com
Covers all aspects of ocean voyaging in powerboats and sailboats, emphasizing technology, navigation, destinations and route planning, personal voyage accounts, general maritime news and events.

Blue Water Sailing
170 Aquidneck Avenue
P.O. Box 268
Newport, Rhode Island 02840
401-847-7612
Fax 401-845-8580
E-mail: georged@bwsailing.com
http://www.bwsailing.com
Offshore sailing, voyaging, and world cruising.

Latitude 38
15 Locust Avenue
Mill Valley, California 94941
415-383-8200
Fax 415-383-5816
http://www.latitude38.com
Popular West Coast cruising publication with world cruising coverage.

Sail
84 State Street
Boston, Massachusetts 02109-2202
617-720-8600
Fax 617-723-0911
Sailboat cruising, racing, and technology.

Yachting
2 Park Avenue
New York, New York 10016
212-779-5300
Fax 212-725-1035
http://www.gsn.com/yachting.net
Short- or long-term cruising under power or sail.

OTHER PERIODICALS
Many other magazines provide less direct coverage of issues relating to fishing aboard cruising vessels, including *Ocean Realm, Sport Diver* (another product of World Publications, Inc.—see previous contact information), *SkinDiver*, even *National Geographic*.

Organizations and Associations
Organizations and associations of interest to fishing cruisers include clubs that disseminate general, voyaging, and fisheries information. We mentioned the IGFA in chapter 2; membership fee includes a newsletter and annual soft-cover book.

International Game Fish
Association (IGFA)
300 Gulf Stream Way
Dania Beach, Florida 33004
954-927-2628
Fax 954-924-4299

E-mail: IGFAHQ@aol.com
http://www.igfa.org

For practical worldwide cruiser information

Seven Seas Cruising Association (SSCA)
1525 South Andrews Avenue, Suite 217
Fort Lauderdale, Florida 33316
954-463-2431
Fax 954-463-7183
E-mail: SSCA1@ibm.net
http://www.ssca.org

International cruisers can get invaluable world health information from the

International Association for Medical Assistance to Travelers (IAMAT)
417 Center Street
Lewiston, New York 14092
716-754-4883

Those bound for the Indo-Pacific may wish to contact

The Secretariat of the Pacific Community (SPC)
Marine Resources Division, Information Section
B.P. D5, 98848 Noumea Cedex, New Caledonia
687-262000
Fax 687-263818
E-mail: cfpinfo@spc.org.nc
http://www.spc.org.nc
The SPC publishes newsletters and has numerous useful publications relating to regional fisheries and techniques.

Billfish aficionados might wish to join

The Billfish Foundation
P.O. Box 8787
Fort Lauderdale, Florida 33310-8787

954-938-0150,
800-438-8247
Fax 954-938-5311
http://www.iwol.com/billfish
This organization advocates research and education relating to billfish conservation and is a source of fish-tagging kits and information.

Another excellent conservation organization is

The American Littoral Society
National Headquarters
Sandyhook
Highlands, New Jersey 07732
732-291-0055
E-mail: als@netlabs.net
ALS members receive newsletters and a quarterly magazine, *Underwater Naturalist*, and can participate in the popular ALS fish-tagging program—inexpensive tagging kits available on request.

Perhaps the largest body of information on organisms of interest to fisheries throughout the world resides at

Food and Agriculture Organization of the United Nations (FAO)
Via delle Terme di Caracalla
00100, Rome, Italy
39-6-570051
Fax 39-6-57053152
http://www.fao.org

For information on fish-tagging programs, billfish aging, and other kinds of fisheries research, contact

Dr. Eric Prince
U.S. National Fisheries Service
Southeast Fisheries Science Center (NOAA Fisheries)
Miami Laboratory
75 Virginia Beach Drive
Miami, Florida 33149
305-361-4248

Fax 305-361-5761
E-mail: eric.prince@noaa.gov
http://www.sefsc.noaa.gov
http://www.aoml.noaa.gov/general/lib/sefcw.html

Other Sources
For live-well design review and other discussion (chapter 8):

Palmer Bannerot
213 Morgan Center
Butler, Pennsylvania 16001
724-282-8611
Fax 724-287-1885

For dive accident information and emergencies (chapter 10):

Divers Alert Network
Phone toll free: 800-684-8111 (U.S.)

For the latest information on use of beta-blockers and diving risks (chapter 10):

Dr. Simon Mitchell, Director
Wesley Center for Hyperbaric Medicine
P.O. Box 2056
Milton Q4064, Brisbane, Australia
61-7-3371-6033
Fax 61-7-3371-1566
E-mail: smitchell@wesley.com.au
Dr. Mitchell is vice president of the Undersea and Hyperbaric Medicine Society, former director of hyperbaric medicine for the Royal New Zealand Navy, and coauthor of the first research paper noting the connection between beta-blockers and pulmonary edema cases in scuba divers (see Grindlay and Mitchell, appendix 5). Readers may also wish to contact his colleagues Dr. Joanne Grindlay or Dr. Anthony Holley, Auckland Hospital Emergency Department, Auckland, New Zealand, 64-9-379-7440.

Appendix 3

The Wonderful World of Fly-Fishing

Many folks are put off from trying out fly-fishing by old stereotypes or intimidation. Admittedly, this method does normally occur somewhat down the line of most fishing careers, because it often does not produce fish at the same rate as other techniques. If a fisher is unsatisfied with or would be intolerant of production less than that available from application of "maximum legal fishing power," they are not likely to pick up a fly rod except where streams, rivers, or lakes are designated "fly-fishing only."

Why, then, has this sport become immensely popular in salt water as well as classic freshwater venues, and grown to include a much larger slice of the general fisher population than a few crusty old bluebloods? The reasons are many.

- ◆ Fly-fishing is not difficult to learn—the truth is, just about anyone can do it.
- ◆ Fly-fishing equipment for a huge range of purposes has now become widely available, and includes *fairly* reasonably priced, affordable products that work well.
- ◆ The increase in fly-fishing technology has vastly improved the effectiveness of this gear—never before have fly fishers been able to deploy realistic flies at so many depths, current velocities,

and bottom configurations.
- ◆ Fly gear permits presentation of detailed, delicate, extremely lifelike imitations of insects, crustaceans, fish, and many other food items, as well as unique, light, pulsating, and darting lure actions difficult or impossible for other gear.
- ◆ Consequently, the number of situations where a fly can compete with or out-fish other hook-and-line methods has grown.
- ◆ If the aesthetics of fishing appeal to you, keep in mind the potentially valid argument that no other fishing method permits the degree of solitude, silence, beauty, challenge, and satisfaction possible from fly-fishing.

What does all this mean? That it's time to make another one of our bets. I bet that if you enjoy any form of fishing, you'll thoroughly delight in fly-fishing, *given the right exposure*. Ah-ha, you say, he's trying to hedge with that last phrase. Here's exactly what I mean by "right exposure":

- ◆ Cut the complication of technicalities to a minimum, across the board . . . *keep it simple*.
- ◆ Fly fish when it's a reasonable strategy—that is, when it is an effective means of getting a strike.

- ◆ Use rugged, versatile gear appropriate to a wide spectrum of fishing situations and conditions.

You can specialize all you want later. Stick to these principles, get started somewhere you won't flog yourself to death with hundreds of casts per strike, and you'll have a great time. If you choose to consult books or videos *before* you hit the water and feel yourself getting overwhelmed by all the detail, then close the book, switch off the VCR, and go have some fun. The purpose of this appendix is to succinctly describe one bare-bones way to do just that. This crash course is nonetheless designed to be complete: get the equipment, follow the instructions, and hit the water; there's no reason you shouldn't have a ball.

Inexpensive Fly Gear That Will Catch Just about Anything

Recall that it's the weight of the *line*, not the lure, that carries a fly cast. Thus, fly lines and the rods that throw them are classed according to weights ranging from 2 (lightest) to 15 (super heavy) or so. These lines either float or sink at various rates (fast, slow, intermediate), and they aren't very long—not much over 100 feet (30 m), or less. Thus, you tie the reel end to 250 yards (229 m) of nonstretch Dacron backing so you have enough capacity to play strong fish. The fly reel must be large enough to accommodate the fly line and backing and have a drag system.

Table A3-1 recommends specific gear for a cruiser who'd like to start fly-fishing. Get an 8-weight outfit to begin, the approximate fly gear equivalent to your 10-pound (4.5 kg) test spinning outfit—it will catch bonefish, trout, salmon, trevally, small tuna and mackerel, mahi mahi, striped bass, bluefish, redfish, small tarpon, jacks, and a host of other species. Get a three-piece rod and you can stick it in a backpack and hike inland or along a shoreline. Buy a readymade fly selection from one of the catalogs. You'll tie your own leaders from monofilament supplies already aboard. See appendix 1 for sources (check out Captain Harry's, Offshore Angler, World Wide Sportsman, Cabela's, and Bass Pro).

Darn, that's 435 bucks . . . well, you only go around once and you can't take it with you, and this is cheap by fly-fishing gear standards. If the fly-fishing bug bites hard, add the items in table A3-2.

Assemble Your Gear and Load the Line

Clamp the reel to the reel seat on the rod. Set up the backing line spool just as you did to fill any revolving-spool reel in chapter 2. Tie the backing to the reel spool with a uni-knot (see chapter 2) and wind just under half of the 500-yard (457 m) spool onto the reel evenly and under tension (240 yds./219 m is perfect). Now tie the fly line (thin end, intended to go on the reel) to the backing line with a nail knot (figure A3-1), and wind it on evenly and under tension. Tie 4 feet (122 cm) of 60-pound (27 kg) test monofilament to the end of the fly line with a nail knot, then add 4-foot (122 cm) sections of 30-pound (13.6 kg) and 20-pound (9 kg) test with line-to-line uni-knots, tie on a fly with a uni-knot, and you're done!

Stretch Your Fly Line

New fly line, or fly line that has been cooped up on your reel for a while, develops memory or kinks that make casting and detecting bites more difficult because all of those little meanders must pull tight before you feel the fish. Strip all of the fly line off the reel, have someone get on the other end, then each of you grasp the line in one hand, pass it across the middle of your rear end, and grasp it in the other hand. Now, walk apart until it's suspended in the air, and then pressure it to a straight horizontal line, taking the strain across your buttocks (commercial longliners call this "puttin' some ass on it," and that's how they cinch blood knots in 700 lb./318 kg test monofilament mainline). You'll *feel* the line stretch—lean into it a few times, but don't get excessive, and you're all set—crank the line back onto the reel and go fishing. If you're alone, wrap several turns of the *backing* end of the fly line around a fairly large-diameter, smooth tree trunk (coconut palms are perfect) or post, and put the leader end across your buttocks to stretch the line.

Practice Casting

Figure A3-2 demonstrates exactly how to fly cast using a double haul. It's a simple matter of timing and coordi-

---

TABLE A3-1. SPECIFIC GEAR CHECKLIST FOR A CRUISER'S INITIAL FLY OUTFIT

Item	Specific Recommendation	Approximate Price
Travel fly rod, 8 weight	Gold Cup IM-6 graphite 3-piece, 8/9 weight line	$170
Fly reel	Scientific Anglers System 2, Model 78	$158
Floating fly line	Cortland 444SL, WF8F	$45
Backing line	Magibraid 20 lb. (9 kg), 500 yds. (457 m)	$14
Flies	pick a boxed catalog selection	$20 and up
Poppers	pick a boxed catalog selection	$28

TABLE A3-2. ADDITIONS THAT ENHANCE FLY-FISHING VERSATILITY

Item	Specific Recommendation	Approximate Price
Additional fly lines		
Fast sinking	Scientific Anglers Wet Cel IV, WF8S	$35
Intermediate sinking	Scientific Anglers Wet Cel II, WF8S	$35
Additional backing line	Magibraid 20 lb. (9 kg), 500 yds. (457 m)	$14
Additional reel spools	for Scientific Anglers System 2, Model 78	$67 each

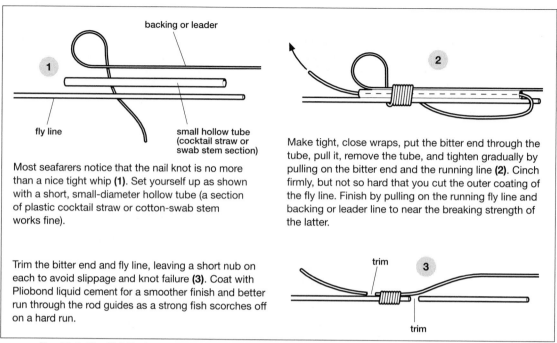

backing or leader

1

fly line

small hollow tube
(cocktail straw or
swab stem section)

Most seafarers notice that the nail knot is no more
than a nice tight whip **(1)**. Set yourself up as shown
with a short, small-diameter hollow tube (a section
of plastic cocktail straw or cotton-swab stem
works fine).

2

Make tight, close wraps, put the bitter end through the
tube, pull it, remove the tube, and tighten gradually by
pulling on the bitter end and the running line **(2)**. Cinch
firmly, but not so hard that you cut the outer coating of
the fly line. Finish by pulling on the running fly line and
backing or leader line to near the breaking strength of
the latter.

Trim the bitter end and fly line, leaving a short nub on
each to avoid slippage and knot failure **(3)**. Coat with
Pliobond liquid cement for a smoother finish and better
run through the rod guides as a strong fish scorches off
on a hard run.

trim

3

trim

Fig. A3-1. The Nail Knot.

nating the actions of your rod arm, wrist, and hand with your line hand. Like cast-netting, you can get decent enough results the first session to catch fish, and then spend months perfecting your casts. Here are two examples. My brother-in-law Marshall came to visit us in New Zealand and longed to catch a decent trout on a fly, but had never fly fished. We dinghied in to a broad, shallow, sandy bay at Lake Waikaremoana. We reviewed figure A3-2 with him for maybe fifteen minutes, until he was at least getting the timing enough to send the line out 40 feet (12 m). Not wanting to pester, I wandered away to climb a large rock that provided an excellent fish-spotting platform. I wasn't there ten minutes before I picked out the distinct shape of a large brown trout cruising over the sand toward Marshall. A quick glance revealed that he'd just cast, and I told him to leave the fly right there on the bottom. When the trout slowly meandered to a position 10 feet (3 m) from the fly, I told Marshall to give it a quick twitch. The hefty brown surged for-

ward and inhaled the fly—Marshall saw the take, felt a tug, and raised the rod, setting the hook. The beautiful fish weighed just over 5 pounds (2.3 kg), a heck of a first trout for the first five minutes of fly-fishing!

Hey, that was good fortune, although a local friend had loaded the deck by earlier showing me the spot and even tying just the right fly for that location, but the point still holds. Another time, while at Palmyra Atoll in the central tropical Pacific, commercial tuna captain Mike Needham asked me to take him for a first stab at fly-fishing for bonefish. Using the same rod that later caught Marshall's trout, Mike and I went through the double-haul lesson on a shallow sand flat that tended to load up with bonefish as the tide rose. Soon small packs of bonefish began to appear, just as Mike was getting the rhythm. I spotted a bunch on a suitable approach course, and an almost identical sequence of events to the trout episode resulted in Mike's first bonefish on fly, to which he added three more.

Obviously, these were two great fishing locations—with little or no wind, no place to tangle the back cast or loose line coils—and good visibility, not to mention plain good luck. Yes, folks fly cast for years trying to experience what those guys did in their first half hour, but you can catch any number of different species on your first outing as well. Find any school of surface-feeding fish, chuck out a reasonable facsimile of what they're feeding on, strip the fly line between your forefinger and middle finger of the rod hand in erratic, 6-inch (15 cm) hops, grasp the line lightly and raise the rod abruptly when you feel life—and you're hooked up. Allow any loose line coils to slide under tension through the thumb and forefinger of your line hand until it is running off the reel spool (a process called "clearing the line"). The rest of the fight resembles other kinds of fishing rods and reels—lift and wind, tire the fish, and play it to the net. Release after photos if you don't need it for food.

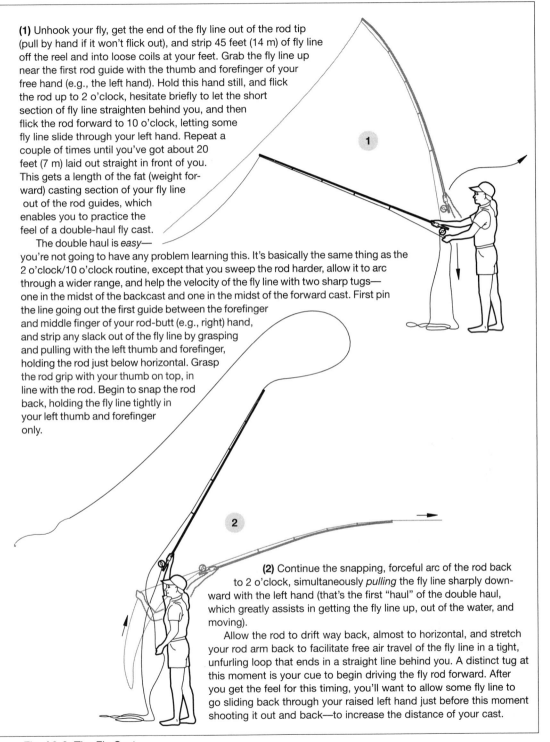

(1) Unhook your fly, get the end of the fly line out of the rod tip (pull by hand if it won't flick out), and strip 45 feet (14 m) of fly line off the reel and into loose coils at your feet. Grab the fly line up near the first rod guide with the thumb and forefinger of your free hand (e.g., the left hand). Hold this hand still, and flick the rod up to 2 o'clock, hesitate briefly to let the short section of fly line straighten behind you, and then flick the rod forward to 10 o'clock, letting some fly line slide through your left hand. Repeat a couple of times until you've got about 20 feet (7 m) laid out straight in front of you. This gets a length of the fat (weight forward) casting section of your fly line out of the rod guides, which enables you to practice the feel of a double-haul fly cast.

The double haul is *easy*— you're not going to have any problem learning this. It's basically the same thing as the 2 o'clock/10 o'clock routine, except that you sweep the rod harder, allow it to arc through a wider range, and help the velocity of the fly line with two sharp tugs— one in the midst of the backcast and one in the midst of the forward cast. First pin the line going out the first guide between the forefinger and middle finger of your rod-butt (e.g., right) hand, and strip any slack out of the fly line by grasping and pulling with the left thumb and forefinger, holding the rod just below horizontal. Grasp the rod grip with your thumb on top, in line with the rod. Begin to snap the rod back, holding the fly line tightly in your left thumb and forefinger only.

(2) Continue the snapping, forceful arc of the rod back to 2 o'clock, simultaneously *pulling* the fly line sharply downward with the left hand (that's the first "haul" of the double haul, which greatly assists in getting the fly line up, out of the water, and moving).

Allow the rod to drift way back, almost to horizontal, and stretch your rod arm back to facilitate free air travel of the fly line in a tight, unfurling loop that ends in a straight line behind you. A distinct tug at this moment is your cue to begin driving the fly rod forward. After you get the feel for this timing, you'll want to allow some fly line to go sliding back through your raised left hand just before this moment shooting it out and back—to increase the distance of your cast.

Fig. A3-2. The Fly Cast.

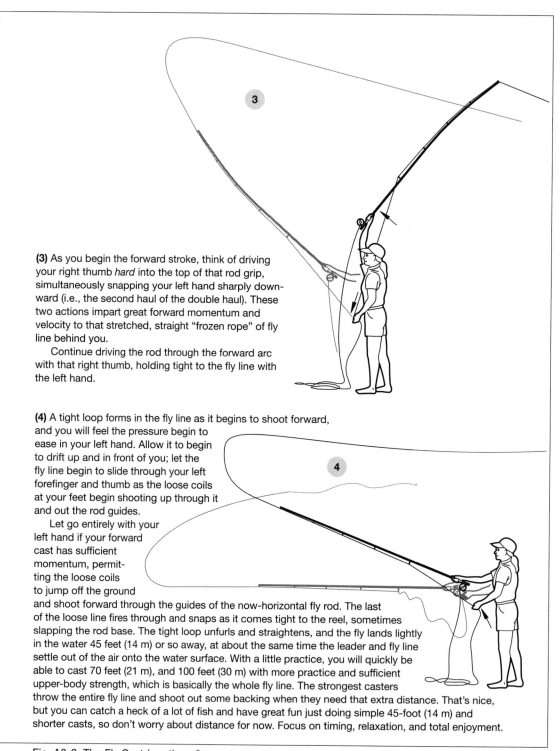

(3) As you begin the forward stroke, think of driving your right thumb *hard* into the top of that rod grip, simultaneously snapping your left hand sharply downward (i.e., the second haul of the double haul). These two actions impart great forward momentum and velocity to that stretched, straight "frozen rope" of fly line behind you.

Continue driving the rod through the forward arc with that right thumb, holding tight to the fly line with the left hand.

(4) A tight loop forms in the fly line as it begins to shoot forward, and you will feel the pressure begin to ease in your left hand. Allow it to begin to drift up and in front of you; let the fly line begin to slide through your left forefinger and thumb as the loose coils at your feet begin shooting up through it and out the rod guides.

Let go entirely with your left hand if your forward cast has sufficient momentum, permitting the loose coils to jump off the ground and shoot forward through the guides of the now-horizontal fly rod. The last of the loose line fires through and snaps as it comes tight to the reel, sometimes slapping the rod base. The tight loop unfurls and straightens, and the fly lands lightly in the water 45 feet (14 m) or so away, at about the same time the leader and fly line settle out of the air onto the water surface. With a little practice, you will quickly be able to cast 70 feet (21 m), and 100 feet (30 m) with more practice and sufficient upper-body strength, which is basically the whole fly line. The strongest casters throw the entire fly line and shoot out some backing when they need that extra distance. That's nice, but you can catch a heck of a lot of fish and have great fun just doing simple 45-foot (14 m) and shorter casts, so don't worry about distance for now. Focus on timing, relaxation, and total enjoyment.

Fig. A3-2. The Fly Cast (*continued*)

The poppers mentioned in table A3-1 are fly-fishing's equivalent of surface plugs. Fish them the same way, making them pop and chug, pause at times, keep the rhythm irregular, and speed it up for species that seem to lose interest in slower action. You'll elicit the same spectacular surface takes that you did with your spinning gear. The variety of potential fish species is vast, including marlin, sailfish, and (recently offshore of Kenya) even a broadbill swordfish! You'll need a little beefier fly gear, however, at this end of the spectrum.

So You Want to Learn More

Check out the fly-fishing sections of the previously mentioned catalogs for videos and books. For marine environments, we recommend Lefty Kreh's *Fly Fishing in Salt Water* and any of his other books on the topic (available from World Wide Sportsman—see appendix 1).

Several excellent magazines also address fly-fishing in environments common to cruising seafarers.

Saltwater Fly Fishing
Abenaki Publishers, Inc.
160 Benmont Avenue
Bennington, Vermont 05201
802-447-1518
Fax 802-447-2471
http://www.flyfishmags.com
U.S. and international coverage of destinations, fisheries, technical information, and news. Other fly-fishing magazines of interest by the same publisher are *American Angler*, *Fly Tyer*, and *Warmwater Fly Fishing*.

Fly Fishing in Salt Waters
2001 Western Avenue, Suite 210
Seattle, Washington 98121
206-443-3273
Fax 206-443-3293
http://www.flyfishinsalt.com
Coverage similar to *Saltwater Fly Fishing*, also entirely marine; many aficionados subscribe to both.

Fly Rod & Reel
Down East Enterprises, Inc.
Outdoor Group Publications
P.O. Box 370
Camden, Maine 04843
207-594-9544
Fax 207-594-5144
http://www.flyrodreel.com
Focus is on cold-water salmonid fishing in U.S. and international locations (freshwater and sea run trout and salmon), also with good coverage of marine and other environments. Many of the situations are typical of those encountered by temperate latitude cruisers, where fly gear is often an excellent or the only legal choice.

Appendix 4

Fishing-Reel Maintenance and Repair

Occasionally your fishing reels will demand more thorough attention than rinsing, scrubbing externally with detergent and a toothbrush to discourage buildup of salt deposits, and spraying with light oil like Pennz-Guard, CRC, or WD-40. Drags get sticky; minor internal mechanical wear and failure occurs, requiring disassembly and replacement of faulty parts. This appendix outlines common eventual failures for representative recommended reel models, the spare parts you should carry, and procedures for making these repairs.

Spinning Reels

Spinning reels are simple to dismantle and put back together. You won't have any problem rebuilding them once in a while, in between the capture of hundreds of fish per repair. We pick up where we left off in chapter 2, using the Penn 850SS as a model. We already discussed replacement and periodic lubrication of the drag washers; only two other problems generally arise with any frequency: failure of the main gear and failure of the bearings.

Main Gear

Main-gear failure occurs because of tooth wear from pressure exerted on the reel handle transmitting through the main gear (8N) to the pinion (19) (see fig. 2-9). One day you'll be fight-

ing a fish, hear a ratcheting sound, feel a grinding vibration and binding as you attempt to turn the handle, and you'll no longer be able to gain line on the fish. Usually you will have some warning well before outright failure—as soon as you hear or feel the symptom, replace the main gear or it may cost you a fish. If you experience catastrophic failure during battle, all is not necessarily lost. Grab another fishing rod and cut off any terminal tackle. Allow the fish to become settled, loosen the drag, feed plenty of slack, cut the line, and quickly uniknot it to the cut end of the standby rod line. You're back in business.

Replacing the main gear is simple—remove the handle (15) by turning it backwards with the anti-reverse lever (6E) on, remove the three housing-cover screws (46), lift off the housing cover (45), remove and replace the main gear (8N), and reassemble. If you note significant salt deposits or internal corrosion, disassemble the reel completely, placing all parts in a small plastic container of mineral spirits. Scrub each with a toothbrush, coat with a film of Penn Muscle Grease or Diawa Blue Grease, reassemble, and smear a protective layer of grease on the assembled internal parts before replacing the housing. Carry one or two spare main gears per spinning reel.

Bearings

Penn uses the same bearing (20) in three places on SS series spinning reels: one on either side of the housing for the reel handle pivot (15B or 15BL), and a main or head bearing (20) to effect the rotation of the pinion (19) (see fig. 2-9). The main reason these bearings may freeze is saltwater submersion of the reel, which allows corrosive seawater to enter the bearing case and rust the steel bearing balls. Symptomsinclude increasing resistance to turning the reel handle. Any time you accidentally dunk a spinning reel, take off the housing cover and flush it well with freshwater, dry, and spray it heavily with light anticorrosion oil (Corrosion Block is best for this). If you later detect resistance, disassemble and find and replace the bearing(s) responsible. Carry three spare bearings per spinning reel.

Penn International Big-Game Reels

Larger revolving-spool reels of the sort you might have on a stand-up outfit are slightly more complex than spinning reels to completely disassemble and reassemble, and degree of difficulty varies between models. Penn Internationals are fairly straightforward, and full disassembly is infrequently necessary. Using the Penn International 50TW as a model, the first malady you'll likely experience is drag stickiness, requiring partial disassembly and light sanding of the fiber drag washer shown as one part with drive plate 117—this is actually two entities—see fig. A4-1. If the metal drag washer (7) is pitted, sand carefully to restore it, or replace. A less common failure, usually after catching many large strong fish, is worn-out quadrant bushings (157), which may cause binding as you attempt to turn the reel handle. The following thorough service procedure, performed annually or so, is adequate for most cruisers (refer to fig. A4-1). Apply Penn Muscle Grease, Daiwa Blue Grease, or a similar product for all instructions calling for grease. Carry spare quadrant bushings (157), fiber drag washers (117), and at least one metal drag washer (7) for each of your Penn Internationals.

1. *Keep retaining screws corrosion-free.* We first reemphasize the importance of ensuring that salt deposits do not build up on and around the frame screws (38). Remove and first coat them with Duralac, allow them to dry, and then coat again with grease. Doing this *straight out of the box prevents* galvanic corrosion between the stainless steel fasteners and the anodized aluminum housing that surrounds them. Repeat any time you disassemble the reel. Arduous maintenance adventures always seem to begin with corroded and frozen screws.

2. *Remove the right-side plate assembly.* Set the reel on its side, handle up. Remove the three quadrant-ring screws (31, 32, 38C) from the quadrant ring (2). Carefully lift off the quadrant ring, taking care to collect the two quadrant-ring bushings (157) that mount on screws 31 and 38C. Remove the four screws (38) that hold the right-

side plate assembly (1) to the tube frame (183). Lift the right-side plate from the tube frame and set it aside.

3. *Dismantle the right-side plate assembly.* Remove the handle-lock screw (110) and lift off the handle-locking plate (110A). Place the socket of the Penn special wrench supplied with your reel over the handle screw (23) and remove it. Then lift off the handle (24), gear-stud washer (134A), and handle-spacing sleeve (9). Now remove the three bridge-cover screws (39) from the bridge cover (124). Lift off the bridge cover. Now you can remove the strike (eccentric cam) lever (21) and backing washer (60), and extract the main gear (5) and gear stud (134) from the right-plate assembly (1). Place the main gear and gear stud in a plastic container of mineral spirits,

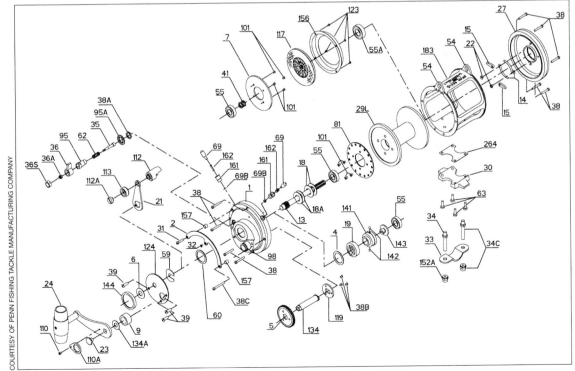

Fig. A4-1. Parts diagram and list for Penn International Models 30T–50T-TW.

clean with a parts brush to remove old grease, and set aside on a clean rag to drain and dry. Also dip the right-side plate assembly in the thinner bath and brush away all old grease and debris, particularly from the inner side of the plate where the preset assembly sits.

4. *Separate, dismantle, and clean the preset assembly.* Hold the right-plate assembly (1), push a forefinger into the central opening from the handle side, and the preset assembly (consisting of parts 19, 141, 142, 143, and 26) will drop out as a unit. Reach in the back side of the right-side plate assembly and extract the cam-thrust washer (4). Now you can take the preset assembly apart—pull the eccentric cam (19) off of the cam follower (141), and pull out the two cam-follower pins (142) from the cam follower. Replace these with new ones if you see any signs of distortion and wear. Take out the spool bearing (55) from the cam follower (141) by turning the adjusting screw (143) *clockwise* until the spool bearing separates from the cam follower. Spray the spool bearing with Corrosion Block and set it aside—don't use any anticorrosion sprays that might penetrate and leave a paraffin residue inside on the steel bearing balls. Place the rest of the preset assembly in a plastic container of mineral spirits; dab and stroke each component with a parts brush to remove all old grease, salt, and grit; and set them aside on a clean rag to drain and dry.

5. *Lubricate and reassemble the preset assembly.* Smear the cam follower (141), adjusting screw (143), spool bearing (55), two cam follower pins (142), and eccentric cam (19) thoroughly and evenly with grease (give this job to a young bystander, they love it). Fit the adjusting screw (143) and cam follower (141) back together, insert the spool bearing (55) into the cam follower, place the cam follower pins (142) into their cavities in the cam follower, and fit the eccentric cam (19) back into place over the cam follower.

6. *Lubricate and partially reassemble the right-side plate assembly.* Apply a moderate film of grease to the inner side of the right-side plate assembly (1), main gear (5), and gear stud (134). Insert first the cam-thrust washer (4) and then the preset assembly into its housing on the inner side of the right-side plate assembly (1). Insert the main gear (5) and gear stud (134) into place on this same side of the right-side plate assembly (1). Set this partially reassembled unit aside, and neatly array all other parts in the same area on a clean rag.

7. *Remove the spool from the tube frame of the reel.* Lift the spool (29) and pinion gear (13) as a unit out of the tube frame (183). Pull the pinion gear (13) out of the spool, without losing or separating the four disc clutch springs (18 and 18A) from the shaft of the pinion gear. Remove all old grease in the thinner bath and set aside to dry on a clean rag.

8. *Remove, inspect, clean, lubricate, and replace the left-side plate assembly.* Remove the five frame screws (38) and separate the left-side plate (27) from the tube frame (183). Clean all of the screws and coat them with Duralac. Turn your attention now to the inside of the left-side plate assembly—inspect the action of the dogs (15) by flicking them and ensuring they snap back into place. Excess grease and debris, or fatigued dog springs (14), can cause their anti-reverse function to fail on a hard, fast fish run, resulting in a bird's nest and break-off. Don't clean with mineral spirits due to the proximity of the left-side-plate ball bearing (55A), but carefully remove all excess grease and grit with a clean rag and recoat with a thin new film. Spray a shot of Corrosion Block onto the ball bearing (55A). Coat all frame screws (38) with grease and reinstall the left-side plate (27).

9. *Dismantle, inspect, treat, and lubricate the drag assembly.* Press down and hold the drag cover (156) while you remove the four drag-cover screws (123) from the outer rim of the drag cover. Then slowly ease the downward tension and lift the drag cover (156) and drive the plate (117) off the left-side bearing spring (41). Remove the bearing spring (41) and then separate the fiber drag washer (shown as 117—this spearates from the drive plate) from the metal drag washer (7). Clean the metal drag washer with mineral spirits. Examine the surface of the fiber drag washer for salt deposits, distortion, and rough areas. Carefully remove loose debris with a toothbrush, and lightly sand the surface smooth with 220 grit or finer sandpaper, then wipe the surface clean with a rag dampened with mineral spirits. Similarly remove corrosion and smooth out light pitting on all metal drag surfaces. Fiber drag washers can be salvaged from considerable wear for another round; metal surface defects more often dictate replacement of the part because the pitting only rescores the fiber washer. Paint all of the drag-cover screws (123) with Duralac. Smear a thin coat of grease onto the fiber washer (half of 117) and wipe off any excess.

10. *Put the drag assembly back together.* Reassemble the fiber drag washer (half of 117) and metal drag washer (7), and spray a shot of Corrosion Block onto the spool ball bearing (55) on the left end (drag side) of the spool. Set the left-side bearing spring (41) in place, then rest the drive plate (117) and drag cover (156)—with drag-cover screw holes aligned—over the spring. Cover the four drag-cover screws (123) with grease. Now press down evenly on the drag cover (156) until it is flush to the mounting surface, hold in place, and install the four drag-cover screws (123).

11. *Clean, inspect, lubricate, and reinstall the spool in the tube frame.* Wipe off any excess grease or debris from the spool bearing (55) in the right end of the spool and give it a shot of Corrosion Block. Apply a light film of grease to the entire pinion gear (13) and the four disc clutch springs (18) mounted on the shaft of the pinion gear. Reinsert the pinion gear (13) in the spool (29). Now slide the assembled spool into the tube frame (183), pressing lightly and rotating the pinion gear counterclockwise to allow the spool to snap properly into place.

12. *Reinstall the right-side plate assembly in the tube frame.* All retaining screws (38, 39, 31, 32, 38C) should sport a dry coat of Duralac. Now coat them with grease. Begin by installing a frame screw (38) through the right-side plate assembly (1) and into one of the upper threaded holes of the tube frame (183). Now install two frame screws (38) into the two lower threaded holes on the tube frame. Tighten these three frame screws (38), pausing to turn the spool to ensure that the gears are properly meshed as the screws seat firmly.

Now you've got it made. Rest the two quadrant-ring bushings (157) in place, and then set the quadrant ring (2) upon them. Install first the small center quadrant screw (32), and next the short quadrant screw (31)—note from figure A4-1 that this should go at the "free spool" end of the quadrant. Then install the long quadrant screw (38C). Last, insert and tighten the fourth frame screw (38) into the hole beside the short quadrant screw (31).

13. *Put the bridge assembly, eccentric cam lever, and handle back on.* Grease the backing washer (60), insert into the outer central housing of the right-side plate assembly (1), and replace the eccentric cam lever (21), ensuring that it is in the "free-spool" position. Align the preset knob (144) with the adjusting screw (143) as you reinstall the bridge cover (124) with the three bridge cover screws (39). Place onto the gear stud (134) the spacing sleeve (9) and then the gear-stud washer (134A). Seat the handle (24) onto the end of the gear stud (134). Install the handle screw (23) firmly with your Penn wrench. Place the handle-locking plate (110A) over the handle screw (you might need to adjust the handle screw slightly to align the holes in the plate and in the handle). Install the handle-lock screw.

Other Reels and Winches

Alvey commercial deck winches require less maintenance than sportfishing reels. If the drag gets sticky, dismantle the stack of alternating fiber and metal drag washers. Clean, recondition, and apply a thin coat of grease, wiping away any excess, just as you would for your extremely similar spinning-reel drag. Carry spare fiber drag washers and a few extra metal drag washers for cases of scoring, distortion, or corrosion that are beyond reasonable help.

The more expensive fly reels have a stacked washer-drag system quite similar to the Alvey commercial deck winches. Less expensive models, like the Scientific Anglers System 2 Model 78, have only a simple adjustable brake-plate device that acts on the central reel spindle or, in some cases, a brake shoe. Carry spare drag washers for the better reels. The simpler systems are incapable of exerting much pressure and, as a result, don't seem to need much attention other than keeping rinsed, clean, and lightly sprayed with anticorrosion oil.

A Few Last Tips

We have purposely used exploded diagrams (figs. 2-9 and A4-1) to orient you to disassembly and reassembly procedures. Learning to envision how it all goes together in this form more accurately duplicates the reality of a scattered array of parts laid out after cleaning and lubrication.

You might still wonder about getting lost as you attempt to refit all of these components into a functional entity. The models shown aren't too bad, and using this appendix as a guide should keep you out of trouble. Other reel makes and models (e.g., Penn Senators) aren't quite as easy because they depend on spring-loaded tensions developed from assemblies that tend to blow apart as you dismantle them. Such models often stay dismantled until the owner finds a tackle repair center to reassemble the parts. Even the pros use the following trick: Have two reels of the same model, and leave one assembled at all times. If you get stuck somewhere along the way on the rebuild, carefully disassemble the second reel to the sticking point to see exactly how the parts should be oriented. Diagram these orientations as you go through the procedure the first time, and all subsequent maintenance rounds will go faster.

Appendix 5
References

Abbott, R. T. *American Seashells.* 2nd ed. New York: Van Nostrand Reinhold, 1974.

Abdula, Rabia. "A Summary about Holothurians in Mozambique." *SPC Bêche-de-Mer Information Bulletin* 10 (1998): 34–35.

Allen, Gerald R. *Reef Fishes of New Guinea.* Madang, New Guinea: Christensen Research Institute, 1992.

Allen, Gerald R. "Snappers of the World: An Annotated and Illustrated Catalogue of Lutjanid Species Known to Date." *FAO Fisheries Synopsis* 6, no. 125 (1985).

Allen, Gerald R., and Roger Steene. *Indo-Pacific Coral Reef Guide.* 3rd ed. Singapore: Tropical Reef Research, 1996.

Allen, Gerald R., and Ross Robertson. *Fishes of the Tropical Eastern Pacific.* Honolulu: University of Hawaii Press, 1994.

Allen, Gerald R., and R. Swainston. *Marine Fishes of Northwestern Australia.* Perth: Western Australia Museum, 1988.

Ayling, Tony. *Collins Guide to Sea Fishes of New Zealand.* Auckland: William Collins Publishers, 1982.

Bagnis, Raymond, Philippe Mazellier, Jack Bennett, and Erwin Christian. *Fishes of Polynesia.* 2nd ed. Singapore: Les Éditions du Pacifique, 1987.

Baine, Mark, and Bobby Forbes. "The Taxonomy and Exploitation of Sea Cucumbers in Malaysia." *SPC Bêche-de-Mer Information Bulletin* 10 (1998): 2–7.

Barnes, Robert D., and Edward Ruppert. *Invertebrate Zoology.* 6th ed. Philadelphia: W. B. Saunders Company, 1993.

Beilan, Michael H. *Your Offshore Doctor: A Manual of Self-Sufficiency at Sea.* New York: Dodd, Mead, & Company, 1985.

Bell, Lori J. "Mariculture Prospects for the West Indian Topshell, *Cittarium pica.*" *Proceedings of the Gulf and Caribbean Fisheries Institute* 44 (1998): 499–503.

Blanc, Michel. *On-Board Handling of Sashimi-Grade Tuna: A Practical Guide for Crew Members.* Noumea, New Caledonia: Secretariat for the Pacific Community, 1996.

Bligh, E. Graham, ed. *Seafood and Science Technology.* London: Blackwell Scientific Publications, 1992.

Bliss, Dorothy E. *Shrimps, Lobsters, and Crabs: Their Fascinating Life Story.* New York: Columbia University Press, 1990.

Bohlke, J. E., and C. C. Chaplin. *Fishes of the Bahamas and Adjacent Tropical Waters.* 2nd ed. Austin: University of Texas Press, 1992.

Bond, Carl E. *Biology of Fishes.* Philadelphia: W.B. Saunders Company, 1979.

Bone, Q., N. B. Marshall, and J. H. S. Blaxter. *Biology of Fishes.* 2nd ed. London: Chapman & Hall, 1995.

Brusle, Jacques. *Ciguatera Fish Poisoning, A Review: Sanitary and Economic Aspects.* Paris: Les Éditions INSERM, 1997.

Burgess, Warren, and Herbert R. Axelrod. *Fishes of Sri Lanka, Maldive Islands, and Mombasa.* Neptune City, NJ: T. F. H. Publications, 1973.

Burukovskii, R. N. *Key to Shrimps and Lobsters.* New Delhi: Oxonian Press, 1982.

Carpenter, Kent E. "Fusilier Fishes of the World: An Annotated and Illustrated Catalogue of Caesionid Species Known to Date." *FAO Fisheries Synopsis* 8, no. 125 (1988).

Carpenter, Kent E., and Gerald R. Allen. "Emperor Fishes and Large-Eye Breams of the World (Family Lethrinidae): An Annotated and Illustrated Catalogue of Lethrinid Species Known to Date." *FAO Fisheries Synopsis* 9, no. 125 (1989).

Cohen, Daniel M., Tadashi Inada, Tomio Iwamoto, and Nadia Scialabba. "Gadiform Fishes of the World (Order Gadiformes): An Annotated and Illustrated

Catalogue of Cods, Hakes, Grenadiers, and Other Gadiform Fishes Known to Date." *FAO Fisheries Synopsis* 10, no. 125 (1990).

Collette, Bruce B., and Cornelia E. Nauen. "Scombrids of the World: An Annotated and Illustrated Catalogue of Tunas, Mackerels, Bonitos, and Related Species Known to Date." *FAO Fisheries Synopsis* 2, no. 125 (1983).

Compagno, Leonard J. V. "Sharks of the World: An Annotated and Illustrated Catalogue of Shark Species to Date. Part 1: Hexanchiformes to Lamniformes." *FAO Fisheries Synopsis* 4, no. 125-1 (1984).

Compagno, Leonard J. V. "Sharks of the World: An Annotated and Illustrated Catalogue of Shark Species to Date. Part 2: Carcharhiniformes." *FAO Fisheries Synopsis* 4, no. 125-2 (1984).

Conant, Roger. *A Field Guide to Reptiles and Amphibians of Eastern and Central North America.* Boston: Houghton Mifflin Company, 1975.

Cowx, I. G., and P. Lamarque, eds. *Fishing with Electricity.* Oxford, England: Blackwell Scientific Publications, 1990.

Craig, Jeanne. *Fishing Fame: How to Catch a World Record Fish.* Camden ME: Ragged Mountain Press, 1999.

Crawford, Ray, ed. *1997 World Record Game Fishes.* Pompano Beach FL: International Game Fish Association, 1997.

Dahlem, Ted. *How to Make and Mend Cast Nets.* St. Petersburg FL: Great Outdoors Publishing, 1968.

Davis, Richard A., Jr. *Principles of Oceanography.* 2nd ed. Reading MA: Addison-Wesley Publishing Company, 1977.

Dawson, Elliot W. "King Crabs of the World (Crustacea: Lithodidae) and Their Fisheries: A Comprehensive Bibliography." *Miscellaneous Publication* 101, New Zealand Oceanographic Institute, Wellington, 1989.

Dore, Ian. *Shellfish: A Guide to Oysters, Mussels, Scallops, Clams, and Similar Products for the Commercial User.* New York: Van Nostrand Reinhold, 1991.

Earp, Samuel A., and William J. Wildeman. *The Blue Water Bait Book: Secrets of Successful Big Game Fishing.* Boston: Little, Brown, and Company, 1974.

Eastman, Peter F. *Advanced First Aid Afloat.* 3rd ed. Centreville MD: Cornell Maritime Press, 1987.

Evans, David H., ed. *The Physiology of Fishes.* Boca Raton FL: CRC Press, 1993.

Ferrell, Dave. "In Broad Daylight." *Marlin* (Dec./Jan. 1999): 56–59.

Francis, Malcolm. *Coastal Fishes of New Zealand: An Identification Guide.* Auckland: Reed Publishing, 1996.

Garner, John. *How to Make and Set Nets: The Technology of Netting.* Surrey, England: Fishing News Books, 1986.

Goadby, Peter. *Saltwater Gamefishing: Offshore and Onshore.* Auckland: Collins New Zealand, 1991.

Grainger, R. J. R., and S. M. Garcia. "Chronicles of Marine Fishery Landings (1950–1994)." *FAO Fisheries Technical Paper 359,* 1996.

Grindlay, Joanne, and Simon Mitchell. "Isolated Pulmonary Edema Associated with Scuba Diving." *Emergency Medicine* 11 (1999): 272–76.

Gunson, Dave. *A Guide to the New Zealand Seashore.* Auckland: Penguin Books, 1993.

Hall, G. M., ed. *Fish Processing Technology.* New York: VCH Publishers, 1992.

Halstead, Bruce W. *Poisonous and Venomous Marine Animals of the World.* 2nd revised ed. Princeton: Darwin Press, 1988.

Harrison, Peter. *Seabirds: An Identification Guide.* Boston: Houghton Mifflin Company, 1983.

Heemstra, Phillip C., and John E. Randall. "Groupers of the World (Family Serranidae, Subfamily Epinephelinae): An Annotated and Illustrated Catalogue of the Grouper, Rockcod, Hind, Coral Grouper, and Lyretail Species." *FAO Fisheries Synopsis* 16, no. 125 (1993).

Hillhouse, Darrell. "Rigging & Tackle: Heavy-Duty Loop." *Sport Fishing* (July/Aug., 1998): 27.

Hokama, Y., J. S. M. Ebesu, K. Nishimura, S. Oishi, B. Mizuo, M. Stiles, B. Sakamoto, W. Takenaka, and H. Nagai. "Human Intoxication from Hawaiian Reef Fishes Associated with Diverse Marine Toxins." *Journal of Natural Toxins* 5, no. 2 (1996): 235–47.

Holthius, L. B. "Shrimps and Prawns of the World: An Annotated Catalogue of Species of Interest to Fisheries." *FAO Fisheries Synopsis* 1, no. 125 (1980).

Humann, Paul. *Reef Creature Identification: Florida, Caribbean, Bahamas.* Jacksonville FL: New World Publications, 1992.

Humann, Paul. *Reef Fish Identification: Florida, Caribbean, Bahamas.* Jacksonville FL: New World Publications, 1992.

Humann, Paul. *Reef Fish Identification: Galapagos.* Jacksonville FL: New World Publications (1993).

Jefferson, Thomas A., Stephen Leatherwood, and Marc A. Webber. *FAO Species Identification Guide: Marine Mammals of the World.* Rome: Food and Agriculture Organization of the United Nations, 1993.

Jenkins, R. J. *Mussel Cultivation in the Marlborough Sounds (New Zealand).* 2nd ed. Wellington: New Zealand Fishing Industry Board, 1985.

Jimenez, Jorge Arturo. *Los Manglares del Pacifico Centroamericano.* Heredia, Costa Rica: Editorial Fundacion Universidad Nacional, 1994.

Johnson, R. H. *Sharks of Polynesia.* 3rd ed. Papeete, Tahiti: Société Nouvelle des Éditions du Pacifique, 1990.

Jones, Diana, and Gary J. Morgan. *A Field Guide to Crustaceans of Australian Waters.* Chatswood, NSW, Australia: Reed, 1994.

King, Marita M. "Oysters, Solomon-Islands Style." *Cruising World* 24, no. 10 (1998): 33–34.

Kuiter, Rudie H. *A Photographic Guide to Sea Fishes of Australia.* London: New Holland, 1997.

Lange, W. Robert. "Ciguatera Fish Poisoning." *American Family Physician* 50, no. 3 (1994): 579–84.

Larson, David E., ed. *Mayo Clinic Family Health Book.* New York: William Morrow and Company, 1990.

Last, P. R., and J. D. Stevens. *Sharks and Rays of Australia.* Australia: CSIRO, 1994.

Levine, David Z. "Ciguatera: Current Concepts." *Journal of the American Osteopathic Association* 95, no. 3 (1995): 193–98.

Levinton, Jeffrey S. *Marine Ecology.* Englewood Cliffs: Prentice-Hall, 1982.

Lieske, Ewald, and Robert Myers. *Coral Reef Fishes: Caribbean, Indian Ocean, and Pacific Ocean, Including the Red Sea.* New York: HarperCollins, 1994.

Lippmann, John, and Stan Bugg. *The DAN Emergency Handbook: A Guide to the Identification of and First Aid for Scuba (Air) Diving Injuries.* 2nd ed. Victoria, Australia: J. L. Publications, 1989.

Logsdon, Gene. *Getting Food from the Water: A Guide to Backyard Aquaculture.* Emmaus PA: Rodale Press, 1978.

Marquez, M. R. "Sea Turtles of the World: An Annotated and Illustrated Catalogue of Sea Turtle Species Known to Date." *FAO Fisheries Synopsis* 11, no. 125 (1990).

Masuda, H. K., C. Araga, T. Uyeno, and T. Yoshino. *Fishes of the Japanese Archipelago.* Tokyo: Tokai University Press, 1984.

McKay, Roland J. "Pearl Perches of the World (Family Glaucosomatidae): An Annotated and Illustrated Catalogue of the Pearl Perches Known to Date." *FAO Fisheries Synopsis* 17, no. 125 (1997).

McKay, Roland J. "Sillaginid Fishes of the World (Family Sillaginidae): An Annotated and Illustrated Catalogue of the Sillago, Smelt, or Indo-Pacific Whiting Species." *FAO Fisheries Synopsis* 14, no. 125 (1992).

Mead, Paul. "The Deep Sea Development Project's Report on Second Visit to Fiji." *SPC Unpublished Report 1.* Noumea, New Caledonia: Secretariat of the Pacific Community, 1997.

Mead, Paul. "Report on Third Visit to Niue." *SPC Unpublished Report 8.* Noumea, New Caledonia: Secretariat of the Pacific Community, 1997.

Mead, Paul, and L. Chapman. "Report on Fourth Visit to Tonga." *SPC Unpublished Report 27.* Noumea, New Caledonia: Secretariat of the Pacific Community, 1998.

MEDPC. *Physicians' Desk Reference.* 49th ed. Montvale NJ: Medical Economics Data Production, 1995.

Michael, S. W. *Sharks and Rays of the World.* Monterey: Sea Challengers, 1993.

Moore, Abigail. "Preliminary Notes on the Exploitation of Holothurians in the New Wakatobi Marine National Park, Sulawesi, Indonesia." *SPC Bêche-de-Mer Information Bulletin 10* (1998): 31–33.

Morey, Shaun. *Incredible Fishing Stories.* New York: Workman Publishing, 1994.

Myers, Robert F. *Micronesian Reef Fishes.* 2nd ed. Guam: Coral Graphics, 1991.

Nakamura, Izumi. "Billfishes of the World: An Annotated and Illustrated Catalogue of Marlins, Sailfishes, Spearfishes, and Swordfishes Known to Date." *FAO Fisheries Synopsis* 5, no. 125 (1985).

Nakamura, Izumi, and Nikolai V. Parin. "Snake Mackerels and Cutlassfishes of the World (Families Gempylidae and Trichiuridae): An Annotated and Illustrated Catalogue of the Snake Mackerels, Snoeks, Escolars, Gemfishes, Sackfishes, Domine, Oilfish, Cutlassfishes, Scabbardfishes, Hairtails, and Frostfishes." *FAO Fisheries Synopsis* 15, no. 125 (1993).

Nelson, Joseph S. *Fishes of the World.* 2nd ed. New York: John Wiley & Sons, 1984.

OECD. *Organization for Economic Co-operation and Development Multilingual Dictionary of Fish and Fish Products.* 2nd ed. Surrey, England: Adlard & Son, 1984.

Parsons, Timothy R., Masayuki Takahashi, and Barry Hargrave. *Biological Oceanographic Processes.* 2nd ed. New York: Pergamon Press, 1977.

Paul, Larry. *Marine Fishes of New Zealand 1: Shoreline and Shallow Seas.* Auckland: Reed Publishing, 1997.

Paul, Larry. *Marine Fishes of New Zealand 2.* Auckland: Reed Publishing, 1991.

Poveromo, George. "Tactics & Tackle: High-Speed Planers Deadly Offshore." *Salt Water Sportsman* (Aug. 1998): 14–16.

Preston, G., L. B. Chapman, P. D. Mead, and P. Taumaia. *Trolling Techniques for the Pacific Islands: A Manual for Fishermen, SPC Handbook 28.* Noumea, New Caledonia: Secretariat of the Pacific Community, 1987.

Randall, J. E. *Diver's Guide to Fishes of the Maldives.* London: IMMEL, 1992.

Randall, J. E. *Red Sea Reef Fishes.* London: IMMEL, 1983.

Randall, J. E. *Sharks of Arabia.* London: IMMEL, 1996.

Randall, J. E., G. R. Allen, and R. C. Steene. *Fishes of the Great Barrier Reef and Coral Sea.* Honolulu: University of Hawaii Press, 1990.

Randall, J. E., and A. Ben-Tuvia. "A Review of the Groupers (Pisces: Serranidae: Epinephelinae) of the Red Sea, with Description of a New Species of *Cephalophosus.*" *Bulletin of Marine Science* 33, no. 2 (1983): 373–426.

Rizzuto, Jim. *Fishing Hawaii Style: A Guide to Saltwater Angling Volume 1.* Honolulu: Hawaii Fishing News, 1983.

Robins, C. Richard, and G. Carleton Ray. *A Field Guide to Atlantic Coast Fishes of North America.* Boston: Houghton Mifflin, 1986.

Romashko, Sandra. *The Complete Collector's Guide to Shells and Shelling.* Miami FL: Windward Publishing, 1984.

Roper, Clyde F. E., Michael J. Sweeney, and Cornelia E. Nauen. "Cephalopods of the World: An Annotated and Illustrated Catalogue of Species of Interest to Fisheries." *FAO Fisheries Synopsis* 3, no. 125 (1984).

Rosman, I. *Fishing with Bottom Gill Nets.* Rome: Food and Agricultural Organization of the United Nations (FAO), 1980.

Russell, Barry C. "Nemipterid Fishes of the World (Threadfin Breams, Whiptail Breams, Monocle Breams, Dwarf Monocle Breams, and Coral Breams) Family Nemipteridae: An Annotated and Illustrated Catalogue of Nemipterid Species Known to Date." *FAO Fisheries Synopsis* 12, no. 125 (1990).

Safina, Carl. *Song for the Blue Ocean: Encounters along the World's Coasts and beneath the Seas.* New York: Henry Holt, 1997.

Sainesbury, John C. *Commercial Fishing Methods: An Introduction to Vessels and Gears.* 2nd ed. Surrey, England: Fishing News Books, 1986.

Salvat, B., and C. Rives. *Shells of Tahiti.* Papeete, Tahiti: Société Nouvelle des Éditions du Pacifique, 1984.

Schatman, Ron. "Sportfishing for Broadbill Swordfish." *The Big Game Fishing Journal* 10, no. 4 (1997): 34–43.

Sedgwick, Stephen D. *The Salmon Handbook: The Life and Cultivation of Fishes of the Salmon Family.* London: Andre Deutsch, 1982.

Thomson, Donald A., Lloyd T. Finley, and Alex N. Kerstitch. *Reef Fishes of the Sea of Cortez: The Rocky-Shore Fishes of the Gulf of California.* New York: John Wiley & Sons, 1979.

Tinker, Spencer W., and Charles J. DeLuca. *Sharks and Rays: A Handbook of Sharks and Rays of Hawaii and the Central Pacific Ocean.* Tokyo: Charles E. Tuttle, 1973.

Tolmazin, D. *Elements of Dynamic Oceanography.* Boston: Allen & Unwin, 1985.

Tomczack, M., and J. S. Godfrey. *Regional Oceanography: An Introduction.* London: Butler & Tanner, 1994.

Veitayaki, Joeli. *Fisheries Development in Fiji: The Quest for Stability.* Suva, Fiji: Institute for Pacific Studies, University of the South Pacific, 1995.

Von Brandt, Andres. *Fish Catching Methods of the World.* Surrey, England: Fishing News Books, 1984.

Werner, David. *Where There Is No Doctor.* 2nd ed. Palo Alto CA: Hesperian Foundation, 1992.

Whistler, W. Arthur. *Polynesian Herbal Medicine.* Kauai HI: National Tropical Botanical Garden, 1992.

Whitehead, Peter J. P. "Clupeoid Fishes of the World (Suborder Clupeoidei): An Annotated and Illustrated Catalogue of the Herrings, Sardines, Pilchards, Sprats, Shads, Anchovies, and Wolf-Herrings. Part 1—Chirocentridae, Clupeidae and Pristigasteridae." *FAO Fisheries Synopsis* 7, no. 125-1 (1985).

Whitehead, Peter J. P., and Gareth J. Nelson. "Clupeoid Fishes of the World (Suborder Clupeoidei): An Annotated and Illustrated Catalogue of the Herrings, Sardines, Pilchards, Sprats, Shads, Anchovies, and Wolf-Herrings. Part 2—Engraulidae." *FAO Fisheries Synopsis* 7, no. 125-2 (1988).

Yasumoto, Takeshi, and Michio Murata. "Marine Toxins." *Chemical Reviews* 93, no. 5 (1993): 1897–1909.

Index

Index of Scientific Names